CAMBRIDGE LIBRAI

Books of enduring sch......., ...

Linguistics

From the earliest surviving glossaries and translations to nineteenth century academic philology and the growth of linguistics during the twentieth century, language has been the subject both of scholarly investigation and of practical handbooks produced for the upwardly mobile, as well as for travellers, traders, soldiers, missionaries and explorers. This collection will reissue a wide range of texts pertaining to language, including the work of Latin grammarians, groundbreaking early publications in Indo-European studies, accounts of indigenous languages, many of them now extinct, and texts by pioneering figures such as Jacob Grimm, Wilhelm von Humboldt and Ferdinand de Saussure.

An English–Cornish Dictionary

Cornish had all but died out as a spoken language by the middle of the eighteenth century. However, it experienced a slight resurgence in the nineteenth century, spurred by increased scholarly interest. Published in 1887, this dictionary played a role in preserving Cornwall's linguistic heritage. Compiled by Frederick W.P. Jago (1817–92) and intended as a supplement to existing Cornish word lists and glossaries, it was the first resource to provide Cornish translations for English words and phrases. Jago attempts to provide literary citations for the entries wherever possible, but does not manage to do this throughout, observing that 'life is short, art is long'. Appendices include literal translations of biblical texts such as Genesis and the Ten Commandments. Jago's *The Ancient Language, and the Dialect of Cornwall, with an Enlarged Glossary of Cornish Provincial Words* (1882) is also reissued in the Cambridge Library Collection.

Cambridge University Press has long been a pioneer in the reissuing of out-of-print titles from its own backlist, producing digital reprints of books that are still sought after by scholars and students but could not be reprinted economically using traditional technology. The Cambridge Library Collection extends this activity to a wider range of books which are still of importance to researchers and professionals, either for the source material they contain, or as landmarks in the history of their academic discipline.

Drawing from the world-renowned collections in the Cambridge University Library and other partner libraries, and guided by the advice of experts in each subject area, Cambridge University Press is using state-of-the-art scanning machines in its own Printing House to capture the content of each book selected for inclusion. The files are processed to give a consistently clear, crisp image, and the books finished to the high quality standard for which the Press is recognised around the world. The latest print-on-demand technology ensures that the books will remain available indefinitely, and that orders for single or multiple copies can quickly be supplied.

The Cambridge Library Collection brings back to life books of enduring scholarly value (including out-of-copyright works originally issued by other publishers) across a wide range of disciplines in the humanities and social sciences and in science and technology.

An English–Cornish Dictionary

Compiled from the Best Sources

FREDERICK W.P. JAGO

CAMBRIDGE
UNIVERSITY PRESS

CAMBRIDGE
UNIVERSITY PRESS

University Printing House, Cambridge, CB2 8BS, United Kingdom

Cambridge University Press is part of the University of Cambridge.

It furthers the University's mission by disseminating knowledge in the pursuit of
education, learning and research at the highest international levels of excellence.

www.cambridge.org
Information on this title: www.cambridge.org/9781108071628

© in this compilation Cambridge University Press 2014

This edition first published 1887
This digitally printed version 2014

ISBN 978-1-108-07162-8 Paperback

This book reproduces the text of the original edition. The content and language reflect
the beliefs, practices and terminology of their time, and have not been updated.

Cambridge University Press wishes to make clear that the book, unless originally published
by Cambridge, is not being republished by, in association or collaboration with,
or with the endorsement or approval of, the original publisher or its successors in title.

DOLLY PENTREATH. MOUSEHOLE.

DOLLY PENTREATH'S HOUSE. MOUSEHOLE.
FROM A SKETCH BY MISS MINNIE JAGO 1882.

AN

ENGLISH-CORNISH

DICTIONARY.

COMPILED FROM THE BEST SOURCES

BY

FRED. W. P. JAGO, M.B. Lond:

AUTHOR OF "A GLOSSARY OF THE CORNISH DIALECT."

LONDON:

SIMPKIN, MARSHALL & Co., STATIONERS' HALL COURT.

PLYMOUTH:

W. H. LUKE, PRINTER AND PUBLISHER, BEDFORD STREET.

1887.

DEDICATION.

THIS

ENGLISH-CORNISH

DICTIONARY

IS GRATEFULLY DEDICATED BY THE AUTHOR TO HIS OLD AND
VERY DEAR FRIEND

Dr. W. T. A. PATTISON,

FORMERLY OF

DUPORTH, NEAR St. AUSTELL, CORNWALL.

CONTENTS.

INTRODUCTION.

L HUYD says, "that to preserve any old language in print is, without all doubt a most pleasant and obliging thing to scholars and gentlemen, and altogether necessary in the study of antiquity."

This remark is peculiarly applicable to the ancient language of Cornwall, the remains of which are so well worth preserving. We call it the ancient language of Cornwall, but in reality the remains are those which were once spoken far beyond the limits of the most westerly county of England. A language only recently extinct, and dating from almost unknown time.

"The Celts, says Max Muller, seem to have been the first of the Aryans to arrive in Europe; but the pressure of subsequent migrations, particularly of Teutonic tribes, has driven them towards the westernmost parts, and latterly from Ireland, across the Atlantic. The only remaining dialects are the Welsh, the Cornish, lately extinct, the Armorican of Brittany, the Irish, the Gaelic of the West Coast of Scotland, and the dialect of the Isle of Man."

"Gaul, Belgium, and Britain were Celtic Dominions, and the North of Italy was chiefly inhabited by them. In the time of Herodotus, we find the Celts in Spain; and Switzerland, the Tyrol, and the country south of the Danube, have once been seats of Celtic tribes. A Celtic colony settled in Asia, and founded Galatia, where the language spoken at the time of St. Jerome was still that of the Gauls."

As to the Cornish branch of the ancient language of the Celts, Drew (Hist. of Cornwall, vol. 1. p. 218) remarks that, " the Cornish tongue is generally admitted to be a dialect of that language, which till the Saxons came in, was common to all the western parts of Britian, and more anciently to Ireland and Gaul."

In latter times we find the Cornish language still struggling for existence, and retreating across the banks of the Tamar. Polwhele, (Hist. of Cornwall, vol. 3. pp. 28. 29. Ed. of 1803) says, " the Conqueror and his followers, as soon as they were settled in this country made every effort to substitute the Norman-French for the Anglo-Saxon, which was generally spoken in England. In their attempts, however, to recommend their own language to the attention of the English, both themselves and their successors were for several generations unsuccessful. The Saxon prevailed in every part of England excepting Devonshire and Cornwall. In Devon indeed, it became fashionable among the superior orders of the people, though the inferior classes adhered firmly to their old vernacular tongue. Not that the Cornu-British was abandoned by every Devonian of rank or education. It was certainly spoken in Devonshire by persons of distinction, long after the present period."

At length the language of the Cornish Celts was beaten back towards the extreme west where it has ceased to be spoken almost within living memory.

There were many causes tending to hasten the time when the old tongue would become extinct, and writers of Cornish history, although agreeing in general statements, differ from each other in some particulars.

About the time of the Reformation a fatal blow was given, when the Cornish language was disused in the services of the Church.   How this was done is variously stated.   Borlase (Nat. Hist. of Cornwall, p. 315) asserts that, " when the liturgy at the reformation was appointed by authority to take the place of the mass, the Cornish *desired* (Scawen, p. 49), that it should be in the English language, being apprehensive that it might be injoined them in their mother tongue, as it was with regard to the Welsh.   By this means, and the gentry mixing gradually with the English, the Cornish language lost ground, in proportion as it lay nearer to Devon."

This statement of Borlase, the clever but dogmatic Whitaker (Anc. Cathedral of Cornwall, vol. 2. p. 37), emphatically contradicts. He insists that, " the English too was not *desired* by the Cornish, as vulgar history says, and as Dr. Borlase avers ; but, as the case shews itself plainly to be, *forced* upon the Cornish by the tyranny of England, at a time when the English language was yet unknown in Cornwall.   This act of tyranny was at once gross barbarity to the Cornish people, and a death blow to the Cornish language."   Alluding to the first use of the English service in Menheniot church, Mr. Whitaker says, " that had the liturgy been translated into Cornish as it was in Welsh, the Cornish language would have been preserved to the present moment."

But other causes were at work to which I will allude in my summary of Scawen's treatise on this subject.

Another version is given in Lake's Parochial History of Cornwall (vol. 1. p. 103), thus :—" Humphrey Arundell, the leader of the Cornish insurgents in 1549, resided at Helland, near Bodmin.   He was governor of St. Michael's Mount, and a man of some military reputation.   The Cornishmen in this rebellion were probably as much instigated by the attempt of the government to displace the old language in the service of the church as by the other innovations made upon their religion.

" Among the fifteen articles insisted upon by Arundell and his fellow rebels as the price of their submission, the eighth stipulates that, " we will not receive the new service, because it is but like a Christian game; but we will have our old service of Latin as it was before.   And so we Cornishmen, whereof certain of us understand no English, utterly refuse this."

One thing is certain that when the English service was first used in Cornwall, at the end of the reign of that pious king Henry VIII, (1509-1547), Cornish was known and spoken from the Tamar to the Land's End.

It was in Menheniot church that the English service was first used, about 1540. Dr. Moreman who was the Vicar, was the first minister who taught his parishioners the Lord's Prayer, the Creed, and the Commandments, in English.   It is evident in thus teaching the parishioners English, about the year 1540, at Menheniot, and not far from the Tamar, that Cornish was then the common speech in use among the people of that district.

The English service, though first used in Menheniot church, was not universally read in the Cornish churches. Hals (Paroch. Hist., p. 133) says, " the Cornish tongue was so long retained in this parish (Feock) by the old inhabitants thereof till about the year 1640, that Mr. William Jackman, then vicar thereof, Chaplain of Pendennis Castle, at the seige thereof by the parliament army, was forced for divers years to administer the sacrament to the communicants in the Cornish tongue, because the aged people did not well understand the English, as he himself (says Hals), has often told me."

Drew's (Hist. of Cornwall, vol. 1. p. 224), remarks that, " although the Cornish language appears to have been excluded from all our Cornish churches, except Feock and Landwednack, so early as the year 1640, yet it was not driven from common conversation until a much later period. So late as 1650, the Cornish language was currently spoken in the parishes of Paul and St. Just ; the fish-women and market-women in the former, and the tinners in the latter, for the most part conversing in their old vernacular tongue."

It is stated by Scawen, " that the Rev. F. Robinson, rector of Landwednack preached a sermon to his parishioners in the Cornish language only." This was about the year 1678, and appears to be the record of the last sermon in Cornish.

But Cornish was not yet extinct, as the following statement will prove.

Lhuyd, who has done so much for ancient Cornish, gives us in his learned work the Archæologia Britannica, (p. 153), a glimpse of the state of the Cornish tongue. The spelling of the names of places is here given as he wrote them. Writing about the year 1707 Lhuyd informs us that, " the places in Cornwall that at this day retain the ancient language are the parishes of St. Just, St. Paul, Burrian, Sunnin, St. Lavan, St. Krad, Morva, Maddern, Sunner, Tewednok, St. Ives, Lelant, Leigian, Kynwal, or (as now, 1707, pronounced) Gylval; and all along the sea-shoar from the Land's End to St. Kevern's near the Lizard point. But a good many of the inhabitants of these parishes, especially the Gentry, do not understand it; there being no necessity thereof, in regard there's no Cornish man but speaks good English."

We come now to a later period. The familiar name of Dolly Pentreath reminds us that we have reached a period when the old language was all but quite dead. A good deal of doubt has been created respecting the truth of the tales about Dolly Pentreath. Into the controversy it is not necessary for me to enter. I will only say that I obtained, in the summer of 1882, valuable, and reliable information from Mr. Bernard Victer, of Moushole, near Penzance. He is the grandson of George Badcock, who was the undertaker at old Dolly's funeral. Mr. Victor remembers his grandfather, George Badcock, from whom the information was orally given to him. The full particulars are given about Dolly in my " Glossary of the Cornish dialect," and they would take too much space to be recorded here. The main facts, as I believe them to be, are these, viz : that Dolly died on December 26, 1777, aged 102 years; that she was the last known person *whose mother tongue was Cornish*, and that she knew no other language until she was a grown woman ; that those who lived after her time, although they could converse more or less perfectly in Cornish, yet they were born and brought up when children to speak English.

That Cornish was known to some after Dolly died, is proved by the epitaph written in the old language, and never, so far as is known, placed on Dolly's grave about the time of her burial.

From the foregoing sketch we may see how surely, if slowly, the ancient language became extinct.

Even now, some remains of the old tongue are remembered quite apart from books.

In the *Cornishman* (a newspaper published in Penzance), there were in 1879, lists of old Cornish words, one by Mr. Bernard Victor above mentioned, and another by Mr. Pentreath. Each list contained about 150 words which each gentlemen had orally learnt.

I alluded, in a previous page, to the interesting treatise by Mr. Scawen, of Molenick (he died aged about 84 in 1689), on " The causes of the Cornish Speech's Decay."

Scawen's dissertation is given in full in D. Gilbert's " Cornwall," (vol. 4. pp. 190-221), and also in Grose's " Antiquarian Repertory," (1807-9), vol. 3. pp. 208-234.

The following is a summary account of the causes which, according to Scawen, brought to an end the use of ancient Cornish :—

1. The want of letters, or " of a character," and of authors or writers, as in the cases of Rome and Greece, to hand the language down.

2. The custom of the Druids to depend on memory only, and rarely on writings.

3. The great loss to us of Armorica (Brittany), whose people were so closely allied to us by race and language, and the decreasing of the mutual interchanges between that country and Cornwall.

4. The gradual cessation of the Miracle Plays being acted and recited before multitudes of Cornish in their " Rounds " or Plaen an Gwaré.

5. The loss of the old stories and traditions of the Ancient Cornish.

6. The loss of ancient records " which some affirm were burnt, and others lost in the ancient ruins, as of Restormal, and other castles."

7. " Disuetude, or want of a continual use."

8. " A general stupidity," or ignorance and indifference as to the past.

9. The decay of what learning there was after the suppression of the Druids, and " no reparation thereof when the supposed saints " came to Cornwall; and for latter times learned men who came among us, " seeing our own neglect of our tongue," did not think it worthy of being studied by them.

10. The speech " invaded," and " eaten up " by the use of Saxon words for ancient names.

11. The near vicinity to Devon, and the Saxons, whose influence extended to the west and corrupted the language.

12. The gentry, who anciently kept themselves in their own county, marrying out of it, and so admitting more " Saxonage."

13. The coming in of all sorts of strangers upon us.

14. Not having the church service continued in the ancient tongue, as it was in Wales.

15. "The little or no help, rather discouragement" of the gentry who in Cromwell's time rather laughed at the poor who persisted in speaking it.

16. The want of writing it is the great cause of its decay, for the characters "now in use," would have saved it. And, says Scawen, "here I cannot but lament the want of such persons, books, records, and papers, *which were late in being*, and not now to be had, and my misfortune in not having translated them," as for instance, the MS. of Anguin, and "a Cornish Accidence . . . . . which was destroyed by children before it could be brought to me," and a "Matins in Cornish . . . . . but I could never attain to it."

"The language, says Drew (Hist. of Cornwall, vol. i, p. 218), which was once spoken in this county by our British ancestors, awakens our solicitude from motives of local attachment, and becomes particularly interesting from the singular circumstance of its being now no more. At present we behold its mighty shadow in the pages of our history, and even this is gradually disappearing. The only scattered remnants which have survived its oral existence, may be found in those provincial phrases, and local names for which Cornwall is so peculiarly remarkable."

THE REMAINS

OF

CORNISH LITERATURE.

AFTER the account which has been given of the causes of the decay of the Ancient Cornish Language, an inquiry as to the remains of Ancient, or Celtic Cornish Literature naturally follows.

There is no evidence to prove that anything was ever printed in Cornish before 1707, when the Archæologia Britannica by Lhuyd was published, "giving some account additional to what has been hitherto published of the Languages, Histories, and Customs of the Original Inhabitants of Great Britain from Collections and Observations in Travels through Wales, Cornwall, Bas Bretagne, Ireland, and Scotland, by Edward Lhuyd, M.A. of Jesus College, Keeper of the Ashmolean Museum in Oxford, April 9th, 1707." This learned work contains a Cornish Preface, a Cornish Grammar, and a great number of Cornish words. A reference to the preface to Pryce's Cornish Dictionary, (given in the appendix of this book) will help the reader to judge how valuable were the labours of Lhuyd.

In the year 1754 was published the first, and in 1769 the second edition of the "Antiquities, Historical and Monumental of the County of Cornwall," by William Borlase. Each edition has a Cornish-English Vocabulary which contains about 4000 Cornish words. Borlase in the preface to this Vocabulary says " The Helps I have received I must acknowledge chiefly owing to the Archæologia of the late Mr. Edward Lhuyd. . . . . who has published a Grammar of the Cornish, and therein preserved the Elements of this Language, which had otherwise wholly perished with him, and his friend Mr. John Keigwyn, who was indeed Mr. Lhuyd's Tutour in this Point of Learning, and died a few years after him. . . . . Besides Mr. Lhuyd's Works, I have been favoured with the perusal of a curious MS. written by the late Mr. Scawen of Molinek, in Cornwall, in which, first, there was a Part of a Cornish MS. called Mount Calvary, with a Verbal English Translation (no small Help to a beginner). . . . .

" I had the favour of perusing what the late William Gwavas, Esq ; (after Mr. Keigwyn ; and Mr. Lhuyd, the most knowing of his Age in the Cornish Tongue) left behind him ; and a few MSS. of the late Mr. Boson ; part of Mr. Hals's Cornish Vocabulary, and some Translations of several parts of the Holy Scripture. Lastly I have inserted the Cornish Vocabulary, which is in the Cotton Library, London ; a MS. Mr. Lhuyd thought, about seven hundred years old."

In 1790, William Pryce, M.D., of Redruth, Cornwall, caused to be published the "Archæologia Cornu-Britannica, or, an Essay to preserve the Ancient Cornish Language, containing the Rudiments of that Dialect in a Cornish Grammar, and Cornish-English Vocabulary, compiled from a variety of materials which have been inaccessible to all other authors, wherein the British Original of some Thousand English Words in common use is demonstrated; together with that of the Proper Names of most Towns, Parishes, Villages, Mines, and Gentlemen's Seats and Families, in Wales, Cornwall, Devonshire, and other Parts of England."

It should be mentioned that Pryce used the MS. compilations of Tonkin and Gwavas, done about fifty years before Pryce's time, or about the year 1730.

Severe strictures have been made on Pryce, but whether the charge of plagiarism be true or not, still Pryce *worked*, and this should cover a multitude of sins; and we have to thank Pryce for getting the Archæologia Cornu-Britannica printed. In the Appendix to this book will be found Prince Napoleon's letter in which Pryce is called a "plagiate." I have also given a verbatim copy of Pryce's preface, so that those who read it may judge whether the charge of plagiarism is just or not.

The Vocabulary in Pryce's book contains about 4000 words. The other contents will be noticed further on under the heading "Minor Remains."

In the year 1826, Mr. Davies Gilbert caused to be published the Cornish Drama, called "Mount Calvary," but it was issued so abounding in typograhical errors as to be all but useless. In the year 1862, a corrected copy "under the care of a most able scholar," Mr. Whitley Stokes, was published for the Philological Society.

The MS. of Mount Calvary was written in the fifteenth century. Williams in the Preface to his Lexicon Cornu-Britannicum thus describes it. "It contained 250 stanzas of eight lines each in heptasyllabic metre with alternate rhymes. The subject of this Poem is the Trial and Crucifixion of Christ. There are four copies of this manuscript, the oldest being in the British Museum, and the other three appear to be copies taken from it. Two of them are in the Bodleian Library, and in these a translation by John Keigwin is written on the opposite page.

Norris (*Cornish Drama*) says, "a third paper copy has recently been found in Cornwall; it is in folio, and has the English Translation, which is not carried quite to the close of the work. This copy is now (July, 1858) in the possession of Mr. Hotten, bookseller of Piccadilly. This volume contains also the "Creation" of William Jordan, and a translation of Lhuyd's Preface to his Cornish Grammar in the Archæologia Britannica, made by the joint labours of Gwavas and Tonkin; it is the one printed by Pryce in the Archæologia Cornu-Britannica."

In 1827 was published "The Creation of the World with Noah's Flood," written in Cornish in the year 1611 by William Jordan; with an English Translation by John Keigwin. This Edition was edited by Mr. Davies Gilbert, but it also is nearly useless because of the numerous typographical errors it contains. At the end are the First Chapter of Genesis, and other miscellaneous pieces written in Cornish. A correct edition, with a translation on the opposite pages, and notes at the end of the book, was published by the Philological Society in 1864. This edition is entitled "Gwreans an Bys, The Creation of the World, a Cornish Mystery," edited with a translation and notes by William Stokes.

This play contains 2548 lines.   The Cornish is that of the Language in its decay, and mixed with many borrowed words from the English.

In the year 1859 "The Ancient Cornish Drama" edited and translated by Mr. Edwin Norris, Secretary, R.A.S. was published at the University Press, Oxford.   It is in two volumes 8vo.   The first volume contains the "Ordinale de Origine Mundi," or the Beginning of the World.   There are 2846 lines.   The next is the "Passio Domini nostri Jhesu Christi," or the Passion of our Lord Jesus Christ.   This contains 3242 lines.

The second volume begins with the "Ordinale de Resurrexione Domini nostri Jhesu Christi," or the Drama of the Resurrection of our Lord Jesus Christ.   This extends to 2646 lines.   The translations are given on the opposite pages.

The second volume contains also Notes, a Sketch of Cornish Grammar, and the Ancient Cornish Vocabulary in alphabetical order.   An Appendix of more than 70 pages ends the work.   The Old Cornish Vocabulary in this work is also in the Grammatica Celtica of Zeuss but without alphabetical arrangement.

The MS. of this old Vocabulary entitled "Vocabularium Wallicum" was first proved to be Cornish and not Welsh, by Lhuyd, who mentions it in his Archæologia. Williams speaks of it as being "of great philological importance."   It was written in the thirteenth century, and may be, says Williams, a copy of an older original.

The three Dramas above mentioned are very valuable remains, and equal in amount all the rest of the old Language.   The Cornish in them is of great purity.   These Dramas are of the same age as "Mount Calvary."

In the year 1865 was published in quarto, pp. 398, that fine work the Lexicon Cornu-Britannicum, "a Dictionary of the Ancient Celtic Language of Cornwall, in which the words are elucidated by copious examples from the Cornish works now remaining, with translations in English.   The synonyms are also given in the cognate dialects Welsh, Armoric, Irish, Gaelic, and Manx, shewing at one view the connection between them.   By the Rev. Robert Williams, M.A."   This is indeed a grand addition to the Celtic Literature of Cornwall.   For such a work philologists, and Cornishmen, will be for ever grateful.

About four years after the publication of the Lexicon Cornu-Britannicum another interesting and valuable manuscript was discovered, entitled Bewnans Meriasek, or the Life of Saint Meriasek.   This Cornish Drama was published in 1872, and ably edited, with a translation and notes, by Mr. Whitley Stokes.   It contains 4568 lines of which a translation is given on the opposite pages.

The following is from the Preface by Mr. Stokes.

"The drama of the Life of St. Meriasek, Bishop and Confessor was found about the year 1868, (Mr. Stokes, in 1872, said "about three years ago") among the Hengwrt MSS. by Mr. Wynne of Peniarth.   The first thirty six lines were printed in the Archæologia Cambrensis for 1869, p. 409, by the Rev. Robert Williams of Rhydycroesau, but the remainder is now (1872) for the first time published.

"The manuscript is a small paper quarto, measuring eight and a half inches by six, in an old brown leather binding now labelled on the back '310, Cornish Mystery,' and on the top side 'Legendary &c. Lives of Saints, No. 2, 7 books, 310.'   Inside the cover is a yellow label on which is printed 'R. Wmes. Vaughan Hengwrt.'   It contains 90 leaves paginated in pencil, and a leaf six and a quarter inches by six (marked 91ᵃ , 91ᵇ) inserted immediately before the forty sixth leaf.   The versos of leaves 49 and 90 are occupied with rude plans of the stage.   Half of p 97, and three fourths of p. 179 are blank.   The colophon states that the MS. was finished by 'Dominus Hadton,' in the year 1504 . . . . .

The MS. has suffered little (ff 11 and 13 have lost a small portion of the margin), and is carefully preserved at Peniarth, near Towyn, Merionethshire."

"Except a few English, French, and Latin oaths, curses, and other phrases scattered through the play, its language is Middle Cornish, but rather more modern than that of the " *Passion*," and of the Dramas published by Mr. Norris.

Thus loanwords from the English are somewhat more numerous than they are in Mr. Norris's Dramas.   Again, the vowels *e* and *o* have often become *a*. . . . .   But there are more phonetic corruptions.   The Grammar of the language is pure Middle Cornish. . . . .   The Syntax is that of the older Dramas save that the future of the verb substantive is sometimes used for the present.   It stands between the 14th century Oxford plays and the " Creation."

<hr>

THE MINOR REMAINS OF CORNISH LITERATURE.

IN addition to what has been already stated, it may be useful to give lists of what may be called the minor remains of Cornish Literature, together with any information connected with them.

In Pryce's Dictionary, already noticed, are also the following, viz :—The Lord's Prayer, the Creed, and the Ten Commandments, all of which are given in Ancient and Modern Cornish.   Also a collection of Proverbs, Mottoes, Rhymes, and Songs in the Modern or Vulgar Cornish.   These are followed by Numbers, and the names of the months.   Next to these are :—

1.   One Parson's Certificate to another to marry a person whose Banns have been called.

2.   On the verdict of the twelve honest men of the County of Middlesex ; and the judgment of the four Barons thereon.

3   To Neighbour Nicholas Pentreath.

4.   Advice from a Friend in the Country, to his Neighbour that went up to receive £16,000 in London.   By Mr. John Boson, of Newlyn.

5.   On a Lazy Idle Weaver.

6.   Verses on the Marazion Bowling-Green, and Club.

7.   Advice to all Drunkards, and Company.

8.   A Cornish Riddle.

9.   Advice to all Men.

10.   Another.   (Advice).

11. A concluding one. (Advice).

12. A Cornish Song.

All those numbered above have translations in English on the opposite columns.

In pp. 55-64, Pryce has also given a "Specimen of the Modern Cornish, collated with the Welsh, with an English translation."

The book ends with letters from Lhuyd to Tonkin. They are very interesting as may be supposed. One of the letters has a long poem in Cornish and Latin entitled, " In Obitum Regis Wilhelmi 3tü Carmen Britannicum, Dialecto Cornubiensi; Ad Norman Poetarum Secnli Sexti."

In the *Western Morning News* of August 2nd, 1871, an excellent list of the Gwavas manuscripts may be found. It is so good that it will suitably conclude this acoount of Cornish Remains.

THE GWAVAS MANUSCRIPTS.

" THE Gwavas manuscripts were formerly in the possession of the Rev. William Veale, of Trevaylor. After his decease they passed to the Rev. William Wriothesley Wingfield, the Vicar of Gulval, by whom they were presented to the British Museum. They are in a bound volume, lettered Gwavas MSS. and are known as ' British Museum Additional MSS. 28.554.'

Letter from Davies Gilbert, dated East Bourne, 22nd, July 1836, to Rev. W. Veale; p. 1.

Three letters from John Boson, dated Newlyn, 1709, 1711, 1720, to W. Gwavas, Brick Court, Middle Temple, London; pp. 2. 10. 12.

Letter from W. Gwavas, dated 1711 to Oliver Pendar, Merchant, Newlyn; p. 3.

Letter from O. Pendar, dated Newlyn, 1711, to W. Gwavas, London; p. 4.

Letter from W. Gwavas, dated Middle Temple, 1711, to J. Boson, Newlyn; pp. 8-9.

Letter from W. Gwavas to——, dated March 1731, ætate 55; p. 11.

Three letters from Thomas Tonkin, dated Polgorran, 1735, to W. Gwavas, Penzance; pp. 14. 18. 22.

Three letters from W. Gwavas, dated Penzance, 1735, 36, to T. Tonkin; pp. 16. 20. 23.

Copy of " The Creation, finished by J. Keygwin, gent. in ye year 1693 ;" pp. 24-49.

Copy of " Mount Calvary," amended and corrected by W. H. 1679-80; pp. 51-58.

The Lord's Prayer in Cornish; p. 50.

Cornish Glossary—A. to c L.; pp. 59-78.

Cornish Vocabulary—A. to w.; pp. 80-89.

" Mr. William Gwavas was the son of William Gwavas, and was born in 1676. He became a barrister of the Middle Temple, where he resided for some time in Brick-court. He was impropriator or lay vicar of Paul, and in that capacity had various disputes with the fishermen of that parish respecting the tything of fish."

Sometime ago there was published "Some observations on the Rev. R. Williams's preface to his Lexicon, by Prince L. L. Bonaparte, (London, May, 1865,) s. sh. 4to." This work contains "A copy of a letter from the Rev. (sic) W. Gwavas to T. Tonkin," dated Penzance, 25th January, 1732, and is as far as we know, the only other document referring to Mr. Gwavas besides those already mentioned. Some of Mr. Gwavas's Cornish writings have been printed by Borlase, Pryce, and Polwhele. Mr. Gwavas died in 1741, and was buried at Paul, near Penzance, on the 9th January in that year."

It is stated (*Biblioth Cornub.* Veale, Eliz[h].) that the first and third chapters of Genesis in Celtic Cornish were written by Mrs. Elizabeth Veale the eldest daughter of William Gwavas.

There is a curious paragraph in an old newspaper called " Brice's Weekly Journal," formerly published at Exeter.

In it, June and July, 1727, appeared " The Exmoor Scolding," in which occurs this passage : " And I hear of a gentleman in Cornwall (in Antique Age Renowned —for Love to *Saints* , and *Shipwrecks !)* who has taken noble mighty pains in translating the Bible into Cornish, or Cornubian Welsh "—I do not know of any MS. translation such as Brice speaks of. Perhaps the phrase " translating the Bible " may only mean such parts as have been before noticed.

It has been, and still is, a popular belief that there is not much of the old language left. The catalogue of remains here given goes far to prove that the popular belief is wrong. It should be remembered that besides the printed books in Cornish, there are numbers of ancient Cornish words still in use. Then, again, the names of persons and places, derived from the old tongue, amount to at least 20,000 words. These may be seen in " The Glossary of Cornish Names " by the Rev. John Bannister. Roughly counted there are about eight thousand Cornish words in Dr. Williams's Lexicon, four thousand in Pryce's vocabulary, and about four thousand in that of Borlase.

These numbers must not be added together. Excluding the names of persons and places, and numbering from all other remaining sources, it may be stated that about fifteen thousand words of the Celtic language of Cornwall have been saved to us. Borlase has many words not to be found in Pryce, and *vice versa.* There are also many words in Pryce and Borlase not to be found in Williams. Such works in Cornish as are preserved are valuable, because we find in them specimens of the language in its various stages of purity and decay. Although the books are not numerous and would occupy but a small space in a library, yet the words and phrases are sufficient to express almost every form of thought.

It has been said that the husbandman expresses all his thoughts by using four or five hundred words, and Shakspere used about 15,000 words. Thus it may be seen that the " remains " of Celtic Cornish stand far beyond the vocabulary of the rustic, and rival in their amount the words of Shakspere. Still, we have to lament that much of the old tongue is quite lost to us, and especially in regard to the *names of things.* In making this compilation the following rules appeared to be the best, and most practical, viz :—

1. To collect all the words which should find a place in an English-Cornish Dictionary.

2. To quote some Cornish phrases for the sake of illustration.

3. To give the various forms or spellings of the words just as they are found in the remains of ancient Cornish, *without constructing a single word, or phrase, and without alteration or addition.*

4. To place the various spellings of the words in a gradational form, for the sake of their being more easily compared.

5. To give *one* authority at least for each word and phrase, for the sake of an easy reference to the originals.

These rules have been followed, and the scholar will well know how to judge of what rests on the authority of Williams, or Borlase, or Pryce, or others. All Cornish words known to me as still in oral use in the Cornish dialect are here included. Some of these are doubtful, but it is safer to keep than to lose them.

It seemed an endless and a hopeless task to bring the chaos of Cornish orthography into anything like order.

However, by adopting a gradational arrangement of the various spellings, there is the satisfaction of finding that words, which when apart were hardly to be known, so uncouth is the spelling, become, when grouped or placed in gradational order, explanatory of one another

All through the book there are four principal reference letters, viz. :   W.N.P. and B, which are used to indicate that words so marked may be found somewhere or other in the pages of Williams, Norris, Pryce, or Borlase.

There are letters, and also figures, of which information is given in the " Explanations," Q.V.

Some plurals of nouns are given, sometimes separately, and occasionally immediately after the nouns.

Participles are not often written. The student will know how to form them, and therefore a frequent admission is not required.

The grammar is from the Lexicon Cornu-Britannicum of Williams, and given here as in his work.

It was intended to illustrate *each* word by at least one Cornish quotation, but life is short, art is long.

I have been able to find many words, and to quote many Cornish phrases from the Beunans Meriasek, which was printed after Dr. Williams's Lexicon was published.

It may be asked, what is the use of an English-Cornish Dictionary ? Is it a literary want ? Will it fill a gap in Celtic Cornish literature ?

When we remember the labours of Lhuyd, Keigwyn, Gwavas, Tonkin, Pryce, Borlase, Polwhele, Williams, Norris, Stokes, Bannister, and others, there cannot be a doubt that the reply should be in the affirmative. If such men thought it necessary to take so much trouble in preserving the remains of Ancient Cornish then surely this effort of mine needs no apology.

Whether the Celtic Scholar will care for such a work as this is not for me to say, but I am very sure that Cornishmen especially, and many who are not natives of Cornwall, heartily encourage everything which helps to preserve what is left of the old language of Cornwall.

Borlase (Antiq. of Cornwall, 1st Ed.), in the Preface to his Cornish Vocabulary, says, "I hope tho' what follows is not compleat, it may lay a foundation, and provoke some one of more leisure, *to add to it an English-Cornish Vocabulary.*"

Such a hope from so eminent a Cornish writer acquires the force of a command, and not only deserves respect, but demands fulfilment.

My much regretted friend Dr. Bannister began an English-Cornish Dictionary, but he did not live to complete it, and the unfinished MS. lies buried in the British Museum. Dr. Bannister, like Borlase, considered such a book as this a literary want.

A Cornish Dictionary without the English-Cornish part of it is like a bird with one wing. The missing wing, imperfect it may be, I have attempted to supply.

What should we say of a Latin Dictionary without an English-Latin division?

My wish has been to compile a handy dictionary, so that anyone might find, so far as the remains of the ancient language will allow, what is the Cornish for an English word.

The labours of others have made such a task comparatively easy; indeed, without the works of Williams, &c., this compilation would have been impossible to me, and I have to acknowledge the invaluable assistance derived from all sources.

This is simply a piece of literary drudgery, which, to use the words of Borlase, "will I hope, be useful to my countrymen, and satisfactory to all who will not be too scrupulous and critical."

FRED. W. P. JAGO.

Belle Vue House, Saltash, and
Lockyer Street, Plymouth.

EXPLANATIONS OF THE LETTERS IN THE TEXT.

W.	Words and phrases from the Lexicon Cornu-Britannicum.
P.	Words and phrases from the Archæologia Cornu-Britannica.
B.	Words and phrases from Borlase's Cornish Vocabulary.
N.	Words from the Cornish Grammar of Norris.
B.V.	Ancient Cornish words still known apart from books to Mr. Bernard Victor, of Moushole, near Penzance.
W.F.P.	Ancient Cornish words still known apart from books to Mr. W. F. Pentreath, of Newquay, Cornwall.
D.	Ancient Cornish words still used in the Provincial Dialect of Cornwall.
C.W.	Words and phrases from "The Creation of the World."
M.C.	Words and phrases from "Mount Calvary."
O.M.	Words and phrases from the "Origo Mundi."
P.C.	Words and phrases from the "Passio Christi."
R.D.	Words and phrases from the "Resurrectio Domini."
M.	Words and phrases from the "Beunans Meriasek."
Figures.	The figures point to the number of the line quoted in any of the Cornish Dramas which are indicated by the letters given above.

ABBREVIATIONS.

adj.	Adjective.
adv.	Adverb.
conj.	Conjunction.
i. e.	Id est, that is.
id. qd.	Idem quod, the same as.
imp.	Imperative.
imperf.	Imperfect.
interj.	Interjection.
irr.	Irregular.
Lat.	Latin.
Lit.	Literally.
part.	Participle.
pl.	Plural.
pluperf.	Pluperfect.
poss.	Possessive.
prep.	Preposition.
pret.	Preterite.
pron.	Pronoun.
q. v.	Quod vide, which see.
s.	Substantive.
sing.	Singular.
subj.	Subjunctive.
superl.	Superlative.
v.	Verb.
ê.	The ê not silent.

AN
ENGLISH-CORNISH DICTIONARY.

A or **AN**, *indef. art.* Un, *un pols*, a while, *un map*, a son; *un* is not often used, N. In Cornish manuscripts also written *a* and *y*, P.

ABATE, *v.* Accoÿés, B; bassé. bashé, w.

ABATEMENT, *s.* Alloys, P.

ABBOT, *s.* Abat, w.

ABIDE, *v.* Gortos, wortos, P; revewsé, revesé, B; trega, tregé, triga, trigé. trigia. w.; tregowhé, c.w. 176; trussen, P.

ABJECT, *adj.* Trôt, trôth, B

ABLE, *adj.* Covaithac, cefuidoc, cyvethidog, w.; kyvethidog, galluidoc, gallydhog, B.; galhydock, P.; gallosek, gallosec, galluzack, gallozek, gallogec, galluster, B.; gallas, P.; gew, gyu, B.; gyw, gwyw, w.; yrvyrys, P.

TO BE ABLE, MAY OR CAN, *v.* Gally, w.; galsé, galso, galsy, hÿllÿ, kally, P.; medry, w.; wôs, yrvyry, yl, P.; bôz, talvez. B

I AM ABLE. Ellam, ellim. *Ello why clapier kernuak?* Can you speak Cornish? *Me ellam*, I can, w.

ART THOU ABLE? Allosti? w.

YE ARE ABLE. Gellouch, ellouch, elloh, w.

I HAD BEEN ABLE. Alsen. A mutation of *galsen*, 1 pers. s. plup. of *gally*, to be able, w.

THOU HADST BEEN ABLE. Alsest. A mutation of *galsest*, 2 pers. s. plup. of *gally*, to be able, w.

HE HAD BEEN ABLE. Alsé. A mutation of *galsé*, 3 pers. s. plup. of *gally*, to be able, w.

THEY HAD BEEN ABLE. Alsens. A mutation, of *galsens*, 3 pers. pl. plup. of *gally*, to be able, w.

HE IS ABLE. Or. A late form of *wôr* w.

I MAY BE ABLE. Allan, hallan. Mutations of *gallan*, 1 pers. s. subj. of *gally*, to be able, w.

I MAY BE ABLE. Gyllyff. 1 pers. s. subj. of *gally*, w.

I MAY BE ABLE. Hyllyf. A mutation of *gyllyf*, 1 pers. s. subj. of *gally*, w. Also written *hilliv*.

THOU MAYEST BE ABLE. Hylly. A mutation of *gylly*, 2 pers. s. subj. of *gally*, w.

HE MAY BE ABLE. Allo. A mutation of *gallo*, 3 pers. s. subj. of *gally*, w.

HE MAY BE ABLE. Hallo. A mutation of *gallo*, 3 pers. s subj. of *gally*, w.

WE MAY BE ABLE. Hyllyn. A mutation of *gyllyn*, 1 pers. pl. subj. of *gally*, w.

THEY MAY OR MIGHT BE ABLE. Allons, hallons. Mutations of *gallons*, 3 pers. pl. subj. of *gally*, w.

I MIGHT BE ABLE. Callen. A mutation of *gallen*, 1 pers. s. subj. of *gally*, w.

HE MIGHT BE ABLE. Callé, hallé. Mutations of *gallé*, 3 pers. s. subj. of *gally*, w.

YE MIGHT BE ABLE. Calleuch. A mutation of *galleuch*, 2 pers. s. subj. of *gally*, w.

I SHALL BE ABLE. Callaf, allaf, hallaf. Mutations of *gallaf*, 1 pers. s. fut. of gally, w.

THOU SHALT OR WILT BE ABLE. Yllyth. A mutation of *gyllyth*, 2 pers. s. fut. of *gally*. Also written *cyllyth* and *kyllyth*, w.

HE SHALL OR WILL BE ABLE. Gýll, gýl, and in construction *ýll*, *ýl*, 3 pers. s. fut. of gally. Also written *hýl*, a mutation of *gýl*; and *ill* a mutation of *gill*; other forms are, *alla*, (a mutation of *galla*, 3 pers. s. fut. of *gally*), and *cýll*, *kýll*, *ell*.

WE SHALL BE ABLE. Cyllyn, kyllyn, yllyn. Mutations of *gyllyn*; and cellyn, kellyn, mutations of *gellyn*, 1 pers. pl. fut. of *gally*, to be able, w.

YE SHALL BE ABLE. Hallouch. A mutation of *gallouch*, 2 pers. pl. fut. of *gally*. Also written *yllouch*, a mutation of *gyllouch*, 2 pers. pl. fut. of *gally*, w.

I SHOULD BE ABLE, Halsan. A mutation of *galsan*, 1 pers. s. pulp. of *gally*, w.

HE SHOULD BE ABLE. Cyllé, kyllé. Mutations of gyllé, 3 pers. s. subj. of *gally*, w.

I WAS ABLE. Gellys, ellys. Also yllyn, a mutation of *gyllyn*, 1 pers. s. impcrf. of *gally*, w.

HE WAS ABLE. Allas. A mutation of *gallas*, 3 pers. s. preter. of *gally*, w. Hylly, ylly, mutations of gylly, 3 pers. s. imperf. of *gally*. Also written, gellé and ellé, w.

WE WERE ABLE. Gelsin, elsin. Also ylsyn, a mutation of *gylsyn*, 1 pers. pl. preter. of *gally*, w.

YE WERE ABLE. Gelsich, elsich, elsih, w.

THEY WERE ABLE. Yllens. A mutation of *gyllens*, 3 pers. pl. imperf. of *galty*, w.

ABOUNDING. *aaj.* Lên, leana, leun, luen, w. *Mab Marea leun a rás*, the son of Mary (full of) or, abounding in grace. M.C. 9.

ABOUT. Cerchen, kerchen, kerchyn, cerhyn, kerhyn, gerchen, w. *Awos gwyské an queth a fue yn kerchyn Ihesu*, because of wearing the cloth that was about Jesus. R.D. 1937; ter, *Ter i hodna*, about her neck. *Lhuyd*, p. 249, Adrô, a dhe drô, a dre drô, w.; adres. P.; tro, dro, w.

ABOVE. Avan, a van, a vadna, aban, yn ban ; awartha, wartha, auch, w.; augh, haugh, hagh, juh, yew, P.; iuh, w.; yuh, P.; a uch, uch, uchel, huch, huhel, huhon, uchon, uchan, yûs, ûs, w.; uge, B.; uhal, hual, chual, hychol, a hugh, P.; ahueh, w.; auyche, auoz, uban, âr, hâr, P.

ABOVE ANYTHING. Auoz travyth. P.

ABOVE ME. *pron, prep.* Aughaf, P.; uchaf (uch-mi), yuhaf, w.

FROM ABOVE. Reworro, P.

ABROAD. A mês, yn mês, emês, a vês, avês, w.; emêz, P.; emeas. evez, B.; amês, avês, adrês, alês, w.; alêz, P.; alees; *Gans tha lagusowe alees*, with thy eyes abroad, c.w. 694.

ABROAD. (Out, outside.) Dyveas. *Dho towla uyveas*, to throw out. *Lhuyd*, p. 51.

ABROAD. (Spread abroad.) Unlês, (un-lês), P.

ABROAD. (Wide open.) Leas, lees, leys, lês, P.

ABSCESS, *s.* (*An alveolar abscess.*) Fellen, fellon, vellon, D.

ABSOLUTELY, *adv.* Porrys. *Ytho why a vyn porrys*, then you wish absolutely, P.C. 2359.

ABSORB, *v.* Dena, dené, deny, tené, tena; lency, lenky, dadlyncy, w.

ABSURD, *adj.* Gocy, goky, gokky, gucky. In construction *woky*, w.

ABSURDITY, *s.* Gocyneth, gokyneth, w.

ABUNDANCE, *s.* Gulloar, B.; leasder, liastre, P.; liasder, w.; lower, c.w., 363; peth, B.

ABUNDANT, *adj.* Caugant, crêf, crif, B.; luen, leun, w.

ABUNDANTLY. *adv.* Laur, P.; Mêr amês, B.

VERY ABUNDANTLY. *Púr vear*, w.

ABUSE, *s.* Belyny, velyny, vylyny, w.; hûs, P.

ABUSE. *v.* Provycha, P.

ABYSS, *s.* Lûr. *Gynen may teffo the'n lûr*, to come with us to the abyss, R.D. 2330.

ACCEPT, *v.* Cemerés, chymerés, hemerés, hymerés, kemerés, w.; kymeraz, P.; gemerés, w.

ACCEPTABLE, *adj.* Lués, luhés, w.

ACCIDENT, *s.* Lam, w.

ACCOMPLISH, *v.* Dewedhy, dewedhé, dhewedhé, dewethé, diwedhé, dywedhé, w.; dho diuadha, P.

ACCOMPLISHMENT, *s.* (Fulfilment.) Coweras, w.

ACCORDING TO. Heruyth, herwyth, P.; herweth, N.; *Herwyth y volungeth ef*, according to his will O.M. 1320. *Herwith the grath*, according to thy grace, O.M. 2253; rên, uar, P ; warlergh, N.

ACORN, *s.* Mesen, w.

ACCOUNT, *s.* (Esteem, value.) Bry, brys, w.; brêz, B.; pris, priz, prys, vry, w. *Dén a brys*, a man of account, B.

ACCOUNT, *s.* Ous, ovs, P. *Sur wâr nep ovs*, surely on any account, R.D. 1368.

IN ACCOUNT. Yn whare, B.

ON ACCOUNT OF. Râg, w.; awôs, w.; awoos, c.w. 1133; auôz, P.

ON ANY ACCOUNT. Awôs heghen, PC. 1474.

ACKNOWLEDGE, *v.* Dho gothy, P.

I ACKNOWLEDGE. Whôn. The aspirate mutation of *gón* I know, w.

ACCURATELY, *adv.* Púr eûn, P.

ACCURSED, *adj.* Goef, gweve, P.; mollethec, molethek, w.

ACCURSED! *interj.* Soweth! P. *Soweth an prys*, accursed be the time, w.

ACCURSED, *part.* Emscumunys, w.; emskemmunys, B.; omskemynés, P.; ymscemunys, w.; skemynys, c.w. 212, schumunys, M. 2430 ; mylegés, mylygys, w.; mylygés, mylygé, P.; malegas, melegés, w.; melagas, c.w. 305, vylygés, w.

ACCURSEDLY, *adv.* Yn soweth, B.

ACCUSE, *v.* Achesa, B.; cuhudhé, cuhudhas, cuhudha, cyhydha, w.; kyhydha, B.; gyhydha, w.; guhutha, guhytha, guhuthas, P.; cuhuthé, P.; huhuthas, B.; sclandry, w.

ACCUSATION. *s.* Achos. (Pl. Acheson.) Acheson, ceson, cheson, ceyson, cheyson, keyson, w.

ACCUSER, *s.* Cuhuhudioc, perhaps, more correctly, cuhudhadioc, w.; cuhupudioc, cuhuthudioc, B.

ACCUSTOMED. (To be accustomed.) Yuzia, P.

ACKNOWLEDGE, *v.* Aswonvos. *Aban wreth y aswonvos*, since thou dost acknowledge it, P.C. 1499.

ACQUAINTANCE, *s.* (Friend.) Speal, B.; sôs, D.

ACQUAINTED, *part.* Cowethys. *Gans Christ ythe cowethys*, with Christ he was acquainted, w.

TO BE ACQUAINTED. Pryery, P.

TO BE ACQUAINTED WITH, *v.* Aswon, aswonvos, w.; aswony, aswonyn, P.; godhvos, godhfos. In construction changed into *wodhvos*, w.

I AM ACQUAINTED WITH. Adzhan, azwen. These are late corruptions of *aswon*, to know, w.

ACRE, *s.* Eru, w.; erw, eri, P.

ACROSS. Drûs, drues, adrûs, adrês, drês, dreis, dreys, dris, drys, w.; adrues, N.; a leas, c.w. 2269.

ACT, *s.* (Or motion.) Gwyth, gueid, w.

ACT, *s.* (Or deed.) Prat, pratt, bratt, w.; takel. *Pl.* tacklow. *Tacklow privie*, private actions or things. P. Culeth, knleth, coleth, are only used with *dróc*, evil, as *drócoleth*, an evil deed, w.

ACT, *v.* (To set about a thing.) Gruthyl, w.

ACT, *v.* (As in a play.) Gwaré, gwary, w.; guaré, P.; huaré, B.

ACTION, *s.* Gwŷthrés, wŷthrés, w.; wŷth, P.

ACTIVE, *adj.* Bew, biu, byw, vew; stric, strik, w.

ACTOR, *s.* Bardh, barth, w.

ACUTE, *adj.* Glew, lym, w.

ADDER, *s.* Nader, w; nadar, naddyr, B.

THE CAST SKIN OF AN ADDER. Glenader, D.

ADDER'S-TONGUE, *s.* (The herb.) Tavas nader, w.

ADDRESS, *s.* (Speech.) Progath, pregoth, B.

ADHERE, *v.* Glené, glyné, gleny, w.; glenaz, dho glenys, sesé. P.

ADIT, *s.* (A mine level.) Ty. P. A name still used. The open cutting at the entrance to an adit is called *lost lovan*, D.

ADJURE, *v.* Tiah, tyé, toy, w.

ADJUST, *v.* Ewné, ewnné, w.; euna, B. *A wottense ewnys da*, behold it well adjusted, P.C., 3212.

ADMIRED, *part.* Veras, B. See TO BEHOLD.

ADOLESCENCE, *s.* Yowyncneth. *Lit.* YOUTHFULNESS, *qd. v.*

ADORE, *v.* Coly, P.; gordhy, gordhyê, gordhya, gwerdhya, gurria, w.; guria, gworria, gwerthya, worth, P.; wordhyé, worria, urria, w.; worthé, B.

ADORATION, *s.* Gordhyans, gorryans, w.; guoryans, gurthyans, gorty, P.; wordhyans, w.; worthyans, P.; urria, B.

ADORN, *v.* Kaerat, afyny, P.; *Avell eall wheake afynés*, like a sweet angel adorned, c.w. 537.

ADVANCE, *v.* Avonsyé, *Sol-a-thyth the avonsyé*, for a long time to advance thee, O.M. 2612.

ADVANTAGE, *s.* Gwayn, w.; guayn, B.; prow, lês, w.; leys, M. 3387. *Ne veth ov lés*, it will not be to my advantage. M. 774.

ADVERSE, *adj.* Três, w.; gorth, M. 3394. *Thum du ny vanna boys gorth*, to my God I will not be adverse, M. 3394.

ADVERSARY, *s.* Yskerens, P.C. 737.

ADVICE, *s.* Brys, brês, brêz, w.; brûs, brues, P.; vrys, w.; gydhaz, B.; Cusul, cyssyl, w.; cusyl, P.; cusyll, kyssel, B.; gusul, w.; gusyl, P.; husul, w. See JUDGMENT and OPINION.

ADVISE, *v* Cusulyé, cusyllyé, cossylya, w.; cusullyé, P.C. 567; gusulyé, husulyé, husullyé, w.; gesul, P.; cesulyé, w.; daryvas, dharyvas, P.

HE WILL ADVISE. Gesul. A mutation of *cesul*, 3 pers, sing, fut. of *cesulyé*, w.

AFAR. Peldar, c.w., 1384. *Peldar adro in byes*, afar, round in (the) world, c.w. 1384.

AFAR OFF. Abell, a bel, obel, w.; bel, pel, P.

AFFECTED, MINCING, *adj.* Foo-ty, D.

AFFECTION, *s.* Brena, P.; carenga, w.; carenza, karenza, garenga, P.; cerensé, herensé, w; kêr, keer, carer, kêrd, B.; kefyans, M. 3076, *Rag dendel dyso kefyans*, for gaining to the affection, M. 3076; pythays, M. 918. *Ortheff na wyla pythays*, of me seek not affection, M. 918.

AFFECTIONATE, *adj.* Cescer, w.

VERY AFFECTIONATE, Chefcar, w.

AFFLICT, *v.* Duwanhé, dewhanhé, grevya, w.; greffya, R.D. 502.

TO BE AFFLICTED. Huthy, P.

AFFLICTION, *s.* Cûth, hûth, govid, w.; govis, govys, P.; gossythyans, c.w., 1122.

AFFLICTIONS, *s.* Govidion, govigion, govidzhion, govegion, w.

AFFORD, *v.* Drei, dho drei, B.

AFORESAID, *part.* Râgleverys, w.

AFRESH. Whâth, whêth, huâth, B.

AFTER, or BEHIND. Adhelhar, *Adhethar dyn remanat* behind the remainder, P.

AFTER, AFTERWARDS. Wôs, P.; wose, w.; uoze, P.; udzhe, woge. w.; gwose, w.; guoze, B.; gooze, P.; wage, P.; wege, w.; wosa, M. 22; woza, uoza, P.; odzha, udzha, odgha, gwodzhi, w.; guodzhi, B.; guzdzhi, P.; lyrgh, B.; dogha P. *Sythyn wose hemma*, a week after this, O.M. 1026. *Woge soper*, after supper, P.C. 834; warlerch, warlyrch, w.; warlergh, uarlergh, warlyrgh, P.; uarlyrch, uardhalyrk, B.; warlerth, c.w. 1864; warler, w.; uarler, B. *Sau me warlergh drehevel*, but I risen *after*, P.C. 876; but I risen *afterwards*, P.C. 896.

AFTER THAT. Enmên, B,; gwosé na, udzhena, w.; ylergh, P.

AFTER THEE. War-the-lergh, P.

AFTER THIS. Woge hemma, o.m., 1427.

AFTERWARDS. Odzha henna, w.; odgha uena, udzhehenna, udzehedda, P.; udzhena, guozena, B.; lyrgh, P.; warlergh, N. See AFTER or AFTER-WARDS for other forms.

AFTERNOON, s. Dochageydh, w.; dogha geyth, P.; dehadzhedh, w.; dohadzheth, B.; dyhodzhadh, P.; dyhodzhedh, dyhodzhydh, w.

AGAIN. Arté, w.; arta, c.w. 350. *Ny'm guelyth arté*, thou shalt not see me again, o.m. 244. Wheth, w.; whet, p.c. 1115; what, P.; *wheth ow cufyon dyfunough.* again my wise ones awake, p.c. 1075; nês, w.; neys, m. 3619. *Maria me a weyl neys*, Mary, I see again, m 3619.

AGAINST. Bidn, dyag, tyag, P.; drês, dreis, dreys, dris, drys, enap, enep, erbyn, w.; erybyn, P.; erdhabyn, orthebyn, enuoch, fin, fyn, rego, B.; worth, orth, warbyn, warbidn, w.; uar bidn, P.; warben, B.; adrús, adrues. N. *Kyn whrylly cous adrús*, though thou do speak against it, R.D. 1792. *Erbyn a laha*, against the law, p.c. 572. *Erbyn hâf*, against summer, o.m. 31. *The trôs worth mên*, thy foot against a stone, p.c. 98.

AGAINST HER. Er y fyn, w.

AGAINST HIM. Er y byn, w.

AGAINST THEE. Er dhe byn, w.; erthebyn, m. 2302. *Drehevys sûr erthebyn*, risen surely against thee, m. 2302.

AGAINST THEM. War aga phidn, er aga fyn, w.

AGAINST US. Er agan pyn, w.

AGAINST YOU Er agas pyn, w.; er agas pyn huy, N.

AGAINST SUMMER. Erbyn hâf, N.

AGE, s. Huis, w.; huys, hyeis, wz, B.; uz, uze, oose, oze, oys, og, P.; oydge, oge, w. Same as the Latin *seculum*. Also used as to the duration of life, as *henys* (*hen oys*), old age, m. 167.

AGE, or GENERATION, s. Hoedel, henath, B.

AGITATION, s. (Excitement.) Por, pore, poar, kilter, quilter, D.

AGONY, s. Pyn, peyn, poan, poen, w.

AGGRAVATION, s. Velyny, P. See ABUSE.

AGREE. r. (To suit with.) Blegedow. *Bosdy gewsys ny blegedow*, but the speeches did not agree, P.

AGREED. (Of one mind.) Unver, w.

AGREED. (Or bargained for.) Bargidnias, P.

AGREEABLE, *adj.* Plegadow, plygadow, w. *A wren re bo plygadow;* which we do, be it agreeable, o.m. 1008; blek, P.; kyvadhas, B.; têg, têc, têk w.; teck, teage, thêk, P.

AGREEMENT, s. Agreanz, P.; olegaddow, B.; ce-senyans, w.; kesenyanz, P.; gorholeth, w.

AGGRIEVE, *v.* Dygnas, w.

AGUE, s. Lêauch, w.; lêauh, P.

AH! *interj.* A, *a dâs*, ah! father; *a venen*, ah! woman, w.; ha! P.

AHA! *interj.* Ow, w.; used to call attention.

AH UNHAPPY! *interj.* A soweth, w.; a syweth, a syeudh, P.; a siueth, B.

AID, s. Fors, gweras, gwerés, werés, w.; uerraz, P.

AILMENT, s. Whêr, w.; whear, wêr, P.

AIR, s. Ayr, yer, w.; awyr, aruit, B.

ALAS! *interj.* Ellaz, B.; ellas, m. 363; aylace, c.w. 1118; ethlays, c.w. 1040; oge, P.; trew, tru, w.; sioas, B.

ALAS, WOE IS ME! *interj.* Sowêth, w.; syweth, syuedh, P.; siueth, B.

ALAS, SAD! *interj.* Govy, gony, gwae, P.

ALAS, WOE, OH! *interj.* Eychan, eyhan, w.

ALBEIT. Syl, w.; lyn, P.

ALCOVE. (?). A raised alcove for a bed is called a *talafa:.* D.

ALDER, s. (Tree.) Gwern, guern, wern, w.; warne, P.; gwernen, guernen, wernen, warnen, w.; guernan, P. *A place of alders.* Gwern, B.

ALE, s. Côr, w.; kôr, B.; coref, coruf, w.; koruv, B.; corff, m. 661.

ALEHOUSE, s. Tshyi tavargn, P.

ALIKE, *adv.* Awedh, auedh, aweeth, awyetha, P.; cepar, kepar, w.; kekyffrys, B.; avel, havel, w.; haval, havan, P.; kevelep, P.; hevelep, hyvelep, w.

ALIKE, *adj.* Mal, val, w.

ALIVE, *adj.* Bew, w.; beu, yn beu, P.; biu, byw, vew, w.; veu, yn vêu, in vêu, P.; few, w.

ALIVE, TO BE ALIVE, *v.* Bewé, pewé, w.

ALL, s. Myns, w. *Myns a vinno*, all that he will, N., mêns, w.; ôl, *Hag ól*, and all, N.; oll, hol. Pup, pub, pyb, peb, bub, bup, w.; pop, pob, P.; pup ol, N. *Pup dén ol*, all men. N.

ALLOW, *r.* Gesy, gyssy, gosheny, preva, dho prêf, P.

ALLY, s. Câr, w.; kâr, B.

ALMIGHTY, *adj.* Cefuidoc, w.; chefitodoc, P.; chefindoc, B.; olgallusec, olgalluster, w.; goilousacke, c.w. 13.

ALL ABROAD, ALL TO PIECES. Dewscol, dewscoll, w.; dowstoll. (*Stokes.*); ayle, P.

ALL BUT. Namna (before consonants), namnag (before vowels), w.

ALL DAY. Têtholl, B. A form of *dêdh*, day, and *oll*, all.

ALL-HEAL, s. Guthyl; kefyl (p. 307), B.

ALL OF US, s. Pup huny, huny, P.

ALL SAINTS' DAY. Dew halan gwâv, deu halan guav, w. *Lit.* The calends of winter.

ALL THAT. Ol hedda, P.

ALL TIMES. Pubtermin, B. For other forms see TIME.

ALEXANDERS, *s.* (Name of a plant.) Skit. D. The Alsanders, or *Smyrnium olusatrum.* A doubtful *Cornish* word.

ALLIANCE, *s.* Nès, M. 2590. *Na russen nês,* nor should I make alliance, M. 2590.

ALLOW, *v.* Gasé. *Part.* Gesys, w.

ALLOW YE. Gerro, a late corruption of *gesouch,* w.

ALLUREMENT or BAIT, *s.* Peecher, W.F.P.

ALMOST. Namna, N. *Namna'n dallus,* almost blinded us, R.D. 42; namnag. *Namnag yv ow colon trogh,* almost is my heart broken, P.C. 3185.

ALMS, *s.* Alusyon, M. 536 *Regh dym agis alusyon,* give me your alms, M. 536; alesonov, M. 1829.

ALONE, *adj.* Sol, P.; unsel, unsol; ednac, w.

ALONG. Aber, P.; a ber, P.; a hys, a heys, N. *Groweth a heys,* lie along, O.M. 1134.

ALOOF. A bel, obel, w.

ALPS, the ALPS, *s.* Mynneu, B. See *Lhuyd.*

ALREADY. Esos, w.; esoz, B.; esou, P.; eredy, yredy, B.

ALSO. Awedh, w.; enuedh, B.; enwedh, inwedh, w.; in weth, P.; ynwedh. w.; ynweth, B.; yn weth, P.; yn weyth, N.; yn wys, P.C. 2432. Weth, wethe, P.; weydh, weyth, w.; queth, quct, P.; yc, yk, w.; euth, ruth, B.; ceceffrys, w; kekeffrys, B.; cefrys, cyffrys, cyfrevs, keffryz, keheffrys, kevery, keverys, P.; magata, B. *Ha ty wethe,* and thou also, P. *Hag inweth gvra the'th worty,* and also make to thy husband, O.M. 199.

ALTAR, *s.* Alter, altor, w.

ALTAR-PLATE, or PATTEN, *s.* Engurbor. w.

ALTHOUGH. Adal, cen, ken, cyn, kyn, w.; keen, P.; gen, ce, w.; key. P.; lyn, mar, P.; pe, B.; syl, w.; drefen, drevan, drefan, drethan, P.

ALTHOUGH, IF. Cra, cueia, w; kueia, B.

ALTHOUGH HE IS. Centhew, kenthew, w.

ALTHOUGH THOU ART. Kynthota. c.w. 2306.

ALTOGETHER. Prechyons, preshyons, w.; precins, O.M. 918. *Precins haval thy'm certen,* altogether like myself certainly, O.M. 918. Warbarth, warbarh, B.; *Ython warbarth myshevyys,* we are altogether destroyed, O.M. 1704; ha heys, P.; haheyz, B.; yn tyan, M. 171; yn tean, c.w. 1078.

ALWAYS. Bys, byth, vyth, bynytha, vynytha, bythqueth, vythqueth, byner, vyner, w.; vynerre, O.M. 2196; bepprês, w.; bepprêz, P.; bypprys, buprys, w.; pupprys, B.; pyprys, w.; pub pryes, pup preis,

c.w. 44; 911.; pup preys, P.; pub preyse, pub eare, c.w. 21, 228; kympez, gympes, gymps, P.; prest, stella, jammes, w.; jammas, г.

AM, *v.* Tho, etho, B.

I AM. Assoma, esôf. a reduplicate, form of *ôf,* as also ezhôf, w.; adzhaf, adzhav, w.; bosâf, bosef, bonés, dhera, thera, thyra, thesaf, P.; thom. *Thom kimerez,* I am taken, B.; etho ve, B; ithoff, M. 2513; serf, P. *Mur serf ef bad y vester,* if I am he, a bad master, P.; veyf, vyf, vev, P.; ôf, ôv, ovv, w.; uav, P.; oma, osav, ossav, ossam, w.; pethaf, P.; ÿ'm, O.M. 1; me yv, M. 2682. *Me yv yurle in venetens,* I am Earl in Vannes, M. 2682; me ewe, c.w. 124; me yw, w.; ydzhiz, B.; ydhema, a reduplicate form of *oma* an enlarged form of *ôf* 1 pers. s. pres. of *bós.* to be; ydhama, also a reduplicate form of *oma,* w.; ydhof, w.; ythôf, ythove, c.w. 1436, 1574; ydhesaf, w.; ythesaf, c.w. 1667; yethesaf, c.w. 1696. The last six are reduplicate forms of *ôf,* 1 pers. s. pres. of the irr. verb *bós,* to be. Also these variations viz., assof, yssof, sof, thof, N.

I AM NOT. Nagoff, B.; ny vethaf, c.w. 1517.

AMAZE, *v.* Stumuny (?) *To be amazed.* Omstumunys, P.

AMAZED, *adj.* Muscoe, museok, muskegvi, mustok, P.; mescat, w; meskat, B.

AMEN. (So be it.) Andella re bo, andellna rebo, yn della re bo, andel na ra bo, andellarbo, P.

AMEND, *v.* Euna, owna, w.; ouna, P.; gwella, guella, B.

AMENDING, POORLY. Palch, w.; palchy, D. This word is still used in Cornwall for one who is in weak health. "He is very palchy," "he is only palched up," i. e. badly restored to health, are common phrases.

AMERCEMENT. *s.* Spâl, B. In the Cornish dialect " to be spaled," means " to be fined " for loss of time in mine work, &c.

AMERICA, *s.* Lollas, B.

AMIABLE, *adj.* Hegar, w.

AMONG, AMONGST. Emêsc, w.; yn mêsc, w.; yn mesk. yn mysk, P.; yn myske, c.w. 539; mesk, B.; mysk, M. 8; yntre, P.; ynter, w.; trelhow, P.

AMONG THEM. Trens, B.; trethé, B; yntredhé, w.; yntrethé, N. *Yntrethé gasaf ow ras,* among them I leave my grace, R.D. 1584.

AMONG US. Yntredhon, w.

AMONG YE. Yntredhouch, ynterdhoch, w.; yntrethow, B.

AMPLE, *adj.* Ledan, w. *Bras ha ledan,* great and ample, O.M. 2261.

AMULET or CHARM, *s.* Soon, D. From *sona,* to charm.

AMUSE, *v.* Dydhané, dhydhané, w. ; thythané, o.m. 152. *A russe the thythané*, it would amuse thee, o.m. 152.

AN, *indef, art.* See A or AN.

ANCESTOR, *s.* Rhagdas, w. ; rhagadaz, p. ; wâd, o.m. ; hendas, hengyke, p. *Pl.* rhagdazu, ragdazu, henlasou, p. ; wadow, o.m. 1624.

ANCHOR, *s.* Ancar, angor, b. *A stone anchor*, (a stone used as an anchor,) killeck, d. *A frame for the stone anchor.* Ludas, b.v.

ANCHORITE, *s.* Ancar, w.

ANCIENT, *adj* Côth, gôth, coyth, w. ; kôth, cooth, p. ; côz, b ; hén, w. ; hean, hane, p. ; henn, b. ; henwys, hennawys, p.

AND. A, ha, w. ; haw, c w. 707 ; hawe, p. These forms are used before a word beginning with a consonant ; as, *máp ha tás*, son and father, p.c. 297 ; gu, p. ; ag, hâg, w. ; hage, hach, p. These forms are used before a word beginning with a vowel, as, *hág yn tyr*, and in the earth, o m. 27. The common forms are *ha* and *hag*. *Ha* is used with *kepar* (like, as), thus *kepar ha dew*, like a god, and is commonly joined to other words as *han*, i e. *hán*, or *ha an* ; other examples are given below.

AND ALSO. Hagen zôl, p.

AND ME. Hammy (ha-my), w.

AND MY. Haw (*ha'w* i.e. ha-ow), w. Also written *how*, i.e. how, ha-ow, w.

AND OUR. Hain, w.

AND OF IT. Hay, i.e. *ha'y*, ha-hy, b.

AND THAT. Hai, p. ; hay, b.

AND THE. Ha'n (ha-an), b.

AND THIS. Hath, p., ha'th (ha-ath).

AND THY. Hâth, ha'th (ha-ath) ; hâd. w.

ANEW. Whath, wheth, hueth, w.

ANGEL, *s.* El, eal, w. ; eall, eale, c.w. 43, 134 ; eyl, w. ; ail, b.

ANGEL'S, *s.* Eleth, m. 215 ; elâth, elâthe, c.w., 27, 140 ; eledh, p.

ANGELICA, *s.* (The herb). Coiclinhat, w. ; coiclinat, p. ; coillinhat, b.

ANGER, *s.* Fôr, p. (? sor) ; frôth, gewar, sôr, sorras, w. ; guith, b *Na theqovgh sor yn colon*, do not bear anger in heart, p.c. 539.

ANGER, *v.* Serry, sorry, w.

ANGERED. Serrys, w

ANGLE, OR ELBOW, *s.* Elin, elyn, w. ; kornat, p.

ANGRY, *adj.* Serry, p. sorras, b.

VERY ANGRY. *Resorras*, b., litiauc, b. *Ov arluth pan wruk serry*, when I made my lord angry, o.m., 352.

ANGRY, *v.* TO BECOME ANGRY, TO BE ANGRY, Perthegés, serry, sorry, w. ; sorren, p.

ANGUISH. *s.* Angos, p. ; angus, w. ; ankinsy, p. ; câs, gâs, w. ; *Hep joy prest maysteffo câs*, without joy always, that anguish came to them, r.d., 160 ; cên, kên, chên, galar, gelar (?), gloys, glôs, w. ; glous, p. ; peyn, pyn, poan, poen, w.

ANIMAL, *s.* Mil, bêst, eneval, w. ; gurtfill, p. ; gurthvil, ourthvil, b. *A she beast.* Enevalés, w. *A very small animal, or worm.* Prîf, prêf, prev, pryf, w.

VERY SMALL ANIMALS. Pryvés, w.

ANIMOSITY, *s.* Mican, mikan, w.

ANKLE-BONE, *s.* Lifern, livern, ufern, w

ANNOY, *v.* Coddros, koddros, goddros, w.

ANOINT, *v.* Uré, huré, iré, w. ; ira, p. ; untyé w. ; yontyé, b. ; ylyé, w.

ANOINTED, *part.* Untye, b. ; vngijs, m. 4282 ; *Ungijs gans henna defry*, anointed therewith certainly, m. 4282.

ANON. Wharé, p. ; wharee, m. 1431. *Omma wharee*, here anon, m. 1431.

ANOTHER, *adj.* Arall, w. ; aral, eral, p. ; areyl, m. 414 ; beyn, byn, p. ; eil, eyl, neyl, yll, w. ; gele, gyle, p ; ken, r d., 346. *Ha gyllys the ken tyreth*, and gone to another country, r.d., 346.

ANSWER, *s.* Gorib, gorryb, gortheb, wortheb, gorthyp, worthyp, w. ; gorthib, c.w. 1754. *Me a re scón gorthyp thy's*, I will soon give an answer to thee, p.c. 512 ; wother, p.

ANSWER, *v.* Gortheby, wortheby, gorthyby, worthyby, goriby, gorriby, gweriby, w. ; gorthybi, gorthebi, awother, p.

ANSWERED, *part.* Awothebys, b.

ANSWERING, Owav. *Answer ye*, Gorrybowhe. p.

HE ANSWERED. Wothebys, worthybys. Mutations of *gorthebys*, and *gorthybys*, 3 pers. s. preter, of *gortheby*, and *gorthyby*, w.

THOU SHALT ANSWER. Worthebyth A Mutation of *gorthebyth* 2 pers, s. fut. of *gortheby*, w.

HE WILL ANSWER. Worthyp. A mutation of *gorthyp*, 3 pers. s. fut of *gorthyby*, w.

ANT, *s.* Meuwionén, meuionên, mevionên, murianean, b. menwionen (?) ; murrianên, w. ; *pl.* Murriân, w.

ANT-HILL, *s.* Crig murrian, w.

ANTIQUE, *adj.* See ANCIENT.

ANVIL, *s.* Anuan, anwan, w. ; anvan, b.

ANXIETY, *s.* Dûr, duer, dour, der, fyenas. *Pl.* Fyenasow, w. *Mûr yv ow fyenesow*, great are my anxieties, p.d. 17. ; preder, pryder, w. ; pridar, p.

ANXIOUS, *adj.* Predar, c.w. 1193.

ANY. Nep, b. *Yn nep pow*, in any country, b. ; byth, vyth, vyt, p. ; vith, b. ; veth, fyth, p. *Dên byth oll*, any man whatever. Dên vyth, (or *fyth*), any man, p. ; neb, w.

ANY AT ALL. Bythwell.

ANYONE. Nebyn, vethol, vethyl, vythyl, P.

ANYTHING, s. Gonon, P.; néppeth, nép-peyth, travyth, (tra-byth), trevyth, tryveth, w.; tryvyth, tramyn, P.

ANYWAY. Cammen vyth.

ANYWHERE. Pylek, P.c. 681.

ANY WORD. Gêr vyth, P.

APOLOGIZING. Ov teharas, M. 3344. *Bys may fons ov teharas*, till they be apologizing, M. 3344.

APPAREL, s. Dillas, w.; dillaz, dyllas, dhyllas, (thillas), delles, M. 1674; dillad, dillat, dilladas, dilladzas, dilladzhaz, P.; gweth, kueth, B.

APE, s. Sim, B.

APPEARANCE, s. Goloc, golok, woloc, semlant, w.

APPELLATION, s. Hanow, anow, w.

APPETITE, s. Dsvotter, whans, w.; whanz; P.; dwans, w.

APPLE, s. Aval, w.; avall, c.w. 706; avell, B. *A double-shaped apple*, loder, D.

APPLES, s. Avalow, w.; avalou. P.; avallow, c.w. 831; lavalow, w.; lavalou, B. *Avalow*, is the plural for all kinds of fruits, w.

APPLE-CAKE, s. (The pressed mass in the cider press), mock, D.

APPLE-TREE, s. Avallen, gwedhan lavolcw, gwedhan avalow, w.; guedhan lavalu, P.

APPLE OF THE EYE (The pupil). Biu an lagat, P.; biu en lagat, B.

APPOINT, v. Ordené, ordeyné, ordyné, ordné, w.; ordnés, ordnys, ordnen, P.; gorthrodhy, w.

APOSTLE, s. Apostel, abostel, w.; abestel, P. (*Pl.* Abestely, abesteledh, P.; abesteleth, w). Cannas; *pl.* cannasow, w., canasow, B.

APOSTLES' CREED, s. Credgyans an abesteleth. See BELIEF, or CREED.

APRIL, s. Ebral *Mis Ebral*, the month of April. Miz Ebrall, i.e. the primrose month, "when the Gauls and Normans set out to go to sea for catching mackerel." P

APPROACH, v. Nessé, P.; dôz ogoz, P.

APRON, s. Apparn, lavrok-pan; goul and guns. *Lit.* a veil for a *vagina*, P. In the Cornish dialect, a coarse apron is called a *towser*; and a fisherman's leather apron, *barwell, barvil*, from *barvas*, a codfish.

APPREHEND, v. Sensy, sensye, w.; sinsy, P.; synsy, w.; sensa, sansa, syngy, dho sendzhé, P.; sendzha, w.; sindzha, P.

APPREHEND, v. (Seize on). Askemery, dicemmer, P.

APT, adj. Gwyw, w.; habal, able, P.

ARABIA, s. Araby. *Yn Araby*, in Arabia, o.m. 1930.

ARATOR, s. Araderuur, w. See PLOUGHMAN.

ARE, v. Ow, ou, ov, idzhaw, yr. *Ov ry*, are giving, P.

ARE YOU? Erouh? Era why? P.

THEY ARE. Asens, ens, gens. *Na gens*, (properly *nag ens*) they are not; mons, used with plural nouns, as *ma* is with singular nouns; yns, w. Yns, monz, P.; mowns, w.; ynz, B.; ymons, y mons, used with nouns plural as *yma* is with nouns singular, w.; ytowns, ydhyns, ydzhens, w.

WE ARE. On, ony, oni (ôn-ni) assôn, esôn, idzhin; ydhon, a reduplicate form of *ôn*, 1 pers. pl. of *bos*, to be, w.

YE ARE. Ough, N.; ouch, och, oh, o, aso; asouch, esouch, ysouch, ydhouch, w.; yzouch, B. These last five words are reduplicate forms of *ouch*, 2 pers. pl. pres. of *bós*, to be. Odzhi, w.; a late corruption of *ysouch*.

ART, v. Os, P. Properly, thou art.

ART THOU? Ose, otese, B.

THOU ART NOT. Ny pûs, P.

IF THOU ART. Marsew, c.w. 1650; mar sôs, mar sosa, mar sose, mar a sose, mar soge, w.; mar sota, P.

THOU ART OR WERT. Festa, fasté, P.

THOU ART. Bosta, ôs, w.; ôz, P.; osy, ose, oge, osa, sôs, w.; sota, B.; ota, oté, assós, ossôge, w.; ôzhôz, P.; assosa, assota, ettogé, esós, yssos, ydhos, w.; ydhoz, B; ydhose, w; ythose, P.; ythoes, c.w. 2303; ythoge, P.; ydhosta, w.; y vosta, c.w. 2295. Several of the above forms of Cornish for "thou art" are reduplicates of *ós, óse*, or *ósta* (*ós-te*). 2 pers. s. pres. of the irr; verb *bós*, to be.

ARCH. s. Guarrak. B.

ARCHANGEL. s. Archail, ẇ.

ARCHANGEL, s. (The herb). Coichlinhat, coiclinat, P.

ARCHBISHOP, s. Arch-escop, arch-ispak, P.

ARCHER, s. Saithor, sethar, zethar, w.

ARCHITECT, s. Bysterdên, vysterdên, mysterdên, w.; peidwurty, peidwura, B.

ARGUMENT, s. Bresel, bresell, bresul, w.; bressell, P.; vresyl, w.; scyle, P.

ARIGHT. Poran. *Te aseathe poran*, thou shalt sit here aright, c.w., 54.

ARISE, v. Dasserchy, tasserchy, dasserhy, tasserhy, w.; erigea, B.; sordya, *Sordyas bressel*, arose a contest, P.

ARK, s. Gurchel gurhal, gorhel, w.; gorhall, P.; gorhyl, o.m. 1074; gorthell, c.w. 2255; worhel, w.; *Lemyn noy y'th worhel ke*. Now Noah go into thy ark. o.m. 1017

ARM, s. (Weapon) Arv. *Pl.* Arvow. P.

ARM, *s.* Brêch, brêh, vrêch, vɪêh, w. ; brêgh. vrêgh, p. (In the o.m. 262, for the *pl.* Bregh) ; anchel, B.

ARMS *s.* (The two arms). Dewvrêch, dywvrêch, dibrêh, defrêch, dhefrêch, dheffrêch, w.; dywvregh, N.; thefrêgh, B.; thyw-vrêg, P c 1179. *Kelmeugh warbarth y thywvrêg*, bind his (two) arms together, P.C. 1179.

ARMS, *s.* (Of the body). Sely, B.

HIS ARMS. *Ysely.* B.

ARM OF THE SEA, *s.* Trôt, p.

ARMED. Arveth, ervys. P.; ervyz, yrvyz, B.; yɪvys, w. *Tûs ervys*, armed men.

ARMORIC, *adj.* Brezzonnek, Lezow, B.

ARMOUR, *s.* Mael. B.

ARMPIT, *s.* Ascal, casal, cazal, cesal, w. ; kazal, p.; gazel, M. 1419. *Lemmyn a'n caffen er an ascal*, now I would take him by the armpit, R.D. 289. 290. *Dôkhy indan the gazel*, carry it under thy armpit, M. 1419.

ARM-WRIST, *s.* Codna brêh, kodna brêh, P.; cona brêch, w.; conna brêgh, P.O. 2762. *Lit :* The neck of the arm.

ARMY, *s.* Lu, luu, llu, ly, lhy, ôst, w.

AROUND Adro, adrês, adrê, N. *In pow adro*, in the countɪy round, o.m. 189. *A'n beys ôl adrv*, of the world all round, o.m. 404. A dhe dro, a dre drô, N. Ter. w. *Ter. i hodna*, around her neck. Lhuyd, p. 249.

AROUND. (THEE). Kerhyn. *Yth kerhyn*, around thee. M. 3003.

ARRAS, *s.* (Cloth of) Kyulat. p.

ARRAY, *s.* Atheray, P.

ARRAYED. Taklays, M. 3004. *Genen te a veth taklaÿs*, by us shalt thou be arrayed, M. 3004.

ARRIVE, *v* Dôs, donês, w.

ARRIVED, *part.* Devedys, dyvythys. w.

ARROGANCE, *s.* Terros, P.C. 43. *Penys a reys râgh y terros*, penance is necessary, that his arrogance, P.C. 43.

ARROW, *s.* Sêth, w.; zêth, zeath, B. ; zeah, P.; sêgh, c.w , 1573; sethan, zethan, w. , harau, P. *Pl.* Sethaw, c.w. 1491.

ART, *s.* Crêft, w.; krêft, B.; scient, sceans, skeans. skeÿcns, scians, skyans, skyens, skeÿens, w.

ARTEMISIA, *s.* (The herb) Lodés, B.

ARTICLE, *s.* (Or thing). Pêth, peyth, pɪth, w. *Pl.* Pethow, things ; also meaning riches, wealth, w.

ARTIFICER, *s.* Creftor, w. ; ceard, keard, B. ; sair, w.

ARTIFICE, *s.* Coyntis, goyntis, w.

ARTISAN, *s.* Sair, w. See ARTIFICER.

AS. Avêl, w.; avele, c.w. 137. *Avêl gôs*, like blood, R.D. 2500 ; *Maga whyn (guyn) avêl an têth.* as white

as the milk, P.C. 3138, *Maga vrâs ove avele dew*, as great am I as God., c.w. 137. vel, mel, mal, w. ; mar, mor, P ; maga, P.C. 3138 ; cetel, kettel, kettyl, w.; ketwel, P.; kettoth, B.; cepar, kepar, w. ; pekar, P.; pecâr, pocâr, w. ; pycar, pykar, B.; pocara, w.; pokara, P.; yn N. *Yn felon*, as a felon, N.

AS, LIKE AS, THAN, SO. Del, w.; par del, M. ɟl76 *Maga têk bythqueth del fue*, as fair as ever he was. R.D. 1659.

AS, ACCORDING TO. Rên, P.

AS. Cy, ky, car, cara, caman, camen, cammen, tra, tre, dre, tro, trɪy, maga, magata, mâl, mân, (ma-yn) w.

AS FAR AS. Trebé, trybo, w. ; trehé, terebah, P. ; bet, bes, bys, w. dha'n, B.

AS IF. Cara, kara, B. ; pocar, pokar, B.

AS IF NOT. Kyné, kynna, p.

AS IS. Pare dell, c.w. 43. *Pare dell ywe owe bothe nefra*, as is my will ever, c.w. 43.

AS IT WERE. Haval, havel, P.

AS LONG AS. Byzpan, P.; cêth, kêth, w,; entermen, P.; hedré, w. ; heddré, B. *Hedré veyn beu*, as long as I am living, P.c 115.; spâs, B.; tro, tra, trɪy, w.

AS MANY. Myns, B.

AS MANY AS. Cenefra, ceniver, keniver, cenifer, cenyver, kenyver, kynyver, cenever, cyniver, w. kyniver, N.; kenifer, hynifer, P.; pezealla, B; cecemmys, kemmys, w.

AS MUCH. Maga, w.; vrer, P, a doubtful word.

AS MUCH AS. Cecemmys, w.

AS OFTEN AS. Pesgwyth. w. Pesguythe, as *soon* as P.

AS SOON AS. Cetel, kettel, kettyl, cettoth, w. ; ketoth, kettoth, kettuth. kettost, ketwel, P.; mar scôn, B.; mar skan, pesguythe, P.

AS WELL. Ceceffrys. P.; kekeffrys, B.; cefrys, cyffrys, cyfreys, keffryz, kevery, keverys, magata, P.; magé ta. o.m. 972. *Lath ny gansé ta*, kill us with them as well, o M. 972.

ASCEND *v.* Uchellé, uchellas, ychellas, euhelle, yuhellas, w. ; yuhellaz, P. ; ascen, ascenna, w. yskvn, yskynna, P.; yscynné, escynya, w.; eskynna, P.

ASCENT, *s.* Als. w.

ASHAMED. To be ashamed. Mêdha, w. ; dho methé, P.

ASHAMED, *part.* Cudhygic, cudhygik, w. cuthygyk, R.D. 1521. *Ty a yl bôs cuthygyk*, thou mayest be ashamed. R.D. 1521.

ASH-COLOURED. *adj.* Glâs, w.; glase, glaze, P. ; glayis, lays, B.

ASH, *v.* (*Tree*). On. A name in general.

A SINGLE ASH TREE. Onnen, enwedhan. w.; enued-han, P.; enwyth, B., but this is a plural. *Pl.* En-with, enwyd, P.

ASHES, *s.* (From combustion). Losow, w.; lozou, P.

ASK, *v.* Govyn govynny, wovyn, wovynny, gofen, w.; wouyny, P.; gophon, B.; gefen, goffen, gofyn, goven, gophidn, P.; gelwel, gylwel, celwel, w.; gulwel, dymandia. P.

I SHALL ASK. Covynnaf, cofynnaf. Mutations after *mara* of govynnaf. w.

HE SHALL ASK, or COMMAND. Erch. w.

ASK, ENQUIRE. Cott govena. P.

ASKED. Govynnas, govyn, P.

ASKING, *s.* (An asking). Govynnad, w.

ASK FOR, *v.* Cria, creia, greia, dho greia râg, w.; greiah, P.

ASK or LOOK FOR, *v.* Huila, B.

ASK or INSIST, *v.* Archa, w. See COMMAND, *v.*

I ASKED FOR Yrhys; a softened form of *yrchys,* 1 pers. preter. of *archa.* Also used for the 3 pers. w

HE ASKED FOR. Yrchy. 3 pers. s. imperf. of *archa,* w.

ASPECT *s.* Miras, w.; miraz, P.; goloc, golok, woloc, tremyn, w.

ASPEN, *s.* (Tree). Bedewen, bezo, bedho, w.

ASS, *s.* Asen, w.; asan, c.w. 406 ; azen, onager, w.; moguz. mogust, D.

A HE-ASS, Rounten, D.

A WILD ASS, Asen guill, w.; asenguil, B.

AN ASS COLT, Asenza, B.

ASSAULT, *v.* Tria, B.

ASSEMBLY, *s.* Cetva. w.; chetva, ketva, P.; chetua, w. But these words seem to mean the *place* of assembly. Bagat, cuntellet, cuntully, P.; sened, senedh, B.

ASSERTER. *s.* Dadloyar, dadloyer, dathluur, P.

ASSIST, *v.* Gwerés. werés, w.; guerés, P.; amwyn. B.

ASSISTANCE, *s.* Gwerés, gwerés, w.; gwerras, gweret, P.; werés, w.; uerraz, P.

ASSISTANT, *s.* Aber, w.

ASSOCIATE, *v.* Gustlé, w.

ASSUAGE, *v.* Accoyés, B.; dho aizia, P.; difydhy, defydhy, dufydhy, difythé, P.; lyha, o.m. 1772. *Ha sur y lyha the grêf,* and he will surely assuage thy pain, o.m. 1772.

ASSURED. Yskerens, P.

ASSUREDLY. En dhiougel, en dhiûgel, w.; diogel, diougel, P.

ASTHMA, *s.* Beranal, w. Pôs, D.

ASTONISHED. Omstumunys, P. *Astonished him.* Om-stumunys, B.

ASTONISHMENT, *s.* Thir, P.

AT. Worth, orth, ord, w.; bez, tâm, P.; yn, N. *Yn pup termyn,* at all times, R.D. 1040.

AT ALL. Byth, vyth, bêth, vêth, w.; this, B.

AT ALL ADVENTURE. Dro. P.

AT FIRST. Wostalleth, N. *Wostalleth na wosteweth,* at first not at last, o.m. 2762. (Not found elsewhere.)

AT HAND. Ogas. M. 2643. *Mar sus drók sperys ogas,* if there be an evil spirit at hand, M. 2643.

AT LAST. Teua, a deweth, B.; woleweth, wosteweth, P. *Wostalleth na wosteweth,* at first not at last. o.m. 2762.

AT LEAST. Euliock, dhanleiah, B.; dan leiah, en leiah, P.

AT LENGTH. Breman.

AT PRESENT. Luman, lebmyn. For other forms of these words see NOW, (luman).

ATEST. (Thou atest). Attebrés. w. See EAT *v.*

ATHLETE, *s.* Kan-pûr.

A FEMALE ATHLETE. Kan-wûr, B.

ATHWART. Drûs, drues, adrûs, w.; adrues, N., *Adrûs musury,* measure athwart, o.m 393 ; wâr gam; P.C. 2735.

ATONE, *v.* (To atone for). Prenna, P.

ATONEMENT, *s.* Dewellens, w.; dewelyans, M. 1828; dewyllyens, dewhyllyans, w; dewhillyans, c.w. 2480. *In dewelyans am pehas,* in atonement of my sin, M. 1828.

ATTACHED, *adj.* (Loving). Serchog, cescer, w.

ATTAIN, *v.* (To attain to). Drehedhy, w.

ATTEMPT, *v.* Astel. lavasy, w.

ATTEMPT, *s.* (A bold attempt) Antell, w.

ATTENDANCE, *s.* Gwasanaeth, w.; guasanaeth, P.; herwith, B.

ATTENDANT, *s.* Goneseg, gonidoc, w.; gonidog, B.; acectour, M. 3532. *An iovle agis acectour,* the devil be your attendant, M. 3523.

AUDACIOUS, *adj.* Drès, drews, w.

AUGER, *s.* Tarad. tardar, w.; thardar, o.m. 1002. *Ov thardar ha'm morthelow,* my auger and my hammers o.m. 1002.

AUGUR, *s.* (Soothsayer). Cuillioc, w.; kuillioc, B.; chuilliôg, P. *A female soothsayer,* cuillioges, chuillio-gés, P.

AUGUST, *s.* East, mis east, w.; miz east, i.e. *eausti,* the month to get in harvest, P.

AUNT, *s.* Modereb, w.; modryb, modrap, B.

AUNT ON THE MOTHER'S SIDE. Modereb abarh mam, w.; modereb a barth mam, moderebat barth mem, P.

AUNT. ON THE FATHER'S SIDE. Modereb abarh tat, w.

AUTHORITY, *s.* (Power). Gallos, gallus, galloys, w.; othoredzhek, P.

AUTHORITY, *s.* (Dominion). Arthelath, w. See LORDSHIP.

AUTUMN, *s.* Cyniaf, w.; kyniaf, P.; kyniav, w.; kyniau, B.; cidniadh, w.; kidniadh, cidniaz, P.

AVAILING. Yrvyrys, P.

AVALONIA, *s.* (Herb). Gouiles, B.

AVENGED. Dylies, dyliez, w.

AVERSE, *adj.* Destotha, P.

AWAIT, *v.* Gortos, wortos, w.

AWAKE. *v.* Defena, devina, difuné, dyfuné, dyfuny, w.; tefeny, P.

AWAKE, *adj.* Difun, dhyfun, dufun, dyfun, w.; teffen, en teffen, B ; thyfun, P.C. 2204. *Rág me an guelas dufun,* for I saw him awake, R.D. 524.

AWAKE YE. Dufunugh, M. 1526.

AWN, *s.* (The beard of corn). Côl, w.

AWARE, (To be aware of). Dho wâr, P.

AWARE OF. Wâr, P.

AWARE, *adj.* Dous, P.

AWAY. Cer, ker, kerr, w,; in ker, c.w. 2127; kar, P.; cerdh, kerdh, w.; kerth, P.; in kerth, M. 813; yn kergh, N.; kergh, kyrgh, kyrhas, omelys, P.; towl, B. *Duen ny in kerth,* let us come away, M. 813. *Ke yn kergh dywhans,* go away quickly, R.D. 116; the ves, M.; vezy, B.V.

AWAY, BEGONE. Wêr, P.

AWFUL, *adj.* Uthec, ûthek, ûthyc, ûthyk, w.; ûter, B.; ethuc, ethec, ethic, ethyc, ythec, w.

AWFULNESS, *s.* Uth, euth, uthecter, w.

AWHILE. Pôls, P. *Pôls the powés,* awhile to rest, P.C. 1873.

(AWOKE,) HE AWOKE, *v.* Tefenas. A mutation of *defena*, 3 pers. s.; preterite of *defena,* id. qd. *dyfuny,* to awake, w.

AWRY, *adj.* Crum, crom, P.

AXE, *s.* Bûl, bool, boell, bial, biail. bony, pony, w.; bogl, B.

AN AXE, USED BY MINERS. Dag, D.

AXLE, *s.* Mellier, D. This name is for the axle of a frame used in the washing of tin by tinners.

AZURE, *s.* and *adj.* Glâs, w.; glase, glaze, P.; glayis, lays, B.

B.

B, has the same sound in the Celtic languages as in English.

It is both a radical or primary consonant, and a secondary When radical it changes into V, as *bara,* bread; *y vara,* his bread . . . .

The Cornish also changes the sonant B into the surd form P, as *bewé,* to live, *ow pewé,* living . . . .

When secondary, B is a mutation of P, as *pen,* a head, *y ben,* his head. *W. Lex. Corn. Brit.*

BABE, *s.* Baban, maban, w.

BACK, *s.* (Of the body). Cein, w.; kein, P.; gein, hein, ceyn, keyn, geyn, w.; heyn, P.C. 220; hyen, P.C. 1114; chein, B.; cheim, P.; cevn, B.; cyn, kyn, gyn, cil, kil, chil, cyl, kyl, kyll, w.; kylban. c.w. 1114; y kylbyn, c.w.; dywen, P.C. 1368; *War an aywen,* on the back, P.C. 1368; halen, yenter tor, B.; leyta, leth, lyth, P. *Ha whys pup góth ôl ha lyth,* and sweat all my neck and back, P.C. 2512. *Cil, kil, cyl,* and such forms, more correctly mean the nape, or back of the neck; and *cein* &c., the loins.

BACKBONE, *s.* Asgarn an hein, w.

BACK OF THE HAND, *s.* Kein-dorn, P.

BACK, *s.* (The upper part of a mineral lode). Broil, bryle. D.

BACK, BACKWARD, BACKWARDS, BEHIND. Der, *Der devethys,* come back, P.; delhar, dhellar, w.; thellar thellurgh, B ; dellarch, a dhelhar, w.; a theler, P.; war dhelhar, w.; uar dhelar, P.; war dhellar, w.; warthellurgh, B.

BACK-BITING, *adj.* Drôgdavasec, w.; drôkdavazek, B.

BACON. *s.* Cig moh, w.

BACON FAT, LARD, *s.* Mehin, w.; mord, mort, D. See LARD.

BAD, *adj.* Drôc, drôk, drôg, w.; thrôg, c.w. 1411; *Why as byth drôg vommennow,* you will have bad blows, O.M. 2324.

BAD, *adj.* (Naughty). Lac. w.

BAD, *adj.* (Unwell). Aniach, w.; aniak, B.

BAD-LUCK, *s.* Meal, meawl, w.

BADGER, *s.* Brôch, w.; brogh, M. 1260; gale, w.; brakgye, w.; brathkye, P.; grey, brock, bawson, D.

BAG, *s.* Côrs, siglen, B.; sâch, zâh, zêh, pot, w.

BAG-PUDDING, *s.* (White pudding). Pot guidn. P.

BAIL, *s.* Mach. *To be bail for anyone,* Machenno, B.

BAIT or ENTICE, *v.* Clithio, B.

BAIT or ALLUREMENT, *s.* Peecher, w.f.p.

BAIT. *s.* (Cut from a fish), Scethen. This cut up and ready to put on the hooks, *trestrem,* w.f.p.; scethen, B.V.

BAIT, *s.* (Cut from the tail of a mackerel). Lash. D.

BAKE, *v.* Poba, pobas, dho pobas, w. ; pobaz, uyroz, P.

BAKED or BOILED. (Prepared to be eaten). Paret. B.

BAKER, *s.* Peber, w. ; pebar, B.

BAKE-HOUSE, *s.* Ti pobas, popti, w. ; pob-ti B. ; tshyi pobaz, tshyi vorn, P. ; chy vorn (*ch* is soft) w.

BAKESTONE, *s.* Mân pobas, w. ; mên pobaz, B. ; mean pobaz, P.

BAKING-DISH, *s.* Tolyer predn. B.V. This name is also used for a large wooden platter.

BAKING POT, or BAKER, *s.* Wilver, D.

BALD, *adj.* Moel, w. ; leven, B. ; pilés, pilez, peléz, pyllés, w. ; nôth, noath, noeth, nooth, noyth, B.

BALD-HEAD, *s.* Pen pilez, pedn pilez, B ; pedn pelez, w.

BALD-OATS, *s.* Pillés, w. ; pillez, B. The *avena nuda*, of Ray.

BALL, *s.* Pel, pelen, B. A ball of thread, yarn, &c., is simply called *pellen, pellan,* w.

BALLAD, *s.* Caniad, B.

BALLAST, *s.* Gro, B. Pronounced *grou.*

BAND, *s.* (Fillet). Colmen, celmen, gelmen, funen, w.

BAND, *s.* (Or tie). Ere, B.

BAND or COMPANY, *s.* Byddin, B ; lias, P. ; liaz, B. ; lyes, P.C. 557. *May ma lyes gvrek ha govr,* that the band of men and women may be, P.C. 557.

BANDY-LEGGED, *adj.* Gargam, gargabm, w. ; gar cam, P.

BANG or THUMP, *v.* Croncyé, w. ; cronkyé, cronkya, P. ; groncyé, w.

BANISH, *v.* Didirio, difroi, B.

BANISHED. Exilys, P. ; pelleys, M. 2083. *An ladron a veth pelleys,* the robbers shall be banished, M. 2083.

BANISHENT. *s.* Difroedd, B.

BANK, *s.* (Of earth). Bancan, w. ; bankan, P. ; ladn, B.

BANK or RAMPART, *s.* Tuban, w. ; tuban-agger, P.

BANK, SIDE, or BRINK OF A RIVER, *s.* Glân, glând, w. ; aut, brôch, B. ; an avan, torneuan, P. ; torlan, B. The words *glân,* and *gland* are still in frequent use for a bank.

BANK or PUBLIC STOCK, *s.* Tryssor, B.

BANKER, *s.* Bathor w. ; bather, B.

BANNER, *s.* Baniel, B. ; baner, vancr, w.

BANNS OF MATRIMONY, *s.* Gôsteggion, B.

BANQUET, *s.* Prez-buz, B. ; sant, w. ; saut, B.

BAPTIZE, *v.* Bedidhia, w. ; bedidio, B. ; bysydhia, bysydha, bedzhidhia, bidbyzi, w. ; vygythy, P.

BAPTIZED, *part.* Bysydhys, bygydys, vygydys, w. ; begythys, M. 1821.

BAPTISM, *s.* Bedidhians, w. ; bedzhidian, P. ; bedzhidia, B.

BAR or BOLT, *v.* Bara, prenné, w. ; prenny, P.C. 3033 ; *The prenny agan yettys,* to bar our gates, P.C. 2038 ; sparla, B.

BAR or BOLT, *s.* Attal, baar, claust, cloist, B. ; gyst, P. ; trossol, B.

ONE OF THE BARS OF A GATE. Shivver, D.

BAR or HINDRANCE, *s.* Cluddias, B.

BAR, *s.* (In a court of justice). Gorseddaddleu, B.

BARBAROUS, *adj.* Creulon, B.

BARBARISM, *s.* (In speech). Lediaith, llediaith, lligruer, B.

BARBEL, *s.* (Fish). Mehil, mehall, meill, B.

BARBER, *s.* Barbar, B.

BARD, *s.* Bardh, barth, w.

BARE, *adj.* Moel. *Moel vrê,* the bare hill, w. ; leven, B. ; nooth, P. ; nôth, noath, noeth, noyth, pilés, pillez, pyllés, w.

BARE, *adj.* (Ill-clad). Fernoyth, ferneth, B.

BARGAIN, *v.* Bargidnia, dho bargidnia, P.

BARGAINED FOR. Bargidnias, P.

BARGAIN, *s.* Ambos. *Yn dun ambos ythesés,* under a bargain thou art, P.C. 2259 ; chyffar, *an chyffar,* the bargain, B. ; nuur, P. ; thyfar, unver, B.

BARGE, *s.* Ceibal, B.

BARK, *v.* (Like a dog). Harthy, harha, harrah, pefyr, B. ; ullia, w. ; uolé, P.

BARK, *s.* (Of a tree). Gwisc-pren, B. ; risc, rusc, ruscen, w. ; risk, P. ; rusken, O.M. 778 ; *Hag adro thethy rusken,* and around it bark, O.M. 778 ; levar, liver, B.

BARKED, UNRINDED. Dyruskys, P.

BARLEY, *s.* Haiz, haidh, P. ; heid, B. ; barlys, barliz, P. The common name is *haiz.*

BARM or YEAST, *s.* Burm, w. ; burman, gweal, gwêl, B.

BARN, *s.* Scaber, sciber, skiber, scibor, skibor, w. ; scaberias, P.

BARON, *s.* Erelyr, breyr, B.

BARRED, *part.* Degés, dygés, w.

BARREL, *s.* Balliar, tonnel, w. ; tonnell, P. ; tonwell, B.

BARREN, *adj.* Thrês, P.

BARREN, *adj.* (As of children). Anvab, w.

BARRENESS, (As of children). Anvabat, w.

BARROW, or HANDBARROW, *s.* Gravar, gravar dhula, w. ; gravar dowla. B.

BARROW, *s.* (Of stones). Creeg, w. ; crig, D. ; crûk, crûc, cryk, w. ; crûg, D.

BARROW PIG. *s.* (A castrated pig). Porhal, P. Borlase uses this word and *porchel* for a little pig.

BARTER, *v.* Newidio, B. ; scôs or scoce, D.

BASE, *adj.* (Wicked). Acr.

A BASE FELLOW, Cauchwâs, w. ; caughwâs, casadow, P.

BASE, *s.* (Foundation). Goden, sil, seil, seyl, scyle, sôl, w.

BASE or STEM. *s.* Bên, w. ; dulw, B.

BASE, *s.* (In music) Faborden, w. See BASS.

BASENESS, *s.* Eselder, M.C. 1166.

BASHFUL, *adj.* Mêth, môth, mûl, mûlder, yswil, B.

BASHFULNESS, *s.* Médh, mêth, w.

BASKET, *s.* Basced, P. ; bascaeid, B. ; bascauda, P. ; cawal, cauwel, cowal. cowel, w. ; kaval, B. ; costan, D, a name still for a basket used for straw and brambles ; guisetti, B. ; kanstal, muys, B. A fish basket is still called a *cowel.*

BASIN. *s.* Bathon, bathyn, cawg, ysgal, B.

BASS, *s.* (In music). Faborden, R.D. 2359. *Kenough why faborden brâs,* you sing a great bass. R.D. 2359.

BAST or BEAT, *v.* Marthu, B. *Lit.* To hammer ; fûsta, fysta, w.

BASTARD, *s.* Bastardh, w. ; pagva, M. 2393 ; *Pagva mergh es,* a girl's bastard thou wast. M. 2393.

BASTARD'S BASTARD, *s.* Hingerlin, B.

BAT, *s.* (The animal). Sgelli-grehan, w. ; skelli-grehan, B. ; asgelly-grohen, hisommet, hihsomet, w. ; *Lit,* meaning, leather wings. In Devon, *sgerligrehan,* a name also used by Borlase. Ystlym, P.

BATCHELOR, *s.* (Unmarried man). Gwyrif, B.

BATH, *s.* Golch, B.

BATTLE, *s.* Ar, hâr, w. ; heir, P. ; cad, câs, gâs, w. ; gwaeth, B.

BATTLE-FIELD, *s.* Gwaeth, B.

BATTLE ARRAY, *s.* Luid, w.

BATTLEDORE, *s.* Pelegyp, B.

BAUBLE, *s.* Gwailbeth, B.

BAWD. *s.* Buttein, muyglen, B.

BAWDY-HOUSE, *s.* Puttendy, tshyi hora. B.

BAWL, *v.* (To cry out). Bloeddio, gwaeddi, B.

BAY, *v.* (Like a dog). Harthy, harha, w. ; harrah, B.

BAY, *s.* Hean, P. ; gwic, porth, w. ; zanz ; hence, says Pryce *Penzance,* the head of the bay, and not the Saint's head, as some imagine.

BAY, *s.* (Of a building). Cowlas, B.

BE, *v.* (To be). Bôs, w. ; bôz, dho bôz, boes, bûs, bas, baz, P. ; pôz, B. ; bonés, w. ; bonez, B. ; bonas, bosa (poetically), w. ; rebôs, rebue, râg û, P. ; vôs, w. ; vose, B. ; voos, C.W. 2383 ; vea, voy, the voy, P. ; vonés, w. ; wôs, B. ; moy, ez, P.

THEY BE. Vons, sens, B.

THAT HE BE. A wôs, B.

IT MUST BE. Porris, B.

THOU BEEST. Sôs, B.

IF IN ME BE. Kenymbo, *(ken ym bo),* P.

BE IT. Rebo, rubo, reby, rebee, P.

BE HE. Beva, w.

BE THOU. Byth, N. ; bêdh, bydh, bêz, by, w. ; beva te, bethys. P. ; fydh, w. ; soge, B. ; vêdh, vydh, mutations of *bédh* and *bydh,* 2 pers. s. imp. of *bós,* to be, w.

BE YE. Bedhouch, bedhowh, bedheuch, bydhouch, pethouch, pethough ; vedhouch, a mutation of bed-houch, 2 pers. pl. imp. of *bós,* to be, w. ; bethough N.

BE TO ME. Byma, P.

LET HIM BE. Boes, bedhés, bydh, bis, w.

LET IT BE. Fôn, reth fo, wreth fo, P.

LET THEM BE. Bedhens, bedhans, w. ; bethens, N.

LET US BE. Bethon, N.

YE BE. Sew, B.

I HAVE BEEN. Bym, P. ; bûf, buef, fûf, fuef, w

THOU HAST BEEN. Bûs, vûs, fûs, bues, vues, fues, besté, vesté, festé, w.

HE HAS BEEN. Bué, fué ; fuvé, after *del ;* vuvé ; rebé, 3 pers. s. preterite of *bós,* to be, with the particle *re* prefixed, w.

WE HAVE BEEN. Bên, buen, fuen ; *rebén* with the particle *re* prefixed, 1 pers. pl. preterite of *bós,* to be,w.

YE HAVE BEEN. Bùch, fûch, beuch. feuch, w. ; byoh, huei a vyogh, P. *Vyogh* is a mutation of *byoh,* a late form of *beuch,* 2 pers. pl. preter of *bós,* to be, w.

THEY HAVE BEEN. Byonz, B.

I HAD BEEN. Veadzhen, a corrupt form of *veasen* a mutation of *beasen,* 1 pers. s. plup. of *bós,* to be, w.

THOU HADST BEEN. Beasés. The 2 pers. s. plup. of *bós,* to be, w.

HE HAD BEEN. Beasen, w. ; 3 pers. s. plup. of *bós,* to be, w. Also written *rebye,* the particle *re* prefixed.

WE HAD BEEN. Beasen, w. ; 1 pers. pl. plup. of *bós,* to be.

YE HAD BEEN. Beasch, 2 pers. pl. plup. of *bós,* to be, w.

THEY HAD BEEN. Beasens, 3 pers. pl. plup. of *bós,* to be, w.

HAD IT NOT BEEN. Na via, b.

I MAY BE. Bon. ben, byf, beyf; ven, a mutation of *ben*; vyf, a mutation of *byf;* veyf, feyf. mutations of *beyf;* byma (*byf ma*); vyma. a mutation of *byma*, comp. of *byf* 1 pers. s. subj. of *bós*, and *me*, I, w.

THOU MAYEST BE. Bes, bey, by, and their mutations, ves, fes, vey, fey, vy, fy. Also vysé, a mutation of bysé, composed of *by* and *se*, for *te*, thou, w.

HE MAY BE. Be, pe, ve; bo, vo, fo; bova, fova. (*Pe* and *ve* are mutations of *be*; *fo* and *vo* of *bo*; *fova* of *bova*). The 3 pers. s. subj. of *bós*, to be, w.

WE MAY BE. Bên, been, beyn, byyn, w. Their mutations are, vên, fên, veen, feen, veyn, feyn, vyyn, fyyn, 1 pers. pl. subj. of *bós*, to be. Also *veny* comp, of *vén*, a mutation of *bén* and *ny*, we.

YE MAY BE. Beugh, n.; beuch, byuch. their mutations are veuch, vyuch, 2 pers. pl. subj, of *bós*, to be, w.

YOU MAY OR CAN BE. Hallough, yllough, b.

THEY MAY BE. Bôns, byns, their mutations are vôns, fôns, vyns, fyns. Also written *bens*, w. The 3 pers. pl. subj. of *bós*, to be.

THERE MAY BE TO ME. Bomé, w.

MAY BE. Fons, b.

WHEN THERE IS OR MAY BE. Pa fo, po, w.

THAT THEY MAY BE. Mollough. For, may yllough, b.

MAY IT BE YOURS. Ragas, w.

MIGHT OR COULD BE. Thellé, dellé, vyo. b.

THAT HE MIGHT BE. Resteffo. b.

I SHALL OR WILL BE Byvé, bydh; bedhaf. The mutations are pedhaf, vedhaf, fedhaf, vethaff. The 1 pers. s. fut. of *bós*, to be, w.; bythaf, bethaf, n.

THOU SHALT OR MAYEST BE. By. The mutations are, vy, fy, w.

THOU SHALT OR WILT BE. Bedhyth, and it mutations, vedhyth, fedyth; bydhyth, and its mutations vydyth, fydyth. *Vydyth* after *ny*. the 2 pers. s. fut. of *bós*, to be, w.; bethyth, bythyth, n.

HE SHALL OR WILL BE. Bêdh, its mutations are pêdh, vêdh, fêdh; byth, n.; bêth, w.; fêth, b.; fêt, w.; fyt, b.; bydh, its mutations are pydh, vydh, fydh; beydh, its mutations are veydh, feydh; veys; bedho, and its mutation *vedho*, the 3 pers. s. fut. of *bós*, to be.

WE SHALL OR WILL BE. Bedhyn, its mutations are pedhyn, vedhyn; bydhyn, its mutations are vydhyn, fydhyn. Read *vydhyn* after *ny*. The first pers. pl. fut. of *bós*, to be, w.; bethyn, n.

YE SHALL OR WILL BE. Bydheuch, bedheuch, bedhouch, pedhouch, 2 pers. pl. fut. of *bós*, to be, w.; bythough, n.

THEY SHALL OR WILL BE. Bedhens, bydhens, bedhons, bydhons. Mutations. vedhens, fedhens, vydhens. fydhens. vedhons, fedhons, 3 pers. pl. fut. of *bós*, to be, w.; bethens, bythons, n.

IT SHALL BE. Reth fo, wreth fo, p.

SHALL BE. A' vea, avit, avyth, robo, bonex, p.

I SHOULD OR WOULD BE. Bên; fên, mutation of *bén*; bean; vean, mutation of *bean*; byen, its mutations vyen, fyen; bein, b.; bef, its mutation vef; beva, its mutation feva; bedhan, its mutations vedhan, fedhan; vethan. c.w. 1640; fethan, c.w. 1637. The 1 pers s. subj. of *bós*, to be, w.

THOU SHOULD'ST OR WOULD'ST BE. Bês. Its mutations are pês, vês, fês; beis; byes, its mutations vyes, fyes; bydhé, its mutation fydhé. Read *vyes* after *ny*. The 2 pers. s. subj. of *bós*, to be, w.

HE SHOULD OR WOULD BE. Byé, its mutations vyé, fyé; bia, its mutation via; bea, its mutation vea; bedhé, bedha. their mutations, vedhé, fedhé, pedha. The 3 pers. s. fut. of *bós*, to be; bethé, bythé, n.

IT SHOULD OR WOULD BE. Assevyé, vyé; peva, a mutation of bé, 3 pers. s. subj. of *bós*, to be, and *va* for *ve*, he, w.

WE SHOULD OR WOULD BE. Bên, been, bein, byen, beyn, bôn. Mutations, fên for *bén*; feen for *been*; pôn for *bon* The 1 pers. pl. subj. of *bós*, to be, w.

SHOULD BE. Bonés, bonas, vyé, p.

YE SHOULD OR WOULD BE. Byeugh, n.; byeuch, its mutation fyeuch, w.; besch, bedhech, bese, p.; beze, bezech, beuch, b. The 2 pers. pl. subj. of *bós*, to be; beugh, n.

THEY SHOULD OR WOULD BE. Byens, n.; bens, its mutations, vens, fens; bôns, its mutations, vôns, fôns; bedhens, w. The 3 pers. pl. subj. of *bós*, to be.

BEACON, *s.* Huyl-bren, b.

BEAD, *s.* Beder, peder. *Pl.* Bederow. pederow, w.

BEAK, *s.* (Of a bird). Gelvin, w.; gelvyn, gilbin, b.; gylfin, pyg, p.

BEAM, *s.* Ten. *Pl.* Tennow, w.

BEAM or RAFTER, *s.* Ceber, w.; keber, p.; gyst, jyst. (*Pl.* Jystys, w.); troster, trester. w.; traust, b.

BEAN, *s.* Favan, w.; fa, m. 2616; ponar, b. (*Pl.* Fâv, w); fave, fava, p.

BEAN-PODS, or BEAN-COD̃S, *s.* Cûthû fâv, w.

BEAN-STALK, *s.* Gwelltfa, b.

BEAR, *s.* (The animal). Ors, w.; orth, arth, b. Borlase gives *ors* for a he-bear.

BEAR or CARRY, *v.* Dôn, doen, w.; doan, b.; dûn, down, doyn, tûn, toon, w ; teen, p.; doga, degy, w.; dregy, degyn, thegyn, p.; thegis, thek, b.; tocka tocké, thogga, teigé, p.; torry, w.; rethokko, p., caria, w.; porthy, perthy, prethy, w.; aborth, p.

BEAR or BRING, *v.* Drey, dho drei, dry, dyrey, P.

BEAR or BRING FORTH, *v.* Dynythy. *Dho dynythy map*, to bear a child, P.; ethon, B.

BEAR WITNESS, *v.* Dustuné, dystynyé, tustuné, w.; tystio, B.

BEAR. SUFFER or ENDURE, *v.* Codhaf, godhaf, wodhaf, codhevel, godhevel, w.; perthegy, P.; perthegés, porthy, perth., prethy, w.

BEAR THOU. Dôg, dôc, dôk, w.

BEAR YE. Thegough, B.

HE WILL BEAR. Pyth, 3 pers. s. fut. of *perthy* to bear or carry, w.; dêg, dêc, dêg, w.

SHE BORE. Rugfi, B.

BEAR REMEMBRANCE, BEAR THOU REMEMBRANCE. Percou, w.

BEARD, *s.* Barf, baref, w.; bar, P. *Pl.* Barwou, barvou, M. 2309, 2313. *Y a schaky age barwou*, they shall shake their beards, M. 2313.

BEARD, *s.* (Of corn), Colyd, B. *Pl.* Colow, culhu, w.; kulhu, B.

BEAST, *s.* Mil, bêst, eneval, w.; gurtfill, P.; gurthvil, ourthvil, B. *A she beast.* Enevalés, w. *A beast of labour.* Yscrybel, w.

BEASTS, *s.* Bestés, N.; bestez, bestaz, P.

BEAT or BAST, *v.* Marthu, B. *Lit.* To hammer; fûsta, fysta, w. For the various forms see STRIKE, *v.*

BEAT EACH OTHER, *v.* Ymnoucé.

BEAT UP, *v.* Gwaythy, gwethé, w.; guethé, P.; fethy, w.

BEATEN SOUNDLY. Lam to rez, B. A corruption of *terhi.*

BEATING, *s.* Coot, D. The Cornish call a blow, a *coot*, and a "good thrashing," a "good cooting."

BEAUTIFUL, *adj.* Caer, faidus, w.; gortas, P.; tec, têk, w.; teek, thêk, teage, P.; têg, w.; gwen, wen, B. *Most beautiful*, Ailla, *Pl.* Aluin, B.

BEAUTIFY, *v.* Kaerat, P.

BEAUTY, *s.* Cârdêr, cairder, tecter, tekter, w.; tectar, c.w. 288; ailne, B.

BEAVER, *s.* Lostlydan, B.; befer, P.

BECAUSE. Aban, N.; *Aban golsté worty hy*, because thou hearkenedst to her, O.M. 269; râg, râc, râk, w.; râgh, rhâgh, P. *Râg orty ty dhe golé*, because thou harkenedst to her, O.M. 324; urt, P. Awos, drefen; drevan, w.; drevon, c.w. 847; drefan, drevan, P.; *Drefen, ow bôs noeth hep queth*, because I am naked without a cloth, O.M. 259. *Râg dhe offryn kêr*, because of thy dear offering, O.M. 507. See NOTWITHSTANDING.

BECK or NOD, *s.* Amnuid, B.

BECKON, *v.* Amneidio, B.; gogwyddo, P.; *Gogwyddo pen*, to nod the head, P. Or shake the head.

BECOME, *v.* Cylly, gylly, geli, gyll, P.

TO BECOME CLEAN. Omlana, w.

TO BECOME FULL. Lenwel, w.

TO BECOME ONE. Yunnyé, w.; Yunnyy, P.

BECOME. Kelés, *Ny dal kelés*, I am become blind, P.

I AM BECOME. Galsôf, w.

IT BECOMES. Degôth, dhegouth, w.; thegôth, P.; dogôth, w.

IT BECOMES THEE. Awys thy, B.

IT WOULD BECOME. Gôtho, w, The subj. mood of gôth.

IS BECOME. Dyvotter, (?) w.

BED, *s.* Gwely, w.; guely, P.; guelé, B.; gueli, P.; gwili, w.; guili, B.; gwillé, w.; gwelly, P.; wili, w.; uili, P.; gluth, loven, B.; tie, tye, D.; *Tie* or *tye*, means a feather bed.

BED, *s.* (Of a river). Trôt, P.

IN BED. Crowethé, crywedhé, krywethé, kryvedé, B.

BED-CHAMBER, *s.* Gwelyfod, glûth, tshomber, B.

BED-CLOTHES. *s.* Dillat gueli, w.; pensgruet, B.

BED-FELLOW, *s.* Cywelu, B.

BEDLAM, *s.* (A bedlam). Cynderiog, B.

BED-LINEN, *s.* Lien gueli, w.

BED-RIDDEN, *adj.* Gueli-croueth, P.

BED-ROOM, *s.* See BED-CHAMBER.

BED-SHEET, *s.* Lian-gwili, w.; lian gueli, B.; lien-gueli, P.

BED-SICKNESS, *s.* Gwelly gluyan, gwelligluyan, w. gorthewyth, B.

BEDUNG, *v.* (*Concaco, Lat.*). Ymgachu, B.

BEE, *s.* Gwenenen, guenenen, gwenynen, gwanau, w.; guanan, P. *Pl.* Gwenyn, guenen, w.; guenyn, w.

BEE-HIVE, *s.* Cawal gwanan, w.; caul guanan, P.; butt, D. It is still commonly called a bee-butt.

BEEF, *s.* Bowin, bowen, boen, w.; bouin, bouyn, P.

BEER, *s.* Côr, coref, coruf, w.; kôr, P.

BEER. *s.* (As synonymous with *drink.*) Dewés, dewas, dywés, dhewas, w.

BEST BEER. Côr-guela, korguella, P.

STRONG BEER. Dewas creev.

STALE BEER. Dewas côth, w.; *Lit.* Old drink.

THIN, WEAK, OR POOR BEER. Swipes, D.; (?)

BEES-WAX, *s.* Corgwenyn, B.

BEST, *adj.* Gwella, wella, w.; guella, P.

BEETLE, *s.* (Insect). Hwilen, w.; hwillaen, huilen, P.; huilan, B.; willen, D.

BEETLE, *s.* (Mallet). Gybeddern, w. This name is used by Borlase for a little hammer.

BEFALL, *v.* Digwydha, w.; digwyddo, B.

BEFOOL, v. (*To befool one*). Gwawdio, B.

BEFORE. Râg, râc, rág, rhâg, w.; rágh, rhâgh, P.; dyrâg, adhyrâk, w.; thyràg, a thyràg, B.; theragôn, M. 1217. Cén, kén, w.; keen, P.; cyn, w.; kyn, P.; gén, cens, kens, w.; kenz, P.; gens, hens; cins, w.; kins, P.; cyns, kyns, w.; kynz, P.; gyns, cyngys, kyngys, w.; âr, hâr, P; arâg, w.; arâk, M. 285; a râk, N. *Kyn gys merwel*, before you die, P. *Kyns vyttyn*, before morning, O.M. 1641. *Y fue kyns y vôs gurys*, there were, before it was done, P.C. 350.

BEFORE DAY. Hyns vythyn, P.; kyns vythyn, O.M. 1644.

BEFORE-HAND. Cens, kens, cyns, kyns, gen, hens, w.

BEFORE HER. Ryghty, (râg hy), deryghthy dheryghthy, dyraghthy, w.

BEFORE HIM, OR IT. Dyragtho, a dhyragtho, w.; theragtho, M. 280.

BEFORE ME. Adhyragof, athyragof, w.

BEFORE MENTIONED. Rágleverys, w.

BEFORE NOW. Censemmyn, w.; kenzemmyn, P.

BEFORE THEE. Dyragos, a dhyragos, adhyragos, w.; athyragos, athyragtho, P.

BEFORE US. Deragôn, dyragôn, dheragôn, adhyragôn, w.; athyragoon, P.; theragôn ny, M. 1217; aragôn, ragôn nyi, ragôn, P.

BEFORE YOU. Dyragouch, a dhyragouch, w.; thyrageugh, athyragough, ragas, ragôs, ragôn, P.

BEG, v. (Or supplicate). Pesy, pisy, pysy, pidzhi, pigy, pygy, w.

BEG, v. (Seek alms). Cârdotta, B.

BEGGAR, s. Cardottin, B.; bothosek, M. 779. *Covs, ty bothosek*, speak. thou beggar, M. 779; brebour, M. 1400; gwilliew, w; guillein, P. guilleia, B.

BEGGARLY, *adj.* Haru, B.

BEGET, v. Dynythy, w.; gynez, P.

BEGIN, v. Astel, w.; rebea, P.; dalleth, dallath, dhallath, dallethy, talleth, w.; thesefsé, P.

BEGINNING, *part.* Ow talleth, w

BEGINNING, s. Dalleth. dallath, dhalleth, w.; talleth, P.; dallathvas, dallathfas, dhallathfas, w.; thallatheas, P.; thalathfas, C.w. 1987.

BEGINNING, s. (Head, chief) Pen, pedn, pyn, w.

BEGONE. (Away with you). Wér, P.; a voyd, C.w 1292. *A voyd dama*, begone mother, C.w. 1292.

BEGOTTEN. Denethys, B.; dynythys, w.; genys, B.

BEGUILE, v. Tollé, tolla, twyllo, gurra, B.

BEHALF, s. Abreth, M. 2010. *Bohogogneth abreth du*, poverty on behalf of God; leys, M. 3868. *Peys rág ov leys*, pray on my behalf, M. 3868.

BEHAVE, v. (Well or ill). Ymdowyn, B.

BEHAVIOUR, s. Arweddiad, B

BEHEAD, v. Dibenna, w.

BEHEADED. Debynnys, M. 1353

BEHIND. Adryff, dellarch, dylarg, delhar, dhelhar, a dhelhar, w.; adelhar, P.; war delhar, w.; uar delhar, dislarg, B.; disler, w.; dislor, B.; a theler, P.; weath, awheath, ynolwedhi, B.

BEHOLD, v. Meras, miras, myras, w.; miraz, mira, P.; veras, w.; dho viroz, da viraz, P.; medra, w., a late corruption of *mira*. Gwelés, gwelas, w.; guelaz, guella, P.; welés, w.; wellas, P.; avycya, c.w. 1803; sylly, w.

BEHOLD THOU. Avicé, c.w. 1799. *Avicé pub tra ha lavar*, behold everything and say. c w. 1799; myrough, myrugh, w.; mere, meir, merrow, P.

BEHOLD! LO! *Exclam.* At, M. 599, *At eve fast bys in top* behold! it is quite up to the top. Otté, w.; oté, ota, osé, P.; os, otevé, B. wetté, P.; wetta, B.; wotta, awot, awatta, w.; awetté, awottué, P.; yta, w.

BEHOLD HER. Ottensy, w.

BEHOLD HIM. Ottevé, ottevé, ottensé, wottevé, w.

BEHOLD IT. Ottensy, wottensé, w.

BEHOLD THEM. Ottensy, ottengy, w.

BEHOVETH, IT BEHOVETH, IT OUGHT, IT IS DUE. Dâl, dayl, e dâl, gôth, côth, degôth, deleth, teleth, telet, w.; thegôth, P.; tegôth, M. 1299; reys, rêz, P.; buddiol yw, B. *Teleth, telet*, are mutations of *deleth*, 3 pers. s. fut of *dely*, to owe, w.

IT SHOULD BEHOVE. Cothfo, a mutation of *gothfo*,w.

BEING, s. (Nature, profession). Drês. *Ladrón dres*, thieves by profession, B.

BELCH, v. Bytheirio, B.

BELFRY, s. Clechti, w.; clecha, lucar, B.

BELIE, TO BELIE ONE, v. Camgyhuddo, B.

BELIEF, s. (Creed or faith). Fydh, fèdh, crêd, crês, krêz, grês, crygyans, kredzhanz, credzyans, credzhyans, credgyans, w.; kredzhans, B.; grygyans, w.; gregyans, c.w. 176; grydgyans, c.w. 2317; gris, grez, B. (The g is sounded as *j*).

BELIEVE, v. Credy, cregy, w.; crugy P.; credzi, w.; credzhi, credzha, P.; criedzy, B.; cresy, crysy, crygy, w.; kresy, kridzhi. crydgy, P.; gregy, grygy, w.; creis, creiz, agris, agrys, P.; grys, B.; tibias, tybias, tybyas, fydhyé, w.

BELIEVE THOU. Crês, creys, crys, w.

HARDNESS of BELIEF. Anghygred, B.

1 DID BELIEVE. Gresyn, a mutation of *cresyn*, 1 pers. s. imp. of *crésy*, to believe, w.

I WILL BELIEVE. Gresaf, grysaf, mutations of cresaf, crysaf, 1 pers. s. fut. of *crésy*, to believe, w.

THOU WILT BELIEVE. Gresyth, a mutation of *cresyth*, 2 pers. s. fut. of *crésy*, to believe, w.

HE WILL BELIEVE. Crês, crêys, crys. Also the mutations of the proceeding words into, grês, grêys, grys, the 3 pers. s. fut. of *crêsy* and *crysy*, to believe, w.

HE MAY BELIEVE. Gresso, grysso, the mutations of *cresso*, *crysso*, 3 pers. s. subj. of *crêsy*, and *crysy*, to believe, w.

YE WILL BELIEVE. Gresouch, a mutation of *cresouch*, 2 pers. pl. fut. of *crêsy*. to believe, w.

BELL, s. Clôch. w.; klôch, B.; clôh, w.; klôh, B.

A LITTLE BELL. Cledhic, w.; kledhic, B.

A GREAT BELL. Clôchmuer, w.; clôch mûr, P.; clôchmaur, B.

BELLOW, v. (Like an ox). Pedhigla, w.; bedhigia, B.

BELLOWING, *part.* A pedhîgla, w.

BELLOWS, s. Megin; meginow, w.; meginou, P.; mygenow, miginau, B.

BELLMAN, s. Dên an clôc, B.

BELLADONNA, s. (The plant). Scaw-coo, D.

BELLY, s. Tor, dor, torr, thor, w. *Lenow ov thor*, my belly is full, w. *Cosk wâr the tor ha powes*, sleep on thy belly and rest, o.m. 2070; talon, bôl, w.

A GREAT BELLY. Bolitho, w.

BELOVED, *adj.* Cêr, kêr, cyr, gêr, cûf (*Pl.* Cefyon, cardow, garadow, w.; meadow, P.); hueg, huegol, B.

BELOVED, *part.* Cyrys, kyrys, w.; thermaz, B.

BELOW. Dan, tan, dhan, dadn, yn dan, weath, awheath, wollas, B.; a wollas, c.w. 18; wolaz, B.; a wolas, c w. 59; warwolês, w.; uarolez, B.; uarnolés (? uarwolés), P.; icol, isod, isot, B.

BELT, s. Grugis, grigis, grigiz, grygis, w.; grygys, grwegus, grug, gouris, guris, cleddif, B.; vallok, o.m. 2967. *Na lader by my vallok*, he shall not steal, by my vallok, o.m. 2967. *Vallok* seems a form of *ballok*, a word used by the vulgar for the *scrotum* and *testés*; "by my vallok." being a coarse phrase. Norris translates it, *belt*.

BENCH, s. Benc, benk, bync, vync, w.; scavel, scavell, skaval, P.

BENCH or CHAIR, s. Ysgobeth, B. *A high bench or seat*, soler. B,

BENCH OF LIES. Scavell an gow, skaval angow, P.

BEND, v. Plegyé, w.; plegya, P.; plekgyé, pleghyé, w.; gwyrê, B.; camma, gamma, w.; cabmy, P.

TO BEND ONE'S SELF. Omgamma, w.

TO BEND, BOW OR NOD. Gogwyddo, B.

BEND, s. Plêg, plêth, w.; plêk, P.

BENDING, *adj.* Crum. crom, w.; krom, crobm, croum, B.

BENEATH, *prep.* See BELOW.

BENEFICIAL, *adj.* Mâs, w.; mâz, P.; vâs, fâs. mâd, mât, w.

BENEFIT, s. Lês, w.; leys, M. 3194. *Maria wek myr thy lêys*, sweet Mary, see to his benefit, M. 3194.

BENEVOLENCE. s. Cariad, B.

BENT or SEA RUSH, s. Starr, D.

BENUMBED. (With cold). Clum, D.

BEQUEATH, v. Cemynny, kemynny, cymmyny, w.; kemynni, P.; cymmuno, B.

BERRY, s. Bail, grawn, gronen, B.; moran, *Pl.* moyr, môr, moyar, w.

BESEECH, v. See, TO PRAY.

BESET, v. Gylchynu, restoua, B.

BESIDE. Drês, dreis, dreys, dreyz, drêz, drys, drîs, P.; reb, rip, ryb, ryp, N; *Me a gosk ryp y pen*, I will sleep beside his head, R.D. 418; juh, N.

BESIDES. Mernas, menas, w.; menes, P.

BESMEAR, v. Ysbryshu, B. See BEDUNG. *Lit.* To *clay*, one's self.

BESOM, s. See BROOM.

BEST, *adj.* Gwella, wella, w.; gwelha, c.w. 1957; guella, N.; guela, P.

BESTOW, v. Ro, roi, w.; roy, P.; zhoi, (? rhoi) B.; ry, rei, rey, w.

BETHINK, v. Thugy, P. *They bethought.* Y chugfyons, B. (? thugfyons). See CONSIDER.

BETHOUGHT HIMSELF. Prederys, brederys, B.

BETIMES. A dermyn, P.; y bore. y fore, B.

BETOKEN, v. Arwyddocan, B.

BETONY, s. Lês dushoc, w.

BETRAY, v. Thrayta, thragta, B.; towith, kuhuthé, kyhyda, P.

BETRAY, v. (*To betray a secret*). Datguddio, B.

BETRAYER, s. Traytour, thraytor, B.

BETROTH, v. Dyweddio, B.

BETTER. *adj.* Gwell, w.; guel, P.; guella, N.; wel, w.; bythwell, gallas, martha. *q.d.* so good, P.

FOR THE BETTER. In'wall, P.

HE MAY BETTER. (Improve). Wella, a mutation of *gwella*, id. qd. *gwello*, 3 pers. s. subj. of *gweila*, w.

IT IS BETTER. Guel yu, guello, P.

BETWEEN. Ynter, inter, yntre, etre, entre, tre, w.; trethow, in, en, P.; drethough, keffrys, kystris, hanter, B. *Yntre an môr ha'n tyryow*, between the sea and the lands, o.m. 26.

BETWEEN HIM. Yntredho, w.

BETWEEN THEM. Yntredhé, ynthrethyns, w.; trethyns, trethynz, P.

BETWEEN US. Yntredhon, yntrethon, trethon, w.; interranye, c.w. 841.

BETWEEN YOUR. Yntre agas. tres, w.; trez, p.

BETWEEN YE. Yntredhouch. w.; ynterthow, N.; ynterdhoch, w.; ynterthogh, N.

BETWIXT. See BETWEEN.

BEVERAGE, s. See DRINK.

BEWAIL, v. Galarow, w.; galarou, B.; gwelvan, olé, holea, w.; hoalea, elow, P

BEWARE, Exclam. Gueyt. queyt, p.

BEWITCH, v. Zheibio, p.

BEWITCHED. Huthick, p.

BEWRAY, or FOUL, v. Sautra, B.

BEYOND. Drês, dreys, d·eis, w.; dreyz, drêz, driz, trez, p.; tre, tra, w.; auyche, juh, p. Drês dyfen ow arluth ker, beyond the prohibition of my dear Lord, o M. 172.

BEYOND THEM. Trens, B.

BID, v. Herghy, arka, p. See TO COMMAND

BIDDING. s. (Charge). Gurchmennis, gorhemmyn, gurhemin, w. See COMMAND or COMMANDMENT.

BIER, s. Geler, elar, elor, w.; vasken, M. 4358. Geresugh orth an geler, help ye at the bier, M. 4487. Yma sûr wâr y vasken, is surely on his bier, M. 4358.

BIG, adj. Mûr, meur, mêr, maur, vêr, veur, w.; veor, p.; brâs, w.; brâz, B.; braos, brawse, p.; vrâs, w.; ûthyk, ûthy, ethek, ethuk. ethyk, ithyk, p.; houtyn. w.; ruth, p. See also, LARGE.

BIGGER, adj. Moy, voy, w.

BIGGEST, adj. Moya, moicha, p.

BIGNESS, s. Brâsder, vrâsder, mourder, w.; moygha, p.

BIG-BELLIED, adj. Torrog, tor brâs, w.; crothacke, c.w. 1105.

BIG-EYED, adj. Legasek, M, 3813. Lauer thymo legasek, tell me, thou big-eyed, M. 3813.

BILL, s. (Of a bird). Gelvin, w.; gelvyn, gilbin, B.

BILL, s. (The tool). Boell, bial, w.; biail, p.; bilw'g, B.

BILL, or NOSE OF LAND, s. Ryn, B.

BILL, v. (As a pigeon). Gwep, B.

BILL-HOOK, s. Filh, voulz, B.

BILLOW, s. (Great wave). Tôn, tûn, B.

BIND, or FASTEN. v. Celmy, kelmy, cylmy, kylmy, w.; kelma, colmye, B.; gelmy, gylmy, w.; lychy, synsia, p.

HE WILL BIND. Gelm, gylm, mutations of celm and cylm, 3 pers. s. fut. of celmy and cylmy, w.

BIND or GIRD, v. Strothé, s·trothy, w.

BINDER. s. (Of corn). Colmûr, w.

BIPARTITE. adj. Dibarh. dhibarh, w.

BIRCH, s. (Tree). Bezula, p.; bezo, be·lou, bedho, bedewen, w.

BIRD, s. Edhen. w.; edhyn, p.; idhen, w.; ydhyn, p.; ethen. B.; eithen, hethen, w.; ezen, B.; yolacit, w.; adglaer, Cott Ms, iq. qd. an eagle; nygethys. w. i e. that which flieth.

BIRDS, s. Ethyn, c.w. 108; edhen, ydhyn. lawan, w.; nethyn, as if an edhen, whence 'n ethen in the plural, p.

A YOUNG BIRD. Idnic, ydnic, w.; idninc, p.

BIRDLIME, s. Glûd, B.

(BIRTH), TO GIVE BIRTH TO, v. Denethy, denythy, dynythy, w.

BIRTH, s. Genegyg, M. 850. Omma an genegygva. of the birth here, M. 850.

BIRTHDAY, s. Nadelec, nedelic, w.; genesygeth, M. 4387. Ay genesygeth defry, from his birthday really M. 4387.

BISHOP, s. Escop, epscop, w.; escob, ebscob, B.; ispac, ispak, w. Pl. Epskobon, epskobou, p.

BISHOP'S SEE, s. Sethe, p

BIT, s. Banne. p.c. 1078. Judas ny gosk vn banne, Judas does not sleep a bit; mân. R.D. 295. Ellas thy'nny ny dal mân, alas! it avails us not a bit R.D. 295; tâm, tabm, o M. 551. Venytho na'n geffo tâm, he shall never have a bit, o.M. 551; skerrik, D.

A GOOD BIT. Polgé, M. 659. Polgé de alema, a good bit (distance) hence, M. 551.

A SMALL BIT OR PIECE. Didjan, midjan, mijum; didgen, (the g is soft) jowd, jowder, D.; peg, p.c. 1182. Den vythol na thovtgans. let not any man doubt a bit; peg p c 1182; peyth, o.M. 521. An peyth a wrehaf ny wra, the bit which I do will not o.M. 521; screed, D.

A SMALL BIT OR QUANTITY. (As of gold &c. found in streamworks). Prill, D.

SMALL BITS OR PIECES OF WRECK. Scubmaw, skubmaw. p.

NOT A BIT. What, whera ban, p.

BITCH, s. (Female dog). Gêst, gyst, w. Pryce gives gesti as a plural for dogs or bitches.

BITE, v. Danta, w; cnoi, deintio, danhedda, dendzall, B.

BITTER, adj. Wherow, hwero, w.; huero, p.; chuero, w.

MORE BITTER. Hwerwa, w.; huerua, huera, p.

BITTER, or CRUEL, adj. Wherow, chuero, w.

BITTER, adj. (Sorrowful, regretful). Tyn, o.M. 402. Daggrow tyn gvraf dyveré, bitter tears I shall shed, o.M. 402.

BITTER PANGS. Galarou, B.

BITTERN, s. Clabitter, w. ; klabitter, B.

BITTERNESS, s. Bestyll, B. This word also means *gall* of the liver. See GALL.

BLAB, s. Tavas re hîr, w. *Lit.* Long tongue.

BLACK, *adj.* Du, diu, dhiu, duw, w. ; dyon *Pl.* of du, w. ; dew, P. ; tew, O.M. 546 *Nefre yn tewolgow tew,* ever in black darkness, O.M. 546 ; thew, teual ; and in names *thew* is changed to *sew,* as Carnsew, P. ; morel, M. 2111, but this is a name for the black cherry whence perhaps the term. *Pyma thym ov margh morel,* where for me is my black horse, M. 2111.

BLACKBERRY, s. Moran dhiu, w. ; moran diu, P. ; moaren, w. ; moras, B. *Pl.* Moyar diu, w. ; môr diu, P.

BLACKBIRD, s. Mola-dhiu, moelh ; in composition it is written *woelh, woof,* P.

BLACKGUARD, s. See SCOUNDREL, or RASCAL.

BLACKISH, *adj.* Pyst. w.

BLACK-MAN, s. Dên diu, w.

BLACK-MONTH, s. The black month. (November). Mis diu. w.

BLACKSMITH, s. Gôf du, B. ; gôf diu, w. ; gov diu, P. ; ferror, heirnior, w.

BLACKSMITH'S SHOP, s. Gofail, govail, w. ; gof-adl, P.

BLACKNESS, s. Duat, diuat, B.

BLACK THORN, s. Spêrnan diu. w.

BLADDER, s. Gysigan, w. ; gyzigan, guzigan, churisigen, B. ; gusigan, w.

BLADDER OF A FISH. Cowl. D.

BLAME, s. Bai, B.

BLAME. v. Airthbear, B.

BLAMELESS, *adj.* Difai. B.

BLANCH or WHITEN. v. Cannu, B.

BLANKET, s. Lên. (*Sagum,* Corn. Vocab), w.

BLASPHEMY, s. Cabledd, serthed, B.

BLAST, s. (Wind). Whêth, hwêth, w. ; huez, P. ; êth, w.

BLAST, s. (Puff). Bremmyn, P. ; êth, w. Bremmyn is the *plural* of *bram,* a fart or puff.

BLASTING, or STROKING WITH A PLANT. (*sic*). Echrys, B.

BLAZE, s Tangés. M. 2106. *Yma ov lesky an coys the vn tangés lel,* the wood is burning to a real blaze, M. 2106.

A SHORT SUDDEN BLAZE. Screech, D. (?)

BLAZE, v. Tewy, tiwy, tywy, w. ; tewé, tewye, P. ; dewy, diwy, dywy, w.

BLEAK, *adj.* (Cold). Oer, P. ; oerni, oich, oerfel, oerder, B.

BLEAK, *adj.* (Bare, exposed). Voel, B.

BLEAR-EYED, *adj.* Primusdoc, w. ; pimuschoch, perhaps more correctly, wimuschoc ; cuic, B.

BLEAT, v. Priva, brivia, w. ; brefu, breferud, B.

BLEB, s. Chusigen, guzigan, B. See also BLADDER.

BLEED. v. (To lose blood). Gwaedu, B. ; dewosa, M. 1575, dewosé, M. 1619.

BLEEDING, (At the nose). Gwaedling, B.

BLEMISH, s. Anav, B. ; gyll ; tull, *Heb tull ny gyll,* without blemish or fault, P. ; nam, w.

BLEMISH, v. Anglod, drygaer, B.

BLESS, v. Soné, sona, zona, w. ; benigia, B. ; fenygia, kesky, kisky, gisky, P.

I BLESS. Bynygaf, w.

YE BLESS. Fenygough, N.

YE WILL BLESS. Benygouch, fenygouch, w.

BLESSED, *adj.* Gwyn, wyn, *Maria wyn,* blessed Mary, M. 3190.

BLESSED, *part, and adj.* Benegés, benygés, benegas, benigas, w. ; benigeys, M. 1191 ; benigays, M. 1117 ; bynegés, bynygés, bynygys, veneges, w. ; bennet, P. ; sonas, B. ; sonys, O.M. 466. *Gans werés du benegeys,* with help of blesssed God. M. 1991. *Awos an tas bynygeys,* because of the blessed father, P.C. 400. *Ov vos sonys hep whethlow,* being blessed without idle tales, O.M. 466. *Bennet sewys,* blessed be thou, P.

BLESSEDNESS, s. Venegycter, M. 203 ; *Luen os a venegycter,* full art thou of blessedness, M. 203 ; venesycter, M. 4495.

BLESSING, s. Benés, benneth, w. ; beneth, M. 31 ; benath, B. ; bennath, banneth, w. ; bednath, P. ; bedneth, M. 198 ; benet, P.C. 3015 ; vanneth, M. 211 ; vennath, w. ; dyson, B. ; son, O.M. 896. *Pl.* Bannethow, w. ; bannothow, M. 46.

BLIND, v. Dalla, w.

BLIND, *adj.* Dall, dal. w. ; thal, O.M. 1056 ; teual, P. ; kuick, B. ; kuk, M. 3481.

BLIND OF ONE EYE. Cuic, w. ; ydn lagadzhak, lygadzhiag, P. The other forms of *cuic* are kuick, B. ; and kuk, M. 548i, in which two last references, *kuik* and *kuk* simply mean blind. See *William's Lex. Corn. Brit.* for *Cuic.*

BLIND-MAN, s. Dal, P. ; an abbreviated form of *dén dal.*

BLINDED, *part.* Dyegrys, M. 3667 *Dyegrys off gans gvynder,* blinded am I by whiteness. M. 3667.

BLINKARD, s. Kuick, B. Borlase also uses this word for *blind.*

BLISS, s. Lowene, lowyne, lowender, lowenna, w. ; dedwyddweh, B.

BLISTER, s. (Bleb or vesicle). Gwenan, w. ; guenan, P. ; chusigen, guzigan. See BLADDER.

BLOCK, *s.* Cyff, boncyff, B. *Block of wood*, Blog, blogon, P.

BLOCKHEAD, *s.* Boba, w. ; dicreft, B. ; lorden, w. ; pen cok, pen pyst, P. ; pen blogh, M. 3828. *Me a pylse the pen blogh*, I will peel thy blockhead, M. 3828 ; talsoch, treuzhan, B. *Treuzhan* in the form of *dreuzen*, or *droosen* is still in use. A "dreuzen headed fellow" means a blockhead, a stupid person. Also zape, zapey, zawker, D.

BLOOD, *s.* Goys, gôs, goos, goosh, w. ; guyzh, B. ; guoys, gudzh, P. ; guydzh, guyd, w. ; guydh, B. ; guit, w ; kues, kueus, P. ; kuevs, R.D. 231 ; cues, crow, w. ; crou, P. ; wôs, woos, w. ; woose, C.W. 2522 ; voys, O.M. 577 ; oys, w.

BLOOD LETTING, *s.* Dilla gudzh, w. ; dilla guyzh, B.

BLOOD PUDDING, *s.* Gudzhygan, w. ; gudzhigan, B.

BLOODY, *adj.* Gooshac, w. ; gooshak, P. ; gosys, B.

BLOSSOM, *v.* Blodeno, B.

BLOSSOM, *s.* Blodon. BLOSSOMS, Blegyow. w.

BLOT or BLUR, *s.* Brych, magl, B.

BLOW, *v.* Whethé, w. ; whethy, P. ; whythé, w. ; wheythy, P. ; hwetha, w. ; huetha, P. ; hwethia, w. ; huethia, P. ; wethe, wyth, B.

TO BLOW THE HORN. Whethé the gorn, B.

BLOW or THUMP, *s.* Bom, bum, bommen, bync, boxses, w. ; bynk, P. ; banc, w. ; bank, B. ; blygh, P. ; tummas, whaf. w. ; wat, what, P. ; scat, B. skat, P. ; skuit, strôc, strocos, stuen, B. ; clout, fôs, P. ; pylt, B ; *Gans morben bom trewysy,* with a mallet, a terrible blow, O.M. 2704. *Ry whaf thethy my a wra,* give a blow to her I will. O.M. 2755. *Me a re clout thotho,* I shall give a blow to him, P. *Pyua rôs thyso an wat,* who gave thee the blow? P. ; coot, tummas. poot D. See also THUMP OR BLOW.

BLOW OR SLAP, *s.* Stlap, stlaf, w. ; For more see SLAP.

A HEAVY BLOW Vumfra. D ; This appears to be the same as *bum brâs,* a great blow.

BLOWS, *s.* Bomennow, vomennow, the *pl.* of *bommen;* boxsesow, pl. of *boxses,* w. ; borow, P. ; blythen, blyzen, B. ; hoxsusow. P.C. 1389. *Ha ren thotho boxsusow,* and gave him blows, P.C. 1389.

BLOWING-HOUSE, *s.* Fôg, w. ; foge, P. (*g* soft). *Carra an stean dha an fóg,* carry the tin to the blowing-house, w. (A blowing-house is the place where tin ore is melted; so called because of the great bellows used for the fire).

BLUDGEON, *s.* Blogon, O.M. 2709 ; uther, B. ; lôr vraoz, P.

BLUE, *adj.* Glâs, w. ; glayis, B. ; glase, glaze, P. ; glays, M. 1445 ; lâs, w. ; lays, B. *Tovle in the wedyr glays,* throw it into thy blue glass, M. 1445.

BLUE. (A light or sky blue). Blou, P.

BLUE. (To become blue). Glasé, w.

BLUE-TIT, *s.* Pridn-prall, D.

BLURR, SMUDGE, or STREAK, *s.* Strôm, D.

BLUSH, *v.* Yswilio, B.

BLUSTERING, *s.* Rôs, P. *Yn ow rôs,* in my blustering. Pryce says *rôs* is from *trôs,* a nose. Curiously enough they call a blusterer a *nosey* fellow.

BOAR, *s.* Baedh, w. ; bahed, B. ; bahet, w. ; baeth, bora, P. ; yerrés, borro, barro, B. ; ors, P.

BOARS-FLESH, *s.* Bahed kyg, B.

BOARD or PLANK, *s.* Plancen, planken, plyncen, plync, w. ; plankan, P. ; astel, w. ; astell, B. ; astull, w. ; astyllen, B.. See PLANK or PLANKS.

BOARD and TABLE, *s.* Bôrd, P.

BOAST, *v.* Bostyé, w. ; gwertha, guerha, P. ; borsach, B.

BOASTER, *s.* Qualloc, w.

BOASTERS, *s.* Bosteryon, vosteryon, w.

BOASTING, *s.* Bôst, bôs, fôs, fâs, w. ; rôs, terrôs, whêth, P.

BOAT, *s.* Côc, w. ; côk, P. ; scâth, schâth, w. ; gurhal bien, P.

BOATS, *s.* Kûkû (coo-coo), scatha, w. ; skatha, P.

BOATSWAIN, *s.* Brenniat, w. ; brennyat, brennat, B. ; leuint, P.

BODY, *s.* (Corpse). Corf, w. ; corfe, B. ; corff, M. ; 523 ; korf, B. ; gorf, O.M. 2367 ; horf, horfe, B. ; trogel, M. 4367. *In trogel in breten suyr,* in a body, in Brittany surely, M. 4367.

A LITTLE BODY. Corfel, B.

BOG, *s.* Cors, tir devrak, w. ; devrak, winnick, whynick, P. ; siglen, B. (? a privy).

BOGS, *s.* Canego, B.

BOG-PLANT, *s.* Corsen, w.

BOGGY, *adj.* Gwinic, w.

BOGGY LAND, *s.* Tir devrak, B.

BOIL, *s.* (*Anthrax*). Cornwyd, gweli, pedn diu, w. ; *Pedn diu* is literally blackhead, the provincial name for a boil or furuncle.

BOIL, *v.* Bredion, bridion, bridzhan, bridzhian, w. ; brudziar, B. ; prydzhan, w.

BOILING, *part.* Brôs, broaze, P. This is still used for anything which is near the boiling point.

AT BOILING POINT. Broaze, B.V.

BOILING, *s.* (A boiling or coction). Bredion, B. ; bredian, P. ; prydzhan, B.

BOISTEROUS, *adj.* Drychinog, tymbestlog, B.

BOISTEROUSNESS, *s.* Uary, P.

BOLD, *adj.* Asper, o.m. 2203; drês, drews, w.; drues, m. 1047; hardh, w.; kriv, vold, B. *My a'd pys may fy asper,* I pray thee to be bold, o.m. 2203.

BOLDNESS, *s.* Hyfder, B.

BOLSTER, *s.* (A long large pillow). Plufoc, plyvog. w.; penguele, gobennudd, B.

BOLSTERS. Claatgueli, B.

BOLSTER or **PILLOW CASE**, *s.* Slip, D.

BOLT, *s.* Attal, baar, trossol, B.

BOLT, *v.* Bara, w.; prenny, p.c. 3038; sparla, B.

BOND or **TIE**, *s.* Colm. colmen, golmen, gelmen, w.

BONDAGE, *s.* (Slavery). Habadin, gwasanaeth, w.; guasanaeth, p.; caethiwed. B.

BONDSMAN or **SLAVE**. *s.* Vehegar, B.; caeth, caid, w.; caith, caid pinid, B.

BONDSWOMAN. BONDWOMAN, or **FEMALE SLAVE**, *s.* Caités, w.; caithés, kaithés, B.

BONE, *s.* Ascorn, asgorn, w.; asgarn, esgar p.; scren, B. The Cornish say, "I hav'nt a *scren*," *i.e.* nothing.

BONES. *s.* Escarn, yscarn, w.; *Yscarn map dev dygavelsys,* the bones of the Son of God laid bare, p.c. 3179; yscren, B.; scren, p.; *Nevera ol ys scren,* number all his bones, p.

BONFIRE, *s.* Tanllwyth, eiriasden, B.

BONY, *adj.* Asgornec, w.; asgorneck, B.

BOOBY, *s.* Boba, w.; bobo, bobba, p.c. 1778, 2385. *Nyn syv lemyn vn boba,* he is not now a booby, p.c. 1778.

BOOK, *s.* Levar, lyvyr, liver, w.; lavar, lyfr, B.; levyr, N.; caiauc, w. *A little book.* Stollof. p.

BOOKS, *s.* Leverow, lyfrow, lyffrow, lyfryow, w.

BOOKCASE, *s.* Levarva, r.

BOOT, *s.* Hôs. (*Lat.* hosa) w.

BOOTH, *s.* Bôth, w.

BORDER, *s.* See EDGE.

BORDER, *s.* (Of a country, or coast). Urrian, w.; yrhian, min, miniog, B.; cûr, gûr, w.; kûr, p.; bro, vro, w.; brou, B.

BORE, *v.* (To bore a hole). Telly, tolla, tylly, w.; tyllou, B.; delly, tardhé, w.; tardha, p.; ebilio, B. *Aban yv an pren tellys,* since the wood is bored, p.c. 2573. *Y delly scon my a wra,* I will soon bore it. p.c. 2570.

BORE, *v.* (To pierce or stab). Guâna, B.

BORED, *part.* Tollys, p.

HE WILL BORE. Tyl, dyl; teyl, 3 pers. s. fut. of *telly*, w.

HE BORED A HOLE. Dollas, a mutation of *Tollas,* preterite of *tolly,* to bore, w.

BORER, *s.* Tarad, tarder, w.

BORN, CARRIED, *part.* Aborthés, degis, p.

BORN, *v.* (TO BE BORN). Geny, w.; *Fflogh byen nowyth gynys,* a little child newly born, o.m. 806.

BORN, BEGOTTEN, *part.* Denethys, B.; genys, gynys, w.; genyz. p. *Genys ha mygys,* born and bred, p.

BORN, *part.* Ffras, B. *To be born.* Inffras. B.

BOROUGH or **CORPORATION**, *s.* Trefraint, B.

BORROW. *v.* Benthygio, B

BOSOM, *s.* Ascra, ascle, B.; hascra, m. 544; devra (n) c.w.; 1837; *Hag in y devra flogh teake,* and in her bossom a fair child, c.w. 1837; bodn, bron, p.; brys, r.d. 191; brodn, w.; brun, B.; pron, w. vrys, p.; *Creator a brys benen,* creatures from the bosom of woman, r.d. 191

BOSOMS, *s.* (The two bosoms, or breasts). Duivron, defran, devran; cluid duyvron, p.

BOSS or **STUD**, *s.* Prumpl, B.

BOTH, *s.* (The two). An diew, diew, w.; an dieu, dieu. p.

BOTHER, *s.* (Worry, perplexity). Crum a grackl, D.

BOTTOM, *s.* (The buttock or breech). Cylbah, kylbah, tyn, teen, tin, patshan, pedren, penclûn, penklyn, w.

BOTTOM, *s.* (The lowest part). Golés, golas, w.; golaz, B.; gollas, p.; gullas, wolés, w.; wolas, B.; izy, p.; isav, B.

THE BOTTOM OF. Iseldor, w.

THE BOTTOM OR GROUND OF ANYTHING, Eigion, B.

BOTTOMLESS PIT, *s.* Pul doun, downder, w.; dounder, B.

BOUGH, *s.* (Of a tree). Sciran, scoren, w.; skiran, scorren, B.; skoran, c.w. 687; bar, baren, p.; varen, w; kerdinen, rhodd, B.; *Many boughs,* Lues scoren, p. *Lit.* Many a bough. *Pl.* Scorennow, o.m. 780; barennow, o.m. 788.

BOUGHT, *part.* Prennas, brennas, prinid, *Caid prinid,* a bought slave. w. See BUY.

BOUND, *v.* (To leap). Lammé, lemmel, w., lamma. p.

BOUND, TIED, or **FASTENED**. Colmas, golmas, B.; renothas, p.

BOUND, OBLIGED. COMPELLED. Sensys, sengys, syngys, dysosys, w.

BOUND, BOUNDARY, or **LIMIT**, *s.* Diwedh, dywedh, w.; diuadh, p.; dyweth, w.; diuath, B.; diua, p.; dewedh, duadh, dywedhva, duwedhva, fen, fin, fyn, w.; geyth, gyst, p.; hars, harz, or, ors, cyffin, B.

BOUND-STONE or **BOUNDARY STONE**, *s.* Mén hars, B. mén-heir.

BOUNDARY, *s.* (Border of a country). Urrian, w.; yrhian, min, miniog, B.

BOUNTIFUL, *adj* Hail, w.

BOUNTY, *s.* Roweth, w.; huelder, B.

BOW, *s.* (For arrows; or that which is bent). Gwarac, guarac, w.; guarrak, B.; gwaracke, c.w. 1466. *Pl.* Guaregov, M. 3911. *Hag archers gan guaregov*, and archers with bows, M. 3911.

BOW, *v.* Vossa, B.

BOW, *v.* (To bow down, to bow down to, to bow the knee). Plegyé, plygyé, blygyé, w.; plegy, P.; plegya, plynché, B.

BOW, *v* (To bow or nod the head). Gogwyddo, gogwyddo pen, B

BOWED or BENT, *adj.* Crum, crom, w.; krom, kroum, crobm, kam, kabm, B.

BOWED or BENT DOWN. Gamma, omgammé, B.

BOWEL, *s.* Colon, w.; koloneion, P.; cylyrion, culurionen, culurionein, w.; enederon, B.; pott, w.; pot, D.

BOWELS, *s.* Enederen, B.; coloneiou, w.; kylyrion, B.; pottis, M. 1272. *Pots* or *potts* is still used for bowels by the vulgar in Cornwall.

BOWL, *s.* Hanaf, hanath, bolla, fiol, w.

BOWL. *s.* (The ball used in the game of bowls). Pellan, P.

BOW LEGGED, *adj.* Divesgergam, w.; i.e. Crooked two shanks.

BOW-LINE, *s.* (In a fishing boat). Vargord, B.V.; vargoard, w.F.P.

BOWSTRING, *s.* Tenewen, denewen, ternewan, tornewan, tyrnewan, w.; tornehuan, P.

BOX, *s.* See BLOW.

BOX, *v.* Boxcusy, w. (To strike blows).

BOX, *s.* (Trunk or coffer). Trôc, trôk, w. *Teleugh ef yn trôk a horn*, cast it in a box of iron, R D. 2162; prenol, B.; cofor, cofer, P.; kopher, kophor, B.; kist.

A SMALL BOX OR CHEST. Kistan, B.

BOX-TREE, *s.* Box, w.; bix, P.; byx, P.C. 26.

BOY, *s.* Mâb, maw, w.; maow, N.; mau, P.; mawe, c.w. 204; vaw, w.; vau, vaow, flôch, flôh, flôgh, hlôh, P.; guas, M. 1884. *Ty vaow*, thou boy.

A LITTLE BOY. Meppig, B.

BOYS, *s.* Meyb, mebion, mebyon, mybyon, mebbion, cosgor, kosgar. *Gen kosgar*, our boys, w.

BRACELET, *s.* Moderuy, w.; modereuy, B.

BRAG, *v.* Bostyé, folie, w.; guerha, gwertha, P.

BRAG, *s.* Bôst, bôs, fôst, fâs, w.

BRAGGART, *s.* Qualloc, w.; quallok, O.M. 2068; guallak, P.

BRAGGARTS, *s.* Bosteryon, vosteryon, w.

BRAGGING, *s.* Bôst, bôs, tôst, fâs, w. *Awos agas tâs ha trôs*, notwithstanding your bragging and noise, P.C. 2.10; rôs, *yn ow rôs*, in my bragging. P.; terros, wheth, P.

BRAID, *s.* Plêth, w.

BRAID, *v.* Plethan. *Polwhele.*

BRAIN, *s.* Empen, w.

BRAINS, *s.* Empinion, impinion, ympynion, empynyon, empynnyou, ympynnyon, empinnion, w.; ompynnen, M. 1274; ompenyon, M. 2996; pidnian, P.; ampydgnyan, a corruption of *empynyon*, w.; nenpynion, i.e. "an empynion, the brain," B. But these are true plurals.

BRAKE, *s.* Redanan, w. Borlase and Pryce use this word for a brake of ferns.

BRAMBLE, *s.* Draenen, dreisen, w.; dreizan, drachen. *Pl.* Drên, drein, drain, drize; dreis, w.; dreyne, c.w. 1091 Borlase erroneously gives dren, drein, drain, and drize, in the singular. Spedhen. *Pl.* Spedhés, w.; spethés, P.

BRAMBLE-BERRY, *s.* (Blackberry). Moran diu, P.

BRAMBLE-BUSH, *s.* Moyr bren. Pryce thought this was the proper name for a mulberry tree; yet he gives it for a bramble-bush.

BRAN, *s.* Talch, w.; eisin, ysgarthion, B.

BRANCH, *s.* (Of a tree). See BOUGH. *Branches*, Palmés, B.

BRANCH, *s.* (Of a river). Savig, B.

BRANCH OUT, *v.* (To branch out). Blaguro, B.

BRAND or MARK, *s.* Arwydd, B.

BRANDED, *part.* (Stigmatized). Omskemynés, P.

BRANDICE, BRAND-IRON, *s.* Tribêdh, trebath, tribet, w.

BRANDISH, *v.* Ysgwydarf, B.

BRANDY, *s.* Dour tubm Franc, B. *Lit.* French hot water.

BRASS, *s.* Brêst, prêst, w.; elydr, elydn, B.; kober, cober, P. *Cober* and *kober* are the proper names for copper.

BRAT, *s.* Spud, D.

BRAVE, *adj.* Dour, M. 4323. *Sensys gans ov flehys dour* held by my brave children. M. 4323.

A BRAVE FELLOW, Guas smat, or briefly *smat*, w. *Dysmyg lemmyn ty guas smat*, declare now, thou brave fellow, P.C. 1382.

BRAWL, *v.* Deragla, w.; ymeirio, B.

BRAWLING, *s.* Bairsighe, B.

BRAWN, *s.* Brawan, P.

BRAY, *v.* Begy, w.

BRAZE, *v.* Elyddu, pressu, B.

BRAZIER, *s.* Gueiduur cober.

BREACH, *s.* Tolva, do va, w.; brêg, gwyth, wyth, with, P.

BREAD, *s.* Bara, vara, w.; varé, o.m. 2186.

WHITE BREAD. Bara gwyn, w.

WHEATEN BREAD. Bara gwaneth, w.

BARLEY BREAD. Bara haiz, w.

OATEN BREAD. Bara kerh, w.

RYE BREAD. Bara sugall, w.

A LOAF OF BREAD. Torth a vara, w.

ANYTHING EATEN WITH BREAD. Sant, w.; saut. B.

A BIT OF BREAD AND BUTTER. Tam, tabm, D.

BREADTH, *s.* Lês, leas, w.; leys P. *Three breadths*, Tryllês, w.

BREAK, *v.* Terry, terhi, terhy, tyrry. w.; torr, N.; torri, P.; torry, trochy, w ; trehy, troghy, P.; trohy, derry, derhy, dyrry, w.; doré, dorré, P.; skuattia, scuattya, sguattia, squattya, dho skuattya, gwaythy, gwethé, w.; guethé, P.; fethy, ranné. w.; recto, *Mara gwrewo un recto*, if I did once break, P.; crakyé, crakya, B.; grachia, P.; grachya, B.

TO BREAK IN PIECES. Brewy, squardyé, squerdyé, w.; squerdya, P.

TO BE BROKEN IN PIECES. Squardyé, squerdyé, w.; squerdya, P.

TO BREAK IN SMALL PIECES Dryllio, B.

TO BREAK OFF. Trochy, trohy, trechy, trehy, tyrry, dyrry, w.

TO BREAK OR BRUISE. Cob, dho cob, B. The breaking up of the stones of ore is called *cobbing*, and those who do this in the Cornish mines are called *cobbers.*

TO BREAK OUT. (As an eruption on the skin). Tardbé, w.

HE MAY BREAK. Dorro, a mutation of *torro*, 3 pers. s. fut. of *torry*, to break, w.

I WILL BREAK. Dorraf. a mutation of *torraf*, 1 pers. s. fut. of *turry*. to break, w.

HE WILL BREAK. Ter, der, 3 pers. s. fut of *torry*, to break, w.

BREAKING, *s.* Terry, terri. *Terri an dédh*, the breaking, or break of day, w.

BREAKING OUT, *s.* (An eruption on the skin). Tardh, tarth, P.

BREAKFAST, *s.* Haunsel, hounsal, halsel, dishunish, B.; dizanhih, P.; boren frwyd, B.; li, w.; ly, P.

BREAM, *s.* Siw, w.; zew, ziu, P.; ziew, B. (*Pl.* Sewion). wyan, P ; shewyan, c.w. 1410; zivion, B. *A bream of a lesser kind.* Lobmas, P.; lobmaz, B. There is a kind of bream which the Cornish call *becker*, D.

A BREAM TWO THIRDS GROWN. Grobman D.

A BREAM HALF GROWN. Plosher, D.

BREAST, *s.* See BOSOM. *Ahanaf ketep map bron*, for me every son of the breast, P.C. 892. *Avel kyns ketep map pron*, as before; every son of the breast, O.M. 1162.

BREAST, PAP, or TEAT, *s.* Tidy, w.; tidi, P. In the dialect, to give a child the breast is expressed by "giving the child some tiddy."

A LITTLE BREAST. Têthan, w.

BREAST-HOOK, *s.* (Of a boat). Gwaith, D.

BREAST-PLATE, *s.* Duyfronneg, B.

BREATH, *s.* (The breath). Alan, anal, anall, B.; anel, M. 4094; *Púr guir gans hy anel poys*, right truly by her heavy breath, M. 4094; huez, spryes, P.; whêth, hwêth, w.; êth, O.M. 1994. *Pan yo mar whek aga eth*, since their breath is so sweet, O.M. 1994.

BREATH or PUFF, *s.* Whêth, hwêth, êth, w.

BREATHE, *v.* Whyth, whethé, B.

BREATHLESS, TO BE BREATHLESS. Dyené, tyené. w. See TO PANT.

BREATHING, *s.* Pregoth, B.

BRED, NURTURED, *part.* Megys, migys, mygys, w.; megyz, mighyz. P.

BREECH, *s.* See BOTTOM.

BREECHES, *s.* Lafroc, lafrog, lavrac, lavrak, w.; lavarrak, lydrou, laudr, B.

BREED, *v.* (Nourish or bring up). Mâg, B.

BREED, *v.* (To be breeding, to become pregnant). Ymdhoyn, humdhan, w.; humthan, P.; eppilio (? an euillio), B.

BREED, *v.* (To breed maggots, or to rot). Centreyny, kentreyny, w.

BREEDER, *s.* Tadvath, tadvat, w.

BREEDING, *part.* Humthan. *Ma hy a humthan*, she here is breeding. B.

BREEZE, *s.* Awel, auhel, w.; awal, P.

BRETHREN, *s.* Breder, vreder, bredereth, brudereth, w.

BREW, *v.* Darlow, gara brihi, B.

BREWER, *s.* Darllawydd, B.

BREWER'S GRAINS, *s.* Seag zeag, w.; seage, zeage, B.; *Lacku vel seage*, worse than grains, B.

BRIAR, *s.* Spedhen. *Pl.* Spedhés, w.; spethés, O M, 275.

BRIARS, BRAMBLES, AND SUCHLIKE *s.* Dréis, w.

BRIBE, *v.* Halogu, B.

BRICK, *s.* Pob-faen, B.

BRIDE. *s.* Bennen priot, benen nowydh, B.; priot, B. *Priot* is a term used for both sexes, as *gûr-priot*, a bridegroom, *bennen priot*, a bride, B.

BRIDEGROOM, *s.* Gur-priot, dên nowydh, B.

BRIDEWELL, *s.* Carchur, carchurdy, B.

BRIDEWOMAN, *s.* Bennen priot, benen nowydh, B.

BRIDGE, *s.* Pons, W.; ponz, B.; pont, pon, P.

A FOOT BRIDGE. Clam, D.

BRIDLE, *s.* Fruyn, W.; frudn, P.

BRIEF. SHORT, *adj.* Cut, cot, W.; cueth, cutta, byr, ber, ver, B.

A BRIEF OR SHORT TIME. Cut termyn, P.

BRIEFNESS, *s.* Breder, berder, vreder, W.

BRIEFLY, *adv.* Breder, brief, W.

BRIGHT, *adj.* Cleyr, clêr, dyblans, dhyblans, W.; *Ow formyé têk ha dyblans,* me create fair and bright, O.M. 87; elyn, C.W. 90. *Rág y wetha pûr elyn* for to keep it full bright, C.W. 90; golow, W; glân, O.M. 34. *Then beys ol golowys glân,* to all the world bright lights, O.M. 34; splân, spladn, B.; splèn, tevery, deverye, P.

BRIGHTNESS, *s.* Fflûr, B.; goleuder, golowder, splander, W.; splandor, P.

BRILLIANCY, *s.* The same as "Brightness," *q. v.*

BRIM or EDGE OF ANYTHING, *s.* Urrian, yrhian, W.

BRIM, *v.* (As a sow). Gydhivaz, B. (*Marem appetere*).

BRIMSTONE. *s.* Mygfaen, ruibht, B.

BRINE, *s.* Gulyber, helu, B.; hyly, W. *Nag yn dour nag yn hyly,* nor in water, nor in brine, R.D. 2318.

BRING, *v.* Dôn, doen, dhôn, tôn, W.; doan, B.; doyn, doga, degy, W.; dregy, P.; doroy, W.; doro, *Doro thym an guyn guella,* bring me the best wine, P.; dyrey, drey, dry, W.; dyg, B.; dyghty, thyghtye, thoro, try, rén, êry, P.; hombroncy, hembryncy, hebrency, W.; hembrynky, P. Cerchés, kerchés, kerghas, cyrchés, cerhés, kerhés, kerhez, kergh, kyrgh, gerchés, gerhaz, P.; cyrhas, gyrhas, W.

BRING FORTH, *v.* Denythy, dynythy, W.; nystevy, P.

BRING TOGETHER, *v.* Dierbyn, dyerbyn, P.

BRING THOU. Dro, drou, W.; drew, P.; doro, N.

LET HIM BRING. Drens, N.

BRING YE. Dreuch, W.; dreugh, P.

HE MAY BRING. Tokko. From *degy,* B.

THAT HE MAY BRING. Mai tokko, from *degy,* B.

HE WILL BRING. Drossa, gerch, a mutation of *cerch,* 3 pers. s. fut. of *cerchés,* W.

WE WILL BRING BACK. Trylyn, dryllin, W.

BRINK, *s.* See BORDER, and BRIM.

BRINK, *s.* (Side of a river, or of a bank or "cutting") Glân, glând, W. This is still in common use with miners, &c.

BRISKLY, *adv.* Broazen. As of a fire burning briskly, P. This term is still remembered by a few.

BRISTLE, *s.* Gurychin, B.

BRITISH, *adj.* Brethonec, W.

BRITON, A BRITON, *s.* Kembra; *Chi an Kembra,* the house of a Briton, P. (*Pl.* Brethon, W.)

BRITTANY, *s.* Lezow, B.; Breton, M. 231; Breten, M. 511; Bryten, M. 1; Bryton vyan, (*Little Britain*) M, 169; Vreten, M. 649. *A vreten,* from Brittany.

BRITTLE, *adj.* Brenoll, brettol, B.; vrotall, C.W. 22.3; hydruk, P.

BROAD. *adj.* Ledan, W.; bredar, B.; rûth P.; lidden, D.

BROAD or O EN, *adj.* Leas, lees, leys, lês, P.

BROAD-FIGS, *s.* Figés ledan, W.

BROIL, *s.* (Tumult). Godoryn, B. See, ROW, UPROAR, FRAY.

BROIL, *v.* Crussu, B.

BROKE or BROKEN. Dorré, B.; troch, brew, vrew, W.; torras, dorras, B.

TO BE BROKEN. Ranné, W.

HE BROKE. Dorras, a mutation of *torras* 3 pers, s. pret. of *torry,* to break, W.

HE HAD BROKEN. Dorrassa, a mutation of *torrasa,* 3 pers. s. pluperf, of *torry,* to break, W.

BROOD, *v.* (To sit on brood). Gorweddar, B.

BROOD, *s.* (Of chicken). Deoriad, B.

BROOK, *s.* Ick, thour, carrog, P.; Karrog is doubt-fully given by Borlase for a river, B.

FULL OF BROOKS. Hêlêk, From *hêl,* a river, B.

BROOM, *s.* (The plant). Banal, banathel, W.

BROOM, *s.* (To sweep with). Bannolan, banolan, bynolan, W.; bynollan, B.; bannal, P.; scubellen, scubilen, yscubell, B.

BROTH, *s.* Brôs, R D. 142. *Yn brôs pûr dêk,* in a very fair broth, R.D. 142; cowl, coul, caul, W.; kaul, P.; kowl, B.; joul, iskel, isgel, P.; ligge, B.V. brawder, B.

BROTHEL, *s.* Tshyi hora, P. *Lit.* Whore-house.

BROTHER, *s.* Broder, bredar, brodar, bruder, W.; brauder, P.; braud, W.; brawd, B.; vroder, vredar, W. *Pl.* Breder, vreder, bredereth, brudereth, W; bredereth, P.

BROTHERHOOD, *s.* Brudereth, W.; brawdoliath, B.

BROUGHT, *part.* Drês, dreys, druyth, drûth, W.; drew, P.; dhrôz, dhroys, dhoroaz, drossen, bronkis, B.

HE BROUGHT. Dûc, dhûc, dùg, dyg, drôs, dhros, W.

WE HAD BROUGHT. Drossen, w.

BROW or FOREHEAD CLOTH, *s.* Talien, koruadh, B.

BROWN, *adj.* Teual, P.; guinenddhy, B. *Lit.* Black white.

BRUISE, *v.* Terry, terhi, tyrry, torry, w.; torri, P.; brewy, w.; bodrethé, P. See BREAK.

BRUISE, *v.* Ysigo, B. (? as of corn).

BRUISED, *part.* Brew, vrew, w.

BRUISE, *s.* Brew, w.; buffon, D.

BRUISES, *s.* Brewyon, vrewyon, bodredhés, w.; bodrethés, P.; potredés, w. *Del veth luen a bodrethés,* that it shall be full of bruises, O.M. 2714.

BRUSH. *s.* Scibia, w.; skibia, P; scaberia, w.; ysgubo, B.

BRUTAL, *adj.* Melen, milen, mylen, velen, vilen, vylen, felen, w.

BUBBLE, *s.* Hwêthvians, w.; huêthvians, P. *Hwêthvians an dour,* a bubble of water.

BUCK, *s.* (Buck goat, he-goat). Bôck, w.; bôc, byk, P.; byck, B.; bocca. P.; bogh, M. 3418.

BUCK'S HEAD, *s.* Pen bogh, M. 3418.

BUCKED MILK, *s.* Buchar, w.

BUCKET. *s.* Kibal, kibbal, ystuuc, B. *Kibble* is in constant use among miners for an iron mine-bucket.

BUCKLE, *s.* Broche, P.; fial, fyal, fual, B.; streing, w.; streig, B.

BUCKLE, *v.* Clymmu, B. When things are stuck together they say they are *clemmed,* D,

BUCKLER, *s.* Costan, w.; kostan, B.; gostan, w.

BUCKSOME, *adj.* Anludd, drythyll, B.

BUD, *v.* Brousta, B.

BUDGET. *s.* Daver, w.; codgroen, B.

BUFFET, *s.* See BLOW, AND BOX.

BUFFOON, *s.* Farvel, B.; bardh, barth, w.

BUG, *s.* Contronen. *Pl.* Contron, w.

BUGBEAR, *s.* Bucca, w.; bucha, P.

BUILD. *v.* Drehevel, dereval, w.; derebal, derevel, direvall, kidha, B.

BUILDER, *s.* Veidvur ti, w.

BUILDING, *s* Adail, B.

BUILDING STONES, *s.* Mein wheal, P.; mein hweyl, w.; meyn wheyl, O.M. 23:9.

BULGE, *s.* Tor, torr, w.

BULL, *s.* (The animal). Tarow, w.; taro, P.; tarw, B.

AN IMPOTENT BULL. Gale, D.

A YOUNG BULL. Ywegés, w.

BULLS, *s.* (The Pope's bulls). Bollys, vollys, M. 2769, 2766. *Yma an bollys parys,* the bulls are ready, M. 2769 *Y vollys a veth screfys,* his bulls shall be written, M. 2766.

BULLFINCH, *s.* Nope, B.

BULLOCK, *s.* Odion, odgan, w; odzhon, ohan, B.; oh, w.; lôn, c.w. 1569; lodn, w.; lond, lodn gwarack, P.; lodn guaracк, dunuvés, denevoit, B. *Any bullock,* Lodzhon, B.

BULLOCKS, *s.* Lodnow, lothnow, ludnow, w.; ludnou, B.

BULLY, *s.* Jannak, jannek, D.

BULRUSH, *s.* Brunnen, brychan, corsfruynen, B.; heschen, haskyn, hoskyn, P.; hesken D. Pryce gives *heschen, haskyn, hoskyn,* for sedge and burr reed, as *goon hoskyn,* the down of sedge, or rushes.

BULWARK, *s.* Brenniat, P.; brennyat, cadarnlé, cadernid, B.; dîn. dinas, dinaz, P.; pill, B. *Pill* is also given in Bonds' History of Looe, note, p. 163.

BUM, *s.* See BOTTOM.

BUN or CAKE, *s.* Fuggan, D.

BUNCH or BUNDLE, *s.* Dylofni, B.; wad, waze, D.

BUNCH, *s.* (A bunch or rise of land). Bôr, P.; *Borlase* in St. Wenn, The green rising, or bunch.

BUNCH, *s.* (A bunch of flowers). Tosh, D.

BUNDLE, *s.* Torchat. B.; puscrn, w. *Me a'n kelm auel pusorn.* I will tie him like a bundle, R.D. 5 12.

A SMALL BUNDLE. (As of hay, straw, &c). Wad, waze, D.

BUNGLER, *s.* Cobbé, D.

BURDEN, *s.* Bê, vê; w.; bedh, P.; carg, w.; karg, P.; sam, saw, w.; pouis, pois, poiys, B.

BURDEN, *s.* (The burden of a song) Pusorn, w.

BURDOCK, *s.* (*Arctium lappa*), Lés-serchoc, lês-enhôc, B.

BURIAL, *s.* Arwyl, B.; ancledhyas, anclydhyas, w.; anclythyas, P.

BURIAL-PLACE. *s.* Clathva, P.C. 1545; cladva, corhlan, w.; korhlan, B.

BURN. *v.* Loscy, losky, lescy, lesky, leyscy, lyscy, w.; lyskye, c.w. 107.; leysky, P.C. 1768; leski, P.; losgi, B.; tewy, w.; tewye, tewé, diwy, P.; dywy, dewy, w.

BURN, *v.* (To burn turf). Kesow, P. Perhaps from *kesan,* a turf. This turf burning is provincially termed, beat-burning.

BURNING, A BURNING, *s.* Losc, losk, losevan, lostvan, w.; lesky, R.D. 170.

A BURNING COAL. Leskyad, B.

A RAPID BURNING. Broasen, B.V.

BURNT OFFERINGS, *s.* Golwyth, B.

BURST, *v.* Squattya, skuattia, scuattya, dho skuattya, sguattia, w.; tarzas, B.

BURY, *v.* Ancledhy, encledhyés, w.; anclethias, M. 1323; bêdhy, w.; daiarou, cluddu, B.; clathna, clethy, P

BU⌢H, s. Loin. w. ; (Pl. Loinou, p. ;) bôs, r.d. 539.
Yn nop bôs tewl py yn sorn, in some bush, hole, or in
a corner. r.d. 539 ; bagas, w. ; bagaz, p. ; bosnos,
o.m. 1398. *An bosnos dywy a wra*, the bush is on
fire, o.m. 1398.

BUSH OF THORNS. Bosnos, p.

BUSHY, *adj.* Lesic, w. ; lesek, lessick, p.

BUSHEL, s. (A bushel or strike). Math armessur, b.

BUSILY, *adv.* Besy, vesy, m. 3374. *Orth ov gorthya
púr vesy*, worshipping me right busily, m. 3374.

BUSINESS, s. Negés, negis, negys, nygys, w. ; gever,
p. Pryce means by *gever*, business or *duty*.

BUSKIN, s. Ffollach, b.

BUSKINS. s. Poltrigas, b.

BUSTLE, s. Trafferth, b.; stroath, stroather, p. The
words *stroath* and *stroather*, for bustle, hurry or excitement, are still used in the Cornish dialect.

BUSYBODY, s. Staver, d.

BUT. Bês, bez, p.; bôs, bôz, buz, b. ; bys, byz, byt,
pôs, pays, prest, mês, mâs, maz, p. *Més mara keusys
yn lel*, but if I have spoken truly, p.c. 1273 ; saw,
sau, p. ; sow, sowe, c.w. 371, 461. *Saw betegyns ragon
ny*, but nevertheless for us, r.d 980. *Sau an ethyn bynegés*, but the blessed birds, o.m. 1067 ; ja, gew, gyu,
whare, b. ; hagen, gorreugh, penag, penag, penegés,
p. ; leman, lemen, lemman, lemmen, lemyn, lemmyn,
lymmyn, luman, w. *Nyn syu gulan lemmyn mostys*,
it is not clean but dirty, r.d. 1927.

BUT THEE. Marnas, o.m. 948. *War pep ol marnas*,
over all but thee, o.m. 943.

BUT IF Po cen, poken, pyken, p.

BUT YET. Hagen, p.

BUTCHER, s. Cugdd, b.

BUTLER, s. Guallofwr, b. ; menistror, spencer, w.
Moy nw arluth es spencer, the lord is more than the
butler, p.c. 802.

BUTT-END, s. Bên, w.

BUTTER, s. Amenen, emenin, manyn, menen, am-
man, w.

BUTTERFLY, s. Ticcidew, w. ; tikki-deu, gloindiu,
gloyndiu, b.

BUTTERMILK, s. Meith, p.

BUTTERY, s. Spens, p. ; trull, b. ; talgel, w.

BUTTOCKS, s. (The two buttocks). Duklyn, m.
3312 ; pedrennov, m. 1422. *Rag esya an pedennov* ;
for easing the buttocks. *May fo claff age duklyn*, that
their buttocks may be sore, m. 3312. See BOTTOM.

BUY. v. Prenné, prenna, prynny, perna, berna, w.;
perhen, p. ; frenné, frenna, w. *Rág i frenna*. To
buy it, p.

HE WILL BUY. Pren, bren. The 3 pers. s. fut. of
prenné, w.

BUYER, s. Pernar, w.

BUZZARD, s. Body-guerni, b.

BY. A, w.; ha. p ; êr, w. ; uorh, b.; dres, p.; der,
dre, tre, dredh, orth, ordh, worth, w. ; bur, kyn, p. ;
gen, gan, gans, cans, w. ; genz, ryby, p. ; ran, m.
399 ; tan, o.m. 2534. *Er an thewen*, by the gods,
o m. 2651. *Gans peder ha iowan parys*, by Peter and
John prepared p.c. 700. *Kyn wylly mûr wolowys*,
by seeing much light, r. *Dre un venen wharevethys*,
wrought by a woman, o.m. 626. *Dre vertu a'n thyr
guelen*, by virtue of three rods, o.m. 1763. *Rân sens
in neff*, by the saints in heaven, m. 399. *Tân ou fêth*,
by my faith, o.m. 2534. Rêb, rîb, ryb. ryp, w.; orta, ordan, b. *Me a gosk ryp y pen*. I will sleep by his
head, r.d. 418.

BY. Re. Used only in imprecations, as, *Re jovyn*, by
Jove. *Re deu an tás*, by God the Father, o.m. 1919.

BY and BY. Wharre, warre, whare, p.

BY MY. Rum, rom, w.

BY HIS SIDE, OR HER SIDE. Aytu (a y tu), w.

BY IT. Anedhy, anethy, annethy, anythy, p.

BY OR NEAR UNTO US. Rybbon, rybon, rebbon, w.

BY OR THROUGH. Drydh, drêdh, w.

BY OR THROUGH HER, OR IT. Dredhy, drydhy, w.

BY OR THROUGH HIM OR IT. Dredho, w.

BY OR THROUGH ME. Dredhôf, w.

BY OR THROUGH THEE. Dredhôs, w.

BY OR THROUGH THEM. Dredhé, w.

BY OR THROUGH US. Dredhôn, w.

BY OR THROUGH YOU. Dredhouch, w.

BY OR THROUGH YOUR. Derrés, w.

C.

C. This letter in all the Celtic languages has exactly
the sound of the English *k*.

In Cornish C is both a primary and a secondary letter ;
when primary it changes in construction into G and
ch, which is generally represented by H, as *colon*, a
heart ; *y golon*, his heart, *y holon*, her heart. When
secondary, C in Cornish, is a mutation of G, as *gallaf*,
I shall be able ; *mar a callaf*, if I shall be able, w.
Lex. Corn. Brit.

CABBAGE, s. (A cabbage). Bresych, ongel, b.

CABBAGE, s. Caol, caul, cowl, cawl, w. ; kaol, b. ;
kavatch, p.

CABIN, s. Overgugol, b.

CABINET, s. (A cabinet). Cib, b.

CABLE, s. Zhaff, b.

CACKLE, v. (Like a hen). Gregar, b.

CAKE. *s.* Tesan, tezan. desan, w. ; dezan, p. ; cacan, w ; kakan, p. (*Pl.* Kakez, p ;) fuggan, fogans, foogans, D.

CALDRON OR CAULDRON, *s.* Pêr, kaltor, kaudarn, B ; caudarn, w.

CALENDS, *s.* (The first day of the month). Calan, kalan, halan, w. ; cala, M. 3339. *Culamé*, calends of May, M. 3339.

CALF, *s.* (The animal). Lôch. leauh, w. ; leauch, p. ; lugh, M. 1557 ; ebol. *Pl.* Ebilli, p.

CALF, *s.* (Of the leg). Logoden fer, w. ; belgar, B.

CALL or CRY, *s.* Crei, krei, cri, cry, gri, gry. w. ; galus, p. ; galow. o M. 1832. *Clew galow an bobyl*, hear the call of this people, o.M. 1832.

CALL, *s.* (A call for the cows). Pruit, pruit pruit, D.

CALL, *v.* (Call, call for, call or cry out). Cria, w. ; kriha, B. ; creia, crya, cryé. crio, gelwel. gylwel, w.; galwy, p. ; galua, B. ; galu, p. ; celwel, kelwel, w.

CALL or NAME, *v.* Henwel, honwa, celwel, kelwel. gelwel, gylwel, w. ; galwy, p ; galua, B. ; galu, p.

CALLED or NAMED, *part.* Henwys, hynwys, honwys, honys, w. ; hylwys, henuelés, p. ; henuelez, B. ; gylwys, gilwys, w. ; gheluyz. ghiluyz, B.

CALL, *v.* (To call for, to ask earnestly). Yrghy, ergh, yrgh, p.

CALL, *v.* (To call to mind). Covio, w. ; perko, perkou, p.

CALM, *s.* Têgauel, avel, B. ; têg awel, awel vâs, auel vâz, p.

CALM, (To be calm). Lluesu, B.

CALMNESS, *s.* Callamingi, kallaminghi, B. ; kallamingi, p.

CALUMNIATE, *v.* Câbly, w.

CALUMNY, *s.* Cabel, w.

CAME. Devethês, dheth, gath, venons, B. See TO COME.

I CAME. Duthe, dhuthe, duyth, dueyth, dhueyth, w.

THOU CAMEST. Duthys, dues, ti a dhês, w.

HE CAME. Dêth, têth, dhêth, duth, dhuth, tuth, dueth. dhueth, tueth, dês. deve, defe, w. ; dothye, B.

YE CAME. Dutheuch, dhutheuch, w.

THEY CAME. Dethons, tethons, w. ; thethons, p. ; dethens, w. ; dothyans, B. ; desons, dhesons, w. ; thesons, p.

CAMEL, *s.* Caurmarch, w. ; kaurvarch, B.

CAMP, *s.* Cadlys. *Lit.* Battle-place.

CAN or FLAGON, *s.* Canna, w. ; kanna, p.

CAN. Kyll. *Mar a kyll*, if he can, B. ; kylle, keller, p. ; eiloh. *Hui eiloh*, ye can ; oar, ôr, B.

I CAN. Allaf, callaf, p. ; worrians, B. ; ylla, p.

I CAN OR MAY. Manaf, p.

I CAN OR KNOW. (*sic*). Mior, B.

AS I CAN. Dell wour, B.

IF I CAN. Mar a callaf, p.

IF HE CAN. Mara kor. p. ; mar a kyll, B.

IF THOU CANST. Mar kylleth, c.w. 1735.

HE CAN. Fol. *A neth pyth fol*, with what force he can. p.

WE CAN. Gyllin, ni a yllin, B.

CANST THOU? Ylta? (yl-te), w.

CANDLE, *s.* Cantuil, cantal. cantl, w. ; kantl, p. kantuil. (*Pl.* Kyntulti, B) ; lugarn, w.; lygarn, p;

CANDLESTICK, *s.* Cantulbren, cantalbren, tshownler, w. tshounler, golou-lestre, B.

CAP, *s.* Capa. *Pl.* Capiez, w. ; kappioz, p.

CAPE, *s.* (Or headland). Rhyn, rûn, pen-ryn, w.

CAPON, *s.* Talbum, w. ; tshappon, p.

CAPTAIN, *s.* Dûf, dêf, w. *Fystyn ov dúf whek avy*, hasten my sweet captain of me, p.c. 989 ; *Ha why annas ov déf kér*, and you Annas my dear captain, p.c. 977.

CAPTAIN, *s.* (Or leader in an army). Hebrenchiat luid. w. ; hebrenchiat luir, p.

CAPTIVE, *s.* Dalhen. w. ; hegar. B

CAPTIVE, *adj* Caeth, w.

CAPTURE, *v.* Cemerés, hemerés, w.

CARD or COMB. *v.* Cribia, w. ; kribia, criba, kriba. kribaz, p.

CARE, *s.* (Keep or keeping). Cûr, o.M. 1620 ; *Guyth ny y'th cúr*, keep us in thy care, o M. 1620.

CARE, *s.* (Anxiety). Dour, duer, dêr, dûr, w. ; *Awos y lathé ny'm duer* for killing him no care is to me, R.D. 1898 ; rach, p.c. 2722. *Ha henna gans múr a rach*, and that with much care, p.c. 2722 ; reonté, *Gans múr reonté*. with much care, p. Williams thinks this may be reouté.

CARE, *s.* (Consideration). Preder, pryder, w. ; pridar, p.

CARE, *s.* (Caution). Gwith, gwyth, guyth, w. ; guet, o.M. 1784 ; with. wyth, wihith, w. ; vihith, B. *Saw guet may wrylly cresy*, but take care that thou do believe, o.M. 1784.

CARE FOR, TO CARE FOR, *v.* Dhowlyth, thowlyth p. ; gorwythy, w. ; gorwith, gorquith, p.

BE CAREFUL. Gorquyth, gorwyth, w. ; gorguith, B.

CAREST. Thoutyth, thowtyth, B. *Ni thowtyth du*, carest thou not for God? B.

HE WILL TAKE CARE. Wyth, a mutation of gwyth, 3 pers. s. fut. of *gwythé* or *gwithé*, w.

CAREFUL, *adj.* (Cautious). Fûr, fêr, feer, w.; fyr, p.; fîn, w.; wâr, p.; ystig, B.

CAREFUL, *adj,* (Considerate). Prederys, priderys, pryderys, w.

CARE-TREE, *s.* (The mountain ash). Cerden, w.; kerden, p.

CAREER, *s.* Hins, w.

CARGO, *s.* Carg, w.; karg, p.

CARNAGE, *s.* Calanedh, w.

CARP, *s.* (The sea carp). Cunner, D.

CARPENTER, *s.* Sair-pren. *Lit.* Sawer of wood, w.; cafenter, D.

CARPENTER'S MEASURE. *s.* Scanteloun. w.

CARPETING, *s.* Elestr, B.

CARRIAGE or CART, *s.* Carios, w. See CART.

CARRIED, *part.* Cerrys, kerrys, w.; gurys, B.; aborthés, degis, p.; degys, dregy, thoké, B.; rafsys, w.; rassys, p.

CARRION, *s.* Carynnyas. O.M. 1103. *Mar kyf carynnyas certan,* if it finds carrion. certainly. O.M. 1103.

CARROT, *s.* Caretys, p. . karetys, B. Borlase gives the same name for a parsnip.

THE WILD CARROT OR PARSNIP. Kager, keggas, kai-yer, D. The ancient Cornish called hemlock, *kegas.*

CARRY, BEAR, BRING, *v.* Dôn. doen, w.; doan, B.; doyn, dûn. tôn, toen, w.; teen, p.; doga, degy, w.; dregy, p.; thegis, thêk. B.; porthy, w.; aborth, p; perthy, prethy, berthy, cerchés, kerchés, cyrchés, cerhés, kerhés, w.; kerhez, kergh, kyrgh, gerhaz, p.; caria, w. See also TO BEAR OR CARRY.

HE CARRIED. Duk, dug. N.

HE SHALL CARRY. Dek, deg, N,

THAT HE MAY CARRY. Dogo, N.

CARRY THOU. Dok, dog, doga, N.

LET HIM CARRY. Degyns, N.

LET US CARRY. Degen, w. From *degy.*

CARRY YE. Degeugh, w.

CARRYING. Ou toon, ou ton, N.

CARRIED. Degys, N.

CARRY AWAY, *v.* Hethas, p.

CART, *s.* Cert, kert, w.; carios, P.C. 2266.

CARVE, *v.* (Cut, engrave). Gravio, w.; gravia, p.

CARVER or ENGRAVER, *s.* Gravior, renniat, w.

CASE, *s.* (In that case). Kâz, B.

CASH, *s.* Sols, vonés, voné, monnah, B.

CASK, *s.* Tonnel, w.; tonnell, p.; tonwell, B.; balliar, w.

A SMALL CASK. Perseit, B; This is also a name given to a jug with two ears. (*Amphora*).

CAST, *s.* (A throw or fling). Toul, tewl, teul, w.; doul, dowle, p.

CAST. *s.* (A throw). Fauns, B. A wrestling term.

CAST, *v.* (Throw, throw down, cast out, fling). Towla, toula. w.; dowla, doulla, teuly, p.; tewlel, w.; tiulel, p.; tywlel, w.; tyulel, B.; towlal, toleugha, p.; stlapa, B.

CAST or THROWN Tewlas, dewlys, B.

I CAST MYSELF DOWN. Umhelaf, p

CAST YE. Telywch, from *teulel,* to cast or throw, p.

CAST or THROW AWAY, *v.* Redeuly, p. *Cast out,* Lamas, p.

CASTLE, *s.* Caer, câr, w.; kaer, p.; din, tin, castel, w.; kastal,; kestell, p. *Pl.* Cestel, w.; kestel, p.; castylly, M. 305; kastilli, p.

CAT, *s* Câth, w.; kâth, kât, p.; cât, gâth, w.

A HE-CAT. Gûrcâth, w.; gûrkath, gûrgâth, p.

A WILD CAT. Koid-gâth, w; koith-gâth, B. *Lit.* A wood-cat, or cat of the wood.

CATCH, *v.* (Hold or seize). Sensy, synsy, sinsy, sensyé, sendzha, w.; sindzha, dho sendzhé, sensa, sansa, syngy, p.

CATERPILLER, *s.* Cafor, w.; prif-pren, prev-pren, B. *Lit.* Twig-worm, as if so called from its shape.

CATTLE, *s.* Ludnow, lodnow, w.; ludnou, lodnou, B.; ehal, gwarthec, gwarrhog, w.; guarrhog, p.; guarthek, O.M. 1065; tshattal, B. *Mergh, guarthek, mogh, ha devés,* horses, cattle, pigs, and sheep. O.M. 1065.

CAULDRON, *s.* See CALDRON.

CAUSE or REASON, *s.* Ceyson, keyson, cheyson, cheson, ceson, w. *Na allons caffus cheson,* let them not be able to find cause, O.M. 1835; cûs, p.; kâz, B.; kên, O.M. 1826; R.D. 2153. *Kafus kên the thyscrysy,* find cause to disbelieve. O.M. 1826. *Leuereugh an kên,* tell use the cause, R.D. 2153; rys. *Rysyw,* there is cause, B.

CAUSE or LAWSUIT, *s.* Kên, cên, chên, w.

CAUSE. *v* Scylé, w ; gwra, gura, wra, ry, B.

CAUSED, *part.* Grew wra, wre, B.

CAUSE QUIET, TO CAUSE QUITE, *v.* Hêdhy, w

CAUTION, *v.* Gwarnya, w.; guarnya, B.

CAUTION, *s.* See CARE and also PRUDENCE.

CAUTIOUS, *s.* See CAREFUL. *Ha bethough war colonuw,* and be of cautious hearts, P.C. 879.

CAVALIER, *s.* Marrec, marheg, w.; marhag, p.; marchec, w. *Pl.* Marregion, marreggycn, marrogion, marrougion, w.

CAVE or CAVERN, *s.* Vûg, vûgh, vûgga, vooga, fogou, fogo, googoo, hugo, vou, fow, fou, ogo, ogov, kaff, kaou gwâg. The word vûg, and those similar to it, as in the above, are still in use for a cave, or cavern. A hollow place or cavity in a mine is so called.　The word *gwâg* is also still used for an empty or hollow place.　For other words see DEN.

CAVIL, *v.*　Cably, w. ; cubla, P.　*Part.* Cablas, cublas, scablé, B.

CAVITY OR VAULT IN A MINE.　Gunny, D.

CEASE, *v.*　Hassa, hedhy, pegya, sestya, P.

CEASING, *s.*　Dylly, B.

CELL, *s.*　Gwâg.　*Pl.* Gwagion, w.

CELLAR, *s.*　Selda, w.

CENTRE, HEART, MIDST, *s.*　Crês, crêd, w. ; crez, krez. B. ; creys, crys, greys, w.

CENSER, *s.*　Encoislester, toislester (?), w. ; inkoislestr, B.

CENTURION, *s.*　Pencanguer, B. ; pen canguer, w.

CERTAIN, *adj.*　Diogel, dyogel, dyougel, dyowgel, dyhogel, diougel, tyowgel, w.

CERTAINLY, *adv.*　This adverb is formed from the adjective *certain* by the prefix *en* or *yn*.　Thus among the many forms we have, en diogel, en dhiougel, en dhiugel, yn diogel, yn dougel, &c.　Sometimes without any prefix. as, diogel, diougel, P. ; dyogeyl, M. 413 ; thyvgel, M. 823 ; thyogeyll, M. 2187 ; also, eredy, yredy, B. ; pur wyr, P. ; sûr, B. ; serten, c.w. 228 ; yn certen, c.w. 52 ; in certen, c.w. 24 ; ywys, c.w. 124.

MOST CERTAINLY.　Pûr pury, P.

CHACE, *v.*　Chasy, B,

CHAD, *s.*　(Fish).　Lobmaz, P.

CHAFE or FRET, *v.*　Rhittia, rhyttia, B.

CHAFF, *s.*　(Of corn), Usion, ision, w. ; ûs, pilm, kuthu, kulin, B. ; culin, colow, culhu, w.　*Colow* and *culin* are the plurals of *côl*, the awn or beard of corn.　See HUSKS OF CORN.

CHAFFINCH, *s.*　Tink, D.

CHAFING-DISH, *s.*　Tshofar, P.

CHAIN, *s.*　Chaden, B.　The plural *chaynys* is from the English.

CHAIN-LINK, *s.*　Merle, D.

CHAIN-SHAKLE, *s.*　Ettaw, D.

CHAIR, *s.*　Cadar, w. ; gadar, P. ; tutton, B., hence *tutts* or hassocks, sichen, B. ; kader.　*Kader Migel*, Michael's chair.

CHAIR or BENCH, *s.*　Ysgobeth, B.

CHAIR or ROSTRUM, *s.*　Pyrcat, B. ; pyrkat, P.

CHALICE, *s.*　Celegel, w. kelegel, P.

CHALLENGE, *v.*　Iskinat, B.

CHAMBER, *s.*　Stevel, steuel, w. ; tshomber, B.

CHAMBER-POT, *s.*　Pitshar pisa, w. ; pitshar piza, B.

CHAMPION, *s.*　Codwûr, w. cadgûr, P. ; campier, w. ; kampier, P. ; campûr, ymdowlûr, w. ; ymdoulûr, B. ; ymdoular, P.

CHANCE, LOT, *s.*　Lam, w. ; prân, prên, P.

CHANGE, *v.*　Treylé, treylyé, trylé, trylyé, legria, w.

CHANGE, *s.*　Legriaz. scôs, B.

CHANGED, *part.*　Legrys, legryz, gangys, B.

CHANGING, A CHANGING, *s.*　Legradz, P.

CHANNEL, *s.*　Frôt, shanol, w. ; rhyn, B.

CHANNEL or ARM of THE SEA, *s.*　Gannel, savas, B. ; *Pensavas*, head of the channel.

CHANNEL OF A RIVER, *s.*　Ruan, ryne, w. ; rine, rîn, P.

CHAPEL, *s.*　Tshappal, P.

CHAPTER, *s.*　Cabydul, B.

CHARACTER, *s.*　Lyble, B.

CHARACTERISTIC, *s.*　Nôd, nôs, nôz, w.

CHARGE, *v.*　Doreganas, B.

CHARGE, ENJOIN, COMMAND, *v.*　Archa, w. ; argha, P. ; ryghté, B.

HE CHARGED. (Commanded).　Yrchys, 3 pers. s. preterite of *archa*, to charge or command, w.

CHARGE YE.　Ynyough, B.

CHARGE, *s.*　(Command).　Gurchmennis, gurhemin, gorhemmyn, w. ;　See COMMAND or COMMANDMENT.

CHARGE, *s.*　(Cost).　Côst, w. ; sam, D.　"I'll stand sam " is often heard said in Cornwall.

CHARGE, *s.*　(Load).　Carg, w. ; karg, P. ; sam, saw, B

CHARGE, *s.*　(Accusation).　Ceyson, keyson, cheyson, cheson, ceson, acheson, w.

CHARIOT, *s.*　Car, B. ; kert, R.D. 236.　*Me a fue yn kert a tân*, I was in a chariot of fire.　R.D. 236.

CHARIOTEER, *s.*　Kyncar, B.

CHARITY, *s.*　Gêr, B.

CHARM, *v.*　Sona, soné, zona, w.

CHARM or AMULET, *s.*　Soon, D.　From *sona*, to charm

CHARTER, *s.*　Guarrac, w. ; guarack, P.

CHASM or GULPH, *s.*　Swallet, D. ;　See GULPH OR CHASM.

CHASTE, *adj.*　Guaf, w. ; dianaff, B.

CHASTISE, *v.*　Cara, w. ; vensy, chasty, B.

CHASTISED, *part.*　Kerethys, M. ; 3251.　*Ha kerethys eredy*, and chastised readily, M. 3251.

CHAT, *v.*　Cewsel, cows, dho kouz, cous, cousa, P. ; cowsy, coosy, D,

CHATTER, *v.*　Flattré, flattryé, w.

CHATTER, *v.* (As from cold). Krehylly, p.c. 1218; *Ma thew krehyllys ov dyns,* my teeth are chattering, p.c. 1218.

CHATTER, " GAB." *s.* Wob, D.

CHATTERER, *s.* Cowser, flattor, w.

A FEMALE CHATTERER, Flattorés, w.

CHATTERING, *s.* Scaval-an-gow, D. *Lit.* A bench of lies.

CHATTELS, *s.* Mebyl. *Hag ol ov mebyl dyblans,* and all my chattels, clearly, M.

CHEAT, *v.* Dilla, dolla, B.

CHEEK, *s.* Bôch. bôh, w.; bock, bok, chal, p.; vôch, vôh, w.; grûd, grydh, (check or jaw) B.

CHEERFUL, *adj.* Lowen, w.; louan, lawen, B.; luenek, leunik, p.; leuenik, louenak, lauenik, lowenic, lawenic, lewenic, lawennek, lowenec, B.

CHEESE, *s.* Cês, kês, caus, cos, w.; kez, keas, p.

A CHEESE, *s.* Kêzn, kêz, p.

CHEMISE or SHIFT, *s.* Creis, crys, w.

CHEST, *s.* Cist. (*A small chest or box.* Kistan, B.); logel, logell, logol, w.

CHEST or COFFER, *s.* Arch, w.; argh, M. 3401. *Tan ha gore in the argh,* take and put in thy chest, M. 3401; cofor, w.; cofer, p.; kophor, kopher, B.

A GREAT CHEST. Kopher brâz, p.

CHESNUT, *s.* Cistinen, w.

CHICK or A CHICKEN, *s.* Edhenic, idnic, ydnic, w.; idninc, p.; ydnungk, ebol, mâb giar, B.

CHICKWEED, *s.* Glêdh, w.; felen, D. "Fellen herb" is often used in Cornwall.

CHIDE, *v.* Canvas, w.; kanvas, B.; flout, deragla, w.; omdhal, p.; ymeirio, B.

CHIEF, HEAD, BEGINNING, *s.* Pen, pyn, w.; pedn, p.

CHIEF or FIRST, *adj.* Censa, kensa, cynsa, w.; kenza, kynsa, kynsé, B.; kinsa, p.

CHIEF, UPPERMOST *adj.* Pennaeth, B.; warrah, w.; uarrah, p.

CHIEF MAN, *s.* Pendevig, pensevic, penzivik, pednzhivig, w.; penzhivik, pendefig, p.

CHIEF PEOPLE, *s.* Pennow ties, w.; guelheven, M. 2797; guelhevyn, M. 2929. *Guelhevyn an pow,* chiefs of the country, M. 2929.

CHIEFLY, *adv.* Pôrth, p.

CHILD, *s.* Flô, flôh, hlô, hlôh, w. *An hlô na,* that child. *A'n hlôh,* of the child, w.; flôch, flogh, p.; floghe, c.w. 1230.; mab, maw, w.; bearn, p.; gruffler, D.

A LITTLE CHILD. Floch byan, w.; flehessig, flehessi, p.; flechet, B.; meppig, baban, maban.

A RESTLESS CHILD. Ruxler, wroxler, D.

A WEAKLY OR UNDERGROWN CHILD. Kinak, kenack, D.

CHILDBED, *s.* (In childbed). Golovas, w.; *Benen in golovas,* a woman in childbed.

CHILDISHNESS, *s.* Yowynkneth, p.c. 434. *Yn yowynkneth mûr notye,* utter in very childishness, p.c 434.

CHILDLESS, *adj.* Anvab, w.

CHILDREN, *s.* Cosgor, cosgar. *Gen kosgar,* our children, w. Flechés, flechys, flehés, flehys, flechet, w.; flehas, N.; flehesou, flehezou, flehez, fleghys, flogholeth, flogheleth, p.; fledgiow, B.; fleghas, p.c. 1924; floghe, c.w. 900.

LITTLE CHILDREN. Flehesyggow, flehysygow, w.; flehyggyov, M. 1515.

CHILL, CHILLINESS, *s.* Anwos, w.; anwous, p.c. 1222.

CHILL, CHILLING, *adj.* Jein, p.; jên, B.; yên, p.; eyn, w.

CHIMERA, *s.* Tarofan, tarosfan, w.; tarnytuan, p.; tarnatuan, B.

CHIMNEY, *s.* Shimbla, w.; tshimbla, p.

CHIN, *s.* Gên, w.; gene, B.; elgeht, w.; elgent, p.; grydh, B.

CHIP, *s.* Sobman, scobman, B. *A little chip.* Sobman vian, scobman vian, B.

A CHIP OF METAL OR STONE. Spall, D.

CHIRP, *v.* (As a bird). Scloqua, B.

CHIVE, *s.* Cinin, w.; kinin, p.; cenin, w.

CHOICE, *s.* (Selection). Thewsys, B.; theusys, p.

CHOIR, *s.* Coer, carol, w.; karol, p.

CHOKE, *v.* Megi, w.; megy, p.; taga, w.; tagou, B.; tagé, p.c. 1528.; devidhy, w.

CHOKED, *part.* Tegés, w.; tegez, p.; teghez, B.; tegys, p.

HE WILL CHOKE. Meec, tâc, 3 pers. s. fut. of *megi* and *taga.*

CHOKING, A CHOKING, *s.* Ardac, tâg, w.; tage, p.

CHOKE-SHEEP, *s.* (A term of contempt for a mean fellow). Deveeder, B.

CHOOSE, *v.* Diwys, dywys, dewesy, w.; dewys, p.; dethewy, B.; cuntel, w.; kyntil, p.; guntel, w.

CHOSEN, *part.* Deuesys, B.; dewesys, w.; dethewys, B.

CHOP, *v.* Trehé, B.

CHOUGH, *s.* Palorés, tshauha, B.

CHRIST, *s.* Grest, Grist, B.; Cryst, M. 532.

CHRISTENING, *s.* Bedidhians, w.; bedzhidian, p.; bedzhidia, B.

CHRISTIAN, *s.* Cristyon, crystyon, w.; crystyen, M. 1327.

CHRISTIANS, s. Cristenyon, cristonnion, w.; crystunnyon, crystenyon, w.; crustunyon, M. 539; kristonion, krestudnian, B.; grystonnyon, R.D. 1544; crystynnyon, R.D. 1583; kristionnion, P.

CHRISTMAS DAY, s. Deu nedelic, deu nadelic, w.; deu nadelik, P.

CHURCH, s. Eglos, eglés, eglis, w.; egliz, P.; eglys, lan, tempel, w.

CHURCH-YARD, s. Corhlan, w.; korhlan, B.; corlan, gorlan, w.

CHURL, s. A gôg, B.

CHURLISH, adj. Gocy, w.; goky, P.; wocy, w.; woky, B.

CIDER, s. Sicer, w.

CIRCLE, s. Rôs, w.; rôz, P; tro, w.; clôs, P.; bondhat, w.; vyrongen, P.C. 1007. Kychough ef yn vyrongen, ye catch him in a circle, P.C. 1007.

CIRCULAR, adj. Cren, w.; kren, kern, P.

CIRCUMSPECT, adj. Fìn, w.

CITADEL, s. Guarth, B.

CITY, s. Caer, câr, w.; kaer, P.; dinas, w.; dinaz, P.; drey, B.

CLAD, part. Gueskys, B. Poorly clad, fernoyth, ferneth, B.

CLAIM, s. Clém, P.; chalyng, M. 2371. Tytel na chalyng dyblans, title and claim distinctly, M. 2371.

CLAMOUR, s. Cri, cry, crei, krei, gre, gry, trôs, trôz, w.

CLAP, s. (As a thunder-clap). Crac, w.; crak, R.D. 294. Krak taran, a clap of thunder, R.D. 294.

CLAPPER, s. (Of a bell). Clicket, B.

CLARION, s. Tollkorn, B. This is also used for a flute, or fife. Lit. it means a holed horn.

CLASP, s. (Fastening, as of a buckle, &c). Broche. streig, P.

CLAW, v. Scrivinas, w.; skrivinas, B.

CLAW, s. (?). Having claws or nails. Ewinog, w. Perhaps ewin or juin for claw, as also for nail, q. v.

CLAY, s. Pri, pry, w.; pryi, B.; bry, vry, pol, bol, bowl, w. A bol hag a lyys formys, made of clay and mire, O.M. 1070.

CLAY-PIT, s. Polpry, w.

CLAYEY-GROUND, s. Prian. w. Among the miners a clayey lode is commonly called a "prian lode."

CLAY-SLATE, or SCHIST, s. Killas, D. This word is still in constant use,

CLEAN, adj. Pûr, w; dinam, B.; elyn, ylyn, w. Yn nep plath têk ha ylyn, in some fair and clean place O.M 2080; glân, w.; glane, P.; gulân, wlân, lân, w.; glannith, P. Dén ow tón pycher dour glán. a man carrying a pitcher of clean water, P.C. 629.

CLEANLINESS, s. Glannithder, w.; glanithder, glannuthder, P.; glendury, lendury, w.

CLEANLY, adv. En lannith, w.

CLEANSE or CLEAN, v. Glanhy. To cleanse one's self. Omlana, w.

CLEAR, v. Carthu, P.

CLEAR, adj. (Evident). Uredy, P.

CLEAR, adj. (Open). Lawn, w.; lan, M. 3715. Forth lan, a clear way, M. 3715; gare, P.

CLEAR, adj (Bright). Splân, splâdn, w.; splên, P.; têc, têk, w.; teek, thêk, teage, P.; têg, w.; tevery, deverye, P.

CLEAR, adj. (Serene). Cuzal, P.

CLEAR, adj. (Clean, transparent). Cleyr, clêr, glân, wiân, w. An dewés yv da ha cler, the drink is good and clear, O.M. 1918.

CLEARLY, adv. Apert, P.C. 1410; fas, yn fas, B.; dyowgel, O.M. 1369. Lauar thy'mmo dyowgel, speak to me clearly, O.M. 1369; scyle, P.; dibblance, C.W. 1839; thibblans, thybblance, C.W. 1985, 1932.

CLEARNESS, s. (Fairness, beauty). Tectcr, tekter, w.

CLEARNESS, s. (Brightness). Splander, w.; splandor, P.

CLEAVE, v. (Or split). Fallia, feldzha, w.; fellia, P.

CLEAVE, v. (To cleave to). Gleny, glené, glyné, w.; glenys, glenaz, P.

CLEFT, s. (Or gap). Rigol, B.

CLERK or CLERGYMAN, s. Cloirec, w.; cloireg, P.; mâb lyen, w. Mâb lyen is, literally, the son of linen. Perhaps from the surplice,

CLERKLINESS, s. Clergy, M. 1378; Súr in clergy, surely in clerkliness, M. 1378.

CLEVER, adj. Fûr, fîr, feer, fyr, sotel, w.

CLIENT, s. Undamsi, dên cosgor, w.; dêncoskor, B.

CLIENTS, s. Cosgor, kosgar, dên cosgor, w.

A LITTLE CLIENT. Caidwanid, P.

CLIFF, s. Als, w.; aules, owels, aul, owel, voel, B.; ledr, ledra, lam ledra, w.

A HIGH CLIFF. Alsa, P.

A CLIFF-LIKE ROCK. Clegar, cleghar, cligga, clicker, w.

CLIFF CAVE. Ogo, goog. See CAVE and DEN.

CLIFFS, s. Carnsow, uauffow, B.

CLIMB, v. Grambla, dho grambla, w.

CLING, TO CLING TO, v. Glené, gleny. glyné, w.; glenys, glenaz, P.

CLIP or SHEAR, v. Cynivias, w.; kynivias, P.

CLOAK, s. (The garment). Hûc, hûk, hûgk, clôc, glôc, côp, w.; nanyl, P. Ha nep nan geffo nanyl.

and he who now hath a cloak, P.; scuidlien, sguthlien. B.; mantel, W.; vantel, M. 1186; *The vantel gâs yn gage*, leave thy cloak in pledge, M. 1186; lên, W.; *Guerés dym ser yurle y lén*, keep for me, Sir Earl, his cloak, M. 4536; ulair, W.

CLOCK, *s.* Clechic, B.

CLOD, *s.* (Or bit of turf). Kezan, P. *Of earth*, Tubban, D. The Cornish call a clod or bit of turf a *tab*.

CLOISTER, *s.* Claustr, P.

CLOSE, *adj.* (Near). Liaz, B.

CLOSE OR SHUT, *v.* Teen, D.

CLOSE, CONFINED, *adj.* Hardh, harth, P.

CLOSED, *part.* Degés, dygés, W.

CLOSELY, *adv.* Hardlych, W.

CLOSURE, *s.* (Joining, seam). Enniou, W.

CLOT-BUR, HOG'S HERB, *s.* Serchôg, lêsserchôc, lês-en-hôc, W.

CLOTH, *s.* Pân. (*Pl.* Pannow, R.D. 1509;) pâdn, W.; pad, B.

CLOTH, *s.* (A cloth). Guêth, P.; gwêth, cwêth, quêth, W. *Guartha a'n gorhyl gans quêth*, the top of the ark with a cloth, O.M. 1074.

CLOTHS, *s.* Lysten, O.M. 808.

CLOTHES, *s.* (Or clothing). Dillas, W.; dillaz, P.; dellés, M. 1674; dyllas, dhyllas, W.; thillas, B.; dillat, dillad, dilladas, W.; diladzhaz, dilladzhaz, delagôn, P.; guisc, guisk, guest, B.; gvest, O.M. 36. *Râg fout gvest ha gostotter*, for want of clothing and shelter, O.M. 36; gwéth, gueth, kueth, kuethiou, B.

CLOTHE, *v.* Gwiscy, gwiscé, gwesca, gwesga, W.; guesga, P.; guesky, B.; wiscy, wyscé, W.; wyska, c w. 1585; quetha, c.w. 978.

CLOTHING, *s.* See CLOTHES.

CLOUD, *s.* Couat, W.; ebron, uibren, huibren, W.; nuibren, P.; gorthuer, goruer, W. *A little cloud.* Niul, W.; niull, B.

CLOUDY, *adj.* Comolec, W.; comolek, P.; komolek, B.

CLOUT, *s.* (A cloth or rag). Clût, W.; klût, B.

CLOVER, *s.* Quillet, D.

CLOWN, *s.* Lorden, W. *A rustic or clown.* Trevedic, P.; dên pow.

CLUB or BLUDGEON, *s.* Fûst, vûst, W.; ûther, B.; lôr vraoz, P.

CLUMP or CLUSTER, *s.* Bagas, W.

A CLUMP OR CLUSTER OF SPROUTS OR SHOOTS. Luworchguit, P.

COAL, or A COAL, *s.* Colan, W.; kolan, P.; glow, B.

A LIVE COAL. Colan bew, W.; kolan beu, P.; reightên, glow, glaouen, B.

COAL-ASHES, *s.* Glow lusow (*or* lusew), W.

COAL-PIT, *s.* Hwêl glow, W.

COARSE or GROSS, *adj.* Brâs, vrâs, W.

COAST, *s.* See BORDER and BOUNDARY.

COAT, *s.* Pows, W.; powes, B.; bows, fows, W.; pais, peid, pidde, kota, B.; cota, W.

COB or CLOB, *s.* Tryan, (? pryan) B. This is a mixture of coarse clayey earth and straw for building *cob* walls.

COBBLER, *s.* Cereor, W.; chereor, B.; cherior, P.

COBBLER'S AWL, *s.* Benewés, W.; beneuez, P.

COCK, *s.* (Male bird). Celioc, colyek, W.; chelioc, kelliog, P.; kelioc, B.; cullyec, kullyek, kuliog, kuliak, kulliag, W.

COCK'S COMB, *s.* Criban kuliog, W.

COCKLE, *s.* Cyligi. W.; kyligi, P.

COCKLE-SHELLS, *s.* Kylighi, B.

COD-FISH, *s.* Barfus, barvas, W. *Pl.* Barfusy, P.; towrag, D. A corruption of *dour*, water, and *hoch* a hog, *Lit.* Water-hog.

NEWFOUNDLAND CODFISH. Neflin, D.

COD'S HEAD, *s.* Pedn barvas, pedn barfus, P; pedn borbas, D.

COERCE, *v.* Pela, c.w. 1443.

COFFER, *s.* See CHEST or COFFER.

COFFIN, *s.* Geler, W. *Yn geler horn gorrys dovn*, in a coffin of iron put deep, R.D. 2320; logel, logell, logol, W.

COGNIZANT, TO BE COGNIZANT OF. Godhvos, godhfos. In construction it changes into *wodhvos*, W.

COIN, *s.* Bath, B. *A coin of small value.* Scût, B. The word *scút* is still used, "I hav'nt a scute left."

COINER, *s.* Bathor, W.; bather, B.

COLD, *adj.* Jein, P.; jên, B.; yên, P., yein, W.; yeyn, M. 3042; yne, M. 1145; yeyne, c.w. 1262; eyn, ewen, P. *Guyls ha yne*, wild and cold, M. 1145; riou, B.

COLD, *s.* Wôs, B.; anwôs, annez, (a corruption of *anwos*) W.; anwyd, B

A COLD. Anwôs, W.

A GREAT COLD. Yeinder, P.

COLD, COLDNESS, EXTREME COLD, *s.* Iender, yeinder, yênder, W.

COLD, TO BE COLD. Riua, B.

(COLD). TO CATCH COLD, TO BE VERY COLD. Stervys, stevys.

COLD, *s.* (A cold in the head). Pas, paz, pawse, D.

COLD WEATHER. Yein kuer, P.

COLEWORT, *s.* Magdulans, ungle, B.; caul, caol, cowl, cawl, W.

COLLAR, *s.* Gwiden, w.

COLLATE, *v.* Cetgorra, getgorra, w.

COLLEAGUE, *s.* Coweth, cowyth, cywedh, w.; kywedh, p.; **kyuedh**, b.; cywedhiad, w.; kywedhiad, p.; **kyvadhas**, b.

COLLECT, *v.* Cuntel, guntell, w.; kyntl, b. *Me a guntel*, I will collect, (or gather) w.

COLLECT TOGETHER, *v.* Cronny, w.

COLLECTION or GATHERING TOGETHER, *s.* Cuntell, contell, cuntellet, cuntellyans, contellyans, w.; cuntillyans, p.

COLLEGE, *s.* Colgy, m. 2699. *Ha the oll agys colgy*, and to all your college, m. 2699.

COLOUR, *v.* Liué, w.

COLOUR, A COLOUR, *s.* Liu, lyw, w.

OF ONE COLOUR. Unliu, w.; ynliu, b·

COLT, *s.* Ebol. ebel, ebal, w.; eball, c w. 2389; marh-bian, p.

COLTSFOOT, *s.* (Herb). Trûs ebal, trûz ebal, w.

COMATOSE, *adj.* (?) *A comatose man.* Cuscadur, p.

COMB, *s.* Crib, criban, b.

A LARGE TOOTH COMB. Flisk, d.

COMB, *s.* (Of a bird). Crîb, grîb, greab, w.

COMB, *v.* Criba, kriba, kribia, kribaz, p.; cribia, w.

COME, *v.* Dôs, w.; dôz, p.; dhôs, doys, dûs, tôs, w.; thôs, those. p.; dué, donés, devôs, dyvôz, tevos, w.; teffy, thyffy, dhyllif, thyllif, thellyf, p.; devonés, tevonés, w.; dynythy, venytha, vynytha, vinsa, p.; môs, môz, mouas, garras, b.

COME THOU. Dôs, dûs, dhûs, dues, dês, w.; dees, p.; dîs, dys, w.; dryz, dûn, p.; deugh, b.; diau, p.

COME YE. Deuch, deuh, deu, w.; deue, p.; diou, w.; deug, n.; deugh, deuus, deen, douɔy, p.

COME, ARRIVED, *part.* Dues, dês, w.; dôs, b.; devedys, p.; devedhys, b.; devethys, p.; dyvythys, b.; dynythys, w.

COME. Jeffo, p.

COME. Venons, b.

COME HOME. (Arrived). Devedhez dre, p.

COME HITHER. Dowethy, p.

COME FORTH. Drevethys, b.

COME WITH ME. Deugh genef ve, p.

COME INTO THE HOUSE. Diau tshyi, p.

COME AWAY. Dun yn kergh, p.

I COME. Ezhov, b.

IT COMES. Due, n.

THOU COMEST. Dhive, b.; dueth, duth, n.

THEY COME. Tyffonz, b.; dethons, desons, n.

I CAME. Duyth, dueyth, n.

THOU CAMEST. Duthys, dues, n.

HE CAME. Duth, dueth, n.

YE CAME. Dutheugh, n.

SINCE I CAME. Aban duthe, n.

COME THOU. Dus, dúes, n.

LET HIM COME. Does, w.

LET US COME. Dùn, deun, dewn, dên, w.; dyûn, b.

LET THEM COME. Déns, doens, w.

THAT IT MAY COME. Dogha, n.

THAT THEY COME. May tyffonz, p.

HE MAY COME. Teffo, a mutation of *deffo*, 3 pers. s. ɛubj of irr. v. *dôs*, to come. Written also teffé, w.

YE MAY COME. Dyffouch. Also *tyffouch*, a mutation of dyffouch, 3 pers. s. subj. of irr. v. *dôs*, to come, w.

THEY MAY COME. Deffons, dyffons. Also *teffons*, and *tyffons*, the mutations of *deffons*, and *dyffons*, 3 pers. pl. subj. of irr. v. *dôs*, to come, w.

HE HAD COME. Dôthyé, dhôthyé, dethyé, w.

THEY HAD COME. Dôthyans, w.

I SHALL OR WILL COME. Dôf, dhôf, tôf, a mutation of *dôf*, to come, w.; thaffe, thaf, p.

THOU SHALT OR WILT COME. Dueth, dûth, dhueth, and *túth*, a mutation of *dúth*, w.

HE SHALL OR WILL COME. Dûn, down, w.; dau, b.; de, te, dué, dhué, dyff, deffo, tufé, w.; 3 pers. s. fut. of irr. v. *dôs*, to come, w.

WE SHALL OR WILL COME. Deffyn, w.; down, b.

YE SHALL OR WILL COME. Deuch, dewch, dhewch, w.; douh, b.

THEY SHALL OR WILL COME. Dôns, w.; dônz, b.; tôns, w.

THOU SHALT OR WILT HAVE COME. Dyffy, w.

HE SHALL OR WILL HAVE COME. Dyffo, w.

HE SHOULD OR WOULD COME. Dothé, deffé, to, w.

TO COME HOME. Maoz dhan dre, p.

TO COME TO. Deffyny, p.

TO COME DOWN, *v.* Descyn, deiscyn, w.; deiskyn, p.; dyeskenné, dyescenné, dyescynné, dyscynné, discynna, w.; diskynné, p.

COME DOWN, *part.* Diskynnys, diwennys, w.

TO COME TO LIFE AGAIN, *v.* Dasvewé, dhasvewé, w.

TO COME TO SHORE, *v.* Teera, tira, w.

COMEDY, *s.* Racca, w.; antɛrlick, b.

COMELINESS, *s.* Cârder, cairder, w.; tecter, tekter, b.

COMELY, *adj.* Dèk, dêg, w.; evall, cârder, p.

COMET, *s.* Sterran leski, w.

COMFORT, *v.* Lowenhé, lowenny, w. ; gomfortyé, B.

COMFREY, *s.* (The herb). Boreles, w.

COMMAND, *v.* Gorhemmyna, gorhemmena, w. ; gorhemmenus, gworhemmen, gorhemen, gormenna, gormenus, gurhemyné, gurchemmyny, P. ; gorchymmia, B. ; archa, w. ; arka, P. ; arha, hyrch, B. ; herghy, yrghy, yrbyr, fythy, P. ; rygthé, w. ; thynarghy, thynherghy, P.

COMMANDED, *part.* Yrchys, yrhys ; gorhemmynys, &c., w.

HE COMMANDED. Hyrchys, yrchys, 3 pers s. preterite of *archa,* w.

THOU HAST COMMANDED. Yrchsys, 2 pers. s. preterite of *archa,* w.

HE HAD COMMANDED Archse, arse, w.

HE SHALL OR WILL COMMAND. Hyrch, herch, erch, 3 pers. s. fut. of *archa,* w. ; worhemmyn, a mutation of gorhemmyn, 3 pers. s. fut. of *gorhemmyna,* to command, w.

COMMAND or COMMANDMENT, *s.* Gorhemmyn, w. ; gurhemmyn, P. ; guorhemmyn, B. ; gurhemin, P. ; gorhemmynnad, gworhemmynias, gurchmennis, gorchymmyn, gorchemmyn. w. ; gorwmyn, B.; goribmyn, w. ; gormen, gormenna, B. ; gormenad, w. ; grân, B. *An deag grân deu,* the ten commandments of God. *Grân* is a contraction of *gormen* or *gormænna,* B. The following are mutations, *viz* ; worhemmynnad, a mutation of *gorhemmynnad,* w. ; worchymmyn, P., a mutation of *gorchymmyn* ; uorhemmyn, worhemmyn, P., mutations of *gorhemmyn.* These are specimens of the plurals, *viz* ; gorhemmynadow, worhemmynadow, w. ; gurhemmynadow, worrymadow, P. ; guraminadou, B. In the " *Ordinale de origine mundi,* "lines 353 and 2414, it is written *worhenmyn,* a command. The following terms are also found for *command* or *commandment, viz.* Archad, arhad, w. ; arhas, arghas, argh, yrghys, vôld, P. ; volder, danvonad, w. *Pl.* Aradow, arhadow, danvonadow, w. ; arhadou, arghadou, P. &c.

COMMENCE, *v.* Dalleth, dallath, dhallath, dallethy, talleth. w.

COMMENCING, *part.* Ow talleth, w.

COMMENCEMENT, *s.* Dalleth, dhalleth, dallath, dallathfas, dhallathfas, dallathvas, w. ; thallatheas, P.

COMMEND, *v.* Eysyé, w. ; eysya, P. ; commena, cemyny, w. ; kemynna, M. 503 ; cymmyny, P. ; gemyn, gymyn, B.

HE SHALL OR WILL COMMEND. Gemyn, gymmyn, the mutations of *cemyn* and *cymmyn* 3 pers. s. fut. of *cemynny* and *cymmyny,* to commend, w.

COMMENDATION, *s.* Gormola, w.

COMMODITY, *s.* (Ware). Waroe, P.

COMMON or DOWN, *s.* Gôn, goon, gwôn, gwen, gûn, woon, oon, rôs, w. ; bounder, vounder, P.

COMMON or JOINT, *adj.* Cês, kês, kys. w.

COMMON, *adj.* Scôch. *Scôch fôr,* the common way, B.

COMMON PEOPLE, *s.* Cêth, kêth, kethe, w. ; tuogu, B. ; tiogou, w. ; pobel tiogou, w. ; pobel tuogu, lu, megganu, mogyon, B.

COMMON PERSON, *s.* Gwâs, guâs, w. ; guaz, B.

COMMONALITY, *s.* (The mob, the vulgar). See COMMON PEOPLE.

COMMUNION, *s.* (Fellowship). Cowethyans, w.

COMPANION, *s.* (Mate, friend). Coweth, cowyth, w.; goweth, c.w. ; gowyth, cywedh, w. ; kyuedh, B. ; cydhman, w. ; kydhman, kyvadhas, B. ; cywedhiad, côthman, gôthman, hôthman. *Ow hôthman,* my companion, w. ; palfat, sôs, B. ; tyrguas, P. ; chêt, celé, gelé, gilé, gylé, w.

COMPANION, *s.* (Female). Cowethés, howethés, w. *Dues ov howethés eva,* come my companion Eve, O.M. 652.

COMPANIONSHIP, *s.* Cowethas, c.w. 383 ; gowethas, M. 4256. *Kyn fo têk an gowethas,* though fair be the companionship, M. 4256.

COMPANY, SOCIETY, *s.* Cowethas; cowethé, w. ; gowethas, B. ; herwydh, w. ; tyrguas, P.

COMPANY, *s.* (Assemblage). Byddin, liaz, lias, chetua, B. ; cetva, chetva, w. ; chettys, P c. 3042. P.C. 3042. *Hag a thylyrf an chettys,* and liberate the company, P.C. 3042. *Cetva* is more correctly the *place* of assembly, w.

A COMPANY OF HORSEMEN. Lhy, P.

COMPARE, *v.* Cetgorra, getgorra, w.

COMPASSION, *s.* Trueth, treweth, triwath, w.; triuath, B. ; truath, P. ; truez, B. ; tregereth, dregereth, yttern, ynten, w. ; pyteth, pyté, byté, vyté. *Yv da ha mûr the bylé,* is good, and great thy compassion, O.M. 1854.

COMPASSIONATE, *adj.* Triwardhec, triaudek, P.

COMPATRIOT, *s.* Tyrguas.

COMPEL, *v.* Aderbyny, drynya, P. ; construyné, P.C. 1512.

COMPLAIN, *v.* Plêntyé, w. ; pleyntyé, B.

COMPLAINT, *s.* Cên, kên, chên, w. *Rôg ny fydh kên dhe perthy,* for there will be no complaint to bear it, O.M. 2208 ; crothval, w *The wruthyl crothval na sôn,* to make a complaint nor a sound, O.M. 1836 ; drêm, w. ; grêf, w. *Thege hep grêf,* the tenth, without complaint, O.M. 497 ; whêr, w. ; whear, wêr, P. ; clûn, P. (?) *Pôs re deulseugh agas clûn,* but cast off your complaint.

COMPLAISANT, *adj.* Cooth, w. ; avlethis, P.

COMPLETE, *adj.* Cowal, w. ; coual, P. ; coul, w; ; coule, P. ; gowal, methen, playn, w. ; playne, P. ; perfeth, perfeyth, pyrfyth, w.

COMPLETELY, *adv.* Cowel, M. 3383. *An turant a vyn cowal*, the tyrant will completely, M. 3383.

COMPLEXION, *s.* (Hue). Lyw, B.

COMRADE, *s.* See COMPANION.

CONCEAL, *v.* Celés, kelés, cudhé, w. ; kuthé, cutha, kitha, P. ; githa, w.

ONE THAT CONCEALS HIMSELF. Cudhygic, cudhvgik, w. ; cuthyguk, P.

CONCEALMENT, *s.* Danva, w.

CONCEALMENTS, *s.* Wrunch, P.

CONCEIT, FANCY or NOTION, *s.* Vang, D.

CONCEITED, FORWARD, *adj..* Prall, D.

CONCEIVE, *v.* (To be conceived, to conceive). Hundham, w. ; humthan, B. ; ymdhoyn, B.

CONCEIVED, BREEDING, Humthan, B.

CONCERN, *s.* (Anxiety). Dûr, duer, dour, dêr, bêrn, bearn, vêrn, w.

CONCERNING or OF ME. Wothaf me, P. ; wovente. B.

IT CONCERNS. Amount, w. ; amourit, P. ; dûr, duer, dêr, dawr, w.

CONCERT, *s.* Carol, w. ; karol. P.

CONCLUSION, *s.* Diwêdh, dywêdh, duoêdh, dhewêdh, w. ; dewêth, dhewêth, thewêth, P. ; tywêdh, diwedva, dywedhva, duwedhva, dowedhyans, gorfen, w.

CONCLUSION, *s.* (An extremity, end). Pen, pedn, w.

CONCORD, *s.* (Unity). Cesoleth, kesoleth, cysolath, cyzaleth, w. ; kyzauleth, kyzalath, B.

CONCORD, *s.* (Agreement). Cesenyans, w. ; kesenyanz, B ; gorholeth, w.

CONCUBINE, *s.* Gwadngyrti, w.

CONDEMN, *v.* Dampnys, thamnys, B.

CONDEMNED, *part.* Skymys. From *skemyna*, to curse, P.

CONDITION, *s.* (State). Le, B. ; chêr, P. *Eua wêk gvella the chêr*, sweet Eve, to better thy condition, O.M. 166.

CONDUCT, *v.* Hombroncy, hembryncy, hebrency w.

CONEY, *s.* Cynin, w. ; kynin, kyningen, P. ; cyningen, w.

CONFEDERATE, *v.* Gustlé, P.

CONFEDERATE, *s.* Confethys, P.

CONFIDE, *v.* Fydhyé, w. ; fythy, P.

CONFIDENCE, *s.* See FAITH and BELIEF.

CONFINED, CLOSE, *adj.* Hardh, harth, P.

CONFIRMED, SETTLED. Regeth, P.

CONFIRMED, ASSURED. Yskerens, P.

CONFLICT, *s.* Câs, gâs, câd, w.

CONFLUENCE, *s.* (Of waters). Aber, w.

CONFUSION ! *Exclam.* Gode. An imprecation, thus, *Gode thous re'th vo*, confusion be to thee, w.

CONGER, *s.* Sleane, B. ; zillidouryr. *Pl.* Syllyas, B. ; syllyes, O.M. 139.

CONGER EEL, *s.* Selya. (*Pl.* Selyas,) P. ; zelli, zilli, silly, D. See also EEL.

CONGREGATION, *s.* Cuntellet, w. ; cuntellyans, cuntillyans, contellyans, P.

CONJECTURE, *v.* Kridzhi, B.

CONJURER, *s.* Hwiliog, w. ; huiliog, P. ; pellar, D.

CONJUX, *s.* Chespar, P.

CONQUER, *v.* Fethé, fethy, frethy, w.

CONQUERED, *part.* Gwythys, fythys, w.

CONQUEST, *s.* Budh, B.

CONSCIENCE, *s.* Keskyans, B. ; keskians, kesenyauz, P.

CONSECRATE, *v.* Soné, sona, zona, sacra, w.

CONSECRATED, *part.* Sans, zanz, P.

CONSENT, *v.* Benidnia, rhei an guella, B.

CONSENT or PERMISSION, *s.* Cesenyans, w. ; kesenyanz, P.

CONSIDER, *v.* Prederi, P. ; predery, predyry, prydyry, prydery, w. ; prydiry, P.C. 2906 ; ervyré, yrvyré, madra, w. ; sybbosia, P. ; sypposia, sybottia, B.

TO CONSIDER OF. Thugy, P.

CONSONANT, A CONSONANT, *s.* Cessonyis, w. ; kessonyis, P.

CONSPICUOUS, *adj.* Hewel, w. ; heuel, B. ; sellic, w. ; guydh, P. ; gwydh, gwydd, B.

CONSTANT, *adj.* Bythol, vythol, w.

CONSUL, *s.* Yurl, B.

CONSULT, *v.* Cusulyê, cesulyé, w.

TO CONSULT ONE ANOTHER. Ymcusyllé, w.

CONSULTATION, *s.* Bagat, P.

CONSUME or WASTE, *v.* Guastia, P.

CONTEMPT, *s.* Dafole, schereweth, P. ; scherewith, B.

CONTEND, *v.* Emlodh, emladh, emladha, w. ; omdhal, P. ; cencia, kennkia, strevyé, scornyé, scorné, errya, w. ; gueskal, B. ; scranny, D.

CONTENDING, *part.* Errya, P.

CONTENTION, *s.* Strêf, stryf, w.

CONTEST, A CONTEST, *s.* Bressel, P. ; bresell, bresel, bresul, bresyl, vresyl, w.

CONTINUAL, *adj.* Bythol, vythol, w.

CONTINUALLY, *adv* Benary, venary, bynary, vynary, bisqueth, bisgueth, bythqueth, bythgweth, bithgueth, byth, bith, jammés, w.; jammas, desem-pit, kympez, gympès, gymps, unary, pub erna, pub eure, P.; stella, bypûr, (*byth pup úr*) w.; pûrpûr, B.

CONTRACT, *v.* (To bargain). Bargidnia, dho bar-gidnia, P.

CONTRACT, *s.* Ambôs, w.

CONTRARY, *s.* (The contrary). Gweyth, P.

CONTRIVE, *v.* Tewlel, w.; teulel, tiulel, P.; tywlel, w.; teuly, towlal, towla, toula, dho doulla, P.; gafé, gafa, cafos, B.

CONTRIVER, *s.* Formyas, formyer, w.; inguinor, B.

CONTUMELY, *s.* Bysmer, vysmer, w.

CONVENIENCE, *s.* (A convenience, opportunity). Daffer. *Pl.* Daver, w.

CONVENTION, *s.* Cetva, w.; ketva, chetva, P.; cedva, w.; kedva, B. More correctly the *place* of convention.

CONVERT, *v.* Treylé, treylyé, trylyé, w.; trylé, P.

CONVEX, *adj.* Crûm, crôm, w.; krôm, kroum, cro-bm, B.

CONVEY, *v.* Hombroncy, hembryncy, w.; hembry-nky, P.; hebrency, w.

CONVICTED, *part.* Confethys, convethys, w.

COOK, *s.* Côg, w.; kôg, kêg, B.

A SHE-COOK, *s.* Keghin, B.

COOK-SHOP, *s.* Tshi côg, tshyi côg, w.

COOK, *v.* Dyghthy. *Dyghthy bós*, to cook meat, P.

COOL, *adj.* Yeyn, P.C. 1622. *Guthyl may fe the wôs yeyn*, that will make thy blood cool, P.C. 1622. See COLD.

COOLNESS, *s.* See COLD, COLDNESS.

COOPER, *s.* Bynciar, bynkiar, w.

COP, *s.* (? tuft). Gu, P.

COPE, *s.* Côp, ofergugol, w.

CO-PARTNER, *s.* See COMPANION, MATE, FRIEND.

COPIOUSLY, *adv.* Dewhans, duwhans, dywhans, w.; dyhuanz, P.

COPPER, *s.* Cober, w.; kober, B.; gueidvur, brêst, prêst, w.

CORD, *s.* (A cord). Lovan, w.; louan, P.; myngar, P.; cord. w.

CORDS, *s.* Cerdyn, kerdyn, w.; kerdy, B.

A SMALL CORD. Lovannan, w.

CORDWAINER, *s.* Cereor, w.; kereor, chereor, B.; cherior, P.

CORK, *s.* Spoue, B.

CORMORANT, *s.* Saithor, shagga. The name commonly used in Cornwall is *shag*.

CORN, *s.* Ys, w.; yees, c.w. 1189; yz, îs, P.; îz, B.; yd, hit, guthot, guyraf, w.; maga, B.; eys, O.M. 1058; *Pl.* Esow, w.; esowe, c.w. 1130.

STANDING CORN. Yd, hit, ys, w.; iz saval, B.

THE BEARD OF CORN. Hile (?) D.

AN EAR OF CORN. Pen ys, w.

THE DUST OR HUSKS OF CORN. Ishan. w.F.P. See CHAFF.

BREAD CORN. Ys bara, w.

BELONGING TO CORN. Isick, P.

ALL MANNER OF CORN. Eys. *Gorre hag eys kemyskys*, hay and corn mixed, O.M. 1058.

THE CORN FEAST. Guledh-iz. B. This name of the corn-feast is still in use in Cornwall.

CORN-DEALER, *s.* Bagur, D.

CORN-SMUT, *s.* Losc, losk, w.; colibran, colbran D.

CORN-STRAW, *s.* Culin, w.; kulin, B.; usion, P., but this is properly *chaff*.

CORNER, *s.* (Or nook). Cor, corn, cornat, cornel, cornal, w.; kornal, P.; sorn, w. *Yn nep bôs tewl py yn sorn*, in some bush, hole, or in a corner, R.D. 539.

A LITTLE CORNER. Dinyan, D.

A CORNER FOR WOOD. Huccaner, D.

CORNER or ANGLE, *s.* Elin, elyn, B.

CORNISH, *adj.* Cernewec, Kernuak, w.

CORNISH, *s.* (The language). Tavaseth Kernuak, w. tavazeth Kernuak, P.

CORNWALL, *s.* Cernow, Kernow, Kernou, B.

CORONET, *s.* Corun, P.; koron, B.

CORPORATION, *s.* (Of a borough). Trefraint, B.

CORPSE, *s.* Corf, corfe, horf, horfe, B.; corf maro, P.; *Pl.* Corfow, marows corfows, P.

CORRECT, *v.* Ewna, owna, w.; ouna, P.; cara, w gwella, guella, B.

CORRECTION OR PUNISHMENT, *s.* Anfugy, enfugy, w.

CORRUPT or BRIBE, *v.* Halogu, B.

CORRUPTED, *part.* Fellet, w.

CORRUPT THING, A CORRUPT THING, Podar, P.

CORRUPTION, *s* Harlutry, w. *Orth harlutry prest pub preys*, from corruption always, c.w. 91.

COSTLY, *adj.* Kêr, B.

COTTAGE, *s.* Bosca, bôthoc, w.; bothog, P.; bôth, w.; havodty, B.; overgugol, P.

COTTAGER, *s.* Trevedic, B.

COUCH, *v.* Plattya, w. *Me a wél un lôdn púr vrás hanys in bush ow plattya*, I see a very great bullock from thee in the bush couching, c.w. 112.

COUCH, *s.* Gwely, gueli, w.

COUGH. *s*, Pâs, pâz, w. In Cornwall they call a bad cold in the head a *pawse.*

COULD, MIGHT. Callo, callé. vennyn, wolas, wothe, B.

I COULD. Kaldzha, kaldzha vi, P.

THOU COULDST. Culsté. *Mar culsté*, if thou couldst, a mutation of *gulsté*, for *galsté*, 2 pers. s. subj. of *gally*, to be able, w.

HE COULD. Callo, a mutation of *gallo*, 3 pers. s. subj. of *gally*, to be able. *Ylla*, B.

COULTER, *s.* (Of a plough). Colter, culter, w.; koultyr, trohar, P.; troher, B.

COUNCIL, *s.* Bagat, P.

COUNSEL, *v.* Cusulyé, cusyllyé, w. *Yn scôn râk y cusyllyé,*soon to counsel her, P.C. 1930; gusulyé. w.; gesul, P.; husulyé, husullyé, cossyllya, c.w. 670; daryvas, dharyvas, P.

COUNSEL, *s.* Cusul, w.; cusyl, P.; kusyl, P.C. 472; cusyll, B.; kyssyl, P.; cyssyl, w.; kyssel, B.; gusul, w.; gusyl, O.M. 1828. *Râg the gusyl yv pûr tha,* for thy counsel is very good, O.M. 1828; husul, w.; husyll, c.w. 667. *Pl.* Kysylgou, P.

COUNSELLOR, *s.* Cusulioder, cyssylier, w.; kyssylier, P.; conseler, O.M. 1566. *Conseler gentyl y'th pysaf,* gentle counsellor, I pray thee, O.M. 1566.

COUNT, *s.* (A noble). Yurl, B.

COUNT, *v.* Nivera, nevera, w.

COUNTENANCE, *s.* (Face). Enep, enap, envoch, w.; eineach, B.; fêth, fâth, fyth, w.; fâs, P.; fysmant, vysmant, w.; mein, P.

COUNTENANCE, *s.* (Air, aspect, look). Lyw, P.

COUNTERFEIT, *v.* Plosé, plosi, P.

COUNTERPANE, *s.* Golo ar gueli, P.

COUNTRY, *s.* (Region, land, province). Pow, R.D. 1135; powe, c.w. 1219; pou, P.; gwlâd, w.; gulâd, B.; gulât, gwlâs, w.; glâs, R D 1171; gluaes, M. 2782; wlâs, O.M. 343; wlays, M. 927; ulâs, P.; terros, terrus, w.; terras, P.; teroge, w.; derrus, O.M. 554; tireth, w.; tyreth, R.D. 346; tyreyth, dyreyth, w.; ruivanedh, P.; (?) *Adro yn pow*, about in the country, R.D. 1135. *Thywortheugh my a thu'm glâs*, from you I go to my country, R.D. 1171. *Dynerugh arlythy an gluaes*, greet ye the lords of the country, M. 2782. *Adam ke yn mês a'n wlâs*, Adam, go out of the country, O.M. 343. *Erbyn ov wlays*, from thy country, M. 927. *The vôs lemmyn the derrus*, to go now to our country, O.M. 554. *Ha gyllys the ken tyreth*, and gone to another country, R.D. 346. *O pa an ruivanedh?* of what country art thou? P.

COUNTRY or KINGDOM, *s.* Glascor, wlascor, glasgarn, w.; gulasker, B.; gwlasc, M. 3.

AN OPEN COUNTRY. Mês, maes, meas, w.

A LOW FLAT COUNTRY. Pow isal, w.; pou izal, P.

COUNTRYMAN, *s.* (A rustic). Trevedic, dên pow, w.

COUNTRYMAN or NEIGHBOUR, *s.* Contrevac, w.; contrevak, P.; centrevac, cyntrevac, w.; kyntrevak, contreva, P.

COUNTY. *s.* Conteth, M 512 *In conteth gelwys kernov*, in a county called Cornwall. M. 512.

COUPLE, *v.* (To join). Dzhiunia, dho dziunia, P.

COUPLE or PAIR, *s.* Dew, dhew, dyw, dhyw, w.; See TWO.

COURAGE, *s.* Weior wecor, P. *Wecor gwân*, faint courage, P.

COURAGEOUS, *adj.* Colannac, w.; kolannak, B.; colannak, kalonek, P.; calonec, colanac, cylednac, w.; kalonk, P.; strik, strie, vold, B.

COURSE, TERM, TURN, TIME. *s.* Gwêth, gweyth, gwyth, w.; guyth, B.; wêth, wyth, w.; vêth. P.; plêg, w.; blêk, P. *Mil blêk*, a thousand times, P.

COURSE or WAY, *s.* Hins, w.; hans, c.w. 1743. *Gwyth in hans compas tha y'est*, keep in a straight course to the east, c.w. 1743; arrez, B.

COURSE, *s.* (Cursus. *Lat.*). Redegus, B.

COURT or HALL, *s.* Lês, lys, lîs, cuer, cûr, w.; clôs, P.C. 3234. *Agy th'y clôs*, within his court, P.C. 3234.

COURT, *s.* (A court of persons). Coer, w.

COURT, *s.* (Of justice). Lês, lys, lîs, w.

COURT, *s.* (Meeting in some hall). Odians. B.

COURTEOUS, *adj.* Triwardhec, w.; triaudhek, P.; cyweithas, B.; gortas, P.

COURTESY, *s.* Goyntys, B.

COUSIN, *s.* Câr. w.

COUSIN GERMAN, *s.* Handeru, w.

COVENANT, *s.* Ambôs, w.

COVER *v.* Cudhé, cuthé. w.; kuthé, huthé, P.; cudha, w.; cutha, P.; hudha, w.; hutha, c.w. 966; cidha, w.; kitha, quethé, githa, P.; gorhery, w.; goskesy, P.; gwarroc, tyldyé, ty, w.

COVERED. Cuthens, P.

HE COVERED. Quudhas. A form of *cûdhas* 3 pers. s. preter. of *cudhé*, to cover, w.

THEY COVERED. Quedhens. A form of *cudhens*, 3 pers. pl. imperf. of *cudhé*, to cover, w.; gorgwethens, B.

COVER OVER, TO ROOF, *v.* Ty, w.

COVER ONE'S SELF. Omgwedhé, w.

COVERT, A COVERT, *s.* Gostotter, P.; guskys, guscys, w.

COVERLET, *s.* Kiulat, B.; kyulat, P.

COVERING, *s.* Gwisc, guisc. w. ; guisk, guesk, p. ; gwesk, w.

COVERTURE, *s.* Golo, b.

COVETING, *s.* Hirath, hireth, hyreth, b.

COVETOUSNESS, *s.* Crefnye, grefnye, w. ; kraf, b. ; havaethiaz, p.

COW, *s.* Bûch, biûch, w.; beuk, b. ; bûgh, o.m. 1185 ; bewgh, c.w. 403 ; biûh, w.; bû, b. ; beuh, byuh, w. *Pl.* Biuh, beugh, b. ; viuh, p. *Ma'n viuh gen leauh*, the cow is with calf, p.

COWARD, *s.* Ownec, ownek, w. ; ounek, p. ; cauchwâs, w.; caughwâs, casadow, p.

COWARDICE, *s.* Gowardy, o.m. 2161. *Ny'm prêf dên wâr gowardy*, no man shall prove me of cowardice, o.m. 216.

COW-DUNG, *s.* Busl, buzl, w.

COW-DUNG, *s.* (Dried and used for fuel). Glôs, c.w. 1107 ; gloas, w.; glôz, glauz, b. ; glose, glow, p. This word is still in use. *Ha glose tha leskye*, and dry dung to burn, p.

COWER, *v.* (To cower over the fire). Screedle, d. (?)

COWHOUSE, *s.* Boudi, w ; boudzhi, p.; chall, d.

COWL, *s.* Cugol, w. ; kugol, b.

CRAB. *s.* (The fish). Kankar, b.; cancer, kanker, cancher, p.; grill, w. *Pl.* Cancrés, cencras, w. ; kenkraz, b.

CRAB-BOX, *s.* Corve, d.

CRAB OR LOBSTER POT, *s.* (A floating one). Weely, d.

CRACK, *adv.* (Suddenly, quickly). Skuat, p.c. 2816. *Yn morter skuat the gothé*, into the mortice crack to fall, p.c. 2816.

CRACK, *v.* Grachia, w. ; grachya, b.

CRACKED, *part.* Grachis, w.

CRADLE, *s.* Lesc, w. ; lesk, p.

CRAFT OR ART, *s.* Crêft, w. ; krêft, b.

CRAFT or CUNNING, *s.* Dewnos, deunos, w. ; deuuys, deskans, p.

CRAFTILY, *adv.* Feyl, p.c. 11. *Agan temptyé pûr feyl a wra*, us tempt very craftily will, p.c. 11.

CRAFTY, *adj* Feyl, w.; fêl, p.; cal, kal, b.; cudnick, kydnick, p.; kudnik, b.

CRAMP, *s.* (Of the muscles). Godrabben, gudrabm, b.

CRANE, *s.* (The bird). Garân, w. ; grew, p.; kraná, b.; crana, p. ; bidnepein, b.

CRATE, *s.* Cluit, w.

CRAWL, *v.* Gwayah, w.; guaya, b.

CRAWLING, *part.* (Like a lizard or a toad). Cranagas, w. ; pedrevanas, m. 4218. *War lûr ov pedrevanas*, on the ground crawling. See LIZARD.

CRAYFISH. *s.* Gaver, d.

CRAZED, *adj.* Muscok, n. See MAD.

A CRAZY PERSON. Bucca gwidden, d. *Lit.* A white ghost.

CREAM, *s.* (Of milk). Dehen, w.

CREATE, *v.* Formyé, gwrey, w. ; gurey, gurei, gurelli, p. ; dho gurel, gil, b.

CREATION, *s* Gwreans, gwryans, wreans, w.

CREATOR, *s.* Creador, creator, w. ; credor, p.; creader, b. ; formyer, formyas, w. *Del ôs formyas the'n nêf ha'n lûr*, as thou art Creator of heaven and earth, r.d. 843 ; gwrear, wrear, w. ; gulwur, p.

CREATURE, *s.* Creater, croadur, w. ; creadur, p.

CREATURES, CREATED THINGS, *s.* Crocadur, b.

CREDENCE, *s.* Crygyans. See BELIEF for many forms of this word.

CREDITABLE, *adj.* (Honorus, *Lat.*) Enir, henir, ynir, b.

CREDITOR, *s.* Kendoner, p.c. 502-3. *Dev kendoner yth ege the vn dettor*, there were two creditors to one debtor, p.c. 502-3.

CREDULITY, *s.* Hygoeled, b.

CREED, *s.* See BELIEF.

CREED, THE CREED, *s.* Cregyans, credgyans, credzyans, w. ; kredzhanz, credzhyans, p. ; kredzhans, b.

CREEK, *s.* Gwic, w.; guik, ick, ik, creeg, p. ; zawn, porth, porh, pôr, b.

CREEP, *v.* (To crawl). Gwayah, w. ; guaya, p. ; cruppya, w.; cramé, p.

CREEP, *v.* Theek. *Dawon yn y gorsa theek*, sorrow into the body of it creep, p.

CREST, *s.* (Summit). Crib, w. ; krib, b.

CREST, TUFT, or PLUME, *s.* Criban, w. ; kriban, b.

CREVICE, *s.* (In a lode). Gunnis, d. The old vaults or cavities found in a mine are called " the old gunnies," d.

CREW, *s.* Bagat, b.

CRICK, *s.* (As of the neck). Pinnick, d.

CRIME, *s.* Cam, w. ; ken, p. ; drôgober, w. ; dyfout, diffout, b.

CRIMSON, *s.* and *adj.* Ridh, rydh, rûdh, rûd, rûydh, rûth, rooz, p.

CRIPPLED, *adj.* Clôf, cloppec, w. ; cloppek, p. ; klôf, kloppek, b.

CROAK, *v.* (Like a raven). Crunk, d.

CROCKERY, *s.* (As tea things, &c.) Daffer. *Polwhele.*

CROOK, *s.* Hîg, lk, w. ; hyc, p.

CROOKED, *adj.* Cam, cabm, w. ; kabm, p.; cham, gam, ham, crûm, w. ; krûm, p. ; crôm, w. ; krôm, croum, b. ; cromb, crobm, p.

CROOKED-SHOULDERED, *adj.* Camsgudhec, cabmsgudhac, w.; kabm-sghudak, B.

CROP, OR STOMACH OF A FOWL, *s.* Kah, B.

CROSS, *adj.* (Froward, unjust). Três, w.; camhinsic, camhilik, P.

CROSS, *adj.* (Thwart). Adrês, trûs, w.

CROSS, A CROSS, *s.* Crows, w.; crous, P.; krouz, B.; grows, w.; grous, P.C. 2576; crois, P.; krois, B.; crow, crou, P.

CROSS-BAR, *s.* Cerble, P.

CROSS-BEAM, *s.* Trûspren, P.

CROSS-BOW, *s.* Albalastr, B.

CROSS-ROAD, *s.* Scochfordh, w.

CROSS, TO GO ACROSS, *v.* Trûssé, w.

CROSS OR THWART, *v.* Omdhal, P.

CROW, *v.* Cané, cana, gana, w.; prania, B. *An kuliak a prania,* the cock crows, B.; keny, P.C. 903.

CROW, *s.* (The bird). Brân, vrân, (*Pl.* Bryny,) w.; marburan, B. See RAVEN.

CROWD, *s,* Stevya, w.; steuya, ruth, P.

CROWN, *v.* Ceruné, keruné, curuné, curuny, coroné, w.; curené, N.

CROWN, *s.* (Coronet or diadem). Curun, w.; curun ray, B.; curyn, w.; corun, P.; koron, B.; curen, M. 2994; kerune, O.M. 2398; cyryn, guryn, gyryn, w.; ghyryn, B.

CROWN OF THE HEAD, *s.* Divaleuuit, w.; dipuleuint, P.

CROWN OF A HILL, *s.* Crousel, B.

CROWNED, *part.* Cerenys, kerenys, cerunys, kerunys, w.

CROZIER, *s.* Vagyl, M. 3007. *Sens the vagyl in the leff,* hold thy crozier in thy hand M. 3007.

CROZIER-BEARER, *s* Crosser, M. 2874; crosyer, M. 3922; crocer, P.C. 1456.

CRUCIFY, *v.* Crowsé, w.; crousé, O.M. 1937. *Rag crousé cryst ov máp kêr,* to crucify Christ my dear Son, O.M. 1937; crowsyé, w.; crousyé, P.C. 2184; crewsy, P.; gundé, w. *The gvndé máb dên defry,* to crucify the Son of man, truly, O.M. 1950.

CRUDE, *adj.* (Rude or raw). Criv, w.; kriv, B.

CRUEL, *adj.* Garow, w.; garou, B.; garo, guariow, P.; wherow, chuero, w.; khuero, B.; milen, melen, felen, velen, hager, w.; hagar, P.; brochi, ithek, brâz, B.

MOST CRUEL. Haccré, R.D. 2005; hakeré, R.D. 2071.

CRUELLY, *adv.* Calas, P. *Punscie y tûs mar calas,* his people punished so cruelly, O.M. 1482.

CRUMB, A CRUMB, *s.* Brewyonen, w.; brouian, B.; bramb, bram, P.; frôth, B.; bruyan, buryan. *Pl.* Browsian, w.; brousian, breyonen, B.

CRUMPLED, *adj.* Crum, crom, P.

CRUSH, *v.* Crehylly, w.

CRUSHED, *part.* Crehyllys, guridnias, B.

CRUSH or FLATTEN DOWN, *v.* Squattia, B.; squattya, skuattia, scuattya, sguattia, w.

CRUST, A CRUST, *s.* Creven, crevan, krevan, B.

A DRY CRUST OF BREAD. Null, D.

CRUST or SCAB OF A SORE, *s.* Hud, D. From *hudha,* to cover.

CRY, CALL, SHOUT, *s.* Garm, w.; carma, galus, galow; crei, krei, cri, cry, gri, gry, P.; lêf, w.

CRY, CALL, SHOUT, *v.* Helwy, hilwy, hylwy, w.; hylwys, B.; ullia, w.; uolé, elow, galwy, P.; galua, B.; galu, P.; ylwy, B.; garmé, w.; garmi, P.; carmé, w.; karmé, carma, P.; cria, creia, crya, kriha, cryé, crio, greia, w.; greiah, P.; léfa, w.; gwaeddi, bloeddio, B.

CRY, WEEP, WAIL, *v.* Wolé, olé, w.; olua, diveré, P.; gwelvan, guelvan, B.

CRY, *v.* (To cry out at one). Harthy, harha, w.

CRY YE OUT TO. Ynyough, B.

CRIED OUT. (Shouted). Ynnyas, ylwis.

HE CRIED. (Shouted). Armas, a mutation of *garmas,* from *garma,* to cry out. 2. Greias, a mutation of *creias,* id, qd, *crias,* from *cria,* to cry out, 3, Gryés, a mutation of *cryes,* from *crya,* to shout or cry out. 4 Ylwys, a mutation of *gylwys,* from *gylwel,* to call, w.

THEY CRIED OUT. Hawlsons from *helwy,* to cry out, B.

HE WILL CRY. Gelow, elow. *Elow,* is the mutation of *gelow,* 3 pers. s fut. of *gelwel,* w.

CRYSTALLIZED, *adj.* Drusy, D. See LODE.

CUBE OR LUMP, *s.* (As of granite). Kam. *C.S. Gilbert.*

CUBIT, *s.* Cevelyn, kevelyn, w.; kevellyn, C.W. 2260; kevellen, C.W. 2262; cyvelyn, w.; kyvelyn, P.; keuelyn, O M. 937; gevelyn, w.; gellon, B.; gelen, gelyn, P; elin, B.

CUCKOO, *s.* Côg, gôg, w.; gogue, gôk, P. *An gôg,* the cuckoo.

CUDGEL, *s.* (A short one). Sparl, B.

CUFF OR THUMP, *s.* Colp, coot, D. See BLOW.

CULTIVATE, *v.* Gonedhy, gonés, gonys, gonethy, conys, wonys, w.

CULTIVATED GROUND. Drevas, B.

CUNNING, *s.* Coyntis, goyntis, dewnos, deunos, descans, w.; deskans, P.; sleyveth, w.; gonycke, C.W. 1406.

CUNNING, *adj.* Coynt, w. *Otté ha coynt o an guas,* see how cunning the fellow was, P.C. 1820; cal, P.;

kal, B.; connek, M. 1427; cudnick, kydnik, P.; fûr,
fir, w.; fyr, P.; feer, fêl, w.; eruryr, eruyer, Г.;
slêv, w.; sotel, P.

A CUNNING MAN. *Dên fêl*, P.C 1886.

A CUNNING FELLOW. Gwâs, guâs, w.; connek,
M. 1427.

A CUNNING TRICK. Prat, bratt, w.

CUP, *s* Hanaf, hanath, bolla, fiol, celegel, kelegel,
keroin, B.

A SMALL CUP. Tôs, M. 80. Hence the English
tot, "a tot of liquor."

CUPS OF SACRIFICE. Minne, D. (*Pocula diis
sacrata*)

CUP-BEARER, *s.* Reunniat, P.

CUPBOARD, *s.* Logel, logell, logol, w.

CURDLE, *v.* Crummy, P.; crunny, B.

CURE, *v.* (To cure, to be cured). Sawyé, w.; guerir, P.; yaghy, M. 1500.

CURED, *part.* Yagh, M. 713; yagheys, M. 1500.
Ha me yv yagh. and I am cured, M. 713. *Ny yllogh
bonès yagheys*, can you be cured? M. 1500.

CURE, *s.* Iag, w.; yagh, R.D. 1671. *Hemma yv iag
a'n pla*, this is a cure of the plague, P.C. 2817.

CURLED, *part* or *adj.* Cryllias, w.; krylliaz. B.
Curled hair, bleu cryllias.

CURLEW, *s.* Gelvinac, w.; gelvinak, gylvinak, P.;
gylvinac, w.; golvinak, B.; golvinac, w.

CURRY-COMB, *s.* Streil, B.

CURSE, *v.* Scemyna, w.; skemyna, P.; omscemyny,
w.; omsceminy, P.; emscumuny, ymscemyny, w.;
ymskemyny, P.; mylygé, molletha, mollethia, molythia, w; voleythy, B.

HE WILL CURSE. Vyllyc, a mutation of *myllyc*, 3
pers s. fut. of *mylygé*, to curse.

CURSED. Mylegés, melegés, malegas, w.; mylygé,
B.; ethlays, w.; omskemynés, P.; soweth, syweth, B.

CURSE, *s.* Molleth, mollath, w.; molath, P,; molloth, w.; molth, B.; mollat, R.D. 2287; vetye, P.;
ansueth, theveth, B.

CURSES, *s.* Mollothow, w.; molothowe, c.w. 1220;
mollathow, w.; molathow, P.; volothowe, c.w. 1486.

CURVE, *v.* Camma, gamma, w.; cabmy, P.

CUSHION, *s.* Plafoc, plyvog, B.

CUSTOM, *s.* Desmos, w.; vsadow, M. 135, (? *Fl.*);
vaner, O.M. 1900, *An vaner a vye da*, the custom is
good, O.M. 1900.

CUSTOMARY, *adj.* Arbednec, arbennec, w.

CUSTOM-HOUSE, *s.* Tolva, B.

CUT, *v.* Trochy, w.; troghy, P.; trohy, w.; trohé,
trehy, P.; trehi, B.; terry, terhi, tyrry, torry, w.;
torri, P.; drehy, w.

CUT, *part.* Trôch, w.; trehez, drohas, B.

CUT OFF, *v.* Scilly. From hence, says Pryce. Scilly
Isles, "cut off from the insular continent."

CUT OFF, *v.* (To cut off mutually). Omladh, emladh, w.

CUT ONE'S THROAT, *v.* Dho lâtha, P.

CUT, *s.* Lâdh, w.; flaw, B.; flookan, B. *Flookan* is
a miner's term. It means a parcel of ground which
cuts off one part of a lode from another.

CUTLER, *s,* Trehés, trahés. *Pl.* Trehesi, trahesi.
Trahesi mein, stone-cutters, w.

CUTTING OFF, *s.* (A cutting off). Lâdh, w.

CUTTLE BONE, *s.* Taghir, B. (Locally *skuttle bone.*)

CUTTLE FISH, *s* Stifac, w.; stifak, B.; stiffak,
stiphak, P.; goil, D.

THE GREAT CUTTLE FISH. Pedalincan, padi-
lincan, D.

CYMBAL, *s.* Choch-dibi, P. (? cloch-dibi).

D.

This letter is both, radical and secondary. When radical it changes in construction into *dh*, which has the
sound of *th* in the English words, *this*, *than*; as *dên*,
a man. *Dew dhên*, two men.

In Cornish (and Armoric) *d* changes into *t*, as *dôs*, to
come, *ow tôs*, coming.

When secondary, *d* is the soft sound of *t*, in the Cornish,
thus, *tás*, a father, *y dás*, his father, w. *Lex. Corn. Brit.*

DAGGER, *s.* Clêdha bian, w. *Lit.* A little sword.

DAILY, *adv.* Poynêdh, boynêdh, w.

DAMP, *adj.* Vady, D.

DAINTIES, *s.* Ferclin, saut, sant, B.

DAIRY, *s.* Laitty, w.

DAIRY PRODUCE. Whitsul. Such as milk, sour
milk, cheese, curds, butter and suchlike as come from
the cow, and ewe, D.

DAISY, *s.* Neonia, w.; neonin, gajah, B.; egr dew, w.

A GARDEN DAISY. Egr dzharn, w.

DALE, *s.* Nans, w.; nance, nantz, P.; glen, glyn,
dôl, w.; rôsh, B.

DAM, *s.* Bancan, w.; bankan, P.; tuban, w.; tuban
agger, P.

A LOW DAM OR RIDGE. Astyllen, D. A mining term.

DAMAGE, *v.* Gwaythy, w.; gwaythé, guethé, P.;
gwethé, fethy, w.

DAMAGE, *s.* (Hurt, loss). Drôc, drôk, drôg,
drôcoleth, dhrôcoleth, drôk-culeth, coll, goll, collet,
w.; kollet, B.; cellad, w.; diopenés, P.; diowenés, B.

DAME, *s.* Dama, w.; damma, dâm, P.

DAMNED, *part.* Skymys, P. From *skemyna*, to curse.

DAMNED, THE DAMNED, *s.* Skymys, P.

DAMP, *adj.* Glêb, gleıb, glib, lêb, glew, gleu, dony, P.

DAMP, *v.* (Discourage). Gwaythy, w.; gwaythé, guethé, P.; gwethé, fethy, w.

DAMSEL, *s.* Morên, moroìn, w.; morain, P.

DANCE, *v.* Lemmel, w.; lemal, B.; lebmal, w.; carolli, P.; korolli, B.; thonssyé, R.D. 2656.

DANCE, *s.* Dawns, B. There was an ancient Cornish dance called *Tremathieves.* Polwhele.

DANCE or JIG, *s.* Galliard, B.

DANCER, *s.* Lappior, D. *Female dancer*, lappiorés, w.

DANDRIFF, *s.* Rummet, D.

DANGER, *s.* Antell perill, peryl, feryl, w.

DANGEROUS, *adj.* Dyantell, dyantel, w.; dyantu, P.

DANGEROUSLY, *adv.* Dyantel, P.C. 94. *Ha dyantel r'em laute*, and dangerously by my truth, P.C. 94.

DARE, *v.* Lavasy, w.

DARK, *adj.* Du, diu, dhiu, tewal, w.; teual, P.

DARK or CLOUDY, *adj.* Comolec, w.; comolek, P.; komolek, B.

DARK, THE DARK, DARKNESS, *s.* Gorthuer, P. *Râk nam nagyvw gorthuer*, for now it is dark; tulder, tewlder, tiwlder, tuylder, w.; tuilder, P,; tyuldar, tulgu, tewolgow, w.; teuolgow, P.; tiwulgou, w.; tiuwegou, P.; dewolgow, w.; dewolgowe, c. w. 322. *Ha dampnys the tewolgow,* and condemmed to darkness, P.C. 2466.

DARNEL, *s.* Ivre, w.

DART, *v.* Pechyé, bechyé, w.

DART, *s.* (Shaft or spear) Gew, w.; gu, geu, guu, P ; guw, giw, gwayw, w.

DAUGHTER, *s.* Myrch, vyrch, myrh, vyrh. merch, merh, much, w.; myrgh, P. *Pl.* Myrhes, myrghes, N.

DAUGHTER-IN-LAW, *s.* Guhit, gwhidh, w.; guhidh, B.; elsés, w. Borlase gives *elsés* for a son-in-law by a former wife or husband.

DAVID, *s.* Dewy, B.

DAWN, *s.* (Daybreak). Terri-andzhêth, B.; terr-andzhêdh, duth-tarth, P.; dydh-tardh, w.

DAY, *s.* Dydh, dêdh, deydh, dzhêdh, w.; dydth, dyth, B.; dêth, dêt, dhê, dê, w.; du, P.; di, deiz, B.; tydh, têdh, gêdh, geydh, gydh, gyth, c.w. 85. *An lôr yn nôs houl yn gêyth*, the moon in night, the sun in day, o.m. 39; gêth, B.; jorna, w.; jurna, dzhyrna, B.; dzhyrna, w.

DAY BY DAY. Cynifar dzhyrna, w.; kynifar, dzyrna, P.

TO-DAY, THIS DAY. Hedhyw, hedhew, hedheu. hydhew, hidhu, hithu, hithou, w.; hithow, P.; hithyou, w.; hetheu, P.; hethow, B.; hethyu, ythew, ytho, P.; hethec, w.; hepou (?) B.; yn dzhedh, w.

THE DAY BEFORE YESTERDAY. De genzhéte, w.; deghenzête, P.

THE DAY FOLLOWING. Ternos, ternoys, w.

THE DAY AFTER TO MORROW. Trensa, trenzha, w.; trendzha, B.

TWO DAYS HENCE Trensa, trenzha, w.; trendzha, B.

THREE DAYS TIME. Triddydh, tryddydh, w.; tryddyth, P.

SIX DAYS SPACE. Whêddydh, w.

THE DAY OF JUDGMENT. Dydh brues, w.; deth brûs, P.C. 1669.

BEFORE DAYLIGHT. Kyn vyttyn, P,; *Lit.* Before morning.

DAZZLING, *adj.* Gurygtion, P.

DEACON, *s.* Diagon, w.

DEAD, *adj.* Marow, w.; marrow, o.m. 2702; maro, P.; merow, B.; varow, w.; verou, vyru, B.; varwa, o.m. 3578. *Marow rág the gerensé*, dead for thy love, o.m. 2138. *Er na varwa eredy*, until she be dead quite, o.m. 3573.

A DEAD BODY. Korph maro, B.

DEADS, *s.* (The refuse in a miℕe). Dyzha. *Pryce's Mineralogia.*

DEAF, *adj.* Bodhar, bother, bothak, bythac, bythak, w.; vother, M. 805; aeke, aege, P.

DEAL BOARDS, *s.* Plancys zaban, w.; plankys zaban, P.

DEALER, *s.* Gwicur, gwiccor, w.; gwicker, c.w. 1143; guikyr, B.; gwicher, P.; gwicgur, guicgur, goccor, w.

A CORN DEALER. Bager, D.

DEAR, *adj.* (Beloved). Cêr, cear, w.; kear, B.; cyr, kyr, kêr, gêr, P.; cûf, cuef, cueff, cefyon, (the plural of *cúf*,) whêc, whêk, hwêc, w ; whêg, B.; hwêg, w.; huêg, B.; whêgol, w.; whêgoll, B.; hwêgol, w. *Mar gêr*, so dear, P.

DEAR MOTHER. Vam whêgoll, B.; *Lit.* All sweet mcther.

DEAR FRIENDS. Caradowyon, P.

DEAR LORDS. Arlythy caradowyon, P.C. 2163.

A DEAR NEIGHBOUR. Câr, P.; kâr, B.

DEAR ME! Aree faa; B.V.

DEAREST, *adj.* Kevarwouth, P.; cerra, kerra, w. *Salamon the váp kerra*, Solomon thy son most dear, o.m. 2341.

DEARLY, *adv.* Thermaz, B.

DEARNESS, *s.* (Costliness). Gêr, B. ;

DEAR, COSTLY, *adj.* Cêr, B.

DEATH, *s.* Ankow, ancow, ancou, B. ; ankowe, c.w. 379 ; ankaw, c.w. 1967 ; ancov (*ancou*) M. 4147 ; anken, o.m. 276 ; ancouyns, B. *War beyn ancov ty belan*, on pain of death thou villian, M. 4147. *Trystyns fast bys yn ancow*, great sadness even until death, P.C. 1023 ; marnens, mernans, W. ; marnans, merual, P. ; vernans. W. *Gothaf mernens yn bysma*, to suffer death in this world, P.C. 1343 ; crow, W. ; crou, P. *Dhom peynyé bys yn crow*, to torture me even to death.

THE DEATH. Deweth, theweth, B. See END.

THE PLACE OF DEATH. Kyvur ancou, P.

A VOILENT DEATH. Latha, P.

DEBATE, *v.* Gueskall, P.

DEBILITY, *s.* Gwander, W. For other forms of this word see WEAKNESS.

DEBT, *s.* Cyndan, W. ; kyndan, P. ; gyndan, w.

DEBTOR, *s.* Cendoner, kendoner, W. *Dev keudoner yth ege the va dettor*, there were two debtors to one creditor, P.C. 502-3.

DECAPITATE, *v.* Dibenna, W.

DECAY, *v.* Difygy, dyfygy, W. ; dyfyg, thyfyk, P. ; thyfyé, R.D. 78 ; potry, P.C. 3200. *Na potré bys vynary*, that it do not decay ever, P.C. 3200.

DECEASE, *s.* See DEATH.

DECEASED, *adj.* Marow. W. ; maro, P.

DECEIT, *s.* Fallad, fallas, fraus, feyntys. W. *Hep feyntys na falsury*, without deceit or falsehood, P.C. 1478 ; tulle, B. ; tûll, teul, towl, toul, W. ; gowegncth, gouegneth, P. ; whethlow, o.m. 2560 ; Whethlow is a plural, meaning *idle tales*, in Cornwall called *widdles*. Norris translates "*hep whethlow*," "without deceit." See o.m. 2560.

DECEITFUL, *adj.* Fals, fouls, gôc, gauhôc, gouhoc, W.

DECEITFULNESS, *s.* Tullor, B. See DECEIT.

DECEIVE. *v.* Tollé. tolla, tullé, tulla, tilla, W. ; thollé, twyllo, B. ; dilla. W. ; dulla, c.w. 472 ; dolla, dollé, W. ; collé, P. ; gurra, B. ; gowhelés, wowheles, baché. W. ; baghé, desehy, dyssantyé, lafurye, P. *Rág ef thym a lafurye*, for he hath deceived, P.

DECEIVED, *part. and s.* Fellyon, B. ; thollé, B.

DECEIVER, *s.* Huder, W. ; hudor, lafurye, P. ; tullor, w.

DECEMBER, *s.* Cevardhiu, mês kevardhiu, mis kevardhiu, W. ; miz-kevardhiu, keuar-diu-mis, P. *Lit.* The month of black storms.

DECENCY, *s.* Honester, M. 261 ; onester, M. 487.

DECENT, *adj.* Onest, w.

DECLARE, *v.* Daryvas, dharyvas, dyryvas, derevas, dherevas, deryfas, teryfas, dascudhé, dyscudhé, disquedha, dysquedhas, dyswedha, dywedhy, W. ; dysquethya,, N. ; dythybia, P. ; lavary. leverel, W. ; thesta, P. ; thysta, o.m. 2543.

I DECLARE. Je vody, P. The French "je vous dis" ?

HE DECLARED. Yttterevys. Composed of *y* and *terevys.* a mutation of *derevys*, 3 pers. s. preterite of *derevas*, W.

DECLARATION. *s.* Daryvas, dheryvas, dysquydhyans, W. ; dysquythyens, o.m. 147 ; dysquythyans, o.m. 1733 ; desquethyans, dowethyans, c.w. 618. *Yn dysquythyens a henna*, in declaration of that, o.m. 147.

DECORTICATE, *v.* Dyrusky, W.

DECREED, *part.* Tewlas, dewlys, P.

DEED, *s.* (Exploit). Deray, W.

DEED, *s.* (Act). Gwaith, gwyth, wyth, W. ; guaith, B. ; gwythrés, wythrés, W. ; whythrés, o.m. 272 ; prat, bratt, W. ; brat, P. ; ober, c.w. 1275 ; obar, c.w. 1177 ; culeth, kuleth, coleth, W. (These three last are only used with *dróc*, evil, as *drócoleth*, an evil deed), Takel. (Pl. Tacklow, P. ; as *Tacklow privie*, private action or things). Wreans, c.w. 1121. *An nór y'th whythrés hogen*, the earth is thy evil deed, o M. 272. *Thy'my ef a wruk an prat*, to us he did the deed, R.D. 605.

DEEMED, *part.* Podeerés, P. A corruption of *prederys*, from *predery*, to consider.

DEEP, *adj.* Down, W. ; doun, vown, P. ; town, W. ; towne, B. *Maga towne*, very deep ; bodo, W. *Ha'y wul hyr ha doun*, and make it long and deep for him o.m. 867.

DEEP, THE DEEP, *s* Dounder, B. ; downder, w. As of the sea or ocean.

DEEP PIT. Pul down, w.

DEEPEST PART. Iseldor, W.

DEEPNESS, *s.* Downder, W. ; dounder, P.

DEER, *s.* Carow, W. ; carau, caro, P. ; carou, karo, karu, caruu, B. ; gollon, P.

DEER OR HIND, *s.* Ewic, euhic, W. ; euig, euhig, B.

DEFAME, *v.* Flamya, W. ; dyflya, P.

DEFAMED, *part.* Flamyas, dyflyas, P.

DEFAULT, *s.* Fall, W. ; fal, gyll, dyfout, P.

DEFECT, *s.* Nam, W. ; gyll, P.

DEFENCE, *s.* Archless, costan, kostan, B. ; clem, W. *Me a leuer thy's ràk clem*, I say to you for defence, R.D. 625.

DEFEND, *v.* Amwyn, B. ; coscasa, kosgaza, W. ; kosgazo, P. ; kosgezys, dyffrés, dhyffrés, W. ; thyffrés, P.C. 2622. *Rág y thyffrés a anken*, to defend him from pain, P.C. 2622.

DEFENDANT, *s.* Diffenor, w.; diffener, B.

DEFENDER, *s.* Dadloyar, dadloyer, dathluur, P.

DEFER, *v.* Cregi, dho cregi, P.

DEFICIENT, TO BE DEFICIENT, *v.* Fallé, w.

DEFICIENCY, *s.* Fawt, w.; faut, P.; fowt, fout, w; fal, P.

DEFILE, *v.* Hagry, w.; schyndy, P.; mostya, w.

DEFILE, *v.* (To defile with ordure). Ymgachu, B.

DEFILED, *part.* Mostys, vostys, w.

DEFILEMENT, *s.* Mostya, M. 3863. *Guyth ov ena heb mostya,* keep my soul without defilement, M. 3863.

DEFLOWER, *v.* (Ravish). Guasga, B.

DEFORM, *v.* Defaleby, dafolé, w.

DEFORMED, *part.* Defalebys, w.

DEFORMED, *adj.* Deffryth, disliu, w.; digliu, hager, hagar, uthek, P.

DEFORMITY, *s.* Hacter, w.; hactar, P.

DEGREE, *s.* (Step, measure). Grât, gry, P.

DEGREE, *s.* (Rank). Pryckna, pruckna, gre, P. *Neb a vo moghya gre,* he who is in the highest degree, P.C. 777.

DELAY, *v.* Lettya, hocyé, hokyé, w.; hethy, cregi, dhelledzha, P.; dalea, N.

DELAY, *s.* Gorholeth, w.; gortos, R.D. 2146; let, w.; lettye, o.M. 1194; hockye, P.; hokkye, P.C. 2828; hokye, o.M. 191; hethy, hâs, dyweth, dywyth, P. *Orth agas gortos,* by your delay, R.D. 2146. *My a offryn hep lettye,* I will offer without delay, o.M. 1194. *Heb hokye fast hane ydo,* without delay quickly have done it, o.M. 198.

DELICIOUS, *adj.* Hueg, B.

DELIGHT, *s.* Lowene, lawenés, w.; lauenez, lauen, P.; whecter, w.; whekter, o.M. 359; megyans, M. 25. *Yn més a'n ioy ha'm, whekter,* away from my joy and delight, o.M. 359. *Ha than ena sûr megyans,* and to the soul a sure delight, M. 2025.

DELIRIUM, *s.* Trangiak, galdrum, B.

DELIVER, *v.* Dascor, thascor, dylyr, P.; dilvar, B.

THEY WOULD HAVE DELIVERED. Delyrsens, w.

I WILL DELIVER. A rogolley, P.

DELIVERER, *s.* See SAVIOUR and REDEEMER.

DELUDE, *v.* See DECEIVE.

DELUGE, *s.* Deall, dial, dyal, dhyal, diel, kyel, lîf, lyf, lyv, w.

DELUSION, *s.* Hûth, P.

DELVE, *v.* Palas, balas, w.; ballas, c.w. 982.; balés, o.M. 414; baly, P. See DIG.

DEMAND, *v.* Govyn, govynny, wovyan, wovynny, gulen, w.; dymandia, cria, creia, greia, greiyh, dho greiah râg, P.; huila, B.

DEMAND, *s.* Govynnad, wovynnad, w. *Sûr ôl the wovynnadow,* surely all thy demands, P.C. 599.

DEMENTED, *adj.* Ascient, guan, B.

DEMONIAC, *s.* Sach-diavol, P.; sach-diauol, B.

DEMONSTRATION, *s.* Deskydhyans, dysquedhyans, discwedhyens, w.; disquethians, diskuedhyans, P.

DEMUR, *s.* Ardak, P.C 1870. *By's dys omma hep ardak,* to thee here without demur, P.C. 1870.

DEN, *s.* Cors, kavarn, B.; fow, w.; fou, ffau, vau, vou. *Pl.* Fouyz, P.; fouiz, B.; fowys, P.C. 336. *Ha fowys the laddron plôs,* and dens of foul thieves, P.C. 336. See CAVE or CAVERN.

DENIAL, *s.* Innias, ynnyas, ynny, w.; ynnyad, P. *Pl.* Inniadow, w.; inniadou, P. *Del degoth thy'm hep ynny,* as it becomes me without denial, o.M. 1942.

DENIED, *part.* Nehys, w.; neghys, P.

DENOTE, *v.* Notyé, w.

DENY, *v.* Naché, nahé nacha, naha, nea, w; neghy, nagha, naghé, P.; dynaché, w.; dygnahas, ynnya, ynny, P.

DENY, *v.* (Refuse). Sconya, sconyé, w.; reneag, P.

DEPART, *v.* Dilecha, w.; dewedhy, dewedhé, dhewedhé, dewethé, P.; thewethé, o.M. 686. *An termyn the thewethé,* the time to depart, o.M. 686; omdena, P.; voydya, c.w. 2345; tremené, dremené, w.

DEPARTED, *part.* Degenow, dagenow, w.

DEPENDENT, *s.* Undamsi, w.; dên coscor, B.

DEPENDENTS, *s.* Cosgor, kosgar, w.

DEPENDING, *part.* Koskor, B.

DEPOSIT, *s.* (*Detritus*). Lig, liggan, D.

DEPOSITORY, *s.* Logel, logell, logol, w.

DEPRIVE, *v.* Difyddio, B.

DEPRIVED. Gwedho, w.; guedho, P.; guedeu, w.; guetho, P.

DEPTH, *s.* Downder, w.; dounder, P.

DERIDE, *v.* Dyalé, w.; dyalas, dhyallas, P.; dafolé, gescy, w.; gesky, P.

DERISION, *s.* Dafole, schereweth, P.; scherewith, D.

DESCEND, *v.* Descyn, deiscyn, w.; deiskyn, P.; dyscynné, dyskynné, w.; diskynné, P.; dyescenné, dyeskenné, dyescynné, w.; dyskynnya, c.w. 75; dyiskynya, c.w. 234; dyskyna, B.; discynna, scydnya, skydnya, degensywé, tegensywé, w.

DESCENDED, *part.* Diskynnys, diwenys, &c.

DESCENDING, *part.* Dywenys, &c.

DESCENT, PARENTAGE, *s.* Goys, guydh, gudzh, B. These are some of the forms for *blood, q.v.*

DESCENT, *s.* (A coming down). Tharvivas, P.

DESCRY, *v.* Guydher, P.

DESERT, A DESERT, *s.* Defyth, difeid, devyth, w.; deveth, P. *Yn defyth yn tewolgow,* into desert into darkness, P.C. 142.

DESERT, *s.* (Merit). Rêth, P.

DESERVE, *v.* Dylly, dely, dendel, dyndyly, thyndyly, w.; rêthy, P.

DESERVED, *adj.* Mall, B.

DESERVING, *adj.* Gweff, gyw, gwyw, w.

DESIGN, *v.* (Intend). Arveth, w.; faes, P.; tewlel, w.; teulel, tiulel, P.; tywlel, w.; tyulel, B.; towlal, teuly, P.; towla, toula, w.; doulla, P.

DESIGN, *s.* (Intention). Dowl, dowle, P.

DESIGNED, *part.* Tewlas, dewlys, B., &c.

DESIRE, *s.* Duwhans, dywhans, P.; whans, hwans, w.; whanz, hyreth, herath, P.; wl, w.; youall, B.; yeues, w. *Môs thotho yv ov yeues,* it is my desire to go to him, P.C. 1046; mal, w. *The gafus gynen yv mal,* it is our desire to take thee, P.C. 1178; merth, B.; plegad, w.; blonogeth, C.W. 96; dakkroter, dacroter, P. *Guas dacroter,* a hungry desire, P.; luyst, M. 1824. *Penys purguir yv ov luyst,* to do penance right truly is my desire, M. 1824; omnadow, M. 30.

A DESIRE OR REQUEST. Orphennyaz, P.

A STRONG DESIRE. Awel, hireth, hyreth, w.; hirath, B.

WITHOUT DESIRE. De-whanz, P.

DESIRE, *v.* Desef, yeuny, w.; vedn, P.

THEY DESIRED. Yttasefsons, w. Composed of *y* and *tesefsons,* a mutation of *desefsons,* 3 pers. pl. preter. of *desef,* w.

DESIROUS, *adj.* Dywysic, plegadow, plygadow, whansec, w.; whanseck, P.; whansek, N.; whansack, C.W. 1774; volynzhedhek, P.

DESIST, *v.* Sestya, w.; dho hassa, P.

DESPATCH, *s.* (Haste). Tôth, tooth, towth, touth, toysh, dôth, w.

DESPISE, *v.* Dispresy, dyspresy, w.

DESPISED, *part.* Dyspresyas, B.

WILLING TO BE DESPISED, *adj.* Spernabyl, w.

DESPITE, *s.* Despyth, dyspyth, w.; dyspyt, P.

DESTITUTE, *adj.* Gwedho, w.; guedho, P.; gueden, w.; heb ken, P.

DESTITUTE OF. Noeth, noath, nôth, w.; nooth, P.; noyth, w.

DESTROY, *v.* Disil, diswrey, w.; dyswrey, diswreys, diswel, P.; dyswel, diswul, dyswul, dhyswul, w.; dho diswrug, dyswruthyl, dyswythyl, P.; destrewy, dhestrewy, w.; dystrewy, P.; dystrywy, w.; tystrywy, P.; thistrewy, B.; destria, destra, w.; gwaythé, P.; gwaythy, gwethé, w.; guethé, P.; fethy, w.; treythé, P.; golli, guastia, vensy, B.; brosy, w.; dho toula diveas, B.

HE DESTROYED. Diswrûg, dhyswrug, w.

THOU WOULSDT DESTROY. Tystrewys, a mutation of *dystrewys,* 2 pers. s. subj. of *dystrewy,* w.

DESTRUCTION, *s.* Marnans, mernans, merual, P.

DETAIN, *v.* Thuethy, P.

DETECTION, *s.* Myc, w.; mycke, sogote, P. *Ha ryb tha sogote wre,* and by making this discovery (or detection), P.

DETERMINE or END, *v.* Dhyfyk, P.

DETECT, *v.* Casé, w.

DETESTABLE, *adj.* Ahas, O.M. 1081; cesadow, casadow, w.; kesadow, P.; gasadow, w.

DETRACTION, *s.* Cabel, w.

DETRITUS or DEPOSIT, *s.* Lig, liggan, D.

DEVICE, *s.* Thavys, C.W. 466.

DEVIL, *s.* Diawl, w.; diaul, P.; dioul, B.; diowl, dyawl, w.; dyowl, O.M. 301; deawl, w.; deaul, R.D. 2104; dyallas, dewol, P.; diavol, dzhiawl, w.; dzhiaul, P.; jawl; jowl, joul. iawl, w.; iovl, M. 159; jevan, malan, pla, w. The following are some of the plurals, *viz.,* Dewolow, dywolow, w.; dywolou, B.; dewlugy, w.; deulugy, P.; thewollow, C,w. 481; thevollow, C.w. 2010; tybyles, P.; joulou, B.

DEVILRY, *s.* Devlugy (*deulugy*), M. 2096. *Hennyv rág an devlugy,* that is for the devilry, M. 2096.

DEVISE, *v.* Ervyré, yrvyré, w.; tewlel, teulel, tiulel, tywlel, teuly, towla, toula, towlal, P.

DEVONSHIRE, *s.* Dewnans, w.; Drunanz, P.

DEVOUT, *adj.* Dywysyc, w.

DEW, *s.* Glûth, w.; thew, P.

DEW-SNAIL or SLUG, *s.* Molhuiden, molhuidzhon, melyen, w.

DIADEM, *s.* Curun, curyn, cyryn, guryn, gyryn, w.; curun ray, B.

DIAMONDS, *s.* (?) CORNISH DIAMONDS. Morion, D.

DIARRHŒA, *s.* Girr, P.; gyrr, gerdin, B.

DICE, TO THROW DICE, *v.* Teulel prên, P.C. 2847, *Lat.* To throw wood.

DICK, *s.* (Richard). Hecca, w.; Hecka, P.

DICTIONARY, *s.* Gerlever, w.

DID, (*pret.* of *do*). Wra, wre, wryk, rig, ryg, reeg, B.; rewrûk, gallus, P.; gusel, B.

DIDST COME. Wrafys, B.

I DID WRITE. Me re wryk skrife, B.

THEY DID PUT. Y a reeg gore, B.

DID SAY. Gallus leverel, P.

DID IT OUT OF ENVY. Gusel dre envi, B.

HE DID. Wruge, a mutation of *grúg,* 3 pers. s. preter. of irr. v. *gwrey,* e added in a subjunctive construction, w.; rûg, ryg, wrûc. *Wruc,* a mutation of *grúk,* from *grugé,* to do or make.

THOU DIDST, HAST, DONE OR WOULDST DO. Wrussys, a mutation of *gwrussys,* 2 pers. s. preter. of *gwrey,* w.

THOU DIDST. Whrusté. The aspirate mutation of *grusté*, composed of *gwrus*, i.d. q.v. *gwrês*, 2 pers. s. imperf. of *gwrey* and *te*, thou, w.

WE DID OR MADE. Wrussyn, a mutation of *gwrussyn*, pers. pl. preter. of *gwrey*, w.

YE DID OR HAVE DONE. Wrussouch, a mutation of *gwrussouch*, 2 pers. pl. preter. of *gwrey*, w.

THEY DID. Whrussons. The aspirate mutation of *grussons*, 3 pers. pl. preter. of *gwrey*, w.

THEY DID. Wrens, a mutation of *gwrens* 3 pers. pl. imperf. of *gwrey*, w.

DIE, *v.* Merwel, verwel, w.; meerveil, B.; meruel, veruel, myruel, myrwel, marwel. myrul, maruel, muruel, maro, P.; maru,maruo, varuo, B.; myrav, P.; merwye, B.; mirwy, P.; verwy, B.; firwy, P.; ferue, B.; tremené, dremené, w.

I DID DIE, I SHOULD DIE. Varwen, a mutation of *marwen*, 1 pers. s. imperf. of *marwel*, w.

I MAY DIE. Vyrwyf, a mutation of *myrwyf*, 1 pers. s. subj. of *myrwel*, w.

HE DIED. Verwys, a mutation of *merwys*, 3 pers. s. preter. of *merwel*, w.; ev a veruys, P.

HE MAY DIE. Merwé, marwé, ferwé, farwé, w.

HE WOULD DIE. Myrwy, fyrwy, w.

HE SHALL OR WILL DIE. Verow, vyru, mutations of *merow* and *myru*, 3 pers. s. fut. of *merwel* and *myrwel*, w.

HE SHALL HAVE DIED. Varwo, a mutation of *marwo*, 3 pers. s. fut. of *marwel*, w.

WE SHALL DIE. Vyrwyn, a mutation of *myrwyn*, 1 pers. pl. fut. of *myrwel*, w.

DIET, *s.* See FOOD. *Coarse diet.* Labscou, B.

DIFFERENT, *adj.* Cên, kên, w.; keen, P.; cyn, kyn, gên, w.

DIFFICULT, *adj.* Calés, calas, cals, calys, w.; callys, kallishc, B.; calish, callish, galés, w.; uhal, hual, ughel, B

DIFFICULTY, *s.* Trangiak, B.

DIG, *v* Palas, balas, w.; balés, O.M 414; ballas, c.w. 975; baly, P. *Ty the honan balas*, thou thyself to dig, O.M. 345.

DIGGER, *s.* (Miner.) Derrick, D.

DIGHT, *v.* (To prepare one's self.) Omdhychtyé, w.

DIGNITY, *s.* Aynos, dynyté, P.

DILATORY, *adj.* Hîr, hyr, w. *To be dilatory.* *v.*; Hocyé, hokyé, w.

DILIGENCE, *s.* Reonte, P.

DILIGENT, *adj.* Bysy, vysy, w.; bysythyys, R.D. 2467; hewil, heuil, prederys, priderys, pryderys, brederys, w.; brederez, P.; wâr, P.; gwas bathor, B. (See *Bather* in Borlase's Vocabulary).

DIMINISH, *v.* Lehé, w.; lehy, leihy, P.; leyhy, leyhé, lyha, lyhy, w.; lygha, P.

DIMINUTION, *s.* Alloys, P.

DIMINUTIVE, *adj.* Bêr, ver, w.

DINE, *v.* Cenewal, w.; keneual. kyneual, P.; kynewal, w.; kidnow, P.; guneual, B.; lyvya. M. 113; lefya, M. 3926. *Dho guneual gondzha*, to dine with him, B. *Ny yllyn lefya kyn moys*, that we may not dine before going, M. 3926.

DINGLE or VALLEY, *s.* Cûm, w.

DING-DONG. (As of the sound of bells) Whymwham, P.C. 2734. *Otte del wysk-whym-wham*, see how he strikes ding-dong, P C. 2734.

DINING ROOM, *s.* Stevel, steuel, w.

DINNER, *s.* Cidnio, w.; kidnio, B.; ciniow, cynyow, kynyow, w.; kidnian, P ; lein, B.

DINNER CAKE, *s*, Fuggan, hoggan, hôgan, hobben, D.

DIP, *v.* (As in water). Bidhyzi, bedidhia. See BAPTISE.

DIPLOMA, *s.* Guarac, w.

DIRECT, *v.* Rowlia, w.; roulia, P.

DIRECT THOU. Cevarwoudh, kevarvoudh, w.

DIRECTION, *s.* See COURSE or WAY.

DIRECTLY, *adv.* Dewhans, duwhans, dywhans, w.; dyhuanz, P.; dystouch, dhystouch, w.; dystough, P.; thystough, R.D. 1239.

DIRT, *s.* Caillar, w.; cagal, B.; casa, gasa, gasow, P.; lued, lys, lyys, mostethés, vostcthés, w.; votêhés, mosthés, B. *Dre an mostethés hep fal*, through the dirt without fail, O.M. 2809; plôs, w. *May fons gulan a pup plôs ôl*, that they may be clean from all dirt, P.C. 844; pul, pol, teil, w.; tyle, B.

DIRTY, *adj.* Casa, gasa, gasow, casalek, cawys, caugh. cough, P.; caugeon, R.D 137. *Ha my caugeon lawethan*, and my dirty friends, R.D. 137; gassic, geagle, w.; gagle, P.; mostys, vostys, w *Nynsyv gulan lemmyn mostys*, it is not clean, but dirty, R.D. 1927; plosek, R.D. 1847. *Plosek cnugyan*, a dirty messer or mess-maker, M. 3255; slovan, B. *Loh slovan*, dirty pool, B. *Cawys pous*, a dirty gown, P.

DIRTY AND WET. See WET AND DIRTY.

DIRTY FELLOW. Plosek, R.D. 847. *Plussyon*, dirty fellows, w.

DISABLED, *adj* Effredh, evredhec, w.

DISAGREEABLE, *adj.* Ahas, O.M. 1081. *Ota cowes pûr ahas*, see a shower very disagreeable, O.M. 1081.

DISAPPOINTMENT, s. Draffa, W.F.P.

DISAVOWED, *part.* Nehys, w.; neghys, P.

DISBELIEVE, *v.* Discrythy, P.; dyscrysy, dhyscrysy, w.

DISCHARGE, *v.* (As from a gun). Dellé, dyllo, duello, w.; thello, thelly, P.

DISCIPLE, *s.* Discebel, w.; discibel, P.; disgibl, desgibl, dyscibel, discybel, w.

DISCIPLES, *s.* Dyskyblion, thistyplys, B.; tyskyblon, P.C. 636.

DISCLOSE, *v.* Dysquedhas, dyscudhé, agery, egery, ygery, ugory, ugery, w.; uger, P.

DISCOLOURED, *adj.* Disliu, w.

DISCORD, *s.* Avey, avy, aui, P.

DISCOURSE, *s.* (Talk). Cows, w.; kouz, koums, B.; cowms, cews, gows, w.; gews, B.

DISCOURSE, *s.* (A talking, or speech). Cowsys, cowsés, gowsys, w.

DISCOVER, *v.* Convedhas, w.; convethas, convethy, confethy, daryvas, dharyvas, P.; discudhé, dyscudhé, dhyscudhé, dysquedhas, discwedha, w.; disqnedha, P.; diswedha, dyswedhy, w.; dyswethy, discuthé, mygy, ryguelaz, P.

DISCOVERED, *part.* Confethys, convethys, w.; gothvethys, gôth, P.

DISCOVERY, *s.* Discwedhyans, dysquydhans, dysquedhyens, w.; disquethians, daryvas, P.; descotha, C.W. 1369; myc, w.; mycke, P.

DISCREET, *adj.* Kefyon, P C. 1026. *Ov kefyon kêr colonow*, my discreet dear hearts, P.C 1026.

DISDAIN, *s.* Gowal, P.

DISEASE, *s.* Clevès, clevas, w.; klevas, B. clevaz, klevaz, P.; clevel, w.; clewet, P.; cluyan, gluyan, w.

DISEASE, THE DISEASE, A POX, *s.* Pocvan, w. *Lemmyn pocvan ha lesky*, but disease and burning, R.D. 170.

DISEASELESS, *adj.* Dealer, M. 3086. *Saw ha dealer yv lel*, whole and diseaseless it is truly, M. 3086.

DISFIGURE, *v.* (To disfigure, to be disfigured). Defaleby, w.

DISGRACE, *s.* Belyny, velyny, bylyny, vylyny, w.; basnet (?) w.; meule, M. 1166. *Peyn ha mevle*, pain and disgrace, M. 1166.

DISGRACED, *part.* Dyflyas, P. (? disgusted.)

DISGRACEFUL, *adj* Dyflas, dhyfflas, w.

DISGUST, *v.* Dyflasé, dyflasé, w.

DISH, *s.* Scudel, w.; scudell, skudel, skydel, B.; skidal, P.; scala, w.; skival, B.; padel, padal, P.; engurbor, B.

A LITTLE DISH. Podzher, w.; podzhar, P.; scidal, w.; skidal, P.

A LARGE DISH. Tallyour, w.; talhiar, B.

A BROAD DISH. Talhiar, gurbor, B.

AN EARTHEN DISH. Podzher, podzhar, P.

A WOODEN PLATTER OR DISH. Tolyer predn, D.

DISH-BEARER, *s.* Reiniat, reunniat, P.

DISH-CLOTH, *s.* Clût-lestri, w.; klût lestre, B.

DISH, *s.* Lester, lestre, B. This term is used of anything that holds or receives another thing, as *cantuil-lestre*, a candlestick. See for this word VESSEL.

DISLIKING, A DISLIKING, *s.* Anvôdh, w.

DISLOYAL, *adj.* Dislaian, w.

DISMAL, *adj.* Thyveth, B.; wisht, whisht, D.

DISORDERED, *adj.* (Ill). Clâf, clâv, w.; klav claff, clêf, clevas, clevys, B.

DISPATCH, *s.* See HASTE. *Tooth brâs*, great dispatch, P.

DISPENSE, TO DISPENSE WITH, *v.* Hepcor, w.

DISPERSE, *v.* Keskar, cescar, w.

DISPLAY, *v.* Dysplevyas, dhysplevyas, dyspleytyé, dhyspleytyé, w.; discavyssy, P.

DISPLEASE, *v.* Dyflasé, dhyflasé, w.; dysplesy, M. 119; thyflasé, P. c. 901.

DISPLEASING, A DISPLEASING, *s.* Anvôdh, w.

DISPLEASURE, *s.* Anvôdh, w.

DISPOSE, *v* Dythgthtya, w.; thyatyè, B.

DISPOSE OF, *v.* Guerha, gwertha, gwetha, P.

DISPUTE, *s* Bresell, bresel, w.; bressell, B.; bresul, bresyl, vresyl, trawaran, w.; saunt, P.; "what a *saunt* is he? D.

DISQUIET, *s.* Ancres, w.

DISAPPOINTMENT, Draffa, W.F.P.

DISSEMBLE, *v.* Plosé, plosi, dissembla. *Dho laol gou*, to tell a lie, P.

DISSEMBLER, *s.* Whetlow, P. i.e., a teller of idle tales.

DISSENSION, *s.* See DISPUTE.

DISSOLUTION, *s.* (The dissolution or end of the world). Worvan, P.

DISSOLVE, *v* Tedha, w.

DISTAFF, *s.* Cegel, kegel, cigel, kigel, cygel, gigel, gygel, w.; gigal, B.; kiggal, D.

DISTANCE, *s.* Pellder, pelder, w.

DISTANT, *adj.* Pell, pel, bell, w.; vel, velha, B.; vezy, B.V.

DISTINCT, *adj.* Dibblans dyblans, dhyblans, w.

DISTINCTLY, *adv.* Dyblans, M. 2371. *Tytel na chalyng dyblans*, title ncr claim distinctly, M. 2371.

DISTINCTION or DIFFERENCE, *s.* Deberthva, deberth, dybarth, w.

DISTORTED, *adj.* Cam, cham, cabm, w.; kabm, P.; gam, w.

DISTRACTED, *adj.* Muscok, P.; muscoc, mescat, w.; meskat, B.; mustok, muskegvi, P.

DISTRIBUTE, *v.* Ranné, radna, w.

DISTRIBUTOR, *s.* Reiniat, P.

DISTRUST, *v.* Descrisa. P.; descrissa, dyscryssy, dyscrysy. dhyscrysy, w.; dezkryssa, B.; thyscryssy, P.

DISTRUST, *s.* Gorgys, w. *Yma thy'mmo gorgys brâs,* that is to me a great distrust, R.D. 1499

DISTURB, *v.* Coddros, koddros, goddros, w.; dreyny. P.

DISTURBANCE, *s.* Touse, B. Still in frequent use.

DITCH, *s.* Clêdh, klêdh, w.; cleath, c.w. 1140; glêdh, clawd, kleudh, cleuth, B.; fôs, w.; foze, foza, voza. P.; vossa, w.; rôs, P.; pullan troillia. w.; graff, D. *Graff,* says Borlase, is the name for the ditch, which surrounds a circular Cornish castle.

DIVER, *s.* (The bird). Saithor, w.; sarthor P.; shagga, w

DIVIDE, *v.* (Part) Deberthy, dybarthy, deberhy, w.; deberhé, deberheé. P.; dheberhy, w.; dyberheé, diberh, fysky, P. *An dour ou fyskya lés,* the water is dividing abroad, P.; parrí, parhy, barri, barhy, w.

DIVIDE, *v.* (Share). Ranné, w.; radna, B.; ranna, P.

DIVIDED, *part.* (Parted). Debarris, diberh, B.; theberaz, theberha, P.

DIVIDED, *part.* (Shared). Rynnys. From *ranné,* to divide or share, w.

DIVINER, *s.* Cuillioc, w. *A female diviner.* Cuilliogés. chuilliogés, w.; kuiliogés, B. See SOOTH-SAYER

DIVINITY, *s.* (Godhead) Dusés, dewsys, dowsés, w.

DIVINITY, A DIVINITY, *s.* Dû, dew, duy, w. See GOD.

DIVISION, *s* (Part. or parting). Deberth, dybarth, deberthva, parth, parh, w.; part, P.

DIVISION, *s* (Share). Rân, râdn, w.

DO, *v.* (To do or make). Gûl, w.; gull, B.; gwîl, w.; guil, B.; gweyl, w.; gwyl, geil, P.; geel. gil, cûl, w.; kûl, wûl, P.; huil, B,; whul, hwil, wil, il, w.; wyth, R.D. 2250; wyny, craf, P.; gwregé, gwrugé, grugé, crugé, krugé, gwrey, w.; gwra, gura, ara, B.; gwyll, gwrellé, gwethé, gwethyl, gwruthyl, gruthyl, gwrythyl, gwrithyl, g'rithil, w.; gurithil, gurythyl, P.; guthal, guthyl, kuthyl, cuthyl, wuthyl, w.; wuthell, B.; wuthul, R.D. 2252; wathyll, wethyl, B. The variety of ways in which the verb "to do or make" is expressed in Ancient Cornish is extraordinary, and it is not certain that even the above list is quite completed. The mutations are numerous and perplexing. *Il* is a mutation of *gil*; *whûl* is the aspirate mutation of *gûl*; *hwil* is a corruption of *wûl,* the regular mutation of *gûl*; *gweyl* is

another form of *gûl.* *Gwethé* is from *gwéth, id. qd., gwyth,* a work or deed. Further illustrations are given below, and more may.be found in the Lexicon Cornu-Britannicum of Williams. The examples here given may be useful to the student of Ancient Cornish. For more, see MAKE OR DO.

I DO. This is expressed in Cornish by *dera,* and it is used as an auxiliary with the infinitive mood, thus, *dera mi ton.* I do carry, w. Borlase gives *ghera vi,* for *I do.*

DO. Grês, B *Dell rethe grês,* so they should do.

DO, I PRAY. Loak, dho loak, B.

DOST THOU ? Sesta ? P.

HOW DO YOU DO ? Fatla ella why giel ? *Well thanks to you,* Dah, durdala dha why.

I MAY DO. 1 Wryllyf, a mutation of *gwryllyf,* 1 pers. s. subj. of *gwrey,* w.

2. Wrellyn, a mutation of *gwrellyn,* 1 pers. s. subj. of *gwrey,* w.

THOU MAYEST DO. Wrylly, a mutation of *gwrylly,* also, whrylly, the aspirate mutation of *gwrylly,* 2 pers. s. subj. of *gwrey,* w.

HE MAY DO. Perfo, 3 pers. s. subj. of a verb— the Welsh *peri,* to cause, w.

YE MAY DO. Wrellouch, a mutation of *gwrellouch,* also, wrylleuch, a mutation of *gwrylleuch,* 2 pers. pl. subj. of *gwrey,* w.

WE MAY OR SHOULD DO. Wrellen, wryllyn. Mutations of *gwrellen* and *gwryllyn,* 1 pers. pl. subj. of *gwrey,* w.

I SHALL OR WILL DO. Wrama, wrâf, râf. *Wrama* is a contingent form of *wrâf.* *Râf,* is an abbreviated form of *wrâf.* a mutation of *gwrâf,* 1 pers. s. fut. of *gwrey,* w. Pryce writes for " I do," raf, wra af, wryffo, and, a wharfo.

THOU SHALT OR WILT DO. 1. Wrêth, a mutation of *gwrêth,* (wrêth is also used in the present tense), 2 pers. s. fut. of *gwrey.*

2. Whrêth, the aspirate mutation of *gwrêth,* 2 pers. s. fut. of *gwrey,* w.

3. Wreta. (*wreth-te*), w.

4. Qurêth, a mutation of *gwrêth,* 2 pers. s. fut. of *gwrey,* w.

5. Querth, incorrectly for *qureth,* w.

6. Quereta, a mutation of *gwra,* w.

7. Urylli, uryssys, B.

HE SHALL OR WILL DO. 1. Gwra, 3 pers. s. fut. of *gwrey,* w.

2. Wra. Used with all persons. A mutation of *gwra.*

3. Ra, an abbreviation of *wra.*

4. Qura, a mutation of *gwra,* w.

5. Qureva, a mutation of *gureva*, composed of *gwra*, 3 pers. s. fut. of *gurey*, and *ve*, he, w.

6. Urello, uryllif, B.

WE SHALL OR WILL DO. Wrên, a mutation of *gwrén*, 1 pers pl. fut. of *gurey*, w. Urellon, B.

YE SHALL OR WILL DO. 1. Wreuch, a mutation of *gwreuch*, 2 pers. pl. fut. and imp. of *grewy*, w.

2. Whreuch, the aspirate mutation (after *y* understood) of *gwreuch*, w.

3. Rellouch, an abbreviation of *wréllouch*, a mutation of *gwrellouch*, 2 pers. pl. fut. of *gwrey*, w.

4. Qureuch, a mutation of *gwreuch*, w.

5. Rygo, a corruption of *wrugouch*, a mutation of *gwrugouch*, 2 pers. pl. fut. of *gwrugé*, w.

HE SHALL OR WILL HAVE DONE. Rella. A form of *wrella*, a mutation of *gwrella*, 3 pers. s. fut. of *gwrellé*, w.

THEY SHALL OR WILL DO. 1. Rân. An abbreviation of *wrân*, a mutation of *gwrân*, 3 pers. pl. fut. of *gwrey*, w.

2. Wrôns, a mutation of *gwrôns*, 3 pers. pl. fut. of *gwrey*, w.

3. Dzhyi a'rân, B.

HE SHOULD OR WOULD DO. 1. Wrello, written also *wrella*, a mutation af *gwrello*, 3 pers. s. subj. of *gwrey*, w. 2. Russé. An abbreviation of *wrussé*, a mutation of *gwrussé*, 3 pers. s. subj. of *gwrey*, w. 3. Wrefé, wrefa, w.

THOU WOULDST DO. Wrês. A mutation of *gwrés*, 2 pers. s. imperf. of *gwrey*, w.

THEY HAD DONE OR WOULD DO. Wrussens, a mutation of *gwrussens*, 3 pers. pl. pluperf. of *gwrey*, w.

DO THOU. Gwra, 2 pers. s. imper. of *gwrey*, w.

DO YE. Reuch. an abbreviation of *wreuch*, 2 p. pl. imper. of *gwrey*, w.

LET THEM DO. Gwrêns, grêns, 3 pers. pl. imper. of *gwrey*, w.

DONE, *part.* Gwrys, wrys, w.; gurys, B.

THOU DIDST OR HAST DONE. 1, Russys. an abbreviation of *wrússys*, a mutation of *gwrússys*, 2 pers s. pret. of *gwrey*, w.; 2, Wrûsta, a mutation of *gwrûsta*, composed of *gwrûs id. qd. gwrés*, 2 pers. s. imperf. of *gurey* and *te*, thou, w.; 3, Guryssys, rewrensys B.

HE HAS DONE. Guraz, B.

WE HAVE DONE. Gureithon, B.; wreithon, a mutation of *gwreithon*, 1 pers. pl. preter. of *gwrey*, w.

I HAD DONE OR WOULD HAVE DONE. Grussen, wrussen, a mutation of *gwrussen*, 1 pers. s. pluperf. of *gwrey*, w.

I HAD DONE. Mi a vryssen, B.

HE HAD DONE. Ev a ressa, B.

HE HAD DONE OR WOULD HAVE DONE. Grussé, 3 pers. s. pluperf. of *gwrey*, w.

TO DO HARM, OR ILL. Droga, droaga, w.; gamwuly. wyll, P.; myschevy, P.

TO DO, OR SOLICIT ANOTHER MAN'S BUSINESS. Pryvia, w.

DOCK, *s.* (The plant). Tavolen, tavolan, w.

DOCTOR, *s.* (Savant)). Descader, deskadzher, w.

DOCTORS, *s.* Doctours, N. From the English.

DOCTRINE, *s* Descas, dhescas, dyskas, dyscas, descés, dyscés, theskas, P.C. 818; tyskés, w. *Râg the theskas yv púr da*, for thy doctrine is very good, P.C. 121; discans, diskans, w.

DOCTRINES, *s.* Diskus, P.

DOG, *s.* Ci, ki, chi, ky, cei, kei, gy, w. *Pl.* cien, kuen, N. See HOUND *A young dog.* Coloin, w. *A great dog.* Kimêr, keimaur, P.

DOG'S-BANE, *s.* (Herb). Goitcenin, w.; goickennin, P.; goitkenin, lodosa, hlodosa, B.

DOGFISH, *s.* Dogga, D.; môrgi, *Lit.* Dog of the sea.

DOG-FLY, *s.* Lewen ki, w.; lewinki, P.

DOLEFUL, *adj.* Trewesy, drewesy, trewysy, w.; trewisy, trys, trûs, P.; trawethac, w.; trauethak, P.; trawedhak, w.; trauedhak, travethak, B.; morethec, morethek. w.

DOLT-HEAD, *s.* Pedn-cooge, c.w. 1090.

DOMINION, *s.* (Authority). Arthelath, w.

DOMINION, *s.* (Royalty, a kingdom). Mychterneth, myhterneth, myterneth, mychternés, w.

DOOMS-DAY, *s.* Dêth brûs, M, 1923. *Prederugh hebma déth brús*, think of this on doomsday, M. 1923.

DOOR, *s.* Daras, darras, darat, w. *Bys yn daras y chy*, even to the door of his house, R.D. 1631. *Pl.* darasow, w.; darazou, P.

DOOR, GATE, ENTRANCE, *s.* Porth, yet. w.

DOORS, GATES, *s.* Jannues, P.

DOOR-KEEPER, *s.* Darador, w.; daradur, B.; darazu, P.; porther, w.; portherer, P.

A FEMALE DOOR-KEEPER. Portherés, w.

DOOR-POST, *s.* Dorn, P.; condura, w.; kunduru, P. *Dnrn*, is frequently used for door-post in Cornwall.

DORMOUSE, *s.* Ystlyn, B.; bat, w.

DORMITORY, *s.* Cuski, B.; cuscti, w.; cuseki, P.

DOUBLE, *s.* (Fold, plait, flexion). Plêg, plêk, plêth, blêg, w.

DOUBT s. Fall, B.; dar, thout, P.; toul, P.C. 285. *Heb fall*, without doubt, B. *Dar de senos a wheugh why?* A doubt of it do you make, P. *Hep tovl púr wyr me a grys*, without a doubt truly I believe, P.C. 285.

DOUBTLESS, adv. Hepmar, hemmar, w.; en dhiougel, en dhiugel, diogel, diougel, P.

DOUBTING, A DOUBTING, s. Mar, w.; teul, P. See DOUBT.

DOUGH, s. Toas, B. See PASTE.

DOVE, s. Colom, colommen, cylobman, w.; kylobman, P.; kydhon, B.; golom, w.; golam, c.w. 2453.

DOVE-COT. s. Clomiar, w.; klomiar, klymiar, P.; clymiar, klymmiar, w.; kilymmiar, B.

DOWN or COMMON, s. Gwôn, gôn, gûn, goon, gwen, w.; guen, P.; wôn, woon, w.; uun, B.

DOWN, DOWNWARDS, adv. Haus, w.; hauz, inhauz, P.; inhans, B.; isot, w.; isod, icot, debar, lour, B.; lowr, lûr, luer, w.; doun, voun, thyons, thous, trogh, P.

DOWN HILL. Guimp, gump. The *Gump* in St. Agnes. In Armoric, *guympo*, P.

DOWNRIGHT, adj. (Sincere). Colanac, colannac, colenec, cylednac, w.; kylednak, B.

DOWNY, adj. (As of a common). Gônic, w.

A DOZE, s. Sog, B. This word is still often used.

DRAG, s. (For a wheel). Dral, P.

DRAG. v. Tena, P.; tenna, tenné, tené, P.; tynné, w.; stlegea, B.; denna, M. 3608; dena, deny, w.; synsy, zingy, B.

DRAGGED, part. Dregas, tregid, B.

DRAGON, s. Druic, dragun, w.

DRAIN or ADIT, s. Tye, D.

DRAKE or MALLARD, s. Kiliagaws, w.; kulliagés, P.; kulliughaz, kuliagaz. B.; celioc hoet, w.; maillart. The name commonly used in Cornwall, is *mallard* or *mollard*.

DRAM, s. (A "nip" of spirit). Tot, D.

DRAUGHT, s. (Drink). Suidnan, w.; tén, tyn, P. *Tên guin*, a draught of wine, P.

DRAW, v. Tena. P.; tenna, tené, P.; tenné, tynné. w.; stleya, B.; denna, M. 3608. *Quartrona ha denna*, quarter him and draw him, M. 3608. Dena, deny, w.; synsy, zingy, B.

TO DRAW IN ANYTHING. Gan-zingy, B.

TO BE DRAWN. Tenné, P. *War beyn cregy ha tenné*, on pain of being hanged and drawn, P.

TO DRAW BACKWARD. Cyldené, w.

TO DRAW NEAR. Nessé, dôz ogaz, P.

TO DRAW ONE'S SELF. Ymdenné, w.

TO DRAW OUT. Dema. P. *Feder war an neyl tenewen demas mes clethe*, Peter on the one side drew out a sword, P.

DRAW-BRIDGE, s. Ponteodi, B.

DRAWER, s. (As of a desk). Logel, logell, logol, w.

DRAWERS, s. (The garment). Lafrocwan, w.; tosunea, P.

DRAWING, s. (A pulling). Tên, tyn, w.

DRAWING, s. (The punishment so called). Tenna, M. 1668. *Warbyn tenna ha cregy*, on pain of drawing and hanging, M. 1668.

DRAWING, part. (Pulling or dragging). Tynys, P.

DREAD, s. Own, oun, w.

DREAD, v. Owna, w.; ouna, P.

DREADFUL, adj. Erchyll, B.; ahas, w. *Rák bós y peyn mar ahas*, for his pain being so dreadful, R.D. 1352.

DREAM, s. Hunrus, w.; hendrez, P.; hemdrez, B.; hvn (*hun*), R.D. 513; trangiak, B.; vewns, P. *Dre ov hvn me a welas*, through my dream, which I saw, R.D. 513. *My re welés hunrvs*, I have seen in my dream, O.M. 1954.

DREAM, v. Henrosa, w.

DREGS, s. Godho, godhas, P.; grushens, B. The following words are still in use in Cornwall for *dregs*, viz. grooshans, growshans, grishens, grudgings, growts, and grownds.

DRESS, s. (Clothing). Gwisc, guisc, w.; guisk, P.; gwesc, w.; guesk, P.;

DRESS, v. (To clothe). Gwisey, gwiscé, gwesca, gwesga, w.; guesga, P.; wyscé, wiscy, w.

DRESS. v. (To cook meat). Dyghthy bòs, P.

DRINK, s. (Liquor, beer). Diot, diwés, dywés, dewés. w. *An dewés yv da ha clêr*, the drink is good and clear, O.M. 1918; deuas, B.; dewas, dhewas, w. *Dewas creev*, strong beer. *Dewas cóth*, stale (or old) beer; devés (*deues*), M. 3578. *Na deves na boys*, neither drink nor food, M. 3578; gwiras, gwyras, wyras, pyment, pymeth, w; eveugh, P.

DRINK, s. (A drink or draught). Tên, tyn, P. *Lit.* A pull.

DRINK, v. Efé, evé, w.; eva, cofua P,; médho. B. *Ry dour thy'nny the evé*, to give us water to drink, o M. 1801.

HE MAY DRINK. Effo, w.

DRINK THOU. Yf, 2 pers. s. imp. of *evé*, w.

DRINK YE. Evough, P.

DRINKING-CUP, s. Hanaf, hanath, w.; anneth, P.; bolla, B.

DRINKING-GLASS, s. Gwidran, gwedran, w.; guedran, B.

DRINK-POT, s. (A drunkard). Harfel, B.

DRIPPING, *adj.* (Moist, wet). Sigyr, zigyr, P.; zigur, zyghir, B.

DRIVE, *v.* (To drive out). Hella, helhia, hellyrchy, w.; hellyrghy, helfia, P.

DRIVE, *v.* (To drive away) Pelly, mosé, vosé, w.; (The Cornish use the phrase, "to vease away.") vyé, B.

DRIVE, *v.* (As to strike a nail). Gwyscy, gwescel, gwyscel, w. *Râg an spykis o garow, pan vons gweskis dh'y sensy,* for the spikes were rough, when they were driven to hold him, M.C. 159.

DRIVEN, *part.* Pellys, P. From *pelly,* to drive away, w.

DRIZZLING RAIN, *s.* Slag, B.V.

DRONE. *s.* (Insect). Sudronen, w.

DROP, *v.* (To fall). Dyveré, B.; devery, dyvery, tevery. *Guraf dyvere,* I should drop, B.

DROP, *v.* (To drip, to trickle down). Devery, dyvery, dyveré, w.; tevera, M. 2608; dylly, P.; peysy, w.; peyi, P.

DROP, *s.* Ban, banna, w.; badna, P.; banne, P.C. 393; dagren, M. 2319 *Marsus dagren,* if there be a drop, M. 2319; loum, B.

A SMALL DROP OR TEAR. Dagren, w.

A DROP (OF WATER). Dewerryan, B.

DROPPED, *part.* Deveras, thiveras, throppys, B.; dyllys, O.M. 24.

DROUGHT, *s.* Sechés, sechter, w; zechter, P.; sychder, sichor, sehar, zehar, w.; zeha, B.

DROVE, A DROVE, *s.* Tonec, tonek, w.

DROWN, *v.* Bedhy, budhy, bidhy, beuzi, w.; bidhyzi, buddal, P.; buthy, C.W. 2330; bethy, C.W. 2441; vudhy, vedhy, w.; vethy, aflythy, P. TO BE DROWNED, *Idem.*

DROWNED, *part.* Budhys, w.; buthys, O.M. 1044; bethys, C.W. 2315; vudhys, w.; vuthys, O.M. 1701; bidhyz, driskyn, B.

DROWSINESS, *s.* Hûn, huyn, possygyon, w. *Possygyon yn pen yma,* drowsiness is in my head, O.M. 1906; sog, B.; entredés, uindrau, P.; vinerau, B.

DROWSY, *adj.* Heen, P.; heene, B.

DRUDGERY, *s.* Wheal ober, P.

DRUID, *s.* Druw, B.

DRUNKEN, *adj.* Medho, vedho, w.

SO DRUNKEN. Cyvedha, w.

A DRUNKEN FELLOW. Gwâs medho, w.

A DRUNKEN SOW. Hôt vedho, w.

HALF DRUNK. Prill, D.

DRY, *adj.* Sech, w.; sekh, B.; seych, seigh, seygh, segh, sygh, w.; seugh, B.; sick, sich, sych, seth, seyh, seh, zeh, w.; crin, heskyz, B. *Beuch heskyz,* a dry (*dried?*) cow, B.

DRY, *v.* (To dry, to be dry, to make dry). Seché, sychy, syché, w.; seghy, dyseghy, P.; sihy, seha, tesehé, zeha, w.

DRY, *v.* (To dry up). Dyseghy, disewythy, P.; guedhra, dho seha, B.

DRIED, *part.* Sechés, sechys, sychés, sychys, syhys, sehys, zehys, seghys. w.

DRYNESS, *s.* Sechter. w.; zechter, P.; sychder, sichor, sechés, sehar, zehar, zahas, zehas, w.

DUCK, *s.* (Bird). Hoet, hòs, w.; hâz, P.; hawz, w; hauz, B.; *Pl.* Higi, w.; heidzhe, hoet, B.

DUCKS AND DRAKES. (The game). Tic-tac mollard, D.

DUE, *s.* Devar, P.; dufer, M. 4513. *Del yv dufer dén worthy,* as is the due of a worthy man, M. 4513.

DUE, *adj.* Gwyw, w.; gew, gyu, B. *It is due, it behoveth,* Gôth, côth, couth, w.

DUG or TEAT, *s.* Tidi. w.; tidy, P.; têth, w. *A little dug or teat.* Têthan, w.

DULCIMER, *s.* Cythol, O.M. 1997.

DULL, *s.* (Stupid). Dicreft, pyst, w.; segerneth, B.; talsoch, w.; talsokh, B.; taltoch, P. See STUPID, for other words.

DUMB, *adj.* Avlavar, a-flavar, w.

A DUMB INFANT. Mâb alavar, mâb a-flavar, P.

DUNE, *s.* Towan, towin, tewen, tuan, tuyn, B.

DUNCE, *s.* Talsoch, B.

DUNG, *s.* (Muck, mire, dirt). Teil, w.; tyle, B.; orrach, P.

DUNG, *s.* (Excrement). Câc, cauch, cau, cauh, w.; kauh, B.; gau, w.

COW'S DUNG. Busl, busyl, w.

DUNGING, *part.* Ow scumbla, M. 3952. *In agen meske ov scumbla,* amongst us dunging, M. 3852.

DUNG-CART, *s.* Butt, w. This name is still much used.

DUNG-FORK, *s.* Heeval, hevval, yewal. yewl, P. This is a three-pronged fork. The names at present in use are, hevval, eval, yewal, yewl, and devil.

DUNG-HILL, *s.* Bidzeon, P.; bidzheon, B.; pil-teil, w.; pil tyil, P.

DUPES, *s.* Fellyon, R D. 1273. *Ysough gokky ha fellyon,* ye are foolish, and dupes, R.D. 1273.

DURATION, *s.* Hêd, hês, hys, heys, hirenath, w.

DUSKY or DARK, *s.* Tewal, w.; teual, P.

DUST, *s.* Pilm, w.; (This word is still in use). Scyl, skyl, scûl, skul, w.; treust, B.; pellum, pillum, D.

DUTY, *s.* (Obligation, office, service). Devar, w.; dufer M. 3171. *The dên yonk ythyv dufer*, to a young man it is a duty, M 3171; diffry, B.; dewty, w.; gever, B. *Et i gever*, in her duty, B.; gruyth, w.; mevstry, O.M. 2164. *Hâg a perfo ov meystry*, and to do my duty, O.M. 2164.

DWARF, *s.* (A male dwarf). Côr, w.; kôr, P.; kêr, B.

DWARF, *s.* (A female dwarf). Corrés, korrés, P.

DWELL, *v.* (Inhabit, abide, stay, tarry). Trega, triga, tregé, trigé, trigia, w.; drega, c.w. 334; dregé, dryk, redrygy, wonys, P.

DWELL, *v.* (To dwell in). Anhedhy, w.; annezo, P.

DWELL, *v.* (To dwell together). Contreva, w.

DWELLER, *s.* Treger. w.; trig, tryck, tryk, P.

DWELLING, *s.* (Dwelling-house, abode). Chi, chy, (the *ch* is soft), tshi. tshy. ti, P.; bôd. w.; bôt, P.; bôs, w.; boss, buyth, vêth, B.; annedh, w.

DWELLING-PLACE, *s.* Trê, trêv, w.; trêga, B.; tregva, trigva, w.; trygva, c.w. 664; trygfa, R.D. 2392; dregva, drigva, w.; drygva, P.

DYE, *s.* (Colour). Liu, lyw, w.

DYER, *s.* Liuor, w.; leuiar, B.; liuyer, P.

DYKE, *s.* Clêdh, klêdh, w.; glêdh, kleudh, cleuth, clawd, tuban, B.

DYSENTERY, *s.* Girr, an gir, P.; gerdin, B.

E.

This letter has only two sounds in Cornish the long and the short. When long it has the sound of *a*, as in the English words, *lane, cane*; thus the Cornish *dên*, a man; *nêv*, heaven, were sounded as the English words, *dane, nave*. The long *e* is distinguished by a circumflex. E short was pronouced as in the English words, *fen, hen, pen*. In Cornish *e* is constantly confounded with *y*, as in *dêdh, dydh*, a day, *dehow, dyhow*, the right, &c.

E is commutable with *o*, as *corn*, a horn; *cerniat*, a horn-blower, w. *Lex Con. Brit.*

EACH, *adj.* (Each one). Pûp, pûb, w.; pôp, pêb, pyb kenifer, P.

EAGER, *adj.* Men, ven, fen, w.

EAGERLY, *adv.* Duwhans, dewhans, dywhans, w.

EAGERNESS, *s.* Awel, w.; galloys, B.

EAGLE, *s.* Er (*Pl.* Erieu, w.); adglaer, B. (See BIRD, Adglaer).

EAR, *s.* Scovarn, scovern, scovorn, scoforn, scevarn, w; scouoron, P.C. 2287; *Pl.* Scovornow, N. *Ow scoforn treghys myrough*, see my ear is cut, P.C. 1144.

EAR OF CORN. Pedn yz, w.

EAR-RING, *s.* Scinen, w.; skinen, scinin, B.; skiney, P.

EARL, *s.* Yerl, yarl, yurl, w.

EARL OF CORNWALL. Pedniz, P.

EARLY, *adj.* Arvis, w.

EARLY, *adv.* Avar, w. *Ha drug avar*, and come early, P.C 3239.

EARN, *v.* Dendel, dyndyly, w.

EARNEST, *adj.* Defry, deffry, dheffry, devry, dywysyc, w.

EARNEST, IN EARNEST. Defry, deffry, dheffry, devry, w.; yn tevery, c.w. 521.

EARNESTLY, *adv.* Fast, P.; hard, B.; ynuen, P.; ynven, B.

EARNING, *s.* (Winning, gaining). Vangin, D.

EARTH, THE EARTH, *s.* Dôr, doer, an doer, doar, daor, an daor, dhaor, aor, an aor, an naor, oar, an oar, nôr, noar, w.; noore, c.w. 18; noer, nooi, ean, ennês, P.

EARTH, *s.* (Land, country). Tîr, tyr, w.; tyre, c.w. 89; thore, c.w. 234; tireth, tyreth, tyreyth, dyreyth, w.

EARTH, THE GROUND, *s.* Gweras, gwyrras, gwered, gweret, gueret, lear, lêr, leur, luer, lôr, lûr, w.

EARTH OR MOULD, *s.* Pri, pry, bry, vry, w.

SIFTED EARTH FOR MAKING MORTAR. Ram, D.

EARTH-NUTS, *s.* Killi-môr, killi-more, D.

EARTHENWARE PAN. Bussa, buzza. D.

EARTHQUAKE, *s.* Dôrgis, dôrgrys, w.

EARTHWORM, *s.* Prêv'nôr, w.; buzuguen, B.; *Pl.* Buzug, B

EASE, *v.* Cosowa, w.; kosoua, aizia, P.

EASE, *s.* Hezuek, B.

EASILY. MORE EASILY, *adv.* Daslyer, D.

EASILY SEEN. Hewel, w.; heuel, B.

EAST, *s.* Duryan, w.; thuryan, thorians, houl dreval, B.

EASTER, *s.* Pasc, w.; pask, Q.; pasch, w.

EASTER-DAY, *s.* Du pasc, w.; du pask, P.; du pasch, B.

EASY, *adj.* (Gentle). Aise, P.; medhal, medhel, meddal, w.

EASY, *adj.* (Feasible). Hêdh, hogul, w.; sadt.

MORE EASILY. Daslyer, D.

EAT, *v.* Diberi, debry, dibry, dibbry, w.; tibri, dibri, P.; dybry, dybbry, dhybry, tebry, w.; tibbry, B.; tybbry, w.; thybry, O.M. 273; thebbry, c.w. 836; thibbry, c.w. 875.

HE MAY EAT. Tebro, deppro, w. *Tebro* is a mutation of *debro*, 3 pers. s. subj. of *debry*, to eat.

THOU WILT EAT. Tybryth, a mutation of *dybryth*, 2 pers. s. fut. of *dybry*, to eat, w.

EATING, *part*. Dhybbry, M. 134. *Kyns eva na dhybbry tam*, before drinking or eating a bit, M. 134.

EATING, *s*. Biner, byner, P. ; bûz, bês, B.

EATING-TIME, *s*. Prez-buz, P.

EATER, *s*. (?) A SMALL EATER. Punick, pewnick, W.F.P. This properly means a person who from debility eats little.

EAVESDROPPER, *s*. Ystiferion, w.

EBB, *s*. (As of the sea). Trîg, w. ; drîg, P. *Mór-trig*. the ebb of the sea.

EBBET, *s*. See EFT OR NEWT.

ECHO, *s*. Clowans, w. ; clowance, P.

EDGE, *s*. Brou, B. ; fyvar, P. ; ochre, B.

EDGE, *s*. (Extremity, margin, border). Mîn, vìn, meen, veen, meyn, w. *Guask war an myn*, smite on the edge, P.C. 2727 ; vyne, w. ; miniog, B. ; yrhian, P. ; ymyl, B. ; urrian, w.

EDICT, *s*. (A royal edict). Gurhemin-ruif, P.

EEL, *s*. Selli, silli, w. ; zilli, P. ; silien, B.

EELS, *s*. Selyés, syllyas, w. ; syllyes, N. ; selyas, C.W. 410 ; siliou, B.

FRESH WATER EELS. Valsen, *Carew*.

EFT OR NEWT, *s*. Pedrevan, pedrevor, predresif, wedresif, w. ; pedreriff, P. ; anau, B. ; anaf, P. Commonly called *an emmet, ebbet,* or *evet*, in Cornwall. See also NEWT.

EFFECT, *s*. Ffrwyth, B.

EFFUSE, *v*. Denewy, dhenewy, w.

EGG, *s*. Oy, w. ; oye, oi, wiy, P. ; uy, w. ; ui, liy, B. *Pl.* Oyow, oiow, w.

BIRDS' EGGS. Oyow edhen, w. ; oyow ethen, P.

EGGSHELL, *s*. Pliscin, w. ; pliskin, P.

EIGHT. Eath, w. ; eyth, N.

EIGHTH. Eathas, ethas, w. ; eythves, N. ; ethaz, P.

EIGHTEEN. Eatag, P. ; eithack, D. ; eythek, N.

EIGHTEENTH. Eath degves, w.

EIGHTY. Padgwar iganz, peswar ugens, N.

EITHER. Po, py, bo, P.

ELBOW, *s*. Elin, elyn, ilin, gelen, gelyn, w.

ELDER, *s*. (Prebyster). Hebrenchiat, hebrenciat, hebryngkiad, w.

ELDER, *s*. (The tree). Scawen, scawan, scavan, w. ; skauan, B. ; skawan, scauan, P. ; skaun, scauorian, yscaun, B. *Pl.* Scaw. *Scawen* is still in use in Cornwall for an elder tree.

ELDER OR ELDEST, *adj*. Côtha, C.W. 1059. *Cayne ythew ov mabe cotha*, Cain is my eldest son, C.W. 1059.

ELECAMPANE, *s*. Baiol, w.

ELECT, *v*. Dewys, P.

ELEGY, *s*. Ancenec, ankenek, w.

ELEMENT, AN ELEMENT, *s*. Elven, B.

ELEPHANT, *s*. Olifans, oliphant, w.

ELEVATE, *v*. Drehevel, dreval, w. ; dhrehuel, trehevel, P.

ELEVEN. Unnec, unnek, ednac, w. ; ednack, idnak, P. ; ydnac, w. ; ydnek, B. ; ignack, D.

ELEVENTH. Unnecves, ydnacvas, ydnacas (?) w. ; ydn-hakvas, P.

ELLICK OR PIPER-FISH, *s*. See PIPER-FISH.

ELM, *s*. Ula, elaw, w. ; elau, elan, P.

ELSE. (Or else, otherwise). Po cen. w. ; poken, wanken, P. ; ken, M. 1308. *Ken warbarth ython leskys*, else together we are burnt, M. 1308. Negatively *ken* is *nahen (naken)*, N.

ELVAN, or ELVAN ROCK, *s*. Hardah, D.

EMANATE, *v*. Tardhé, w.

EMBALM, *v*. Uré, huré, w. *Gas vy lemmyn th'y huré*, leave me now to embalm him, P.C. 3196.

EMBER, *s*. Reighten, B.

EMBRACE, *v* Byrla, w.

EMINENT, *adj* Tâl, w.

EMIT, *v*. Dyllo, w.

EMMET or ANT, *s*. Meuwionen, w. ; mevionen, murianean, murianan, P. ; meuionen, B. Menwionen is an error, w. *Pl*. Murrian.

EMMET or NEWT, *s*. See EFT or NEWT.

EMPEROR, *s*. Emperur. emprour, emperour, w. ; empour, M. 930.

EMPRESS, *s*. Emperr, B. ; emperez, w. ; emperés, P.

EMPTY, *adj*. Gwâg, w. ; guâg, B. ; gwâk, w. ; 'uag, P. ; gwal, B. ; vâg, veag, P. ; segeris, segyr, siger, posigr, B.

EMPTY, *adj*. (Vain). Côc, côk, cooge, cowg, cuic, w. ; cowga, P.

ENCHANT, *v*. (Bewitch). Zheibio, B.

ENCHANTER, *s*. Purceniat, purkeniat, purcheniat, w.

ENCHANTMENT, *s*. Hûd, hûs, w.

ENCHANTMENTS, *s*. Galdrum, B.

ENCLOSED, *part*. Degés, degees, degeys, dygés, w.

ENCLOSED PLACE. Ke, kea, P.

ENCLOSURE, *s*. Alwed, claust, cloist, B. ; parc, park, w.

END, CONCLUSION, *s*. Diwedh, w. ; diuedh, B. ; dewedh, dywedh, dhewedh, w. ; diuadh, deweth, dheweth, P. ; duadh, w. ; diuath, B. ; dyweth, w. ; deweyth, O.M. 856. *Dynythys ev ov deweyth*, my end is arrived, O.M. 856 ; dywyth, w. ; dewath, C.W. 940 ; dywet, P.C. 1830 ; diua, P. ; dueth. *Captain*

Hitchins' Cornish epitaph in Paul Churchyard. tywedh, w.; theweth, P.; gorfen, w. *Bys gorfen bys,* till the end of the world, R.D. 178; gorfan, C.W. 2141; worven, C.W. 2118; worfen, w.; worfyn, P.; fen, w.; fedn, ffenwith, B.; fin, finweth, fynweth, pen, pedn, w.; ben, O.M. 2448; pera, P.

END or HEAD, *s.* Pen, pedn, fen, fedn, B. *The two ends,* neyll pen, M. 4491. *My a vyn dón an neyll pen,* I will carry one of the two ends. M. 4491.

END or TOP, *s.* Tâl, thâl. w.

END, *v.* Dewedhy, dewedhé, dhewedhé, w.; dywethva, N.; dewethé, P.; diwedhé, dywedhé, w.; dho diuadha, dhyfyk. P.; gorfenné, gorfenna, worfenna, gura fen, w.

ENDED, *part.* Due, dywythys, w.

ENDING PLACE. Diwedhva, dywedhva, w.; dywethva, N.; duwedhva, dowedhyans, w.

END. (To the end that). Adriff, w.

ENDEAVOUR, *v.* Astel, w.

ENDEAVOUR, *s.* Echen, hechen, ehen, hehen, w.

ENDURE, *v.* (To bear with, to suffer). Codhevel, godhevel, godhaf, perthegés, perthy, porthy, w.; perthegy, P.; thewer, C.W. 424·

ENEMY, *s.* Agary, escâr, eskâr, w.; escare, M. 163; eskere, M. 1176; envy, M. 1013. *Oges yma ov envy,* near is my enemy, M. 1013. *Pl.* Eskerans, M. 1176; yscerens, w.

ENERGY or STRENGTH, *s.* Sproil, sprawl, D.

ENGAGE, *v.* (Or pledge). Thethywy, P.

ENGINEER, *s.* Inguinor, w.

ENGLAND, *s.* Pou an Zouzn, *i.e.,* the country of the Saxons, B.

ENGLISH, *adj.* (Saxon). Sasnec, zaznek, sowsnac, w.; saesnek, B.

ENGLISHMAN, A SAXON, *s.* Saws, Sows. *Pl.* Sawsen, Sowsen, Zowzen, w.; Zawzen, Zouzon, Sausen, P.

ENGLISH, *s.* (The English language). Sawsnec, w.; Sawsnek, Zawsnak, P.; Zouznak, w.; Zowznak, Zaznak, B.

ENGRAVE, *v.* Gravio, w.; gravia, P.

ENGRAVER, *s.* Gravior, w.

ENGRAVING TOOL, *s.* Coltel, B.

ENJOIN OR CHARGE, *v.* Archa, w.; argha, P.; ervyré, yrvyré, w.

ENJOINED, *part.* Erchys, w.

ENJOY, *s.* Covas, P.; kouaz, B *Hep covas,* without enjoying, P.

ENJOYMENT, *s.* Tekter, P.C. 33. *An tekter asbetheugh why,* the enjoyment you will have, P.C. 33.

ENLARGE, *v.* Mochahé, w.; asten, B.

ENLIGHTEN, *v.* Golowa, w.; goloua, P.; gouloua, gylywi, w.; kylyui, gylyua, P.; colowa, P.

ENLIGHTENING, *s.* Golowas, w.; golouas, P.

ENMITY, *s.* Câs, gâs, w.; torkhan, B.; avey, P.; avy, aui, w. *Ha netre y fyth avey,* and ever shall there be enmity, O.M. 314.

ENOUGH. Lôr, lûr, laur, loar, B.; lower, P.; lour, w.; lowre, C.W. 266.; laver, B.; lyc, w.; lyk, lûc, lûk, luek, honor, mane, vâs, P.

ENQUIRE, *v.* Goyn, govynny, wovyn, wovynny, w.

ENQUIRE. (Ask). Cott govena, P.

ENQUIRE FOR, *v.* Greiah râg, P.

ENSIGN, *s.* (Flag). Baner, w.; baniel, P.

ENTER, *v.* Thello, thellé, P.

ENTERTAIN, *v.* (Admit of). Perthy, porthy, w.

ENTERTAINER, *s.* Yrvyrys, P.

ENTICE or BAIT, *v.* Clithio, B.

ENTIRE, *adj.* Dyen, tyen, w.; tyen, P.; cowal, gowal, cowl, w.; coual, coule, P.

ENTIRELY, *adv.* Cowal, gowal, cowl, w.; coual, coule, P.; yn tyen, N.; yntyen, B.

ENTRAIL. *s.* Colon, enederen, w.

THE ENTRAIL OF A PIG. Nattlin, D.

ENTRAILS, *s.* Coloneiou, kylyrion, B.

ENTRANCE, *s.* (Door, gate). Porth, portal, yet, soler, w.; treuth, B.

ENTREAT, *v.* Pesy, pysy, pisy, pigy, pygy, pidzhi, w.; besy, B.

ENTRY, GROUND-ROOM, GALLERY. Soller, Saller, D.

ENVIOUS, *adj.* Drogbrederys, w.; pedn-drôg, P.

ENVY, *s.* Despyth, dyspyth, w.; dyspyt, vafter, wow, P.

EPIPHANY, TWELFTH-DAY, *s.* Stûl, degl stûl, w.

EPISTLE, *s.* Lither, lether, w.

EQUAL, *adj.* Cehafal, kehaval, haval, avel, hevel, hevelep, hyvelep. *Equal to.* Val, w.

EQUAL or MATCH, *s.* Pâr, parow, w.; *The'th pâr râk kymmerés,* to take her for thine equal, O.M. 104; *Hep parow,* without equal, P. Pâr becomes parow also, in the plural.

EQUALLY, *adv.* Awedh, auedh, aweeth, awyetha, P.; cepâr, kepâr, pocâr, pokâr, pecar, w.; pekar, P.; pycâr, pykâr, B.; pocara, w.; pokara, P.; ceceffrys, cefrys, cyffrys, cyfreys, w.; keffryz, keheffrys, kevery, keverys, P.

ERECT, *v.* Drehevel, w.; trehevel, dreheuil, trwethel, P.; dreval, w.

ERE THAT, *adv.* Censenna, w.; kenzenna, P.

ERR, v. (To err, to make to err). Faellu. B.

ERR, v. Miscemeras, w.; miskymeraz, meskymera, P.

ERRAND. s. Negés, negys, negis, nygys, w.; nagys, thanwell, P.

ERROR, s. Miscymerians, w.; myskymerrians, mystite, guyd, kùlbai, B.

ERUDITE, adj. Discys, diskys, P.

ERUDITION, s. Lyen, w.

ERUPTION, s. (As on the skin). Tardh, tarth. w.

ERYSIPELAS, s. Clevas an mytern, w.; klevaz an mytern, B.

ESCAPE, v. Chuȝvyan, vyvyan, fyé, fué, effyé, deanc, dyanc. w; kavankis. B.; scusv, skusy, w.; skesy, P.; schapȝé, R.D. 2270; ponyé, punnia, poynyé, punnio, punnya, ponȝa. B.

ESCAPE, s. Cavanscis, cavanskis, w.; kauanskis, P.

ESPECIALLY. adv. Pôrth, P.

ESPOUSE, v. Demidhy, dimedha, w.; dimedho, P.

ESQUIRE, s. Squerryon, P. ESQUIRES. Squerryon, B. Pryce also gives squerryou for Esquire. (? Pl.)

ESTEEM, ACCOUNT, WORTH, s. Prês, priz, prys, brys, w.; vry, B; woolack, wow, P.

ESTEEM, v. Settya, ȝensy, sensȝé sinsy, synsy, w.; sensa, sansa, sindzha, P.; sindzhy, B.; sendzha, dho sendzhé, syngy, w.; lymery, P.

ESTEEMED, part. Sensys, sengys. syngys, &c., w; gorrys, B.; priveth, pryveth, P.

ETERNAL, adj. Viskvethek, P.; viskuethek, B.

EVE, s. (The name). Eva, Evef, B.

EVEN. Bys, bis, B.; Bys yn y chy, even to his house, P.C. 648.

EVEN, adj. (Equal). Compos, compés, compys, cympés, kympez, w.; compez, B.

EVEN, adj. (Smooth, level). Leven, w.

EVEN AS, LIKE AS. Cepar, kepar, B.

EVEN AS, AS, SO. Tro, tra, tre, try, w.

EVEN NOW. Lumen, leman, lemen, lemman, lemmen, lemyn, lemmyn, lymmyn, w.; yn nans, B.

EVEN TO. Bês, bys, w.; bis, biz, byz, P.; besyn, bys an, trelebba, w.

EVENING, s. Gorthuer, w.; gorthuar, P.; gothuar, gathewer, gurthuwer. gorthewar, gurthuher, w.; gothihuar, B.; godhuar, godhewar, godhuhar, godhihuar, gydhihwar, w.; gydhihuar, gydiuhar, B.; gydhyhuar, P.; gurchuer, w.; gurchwer, P.; dewedhés, w.; dewethas. dewethés, dewethyans, P.; dochageydh, dohadzhedh, w.; dohadzheth, B.; dyhodzhydh, dyhodzhedh, w.

IN THE EVENING. Gurthuper, B.

EVER, FOR EVER. Bys, by, béth, rêth, byth, vyth, pyth, fyth, bythqueth, bisqueth, bythgweth, bith-gueth, pythqueth, bythcth, vytheth. pythueth, bythweth, w.; bythwathe, c.w. 1265; pythweth, bisqueth, bysqueth, bisgweth, bysgueth. w.; bys vickan, c.w. 7; bys vyckan, c.w. 147; bis vychan, P.; vyketh, M. 893. Kyn feny oma vyketh, though we be here for ever, M. 893; viccen. vicken, vycken, benary. venary, w. Yn ponvotter venary, in trouble for ever, O.M. 898; venarye, c.w.; 514; bys venary. P.; bynary, vynary, w.; unary. P.; benytha, venytha, w.; bys venytha, P.; bynytha, besga, vesga, nevra, nefre, w.; nefere. P.; neffre, N. The gous a bréf neffre, thy speech proves ever, P.C. 1408; ueffre, weffra, yn weffra, P.; jammés, w.; jammas, P.; prest, c.w. 997; whâth, whêth, w; worstan, yth worstan, P.

EVERLASTING, adj. Bythol, vythol, w.; viskvethek, P.; viskuethek, B.

EVERY. (Every, every one). Pûp, pûb, pyb. bûb, bûp, pôp, pôb, ceniver, keniver, cenifer, w.; kenifer, P.; kanifer, kynifar, B.; cyniver. kynyver. cenefra, cetep, ketep, kettep, w.; yn kettep, N. Yn kettep guds, every fellow, P.C. 1350; neb, nep, oll, w.

EVERY ONE. Pyb behan. w; pyb behen, peb ôl, P; pub huny, M. 267; pup huny, O.M. 2323; kynivar uonon. P.; kynifer uynyn, B.; ketep onen, O.M. 2308; kettep onen, P.; kettep pol, P.C. 841.

EVERY DAY, DAILY. Poynêdh, boynêdh, w.; kynifar dzyrna, P.; pubtetholl, B.

EVERY HEAD. Kettep pol, P.

EVERY HOUR. Pûb eure, pûp erol, P.; pûrpûr, B.

EVERY SIDE, ON EVERY SIDE. Propay du, P.; bub tewe, c.w. 49; bub tew, c w. 138.

EVERYWHERE Pup teller, O.M. 579.

EVERY YEAR. Pob bledhan, P

EVET, s. See EFT or NEWT.

EVIDENT, PLAIN, adj. Da, dah, uredy, P.

EVIDENTLY, adv. Lur, scyle, P.

EVIL, s. Drôc, drôk, w.; droke, c.w. 769; drôg, w.; droag, c.w. 1687; trôc. w.; throke, c.w. 987; throog, c.w. 1297; gâl, myschyf, pla, w. Kemys drôk, so much evil, P.

EVIL. adj. Tebel, w.; tebal, P.; teball, M. 163; debel, hager, w.; hagar, gwan. P. Gwan oberowe, evil deeds, P.

EVIL DEED. Drôcoleth, dhrôcoleth, drôk-culeth, drôgober, w.; throog ober, c.w. 1297; gwan ober, P.

EVIL-DOER, s. Drôg-oberor, drôchoberor, P.

EVIL-MINDED, adj. Drôgbrederys, w.; pedn drôg, P.

EVIL ONE, THE EVIL ONE. Malan, w.; pla, P c. 1764. Certan ty yv máp a'n pla, certainly thou art a son of the evil one, P.C. 1764.

EVIL PRINCIPLE. (The evil principle). Malan, w.

EVIL THOUGHT. Camdybians, w.; kabmdybiauz, P.

EVIL WORKER, s. Drôch-oberor, w.

EXACT, *adj.* Ewn, ewen, w.; eun, p

EXACTLY, *adv.* Harlyth, w.; pûr eun, p.; poren, M. 1810. *Harlyth my a'n trehy omma,* I will cut it exactly here, o.m. 2515. *Poren an rena ens,* exactly those they were, M. 1810.

EXACTNESS, *s.* Combrynsy, w.; combrinsy, p. *An combrynsy war the ben,* the exactness on thy head, o.m. 2517.

EXALT, *v.* Hwedhy, hûdhy, w.; hûthé, rysyé, p.; uchellé, uhellé, ychellas, w. *Ow colon yv múr húthys,* my heart is greatly exalted, R.D. 483.

EXAMINE, *v.* Aspyé, w.; TO EXAMINE OR TRY. Cably. *Part.* Cablys, p.

EXAMINATION, *s.* Cabel, p.

EXCAVATION, *s.* (An old one in a mine). Hulk, D.

EXCEEDING, *adj.* Uthec, ithic, w.; ithik, ithig, p.

EXCELLENCE, *s.* Dader, dhadder, w.; deder, B.; tadder, w.; thadder, p.; grâs, râs, w.; râz, p.; *Pl.* Grasow, rasow, w.

EXCELLENT *adj.* Brentyn, bryntyn, w.; gore, M. 3018. *Dêth gore yv devethys,* an excellent day is come, M. 3018; gentyl, o.m. 2153. *A vrry assos gentyl,* ah! Uriah, thou art excellent, o.m. 2153; splan, spladn, trauythés, B.

EXCEPT. Mars, marnas, marnés, marny (*mar-ny*), mernas, menas, w.; menés, p. *War pep ol marnas ty,* over all except thee, o.m. 948; ponag, poni, w.; pony, p.; pini, pyni, B.; lemmyn, N.; saw, w.; sau, B. *Ny hynwys thy'm saw peder,* he named none to me except Peter, R.D. 916.

EXCEPTION, *s.* Nam, w.

EXCHANGE, *v.* Newidio, scôs, B.; scoce, D.

EXCITE, *v.* Desethy, amsevy, w.

EXCITEMENT, *s.* (Of mind). See AGITATION.

EXCOMMUNICATE, *v.* Scemyna, w.; skemyna, p.; omscemyny, ymscemyny, w.; omsceminy, p.

EXCOMMUNICATED. *part.* Emscumunys, ymscemunys, w.; emskemmunys, B.

EXCREMENT, *s.* Câc, cauch, cau, cauh, w.; kauh, B.; gau, w. *To void excrement,* Caca, w.

EXCUSE, *v.* Kaunscusé, p.

EXCUSE, *s.* Cavanscis, cavanskis, w.; kauvanskis, p.; flous, w. *Ef a'n pren súr wythovt flous,* he shall surely pay for it without excuse, P.C. 1346; deslam, B.; distain, p.

EXCUSER, *s.* Diffennor, w.; diffener, B.

EXECRATE, *v.* Molletha, mollethia, molythia, w.

EXECRATING, AN EXECRATING, *s.* Mollethians, w.

EXECUTE, *v.* (Perform, do). Dyswul, dyswyl, p. *Rák dyswyl eistenyon,* to execute justice, p.

EXETER CITY, *s.* Karêsk, B.

EXILE, AN EXILE, *s.* Divrés, w.; diures, p.

EXILED, *part.* Exilys, p. TO EXILE. Fyé, B.

EXIST, *v.* Bew, pew, bewé, bewa, vew, vewé, w.

EXIST or TO BE, *v.* Bôs, bonés, bonas, vôs, bosa (poetically), w.

EXISTENCE or LIFE, *s.* Bewnans, vewnans, w.; beunans, bounaz, vewnas, B.

EXPAND, *v.* Lesé, w.

EXPENSE, COST or CHARGE, *s.* Côst, w.; sam, w.; "I'll stand sam," *i.e.,* I'll pay the cost, is often used in Cornwall.

EXPERT, *adj.* Skientic, w.; skientik, p, slêv, w.

EXPERTNESS, *s.* Sleyveyth, w.

EXPIATE, *v.* Perna, prenné, w.; prenna, pryné; p.; prynny, w. *Ile shall expiate.* Pren, 3 pers. s. fut. of *prenné,* to expiate, w.;

EXPLOIT, *s.* Deray, w.

EXPRESSLY, *adv.* Poran, p.

EXTASY, *s.* Trangiak, B.

EXTEND, *v.* Ystyné, w.

EXTENDED, *adj.* Tôt, w. *Mór tôt,* the ocean, or the extended sea.

EXTENDED THING, *s.* Tenewen, ternewan, tornewan, tyrnewan, w; ternehuan, p.; denewan, w.

EXTENSIVE, *adj.* Ledan, w.

EXTENT, THE EXTENT, *s.* Ewhe, B.

EXTINGUISH, *v.* Defydh, w.; defyth, deveth, p.; dufydh, dufydhy, defydhy, difydhy, w.; difythi, p.

EXTOL, *v.* Eysyé, w.; rysy, B.

EXTREMELY, *adv.* Veyll, B.

EXTREMITY, *s.* (End). Cur, gur, pen, pedn, w.; pednan, p.; mein, min, meyn, w.; meen, B.

EYE, *s.* Lagat, w.; llygud, B.; lagas, w.; legadzho, B.; lagaz, p. *Pl.* Lagasow. (For eyes in general).

EYES, *s.* (*i.e.,* the two eyes). Dewlagas, dhewlagas, w.; dew-lagas, p.

EYED, *adj.* Lagadec, lygadzhac, w.

EYE-BALL, *s.* Byn an lagat, B.

EYE, *s.* (The weather eye). Lagas auel, B.

EYEBROW, *s.* Abrans, B.

EYEBROWS, *s.* Bleu an lagat, p.; bleuenlagat, B.

F.

This letter in Cornish " is both a radical and a secondary, when radical in early Cornish it was also immutable. When secondary it is the aspirate mutation of *p,* as *pen,* a head; *ow fen,* my head; *aga fen,* their head.

In Cornish, *f*, is also a regular mutation of *b* and *m*, by hardening *v* after certain particles; thus *býdh.* will be; *ty a rýdh*, thou shalt be; *a fýdh ny*, we shall be. *Brás*, great; *yn frás*, greatly; *más*, good; *yn fás*, well.

In the Ordinalia *f* is often found after particles which always soften the initials, and the following sentence furnishes an instance of this confusion.

Nep na crys ny fydh sylwys, na gans Dew ny vydh trygys, he that believes not shall not be saved, nor with God shall he dwell. In these cases *f* had the sound of *v*, as in the modern Welsh, (see *Lhuyd*, 227).

In the latest days of the existence of the language, *f* had a mutation like *b*, and *m*, into *v*. Lhuyd, 241, gives as an instance, *fordh*, a way; *an vordh*, the way. He also mentions another mutation of *f* into *h*, as *flóh*, a child; *a'n hlóh*, of the child; *dhe'n hlóh*, to the child," w. *Lex. Corn. Brit.*

FACE, *s.* (Surface). Bedgeth, w.; badgeth, P.; budgeth, B. *Budgeth an dour*, the face of the deep, (water) B.; veys, O.M. 24. *The'n nór veys may fe dyllys*, that it may be dropped on the face of the earth; fêth, fyth, w.; fath, fás, P.

FACE. *s.* (Countenance). Enep, enap, fêth, fyth, w.; fath, fás, P.; mein, B.

FACETIOUS, *adj.* Avlethis, P.; avlethys, w.

FACT, A FACT, *s.* Gwythrés, wythrés, w.; wyth, P.

FACTION, *s.* (Party). Herwyth, P.

FAIL, *v.* Difygy, dyfygy, w.; dyfyg, thyfyk, P.; fyllel, fyllell, fallé, pally, w.

I WILL FAIL. Fallaf, the aspirate mutation of *pallaf*, 1 pers. s. fut. of *pally*, w.

FAIL OR FAILING, *s.* Fall, w.; fal, P.; fallas, fallad, w.; falladow, M. 12; fyllel, P. *Hep fal*, without fail, P. *Hep falladow*, without fail, M. 12. *Heb falladowe*, without fail, c w. 107. *Hep fyllel*, without failing, P.

FAILING, *adj.* Mothow, w.

FAIN WOULD. Porris, B.

FAINT, *v.* Clamderé, w.; clamdery, P.; dyené, tyené, lacca, w.; lacka, P.

FAINT OR SWOON, *s.* Clamder, w.

FAINT, *adj.* (Weary). Squyth, scîth, w.; skith, P.

FAINT, *adj.* (Weak and ill). Wingarly, B. This word is still used.

FAIR, *s.* (Mart). Fèr, w.; feur, B.

FAIR, *adj.* (Beautiful, fine). Têc, ték, w. *Ow formyé têk ha dyblans*, me create fair and bright, O.M. 87; teak, B.; teke, c.w. 94; teake, c.w. 412; teek, teage, thêk, P.; têg, dêk, dêg, w.; deke, c.w. 527; gwyn, w.; guyn, gudn, guên, P.; gain, cain, gainor, B.; wên, wyn, P.; glân, w. *Yn hanow dv ty mór glân*, in the name of God, thou fair sea, O.M. 1675; gulân, lân, elyn, ylyn, w. *Maseger ylyn*

wolcum, fair messenger welcome; caer, bel. This last word is the same as the French *belle*, perhaps *bel* is older than *belle*.

FAIRER, *adj.* Têcach, têcah, têcka, têkè, tecké, tekké, w.

FAIREST, *adj.* Têca, têka, têkea, w.

FAIRING, *s.* (Sweets bought at a fair). Fêran, P.

FAIRLY, *adv.* Dygh, P.

FAIRNESS, *s.* (Clearness, beauty). Tecter, tekter, w.; dekter, 2935. *Mar a mynna, dre dekter*, he will through fairness, M. 2935.

FAIRY, *s.* Pisky, B. This is still a common word in Cornwall where they also call a moth a *pisky*. Spriggan, nuggie, D.

FAITH, *s.* Fêdh, fydh, w.; fyth, B., fêth, P.; fey, fay, w.; fás, P. *Rûm fey*, by my faith.

FAITH, *s.* (Belief). Crêd, crés, krêz, grês, w.; grez, gris, B.; crygyans, kridzhans, kredzhanz, P.; grygyans, w. See CREED and BELIEF.

FAITH. (*i.e.*, good faith, loyalty). Lauté, w.

FAITH, TO HAVE FAITH IN. See TO BELIEVE.

FAITHFUL, *adj.* Lel, lell, leal, w.

MORE FAITHFUL. Lellé, N.

FAITHFULLY, *adv.* Yn lên, N.; lên, O.M. 1496. *Na allons lên y servya*, that they may not faithfully serve him, o M. 1496.

FALCON, *s.* Falhun, falbun, w.

FALL OR TRIP, *s.* Lithriad, w.

FALL, *s.* Fauns, B. This is a wrestling term.

FALL, *s.* (As from above). Towl. dowl, w.; doul, P.; dowle, c.w 420. *Gallas genaf hager dowle*, there has gone with me an ugly fall, c.w. 420; lam, w.; kedha, B.

A HEAVY FALL. Qualk, D.

FALL, *v.* Côdhé, côdha, w.; kôdha, côtha, P.; cydha, w.; kydha, P.; gôdhé, gôdho, w.; gôtha, P.; bassé, bashé, omdesevy, w.; tremené, P.; skydnya, c.w. 2208.

HE FELL. Gôdhas, a mutation of *côdhas*, 3 pers. s. preter. of *côdha*, to fall, w.

HE WILL FALL. Gôdh, a mutation of *côdh*, 3 pers. s. fut. of *côdha*, to fall, w.

FALL, *v.* (To fall down). Cubma, cumma, w.; kubma, dyskynné, scydnya, skydnya, w.; desef, P.

FALL, *v.* (To occur, to fall out, to happen). Dygwydha, w.; digwyddo, B.; wharfos, w.

FALLEN, *part.* Cothys, cothas, kydhas, gothys, B.; desefys, P.; clathorée, B.

FALLOW DEER, *s.* Da, ewig luyd, w.

FALLOW GROUND, *s.* Tôn, tôdn, P.

FALSE, *adj.* (Lying). Guac, gow, fals, fouls, w.; falge, M. 777.

FALSE, *adj.* (Spurious). Basa, P. *Basa dow*, false gods, P.

FALSEHOOD, *s.* Gowegneth, w.; gouegneth, P.; gouegueth, B.; (?) *Râk gowegneth ny garaf*, for I do not love falsehood, R.D. 906; falsury, w.; fallsurye, C.W. 533; falsney, B. *Hep feyntys na falsury*, without deceit or falsehood, P.C. 1478.

FALSEHOOD, *s.* (A lie, a falsehood). Gow, gou, w.; gowe, C.W. 65; wow, ow, w. *Pl.* Gewan, w.; geuan, P.; stram. D.

FALSIFY, *v.* Gowea, w.; gouea, B.; gova, w.

FALSELY, *adv.* Falslych, w.; falsury, B.

FALSENESS, *s.* Fallad, fallas, w.

FAME, *s.* Gerda, w. (*Ger da*, a good word).

FAMILIAR, *adj.* Cooth, w.

FAMILY, *s.* (Household). Cosgor, kosgar, w.; goscorthi, P.; goskordhy, B.; teilu, teulu, w.

FAMILY, *s.* (Sort, kind). Echen, hechen, hehen, ehen, w.; ehin, P.

FAMILY, *s.* (Tribe). Leid, leith, luyte, w.; lwyth, tûs, tûz, têz, tîs, tîz, dûz, dîz, B.

FAMOUS, *adj.* Gerûtda, w.

FAN, *s.* Guinzal, P.; *q.d.* all wind.

FANCY, NOTION. or CONCEIT, *s.* Vang, D.

FAR, *adj.* (Distant, remote, long). Pell, pel, bell, w.; vel, velha, B. *Yma moyses pel gyllys*, Moses is far gone, O.M. 1682.

FARNESS, *s.* Peldar, C.W. 1361.

FAR OFF. Cer, ker, kerr, cerdh, kerdh, kerth, P. (A journey, quite a journey.)

FAREWELL, FARE THEE WELL. Anoure, oure, B.; bene-tu-gana, w.

FARDLE, *s.* Pusorn, w.

FARM, *s.* Gwêl, gweal, gueal, B. *A small farm or homestead*, Dijey, D.

FARMER, *s* Tyac, tiak, w.; tyack, P.; tioc, tyoc, dyac, dyack, gonedhic, gonydhic, w.; gonethick, P.; gonythick, w., guikyr, B. See DEALER for this last word.

FARRIER, *s.* Ferror, w.

FART, *v.* Brammé, vrammé, w.

FART, *s.* Bram. *Pl.* Bremmyn, w.

FARTHER. Pellach. pell, felha, velha, w.

FARTHEST, *adj.* Gwarrah, B.V.

FARTHING, *s.* Peuare, P.

FASCINATION, *s.* Hûth, P.

FASHION, *v.* Formyé, dythgthtya, w.; schapy, P.; wonys, B.

FASHION, *s.* (Shape, form). Gwêdh, w.

FASHION, *s.* (Manner). Fest, P.

FASHIONABLE, *adj.* (Honorus, *Lat.*) Enir, henir, ynir, B.

FAST, *v.* (As penance). Penys, P.

FAST. (Eagerly, quickly). Duwhans, dewhans, dywhans, w.

FAST, SECURE, *adj.* Thewhans, tewans *Per thewans, per tewans*, very fast or secure. B.; start, B.

FAST, *adj.* (Quick)). Fast, fest, stric, strik, w.

FAST, *s.* (Fastness). Fastsens, B.

FAST, *s.* (A fasting). Tynys, P.

FASTEN, *v.* Fasté, fastyé, lacié, w.; lychy, P.

FASTEN, *v.* (To bind). Celmy, kelmy, cylmy, kylmy, w.; kelma, colmye, B.; colma, gylmy, w.

FASTEN, *v.* (To tack together). Taccié, taccyé, takkyé, w.; takkia, P.

FASTEN, *v.* (As with a bit of wood). Prenné, pyne, w.

HE SHALY FASTEN. Pyn. 3 pers s. fut. of *pyné*. w.

FASTING, *s.* Denseth, P.

FASTNESS, *s.* (Quickness). Fastsens, B.

FAT, *s.* Blonec, blonit, seym, saim, B.

FAT, *adj.* Bor, berric, soath, w.; tew, B.; teu, P.; ithik, B.

FATHER, *s.* Tât, tâd, tâs, w.; tâz, B.; tase, C.W. 12; tace, C.W. 2118; tays, M. 497; thâs, w.; thâz, B.; thays, M. 280; dâs, w.; days, M.; 378; câr. w.; rera. (*Soawen. Ms.*) *Pl.* Tassow. *His father*, y das, N.

FATHER or SIRE, *s.* Sira, seera. As thus, *seera ha damma*, sire and dame, w.

BY MY FATHER! Renothas, w.; renauthas, P.

FATHER-IN-LAW, *s.* Hwigeren, w.; hwegeren, P.; huigeren, altrou, B.

FATHERLESS. *adj.* Diolaeht, dileuchta, B.; dileakta, *A fatherless child*. Diolacht, dileakta, P.

FATHERLY, *adj.* Tâsek, M. 2852. *Thynny ny bonés tâsek*, to us be fatherly, M. 2852.

FATIGUE, *v.* Fêthê, fêthy, w.

FATIGUE, *s.* Squythens, w.; squytzder, B.

FATIGUED, *adj.* Squyth, w.; skêth, scuiz, B. See TIRED.

FATNESS, *s.* Blonek, B.; berri, tewder, w.; teuder, P.

FAULT, *s.* Acheson (? if this be a plural of *achos*,) w; dyfout, diffout, B.; fall, w.; fal, P.; nam, w.; guyd, kûlbai, B.; gyll, P.; gyl, O.M. 2559. *Prên the gyst hep tôl na gyl*, a tree for a beam without hole or fault, o M. 2559.

FAULT-FINDER, *s.* Baiewl, B.

FAVOUR, *s.* Grâth, grayth, grâf, w.

FAWN, *s.* (The animal). Leau-ewig, loch-ewic, B.; loch euhic, P.

FEAR, *v.* Owna, w.; ouna, P.

FEAR, *s.* Own, w.; oun, P.; owne, c.w. 561.

FEARFUL, *adj.* Ounek, N. *Nag awos den vyt ovnek,* not fearful of any man, o.m. 2158.

FEASIBLE, *adj.* Hêdh, hogul, w.

FEASIBLY, *adv.* Hê, hy, ho, w.

FEAST, *s.* Guledh, lein, prez-buz, B.

A SEA-BIRD'S FEAST. Clyne. Mr. Dunn, Mevagissey.

FEAST, *s.* (A merriment). Lît, B. *A tinner's feast.* Troil, duggle, D.

FEATHER, *s.* Pluven, plyven, plyvan, blyven. *Pl.* Plûv, plyv, pliv, w.

FEATHER-BED, *s.* Gwillé plêv, P.

FEBRUARY, *s.* Huevral, *i.e.,* *hu evral,* the whirling month, P.; hwevral, hwerval, w.; (Borlase says it is corruptly written *huerval*) miseheurer, B.

FEE, *s.* Gobyr, gobar, gober, w.; gubar, gobr, guu, gu, P.

FEEBLE, *adj.* Gwan, wan, w.; guan, guadn, P.; trewesy, dreuesy, B.

FEED or LUNCHEON, *s.* Crowst, crouse, D.

FEED, *v.* Methia, cafos, cafus, P.; maga, w.

FED, *part.* Megys, mygys, w.

FEEDING-TIME, *s.* Prez-buz, B.

FEEDING-PLACE, *s.* Methian, P.

FEEDING-GROUND, *s.* (For cattle). Gwerwels, w.; gueruelz, P.; bounder, vounder, w.

FEEL, *v.* Cothewel, gotheuel, wothaf. *The wothaf an streausow,* to feel the strokes, P.

YE FELT. Wethough, P.

FEEL, *v.* (Handle). Dava, w.

FEEL, *v.* (*i.e.,* to feel one's self). Ymsensy, w.

FEIGN, *v.* Plosi, plosé. P.; fekyll, B.; fugio, figio, w.; omwrellé, ymwyl, omwrey, ymwrey, w.

FEIGN, TO FEIGN ONE'S SELF, *v.* Omwreyth, P.

FEIGNED, *part.* Fekyl, B.

FEINT, *s.* Feyntys, w.

FELLOW, *s.* (Mate, colleague, companion). Coweth, cowyth, w.; kywedh, P.; cywedh, cywedhiad, w.; kywedhiad, P.; chet, w.

FELLOW, *s.* (One of two, match). Celé, gelé, gilé. w.; gela, c.w 1053; pâr, w.; hyller (?) P.

FELLOW, *s.* (A low, mean person). Gwâs, w.; gwase, c.w. 158; guâs, w.; guâz, B.; wâs, w.;

wâz, B.; iaudyn, P.C. 1691. *Py hanow yv a'n iaudyn,* what is the name of the fellow? P.C. 1691; Shammick, D.

A WICKED FELLOW. Wâz teble, B.

A DIRTY FELLOW. Caugh wâs, P.C. 2103; kaugeon, P C. 2291.

A TIMID FELLOW. Ownec, ownek, w.; ounak, P.

A MEAN FELLOW. Guaeldgu, boudhyn, B.

A GOOD FELLOW. Cowyth mâs, P.C. 602. *Lauar thy'mmo cowyth mâs,* tell me, good fellow, P.C. 602.

A SILLY OR STUPID FELLOW. Totle, D. See also FOOL.

FELLOWS, *s.* (Mean persons). Gwesion, the plural of *gwâs*; guesyon, M. 3803; guscas, an irregular plural of *gwâs* or *guas*, a fellow.

FELLOWSHIP, *s.* (Communion). Cowethyans, w.; cuntillyans, contellyans, cuntellyans, P.

FELON, *s.* Esquet, B.

FEMALE, *s.* Benen, venen, banen, bynen, vynen, bynyn, vynyn, ben, ven, benaw, benow, w. *Ol ow tûs gour ha benen,* all my people, male and female P.C. 768. *Pl.* Benow, o.m. 1022. *Gorow ha benow defry,* males and females really, o.m. 1022.

A FEMALE. (Any female). Cansgûr, B.

FEMALE-KIND, *s.* Benenriw, w.; benen-rid. B.

FEMALE COMPANION. Cowethés, howethés, w.

FEN, *s.* Cors, tir devrak, w.; devrak, winnick, whynick, P.

FENCE, *v.* (To hedge). Dho kerz, P.

FENCE, OR HEDGE, *s.* Cê, w.; kê, P.; gê, w. *A low hedge or rough fence.* Gurgo, D.

FENCE OR DITCH, *s.* Clêdh, klêdh, glédh, w.; kleudh, klêd, cleuth, clawd, fos, vos, B.

FENCED, *adj.* Vallic, w.; vallick, vallack, P.; gwallic, wallic, w.

FENNEL, *s.* Fenochel, funil, w.

FENNY, *adj.* Gwinic, winnic, w.; winny, P. *Tir devrak,* fenny land, B. *Môrva,* Fenny place near the sea, w.

FERN, *s.* Raden, redan, B. This is given by Williams as a plural for *ferns.*

FERN-BRAKE, *s.* Redanan, B. and P.

FERN-COCK, *s.* Keliok reden, B. This is a provincial name for a small brown beetle used in fishing, sometimes called ferny-cock, and fern-web. It is the *melolontha horticola,* of the naturalist.

FERRET, *s.* (The animal). Yeugen, w.; yeigen, B.; yeochen, P.

FERRUGINOUS EARTH. Gossan, gozan. This is the common name still used by miners. It is the rusty ochre of iron. Gossan is the name for the

course, bed, broil, or back of a lode. Hence the phrase
" keenly gossan," *i.e.*, a promising lode.

FERRYMAN, *s.*   Porthwys, B.

FERTILITY, *s.*   Waltowat, w. ; paltowat, B.

FERVENT, *adj.*   Frêth, w.

FERVOUR, *s.*   Frêth, P.

FESTIVAL, *s.*   Degl, goil, gôl, w.   *Ov gôl a veth suer,*
my festival shall be surely.

FETCH, *v.*   Cerchés, kerchés, cerhés, kerhés, w. ;
kyrhas, N. ; kerhez. P. ; gerhés, w. ; gerhaz, P. ; cyrchés, w. ; kerghas, kergh, kyrgh, P. ; cerchy, w.

HE FETCHED. Gerhas.   A mutation of *cerhas,* 3
pers. s. preter. of *cerhés,* to fetch, w.

HE MAY FETCH. Gercho.   A mutation of *cervho,*
3 pers. s. subj. of *cerchés,* to fetch, w.

HE WILL FETCH. Cerch, 3 pers. s. fut. of *cerchy,*
to fetch, and also meaning, fetch thou, 2 pers. s.
imp.

FETCH, *v.*   (Reach, take). Fethé, fethy, hedhés,
hedhy, w. ; hedha, hethé, hethas, P.   *Devn the
kethas tha banowe,* let us come to fetch him to pains,
c.w. 1714.

FETID, *adj.*   Flerys, w. ; flayrys, c.w. 2248.

FETTER, *s.*   Fu, fual, hual, w. ; carhar, M. 3686.

FETTERS, *s.*   Carharov, M. 3686.   *The orthys an
carharov,* from thee the fetters, M. 3686.

FETTERED, BOUND, *adj.*   Golmas, B.

FEUD, *s.*   (An old family feud). Corrosy, corresy,
corrizee, D.

FEVER, A FEVER, *s.*   Derthen, w.

FEVERFEW, *s.*   Lêsderth, lês derthen, w. ; bothem,
D.   (*Pyrethrum parthenium*).

FEW, *adj.*   Tanow, tanaw, tanau, w.   *Tûs yv tanow,*
are few people, R.D. 2462.

FEW, *s.*   (A few). Nebés, w. ; nebas, c.w. 830 ;
nebaz, P.

FICKLE, *adj.*   Fykyl, P.

FICTION, *s.*   Feyntys, w.

FIDDLE, *s.*   Crowd, w. ; kroude, B.   A word still in
use.

FIDDLE, *v.*   Crowdy, D.

FIDDLER, *s.*   Crowder, w. ; groudel, B. ; harfellor,
w.

A FEMALE FIDDLER   Fellorés, w.; harfellorés, P.

FIELD, *s.*   Gwêl, gweal, w. ; guel, O.M. 1137 ; gueal,
B. ; gueel, P.   *Tyrségh yn guel nag yn prás,* dry land
in field or in meadow, O.M. 1137 ; gwôn, w. ; gwaeth,
weeth, D.   *Prennys da gwôn yn nép lé,* bought a good
field in some place, P.C. 1544 ; gûn, goon, guen, gôn,
mês, w., mêz, P. ; meas, w. ; meys, P. ; maes, vês,
w. ; êr, erw, B. ; eru, parc, w. ; park, P. ; cê, gê, w. ;

kae, têr, B.   Borlase has *kae* but this is probably a
misprint for *kae.*

THE BEST FIELD IN A FARM. Gews, D.

A FAIR FIELD. Er têg, B.

A PLAIN FIELD. Guew, B. ; mês, maes, meas, w.

IN THE FIELD. Amês. w.

BELONGING TO A FIELD. Mêsic, w.

A LARGE FIELD. Wyth, B.

A SMALL FIELD. Weethan, D.

A FIELD UPON THE BOTTOM. Parc erizy, P.
(in a valley).

A FIELD OF FLAX. Kealinec, P.

FIELD-FARE, *s.*   (The bird). Mola-lâs, w. ; mola-
lâz, swellak, swellak, B.   The last name is still used
in the Cornish dialect.

FIELD-MOUSE, *s.*   Logoden, P.

FIEND, *s.*   See DEVIL.   A FEMALE FIEND,
Diowlés, dzhowlés, w. ; dzhoulés, P.

FIENDS, *s.*   Lawan, c.w. 1721 ; lawethan, w.   *Bel-
sebuc ha lawethan,* Beelzebub and fiends, R.D. 128 ;
Ha my caugeon lawethan, and my dirty fiends, R.D.
37.   See DEVILS.

FIERCE, *adj.*   Clôr, glôr, B.   *Kyn teffons y vyth mar
clôr,* though they come ever so fierce, R.D., 392 ;
garow, harow, w. ; garou, khuero, B. ; garo, guariow,
P. ; hager, w. ; hyll, B. ; wôth, frêth, w. ; fûr, P.

FIERY, *adj.*   (Red, bright gold colour, shining).
Oyrec, oyrek, P. ; oyrech, B.

FIFE, *s.*   Tôlcorn.   *Lit.* A holed horn.

FIFTEEN. Pemp-dek, pymthek, B. ; pymthec, pem-
dhac, w. ; pemdhak, pymthag, P. ; pempthack, D.

FIFTEENTH. Pemp degvas, N.

FIFTH. Pempas, w ; pempaz, pempes, P. ; pympés,
w. ; pympas, c.w. 106,

FIFTY. Dêg ha dugans, w. ; dêg ha duganz, P. dek
ha deugans, N.   *Lit.* Ten and two twenties, Hanter cans, N. ; hanter canz, P.   *Lit.* Half a hundred.

FIG, *s.*   Gala, P.

FIGS, *s.*   Figes, w.   *Figés ledan,* Broadfigs.   *Figés an
houl,* Raisins.   *Lit.* Figs of the sun.

FIGHT, *v.*   Emlodh, w. ; hemlodh, P. ; emladh, w. ;
hemladh. P. ; emladha. omdhal, w.

FIGHT, *s.*   Emlodh, B.

FIGURE, *s.*   (Form). Furf, fuw, fu, roath, gwêdh,
wêdh, weydh, wêth, w.

FILAMENT or THREAD, *s.*   Hurle, D.

FILE, *s.*   (Tool). Heschen, B.

FILL, *v.*   (To fill, to fill up). Colenwel, collenwel,
covlenwel, w. ; kovlenuel, P. ; coullenwel, cowlenwel,
gowllenwell, P ; golenwall, c.w. 463 ; lenwell, leana,
w. ; lena, P.

FILLET or BAND, *s.* Funen, snôd, w.

FILTH, *s.* Plôs, lued, luth, mostethes, vostethés, w.; votehés, P.

FILTHY, *adj.* Plosec, plosek, luedic, w.; luedik, gagle, P.; geagle, gassic, caugeon, caugyon, w.; casa, gasa, gasow, caugh, cough, cawys, casalek, P.

A FILTHY FELLOW. Plosek guâs, caugyon, kaugeon, P.; caugeon, cauchwâs, w.; caugh.wâs, casadow, P.

FINAL, *adj.* Fîn, fyn, w.

FINALLY, *adv.* Yn fyn, wostewêdh, w.; wostewêth, P.; wotewédh, w.; wotewéth, P.

FIND, *v.* Cafos, cafus, w.; kauaz, P.; cafés, cavos, w.; cavoz, P.; cavas, cawas, gafus, gafos, w.; café, gafé, B.; rykavaz, P.; dascevian, w.; dazkevian, kefyth, geyfyth, kefer, P.; cafel, cavel, gavel, gaval, cael, w.; kael, P.; gael, trovia, w.; trouvia, cothas, steva, B.; ganno. P. *Na ganno tru,* that he find not sorrow, P. *Ni steva whans,* found no desire, B.

I FIND. Cassaf, P.; gafe, B.; (? cassaf for caffaf, câf'f.)

IF I FIND. Marath cassaf, P.; (? marath caffaf.)

WE FIND. Cafons, B.

HE DID FIND. Gefé, gevé, mutations of *cefé,* 3 pers. s. imp. of *cafos,* to find.

I SHALL FIND. Caffaf, cafaf, cavaf, cyffyth, kyffyth, and the mutations, gaffaf, gavaf, &c., 1 pers. s. fut. of *cafos,* to find, w.

SHALL FIND. Kyff, P.

THOU SHALT FIND. Cefyth, cevyth, and gefyth, gevyth, the mutations of *cefyth, cevyth,* 2 pers. s. fut. of *cafos,* to find, w.

HE SHALL FIND. Gefyth, gevyth, mutations of *cevyth,* 3 pers. s. fut. of *cafus,* to find, w.

WE SHALL FIND. Cefan, cefyn, caffan, kefyn, cyffyn, kyffyn, and the mutations gefyn, &c., of cefyn, &c., 1 pers. pl. fut. of *cafos,* to find w.

YE SHALL FIND. Cefouch, 2 pers. pl. fut. of *cafos,* to find, w.

THAT 1 MAY FIND. May gesso, P.

HE MAY FIND. Caffo, ceffo, and their mutations, gaffo, geffo, w.

THEY MAY FIND. Cefons, kefons, w.

FIND, *v.* (Find fault). Canvas, w.

FIND, *v.* (To find out). Convedhas, w.; convethas, ryguelaz, P.

FINE, *adj.* (Perfect). Fyn, feyn, w.; fein, P.

FINE, *adj.* (Slender, thin). Muin, moiu, moyn, men, w.

FINE, *adj.* (Handsome). Têc, têk, têg, w.; teek, thêk, teage, P.

FINE, *s.* (A fine). Spâl, w. A word still much used.

FINGER, *s.* Bes, w.; bez, P.; bîs, bys, w.; pêz, B. The word is also used for *toe,* B.

FINGERS, *s.* Bosias, w.; bozias, B.; boziaz, P.; bysias, bessi, w.; bess, B.

THE MIDDLE FINGER. Bês crês, w.

FINGER OR TOE NAIL. Ewin, euin, iwin, w.

FINGER-STALL, *s.* Besgan, biscan. *Biscan (and veskin,)* is still used in the Cornish dialect.

FINISH, *v.* Dewedhy, dewedhé, dhewedhé, w.; dewethé, P.; diwedhé, dywedhé, w.; dho diuadha, P.

FINISHED, *part.* Dywydhys, &c., w.

FIR TREE, *s.* Aidhlen, aidlen, adlen, sibuit, saban, zaban. See also PINE.

FIRE, *v.* (?) Pryce gives *tefigia,* but *fire* must be a misprint for tire. See FIRE.

FIRE, *s.* Tân, tane, thân, P.; taen, M. 2093; dân, P. *May tewé an tân wharré,* that the fire may kindle soon, P.C. 1221. *Yma ól an coys gans taen,* all the wood is on fire, M. 2093. *A dân,* of fire, P. *Dour ha thân,* water and fire, P.

FIRE-BRAND, *s.* Tewen, tehen. Williams gives this for a quenched firebrand. Borlase gives *tewyn,* for firebrand. Itheu, w.; a doubtful word.

A BURNING FIRE-BRAND. Colan leskis, w.; kolan leskiz, *or* kolan, P.

FIRE-PLACE, *s.* Fôc, fôk, fôg, w.

FIRE-SHOVEL, *s.* Rêv tân, w.

FIRE-SIDE or HEARTH, *s* Shimbla, w.

FIRE-WOOD, *s.* Cinnis, kinnis, w.; kynnés, B.; cunys, kunys, w.; tân prynner, O.M. 1290.

FIRM, *adj.* (Secure). Start, B.; prive, w.; bolk, D.

FIRM, *adj.* (Steadfast). Tên, tyn. *Yn tokyn tén,* as a firm token, w.; thyaseth, P. *May hallovgh bo thyaseth,* that you may be (firm) steadfast; spernabyll, spernafyll, B.; spernas, P.

FIRMAMENT, *s.* Ebron, ybron, ebarn, ebbarn, w.; yborn, ybbern, P.; fyrvan, firmament, w.

FIRST. (The first, chief). Censa, kensa, kenza, kinsa, cynsa, kynsa, kynsé, w.; kinso, P.; kynso, O.M. 2162; henz, B.

FIRST. (Before, before that). Cen, ken, cyn, kyn, w.

FIRST OF ALL, AT THE BEGINNING. Yn dalleth, w.; en dallah, P.; wostalleth, w.

FISH, *v.* Pisgetta, w.; pysgetta, B.

FISH, *s.* Pisc, pisk, P.; pisch, B.; pesc, pesk, pysc, pysk, pysg, P.; pyzgh, pysga, pusgar, B.

FISHES, *s.* Puscés, puskés, w.; pysgez, B; pysgaz, pysgyz, B.; puskas, c.w. 107.

A DRY SALT FISH. Scalpion, D.

SALT FISH. Pesc sâl, pesk zâl, P.

DECAYED FISH. Mun, D. Used for manure.

A PIECE OF FISH CUT OUT FOR BAIT. (See BAIT). Scethan, D.

THE REPORT OF THE APPROACH OF A BODY OF FISH. Scry, sory, D.

FISH-BLADDER, *s.* Cowl, B.V.

FISHERMAN, *s.* Piscadur, pysgadyr, w. ; pysgadar, retheruid, B.

FISH-DEALER, *s.* (Itinerant). Jowder, jowter, jowster, chowter, D.

FISHING, *s.* (A fishing). Pisgetta, pysgetta, B.

FISH OVERBOILED. Jowder, D.

FISH-HOOK, *s.* Hîg, hyg, îg, w.

FISH-POND, *s.* Hisclîn, pisclyn, B. ; pisc-liri, P.

FISHING-BOAT, *s.* Scâth rûz, w. *Lit.,* A net-boat.

FIST, *s.* Dorn, dhorn, durn, daorn, w. ; pud, D.

FIT, *adj.* (Suitable). Gioyw, w. ; habal, able, P. ; kyvadhas, B.

FITCHET or FITCHEW, *s.* Milgy, P.

FITNESS, *s.* Composter, w.

FIVE. Pemp, pymp, w. ; pym, R.D. 867.

FIVE HUNDRED. Pymp cans, N.

FLAG, *s.* (The plant). Elestren, w.

FLAG, *v.* (To grow weak). Gwedhra, w. ; guedhra, P.

FLAGGING, *part.* Guedrys. In the Cornish dialect a man who is feeling weak says he is *queedy.*

FLAGON or CAN, *s.* Kniskan, B. ; canna, w. ; kanna, P.

FLAIL, *s.* Fûst, fyst, vûst, vyst, w. ; vysk, B. The leather that joins the two pieces of wood in a flail is called the *keveran.*

FLAME, *s.* Flam, w.

FLAME, *v.* Tewé, tewye, P. ; tewy. tiwy, dewy, dywy, w.

FLANK, *s.* Tenewen, denewan, ternewan, tornewan, tyrnewan, w. ; ternehuan, P. ; tarneuhon, B.

FLAP, *s* (A valve; the flap of the breeches). Balloc, valloc, w.

FLAT, *adj.* Plat, w.

FLAT-IRON, *s.* Stile, D.

FLATTER, *v.* Fecyl, sôth, w.

FLATTERY, *s.* Fecylther, flous, w.

FLAX, *s.* Lîn, lyn, w.

FLEA, *s.* Hwanen, w. ; huanen, B. ; whannon, hwadnen, w. ; huadnan, P. ; huadnen, B. ; hyannen, P. *Pl.* Whidden. w.

FLED, *part.* Ombdenas, fyas, B.

FLEE, *v.* Fyé, effyé, gwevyé, chuyvyan, vyvyan, w. ; scusy, skusy, P. ; skesy, B. ; ponyé, P. ; ponya, B. ; poynyé, punnia, P. ; punnya, punnya ker, punnio, B.

FLEECE, *s.* Cnêu, w. ; kneu, P.

A FLEECE OF WOOL. Cnêu, glân, w. ; knêu, glân, P.

FLEET, *s.* Luu lestri, w. *Lit.* A host of ships.

FLESH, *s.* Cîg, kîg, w. ; kyg, B. ; cyc, kyc, w. ; kych, B. ; chîc, gîc, gyc, gyk, w. ; gyke, c.w. 352.

FLESH-BRUSH, *s.* Streil, B.

FLESH-COLOURED, *adj.* Cîgliu, w. ; kîgliu, B.

FLESH-FORK or SPIT, *s.* Cîgver. kîguer, w. ; kinguer, (?) B.

FLEXIBLE, *adj.* Hyblyth, w.

FLEXION, *s.* Plêg, plêk. plêth, w.

FLIGHT, *s.* Fo, w. ; ffo, B. ; huez, P.

A FAR OR HIGH FLIGHT. Pel huez, P.

FLING, *s.* Doul, dowle, P. See also FALL.

FLING, *v.* Stlapa, B.

FLING, *v.* (To fling down). Toula, dowla, doulla, P.

FLINTSTONE, *s.* Maen flent, w.

FLIT or SLIDE AWAY, *v.* Rees, P. The Cornish use the word *comressing* for flitting.

FLITCH of BACON. Anterhuch, w. *Lit.* Half a hog.

FLOAT, *v.* Nygé, (*g* soft), nija, w. ; nijah, P. ; nysé, nyidzha, w. ; nizhyea, P.

FLOCK, *s.* (Drove, herd). Tonec, tonek, w. ; praed, B.

A GREAT FLOCK. Busch brays, M. 3232. *Me a weyll busch brays a dûs,* I see a great flock of people, M. 3232.

FLOOD, *s.* Dial, dyal, dhyal, diel, dyel, w. ; deall, c.w. 2229 ; lîf, lyf, w. ; lyv. P. ; lywe, c.w. 2358. *Râg lyf brâs my a thoro,* for I will bring a great flood, O.M, 981.

FLOODS, *s.* Lyvyow, c.w. 2314 ; levyaw, c.w. 2164.

FLOOD, TORRENT, LANDFLOOD, *s.* Awan, w. ; auan, P. *A great flood,* Auan brâs.

FLOOR, *s.* Lêr, lear, leur, luer, lûr. w. ; luyr, M. 2263 ; lôr, w. *Ha cala lour war hy luer,* and straw enough on its floor, P.C. 680. *Y woys a resek then luyr,* his blood shall run to the floor, M. 2263.

FLOOR. *s.* Suler, B. ; soler, w. In mines a *soler* (still called *soler* or *saller*) is a floor or stage of boards for the men to stand on and roll away broken stuff in barrows. In a footway shaft the soller is the floor for the ladder to rest on, and so, ladder after ladder to the bottom of the mine, from one saller to another.

FLOUR, *s.* (Of corn). Blês, w.; blêz, brou. p.; blôt, w.; huigan, B.

FLOURISH, *v.* (Prosper, thrive). Sowené, sowynné, w.; sowyn, sowyny, P.

FLOURISH, *v.* (As does vegetation). Glasé, w.; glassa, P.

FLOURISHING, *adj.* (As in vegetation). Gwêr, w.; guer, P.; gear, gwirdh, w.; guirt, P.; guedrek, B.; ryth, w.

FLOUT, *v.* Canvas. P.; kanvas, B.; dyalé, dyalas, dhyallas, P.; gescy, w.; gesky, P.

FLOUT, *s.* Gês, geys, w.; flows, M. 190.

FLOW, *v.* Redek, resec, resek, w.; rees, divery, P.

FLOWED, *part.* Resas, B.

FLOWER, *s.* Blodon, bloden, bledhian, B.; bledzhan, bledzhian, w. *Pl.* Blegyow. w.

A LARGE BUNCH OF FLOWERS. Tosh, D.

FLOWING or FLUX, *s.* Frow, w. "Frou-frou."

FLOWING, *part.* Lôys, a loys, B.

FLOWING INTO. Rilan, B.

FLUKES, *s.* Iles, D. (The liver fluke, *Distoma hepatica.*)

FLUOR SPAR, *s.* Cam, cand, D.

FLUTE. *s.* Wibenoul, tolcorn. *Lit.* A horn with holes; pib, w.

A LITTLE FLUTE. Piban, peban, w.

FLUX, *s.* See FLOWING or FLUX.

FLUX, *s.* (The disease). Girr, an girr, w.; gyrr, girdin, B.

FLY, *s.* (Insect). Celionen, w.; kelionen, P.; kilionen, guiban, B.; guiban, huanen, huadnen, B. See also GNAT.

FLY, *v.* Nygé, nija, w.; nijah, niedga, P.; nyidzha, w.; nizhyea, P.; nysé, w.; nys, nygy, P. In these words the *g* is soft.

FLY, *v.* (To run away.) Ehed, P. *Fayn vy ehed,* let us fly, P.

FLY, *v.* (To fly over.) Trenygé (*g* soft), trenydzha, w.

FLY, *v.* (To fly to and fro). Trenydzha, B.

FOAL, *s.* Ebol, ebal, ebel, w. *Hagh ebel yn vn golmen,* and foal in a halter, P.C. 177.

FOG, *s.* Niul, w.; niull. B.

FOLD or PLAIT, *s.* Plêg, plêk, plêth, blêk, w.

FOLD, *v.* Plyé, P.; pleggya, B.

FOLD, *s.* (For cattle). Boudi, w.; boudzhi, P.

FOLK, *s.* Tûz, tues, w.; dûs, M. 3232; duz. B.; tis, w.; tiz, this, P.; diz, w.; têz, P.; ties, tees, w.; dees, dêz, P.

FOLLOW, *v.* Holyé, w.; holya, P.; hyller, B.; rysyé, P. sewyé, sewé, sywé, w.; sewya, sewsya, P.

FOLLOWED, *part.* Hollyas. B.

FOLLOW YE, Holliou, B.

FOLLOW THOU. Sew, 2 pers. s. imp. of *sewyé,* to follow, w.

FOLLOW, *v.* (To follow each other). Ymsywé, w.

FOLLY, *s.* Folneth, w.; foloneth, P.; gocyneth, gokyneth, w.; wokyneth, P.; wocyneth, w. *Rúm fey múr a wokyneth,* by my faith, a great folly, o M. 473; mescatter, muscochneth, w.; muscoghneth, P.C. 1283; mustoghneth, yowynkés, yowynketh, P.; diskians, B.

FOMENTATION, *s.* Tairnant, w.

FOOD, *s.* Bôs, w. *Rágh yma bôs parusys,* for there is food prepared. P.C. 458; bôz, P.; boos, boys. bûs, bûz, buit, w; buyd, B.; bygyens, vygyens, w. *The vygyens dên war an beys,* for food of man on the earth, o.M. 131; vyguons, P.; breuha, B.; croust, o.M. 1901. (This word, *croust,* is still in use for a luncheon or meal.) *Kemerés croust hag evé,* to take food and drink, o.M. 1901; sant, w.; saut, B.

POOR FOOD. Labscou, D.

FOOL, *s.* Côk, cowga, P.; skogan, B; miskoggan, P; miscoggan, w.; foyl, M. 925; fôl, P. *Omma the foyl,* here thou fool, M. 925, zape. zapey, zawker, gommock, duffan. goky, gaupus, dooda, bucca, cobba, pattic, droojy. D.

FOOLS, *s.* Gothoam, P.; gothoan, B; gockyés, P.C. 1149.

FOOLISH, *adj.* Côc, P.; côk, cuic, w.; cooge, cowg, cowga, P.; gocy, goky, gokky, guccy, w.; gucky, c w. 1008; woky, w.; wokky, P.C. 1290; ucky, descians, discient, diskient, w.; diskréf, B.; fôl (*tellyon,* a plural of *fôl*), muscoc, mescat, w.; meskat, B.; trafyl, P.; bâd, w.

FOOLISHNESS, *s.* See FOLLY.

FOOLISH PEOPLE. Gockorion, B.

FOOT, *s.* (Of the body). Trûs, truz, w.; tros, trous, N.; druz, P.; droose. c.w. 20; trôs, trois, troys, truit. w.; troat, B; truyd, P. *Pl.* Treys, treis, treiz. dreys, trys, tryys, w.; tryes, o.M. 873; thrys, troys, P.; trôs, o.M. 262.

THEIR FEET. Aga threys, N.

ON FOOT. A druz, w.

FOOT or PAW, *s.* Paw, baw, w.

FOOT-BRIDGE, *s.* Clam, D.

FOOT-PATH, *s.* Trulerch, w.

FOOT, *s.* (In measure). Tresheys troisheys, troishys, w.

FOOT-SOLDIER, *s.* Squerryon, (squerryou ?), P.

FOOT-STEP, *s.* Ol treys, w.; ool, ol, P.

FOOTSTEPS, *s.* Olow threys, o.M. 760; goleow oleow, owleow, goly, P.

FOOTSTOOL, *s.* Skaval droasa, P.; skavall droose, c.w. 20; tut, D.

FOOT-WRAPPER, *s.* (Pedula, *Lat.*) Paugen, B.

FOR. A, w.; dy, P.; dre, N. *Hy an grúk dre kerensé,* she did it for love, P.C. 549; êr, orth, ord, worth, w; pur, P.; zen, B.; râg, rhâg, P.; râc, râk, w. *Rák eun kerengé,* for real love, P.C. 483. *Teweugh rák méth,* silence, for shame, R.D. 1495.

FORASMUCH. Hane, P.

FOR THE SAKE OF. Awôs, auoz, P.; er, w.

FOR A TIME. Benytha, P.

FOR WHAT. Perâg. prâg, porâg, w.
FOR or TO YOU Deuch, dych, w.

FORBEAR, *v* Perthegés, porthy, perthy, prethy, w.; foilligiu, koilgim, kyrtaz, spiena, P.

FORBEAR. Hoase. *Carew.* Perhaps the same as *hist,* hush.

FORBID, *v.* Defen, dhefen, dyfan, dyfen, dyffen, w.; tyffen, thefan, P.; defenny, w.

FORBIDDEN, *part.* Dyfynnys, tyffen, w.

FORBIDDING, A FORBIDDING, *s.* Defen, deffan, dyfen, defennad, w.

FORCE, *v.* Aderbyny, P.

FORCE, *s.* Nell, nel, nerth, w.; nerh, nerg, B.; verth, harth, P.; fyt, fêth, B.; creys, crys, greys, grys, mestry, meystry, maystry, w. *Ha herthyé gans nerth yn ban,* and thrust it with force upwards, P.C. 3011.

FORCED ALONG. Dregas, tregid, B.

FORD, *s.* Rîd, w.; ryd, rhyd, rêd, basdhour, P.

FORE-CASTLE, *s.* Flurrag, w.

FORE-DOOR, *s.* Darras râg, w.

FOREIGN, *adj.* Tremôr, *i.e.,* beyond sea, w.; voren, voran, P.

FOREIGNER, *s.* Pergrin, pergirin, B.

FOREFATHER, *s.* Rhagdas, w.; rhagadaz, P.; wad, w.; hendas, hengyke, P.

FOREFATHERS. *s.* Ragdazu, rhagdazu, B.; hendasou, P.; wadow, w. *The'n tyr a th'y the wadow,* to the land where thy forefathers went, O.M. 1871.

FORFEITURE, *s.* Spâl, B. *Spalled,* for fined, is still in use.

FOREHEAD, *s.* Côdna-tâl, kôdna tâl, tâl, w.; thale, c w. 1617; tale, c.w. 1628; dale, c.w. 1373. *Ly-skys of a'n kyl the'n tâl,* I am burned from the neck to the forehead, O.M. 1781.

FOREMOST, *adj.* and *s* Ban, van, w.; vadn, vadna, P. In washing (called by tinners *vanning*) a sample of tin ore on a shovel, a dexterous movement causes the tin ore to be near the foremost end of the shovel, and the refuse to be near the base or broad end. The ore so separated is called by miners the *van.*

FORESHEW, *v.* Arwyddocan, B.

FOREST or WOOD, *s.* Coed, coet, w.; coat, P.; coit, w.; koit, B.; coid, koid. coyd, cuit, cuid, cûs, cûz, w.; kûz, P.; cooz, côs, coys, cotelle, lanherch, w.

FORE TEETH, *s.* Dêns râg, P.

FORWARDS. A râg. *A râg ha denewen,* forwards and sideways, O.M. 2063.

FORGE, *s.* Fôk, P.C. 2717. *Ny dryk gryghonen yn fôk,* there remains not a spark in the forge, P.C. 2717,

FORGET, *v* Ancevy, ankevy, w. *Ny vanna y ankevy,* I will not forget him, M. 4024.

FORGOTTEN, *part.* Ancevys, ankevys, w.

FORGETFULNESS, *s.* Angov, B.

FORGIVE, *v.* Andyllas, (a'n dyllas) w.; andylly, P.; ava, (a mutation of gava); gafé, givia, gava, w.; gevé, B.; gavas, gafas, prunny, P.; gafa, N.

I FORGIVE. Gafsé, P.

HE FORGAVE. Avas. A mutation of *gavas,* w.

FORGIVEN, *part.* Gevys, gefys, givys, w.; geffys, P.; prunnys, B.

TO FORGIVE, TO REMIT, *v.* Wâs. *Ha Dew tho-thef a was,* and God to him did remit, P.

FORGIVENESS, *s.* Dewellens, dewhyllyans, dew-yllyens, w.; dehilians, B; gevyans, gyvyans, gef-yans, gyfyans, w.; givians, P.; gevyons, B. See also PARDON.

FORK, *s.* Fôrh, vôrh, w. *An vôrh,* the fork.

A THREE PRONGED FORK. Vôrh trivôrh.

A SILVER FORK. Fôrh arhans, P.

FORLORN, *s.* (A forlorn, a lost person). Collet, B.

FORM, *s.* (Seat). Benk, P.

FORM, *s.* (Shape). Composter, w. *Heb composter,* without form; furf, fu, fuw, w. *Ny allaf guelas an fu,* I cannot see the form, R.D. 741; gwêdh, gweydh, weydh, wèth, w.; lyu, lyv, P.C. 1240; roath, w.

FORM, *s.* (Appearance). Semlant. w.

FORM, *s.* (Semblance or manner). Dèl, w. *Yn dêl-ma,* in that manner, (torm).

FORM, *v.* Formyé, w.

FORMED, *part.* Formyys, B.

FORMER, *s.* (A former). Formyas, formyer, w.

FORMER, *adj.* Kyns. *Guel ys kyns y threheuel,* raise it better than the former, P.C. 1762.

FORMERLY, *adv.* Cens, kens, w.; kenz, kins, P.; cyns, kyns, w.; kynz, P.; gens, hens, w.

FORSAKE, *v.* Descrirya, w.; scryrya. *Prâg thysta ve scryryas,* why hast thou forsaken me? P. gara, garera, esgara, gasé, w.; gesy, gyssy, P.

FORSOOTH! Aketha, D.

FORSWEAR, *v.* Naché, nacha, naha, nahé, w.; nag-hé, nagha, P.

FORT, *s.* Tour, tûr, w.; kastal, kestell, P.; castel, w.; bre, guâl, P. *Guâl hèn.* an old fort.

FORTH. Yn râg, N. *Dûs yn râg,* come forth, O.M. 2403. See FORWARD.

FORTHWITH. Aredy, eredy, yredy, scôn, w.; skân, P. *The yet parathys in scôn*, to the gate of Paradise forthwith, o.m. 691; toythda, p.c. 2. *Pyseygh toythda ôl kês-colon*, pray forthwith, all with one heart, p.c. 2; adhysempyz, dhy sempys, the sempys, p.; fast, b.; dyson, m. 818. *Bethyns dyson*, let it be forthwith, m. 818.

FORTIFIED PLACE. Caer, w.; kaer, p.; câr, dîn, tîn, w. See FORTRESS for other forms.

FORTITUDE, *s.* Frêth, w.

FORTRESS, *s.* Castel, w.; kastal, kestell, p.; kastelh, b.; dîn, tîn, dinas, dinaz, w.; brenniat, p.; brennyat, b; caer, câr, w.; kaer, p.

FORTY. Dugans, w.; duganz, p.; dowgans, b.; dewugens, dewugens, w.; deu ugens, deu hugens, N.; dewigans, w.; deuiggans, b. Literally, all these words mean two twenties.

FORTY-SIX. Dew ugens ha whe, N. *Lit.* Two twenties and six.

FORWARD, *v.* Finney, w.

FORWARD. Arâg, w.; war râg, b.; yn râg, N. *Deugh yn râg ketep onan*, come forward every one, o.m. 2683.

FORWARD, CONCEITED, *adj* Preedy, D.

FOSTERAGE, NURTURE, *s.* Meidrin, meithrin, w.

FOSTER-FATHER, *s.* Tatvat, tadvath, w.

FOSTER-MOTHER, *s.* Mamaid, mammaith, w.

FOSTER-SON, *s.* Mâb meidrin, w.; mâb meithrin, b.

FOSS, *s.* Clêdh, klêdh, w.; clawd, cleuth, b.

FOUL, *v.* (To foul, to bewray). Sautra, b.

FOUL, *adj.* (Dirty). Casa, gasa, gasow, cawys, w.; cough, caugh, gwaw, p.; casalek, gassic, geagle, plosec, plosek, w.; gagle, p.; ploos, c.w. 1116; lowse, c.w. 158. *Gwase lowse*, foul fellow, c.w. 158; uthek, p.; hethek, m. 1853. *Claff anhethek*, a foul leper, m. 1853.

FOUL, *adj.* (Odious). Tebel, w.; tebal, p.; debel, hager, w.; hagar, p.

MORE OR MOST FOUL. Hacré, hacra, w.

FOUL ACT, OR DEED. Matoberur, p.

FOUL-MOUTHED, *adj.* Drôgdavasec. w.; drôkdavazek, b.

FOUL OFFENDER. Casadow, p.

FOUL WORK. Gwaw obar, p.

FOULNESS, *s.* Plosethés, m. 3527. *Falge plosethés crustunyon*, false foulness of Christians, m. 3527.

FOUND, *part. of to find.* Cevys, kevys, cefys, kefys, ceffys, keffys, w.; cafos, b.; gafus, p.; havas, trouviaz, b.

I FOUND. Cefés, 1 pers. s. preter. of *cafos.* In construction, *gefés*, w.

IS FOUND. Cefer, eefer. kefyr, w.

IT IS FOUND. Gefyr. A mutation of cephyr, w.

HE FOUND. Cafas, gafas, gaffas, cevé, gevé, gavas. *Gavas* is a mutation of *cavas*, or *cafas*, 3 pers. s. pret. of *cafos*, to find. *Gevé* is a mutation of *cevé*, 3 pers. s. imp. of *cafus*, w.

I HAVE FOUND. Gefés. A mutation of *cefes*, 1 pers. s. pret. of *cafos*, to find, w.

THEY HAVE FOUND. Cafsons, 3 pers. pl. pret. of *cafos*, to find, w.

FOUND, *v.* (To cause, to lay a foundation). Scylé, w.

FOUNDATION, *s.* (The base, the groundwork). Sêl, seil, seyl, w.; sail, b.; scyle, sol, w.

FOUNDATION STONE. An mean lêr, w. *Lit.* The ground-floor stone.

FOUNDATION or BASE, *s.* Goden, w.

FOUNTAIN, *s.* Fenten, fynten, funten, w.; fenton, venton, p. *Kergh, a'n fenton thy'm dour clêr*, fetch clear water for me from the fountain, p.c. 650; cornant, nant, b.

FOUR. Peswâr, w.; peswere, p.; pedâr, w.; peder pedyr, pider, pesuar, padzhar, p.

FOURTH. Pesweré, w.; peswera, c.w. 100; paswera, pysweré, w.; peswarra, pazuera, padzhuera, p.; padzhwera, w.

FOURTH, *s.* (A fourth or quarter). Kuartan, p.

FOURTEEN. Peswardhec, paswardhac, pazwardhak, w.; pazuardhak, b.; puzwarthack, (peswarthek,) N.

FOURTEENTH. Paswar dêgvas, padzhuardzak, p.

FOWL, *s.* Edhen. For other forms, see BIRD, BIRDS.

A FOWL'S PATH OR WAY. Voryer, D. *Lit.* Hens' path.

FOWLER, *s.* Edhanor, w.; edhenor, b.; idné, w.

FOWLS, *s.* (Birds in general). Lawan, w. *Why drôg lawan*, ye wicked fowls, c.w. 124.

FOWLS' PATH or WAY, *s.* Vôryêr. From *vór*, a way, and *yêr*, hens, D.

FOX, *s.* Lowern, lowarn, luarn, w.; luern, losteig, lostêg, lostec, lostek, b.; lorn, louern, p. *Lit.* Lostek means, fair tail.

A FOX BITCH. Lowernés, w.; lowernez, p.

FRAGMENT, *s.* Dârn, drâl, tâm, temmig, w.; temig, demig, b.; brewyonen, w.; brouian, b.

A FRAGMENT OF THREAD, COTTON, &c. Tifflen, tifle, D.

FRAGMENTS, *s.* Tymmyn, dymmyn, w. *Pls.* of tâm, and dym.

FRAIL. Lous, p. (?)

FRAIL, *s.* (Rush bag or basket). Kiguer, p.

FRAME, *v,* (To frame, to make). Wathyl, wythyl, p.

FRAME, *s.* (For a fisherman's line). Cader, cantor, D.

FRANCE, *s.* Frinc, Vrinc, w. ; Frink, Vrink, P.

FRANKINCENSE, *s.* Encois, inkois, w. (entois) ?

FRANTIC, *adj.* Conerioc, w. ; koneriok, B. ; con-erive, P. ; folterguscé, w. ; foltreguské, folt guské, P. ; guské, B.

FRATERNITY, *s.* Brudereth, w. ; brawdoliath, B.

FRAUD, *s.* Fallad, fallas, fraus, w. ; gouegneth, B. ; tull, w. ; tulle, B. ; teul, toul, towl, w.

FRAY, *s.* (Breach of the peace). Blondewytt, D.

FRECKLE, *s.* Taish, w.

FREE, *s.* (At liberty). Frank, franc, quyth, w.

FREE FROM DIFFICULTY, EASY. Hêdh, hogul, w.

FREE, *v.* (To get free). Scusy, skusy, w; skesy, P. ;

FREEDOM *s.* Wary, w.

FREEZE, *v.* Rewy, w.

FRENCH, *adj.* Frenc, w. *Cynyphan Frenc,* a French nut, (walnut).

FRENCH, *adj.* (Gaulish). Galec, w.

FRENCH LANGUAGE. Frincac, Vrincac, w. ; Vrinkak, P.

FRENCHMAN, *s.* Frinc, w.

FREQUENT, *v.* (To traverse, to frequent a place). Tremenés, N.

FREQUENT, *adj.* (Many, much). Lues, leas, lias, w. ; liaz, P.

FREQUENT, *adj.* (Often, many times). Menouch, w. ; menough, O.M. 1850 ; minouch, w. *Ov gueres menough thethe,* my frequent help to them, O.M. 1850 ; venouch, a mutation of *menouch,* w.

FREQUENT, *adj.* Torrog, P. (?) This word also means big-bellied.

FREQUENTLY, *adv.* (Often, commonly). Menouch, minouch, venouch, w.

FRESH, *adj.* (Late, recent, new). Newedh, newydh, nowydh, w. ; noweth, nowth, nouedzha. pals, P. *Goleou pals,* fresh marks, or stripes.

FRESH, *adj.* Er, P. Williams says *er* means " juicy, full of sap, green, raw."

FRET, *v.* (To chafe). Rhittia, rhyttia, B.

FRIDAY, *s.* De gwenar, w. ; dîdh guener, B. ; de guenar. P. ; dugwener, M. i20 ; guener, M. 4304. *An kyn*⸍*a guener.* the first Friday, M. 4304.

FRIEND, *s.* Câr, w. ; kâr, B. ; chêt, P.C. 3050 ; cooth, P. ; cothman, gothman, hothman, smât, w. ; sôs, B. ; mayn, w. ; meyn, P. *Na ge*⸍*gho alemma chêt,* that he may not carry a friend hence, P.C. 3050. *Ha the cothmên me a véth,* and thy friend I will be, M. 891. *Thotho ef nyn sôs cothman,* thou art not a friend to him, P.C. 2431. *Ha eua ha lyes smât,* and Eve and many a friend, P.C. 3036. *Ow hothman,* my friend, w.

FRIENDS, *s.* Cardowyon, w. ; kardouion, cardenion, P. (? carde*u*ion); cothmans, M. 387 ; mayny, w. ; meyLy, P.

FRIEND, *s.* (A near friend). Ogaz, ogas, oges, ogos, agos, P.

FRIENDSHIP, *s.* Carensé, cerensé, carengé, carenga, garensa, harenga, w. ; karens, yenes, P. See also LOVE.

FRIGHT, *s.* Tarofan, tarosfan, tarnytuan, uth, euth, w.

FRIGHTENED, *part.* Ownakés, P.

FRIGHTFUL, *adj.* Uthec, uthek, uthyc, uthyk, hu-thyc, huthyk, w. ; uter, B.

FRIGHTFULNESS, *s.* Uthecter, w. ; uthekter, N.

FRIGID, *adj.* Jên, B. ; jein, yên, P. ; oerni, oerfel, oerder, oich, oir, B.

FRIGIDITY, *s.* Jender, w. See COLD.

FRINGE, *s.* (As of a curtain, &c). Pillen, willen, B.

FRISK ABOUT. *v.* Skeese, skeyze, skeyce, scouse, D. From *skesy,* to escape.

FRITTER, *s.* (Pancake). Krampothan, P. ; crampod-han, crampedhan, crampessan, w.

FRIVOLITY, *s.* Ufereth. evereth, w.

FRIVOLOUSNESS, *s.* Ufereth, evereth, w.

FROG, *s.* (The yellow and spotted toad). Cuilken, kuilken, cuilcen, P. ; cwilcen, kwilken, w. ; quilkin, quilkey, wilkin, wilkey, D. ; guilkin, guilskin, guils-cin, gwilscin, gwilskin, guilschin, w ; kranag, khranag melyn, kronek melyn, cronek, croinec, croinok, w. ; cronag, cranag, cronec, wronick, wro-nak, wranak, wraneck, P.

THE YOUNG OF THE FROG, THE TADPOLE. Pedn diu. *Lit.* Black head.

FROLICKSOME, *adj.* Lowen, louen, lawen, B. ; leu-nek, leunik, P. ; leuenik, louenak, lauenik, lowenic, lawenic, lewenic, lawennek, B.

FROM. A, w. *A 'y lé,* from its place, N. ; y, i, P. ; dor, B. ; orth, w. ; worthe, uorh, vet, B. *Golou vet an tuyldar,* light from the darkness; dort, dorte, dhort. durt, B ; dhart, thort, thurt, F. ; ador. adhort, w ; adhart, P. *Auhart au dre,* from the town, P. ; adheworth, w. ; athyworth, N. ; deworth, dheworth, dyworth, w. ; dywort, B. ; thyworth, theworth, N. ; râg, rhâg, râc, râk, w. *Guthys râk an bylen,* pre-served from the evil one, P.C. 41 ; kês, P. ; de, dhe, dy, w. In Cornish, *de, dhe, dy,* are only compounded with *worth,* as *dyworth,* &c.

FROM ABOVE. A wartha, w.

FROM, AWAY. Omelys, P.

FROM BY. Adheworth, adhort, w.

FROM HENCE. A lebma, alemma, w.

FROM THAT PLACE. Alena, w.

(FROM ALL PLACES.) Dro, P.

FROM, OUT OF. Mês, N. *Mar seuyh mês a dre*, if you go from home, O.M. 2185.

FROM THEE. Ahanas, hanys, W.

FRONT, IN FRONT. Râg, rhâg, râc, râk, arâg, a râg, W. *War an brest a râg*, on the breast in front, O M. 2717.

FRONT, *s.* (The front). Tâl, thâl, W.

FRONTIER, *s.* Urrian, yrian, P.

FROST, *s.* Iey, W.; ja, jef, B.; glihi, clihi, rew, reu, W.; reaw, C.W. 1668; reau, riou, reui, rhewi, B.

FROTH, *s.* Spoum, W.; spoom, D.

FROTHY, *adj.* (Trifling). Crothac, crothak, W; cro-thacke, P.

FROWARD, *adj.* Drews, drês, três, W.

FROZEN, *part.* Rewys, M. 3057.

FRUGAL, *adj.* Henbidiat, henbidhiat, B.

FRUIT, *s.* (Of any kind, result). Frêch, frût, fruit, W.; ffyrwyth, B.

FRUITS, *s.* (Especially apples). Lavalow, W. *Ha'n gweedh toen lavalow warler e cunda*, and the trees yielding fruit after their kind, M.C. p. 93.

FRUITFUL, *adj.* Voeth, veath, P.

FRUITFULNESS, *s.* Paltowat, P.

FRUMP, *s.* Frig, squeez, D.

FRY, *v.* Fria, W.; frya, B.

FRYING-PAN, *s.* Padelh, B; padel hoern, W.; padel hoarn (*Lit.* an iron pan), P.; letshar, B.; oilet, W. *Oilet* is also a name for a gridiron.

FUEL, *s.* Cinnis, kinnis, cunys, kunys, W.; kynnés, C. *Small or broken fuel.* Brûz, browse. This is still called in Cornwall, *browse* and *brees*, or *breez*.

FUGITIVE, A FUGITIVE, *s.* Fadic, W.

FULL, *adj.* Abal, W. *Arluth merci abal*, Lord of mercy full, P; auf, P. *Auf vu*, a full view, P.; cowal, gowal, W.; coual, coule, P.; coul, W. *Ty a fydh cowal anken*, thou shalt have full pain, P.C. 2530; leun, luen, lên, laun, W.; lwn, B.; leana, W. *Y box rych leun a yly*, her box rich full of salve, M.C. 35. *Ha Christ yn crês luen a ras*, and Christ in the middle, full of grace, M.C. 186; playn, W; playne, P. *Pan deffa an termyn playn*, when the full time shall come, C.W. 138; trôm, P. *Trôm dyal*, a full flood, P.

FULLER or TUCKER, *s.* Tricciar, trikkiar, trycciar, W.; trykkiar, trikkin, B.

FULFIL, *v.* Collenwel, W.; konlenuel, B.; cowlenwel, coullenwel, covlenwel, kovlenuel, P.; golenwel, gow-lenwel, lenwel, W.; leana, P.

FULFILMENT, *s.* (As of a promise). Coweras, W.

FULLY, *adv.* (Entirely, completely). Cowal, coual, coul, coule, P.; cowel, M. 1087; gowal, W. *Coul dreheuel ôl the chy*, fully build all thy house, O.M. 2340.

Cowel ny a weyl, fully we shall see, M. 1087; whet, wheth, P.

FULNESS, *s.* Lanwés, W. *Lanwés leyth ha mel kefrys*, fulness of milk and honey also, O.M. 1430.

FUME, SMOKE, *s.* Môc, môk, W.; môg, P.

FUN, *s.* Gês, B. *Yn gês*, in fun. See JEST.

FUNDAMENT, *s.* (*Anus, Lat.*) Gwèn, W.

FUNERAL, *s.* Arwhyl, P.; ancledhyas, anclydhyas, W.; anclythyas, P.

FUR, *s.* Pluff, pelf, pilf, D.

FUR-COAT, *s.* Pellisther, W.; pellist-ker, pellistgur, pengughrek, pengughret, P.; penguchgrec, W.

FURIOUS, *adj.* Muscoc, mescat, W.; meskat, B.

FURNACE, *s.* Fôc, fôk, fôg, forn, vorn, per, W.; tern, B.

FURNITURE, *s.* (Household goods). Gwadhel, gut-hel, W.; pêth-tshyi, B.

FURROW, *s.* Pollan-troillia, B.; trone, droke, vore, D.

FURTHER, *adj.* Kén, O M. 794. *May callaf guelês kên ta*, that I may see further good, O.M. 794.

FURTHER, *adv.* Pellach, pella, fella, velha, W. *Na fella*, or *na vella*, no further.

FURTHEST, *adj.* See FARTHEST.

FURTHERMORE, *adv.* Hagenzol, W.

FURTHERMOST, *adj.* Vôn. *Y vôn ynys*, the further-most island, B.

FURY, A SHE-DEVIL, *s.* Diowlés, dzhowlés, W.; dzhonlés, P.

FURZE, *s.* (Gorse). Eithin, ythen, W.; ithen, B. A plural aggregate.

A SINGLE PLANT OF FURZE. Eithinen, eithi-nan, ethynen, W.

A FURZE-BUSH. Bagas eithin, W.; bagaz eithin, P.

FURZE DUST. (The broken fuel). Bruss, B.; bruz, B.V. The name is still in use as *browse* or *brees*.

FUSS, *s.* (Row, uproar). Pôr, porr, towse, goss, garm, strôth, strôther, D.

G.

" This letter is both primary and secondary in the six Celtic dialects.

Its sound is the same as in the English words, *gain*, *get*, *give*, go. (It is sometimes soft, F.W.P.J.)

When radical or primary its commutation is formed in Cornish by omitting it altogether, as *gwrêc*, a wife; *an wrêc*, the wife; *gallos*, power; *y allos*, his power.

When however *g* was followed by *o* or *u*, then *w* was prefixed, as *goloc*, sight; *an woloc*, the sight; *gûl*, *dho wûl*, to make.

In certain cases, as after *y*, the Cornish after omitting the *g* aspirates the succeeding vowel :—thus *gallouch, why a allouch*, ye will be able ; *may hallouch*, that ye may be able.

The Cornish, as in Armoric, also changes *g* into *c*, as *gwerthé*, to sell ; *ow cwerthé*, selling. *Grugé mar crugé*, if I do.

When secondary in Cornish and the other dialects *g* is a mutation of *c*, as *cadar*, a chair ; *y gadar*, his chair, w." *Lex. Corn. Brit.*

GAB or **CHATTER**, *s.* Wob, D. ; clap, w.

GABLE, *s.* Punnion, punken, D.

GADFLY, *s.* Swap, D. See also **WASP**.

GADS, *s.* (Small iron wedges used by miners). Gwlezow, w.

GADABOUT, *s.* Lootal, D.

GADUS MINUTUS, *s.* (Fish). Power, D.

GAIN, *v.* Gwaynia, w. ; guaynia, B. ; guainia, P. ; dendely, M. 3076.

GAIN, *s.* Gwayn, w. ; guayn, D. ; guaian, P.

GAIN, *s.* (Advantage). Prow, w. *Annethe ty ny fyth prow*, no gain shall be to thee from them, P.C. 2615.

GAINING, *s.* (A winning, an earning). Vangin, D.

GALE, *s.* Whêth, hwêth, w.

GALL, *s.* (The bile). Bistel, bestel, w. ; bestl, P. ; bystel, bystyl, bestyl, besl, bezl, w. *Bystel eysel kymyskys*, gall and hyssop mixed, P.C. 2979.

GALL, *s.* (As from pressure or friction). Cab-a-rouse, or simply *cab*, D.

GALLERY, *s.* Soler, w.

GALLOWS, *s.* Crôk, M. 1277.

GAMESOME, *adj.* Anludd, drythyll, w. See also **FROLICKSOME**.

GANDER, *s.* Culliag, w. ; godho, kulliag-godho, kuilliog-godho, chelioc-ghod, P. ; celiog-gûydh, celioc-guit, w. ; chelioc-guit, B. ; keliokuydh, P.

GAP, *s.* Rigol, B.

A WATTLED HEDGE GAP. Frith, D.

GARDEN, *s.* Dzharn, w. ; dzarn, B. ; erber, garth, lowarth, luworth, luar, w.

GARDENER, *s.* Guisur. *Pl.* Guyshysy, P.

GARFISH, *s.* Girac, w. ; girak, P. It is still called a *gerrick*.

GARLAND, *s.* Garlont. *An arlant*, the garland, w. ; snôd, B.

GARLIC, *s.* Eynog, kining eyinoc, kenineuynoc, B. ; cenin ewinoc, w. ; kenin eynoc, B.

GARMENT, *s.* (A garment). Gwisc, guisc, w. ; guisk, guesk, P. ; gwesc, w. ; guest, B. ; gweth, w. ; gueth, P. ; queth, M. 1967 ; cweth, w. ; pous, bous, R.D.

1861. *Honna yv y bous nessa*, that is his nearest garment, R.D. 1861.

AN UPPER GARMENT. Penguch, w.

GARRET, *s.* Tallic, tallick, tallack, tallock, P. *Tallet* is used for stable-loft, D.

GARRISON, *s.* Guarth, B.

GARTER, *s.* Carget, w. ; gargat, B. *Pl.* Gargettou, gurgettan, B.

GATE, *s.* Yet, w.

THE BAR OF A GATE. Shivver, D.

GATE, ENTRANCE, *s.* Porth, yet, w.

GATES, DOORS, *s.* Jannues, P. See **DOOR**.

GATHER, *v.* Cuntel, P. ; cuntell, w. ; kyntel, P. ; kyntl, B. ; guntel, P. *Me a guntell dreyn ha spern*, I will gather briars and thorns, w. ; porogga, B.

TO GATHER SHELL-FISH, *v.* Trig, D.

GATHER, TO GATHER TOGETHER, *v.* Cuntell, w. ; dierbin, dierbyn, dyerbyn, P.

GATHERED, *part.* Cuntullys, cuntlé, B. ; kontlez, P.

GATHERING, *s.* (A gathering together). Cuntell, contel, cuntellet, cuntellyans, contellyans, w. ; cuntillyans, P.

GAULISH, FRENCH, *adj.* Galec, w.

GAVE. Dôk, thoke, thuek, a rose, B. See **GIVE**.

I GAVE. Rês, 1 pers. s. pret. of *rei*, to give. Rys, 1 pers. s. pret. of *rei* or *ry*. w.

THOU GAVEST. Ressys, ryssys, russys, w. ; russé, P. ; 2 pers. s. pret. of *rei* or *ry*, to give.

HE GAVE. Rôs, 3 pers. s. pret. of *rey* or *ry*, w.

THEY GAVE. Rosons, 3 pers. pl. pret. of *rei* or *ry*, w.

GAVE GIFTS TO THEE. Rodothyé, B.

GAVE NOTICE. Wornyas, B.

GEESE, *s.* Gôdhow, godho, w.

GENERAL, A GENERAL, *s.* Dûg, B ; hebrenchiat luir, P.

GENERATION, A GENERATION, *s.* Denethyans, denythyans, kinedyl, kinedhel, cinedel, kinethel, w. ; henath, heeneth, B.

GENEROUS, *adj.* Hail, w.

GENTILITY, *s.* Pednzhivikianz, P.

GENTLE, *adj.* (Easy). Hêkh, hogul, w. ; aisé, P.

GENTLE, *adj.* (Tame). Dôf, dôv, dô, w.

GENTLE, *adj.* (Mild, kind). Hynwys, triwardhec, w. ; triaudhek, P. ; triuadhek, B. ; whâr, wâr, w. *Cryst mês an bêth clêr ha wâr*, Christ out of the tomb bright and gentle, P.C. 3242.

GENTLE BREEZE. Auheo, P.

GENTLEMAN, *s.* Pendzhivig. *Pl.* Pendzhivigion, B.

GENTLEMAN'S SEAT. Trê, P.

GENTLENESS, *s.* Medhalder, medalder, w.

GENTLY, *adv.* Yn whâr. w.; ufel (*vfel*), M. 3776. *Hâg vfel am comondyas,* and gently bade me, M. 3776; clour, M. 4332. *The kerhés thymo pûr clour,* to fetch me very gently, M. 4332.

GET, *v.* (Obtain). Cael, cafos, cafus, cafés, cafel, w.; cawas, c.w. 959 ; kouaz, B.; gafus, gafos, gavel, w.; gaval, P.; gaws, B.; geso, P.

GET or EARN, *v.* Dendle, B. *Dendle peth,* to earn riches, B.; dendlé, dyndyly, w.

GET YE GONE   Eugh, eus, P.

GHOST, *s.* Speris, spyrys, spiriz, w.; sprite, spyr, B.

GIANT, *s.* Encinedel, w.; en kinhedhel, B.; enehinethel, escer, esker, w.; gheon, wrath. B.

A GREAT GIANT. Esker brâs, w.

GIBBET, *s.* Croueg, B. See GALLOWS.

GIBLETS, *s.* Kipes, D.

GIFT, *s.* Ro, (*Pl.* Roow, rohow,) w.; roth, P.; pencion, B.; rew, c.w. 2145.

GIGANTIC, *adj.* Caur, w.

GILDED, *part.* Gorovrys, M. 3396.

GILL, *s.* Brink, D.

GILLS, *s.* Dewen. dhewen, dywen, w.

GIMLET, *s.* Tardar, B.

GIN, *s.* (The trap). Maglen, w.

GIRD, *v.* (Bind, wring). Strothé. w.; strothy, P.

GIRDLE. *s.* Grugis, grigis, grygis, grigiz, w.; grygys, gwregus, grug, guris, guriz. gouris, B.; guri, gurey, P.; cledif, B.; giss, geist, D.

GIRL, *s* Moren, morion. w.; morain P.; meroin, B.; mowes, N.; mergh, c.w. 299; voran. R.D. 1044. *An voran re gusys gow,* the girl has told a lie, R.D. 1044.

GIRLS, *s.* Virhas, c.w. 1985.

GIVE, *v.* Ro, roy. P.; roi, rei, rhei. rey, ry, w.; re, r.; rella, B.; rollé, rollo, rogolly, whom, whon, P.; grontyé, w.

I GIVE. Rof, N.

I WILL GIVE. *Me a re,* P.; rôf, roof, w.; 1 pers. *s.* fut. of *rei* or *ry,* to give.

THOU GIVEST or WILT GIVE. Rêth, reith, reyth, 2 pers. s. fut. of *rey* or *rei,* give, w.

HE GIVES. Re, ree, rea, N.

HE WILL GIVE. Ra, re, 3 pers. s. fut. of *rey,* to give, w. This is also expressed by *wront,* a mutatation of *gront,* 3 pers. s. fut. of *gronté, id. qd. grontyé,* to give or grant, w.

WE WILL GIVE. Rên, 1 pers. pl. fut. of *rei,* to give, w.

I GAVE. Res, rys, N.

THOU GAVEST. Ryssys, M.

HE GAVE. Ros, N.

THEY GAVE. Rosons, N.

I WOULD GIVE. Rên, 1 pers. s. subj. of *rei,* to give, w.

HE WOULD GIVE. Rollo, rollé, 3 pers. pl. subj. of *rei,* or *ry,* to give, w.

THEY WOULD GIVE   Rollons, 3 pers. pl. subj. of *rei* or *ry,* to give, w.

THAT HE MAY GIVE. Rollo, N.

MAY HE GIVE. Roy, 3 pers. s. opt. of *rei,* or *ry,* to give, w.

THAT THEY MAY GIVE. Rollons, N.

MIGHT or DID GIVE. Rolla, B.

GIVE THOU. Ro, 2 pers. s. imp. of *rei,* or *ry,* to give, w.

GIVE YE. Reuch, 2 pers. pl. imp. of *rei* or *ry,* to give, w.; reugh, N.

GIVE THEM. Ro dedhe, P.

LET HIM GIVE. Roy, N.

LET US GIVE. Rên, 1 pers. pl. imp. of *rei,* to give, w.

YOU GIVE. Tero, B.

GIVE IT ME. Ro dhym, ro e dhymmo, P.

GIVING, *part.* Reis, reys, roys, w.; gyrheffias, gytheffys, B.

GIVEN, *part.* Ou ry, N.

GIVER, *s.* Reiat, w. *Gueinoin reiat,* a giver of poison.

GIVE AWAY, *v.* (To unloose). Deglené, w.

GIVE IMPROPER MEDICINES, TO QUACK, *v.* Ponster, P. This word is still used.

GIVE LEAVE TO, *v.* Cummyn, gemyn, gymyn, B.

GIVE NOTICE TO, *v* Gwarnya, w.; guarnya, P.

GIVE OVER, TO CEASE, *v.* Sestya, P.

GIVE THANKS, *v.* Grassé, w.

GLAD, *adj.* Hudyc, huthyc, hutyk, w. *Ny vyth hutyk y golon,* nor is his heart glad, o.m. 2813; lowen, luan, w.; louan. lawen, B.; leunek, leunik, P ; leuenik, louenak, lauenik, lowenic, B.; lowenec, lowenek, w.; lawenic, lewenic, lawennek, B.; lowanheys, cw. 957.

GLADDEN, *v.* Lowenhé, lowenny, dydhané, dhyhané, w.; dythané, R.D. 2526.

GLADDER, *adj.* Lowenna, M. 243; lowenné, w.

GLADNESS, *s.* Lowené, lowyné, lowenna, lawenés, w.; lauenez, lauen, P.; lowender, w.; lowendar, c.w. 1428.

GLADLY, *adv.* Lowan, B.; lowen, w.

GLADE, *s.* Lanherch, w.

GLASS, *s.* Gweder. w.; gueder, P.; gwydr, B.; gurys, P.; weder, M. 853; wedyr, M. 1445. *Avel horle der weder a heb y terry*, as (the) sun goes through glass without breaking it, M. 853.

GLASS OF WINE. Gwedran a win, guedran a vin, B.

GLASSY, *adj.* Guedrek, B.

GLAZE or **VARNISH**, *s.* Glidder, D.

GLEANINGS. *s.* (In the harvest-field). Pil-les, W.F.P. *A gleaner's sheaf.* Sang, zang, D.

GLEN, *s.* Glyn, glen, w. Pryce says *glyn* means a *woody* valley.

GLIDE, TO GLIDE ALONG, *v.* Slintya, slyncia, w.; slyncha, P.

GLITTER or **GLISTEN**, *v..* Dewynnyé, dywhynny, tewynnyé, w.; splanna, P.; terlentry, w.

GLITTERING. Ow terlentry, tevery, deverye, P.

GLOOMY, *adj.* Diu, dhiu, du, w.

GLORIFY, *v.* Gworria, w.

GLORIOUS, *adj.* Gwyn, w.

GLORY, *s.* Clôr, glôr, klôs, P.; clôs, w. *Yn paradys deugh thu'm clôs*, in Paradise come to my glory, R.D. 164; gordhyans. gorryans, w.; guorhyans, P.; gworhyans, gwerdhyans, w.; gurthyans, gwerthya, gorty, gworria, P.; wordhyans, w.; worthyans, lowené, lowendar, P.

GLOVE, *s.* Maneg, manag, manak, manek, w.; stollof, cowedliuer, B. *Pl.* Menik, manegou, B.

GLUE, *s.* Glût, w.

GLUT, *s.* Lanwés, w.

GLUTTON, *s.* Cowleck, D.

GNASH, *v.* Discerny, dheskerny, w.

GNAT, *s.* Centowen, B.; stût, guibeden, gwibeden, gwiban. See FLY.

GNAW, *v.* Cnoi, B.

GO, *v.* (To go, walk, proceed). Monas, w.; monés, O.M. 264; monez, P.; mynés, w.; mynez, P.; môs, w.; moz, P.; maos. maoz, moaz, w.; mouas, mauz, P.; mâz, vôs, w.; vâz, P.; cerdhês, kerdhês, w.; kerdhez, P.; gerdhés, w.; gerthés, M. 3966; cerras, kerras, garras, w.; geitho, eu, P.; daos, w.; duwy, fadé, P.

GO, *v.* (To go, to become). Gylly, cylly, w.; geli, gyll, P.; gallous, B.

GO, *v.* (To pass, slide away, run, flow, rush out). Resec resek, redec, w.

GO THOU. Ce, ke, ki, w. *Lemyn noy y'th worhel ke*, now Noah, go into thy ark, O.M. 1017; cêr, kêr, cêrdh, kêrdh, w.; kertheugh, eugh, euch, eus, P.

GO, GET OUT. Eugh, B.

GET YOU OUT. Eugh yn mês, B.

WAS GOING. E, w.

LET THEM GO. Ens, w.

GO YE. Eugh, N.

GO YE ALL HOME. Eus pup tre, P.

LET THEM GO. Ens, N.

HE MAY GO. Ello, w.

HE MIGHT GO. Ellé, v.

I GO. Thof, tof, P.; thât, B.; ythaf, af, N.

THOU GOEST. Eth, ytheth, M.

HE GOES. A, yytha, N.

WE GO. En, ythen, N.

YE GO. Eugh, yytheugh, N.

I WILL GO. Af, av, w.; thât, B.

THOU SHALT GO. Ei, ti ei, êth; ydheta, to be read, *ydh*, aud *éta*, a poetic form of *éth*, 2 pers. s. fut. of irr, v. *môs*, to go. A, yl, 3 pers. s. fut. of irr, v. *môs*, to go, w.

WE WILL GO. En, w.

I MAY GO. Yllyf, 1 pers. s. subj. of irr, v. *monés*, to go, w.

WE MAY GO. Yllyn, 1 pers. pl. subj. of irr, v. *monés*, to go, w.

I SHOULD GO. Een, ellen, N.

GONE. Gilliz, galsé, galso, gulsé, gerys, B.

I AM GONE. Galsof, w.; gallaf, P.

THEY ARE GONE. Galsons, w.

WAS GONE. Galsé, w.

THOU SHALT HAVE GONE. Ylly, 2 pers. s. 2 fut. of the irr, v. *monés*, to go, w.

HE IS GONE. Reseth, regeth, w.

HE HATH GONE. Reseth, regeth, w.

TO GO ABROAD. Daoz meaz, w.; maos a leaz, P.; maoz a leaz, P.

TO GO ACROSS, *v.* Trussé, w.

TO GO APART, *v.* Anneyley, w.

TO GO AWAY, *v.* Gueny, dilecha, P.

TO GO OUT, *v.* Omdena, wary, P.

GONE OUT, or FORTH. Degennow, degennow yn ônés, P.

TO GO TO STOOL, *v.* Caca, w.; poopy, poop, D.

TO GO UP, *v.* Ascen, ascenua, escynya, yscynné, w.; yskynna, P.; euhellé, w.

GOAD, *s.* Arho, garthou, w.; guan, B.; sumbul, P.

GOAL, *s.* (The end aimed at). Diwedh, diweth, dywedh, dewedh, diwedhva, dywedhva, w.; diuadh, diuath, diua, P.

GOAT, *s.* Gaver, gavar, P.; gueffer, B.; lill, w. *Pl.* Geuer, w.; gour, gever, P.

A YOUNG GOAT. Ceverel, keverel, w.; cheverel, p.

A HE GOAT. Boch, w.; boc, byk, bocca, p.

GOAT-FOLD, *s.* Crou an gueffer, b.

GOAT-MOTH, *s.* Maggyowler, maggyowla, madgyowler, d. The *Cossus ligniperda* of the naturalist.

GOBLET, *s.* Scala, b.; scafa, p.

GOBLIN, *s.* Speris, spyrys, spiriz, w.; sprite, spyr, b.; bucka, c.w. 1196. *Bucca*, for a ghost, spirit, or goblin, is still much used.

GOD, *s* Dew, Deu, Du, Dhew, Dyw, Dhyw, Duy, Dea, Dues, w.; Theu, Thu, Thyu, p.; Thev, o M. 1389; Thyw, R.D. 1007.

GODS, *s.* Dewow, w.; deuou, p.; duou, b.; dewyow, w.; deuiou, dewon, b.; deuon, p.; deauon, deuion, b.; thewen, deusys, p.; devyas, w.; duvo, duy, b.

GOD ALMIGHTY, *s.* Deu Chefitodoc, Duy Chefitidoc, p.

GODDESS, *s.* Dués, w.; deuyse, p.

GODDESS OF LOVE. Gwenar, w.; guenar, p.

GODDESS MALAN. Malan, also called Andras. A celibrated British goddess. Invoked with imprecations in perilous times, w.

GODFATHER, *s.* Aultra, altrou, w.

GODHEAD, THE GODHEAD, *s.* Deusys, Dewaes, p.; Dewgés, c.w. 6.

GODLY MAN. Dên-Dew, w.

GODMOTHER, *s.* Commaer, b.; aultruan, altruan, w.

GOLD, *s.* Our, aur, w.; owr, b.; ower, c.w. 129. Grains of gold found in streamworks the tinners call *Rux* and *Hopps.*

GOLDEN, *adj.* Oyrec, w; oyrek, p.

GOLDEN YELLOW, *adj.* (Colour). Mellyn, p.

GOLDFINCH, *s.* Melenec. molenec, w.; eure, p.

GOLD RING. Besaw our, w.

GOLDSMITH, *s.* Eure, w.

GOOD, *adj.* Da. b.; dah, dha. tha, p.; ta, b. (*púr dha, púrtha, pre da,* very good, p.); mâs, w.; màz, p.; whâs, w.; mays, M. 4087; mâd, mât, vâs, w.; vays, M. 919; vaz, p.; vât, fâs, w.; vusy, fusy, B.V. vazy, w.F.P; bonès, p.; mam, b. *Nyn y mam,* I was not good. *Yn fâs,* well. w. *Moysés del oge dên mâs,* Moses, as thou art a good man, o.M. 1767. *The vrusi an drôk han mays,* to judge the bad and the good, M. 4087. *An diz vâs,* the good people, p.

GOOD, A GOOD, *s.* Da, w.; dah, p.; dha, ta, w.; tha. o.M. 1617; lês, w.; thadder, M. 528. *Ahanés covs múr thadder,* of thee much good spoken, M. 528.

GOOD FAITH. Glendury, lendury, w.

GOODMAN, THE GOODMAN, THE HUSBAND, *s.* Dremas, thermas, w.; thênsa, M. 2719. *A thênsa nynson tollys,* in the goodman we are not deceived, M. 2719.

GOODLY, *adv.* Yn ta, b.

GOODNESS, *s.* Dader, dhadder, w.; dadder, M. 4515; deder, b.; tadder, w.; thadder, p.; thader, M. 380. *Dadder the lues huny,* goodness to many a one, M. 4515.

GOODS, *s.* Ferna, w.

GOOD-WIFE, *s.* Wrêthtye, c.w. 942; benynvâs, c.w. 554.

GOOSE, *s.* Godh, goidh, goydh, guydh, w.; gudh, p.; gwydd, b.; guit, w.; goaz, b.

GOOSE-EGG, *s.* Oy godho, w.

GORE, *s.* (Blood). Crow, w.; crou, p.

GORSE, *s.* See FURZE.

GOSPEL, THE GOSPEL, *s.* Awayl, geawail, w. geawell, p.; geauel, b.; awell, M. 393.

GOVERN, *v.* Rowlia. w.; roulia, p.

GOVERNMENT, *s.* Gonyc, w.; ganyck, p.

GOVERNORS, *s.* Roulers, b.

GOWN, *s.* Pows, w.; pous, p.; peus, peis, bows, fows, gûn, w.

GRACE, FAVOUR. *s.* Grâth, grayth, grâf. w.; rays, M. 319. *Dre ov grath dalleth an beys,* by my grace to begin the world, o.M. 6. *Gouerner lich a fúr rays,* governor liege of great grace, M. 319.

GRACE, THANKS, *s.* Grâs, w.; grâz, p.; grass, râs, râz, w.; arâs, p.; rase, c.w. 14.

GRACES, EXCELLENCIES, *s.* Grasow, rasow, w.

GRACELESS. *adj.* Hep râs, o.M. 251; ongrassyas, M. 2242. *A debel venyn hep râs,* O evil graceless woman, o.M. 251. *Tevdar pagan ongrassyas,* Teudor, a graceless pagan, M. 2242.

GRAIN, *s.* (*Granum, Lat.*) Gronen, w.; grawn, b.

GRAIN, *s.* (All manner of grain, as corn, &c.) Yz, is, iz, eys, yd, it, p.

GRAINS, KERNELS, *s.* Sprûs, spûs. *Sing,* Sprûsan, spûsan, w.

GRAINS, *s.* (Brewer's grains). Seag, zeag, w.; zeage, b. *Lacka vel zeage,* worse than grains.

GRAINS OF GOLD. The Cornish tinners call them *rux* and *hopps,* d.

GRANDCHILD, *s.* Noi, b. Pryce says, nephew. (Lhuyd, *nepos.*)

GRANDEE, *s.* Dên maur. *Lit.* Great man.

GRANDFATHER, *s.* Hendat, hendad, hendas, w. *Lit.* Old father. Sira wyn, w.; sira uidn, p.; sira gwydn. tâz guidn, b.; tâs gwyn, w. *Lit.* White father, from the white hair.

GREAT GRANDFATHER. Diwog, dihog? w.; dipog, p.; hengog, *Cott. Ms.*

GREAT GREAT GRANDFATHER. Hengog, gurhhog, w.; gur-hog, p.

GRANDILOQUENT, *adj.* Brâslavar, w.

GRANDMOTHER. *s.* Dama wyn, w.; dama widn, P.; dama widen, B. *Lat.* White mother, or white dame, so named from the hair.

GRANITE. *s.* (?) *Decomposed granite.* Growder, B.

GRANT, *v.* Gronté, grontyé, w.; crowntya, c.w. 1941; ro, roy, P.; roi, rey, w.; re, B.; ry, rhei, rei, w.; rella, B.

GRANT, *s.* Grontys, w.

GRANTED, *part.* Grontys, w.

GRAPNEL, *s.* Grabel, w.

GRASP, *s.* Gavel, w.

GRASP, *v.* Gaval, w.; gouas, P.

GRASPING, GREEDY, *adj* Grefnye, crefnye, w.; krâf. B.

GRASS, *s.* Gwells, gwels, gwelz, guelz, w.; gwyls, P.; lousauen, B.

GRASSHOPPER, *s.* Celioc-reden, w.; keliok reden, P. *Lit.* The cock of the fern. Griggan, D.

GRAVE, *s.* Bêdh, beydh, w.; bêth, P.; vêdh,; vêth, B.

GRAVES, *s.* Bêdhiow, bethow w.; bedhou, P.; gwâgion, this is also the plural of *gwâg,* a hollow or empty place.

GRAVE-DIGGER, *s.* Derric, w.; derrick, P.

GRAVEL, *s.* Grouan, grean, grou, grow, grouder, P. These words are still used for rough gravelly earth.

GRAVEL or SAND, *s.* Treâth, drêath, traith, draith, P.; treas, B.

GRAVEL-PIT, *s.* Pol grean, w.

GRAVING TOOL, *s.* Kolhel gravio, P.

GREASE, *s.* Blonec, w.; blonit, B.; seym, seim, w.

GREASE, *v.* Uré, iré, w.; ira, P.

GREASY, *adj.* Soath, w.

GREAT, *adj.* Brâs, w.; brase, c.w. 88; brays, M. 257; braoz. B.; vrâs, frâs, w.; mogan, maugan, pyrn. P.; hail, B. *Pol maugan,* the great pool. *Hail mên tor,* the great stone tor, B.

GREAT, HUGE, *adj.* Ethuc, w.; ethuk, P.; ethec, w.; ethek, P.; ythec, ethyc, w.; ethyk, ithik, ithyk, ithig, uthik, uthy, P.

GREAT, MUCH, *adj.* Mûr, w.; muer, M. 384; meur, mêr, mear, w.; mere, P.; meyr, maur, w.; moy, P.; vêr. fûr, vûr, luen, lean, w.; magan, o.M. 1749. *Thyworthe magan bo grâs,* from them grace is so great, o.M. 1749.

GREAT MAN. (Big man). Dên brâs.

GREAT MAN. (Grandee). Dên maur.

GREATER, *adj.* Brassah, brassach, brassa, w.; broza, B.; mui bras, w.; mui braoz, P. The same words will stand for the comparative or the superlative.

GREATER, MORE, *adj.* Moy, mui, voy, w.

GREATEST, *adj.* Brassa, brasa, brassé, w. See GREATER.

GREATEST, or MOST, *adj.* Mochya, w.; moghia, moggha, P.; mocha, moicha, moycha, moya, w.

GREATLY, *adv.* Yn frâs, w.

GREATNESS, *s.* Brâsder, vrâsder, braster, broster, mens, myns, mourder, w.; moygha, P.

GREATNESS, *s.* (High degree) Hunelder, R.D. 425. *Rák luen ôs a hunelder,* for thou art full of greatness, R.D. 425.

GREEDY, *adj.* Grefnye, crefnye, w.; krâf, B.

GREEN, *adj.* (Colour). Glâs, w.; glâz, glays, B.; lâs, w.; lâz, lase, P.; lays, w.

GREEN, *v.* (To be green). Glasé, w.; glassa, P.

GREEN, *adj.* (Verdant.) Gwêr, w.; guer, gear, P.; gwirdh, w.; gwird, B.; guirt, P.; guedrak, B.; glâs, w.; glâz, glays, B.; lâs, w.; lâz, lase, P.; lays, w.; verth, vêth, P.

A GREEN BOUGH. Delkio guer, P.

A GREEN, A GREEN PLOT. Glassygyon, w.

THE GREEN TOP or SUMMIT. Lays, w.

A GREEN TREE. Prên lays.

GREET, *v.* Dynerchy, w.; dinerchy, dinyrghy, P.; dynerhy, w.; dynerhi, B.

GREETED, *part.* Dynerchys, w.

GREETING, A GREETING, *s.* Dynnarch, dhynnarch, w.

GREY or GRAY, *adj.* (The colour). Glâs, w.; glase, glaze, P.; glôs, glayis, lays, B.; lâs, w.

GREY, HOARY, *adj.* Lûz, loos, lôs, w.; loose, c.w. 358; luys, ludzh, P.; loys, lous, w.; lowyz, B.; luit, w.

GREYISH-WHITE, *adj.* Luit, w.

GREYHOUND, *s.* Ci hîr, w.; ky-hîr, B. *Lit.* Longdog; milgi, milgy, w. *Pl.* Mylguen, M. 3166. *Mylguen ha rethys kefrys,* greyhounds and nets likewise, M. 3166.

GRIDIRON, *s.* Oilet, B. Also a name for a fryingpan.

GRIEF, *s.* Ancen, anken, w. *Mara quelyn thy's anken,* if we see grief in thee, P.C. 733; ancow, w.; ankow, P.; ancou, ancouyns, B.; ancrés, awher, w.; awer, M. 231; alloys, B.; bern, vern, w. *Me a vyn monés heb bern,* I will go without grief, M. 3176; cavow, cafow, cén, kên, chén, cûth, cueth, kueth, gueth, w.; kuoth, P.; cothys, dewon, dewan, dewhan, duwhan, duan, dhuan, w.; thwan, duwon, duon, P. *Lamys thy'm na wra duon,* James do not cause grief to me, M.D. 375; edrec, edrek, eddrek, w.; eddrak, B.; yddrac, w.; edrege, yddrage, yddraga, P.; gu, gew, wew, gwae, w.; wêr, gâs, P.; galar, govid, w.;

drôg, layne, wryth, P.; poan, B.; moreth, w. *Rdg moreth a wra terry*, for grief will break, O.M. 358.

GRIEF, *s*. (Grievance, complaint). Grêf. *Ytho prâg na lenés ef kafus y dhegé hep grêf*, now, why not leave him to take his tenth without complaint, O.M. 497. " From the English," w.

GRIEVE, *v*. Duwenhé, duwhené, dewhanhé, grevya, grevyé, treynyé, trynnyé, trynya, drynya, troplesy, w.

GRIEVED, *part*. Cuthys, w.; kuef, P.; gweff, B.; morethec, morethek, vorethec, peynys, poenys, w.; poenis, P.; grevys, B.

GRIEVOUS, *adj*. Bysy, vysy, w.; (pysy ?); anken, O.M. 2335. *The vôs dên lâth, yv anken*, to be a man-killer is grevous, O.M. 2335; grêf, P.; grevye, B.; poys, poes, pôs, pûz, w.; powz, B.; powys, P.

GRIMACES, *s*. Mowys, w.

GRIN, *v*. Discerny, dheskerny, w.; theskerny, B.; thyskerny, P.; rynna, scryncyé, skrynkyé, w.

GRIND, *v*. Melias, w.; meliaz, B. *Dho meliaz yz*, to grind corn; pobas, pobaz, P.

GRINDERS, *s*. (Teeth). Dens dhelhar, dens dhelhor, P.

GRIPE, *s*. (A gripe or handful). Manal, w.

GRIPING, *s*. (A griping of the bowels.) Girr, w.; gyrr, gerdin, B.

GROAN, *v* Ega, hynadzha, w.

GROAN, *s*. Hynadzhas, w.; hynadzhan, B.

GROATS, *s*. (Used as food). Brynnian, brydnian, w.

GROIN, *s*. Cetorva, w.; ketorva, P.

GROPE, *v*. Croppyé, w.

GROSS, COARSE, *adj*. Brâs, vrâs, w.

GROSS, FAT, *adj*. Berric, w. *Pronter berric*, a gorbellied priest, P.; tew, B.; teu, P.

GROSSNESS, FATNESS, *s*. Berri, w.; teuder, P.; tewder, w.

GROTTO, *s*. Kavarn, B.

GROUND, *s*. (The ground, the earth). Dôr, doar, doer, daor, dhaor, w.; dour, M. 3228. *Then dour gansa*, to the ground with them, M. 3528. *Hethe the'n dôr my a'd pys*, reach to the ground, I pray thee, O.M. 2521; an'oar, w.; dodnan, B.; gweras, gwyrras, gweret, gueret, gwered. w.; gulan, O.M. 859; hueret, B. *Ov enef ha'm corf tha'n gulan*, my soul and my body to the ground, O.M. 859; leur, lêr, luer, lôr, lear, w.

GROUND, *s*. (Land, country, earth, soil). Tîr, tyr, tyreth, tireth, w.

LOOSE, HOLLOW, SHELFY GROUND, This was said to be *kivully*.

GROUNDS, *s*. (Sediment, as of drink). Godhas, godho. See SEDIMENT.

GROUND-FLOOR, *s*. Lear, lêr, leur, luer, lôr, w.

GROUND-ROOM, *s*. Soler, w.

GROUND-STAY, *s*. Sekerder, P.

GROUND-WORK, *s*. Sêl, seil, seyl, scyle, sol, w.

GROVE, *s*. Cilli, killi, kelli, celli, kelly, gelly, w.; gilli, P.; loin, w.; lhyn, B. *Pellyn*, the head of the grove, B.

GROVE-NUTS, *s*. (Earth-nuts). Killi-môr, P. See BERRY.

GROW, *v*. Tevy, tyvy, w.; teva, tivia, P.

GROWN, *part*. Tevys, tovys, devys, w.

GROWS. Dyf. *Ny dyf guels*, no grass grows, P.

HE MAY GROW. Tefo, 3 pers. s. subj. of *tevy*, to grow, w.

HE WILL GROW. Têf, teyf, tyf, and dêf, a mutation of *tef*, 3 pers. s. fut. of *tevy*, to grow. Also dyf, w.

LET THEM GROW. Tefyns, 3 pers. pl. imp. of *tevy*, w.

TO GROW DISTRACTED, OR MAD, *v*. Muscegy, w.; muskegy, P.

TO GROW TIRED OF, *v*. Dyflasé, dhyflasé, w.

GRUB, *s*. (*Larva*). Buzuguen. *Pl*. Buzug, B.

GRUDGE, *s*. Drôgbrês, sôr, sorras, w.

GRUEL, *s*. Caul, B.

GRUMBLE, *v*. Ascably, P.

GRUMBLING, *s*. Sôr, sorras, w.; wow, B. *Heb wow*, without grumbling, B.

GUARD or RETINUE, *s*. Cosgor, kosgar, w.

GUARD, *s*. (Protection). Wyth, O.M. 1979. *Re worro wyth am ené*, set a guard over my soul, O.M. 1979.

GUARD, *v*. Gorwythy, w.; gorwith, gorquith, P.; gwithé, gwythé, w.; guitha, kuitha, B.; cuitha, P.; wythé, R.D. 336. *Ordyne tús the ythé*, order men to guard, R.D. 336,

GUARDIAN, *s*. Gwithés, gwithias, gwythias, gwythyas, w.; gwethyas, C.W. 368; guithias, cuithias, P.; guythyas, O.M. 692. *The cherubyn un guythyas*, to the cherub, the guardian, O.M. 692; gwithiad, w.; guythyad, guidthiad, B.; guidthiat, w.

GUARDIANS or GUARDS, *s*. Kuithizi, P.; guythysy, N.

GUARDING AGAINST. Gweras, gwerés, w.; gwerras, gweret, P.

GUDGEON, *s*. (One easily imposed upon). Gargesen, M. 2433. *Indellé, ty gargesen*, so, thou gudgeon, M. 2433.

GUERDON, *s*. Gweryson, weryson, w. *Hag an our the weryson*, and the gold thy guerdon, R.D. 1677.

GUIDE or RULE, *v*. Roulla, B.

GUIDE, *s.* Dyskas, B.

GUILE, *s.* Gowegneth, gouegneth, gouegueth, P.; tûll, teul, towl, toul, w.; gyll, c.w. 58.

GUILLEMOT, *s.* (Sea bird). Kiddaw, mûr, murre, mor, D.

GUILT, *s.* Achos. *Pl.* Acheson, w.

GUILTLESS, *adj.* Dibêh, w.

GUINEA-COCK, *s.* Kôk gini. Zar, for cock or hen, P.

GULF, *s.* (Chasm). Downder, w.; dounder, B.; swallet, D.

GULF, *s.* (Of water). Aber, liz, P.

GULL, *s.* (Bird). Saithor, sethar, zethar, gwilan, gwylan, w.; guilan, P.; gullan, w. *Pl.* Guller, P.; gullez, B.

A GREY GULL. Wagel, D.

GULLET or THROAT, *s.* Brangian, briangen, briansen, brianten, brandzhian, w.; brandzian, brangain, B.; brandzhia, branzia, vyrongen, P.; clunker, D.

GUMPTION, SENSE, NOUSE, *s.* Rode, D.

GURNET or GURNARD. *s.* Pengarn, pengurn, B. *Lit.* Rockhead. Perhaps so named from its angularly formed head. In the dialect it is called *elleck,* or *illek.*

GUSH OUT, *v.* Divery, P.; tardhé, B.

GUSHED, *part.* Tarthas, resas, B.

GUST, *s.* (A strong one of wind). Flaw, flaugh, D. From *flaw,* a cut. Also called *teat,* D.

GUSTY, *adj* Auelek, B.

GUT or ENTRAIL, *s.* Colon. *Pl.* Coloniou, kylyrion, B.

GUTTER, *s.* Shanol, w.

H.

"This letter, sounded as in English, is not only an aspiration, but a distinct letter, and has two separate offices.

First, it is employed to aspirate initial vowels after certain words preceding:—thus *gallaf,* I am able; *ny allaf,* I am not able; *may hallaf,* that I may be able; *gallouch,* ye are able; *ny allouch,* ye are not able; *may hallouch,* that ye may be able.

Secondly, in Cornish *h* is frequently used as a substitute for the guttural *ch* :—thus *whêh* for *cl wêch,* six; *marh* for *march,* a horse; *golhy* for *golchy,* to wash; *dh'y huhudha,* for *dh'y chuhudha,* to accuse her; *yn y holon,* for *yn y cholon,* in her heart," w. *Lex. Corn. Brit.*

HABERGEON, *s.* Hobersen, R.D. 2536.

HABITATION, *s.* (A dwelling-place). Tre, trev, regva, trigva, drigva, annêdh, asêdh, w.; chy, F.

HAG, *s.* Diowlés, dzhowlés, w.; dzhoulés, dyallas, diaul, P.

HAGGARD, *adj.* Hager, hagar, P.

HAIL, *s.* (Of weather). Ceser, w.; keser, P.; kezer, kezzar, w.; kezzor, P.

HAIL. (An exclamation). Lowene, o.m. 2211. *Ov anluth lowene thys,* my Lord, hail to thee, o.m 2211.

HAIR, *s.* (A hair). Blewen. *Pl.* Blewennow, vlewennow, w.

HAIR, *s.* (In the mass). Bleu, blew, B.; bleawe, bleaw, c.w. 1666, 1605. *Saw me a's sêgh gans ow blew,* but I will dry them with my hair, P.c. 484; thyu, P. *Syghys y dreys gans the thyu pléth.* thou wipest his feet with thy hair spread, P.; gols, gwalht, w.; gualht, P.; cudiri, kydynnou, B.

A LOCK OF HAIR. Cudin, w.; gols, gwalht, w.; gualht, P.

THE HAIR OF THE HEAD. Blew an peл, w.; bleu an pedn, P.; blewynpen, B.

HAIRY, *adj.* Blewac, bleuak, P.; blewake, c.w. 1586.

HAKE, *s.* (Fish). Denjack, denshocdoar, P.; denshoc dour, w.

HALF, *s.* Hanter, w. *Try deydh ha hanter,* three days and a half.

HALF-PENNY, *s.* Demma, P.c. 2263; hanter diner, w.; hanter dinair, P.

HALF A YARD. Cevelyn, kevelyn, cyvelyn, w.; kyvelyn, P.; gevelyn, w.

HALM, HALM, HAUM, *s.* Soul, zoul, w.

HALL, *s.* Hêl, hêll, w. *Omma gynen bys y'th hêl,* here with us, even to thy hall, P.c. 1203; bindorn, (perhaps *buidorn*) w.

THIS HALL. Hêlma, P.

HALL, COURT, or PALACE, *s.* Lês, lîs, lys, w.

HALLOO or SHOUT, *v.* Helwy, hilwy, hylwy, w.

HALLOW, *v.* Benigia, soné, sona, zona, uchellé, uhellé, w.

HALTER, *s.* Maglen, w.; kebister, B.; colmen, celmen, gelmen, w.; golmen, P.c. 177.

HAMMER, *s.* Morthol, w.; mortholl, morzol, orz, B.

A LITTLE HAMMER. Gybeddern, B.

A MINER'S HAMMER. Bucker, D.

HAMMERED, *part.* Morthelec, morthelek, w.

HAMMERER, *s.* (*i.e.,* A breaker up of ore). Spaller, D.

HAND, *s.* Dorn, dhorn, daorn, w.; doarn, c.w. 1142; durn, w.; darn, dharn, tarn, P.; torn, w. *Ith torn,* in thy hand; thorn, o.m. 205; lau, luef, lôf, lêf, leyf, w.; leff, leyff, layff, lâv, le, la, B.; lêv, lebf, lov, luf, P.

HANDS, *s.* (Hands generally). Dalhennow, P.c. 1126; dornow, N.

HANDS, THE TWO HANDS, *s.* Dewléf, dewlêff, dywlêf, dyulêf, dewluêf, dywluêf, duilôf, dulé, dewlé, deulé, dhewlé, dywlé, dyulé, diwla, dula, dhula, w.; thewlêff, thewlé, B.; thywlé, N.; thevolé, P.

THE PALM OF THE HAND. Dalv, P.

THE LEFT HAND. Dorn glêdh, w.; luef glêth, (cleth), N.

THE RIGHT HAND. Dorn dehow, w.; dorn dyhow, P.; leff dyghow, c.w. 2215.

HAND-BARROW, *s.* Gravar dhula, gravar dula, w.; gravar dowla, B.

A HAND-BARROW FOR FISH. Gurrie, D.

HAND-BASKET, *s.* Basced dorn, w.

HAND-BOOK or MANUAL, *s.* Coweidliver, cow-aithliver, w.

HANDFUL, *s.* Manal, w.; stollof, B.

HANDKERCHIEF, *s.* Follat, B.; hynelep, P.; stollof, w.; nackin, D.

HAND-MILL, *s.* Brou, w.

HANDLE, *s.* Dorn, dhorn, w.

HANDLE, *v.* Dava, w.; dyghty, thyghtyé, P.

HANDLE CARELESSLY. *v.* (To soil, to crumple). Fousse, D.

HANDMAID, *s.* Mowés, o.m. 2071; p.c. 1876.

HANG, *v.* (To suspend, to be hanging, to be hanged). Cregy, gregy, crogi, grogy, w.

HANG, *v.* (To hang one's self). Omgregy, ymgregy, w.

HANGED, *part.* Crogas, crogys, grogyas, P.; kregys, c.w. 2317.

HANGING, *part.* Grogé, P.; cregy, M. 1668. *War beyn tenna ha cregy*, on pain of drawing and hanging, M. 1668.

HANGING. *s.* (A suspension). Crôc, crôk, crôg, w. *Crog r'om bo er an thewen*, hanging be to me by the gods, o.m. 2651.

HANGING, *adj.* Crôc, krôk, creg, w.

HAPPEN, *v.* Codha, codhé, digwydha, w.; digwyddo, B.; wharfôs, hapya, w.

HAPPENED, *part.* Whyrfys. From *wharfos.*

IT HAPPENED. 1. Whyrfys, whyrys.

    2. Ydhapyas. Composed of *ydh* and *hapyas*, 3 pers. s. preter. of *hapya*, to happen, w.

IT MAY HAPPEN. Wharfo, warfo, hwarfo, 3 pers. s. subj. of *wharfos*, to happen or occur, w.

HE WILL HAPPEN. Whyrfyth, 3 pers. s. fut. of *wharfos.*

HAPPINESS, *s.* Clôs, w.; klôs, P.; eyrysder, w.; eyrisder, eurmat, eur, dedwyddweh, B. *Dychlôs*, without happiness.

HAPPY, *adj.* Fodic, P.; garm, B.; gwyn, guyn, guin, guidn, P. *Guin bys*, happy world, P. *Guyn y vys pan ve gynys*, happy is he that is born, o.m. 1479.

HARBOUR, *s.* Pôrth, w.; pôrh, pôr, B.

HARD, *adj.* Calés, calas, calys, w.; callys, kalish, B.; calish, callish, cals, galés, w.; galas, P. *The colon yw calés brás*, thy heart is very hard, o.m. 1525; crêf, o.m. 1490. *Na's gorren y thy whyl crêf*, that I put thee not to hard work, o.m. 1490; serth, w. (stiff, hard). *An spikys serth*, the stiff or hard spikes.

HARDEST, *adj.* Calessa, calassa, calatsha, w.; kalatza, B.

HARD-HEARTED, *adj.* Wherow, chuero, w.

HARDNESS, *s.* Calatter, caletter, w.; kalatter, P.; kaletter, mael, B.

HARDSHIP, *s.* Dûr, wheal ober, P.

HARDY, *adj.* (Strong, vigorous). Crêf, crêv, w.; krêv, B.; crif, cryff, cryf, w.

HARE, *s.* Scovarnec, scovarnog, w.; scovarnoeg, skyuarnak, P.; scywarnac, w. In Cornwall they still use the names *skavarnak, skavarnoeck, scovarnog,* and *scavernick,* for a hare. *Lit.* Long-eared.

HARK or HEARKEN, *v.* See LISTEN.

HARK! LISTEN. Golsow, P.

HARLOT, *s.* Drûth, w.

HARM, *s.* Drôc, drôk. drôg, trôc, anfugy, enfugy, myshyf, w.

HARP, *s.* Telein, w.; harfel, B.

HARPER, *s.* Teleinior, w.

HARROW, A HARROW, *s.* Klodzhaz, rakkan, harau, P. Pryce gives *harau* for arrow, *q.v.*

HARROW, *v.* (To harrow the clods) Klodzhaz, B.; klodzhia, P.

HART or STAG, *s.* Carow, w.; carou, caruu, karo, kara, caro, B.; carov, M. 1618; gollon, B.

HARVEST, *s.* (Harvest time). Cyniaf, w.; kyniaf, P.; kyniav, cidniadh, cidniaz, w.; kidniaz, kyniau, P.

HARVEST, *s.* (The harvest). Hitadver, w.; hitaduer, P.

HARVEST-HOME, *s.* (Harvest-home supper). Nickly-thize, D.

HASH, *s.* Crehy, M. 2418. *Me a ra ath pen crehy*, I will make of thy head a hash, M. 2418.

HASH, *s.* (Of beef and potatoes). Scably-gulyan, W.F.P.

HASTE, *s.* Tooth, tôth, touth, towth, toyth, P.; dôth, w.; adôth, B.; dewhans, tewye, P.; totta, o.m. 1036. *Gans touth brás*, with great haste, P.C. 660.

HASTE, HASTE. (Make haste). Hysty, B.

HASTEN, *v.* (To make haste). Fystyné, fystena, fysteny, fystynny, festena, w.; dho festinna, P.; festynna, w.; dhe tooth, P.; spedyé, B.

HASTILY, *adv.* Cut, cot, w.; got, P.

HASTY-PUDDING, *s.* Jot, pot guidn, P. *Lit.* White pudding. The Cornish use the term "white-pot."

HAT, *s.* Debr dour. *Lit.* Water saddle; hot, hat, w.

HATBAND, *s.* Snôd, B.

HATCHET, *s.* Bial, w.; biail, P.; bool, bûl, bony, pony, w.; dag, D.

HATE, *v.* Casé, w.

HATEFUL, *adj.* Ahas, cesadow, casadow, w.; kesadow, P.; gasadow, w.

HATRED, *s.* Câs, gâs, w.; torkhan, B.; ate, P.

HAUGHTY, *adj.* Gothys, othys, houtyn, w. *May mar houtyn body*, or so haughty his body, R.D. 545.

HAUNCH, *s.* Clûn, penclûn, w.; penklyn, pedrain, B.; pedren, patshan, w.; tarneuhon, B.

HAVE, *v.* Cafus, cafos, cafés, cafel, w.; kaffel, B.; cavel, gavel, gaval, cavos, w.; cavoz, P.; cawas, w.; kauaz, P.; gawas, cowas, w.; kouaz, P.; gowas, w.; gouas, B.; gouaz, P.; gevas, B.; cael, w.; beel, unsa, P. *Unsa moy joy*, to have more joy, P.; vet, fet, P. *Ou crês a fet benary*, my peace thou shalt have for ever, P.; genyth, P. *Ef an genyth war an chal*, he shall have it on the cheek, P.

HAVE. Wull, well, B. *Had*, A well, B.

I HAVE. Ma d'hymmo. *Lit* There is to me, B.; buof, P.

HAVE YOU? Bues why? P.

I HAVE NOT. Numbus, M. 2632. *Numbus bews*, I have not life, M. 2632; nymbés, c.w. 1685.

I DID HAVE. Gyfyn, a mutation of *cyfyn*. 1 pers. s. imperf. of *cafos*, to have, w.

I HAD. Buof, P.

HE HAD. 1. Gavas, a mutation of *cavas* or *cafas*, to have, w.

2. Jevés, a corruption of *gevés*, a mutation of *cevés* or *cefés*, 3 pers. s. preter. of *cafos*, w.

3. Gevé, a mutation of *cevé*, 3 pers. sing. imp. of *cafus*, to have, w.

4. Gevés, gefés, mutations of *cevés*, 3 pers. s. preter. of *cafus*, w.

HE DID HAVE. Cefé, cevé. The mutations are gefé, gevé, 3 pers. s. imperf. of *cafos*, to have, w.

WE HAD. Cafas, cafés. The mutations gafas, gafés.

I SHALL or WILL HAVE. Cafaf, w.

THOU SHALT HAVE. Cefyth, kefyth, cevyth; also gefyth, a mutation of *cevyth*, and gyffy, a mutation of *cyffy*, 2 pers. s. fut. of *cafos*, to have, w.

HE SHALL HAVE. 1. Câv, 3 pers. s. fut. of *cavas* or *cavel*, to have, w.

2. Cêf, 3 pers. s. fut. of *cafos*. In construction gêf, w.

3. Gyf, a mutation of *cyf*, 3 pers. s. fut. of *cafos*.

4. Cyf, kyf. Also, gevyth, gefyth, mutations of *cevyth* and *cefyth*, 3 pers. s. fut. of *cafus*, to have, w.

WE SHALL HAVE. 1. Can, gan. *Gan*, is a mutation of *can*, 1 pers. pl. fut. of *cavas*, to have, w.

2. Cefyn, kefyn, gefyn. *Gefyn*, is a mutation of *cefyn*, or *kefyn*, 1 pers. pl. fut. of *cafos*, to have, w.

3. Ni a gan, w.

YE SHALL HAVE. Geuh, a mutation of *ceuh*, *id. qd.*, *ceuch*, 2 pers. pl. fut. of *cael*, to have, w.

THEY SHALL HAVE. Cans, gans. *Gans*, is a mutation of *cans*, 3 pers. pl. fut. of *cavas*, to have, w.

I MAY HAVE. Bomé, cafen, caffen, w.

HE MAY or SHOULD HAVE. Geffo, a mutation of *ceffo*; gyffé, a mutation of *cyffé*; also written gyfyé; and jeffo, a corruption of *geffo* (by softening the *g*) which is a mutation of *ceffo*, 3 pers. s. subj. of *cafos*, to have, w.

THEY MAY HAVE. Cafons, cefons, w.

HE WOULD HAVE. Caffé, gaffé, cyfyé, gyfyé, 3 pers. s. subj. of *cafos*, to have, w.

HAVEN, *s.* Hean, P.; haun, B.

HAWK, *s.* Bidnethein, w.; bidnepein, bideven, B.; bidnewin, P.; faucon, B.; cryssat, w. Pryce calls a crest hawk *kryssat*.

HAWKER, *s.* (Dealer). Goccor, gwiccur, w.

HAWK-WEED, *s.* (The mouse-ear kind). Felen, D.

HAWTHORN, A HAWTHORN, *s.* Frith, P.

HAY, *s.* Foen, B.; guyraf, gorra, w.; gorré, O.M. 1057. *Gorré hag eys kemyskys*, hay and corn mixed, O.M. 1057.

LIGHT HAY or GRASS. Sprowse, D.

HAZARD, *s.* Antell, P.; cellad, w.

HAZARDING, A HAZARDING, *s.* Antell, w.

HAZARDOUS, *adj.* Dyantell, dyantel, w.; dyantu, P.

HAZEL, *s.* (A hazel tree.) Colhen, B.; colwidhen, colwiden, golwidhen, gwedhan cnyfan, w.; guedhan knyfan, P.

HAZEL-NUT, *s.* In the Cornish dialect it is called a victor-nut.

HAZELS, A HAZEL GROVE, *s.* Cothwyn, gelli, B.; gelly, gilly, w.; gillis, P. *Tregelli*, town of hazels, B. The word *town* is used for *grove*. In Cornwall they call a grove of trees a "town of trees."

HE, *pron.* Ef, e, y, N.; fe, w. A form of *ef* and used generally after the verb. The letter *o* is only used in composition with prepositions, as *ganso*, with him or it; *orto*, to him or it; *ynno*, in him or it. Pryce makes it *so*, as, *Mer Christ marow vena so*, if Christ dead was he. Yth, B.; *Yth ymwanés*, he stabbed himself. Ev, ve, w.; eu, P.; bos, boz, henna, haneth, B.

HE HIMSELF. Evhonnen, P.

HE THAT. Nêb, nêp, sûl, suel, w.; buel, B.

HE WHO. Nêb, nèp, nêf, B.

THAN HE. Agesso, w.

HEAD, *s.* (Top, chief, beginning, the head, end). Pen, pedu, pyn, ben, fen, fin, fyn, fedn. *War the pen y thenewy*, upon thy head I will pour it, P.C. 487. The forms, *pyn, byn, bidn*, are used in the formation of the preposition *warbyn*, against, w. Pryce gives *pednan*, for head.

HEAD or POLL, *s.* Pol, w.

EVERY HEAD. Ketters pol, P.; kettep pol, P.C. 241.

THE BACK OF THE HEAD. Pol kil, B.

HEAD-COVERING, *s.* Penguch, w.

HEAD OF THE FAMILY. Penteilu, w.; penteileu, penteyley, B.

HEAD OF THE TABLE. Pen an voys, M. 281.

HEAD AND TAIL. Pedn ha teen, w.

HEAD or SUMMIT. Pen, pedn, w.; pednan, P.

HEAD or HILL, *s.* Men, P.

HEAD or SOURCE, *s.* Mamen, B.

HEAD OF AN ARROW. Peÿll, c.w. 1560.
Tenhy in ban besyn peyll, drew it (*arrow*) up to the head, c.w. 1560.

HEADLAND, *s.* Penryn (*pen ryn*), trein, tron, w.

HEADS AND TAILS. (A game with pins). Pedn-ameny, pedn-a-mean, B.V.

HEAL, *v.* Iaché, yaché, w.; yaghy, yehés, P.; jehés, O.M. 1794; gwerés, w.; guerés, P.; werés, w.; guerir, dythgya, P.

HEAL, TO BE HEALED, *v.* Sawyé, w.

HEALED, *part.* Saw, w.; sau; zehés, P.

HEALING or CURE, *s.* Yehés, M. 701; yeheys, M. 1835. *Yehés dywy re grontya*, grant healing to you, M. 701; savment (*saument*) M. 1638.

HEALTH, *s.* Yechés, w.; yeghés, R.D. 1716; yaghés, yehas, ehaz, P.; yaz, B.; iachés, iechés, w.; hega-ratyz, B.

HEALTHFUL, *adj.* Sawell (saw-ell), P.; sawsac, w.

HEALTHY, SOUND, *adj.* Iach, yâch, w.; jack, B.

HEALTH TO YOU. Sewena, sowena, P.

HEAP, *s.* Burn, bourn, bern, dìn, grachel, w.; cruc, creeg, cryk, P.

A HEAP OF STONES. Cârn, w.; kârn, B.; kearne, P.; karnedh, B.

A HEAP OF TURF. (A round one). Pooc, pook, pouk, w.; puuk, B. The name *pook* for a round heap of turf cut for fuel, is still in common use in Cornwall.

HEAP or HILLOCK OF SAND. Towan, towin, tewen, towyn, tuan, tuen, tuyn, P. Sand heaps, or hillocks of sand, especially those above high tide near the sea shore, are still commonly called *towans*. Sand mounds covered with grass are also so called, and the sheep fed there are called *towan* mutton.

HEAP UP, *v.* Tholya, P.

HEAR, *v.* Clewas, clewés, w.; reclewés, klyuez, glewas, gleuas, P.; clewo, glewo, B.; klowo, P.; clowés, w.; cloweys, M. 806; glowés, clowas, w.; clowaz, dho glowaz, glouaz, glouas, P.

HEARD. Gleu, glavis, B.

BY HEARING. Worth glowés, w.

I HEARD. Glowys, a mutation of *clowys*, 1 pers. s. preter. of *clowas*, to hear, w.

THOU HEARDEST. Glowsys, a mutation of *clow-sys*, 2 pers. s. preter. of *clowas*, to hear, w.
　　2. Glewas, a mutation of *clewas*, 2 pers. s. preter. of clewas.

YE HEARD. Glewseuch, glewsyuch, a mutation of *clewseuch*, 2 pers. pl. preter. of *clowas*, to hear, w.

I SHALL HEAR. Glewaf, a mutation of *clewaf*, 1 pers. s. fut. of *clewas*, to hear, w.

HE WILL HEAR. Glew, glow, mutations of *clew*, and *clow*, 3 pers. s. fut. of *clewas* and *clowas*, to hear, w.

HEAR THOU. Glu, a mutation of *clu*, id. *qd*. *clew*, 2 pers. s. imp. of *clewas*, to hear, w.

HEAR YE. Glewyuch, a mutation of *clewyuch*, 2 pers. pl. imp. of *clewas*, to hear. Clowugh, M. 1890.

HE MAY HEAR. Glewfo, a mutation of *clewfo*, 3 pers. s. subj. of *clewas*, to hear, w.

HEARKEN, *v.* Golsowas, w.; guzuwaz, B. *Gwel yw guzuwaz*, it is better to hearken; wolsowas, w.; wolsowasy, P.; gola, golé, w.; grilla, P.; cola, colé, w.

HEARD or HEARKENED TO. Colewuys, gyzyuaz, B.

HEARKEN THOU. Golsow, goslow. *Goslow* is a corrupt form of *golsow*, 2 pers. s. imp. of *golsowas*, to hearken. Cool, from *cola*, to hearken, w.

HEARKEN THOU TO ME. Gethym (*ge thym*), cool gethym, P.

HEARKEN YE. Golsoweuch, gosloweuch. The latter word is a corruption of *golsoweuch*, 2 pers. pl. imp. of *golsowas*, to hearken, w.

HEAR, HEARKEN. Oyeth (Norm. French, *Oiez*), w.

HEARING, *s.* (The sense of hearing). Clevet, w.; klevet, B.; clowans, w.; clowance, P.

HEART, THE HEART, *s.* Colon, golon, holon, *Ow holon,* my heart, wholon, w.; collon, gollon, hollon, colan, B.; kolan, P.; colen, O.M. 428; golan, holan, w.; gollan, hollan, c.w. 284, 734. *Ou holan,* my heart. P.

WITH ONE HEART. Kês colon, P.C. 1076. *Ha kês colon ol pesough,* and with one heart all pray, P C. 1076.

A HARD HEART. Colon galas, P.

BEATING OF THE HEART. Pulcolan, B.

THE BLOOD OF MY HEART. Gos ow holon, M.

HEART or MIDST. *s.* Crês, creys, w.; crêz, krêz, B.; crys, crêd, w.

HEARTH, *s.* Olas, w.; olaz, P.; ollaz, oleas, B.; êth, P C. 1244. *Gans y lappa worth an êth,* with his lap to the hearth, P.C. 1244; fôc, fôk, fôg, shimbla, w.

HEARTILY, *adv.* Colonnek, M. 3103. *Monés dotho colonnek,* go to him heartily, M. 3103.

HEARTY. *adj.* (Sincere, jolly, valiant). Colannac, w.; collannak, P. kolannak, B.; colanac, colenec, w.; colonnek, M. 32; kalonek, kaledneck, P.; cylednac, w.

HEAT, *s.* Tumder, tomder, w.; tombder, B.; tomdar, c.w. 1668; toimder, tymder, w.; tunder, (?) B.; tumma, P.; tês, w.; gurés, grés, P. See also WARMTH.

HEATED, *adj.* See HOT.

HALF HOT or HALF HEATED. (As of an oven). Sam, zam, D.

HEATH, *s.* (A heath-field). Rôs, B.

HEATH, *s.* (The plant). Grig, griglan, w.; gryglans, B.

HEATHEN, *s.* Sarsyn. Properly the name for a Saracen, but used for *heathen* also.

HEAVEN, *s.* Nêf, w.; neff, B.; neif, c.w. 139; neyf, c.w. 1430; neef, c.w. 2469; nêv, w.; neve, P.; reu, B. *The heavens, the sky.* The same words as for *heaven.*

HEAVY, *adj.* (As to weight). Poys, boys, pôs, w.; bôs, P.; poes, w.; powz, B.; powys, P.; pûz, w.

HEAVY, *adj.* (Oppressive, sad). Gryvye, O.M. 1921. *Yma hun orth ov gryvye,* sleep is heavy on me, O.M. 1921; trom, O.M. 1209. *Trom dyal war ol an veys,* heavy vengeance on all the world, O.M. 1209.

HEAVINESS, *s.* (Drowsiness). Possygyon, w.

HEAVINESS, *s.* (As to weight). Pysder, w.

HEAVILY, *adv.* Pôs, R.D. 511. *May fe me re goskês pôs,* my faith! I have slept heavily, R.D. 511.

HEBREW, *adj.* Ebbrow, w.

HEDGE, *v.* (To build a hedge). Dho keaz. P.

HEDGE, *s.* Ce, w.; ke, kea, P.; ge, w. The dry stone hedge of a mine, or a clay-work, is called *stillen,* or *stylen,* and the building of it is *stylin.*

A HEDGE, DAM, or LOW RIDGE. Astyllen, D.

A SMALL TURF-HEDGE. Durgy. Probably this word first meant a water dyke, as from *dûr,* water, *ge,* a fence, w.

A LOW HEDGE or ROUGH FENCE. Gurgo, gurgy, D.

A HEDGE GAP. Clût, cluit, D.

A WATTLED HEDGE GAP. Frith, freath, vreath, D.

HEDGEHOG, *s.* Sort, sart, zart, w.; brath-key, P.

HEDGE-SPARROW, *s.* Golvan ge, gylvan ge, w.; gyliangé, B.; the *ge* is pronounced *ghe.*

HEED, *s.* Vihith. *Dho kimeras vihith,* to toke heed, B.

HEEL, A HEEL, *s.* Gueuan, P.

HEEL-BONE, *s.* Lifern, livern, ufern, w.

HEIFER, *s.* Ledzhec, w.; ledzhek, ledzick, P.

HEIGHT, A HEIGHT, *s.* Ban, pan, van, top, thop, w.

HEIGHT, *s.* (Highness, loftiness). Uchelder, uhelder, ewhelder, huhelder, w.; huheldar, P.; euhelder, ughelder, B.

HELD, *part.* Sensys, sengys, syngys, w. See TO HOLD.

HELL, *s.* Ifarn, w.; efarn, c.w. 244; effarn, yffarn, yfarn, w.; yferne, M. 1256; yffran, B. *Bôs yn yfarn ow lesky,* to be in hell burning, R.D. 1457.

HELP, *s.* Gweras, w.; gueras, B.; gwerés, w.; guerés, M. 3106. *Manaff the welés guerés,* I will to seek help, M. 3209; guereys, M. 3190; gwerras, gweret, P.; kewerés, B.; cyweras. w.; kyueras, uerraz, P.; weras, B.; werés, w. *Râk the werés yv parys,* for thy help is prepared, P.C. 2797.

HELP, *v.* Gwerés, w.; guerés, P. werés, w.

LET HIM HELP. Weresés, a mutation of *gweresés,* 3 pers. s. imp. of *gwerés,* to help, w.

HELP ONE'S SELF, *v.* Omweras, ymwerés, w.

HELPFUL, *adj.* Hewerés, M. 3132. *Hewerés prest orth tûs du,* helpful always towards God's people, M. 3132.

HELPLESS, *adj.* Dycklés, c.w. 1031.

HELPMATE, *s.* Cowethés, howethés, w. *An ven cowethés ordnys,* of the true helpmate ordained, O.M. 92.

HELTER-SKELTER. Oodel-doodel, D.

HELVETIAN, A HELVETIAN, *s.* Hiuhvoeliet, B.

HEM, *s.* (Of a garment). Pillen, B.

HEMLOCK, *s.* Cegas, kegas, w.; kegaz. P. See CARROT.

HEMP, *s.* Cûer, w.; kûer, P.

HEN, *s.* Gâr, w.; giar, B.; iâr, jâr, w.; yâr, P. *Pl.* Yêr, w.

HEN'S NEST. Nyth yâr, P.

HEN'S-PATH, or WAY, *s.* Voryer, D.

HENBANE, *s.* (*Hyoscyamus niger*). Gahen, w.

HENCE, *adv.* Alemma, w.; alema, M. 659; alebma, P. *Ffystyn alemma duwhans,* hasten hence quickly, o.M. 169. *Vn pols byhen alemma,* a little while hence, o.M. 1269; ahanen, w.; ahanan, P.C. 465. *Symon júd dún ahonan,* Simon Judas, let us go hence, P.C. 465; lemma, lebma, P.

HENCEFORTH, *adv.* Gwosé - ma, w.; udzhema, udzhe-hemma, udzhena, P.; udzha, B.; udzhé. P.; guozemma, B.; woza-hemma, uoza-hemma, wagé-hemma, ombdina, P.; wose-helma, M. 1073; divetha, P

HER, *pron.* Y, w.; ye, c.w. 914; hye, P.; hy, hi, i, ys, y's, w.; yr, B.; as, a's, a, w.; se, B.

HER'S, *pron.* Y, i, si, u, P.

AND HER'S. Hay (*ha hy*), hath, P.

AT HER. Worty, orty, w.

BY HER. Worty, orty, gynsy, gensy, w.; drythy, N.

FOR HER. Ryghty, w.; râgthy, N. (*râg-ty*).

FROM HER. Ay (*an hy*), anethy, worty, orty, dy-worty, w.

IN HER. Ynny (*yn-hy*), w.

OF HER. Anedhy, anethy, annethy, w.; ay (*an-hy*), P.

TO HER. Thethy, N.; thuthy, thys, B.; dedhy, dhedhy, dydy, w.; dhyddi, P.; dy (*do-hy*), dethy, w.; worty, orty, w.; ortye, c.w. 892; orty hy, c w. 881.

UPON HER. Warnethy N.

WITH HER. Gynsy. gensy, w.

HERB, *s.* (A herb, any herb). Lôs, lús, lês, leys, w.; lushan, lysuan, lyzuan, B.; losowen, M. 1483.

HERBS, *s.* Losow, lusow, lusu, lyswys, losowés, losowys, w.; luzu, lozouez, lyzuyz, P.

HERBAGE, *s.* Gwells, gwels, gwelz, guelz, w.; gwyls, lousaouen, B.

HERCULES, *s.* Erchyll, B.

HERD, A HERD. *s.* Tonec, tonek, w.; praed, B.

HERDSMAN, *s.* Bugel. begel. bigel, bygel, w.; be-gol, bizel, B.; kuithyas, guithiat, P.

HERE, THIS PLACE. Omma, w.; ommé, N. *Ot ommé an guas,* see here the fellow, R.D 1803; oma, M. 2932. *Oma yma meryasek,* here is Meriasek, M. 2932; umma, w.; unna (?), vynna, P.; ymma, yma, obma, ubma, ybma, obba, w.; ubba, P.; hubba, B.; uppa, ybba, w.; helma le, P.; lemma, w. (*A lemma,* from here); lebma, lebba, w.

HERE, THERE. Dêv. dêf. Used indifferently to signify *here* or *there.* *Dêv têk a brên,* there's a fair tree, or here is a fair tree, P.

HERE THEY ARE. Ottengy, P.

HEREAFTER. Gwosé-ma, w.; guozemma, B.; woza hemma, P.; wosé helma, M 1072. *Gelwys vyth wosé helma,* shall be called hereafter, M. 1072; wagé-hemma. P.; udzhema, w.; udzhemma, B.; udzhe-henna, udzhena, udzhedda, P.; udzha, B.; udzhé, divetha, ombdina, P.

HEREUPON. Gans-hemma, gans-hena. B.; alebma, P.

HERITAGE, *s.* Ertech. w.; hertons, M. 2452. *In ov hertons dêth na nós,* in my heritage, day or night, M. 2452.

HERMAPHRODITE, *s.* Gûr-a-vau, B. (*Vulvatus homo, Lat.*)

HERMIT, *s.* Ancar, w.; erhmit, B.; hermit, P.

HERMITAGE, *s.* Ancar. (*Polwhele*).

HERON, *s.* Cerhidh, w.; kerhidh, P.; cherhit kerhés, w.; kerheis, B.

HERRING, *s.* Hernan guidn. *Lit.* A white pilchard, P.; allec, B. A general term also for pilchards; hering, P.

HESITATION, *s.* Let, w.; lettye, P.C. 591 *Govyn worthy'n hep lettye,* ask of us without hesitation, P.C. 591.

HEW, *v.* Squattya, skuattia, scuattya, dho skuattya, sguattia, w.

HIDE, *s.* (Of an animal). Cen, w.; kroin, lezr, B.; krohan, P. See SKIN.

HIDE, *v.* (Conceal). Cudhé, cudha, cutha, cuthé, w.; kuthé, P.; gutha, c.w. 870; hudha, cidha, citha, w.; kith, kitha, P.; kidha, B.; githa, P.; celés, kelés, w.; gellas, c.w. 1245; gorhery, w. *Hay why a pys an runyow th'agas gorhery,* and ye shall pray the hills to hide you, P.C. 2654-5.

HE MAY HIDE. Gudho, a mutation of *cudho,* 3 pers. s. subj. of *cudhé,* to hide, w.

HID or HIDDEN. Gollas, gyld, B.; cuthens, P.

ONE WHO HIDES HIMSELF. Cûthygûk, P.

HIDING-HOLE, *s.* Cuziat, B.

HIDING-PLACE, *s.* Danva, w.

HIGH, *adj.* Uch, huch, uchel, w.; huth, cuth, P.; ard, arth, earth, w.; warth, worth, wurth, P.; gwarth, ewhal, euhel. w.; euhell, P.; huhel. w.; euhal, yuhal, B; uhal, uhall, P.; euhual, uthall, uhan, P.; ban, pan, w.; doun, P.; laé, B.; tal. *Tal carn,* the high rock, w.

HIGH, CONSPICUOUS, *adj.* Guydh, P.; gwydh, gwydd, B.

ON HIGH. Uchon, uchan, ûs, w.; a huhon, hun-helder, P.

SO HIGH. Mar iuhal, w.

HIGHER, *adj.* Gwarra, w.; guarra, uarrah, p.; warthah, w.; wartha, wortha, varth, p.

HIGHEST, *adj.* Gwartha, warrah, w.; uarrah, p.; uhella, n.; uchaf, w.

HIGH-FLOWN, *adj.* Moureriac, w.; moureriak, b.

HIGHLANDER, *s.* Hiuhvoeliet, b.

HIGHNESS, *s.* Uchelder, w.; ughelder, r.; uhelder, huhelder, w.; huheldar, p.

HIGH-PRIEST, *s.* Volaveth, w.; volaneth, p.c. 953.

HIGH-WORDED, *adj.* Moureriac, w.; moureriak, b.

HIGLY PLACED. (That which is highly placed). Tallic, w.; tallick, tallock, tallack, p.

A HIGH PLACE. Galé, b.

HILL. *s.* Brea, bre, brey, bray, bry, pry, vrê. *Moel vrê*, the bare hill; ben, bin, byn, bân, pân, vân, p.; bern, burn, bourn, bryn, w.; den. p.; dîn, w.; (Pryce's meaning for *din*, is a round steep hill, a fortified hill); tyn, b.; dûn, dorn, dhorn, w.; drôn. *Gún drón*, the down's hill; trôn. p.; rhyn (pronounced *reen*), rûn. *Pl.* Rûnyow. *Ha why a pys an runyow th'agas gorhery*, and ye shall pray the hills to hide you, p.c. 2654-5; alt, als, hâl, w.; men, p.

A HILL ON A DOWN. Gûnbrê, b.

A FORTIFIED HILL. Dîn, dinas, dinaz, w.

A LITTLE HILL. Hâl bian, w.

A STEEP HILL SIDE. Reen, d.

HILLOCK, *s.* Rhynan, w; rynen, b.; pil, creeg, cruk, w.; cruc, cryk, p.; kryk, kryb, bryn, brine, kevnen, b.; tuyn, w.

HILLOCK, *s.* (Of sand). See HEAP (of sand)

HILT, *s.* (Of a knife). Cârn colhan, w.; kârn kolhan, b.

HILLY, *adj.* Denick, thenick, p.

HIM, *pron.* E, ef, ev, w.; eu, b.; ve, w.; y, i, ye, ge, p.; a's, a'n (*a* aux, '*n* him), yn, w.; ren, reth, (*the ren*, to him), b.; do, p.; tho, otho, notho, b.; so, p.

AFTER HIM. War-y-lergh, wary-lurgh, p.; wariler, b.

AT HIM. Worto, orto, w.

BY HIM. Dretho, n.; ganso, worto, orto, w.

FOR HIM. Ractha c.w. 2015; ragtha, ragthé, b.; ragtho, w.

FROM HIM. Adhiworto, odhiworto, w.; odhiuorté, b.; deworto, dewhorto, dyworto, diworto, w.; diuorté, dyworry, p ; worto, orto, anotho, annodho, w.

IN HIM. Ynno (*yn-o*), w.; ynny, p.

OF HIM. Annotho, annodho, w.

ON HIM. Dotha, b.

TO HIM. Thotha, c.w. 799; thotho, thuthy, b., thethé, theth, p.; dy, dhy, dodho, dhodo, w.; dhodho, dhodhé, da, dho. dhydé. p.; datho, b.; dotha, c.w. 1017; worto, orto, w.; uorto, snell, b.

UPON HIM. Worto, orto, w.; warnotho, n.

HIMSELF, *pron.* Honon, honan, honyl, b.; dhom, thom (?) p.

HIND or DEER, *s.* Ewic, euhic, w.; euig, euhig, b.

HIND-CALF, *s.* Loch-euhic, w.; loch-euig, leauheuig, b.

HINDER, *v.* Lettya, m. 586. *Súr the lettya*, surely to hinder thee, m. 586; hethy, thuethy, p.

HINDMOST, HINDERMOST, *adj* Vôn, b.

HINDRANCE, *s.* Let, w.; cluddias, b.; hâs, p.

HINGE, *s.* Bah, w. (*Pl.* Bahau, bahow); mediner, b.; medinor, w.

HIP, *s.* Clûn, penclun, w.; klyn, pedrain, morras, morraz, mordhos, morboit, clenniaw, b. (Clenniaw, *Pl.* ?).

HIP-BONES, *s.* Gulbredengu, b.

HIRE, *v.* Goberna, w.; kyrhy, yrvye, p.

TO HIRE WITH GIFTS. Rodothy, p.

HIRED, *part.* Gobernés, w.

HIRE, *s.* Arfeth, w. *Ow arfeth byth na whyla*, my hire I have never seen, p.c. 2262; gober. gobar, gobyr, w.; gobr. gubar, gu, guu, p.; loosech, w.

HIS, *pron.* A, e, i, hy, y, w.; ye, ge, ys, u, p.; huneth, b.

AND HIS. Hay (*ha hy*), p.

OF HIS. Aga, p.

TO HIS. Thy, b.

HISS, *v.* Tithia, w.

HISSING, *adj.* Whyflyn. w. *Yn tán whyflyn éf a séf*, in hissing fire he shall stay, r d. 2311.

HITHER, *adv.* Dhybba, b. See HERE.

HITHERMOST, *adj.* Nessa, nesav, w.; nês, p.

HITHERTO, *adv.* Bet an ûrma, w.

HIVE, *s.* Kaval, b.

HO! *exclam.* Ow, w.; used to call attention.

HOAR-FROST. *s.* Glit, w.

HOARY, *adj.* Lous, loos, lôs, loys, w.; ludgh, p.; luit, w.

HOARD UP, TO HOARD UP, *v.* Derevel, b.

HOARSE, *adj.* Hôz, b.

HOARSENESS, *s.* Hoizias, b.; hoiziaz, p.

HOBGOBLIN, *s.* Bucca, w.

HOG, *s.* Torch, porhal, hôch, w.; yôch, hôh, môh, b.

HOGS, *s.* Porelli, p.

HOGSHEAD, *s.* (Cask). Balliar, w.

HOG'S HERB, *s.* (Clotbur.). Hochwayu, hochvuyu, w.; hochuayu, B.; hochwayw, hochguayw. P.

HOG-STY, *s.* Krou-môh, B.

HOIDEN, *s.* Hoeden, w.

HOLD, *v.* (To hold, to lay hold of, to grasp, to have). Gaval, w.; gevas, gouas, P.; dalhenné, w.

HOLD, *v.* (To hold, catch, seize, esteem, value). Sensy, synsy, sinsy, sensyé, syngy, dho sendzhé, w.; sindzhy, B.; sindzha, sensa, sansa, P.; zingy, B.; sinzhi, P.

HOLD THOU. Sens, syns, P. The 2 pers. s. imp. of *sensy*, and *synsy*, to hold. At present in Polperro, Cornwall, the boys at play with marbles, instead of saying hold or stop, cry out, *sense.*

HOLD THY PRATE. Syns the clap, P.

TO HOLD ONE'S SELF, *v.* Omdhal, w.

TO HOLD ONE'S TONGUE, *v.* Tewel, w.; teuel, P.

HOLD YOUR TONGUE, HUSH. Tau, taw, B.; tausy, P.; chea-chanter, B.V.; cheechonter, w.F.P.

HOLE, TO MAKE A HOLE, *v.* Tulla, B.; teyl, P.

HOLED, *part.* Tollys, P.

HOLE, *s.* Toll, tol, toul, tewl, w.; tull, B.; doll, pol, bol, w.

HOLES, *s.* Tell. The pl. of *toll*, w.; tel, N.

FULL OF HOLES. Tollec, w.; tollek, B. siger, w.; sigr, P.

A HOLE IN A CLIFF. Sawan, w.; zawn, D. This is still used for a hole in a cliff through which the sea passes.

HOLIDAY, *s.* Dêdh goil, dydh goil, w.; dêgôl, dêgl, B.; gôl, w.

HOLINESS, *s.* Sansoleth, M. 137.

HOLLOW, *adj.* Tollec, w.; tollek, B.; siger, w.; sigr, guag, uag, vâg, veag, P.; keu, B.

HOLLY, *s.* Celin, w.; kelin, P.; holm, B.

HOLLY-TREE, *s.* Celinen, w.; kelinen, B.; huluer, D.

HOLLY-GROVE, *s.* Celynnec, w.; kelinnek, B.; kelynack, P.

HOLY, *adj.* San, sans, zanz, sanct, w.; sant, P.; gulan, glan, lan, w.; galh, gol, B.; benegés. venegés, w.; hali, P.

HOLY FAITH. San crêd, w.

HOLY GHOST. Speris sans, B.; spiriz sant, P.

HOME, AT HOME, HOMEWARDS, *adv.* Dre, w. *Dûn ganso the dre warnot*, come with him home speedily, O.M. 559. *Moaz dre*, to go home; tre, O.M. 1632. *Kyns me the troylé the tre*, before I return home, O.M. 1632; teua, B. *Môz teua*, to go home, B.

HOME or HOMESTEAD, *s.* Tre, trêv, tregva, trigva, w.

HOMESTEAD or SMALL FARM, *s.* Dijey. D.

HOMEWARDS. Adrê, w.

HOMICIDE, *s.* Dênlâdh, pagyia, w.

HONE, *s.* Agolan, w.

HONEST, *adj.* Lên, laian, w.; luen, lwn, B.; onest, w.

HONESTLY, *adv.* Yn lêl, P.C. 1273. *Mês mara keusys yn lêl*, but I have spoken honestly, P.C. 1273.

HONEST MAN. Dremas, M. 1103; dremays, M. 1112,

HONEY, *s.* Mêl, w.; meal, P.

HONEY-COMB, *s.* Criban mêl, w.; kriba-mêl, B.

HONEYSUCKLE, *s.* Guydhuydh, B.

HONOUR, *v.* Perthy, parthy, w.; pertha, B.; enora, M 450.; urria, B.; gordhy, gordhyé, wordhyé, w.; worth, P.

HONOUR, *s.* Gorryans, w.; guoryans, P.; gordhyans, gurthyans, P.; wordhyans, w.; worthyans, gorty, anner, enor, enour, P.; annerh, B.; onour, P.; onowr, honou, kadar, B.

HONOURS. Cyfoeth, B.; onours (from the English), N.

HONOURABLE, *adj.* Enir, henir, ynir, sionge, B.; onest, w.

HONOURED, *part.* Grussés, P.

HONOUREDST, THOU HONOUREDST. Worsys, a mutation of *gorsys*, a contraction of *gordhsys*, 2 pers. s. preter. of *gordhy*, to honour, w.

HOOD, *s.* Cugol, scuidlien, w.; sguthlein. *Lit.* A shoulder linen.

HOOF, *s.* Ewincarn, w.; euinkarn, P.; euin-carn, B.

HOOK, *s.* Ig, yg, hig, hyc; bah (*Pl.* Bahow, w.; bahau, B.) *Bah*, is properly the hook or hinge of a gate. In fishing, the space between the hook and the lead is called *cabesta* or *cobesta*, w.F.P. and B.V.

THE BREAST HOOK OF A BOAT. Gwaith, D.

AN IRON HOOK. Yg hôrn, P.

HOOK, *s.* (For reaping). Filh, voulz, w.; uouiz, krobman, B.; crobman, w.

HOOP, *s.* (?) *A little hoop*, Bisow, bezo, w.

HOOTING. Idzhek, B.

HOP, *v.* Lemmel, lebmal, w.; lemal, B.

TO HOP ON ONE LEG. Vogget, D.

HOREHOUND, *s.* Lêsluit, w.; luitlês, lotles, P.

HORN, A HORN, *s.* Corn, w.; korn, B.; kern, P.; gorn, O.M. 207; horn, w. *Pl.* Kern, P.; gernygov, (*gernygou*), M. 3396; cernow, w.

HORN or TRUMPET, *s.* Corn, w.; korn, B.; hirgorn. *Lit.* A long horn, B.

HORN-BLOWER, *s.* Cerniat, cherniat, cernias, w. ; kernias. kerniat, B.

HORNED CATTLE. Gwarthec, gwarrhog, w. ; guarrhog, B.

HORNET, *s.* Hwirnorés, w.; huinerés, kuilkiorés, B.

HORRIBLE, *adj.* Uthec, ûthek, ûthyc, ûthyk, huthyc, huthyk, w. ; uter, B.

HORROR, *s.* Euth, ûth, uthecter, w. ; uthekter. N. ; rhynny, w. *Pocvan pup vr ha rynny,* sickness always and horror. R D. 2343 ; têr, P. ; scrûth, w. But *scrûth* means a horror or shiver.

HORSE, *s.* March, marh. merh. verh, margh, M. 1884; cevil, kevil, w.; keffyl. *Pl.* Merch, merh, w. ; mergh, N.

A BLACK HORSE. Margh morel, M. 2111.

HORSE-BACK, *s.* Geyn margh, M. 1884. *Me a weyl guas war geyn margh,* I see a lad on horse-back, M. 1884.

HORSE-COLLAR, *s.* Myngar. mungar, w. *Mungar* is still in use in Cornwall, and means a straw horse-collar.

HORSE-COMB, *s.* Streil, w.

HORSE-COVERING, or HORSE-CLOTH, *s.* Gwerés, w.; guerés, P.

HORSE-DUNG, *s.* Buzl verh, w. ; glow, D. *Glow* is also a name for *dried* cow-dung, and *dried* horse-dung. A coal (? a lump of fuel) was also called *glow.*

HORSE-HAIR, *s.* Rên, w.; ruen, M. 1968.

A HORSE-HAIR SHIRT. Hevys ruen M. 1968.

HORSE-LEECH, *s.* Ghêl, gêl, B

HORSE-LOAD, *s.* Sawe, B. See BURDEN and LOAD.

HORSE-MACKEREL, *s.* Scad, D.

HORSEMAN, *s.* Marrec, B. ; marrek. O.M. 2204 ; marheg, B. ; marhag, P. ; marhar, B. ; marchec, w. *Avel marrek fyn yrvys,* like a good horseman armed, O M. 2204.

HORSE-MANE, *s.* Rên verh, w.

HORSEMEN, *s.* Marogyon, varogyon, maregyon, marregion, marrogion, marrougion, marregyon, w.

HORSE-POND, *s.* Grelin, w.

HORSE-ROAD, or WAY, *s.* Vôrver, P. *Vôr, vôrdh, fôr,* a way, and *verh,* a mutation of *merh,* a horse, D.

HORSE-SKULL, A HORSE'S SKULL, *s.* Penpral marh, w. ; pedn pral marh, P.

HOSE, *s.* (Stocking). Hosan. *Pl.* Hosaneu, w. (Long hose.)

HOSE, *s.* (Stocking). Loder. *Pl.* Lodrow, lydraw, w.

HOSE, A HOSE, *s.* (? Tube, as for a fire-engine). Trone (an tron), B.

HOST, *s.* (Multitude). Lu, llu, luu, ôst, w. ; oster, P.

HOST, *s.* (As at an inn, &c.) Ost, w. ; oster, P. From the English ; yrvyrys, P.

HOSTAGE, *s.* Guistel, w. ; guystel, B.

HOSTESS, *s.* Ostés, ostez, w. From the English.

HOT, *adj.* Toim, tom. tum, tubm, tybm, dubm, w. ; kinnis, kynnés, grez, guressauk, B. *Mar dubm,* so hot, P.

THE HOT DOWN. N'un grez, P.

SO HOT. Mar dubm, w.

VERY HOT. Poesgys, B.

TO MAKE HOT. Tomma, tumma, tubma, w.

HOT-BATH, *s.* Golchfa, B.

HOUND, *s.* Milgy, brathcy, brathky, brakgye, w.

HOUNDS, *s.* Kuen, M. 3161. *Honter grua pary the kuer,* hunter make ready thy hounds, M. 3161.

HOUR, *s.* Ur, our, ower, owr, w. ; oer, P. ; ouer, B. ; êr, ear, eyr, w. ; ere, c.w. 905.

HALF AN HOUR. Hanter ûr, w.

IN THAT HOUR. In ûrna (in-ûr-na), w. ; yrna, c.w. 200.

AT THIS HOUR. Yn-ur-ma, w.

TO THIS HOUR. Bet an ûr-ma, w.

HOUR, TIME, or PERIOD, *s* Prit, prês, preys, prys, w. ; pris, erna, P. *At all hours,* Pub erna, P.

HOURLY, *adj.* Benary, bynary, bypur (byth pup ûr), venary, w. ; unary, P.

HOUSE, *s* (Abode, dwelling). Chy, chi, ty, P.; thy, gy, w. ; tshy, tshi, tshei, tshey, tshyi, dzhy, P. ; dzhyi, B. ; te. de. P. ; chem, R.D. 1397. *Yn chemma y fue gynen,* in this house was with us, R.D. 1397 ; bôd, w. ; bôt, P. ; buyth, veth, B. ; bos, w. ; boss, B. ; annedh, w. ; anneth, P c. 705. *Crês dev aberth yn anneth,* the peace of God be in this house, P c. 705 ; trev, trew, luan. B. *Ti* or *ty* appear to have been the earliest forms. Williams (*Lex. Corn. Brit.*) says that, " the letter *t* in this word came to have the sound of *ch,* before the vowel *i* or *y,* as in Erse ; the same as in English *church,* and to express this sound *ty* is always written *chy* in the " Ordinalia." Tshi, appears to be the phonetic form of the same word *ti* or *ty,* as also of *chy* We have proof of the soft sound of *chy,* in Chyandour, a name of a place.

THIS HOUSE. Chymma, chemma, tshymma, w.

HOUSES, *s.* Treven, w. ; trefov (*trefou*). M. 305.

HOUSE OF ORE. Carbona, carbonas, bunny, D. These words are in frequent use among miners, and have been handed down from the ancient Cornish. There is a singular use of the word *house,* for an accumulation or collection. The Cornish call a grove, a *town* of trees, a collection of water in a cavity of a mine, a *house* of water, and an enlargement or accumulation of ore in a lode, a *house* of ore, a *carbona, carbonas,* and *bunny.* I incline to the opinion that *carbona* is singular, and *carbonas* plural. In *carbona, car* would seem to be the same as *carn,* a rock, a rocky place, a heap of stones, and *bunny,* a form of *bona. Bona* and *bunny,* may be from *ben,* a butt-end, or enlargement. In the Armoric it is *bonn.* and *bun.* Sanscrit, *Budna.*

HOUSEHOLD, *s.* Teilu, teulu, w.; goskordhy. B.; goscorthé. P.; meny, M. 2277 *Ov meny a luen golan,* my household with a full heart, M. 2277.

HOUSEHOLD GOODS or STUFF. Gwadhel. w.; guadhel, B.; guathel, P.; guthel, w.; gulhel (?), peth-tshyi, B.

HOUSE-SNAIL, *s.* Melwiogel, B.

HOUSEWIFE, *s.* Gwrêgty, wrêgty, w.; gwreghty, c.w. 448.

HOVEL, *s.* Crow, w.; crou, P.; krou, B.; bosca, bôth, bothoc, w.; bothog, P.

HOW. Pattel, patel, patla, fattel, fatel, fatla, fatl, fetiyl, fetyl, fettel, P.; ffatla, c.w. 2319; era, B.

HOW FAR? Pelea era, B.

HOW IS IT WITH YOU? Fatla gan a why, ?

HOW MANY. Cenefra, ceniver, cenifer, cenyver, cenever, cyniver, keniver, kenyver, kynyver, kenifer, kynifer, P.; peualtra, pezealla, B.

HOW MUCH. Pythkemys, pygimmis, myns, B.

HOWL, *v.* Ullia, w.; uolé, olé, holea, hoalea. P.

HOWLING, *part.* Olah, olva, P.

HOWLING, A HOWLING, *s.* Hynadzhas, w.; hynadzhan, B.

HUBBUB, *s.* Touse, tousse, B. Still in common use. See ROW and UPROAR.

HUE. *s.* (Complexion, colour). Liu, lyw, w.; lew, c.w. 1051. *Rág an houl y lyw golow,* for the sun his bright hue, P.C. 3123.

HUG, *v.* Byzla, P. *Kensa bledhan byzla ha baye,* the first year hug and kiss, P.

HUGE. *adj.* Ethuc, ethec, ethyc. w.; ethuk, ethek, ethyk, P.; eithick, B.; ithic, ithik, w.; ithyk, P.; ithig, uthek. w.; uthik, P.; uthyc, w.; uthy, P.; ythec, w.; leadan, hail, hujeth, B. *Hujeth tra,* a huge thing. B.

HUGELY, *adv.* Ithik, ithig, P.

HUM, *s.* (A monotonous sound). Drilgy, B. The words *drilgy, drulgy,* and *drilsy* are still used for the same, D.

HUMANITY, *s.* (Human kind). Densés, densys, w.

HUMANITY, *s.* (Kindness). Denseth, w.

HUMBLE, *adj.* Huvel, hyvel, vuel, w.; evall, P. *Flehys evall ha gentell,* children humble and gentle,

c.w. 1061; esal, P.; isel, ysel, w.; isal, P.; isall, B.; izal, iza, P.; deboner, dyboner, w.

MOST HUMBLE. Hyvela, isella, w.

HUMBLE SERVANT. Gwâs isal, w.; gwâz izal, P.

VERY HUMBLE SERVANT. Pûr evall oberuaz, P.

TO BE HUMBLE, *v.* Hyvla, w.

HUMBLER, *adj.* Isala, w.; izala, P.

HUMBLEST, *adj.* Hyvela, isella, w.

HUMILITY, *s.* Huveldot, w.; huveldor, P.

HUMOUR, *s.* (Serum, *Lat.*) Lyn, B.

HUNDRED. Cans, can, w.; canz, P.; kanz, B.; hans, w. *Hans* is the aspirate mutation of *cans* after *try.*

THREE HUNDRED. Try cans, trey hans, try hans, N.

A HUNDRED MEN. Canguêr, w.

FIVE HUNDRED. Pymp cans.

A HUNDRED TIMES. Canquyth, w.; canquith, P.; kanzuyth, B.

TWO HUNDRED. Dew cans, N.

HUNDRED or CANTRED, *s.* Cantrev, gevern, B.

HUNGER. *s.* Naun, nown, gwâg, w.; guag, treythe, trethe, P.; densys, B.

HUNGRY, *adj.* Naounak, densys, B.; gwâg, gwâk, w.; guas, P.

HUNT, *v.* Hella, helhia, hellyrchy, w.; hellyrghy, helfia, P.; helghya, M. 3160.

HUNTED, *part.* Heltheys, B.

HUNTER or HUNTSMAN, *s.* Helhwur, w.; hellier, P.; helyur, helhiat, helyiat, helyad, B.

HUNTING-POLE, *s.* Hochwayu, hochvuyu, hochwayw, hochguayw, P. More correctly the names for a hog's spear.

HURDLE, *s.* Cluit, w.; kluyd, clifa, B. They still call a hurdle of wattled rods a *cluit,* or *clût.*

HURL, *v.* (Throw or fling). Towla, toula, tewlel, tywlel, teulel, tiulel, teuly, P.

HURL, *v.* (To play the game of hurling). Hyrliau, P.

HURLING, *s.* (The game so called). Hyrliau. *Hyrliau yu ghen guare nyi,* hurling is our sport, B.

HURRY, *s.* (Fuss, a bustle). Stroath, strother, P. These words are often used by the vulgar in Cornwall. Also pôr, or porr, to express the same thing.

HURRY. *s.* (Haste). Fesky, M. 2098; thir, P.; fors, O.M. 2801. *Fraga pendryv an fesky,* why, what is the hurry? M. 2098. *Nynsus fors awos henna,* there is no hurry for that, O.M. 2801.

HURRIED. Rafsys, w.

HURT, *v.* Droga, droaga, golyé, w.; hertia, P.; schyndyé, shyndyé, syndyé, w.

HURT or ANNOY, *v.* Scallyé, sclandry, P.

HURT, *part.* Desefys, P.

HURT, *s.* Drôc, drôk, drôg, w. ;,dregyn, M. 1124; thir, P. *Nag eff nyngeveth dregyn*, nor shall he have hurt, M. 1124.

HURT, LOSS, DAMAGE, *s.* Diopenés, P.; diowenés, B.

HURTFUL, *adj.* Drôc, drôk, drôg, w. ; parkenniat, B.

HURTLEBERRY, *s.* Iz-diu, B.

HUSBAND, *s.* Gour (pronounced *goor*), w *War y gour mar pyth lethys*, to her husband, if to be slain, P.C. 1982 ; goar, gûr, wour (pronounced *woor*). P. *Vethaf the woor*, I will be thy husband, O.M. 2111 ; uour, B. *Dha wour*, thy husband, B.; gôr, gorty, w. *Neb a'm grûk vy ha'm gorty*, he who made me and my husband, O.M. 181 ; worty, w. *Attebrés ty ha'th worty*, if thou didst eat, thou and thy husband, O.M. 175 ; cansfrueg, cansfreg, B.; dremas, w.

THY or YOUR HUSBAND. Gûrty, gorti, P.; gwyrti, worti, B.

A CAREFUL HUSBAND. Gûr prederys, w.

HUSBAND or WIFE. (*i.e.*, spouse or partner). Priés, pryés, pryas, bryés, friés, w. ; fryas, P.

HUSBANDMAN, *s.* Tioc, tiak, tyoc, tyac, tyach, dyac, dyack, gonedhic, gonydhic, gonythick. w.; gonethick, P.; gwyrthiadereu, guyrthiadereu, gunithiat ereu, B.

HUSH, BE SILENT. Tau, B.; taw, tausy, P.

HUSK, *s.* Gwisc, guisc, gwesc, w. ; guesk, P.; plisg, plysg, w.

HUSK or POD, *s.* Cûth, w. ; kûth, B. *Pl.* Cuthow, cuthu, w.

HUSK, *s.* (A husk of corn). Us, w.

HUSKS, *s.* (Of corn). Usion, ision, w. ; kulin, B. The Cornish still use the word *ishan*, for the husks of corn.

HUT or HOVEL. See HOVEL.

HUT CIRCLES. These ancient British remains are called *crellas*, D.

HYDROMEL, *s.* Cregaud, (?) B. See METHEGLIN.

HYPOCRISY, *s.* Scherewyneth, P.; scherewynsy, O.M. 942 ; anfugy, enfugy, P.

HYPOCRITE, *s.* Duffan, D.

HYPOCRITICAL, *adj.* Anfugyk, anfusyg, enfugyc, w. ; anfesug, R.D. 85.

HYSSOP, *s.* Eysyll, P.; eysel, P.C. 2977.

I.

" This letter is immutable. Its proper sound in all the Celtic dialects is the same as in French and Italian.

When short as in the English words, *sin, fin,* and when long as *ee* in *deed, seed.* In the Ordinalia, *y* is constantly used for it with the same sound.

In latest Cornish it was often sounded as the diphthong *ei.* or *i*, in the English words, *fright, sign.* Thus *hwi,* you. became *hwei* ; *tri,* or *try,* three, trei, &c." w. *Lex Corn. Brit.*

I, *pron.* Mi, my, vi, vy, ma, me, ve, w. ; fe, P.; 'm, 'f, w. ; y, O.M. (y'm, I am) ; yth, N.. *Yth arghaf,* I command, N. ; yu, ys, vsse, P. *Ysse fuef goky,* I was a fool, P.; oyv. B. *Oyv a gulez.* I see, B. The form *ma* occurs only in composition. *Me, mi, my,* in construction change into *ve, fe, vi, vy.*

I ALSO. Minné, w.

ICE, *s.* Clihi, w. ; klihi, B. ; glihi, clehé, w. ; clehy, M. 3055. *Menogh gans yrgh ha clehy,* often with snow and ice, M. 3055 ; rew, reu, w. ; rhewi, reui, reig, riou. B.

ICY, *adj.* Iein, eyn, w.

IDIOT, *s.* (Fool, simpleton). Edyack, P.; bobba, P.C. 2385 ; bucca gwidn, B. ; gaupus, gommok, cobba, pattic, D.

IDLE, *adj.* Dioc, lôs, wâst, w.

IDLE, *adj.* (Of no avail). Euereth, R.D. 936. *Rdk, euereth yv the gous,* for idle is to say, R.D. 936.

IDLE FELLOW. Gadlying, w. ; lorel, losel, P., zigur, zighir, B

IDLENESS, *s.* Ufereth, evereth, w.

IDOLATER, *s.* Gadlying, P.

IF. A. *A pe yn della ve,* if it were so, w. ; ay, po, bo, py, P. ; cên, w. ; keen, P. ; cyn, kyn, gên, mar (before a consonant), mars (before a vowel), w. ; mor, sens, syns, vn, ynne, ynno, P.; mara, N. *Mar a'n pesef ef,* if I pray him, P.C. 466. *Mara keusys falsury,* if I spoke falsehood, P.C. 1271.

IF, ALTHOUGH, *conj.* Cueia. w. ; kueia, B. ; cra, w.

IF NOT. Manan (*ma-na'n*) w.; marny, marnes, P.; po ni, ponag, w. ; pensg, peneges. erriam, P.; krana, B.

IF OTHERWISE. Po cen, w. ; poken, pyken, P.

IF THAT. Ma, w.

IF IT. As, a's, w.

IF I COULD. Callé, callow, P.

IF, SINCE. Apé, P.

IGNORAMUS, *s.* Pen pyst, P.

IGNOBLE, *adj.* Ledryn, B.

IGNORANT, *adj.* Discient, diskient, diskref, B.

ILL, *adj.* (Unwell). Claff. *Efrethek ha claff pan en,* maimed and ill when we were, M.

ILL, *s.* See EVIL.

ILL-CLAD, *adj.* Fernoyth, ferneth, B.

ILL-DEED, *s.* Drocoleth, p.c. 1364; dhroloceth, drûk-culeth, w.

ILL AT EASE. Annês, w.

ILL REPORT. Drôgger drôcger, w.

ILL SAVOUR. Drôg sawarn, w.; drôg savarn, b.

ILL SMELLING. Musac, w.; mekiek, mechiek, p.

ILL-TONGUED. Drôgdavasec, w.; drôkdavazek, b.

ILLUMINATE, *v.* Golowa, gouloua, w.; goloua, p.; colowa, w.; gylyua, p.; gylywa, gylywi, w.

ILLUMINATION, *s.* Golowas, w.; golouas, p.

ILL-WILL, *s.* Avy, aui, w.; avey, p.; drôgbrés, sôr, sorras, w. *Ha gans colen hep sôr*, and with good heart, without ill-will, o.m. 428.

IMAGE, *s.* Avain, w.

IMAGINATION, *s.* See THOUGHT.

IMAGINE, *v.* Avani, b.

IMBECILE, *s.* See IDIOT.

IMBIBE, *v.* Efé, evé, w; eva, p.

IMMEDIATE, *s.* Desempys, dysempys, desympys, dysympys, w.; dhysempyys, thesempys, p.; desimpit, w.

IMMEDIATLY. *adv.* Aredy, eredy, yredy, a desempys, a dysempys, a desympys, w.; a thesempys, a thysempys, w.; adhysempyz, dhy sempys, p.; dysempys, n.; desemhys, the sempys, thesympys, p.; thysympys, o.m. 318; dystouch, dhystouch, w.; dystough, p.; thystough, r d. 1243; scôn, w.; skân, toothda, tothetta, tuthta, tôthda, totta, p.; uscys, w.; uskys, ûth, p.; yscys, warnot, w.; wharé. o.m. 2846; fâst, fêst-yn-tye, p.

IMMENSE, *adj.* See HUGE.

IMMERGE, *v.* Beuzi, bedhy, budhy, bidhy, w.

IMPAIR, *v.* Gwaythy, gwethé. The verbal form is *fethy*, w.

IMPASSABLE, *adj.* Hebford, b. *Lit.* Without a road.

IMPEACH, *v.* Cuhudhé, w.; cuhuthé, p.; cuhudhas, guhudhas, huhudhas, w.; guhuthias, p.; achesa, b.

IMPLORE, *v.* Pesy, pysy, pigy, pygy, w.; pidgy, peidgy, pidzhi, pidzha, pys, b.

IMPORTANT, *adj.* Besy, bysy, vysy. w.

IMPOSE, *v.* (Cheat). Gurra, b.

IMPOSTER. *s.* Huder, w.; hydor, hudor, p.; hydol, b.

IMPOTENT, *adj.* Develo, w.

IMPRECATE, *v.* Molletha, mollethia, molythia, w.

IMPRECATING, AN IMPRECATING, *s.* Mollethians, w.

IMPRECATION, *s.* Molleth, mollath, molloth, w.; molath, molth, b.; ty, w. *Pl.* Mollethow, mollathow, w.; molathow, p.

IMPRESS or PRINT, *v.* Graphy, argraphy, dho argraphy, w.

IMPRESSION or PRINT, *s.* Argraphys, w.; graphy, p.

IMPRESSION, *s.* (As of a foot, &c.) Ol, w.; ool, p.

IMPROVE, *v.* Gwella, w.; guella, p.

IMPRUDENT, *adj.* Anfur, w.

IMPUDENT, *adj.* Corrat, toit, d.; diveth, dyveth, deveth, w.

IN, *prep.* Yn. *Yn ow enef*, in my soul, p.c. 1022; y, e, en, ed, et (this is a late corruption of *en*), in, w.; i, p.; itta. *Itta 'o guilt*, in my bed, b.; der, dre, dredh, p.; aber, aberth, abervedh, aperfeth, w.; abervadh, aberneth, p.; meyny, mein. *Oll mein y chy*, all in the house; ord, orth, worth, w.; uarth, uorh, uar. *Uar an diuadh*, in the end, b.

IN ANY WAY, IN ANY WISE. Malbew, w.

IN SHORT, FINALLY. Yn fen, b.

IN THAT PLACE. Ena, enna, eno, w.

IN THEM. Etta, ettans, ynné, w.

IN THIS PLACE, HERE. Omma, obma, obba, umma, ybba, ymma, yma, ma, w.

IN THY. Yth, ith, w.

IN, WITHIN. Adzhyi, dzhyi, w.

INCENSE, *v.* Provycha, b.

INCENSE, *s.* Encois, incois, inkois. Words also used for frankincense.

INCENSE-POT, *s.* Incoise lest, inkois lestr, b.; encoislester, p.

INCEST, *s.* Squenip, p.

INCESTUOUS, *adj.* Sgenip, sguenip, b.

INCISE, *v.* Trochy, trohy, trechy, trehy, w.

INCLINE, *v.* Posé, w.; possé, bossé, p.; plegyé, plygyé ,w.; plegy, p.; plegya, plynché, b.

INCLINE or SLOPE, *s.* Slintrim, d. Perhaps from *slyntia*, to slide or glide.

INCLINED, *part.* (Disposed). Plegadow, plygadow, w.

INCLOSE, *v.* Degy, w.; dygy, p.; gorhery, w.; ceas, keaz, b.

INCLOSURE, AN INCLOSURE, *s.* Cê, w.; kea, p.; gê, lan, w.; alwed, p.

INCOMPARABLE, *adj.* Hepparow, w.; hepparou, hepar, b.

INCONVENIENT, *adj.* Grêf, p.

INCREASE, *v.* Mochahé, w.; kressia, teva, tivia, b.

TO BE INCREASED. Mochahé, w.

INCREASED, *part.* Kreshaz, b.

INCREDULOUS, *adj.* Dyscrygyk, n.

INCUMBENT, *adj.* Teleth, P.C. 3208. *Y worthyé thy'n y teleth* to worship him is incumbent on us, P.C. 3208.

IT IS INCUMBENT, IT BEHOVETH. Gôth, côth, couth, w.

INDEED. *adv.* Eredy, yredy, en wîr, w.; lanté, lenté, (lauté, leuté, P.; relewté, rulewté, relawta, B.; feyst, M. 2144. *Ladra yúr lues feyst,* to plunder very many indeed, M. 2144; defry, dyffry, w.

INDEED! *exclam.* Renothas! w.

INDIA, *s.* Eynda, P.

INDICT, *v.* Cuhudhé, w.; cuhuthé, P.; cuhudhas, guhudhas, huhudhas, w.; guhuthias, P.

INDIVIDUAL, AN INDIVIDUAL, *s.* Onan, onen, onon, w.; onyn, odn, P.

INFAMOUS, *adj.* Drôggerut, drôcgerut, w.; drôg-gerat, P.

INFAMY, *s.* Drôgger, drôcger, w.; queth, P.

INFANT, AN INFANT, *s.* Mâb a flavar, w.; mâb an lavar, P.

INFERNAL, *adj* Effarne, P.

INFIRM, *adj.* Aniach, w.; aniak, B.; develo, gwan, wan, w.; guan, guadn, P.

INFIRMITY, *s.* Gwander, w.

INFLAMMATION, *s.* Losc, losk, w.

INFLICTED, *part.* Warkerd, P. *Brás vy payne war-kerd,* great was the pain inflicted, P.

INFLICTED, *adj.* Darken, B.

INFLUX OF THE SEA. Morlenol, w.

INFORM, *v.* Dyswithy, dysquethas, thyswethas, B.; desky, w.; desgy, P.; desca, desga, w.

INFORMATION, AN INFORMATION, *s.* Daryvas, dheryvas, w.; methegyeth, M. 1487. *Ny won us methegyeth,* I do not know from information, M. 1487.

INGENIOUS, *adj.* Yngn, P C. 1886. *Dên fel mûr yv hag yngn,* a very cunning man he is, and ingenious, P.C. 1886.

INHABIT, *v.* Trega. tregé, w.; dregé, P.; trigé, triga, trigia, w.; trighia, B.; redrygy, P.; anhedhy, w.; kontreva, B.

INHABITANT, *s.* Treger, w.; trig, tryk, tryck, P.

INHERITANCE, *s.* Achta. ehtas, B.

INJUNCTION, *s.* Danvonad, w.; arghad, O.M. 997. See COMMAND.

INJUNCTIONS, *s.* Danvonadow, w.; arghadow, O.M. 997. See COMMAND.

INJURE, *v.* Droga, droaga, myschevy, schyndyé, shyndyé, syndyé, w.

INJURIOUS, *adj.* Camhinsic, P.; camhilik, parken-niat, B.

INJURY, *s* Cam, gam, drôc, drôk, drôg, drôcoleth, dhrôcoleth, drôk-culeth, w.

INJUSTICE, *s.* Cam-hisic, P.

INLET OF WATER. (A creek). Lo, w.

INN, *s.* Cylden, kylden, ostel. w.

INNKEEPER, *s.* Maidor, B.; ôst, w.; ôster, P.

INNOCENT, *adj.* Glân, gulan, gwirion, gwyryon, w.; gwirryon, c w. 1718; guyryon, O.M. 930.

INQUIRE, *v.* Gofen, goven, goffen, gofyn, gophidn, P.

INSANE, *adj.* Discient, diskient, w; dikref, B.; gur-bullog, w.; gurbulloc, B.; bâd, w.

INSANITY, *s.* Mescatter, w.; diskians, B.

INSATIABLE, *adj.* Abarstick, B.

INSCRIPTION, *s.* Acheson, P. *Pylat vynnus screfé a vewnas chrest acheson.* Pilate would write of the life of Christ an inscription (or memorial); lyble, B.

INSECT, *s.* Gwiban, w.; guiban, P.; prif. prêf, pryf, prêv, w.

INSENSIBILITY, *s.* Vindrau, B.; uindrau, P.

INSIDE, WITHIN. Ynbarth, B.; agy (*a chy*), N. *Avês hag agy,* without and within, O.M. 953.

INSISTED, *part.* Ynnyas, B.

INSOMUCH, *adv.* Aban, w.; awos, auoz, P.

INSPECTOR OF TIN BOUNDS. Tollur, D. From *toll.* a pit or hole. Shallow pits mark the boundary of a tin "sett."

INSTANT, AN INSTANT, *s.* Tuch. See TIME.

INSTANTLY. *adv.* Fâst, fêst-yn-tye, P.; warnot, w. See IMMEDIATELY.

INSTRUCT, *v.* Dyscy, dysky, dhysky, w.; descy, desky, desgy, desca, desga, P.; tysky, w.

INSTRUMENT or TOOL OF IRON. Clao, B.

INSTRUMENT, AN INSRUMENT, *s.* Tacel, w.; takel, P

INSTRUMENTS. MONEY, NECESSARIES OF LIFE. Pegans. w.; peganz, P.; fegans, w. In the Cornish dialect they say *fangings* and *vangings.*

INSULT, *v.* Dyspytyé. dhyspytyé, w.; braggyé, M. 3507. *Neb úr braggye an crustunyon,* at any time to insult the Christians, M. 3507.

INSULT, *s.* Despyth, dyspyth, w.

INTEND, *v.* Faes, teuly, towla, toula, tewlel, tywlcl, yflé, P.

INTENTION, *s.* Mynnas, w.

INTER, *v.* Ancledhy. w.; anclethy, P.; encledhyés, w; dhe ancleythyss, clathna, clethy, P.; daiarou, B.

INTEREST, ADVANTAGE, *s.* Lên, w.

INTERLUDE, *s.* Antarlick, P.

INTERMISSION, *s.* Hâs. *Mar a hás,* without intermission; symueth. *Hág ef vye dryk heb symueth.* and he shall tarry without respite (or in-termission), P.

INTIMATE, *adj.* Specyal, B. *Syecyal brás,* very intimate. They still say of intimates that they are "very special."

INTIMATE, *s.* Mayn, w.; meyn, P. *Pl.* Mayny, w.; meyny, P.

INTO, *prep.* Yn, y, w.; vynyn, c.w. 1819. *Vynyn hy rág temptya,* into it to tempt, c.w. 1819.

INTO, WITHIN. Embera, w.

INTO MY. Ym, im, w.

INTOXICATED, *adj.* Medho, vedho, w.

INTOXICATION, *s.* Medhas, w.; medhdas, P.

INTRENCHMENT, *s.* Fôs, fossa, foza, vôs, vossa, vozé, voza (Câr-voza, in Probus), P.; cadlys, w.; bolla, B.

INTRUST, *v.* Kemynna, M. 503.

INUNDATION, *s.* Líf, lyff, w. See DELUGE.

INVALID, *s.* (Sick person). Aneuin, P.

INVENTOR, *s.* Inguinor, B.

INVITATION, *s.* Galow, w.

INVOKE, *v.* Gelwel, gylwel, w.; gulwel, P.; celwel, w.

INVOCATION, *s.* Pesad, pysad, pidzhad, w.

INVOCATIONS, *s.* Pesadow, pysadow, pydzhadow, pyadow, piyadow, besadow, bysadow, fysadow, w.

INWARD PART. (Within). Parvedh (*a bervedh*), w.

IRIS, *s.* (The yellow water Iris). Laister, D.

IRISH, *adj.* Gôdhaléc, w.; Guydhelek, B.

IRISHMAN, *s.* Gwidhal, Gôdhal. *Pl.* Gwidhili, w.; Guidhili, P.

IRELAND, *s.* Uordyn, w.

IRON, *v.* (To iron, or fasten with iron). Wrennyé, hernia, w.

IRON, *s.* Hôrn, hoern, hoarn, hern, w.   *Of or belonging to iron.* Hoarnek, B.

IRONMONGER, *s.* Hoirnier, B.

IRON OCHRE. Gozzan, gozan, w. The term *gozzan,* or *gossan,* is in common use among Cornish miners.

IRON ORE. (A coarse kind). Cal, kal, P.

IRON FRYING-PAN. Padelhoern, B.

IRON PAN. Padel hoern, w.

IRON TOOL, AN IRON TOOL. Clao, B.

IRREGULAR, *adj.* Ufereth, evereth, P.

IRRIGATE, *v.* Douria, dourhi, w.

IS, *v. irr.* Usy, ugy, ygé, a corrupted form of *usy,* that is, w.; ûs, wêtu, yn, P.; gês. *Nyn gés,* is not, gew, gyu, gugy, pew, B.

IS THERE? Es? *Es connés dhiu?* Is there supper to you? Have you supped? w.; Idzha; ydzha? P.

IT IS. Y ma, yma, w.; ythew.; ythewa, c.w. 1569; yv, M.; yu, u, eu, ewe, eve, ebe, peva, pevés, P.

HE IS. Syw, assyw. asugv, ugy, w.; ysy, B.; yw, ew, otté, w.; yta, P.; ydh-yw. yth-yw, ydzhi, w.; ydzhi, B.; yssyw, w.   *Ydh-yw, yth-yw, yssyw,* are reduplicate forms of *yw,* id. qd. *ew,* 3 pers. s. pres. of *bós,* to be, w.

THAT IS. Usy, ysy, yshi, w.

THERE IS. Bues, bûs, ês, w.; ethiaz, B.; ma, y ma, ydhyw, idzha, w.

THERE IS NOT. Nembés, nimbés, w.

ISLAND, *s.* Enys, enés, ennis, ynys, ynés, w.; ynez, P.; ince, w.; en, B. *En maur,* the great island.

THE ISLAND. Nennis, properly *an ennis,* w.

ISLANDS, *s.* Enesou, enesys, enezou, enezyz, P.

ISLANDER, *s.* Enezek, B.

ISSUE, *s.* (Progeny). Affhen, P.

IT, *pron.* E, ef, ev, w.; eu, B.; hy, w. *Kyns hy bós nôs,* before it be night, N.; hi, w.; y, i, P.; ys, yn, y'n, an (*a* aux. *'n,* him), as, a's, w.

ITS, *pron.* Hy, y, a, e, w.; i, P.

FROM IT. Anodho, anotho, deworto, dewhorto, dyworto, w.; diuorté, dyworry, P.

IN IT. Ynno, unna, etten, w.

OF IT. Anedhy, anethy, annethy, w.; anythy, an nethé, nethé, P.; anodho, annotho, w.; h'y, warfo, P.

TO IT. Dy, ty, w.

ITCH, *v.* Cosé, w.; cossé, P.C. 2084. *Cosso,* he may itch, w.; tebri. *My dorn a tebre,* my hand itches, B.

ITCH, THE ITCH, *s.* Debarn, w.; debron, M. 1187; debren, M. 3432.

ITCHING, AN ITCHING, *s.* Debron, M. 1187.

IVORY, *s.* Danz elephant, P. *Lit.* Elephant's tooth.

IVY, *s.* Idhio, w.; hieauven, B.

J.

"This letter was an entire stranger to the Celtic languages, and when it occurs in old manuscripts it is used for I. It is used in a few Cornish words to express a very modern corruption of the sound of *di,* as *jowl* for *diowl;* and in the loan of foreign words," w. *Lex. Corn. Brit.*

JACKDAW, *s.* Tshawc, tshawka, w. So called from its note.

JACKET, *s.* Peis, w.; pais, peid, pidde, B.; peus, w.; powes, B.; pows, bows, fows, hevis, hevez, hems, w.

JACK-SNIPE or JUDCOCK, *s.* Gaver hâl, w.; dameku, hatter-flitter, D.

JADE, *s* (A mean woman). Moren. w. ; morian, P. ; moroin, w. ; voran, P. ; voren, w. *Ha ty voren myrgh, hy ben,* and thou jade, girl, his head, o.m. 2649.

JADED, *part.* Squyth, scîth, w. ; skîth, P.

JAIL or PRISON, *s.* Carhar, w. ; karhar, B. See PRISON.

JAMES, *s.* Jammeh, B. ; Jamys, P.C. 1014.

JANUARY, *s.* Jenvar, genvar, genwar, w. ; genver, P. ; genuer, B. (The *g* soft).

THE MONTH OF JANUARY. Mis Jenvar, mis Genvar, mis Genwar, w. ; mis Genver, *i.e.* Tenaer, cold air month, P. ; mis Genuer, B.

JAVELIN, *s.* Gew, giw, guw, w. ; gu, geu, P. ; gyw, B. *Pl.* Gwayw, guu.

JAW, *s.* Grud, w. ; grydh, B.

JAW-BONE, *s.* Chal. challa, w. ; chala, c.w. 1117. *Tan hemma wâr an challa,* take this on the jaw-bone, o.m 540.

JAW-TEETH, *s.* Dêns dhelhar, dêns dhelhor, P.

JAY, *s.* (The bird). Janner, D.

JEALOUS, *adj.* Sorras, B.

JEER, *s.* Gês, w. ; geys, P. See also JEST.

JEER, *v.* Gescy, w. ; gesky, cuthil-gês, kuthil-gês, P. See JEST.

TO BE JEERED. Gesys, M. 401.

JEERING, *s.* Gês, B.

JERK, *s.* Squych, skwych, scwyth, w. ; skwyth, P. ; squitch, D. The Cornish, when they are troubled with that jerking or restlesness called " the fidgets," say they have " the squitchems."

JERKIN, *s.* Hems, dzherken, P. ; kota, B.

JEST, *s.* Gês, w ; geys, P. ; geas, c.w. 2428. *Hemma yw pûr xcorn ha geys,* that is a very sneer and jest, P.C. 349.

JEST, *v.* Gescy, w. ; gesky, P. ; gellas, w.

JESUS, *s.* Jesu, Ihesu, M. 992.

JEW, *s.* Edhow, w. ; Ethow, P. ; Hudhow, Yudhow, Yedhow, w. ; Yethew, N.

JEWS. *s.* Edheuon, P. ; Ethowon, Edzhewon, B. ; Hudhewon, w. ; Idheoun, Jedhewon, Huthewon, Yuthewon, P. ; Yethewon, N.

JIG, *s.* (Dance). Galliard, P.

JOHN. *s.* Jowan, P. ; Johann, P.C. 1015 ; Dzhuan, P. ; Jakeh, B.

JOIN or COUPLE, *v.* Dzhiunia, dho dziunia, P.

JOINING, *s.* (A joining, a seam). Enniou, w.

JOINT, *s.* (In carpentry). Scarf, w. *Yn evn greys an scarf trohe,* in the just middle cut the joint, P.C. 2530.

JOIN, *v.* (As in carpentry). Scarfé, w.

JOINT or UNITED, *adj.* (In common). Cés, kês, cys, w.

JOINT, *s.* (Of a body). Cefals, chefals, mâl, w.

JOINTS, *s.* (Of a body). Mellow, mellyow, melyow, vellow, w. ; juntis, B. ; hucksen, D.

JOIST, *s.* Gyst, jyst. (*Pl.* Gystys, jystys, w.) Corble, o.m. 2474.

JOKE, *v.* Gellas, w.

JOLT-HEAD, *s.* Pen brâs, w. ; pen braoz, B. ; pedn braos, w. ; pen-maur, B.

JOT, *s.* (Little bit). Tâm, tâbm, banna, w. ; banné, badna, P.

NOT A JOT. Whera bân, what, P. See BIT, MORSEL, PIECE

JOURNEY, *s* (*Iter,* Lat.) Cerdh, kerdh, kerd, w. ; kerth, kergh, gerghen, P. ; veadge, c.w. 807 ; vyadg, c.w. 484 ; vyadge, c.w. 680,

JOVE, *s.* Jovyn, Iew, Iow, Yow, w.

BY JOVE! Jovyn ! Re Jovyn ! P.

JOWL, *s.* See JAW.

JOY, *s.* Lawenés, w. ; lauenez, P. ; lowender, w. ; lowena, M. 207 ; lowenna, w. *Lowenna tekca gothfy,* the fairest joy thou knowest, P.C. 1042 ; lowyné, w. ; lowené, lauen, loane, louen, P. ; lowhen, o M. 2383. *Ffest yn lowhen arlythy,* in great joy lords, o.M. 2383.

JOYFUL, *adj.* Lowenec, w. ; lowenake, c.w 546 ; lowenek, lewenic, w. ; lawennek, lauenik, B., lowena, c.w. 332 ; lawen, lowen, luan, w.

JOYFULLY, *adv.* Lowen, w.

MORE JOYFULLY. Lowenné, w.

JUD-COCK. See JACK-SNIPE.

JUDGE, *s.* Barner, w ; barnyz, P. ; brodit, bresec, w. ; brezek, P.

JUDGE, *v.* Brugy, w. ; brygy, P. ; brusy, vrusy, breysi, w. ; yuggyé, B. ; yuggé, P.C. 1333. *Neb a thus th'agan brugy,* who will come to judge us, P.C. 1668. *Yn yer worth agas yuggé,* in the sky, to judge you, P.C. 1333.

TO JUDGE ONE'S SELF. Ymbreysé, w.

JUDGEMENT, *s.* Brés, w. ; bréz, P. ; breys, brys, breus, brues, w. ; brûz. P. ; breuth, bryge, w. ; bresul, P. ; bresel, bresyl, and the mutations by changing the initial *b* to *v,* as, vrês, vrêz, vreys, vrûs, vresyl, &c. *Hag a wra thy'n drók bresul,* and he will do us an evil judgment, P.C. 1918. *Na pendra a bryge wreugh,* nor what judgment you make, P.C. 444. *Râg gruthyl ol both the vrys,* to do all the will of thy judgment, o.M. 340. *A reth thy'm orth am vresyl,* givest thou to me for my judgment, o.M. 1814 ; cuhudhas, cyhudhas, gyhudhas, gyhydhas, gydhas, w. ; gydhaz, B.

JUDGMENT-DAY, *s.* Déth brûs, P.

JUDGMENT-SEAT, *s.* Gorsedd, B.

JUG, *s.* (A jug with two ears. *Amphora, Lat.*) Perseit, w.

A LITTLE JUG. Parrick, D.

JUGGLER, *s.* Huder, w.; hudol, P.

JUGGLERY, *s.* Hûs, P.C. 2695. *Nep hûs ef re wrûk thothz*, some jugglery he has done to him, P.C. 2695.

JUICE, s. Sygan, w.

JUICY. *adj.* Er, w.

JULY, *s.* Gorephan, Gor-ephan, w.; Gortheren, M. 2070.

JULY MONTH, *s.* Mîs Gorephan, w.; Mîz-Gorephan, *i.e.*, the chief head of the summer-month; Mys Gortheren, M. 2194. Mîs guaré, *i.e.*, play-month, B.

JUMP, *v.* Lammé, w.; lamma, P.; lemmel, lebmal, w.

JUMPER, *s.* Lappior, P.

JUNCTION OF RIVERS. Aber, w.

JUNE, *s.* Ephan, Ephon, Efin, w.; Misuen, B.; Metheven, M. 4303.

JUNE MONTH, *s.* Mîs Efin, Mîs Ephon, Mîs Ephan, w.; Mîz-Ephan, *i.e.*, the summer month, or head of summer, P.; Mîs-Mesuen, B.; Mês Metheven, M. 4303. *In mês metheven*, in the month of June, M. 4303.

JUPITER, *s.* See JOVE.

JURISDICTION, *s.* Arlottés, P.C. 1604. *Mar sywe a'y arlottés*, if he is of his jurisdiction, P.C. 1604.

JUST, *adj.* (Exactly proportioned). Ewn, ewen, eon, w.; eun, P.; evn, O.M. 2530. *In evn greys an scarf trohe*, in the just middle cut the joint, O.M. 2530.

JUST, *adj.* (Upright, honourable). Ewhinsic, euhinsic, gwirion, gwyryon, w.

JUST MAN, AN EXCELLENT MAN. Dremas, w.; dremmas, O M. 864. *Kepar del fuve dremmas*, like as he was a just man, O.M. 864; eunhilik, B.; guerryon, P.; guirion, B.

JUST AS WELL. Magé lel, M. 863. *Magé lel avel y vam*, just as well as his mother, M. 863.

JUST NOW. Agensow, w.; agynsow, N. *Me a'n guelas agynsow*, I saw him just now, R.D. 896.

JUSTICE, *s.* Eistenyon, P.

JUVENILE, *adj.* Yonc, yonk, yync, yowync, w.

K

" No *k* in the British language, says Moyle (Lett., Vol. 2, p. 182), till the year 1200 when the *w* was also introduced.

The *k* is very rare in Cott. Ms., but Mr. Lhuyd often uses it; and by other moderns the *c*, *k*, and *ch*, are indifferently used." *Borlase*, "Antiquities," 1st Ed., p. 394.

KEEN, *adj.* Lym, tyn, dyn, feyn, garow, w.; garou, garo, guariow, P.

KENNEL, *s.* (Gutter). Shanol, w.

KEEP, *v.* Gwithé, gwythé, gwethé, w.; guitha, guith, kuitha, B.; cuitha, dho cwitha, wethé, w.; wetha, anguathy, P.

KEEP, *v.* (Preserve, take care of, guard). Gorwythy, w.

KEEP, *v.* (Hold). Synsy, O.M. 23. *Râk synsy glaw a wartha*, to keep the rain above, O.M. 23.

KEEP BACK, *v.* (Withold). Guitha dhort, B.

KEEP ONE'S SELF, *v.* Omwethé, ymwythé, w.

KEEPER, *s.* Ceiswas, w.; keisuas, P.; gwithés, gwythés, gwythyés, gwithias, gwythyas, w.; guithias, cuithias, P.; guythyas, N.; gwithiad, guidthiat, wythyés, wythés, w. *Py vr fûf vy y wythés*, what time was I his keeper, O.M. 576.

KEEPERS, *s.* Kuithzi, B.

KEEPING, *s.* (A keeping). Gwith, guyth, with, wyth, w.

KEEPING, *s.* (Preservation). Sawment, w.

KEPT, *part.* Guathas, gunthas (?), B.

KERNEL, *s.* Sprusan, C.W. 1852. *Pl.* Sprûs, spruse, C.W. 1855; spûs, O.M. 823. *Kemer tyyr spûs a'n aval*, take three kernels of the apple, O.M. 823. In this quotation there seems to be an error. *Sprúse*, is a plural in C.W. 1855, and *sprusan* a singular in C.W. 1852. A noun in the singular number should follow a numeral.

KESTREL, *s.* Cryssat, w.; kryssat, P.

KETTLE, *s.* Caltor, w.; kalhtor, kaltor, B.; calter, P.; per, B.; chec, chek, w.; kek, P. *Yn dan an chek*, under the kettle, R.D. 139.

KETTLE or POT, *s.* Crochan, crochadn, B.

KETTLE-DRUMS, *s.* Nakrys, O.M. 1998.

KEY, *s.* Ahuel, alhuedh, alwedh, w.; alweth, alwyth, P.; alwhedh, w.; alyek, B.; dialhwedh, dialhwhedh, dialhwet, dial-hyet, w.

KEYS, *s.* Alwedhow, alwhedhow, alwheoh, w.; alwheow, R.D. 650; aluedhou, alhuedhou, P.

KICK, *v.* (Like a horse). Poot, w. This word is now used in the Cornish dialect for a thump or blow.

KICK or WINCE, *v.* Tygly. *May tyglynan tybyles*, that wince (or kick) do the devils, P.

KID, *s.* (The animal). Ceverel, keverel, w.; cheverel, mynnan, P.; mynan, myn, mîn, B.

A MALE KID. Kydiorch, kytiorch, B.

KIDNEY, *s.* Lonath, B.

THE KIDNEYS. Lonath, w.

KIDNEY-FAT, *s.* (Of a pig). Flair, D.

KILL, *v.* Ladhé, w.; lathé, R. 1852; ladha, dho latha, dho ladh, P. *Râg dhe ladhé dên mar qura*, for if a man shall kill thee, o.m. 598 ; destrewy, dhestrewy, dystrewy. destria, destrea, w. *Dho destria an dén cóth*, to kill the old man, w.

KILLECK. In fishing the frame of the killeck is called *ludras*, b.v.

KILLED, *part.* Ledhys, w. ; lethys, lyhys, p. ; lydhys, w. ; ledhaz, b.

WE SHOULD HAVE KILLED. Lytthyn. To be read *lydhyn*, being 1 pers. pl. subj. of *ladhé*, to kill, w.

KILLING, A KILLING. *s.* Ladh, w. ; latha, p.

TO KILL ONE'S SELF. Emladhé, w.

KIND or SORT, *s.* Cendé, kendé, cunda, kunda, w. ; henda (? *kenda*), p. Echen, ehen, hechen, hehen, w. ; ehin, p. ; ehan, eghen, b. ; pâr, riw, riu. *Gurriw*, male kind, w.

KIND, *adj.* Hynwys, w. ; kelednak, kylednak, cyweithias, w. ; ryth. *A vynyn ryth*, Oh! kind woman, p.

KIND SIR. Densa, m. 641 *Densa lowena dywhy*, kind (sir), joy to you. m. 641.

KINDLE, *v* Tewy, w. ; tewyé, tewé, p. ; tiwy, dewy dywy, w. ; tehen, tewyn, b.

KINDLY. DEAR, *adj.* Cuef, cueff, cûf, w.

KINDNESS, *s.* Yenés, p.

KINDRED, *s.* Deskés, p.

KING, *s.* Mychtern, vychtern. w. ; mychteryl, migterne, myghtern, p. ; mighterne. megtern, myhtern. b. ; myghter, p.c. 982 ; matern, matcryn, ruy, rêv, ruif, w.

KINGDOM, *s.* Mychterneth, michterneth, myhterneth, myterneth, mychternés, w. ; mesterngés, b. ; ruifanaid, ruyvanedh, gwlascor, w. ; gulascor, gulasketh, ulascor, ulaskor, p. ; gwlâd, gwlâs, w. ; gulâs, p.c. 726 ; glâs, p.c 808 ; gulan, p. ; gulat, gwlêth, wlêth, wlascor, w. *Re'n kyrho thotho th'y wlêth*, carry him to him to his kingdom, o.m. 2370.

KINGLY, *adj.* Real, ryal, w. ; ryel, p.

KING'S DECREE. Gurhemin ruif, w.

KING'S EVIL, *s.* Clevas an mytern, w. ; clevaz an mytern, p.

KING-FISHER, *s.* Pysgadyr an mytern, w. ; pysgadyr yn mytern, p. ; guilan, b. *Guilan* seems to be the name for a gull.

KINK or TWIST IN A CHAIN, *s.* Grend, w.f.p.

KINSMAN, *s.* Câr, w. ; kâr, carayos, carogos, karogos, b. ; ogas, ogaz, oges, ogos, p.

KINSMEN, *s.* Nessevyn. m. 387.

KISS, *s.* Am, abem. w. ; amane, p. ; bay, vay, w. ; vee. p. (*Pl* Baiou). p *Bythqueth bay thy'm ny ryssys*, never a kiss to me didst thou give, p.c. 522 ; cussin. cysin, w. ; gussin, b. ; impoc, w. ; impog. pokkail, b. ; poccuil, w. ; pokkuil, b. ; poccan, p. ; pocq, b.

KISS, *v.* Amé, ammé, ama, amma, bayé, w. ; regymmy, p. *Thy'mmo ammé*, kiss me p.c. 1106. *Thy'm the ammé*, to kiss me p.c. 1107.

THOU SHALT KISS. Ymmy, 2 pers. s. subj. of *ammé*, to kiss, w.

KITCHEN, *s.* Cegin w. ; kegin, b. ; keghin, gegin, gegen, w. ; gegan, b. ; gegon, w. ; gegyn, m. 3721.

KITE or PUTTOCK, *s.* Barges, w. ; bargez, p. ; bargus, b. ; bargos, w. ; scoul, b. ; skoul, p.

KITTEN, *s.* Chet, p. (The *ch* is soft). This is still a common name in Cornwall.

KNAT or GNAT, *s.* Centowan, contuan, b.

KNAVE, *s.* Adla, losel, lorel, w. ; voran, voren, p. ; fislak, b. *Out warnough a thevv adla*, out upon ye, Oh two knaves, o.m. 1499. *Re thanvonas vn adla*, he sent a knave, p.c. 1686. See RASCAL.

KNEE, *s* Glin, pedn. glîn, penclîn, glyn. gleyn, clîn, clyn, w.

KNEES, *s.* (*i.e.* The *two* knees). Dewlin, dewlyn, dhewlyn, w. ; thewlyn, dowlyn, b. ; deuglyn, n. ; dew glyen, c.w. 188 ; pendew glyn, bendewlyn, p.

KNIFE, *s.* Collan, colhan, w. ; kolhen, kylhan, b. ; kyllhan. p. ; collel, w. ; kollel. b. ; gollan, w. ; golhan, b. ; golen, hollan, w. ; holan, b.

A LITTLE KNIFE. Kethel, b. ; collel, p.

KNIGHT, *s.* Marrec. w. ; marrek, m. 2444 ; marheg, w. ; marhag, marhak, p. ; marchec, w.

KNIGHTS, *s.* Marregion, marreggyon, marrôgion, marrougion, w. ; marrouggyon, n. ; marogyon, m. 294? marogyen, m. 1742.

KNIT, *v.* Gwia, w. ; guia, b. ; plyé, p.

KNITTING, *s.* (A thing knitted). Gwiad, w.

KNOCK, *v.* Cnoucyé, knoukyé, cnakia, w. ; cronkia, cronkyé, p. ; croncyé. groncyé, gwiscel, gwyscel, wyscel, gwyscy, w. ; guisky, guesga. wysk, p.

KNOCKED, *part.* Gnacias, a mutation of *cnacias*, 3 pers. s. preter. of *cnacié*, *id. qd.* cnoucyé, to knock. w.

KNOT, *v.* Colma, celmy, kelmy, cylmy, kylmy, gylmy, w.

KNOT, *s.* Colm, colmen, golmen. w. ; liam, b. *May fastyo an colm wharré*, that the knot may fasten soon, p.c. 1526. *The knot of a bow* (in archery). Peyl, w ; peyll, p.

KNOW, *v.* Godhfos, godhvos, w. ; gothfos, gcthvos, p. ; gothfés, n. ; gothyés, gothyas, p ; gwodhas, w.; guodhaz, p. ; godhas, w. ; govos, n. ; covas, cothfos, p , wodhfos, wodhvos, w. ; wothfos, wothvos, wothvas, wothya, p. ; wodhfyé, othvas, uffya, w. ; aswon, aswony, aswonyn, aswonvos, adzhan, wor, p.; or, ûr, w. ; wore, wose, woth, whow, myn, p. ; gôn, w.

I KNOW. Gothaff, wothaff, b. ; gôn, w. ; guon, b. ; wôn, w. ; mi a uon, b. ; me a wôr, w.

THOU KNOWEST. Wodhas, a mutation of *godhas*, 2 pers. s. pres. of the irr. v. *godhfos*, to know, w.; gothfés, N.; godhes te, w.; custa, a mutation of *gusta*, an abbreviation of *godhés te*; wothés, wethés, P.

HE KNOWS. Gôr, gour, wôr, wour, wyr, ôr, ûr. *Wor* and *wour* are mutations of *gôr* and *gour*. Used with all persons. *Dew a wór*, God knows. *Me a wór*, I know, &c. Or and *úr* are late forms of *wór*. *Ev a úr* (or *ev a ór*), he knows, w.

WE KNOW Wodhan, wodhen, wydhen. w., mutations of *godhan*, &c., 1 pers. pl. pres. of the irr. v. *godhfos*, to know, w.

YE KNOW. Gothough, N.; wodhouch, wodhoch, wedhoh, codhouch, w.; wothogh, P. *Wodhouch, codhough*, and *wodhoch*, are mutations of *godhouch* and *godhoch*. 2 pers. pl. pres. of *godhfos*; the same also of *wothogh*. from *gothfos*, to know; *wedhoh*, is a mutation of *gwedhoh*, a late form of *gwedhouch*, 2 pers. pl. pres. of irr, v. *gon*, to know, w.

THEY KNOW. Wodhons, a mutation of *godhons*, 3 pers. pl. pres. of the irr. v. *godhfos*, to know w.; gothons, N.

I KNEW. Wodhyen, w.; wothyan, wothean, P.; the mutations of *gothyen*, N.; *godhyen, gothyan, gothean*, 1 pers. s. imperf. of *godhfos* or *gothfos*, to know, w.; gothen, N.

THOU DIDST KNOW. Gothfes, gothes, gothas, N.

HE KNEW. Wodhyé, a mutation of *gothyé, godhyé*, 3 pers. s. imperf. of *godhfos*, to know; wyrthewys, a late corruption of *wodhvedhys*, a mutation of *godhvedhys*, 3 pers. s. preter. of *godfos*, w.

WE KNEW. Wedhyn, a mutation of *gwedhyn*, 1 pers. pl. imperf. of the irr. v. *gón*, to know; guythen, N.

THEY KNEW. Wodhyens, a mutation of *godhyens*, 3 pers. pl. imperf. of *godhfos*, to know, w.

WE HAD KNOWN. Gothfen, N.

THEY HAD KNOWN. Gothfons, N.

(IF) I KNOW. Gothefaf, N.

(IF) HE KNOW. Gothfo, N.

I SHALL KNOW. Wodhefaf, a mutation of *godhefaf*, 1 pers. s. fut. of the irr. v. *godhfos*, to know, w.

THOU SHALT KNOW Gothfy, gothfythy, N.; guidhi, P.

HE SHALL OR WILL KNOW. 1. Wodhfo, a mutation of *godhfo*, 3 pers. s. 2 fut. of *godhfos* to know, w.

　2. Wodhfyth, wodhvyth, mutations of *godhfyth* and *godhvyth*, 3 pers. s. fut. of *godhfos* and *godhvos* w.; govyth, gothvyth, N.

　3. Nabow, an abbreviated form of *anabow*, w.

YE SHALL KNOW. Gothfetheugh, N

THOU MAYEST KNOW. Woffas, a contracted form of *wodhfés*, a mutation of *godhfés*, 2 pers. s subj. of *godhfos*. to know, w.

HE MAY KNOW. Woffé, a contracted form of *wodhfé*, a mutation of *godhfé*, 3 pers. s. subj. of *godhfos*, to know, w.; guothvo ev, B.

YE MAY KNOW. Whodhfouch, the aspirate mutation of *godhfouch*, 2 pers. pl. subj. of *godhfos*, to know, w

THAT HE MAY KNOW. Mai guoth ev, B.

MAY HE KNOW. Re woffé, N. (woffé is gothfé)

I SHOULD KNOW. Wodhfen, a mutation of godhfen, 1 pers. s. subj. of *godhfos*, to know, w.

THEY SHOULD KNOW. Godhfons, codhfons, w.

HE WOULD HAVE KOWN. Wodhfyé, a mutation of *godhfyé*, 3 pers. s. subj. of *godhfos*, to know, w:

KNOW, KNOW YE. Gwothemys, gothvethough, B.

KNOW THAT. Oyha hedda, B.

KNOW THIS. Oyha hemma, B.

KNOWN. Côth, cooth, gôth, P.; gothvethys, N.; gothewys, B.; oren, P

NO MAN KNOWS. Ni ôr dên veth, B.

IT IS KNOWN. Wodher, a mutation of *godher*, 3 pers. pl. pass of *godhfos*, w.

KNOWLEDGE, *s.* Sceans, skeans, scians, skians, skyens, skeyens, skyans, skyhans, scient, descans, deskans. *Yw hynwys pren a skyens*, which is named the tree of knowledge, O.M. 82; scenteleth, skenteleth, w.; skyentoleth M. 156; skentyllur, skentyll; askenteleth, adzuanfas, P.; gothfos, M. 1988; gothvos, M. 28; gothvas, C.W. 545. *Ny rúk truspus thum gothfos*, I have not done violence to my knowledge, M. 1988.

KNUCKLES or JOINTS, *s.* Hucksen, D.

L.

" This letter is radical and immutable in all the Celtic languages, except in Welsh where it is secondary, and a mutation of *ll*," w. *Lex. Corn. Brit.*

LABOUR, *v.* Gwethé, quethé, gwaythé, gwythy, gwethel, guthyl, lafuryé, laviri , w.; lavyrrya, C.W. 1073; lafferya, B.; gonedhy, w.; gonethy, P.; gonés, gonys, conys, wonys, obery, w.; gûl, guil, gwyl, gil, geil, geel. dho whûl, dho wheal, whelé, whela, whelas, wharfé, P.

LABOUR, *s.* Lafur, lafyr, lavur, w. *Awos lavur na dwôn*, because of labour nor sorrow, O.M. 2405; lavyr, P.; lafurye, O.M. 1899; lavut, P; lavirians, gwythrés, wythrés, gwaythe, gwyth, w.; guyth, M. 785; gueid, w.; gûl, P.C. 546; gwreans, gwryans, w.; guryans, P.; ober, B.; obar, C.W. 1177; weyll, M. 2322. For other illustrations see WORK.

LABOUR PAINS. (In childbed). Golovas, w.

LABOURER, s. Gunithiat, gonidoc, w.; gonidog. B.; gonesig, goneseg, onesek, P.

LABOURING, adj. Lavirians, w.

LABOURING BEAST or **BEAST OF LABOUR.** Bêst hwêl, w.; best huel, P.; ehal, ysgrybl, B.; yskryble, P.

LACE, TO LACE TOGETHER, v. Lacie, w.

LACK or **WANT,** s. Faut, P.; fawt, fout, fowt, w.

I LACK or **WANT.** Na faut dho, B.

LAD, s. Mâb, maw, w.; mau, vau, vaw, vaow, P.; guas, M. 1884. Pl. Guesyen, M. 1176; guescyon, guesyon, N. See BOY.

LADING, s. (Of a ship). Geladen. Carew.

LADS, s. See BOYS.

LADLE, s. Haddall, B.

LADY, s. Arludhés, arluthés, arlodhés. arlothés. w.; arluidhés, P.

BY OUR LADY! (The Virgin Mary). Revaria! Borlase says this was a common expression of surprise.

LAKE, s. Lyn, lagen. grelin, w.; lûh, lin, llun, B.; stagen, w.

LAMB, s. Ôn, oan, oin, w. Avel ón doff, like a tame lamb, M. 4028. Pl. Eanow, w.; eanés, B.

A LITTLE LAMB. Ôanic, B.

LAME, adj. Clôf, w; klôf, B.; cloppec, w.; cloppek, P.; kloppek, B.; cloppy. D.; effredh; evredhac, mans, w.; vrethek, P.; omlaua. lempia, B.

A LAME PERSON. Clopper, D.

LAMENT, s. See LAMENTATION.

LAMENT, v. Gwelvan, holea, w.; hoalea, olua, P.; olé, wolé, garlarow, w.; galarou. B.; cyny, kyny, w.; thyké, P,

THEY SHALL LAMENT. Y-vyllyk, vyllyk, B.

LAMENTABLE, adj. Trewyth, trewath, drewath, w.; trewathac, trawedhak, trauedhak, travethak, B ; trauethak, P.

LAMENTATION, s. Duwhan, dewhan. duan, dhnan, duwon, duon, w.; dwôn, o M 2405; duehan, drem, galar. w.; ungarme, B.; olva, w.; olah, P ; ollua. B.; croffolas, w Gesough the vés croffolae. leave off lamentation. o.M. 1662.

LAMP, s. Golowlester, w.; gololuester, P ; gololues-tre, B.; cantly, launtier, lugarn, w.; lygarn, P.

A SMALL EARTHENWARE LAMP. Chill, D.

LAMPREY, s. Môrnader, w.; môrnerdyr, B. Lit. A sea adder. Lamper, D.

LAMP-WICK, s. Boobun, B.V.; booba, W.F.P. This is a name for a wick made of a piece of rag, and used in a chill, or small earthen lamp (rarely made of tin).

LANCE, s. Gew, giw, guw, w.; geu, gu, guu, P.; gyw, B. (? if guu, be plural); bêr. vêr, w.

LANCE-FISH, s. Visnans, B.; calcar, D. See SAND-LANCE and SAND-EEL.

LAND, v. Teera, tira. w.

LAND. s. (Earth. soil, ground) Tir, tyr, teer, dôr, doar, doer, oer (an ver). w.; dodnan, B. Rôf thy's ow tyr, I give thee my land, R.D. 857.

GOOD LAND Nôr vaz, P.

HEAVY LAND. Tyr powys, P.

ENCLOSED LANDS. Tyr fyneau, B.

LAND NEAR THE SEA. Morrab, D.

LANDS, s. Terros, terrus, w.; terroz, terras, P.; teroge w.; teryov, M. 385; tyryow, N.

LAND, s. (Territory, conntry). Tireth. tyreth. ty-reyth. dyreyth, w.; terathe. c.w. 2452; lâz, lâs, B.

HIGH LAND Tyreth vhel (uhel). M. 2212.

THE LAND'S END. THE FURTHEST LAND, Vôn laz, B.

LAND, s. (A land or country). Bro, vro, pow, w.; pou, P.

LAND-FLOOD, s. Cahenryd, chahen rit, w.; kahen-ryd, B.; auan, P.

LANDLORD, s. (An innkeeper). Ost, B.; oster, P.; maidor, B.

LANDSMAN, s. Tyrguas, P.

LAND-ROD. s. (For measuring). Gord, B.V. It was 9 feet long.

LANE, s. Bounder, vounder, P. Chy vounder, the house in the lane

A LANE WAY. Vounder vôr, B.

A LONG NARROW LANE. Gurgo, W.F.P.

LANGUAGE, A LANGUAGE, s. Laveryans, w.; laveryanz, P.; tavaseth, w.; tavazeth. P.; tavas, w.; tavaz, P.

LANTERN, s. Launter, B.; lanter, P.C 609; cantyl launtier, gololulester, P.

LAP, THE LAP, s. Devra, P.; barlen, B.

LAPWING, s. Corniwillen, codnawilan, w.; codna-huilan, P.; kodna-huilen, B.

LARD, s. Blonec, P ; blonit, B.; mehin, w.; mord, mort, D.

LARGE, adj. Efan, effan, w.; evan, P. Vn skyber efan yn scón, a large room soon, P.C. 638 ; brâs, w.; brâz, B.; braos, brawse, P ; vrâs, houtyn, mûr, meur, mear, maur, mêr, vêr, veur, veor, w.; vear, vaur, P.; ledan, leaden, uthec, uthic, w ; ithick, ithig, lardzh, P. See also BIG and HUGE.

LARGENESS, s. Brâsder, vrâsder, w.

LARGELY, adv. Ithik, ithig, P.

LARK, *s.* Melhués, velhués, w.; melhuez, velhuez, P.; melhuet, w ; melhuek. B.

LASCIVIOUS, *adj.* Lill, w. This word also means a goat whence perhaps the use of the word.

LASH or SCOURGE, *v.* Lacé, lak, P. *Me ath lak,* I will lash (or lace) thee; scorgyas, krongkia, terhi, B.

LASH, *s.* (Of skin or thong). Crôn, w. See SKIN.

LAST, *v.* (Hold out long). Dirra, B.

LAST, *adj.* Fìn, fyn, w *Râg hemma yv ow gós fyn,* for this is my last blood, P.C. 824.

AT LAST. Diua, teua, B.; tyweth, P.C. 1810; yn dywêth, O.M. 671; wostewêdh, wotewêdh, w.; wotevêth, B.

LATCH, *s.* (Of a door). Cliket, B.

LATE, *adj.* Avar. P.C. 696. *Whet avar prys soper yv.* it is now late time for supper, P.C. 696; dewedhés, dewethés, dewethas, dywethas, diwedhas, diwedha, diuedhas, P.; diuethaz, B.; dowethyans (? lateness), P.; holerch, w.; holergh, P. Williams and Norris give "early" for *avar.*

LATE, *adj.* (Recent, fresh, new). Newedh, newydh, nowydh, w.; noweth, nouedzha, P.

LATER, *adj.* Divetha, P.

LATELY, *adv.* Agensow, agynsow, w.; pocvan, P. *Agensow me an guelas,* I saw him lately R.D. 911.

LATHS, *s.* Lasys, O.M. 2474.

LATITUDE or WIDTH, *s.* Lês, leys, w.

LATTER, *adj.* Direttha, B.

LAUD, PRAISE, *s.* Golochas, w.; golohas, P.; lawe, w.; lau, P.

LAUGH, *v.* Wharthé, warthé, w.; wharthy, P.; wherthy, w.; wherthen, B.; wherthyn. hwerthin, w.; huerthin, P.; huerthyn, B.; huerhin, w.; hwerwin, B.

LAUGH, *s.* (A laugh). Wharth, hwarth, hwerthin, w.

LAUGHING, *part.* A hwerhin, w.

LAUGHTER, *s.* Wharth, hwarth, hwerthin, w.; huerthin, P; huerhen, B.

A FOOLISH LAUGHTER. Giglot, w.

LAW, *s.* Laha, lacha, w.; lagha, P.C. 2383; latha, M. 1629; dedwh, B. *Pl.* Lays, w.; lahez, P.

LAWSUIT, *s.* Cên, kên, chên, w.

LAWN, *v.* (A space of grass ground). Lanherch, P.

LAX, *adj.* Lac, w.; louzall, P.

LAY, *v.* (To bet). Gysenzhi, w.; gusendzhi, P. *Mi vedn gusendzhi,* I will lay.

LAY, *v.* (To place). Gora, gorré, worré, gurra, lathyé, settya, syttya, w.

TO LAY ASIDE, *v.* Hepcor, w.

LAY YE ASIDE or DOWN. Rowmann (*ro-aman*), w.

TO LAY EGGS, *v.* Gueriff, B.

TO LAY HANDS ON, *v.* Guasga dorn, B.

TO LAY HOLD OF, *v.* Gaval, w.; gouas, P.; dalhenné, prenné, perna, w.

TO LAY ON or IMPOSE, *v.* Gurra, P.

TO LAY SNARES, *v.* Baché, baghé, w.

TO LAY UP, *v.* Godr, gora, P.

LAY, *s.* (A lay, as of land). Tôn, todn. w.

LAY, *adj.* Lêc. lêk, w.; leyk, M. 2931. *Pynag vo lettys py lêk.* whoever he may be, lettered or lay, w. *Leyk ha lyen,* lay and learned, M. 2931.

LAYMAN. *s.* Leic, lêc, laig, w.; leig, B.; lêk, M. 290.

LAZY, *adj.* Sigyr, zigyr, w.; zigur, zighir, segernath, diog, B. *An gwâs brâs sigyr-na,* that great lazy fellow. *Zighirna kusga,* this lazy fellow sleeps.

LAZINESS, *s.* (A fit of laziness). Lurgy, B.

LEAD, *v.* Hombroncy, hembryncy, w.; hembrynky, P.; hebrency, ledya, ledia, w.

THEY LED. Hombronkyas, B.

LED, *part.* Hombronkyas, B.

LEAD, *s.* (The metal). Plom, plobm, B.

LEADER, *s.* (Captain or commander). Hebrenciat, w.; hebrenchiat, P.

LEADER OF AN ARMY. Hebrenchiat luid, w.

LEAF, *s.* Delen, delkian, w.; delkio, P.; delc, w.; delk, P.

LEAVES, *s.* Delyow, dylyow, w.; dellyow, C.W. 94; delyou, delkiou, P.; delciow, deel, deil, deyl, w. *Gans deyl agan cuthé gvren,* let us cover ourselves with leaves, O.M. 254.

GREEN LEAVES. Delciow gwêr, w.; deel glâs.

LEAF, *s.* (Of a book). Aden, livan, w.

LEAK, *v.* Sigger, sigure, sygyr, zighyr, D. From *siger,* full of holes.

LEAN or LANK, *adj.* Cûl, w.; kûl, cal, kyl, B.; tanow, tanaw, w.; tanau, P.

LEAN, *v.* Powesy, posé, w.; possé, P.; puza, bossé, B. *Maw na puza,* boy, do not lean. *Bossé y ben,* to lean his head

HE COULD LEAN. Bossé, a mutation of *possé,* w.

LEAP, *v.* Lammé, w.; lamma, P.; lemmel, w.; lemal, B.; lebmal, w.

LEAP OVER, *v.* (To leap over). Drislemmal, drislebmal, w.; driz-lebmal, P.

LEAP, *s.* Lam, w. *A harlot rêth fo drôk lum,* ah! knave, it shall be a bad leap for thee, P.C. 2247.

LEAP or SKIP, *s.* Lanherch, B.

LEAPER, *s.* Lappior, P.

LEARN, *v.* Descy, w. ; deski, desgy, deshy, P. ; dyscy, dysky, dhysky, tysky, desca, desga, w.

LEARNED, *part.* Discys, diskys, &c , w. ; edris, B.

LEARNED, WISE, *adj.* Scentyl, skentyll, scyntyl, w ; skyntyll, B. ; scientoc, w. ; lyen, M. 2931. *Leyk ha lyen*, lay and learned, M. 2931.

LEARNING, *s.* Scient, sceans, skeans, skeans, scians, skians, skyans, skyens, skenteleth, skentuleth, w. ; skentyllur, skentyll, P. ; dyscyans, w. ; dyskyans, dyskans, P. ; disky, tisky, thesky, B. ; lyen, w. ; litherau, B.

LEAST, THE LEAST. Leia, B. ; leiha, P. ; leiah, leiadh, B. *Bythens kepar ha'n lyha*, let him be like the least, P.C. 1794.

AT LEAST. En leiah, dhan leiadh, B. ; en idnak, P.

LEAT, *s.* (Artificial water channel). Lakka, P. They still call a leat or mill-stream a lake, at Lostwithiel.

LEAVE, *v.* (Relinquish, permit). Gasé, w. ; gasa, B. ; gesy, gyssy, gagé, agé, w ; the asé, N.

LEAVE, *v.* (Quit). Gara, garera, esgara, w.

I WILL LEAVE. Assaf, a mutation of *gassaf*, from *gasé*, to leave, w.

HE WILL LEAVE. Âs, hâs, mutations of *gâs*, 3 pers. s. fut. of *gasé*, is leave, w.

LEAVE YE. Gesouch, geseuch, w., from *gesy*.

HE MAY LEAVE. Gasso, from *gasa*, to leave, w. ; assé, a mutation of *gasse*, from *gasé*, to leave, w.

LEAVE, *v.* (To leave by will). Cemynny, kemynny, cymmyny, w. ; kemynni, P.

LEAVE, *s.* (Permission, license). Cemeas, kemeas, cibmias, w. ; kibmias, kibmiaz, P. *Der ez kibmiaz*, by your leave. B. ; cummeas, w. ; kummeas, P.C. 3112 ; cummyas, w. *Ty ary cummyas*, thou shalt give leave. B. ; kummyaz, B. ; cummyés, gummyas, cymmyas, kymmyas, w. ; gymmyas, c.w. 1545; evodh. *Dregyz evodh*, by your leave, B. ; volder. *Dry volder*, by leave, B.

LEAVEN, *s.* Gwêl, B. ; plummin, D. See BARM.

LEAVENED, *adj.* Plum D. Used of bread only.

LEAVENED BREAD. Bara gwêl, B.

LED FORTH. Digthyas, B.

LEECH, *s.* Gêl, ghêl, w.

LEEK, *s* Porran, cinin, cenin, w. ; kinin, P.

LEES, *s.* (As of drink). Godhas, w. ; godhaz, godho, B.

LEFT, *s.* (The left). Clêdh, klêdh, w. ; klêdhe, B. ; clêth, M. 1850'; klêth, P.C. 1380 ; glédh, w.

LEFT HAND or **LEFT HAND SIDE.** Dorn klêdh, dorn glikin, P. ; luef glêth, P.C. 2747.

LEFT AND RIGHT. Clêth a dyov, M. 1850.

LEFT-HANDED, *adj.* Clêdhec, w. ; klêdhek, P. ; dorn glêdh, dorn glikin, w. The Cornish still call a left-handed person click-handed, clikky-handed or clikky.

LEFT, *adj.* Clêth, glêth, P.

LEFT, *part.* Garrés, from *gara*. *Gwell gerrés*, better left, P. ; gesys, w., from *gasé*.

HE LEFT. Asas, a mutation of *gasas*, from *gasa*, to leave, w.

THOU LEFTEST. Gyssys, 2 pers. s. preterite of *gasé*, to leave, w.

YE LEFT. Gysseuch, 2 pers. pl. preter. of *gasé*, to leave, w.

LEG, *s.* Fêr, vêr, bêr. *Logoden fér*, the calf of the leg ; gar, esgar, w.

LEGS, *s.* Garrou, B. ; garrow, arrow, w. *Garrow pûr trogh*, legs all broken, M. 3831 ; worthosow, B.

LEGACY, *s.* Cymmun, B. ; skuat, skuit, D.

LEISURE, AT LEISURE. Gwâg, gwâk, segyr, segyrys, w.

LEISURELY, *adv.* Tyshatas, tys-ha-tas, w.

LEND, *v.* Kular, B.V. Mr. Bernard Victor, of Mousehole, Cornwall. says that '' his grandfather learnt this word from Dolly Pentreath.'' The grandfather was called George Badcock, and he was old Dolly's undertaker. (See my '' Glossary of the Cornish dialects,'' F. W. P. Jago.)

LENGTH, *s.* (Longitude). Hêd, hês, heys, hys. w. ; hyz. hêz, P. *Try heys the bâl kemery*, take three lengths of thy spade, O.M. 392.

LENGTH. (Of time). Heys, hês. hêz, P.

A LENGTH OF TIME. Hirenath, w. ; hyrenath, P.

LEPER, *s.* Clafhorer. B ; claff, M. 2413 (*Pl.* Clevyon, M. 3.30). *Claff deberthys* (M. 1413). A separated leper.

LEPROUS, *adj.* Claforec, clafhorec, w. ; clafhorech, P.

LEPROSY, *s.* Lovrygyan, M. 1356. *Yma ortheff lovrygyan*, there is leprosy on me. M. 1356.

LESS, *adj.* Lea, P. ; le, w. *Me ny vennaf cafus lé*, I will not take less, P.C. 594.

LESSEN, *v* Lehé, w. ; lehy. leihy, P. ; leyhé, leyhy, lyhy, lyha, w. ; lygha, P. ; leghya, M. 2981 ; cosowa, w. ; kosoua, P.

LESSER, THE LESSER, *adj.* Behatna, P.

LEST, LEST THAT, *conj.* Râgoun, w.

LET, *v.* (Hinder). Hethy, thuethy, w.

TO LET FORTH, *v.* Raggory, P.

TO LET or **LOWER DOWN**, *v.* Cyldené, w.

TO LET OUT, *v.*   Dellé, dyllo, duello, w. ; thello, P.

TO LET BLOOD, *v,*   Dylla gudzh, w.

TO LET or PERMIT, *v.*   See LEAVE.

LET US.   Agun.   *Agun byz,* let us pray, P.

LET   Grenz, gwrenz.   *Grenz enna bós gollow,* let there be light, P.

LET or HINDRANCE, *s.*   Hàs, hethy, P.

LETHARGICK, A LETHARGICK, *s.*   Desimpit, B.

LETHARGY, *s.*   Entredés, w.

LETHARGY, *s.*   (The disease).   Huyn-dhe-sympit, B. ; wuin desimpit, P. ; pundesimpit, B.

LETTER, *s.*   (Of the alphabet).   Litheren, letheren, w.

LETTER, *s.*   (Epistle, missive).   Lither, lyther, let-her, scriven-danvon, w. ; scriven-danven, B.

LETTERS, *s.*   Litherow, w. ; litherov, M. 2796.   *Dotho degogh lytherov,* to him bear ye letters, M. 2796.

LETTERED or LEARNED.   See LEARNED.

LEVEL, *adj.*   Leven, w.

LEVER, *s.*   Gyst, P.

LEVITY or LIGHTNESS, *s.*   Scavder, w.

LEXICON, *s.*   Gerlever, w.

LIAR, *s.*   Goak, w. ; goacke, c.w. 2366 ; gûac, gowec, w. ; gûak, P. ; gowek, B. ; gouhoc, w.   *Pl.* Goui-gion, P.

A TELLER OF LIES.   Gow-leveriat, gowleveriat, w. ; gouleveriat, B. ; gouleveria, P.

LIBERAL, *adj.*   Hail, w. ; gortas, P.

LIBERALITY, *s.*   Roweth, w.

LIBERATE, *v.*   Dyllo, w. ; dylyr, P. ; dilvar, B.

LIBERTY, *s.*   Lyfreson, w.   *Ty a fyth the lyfreson,* thou shalt have thy liberty, R.D. 1676.

AT LIBERTY, FREE.   Wary, w. ; uary, B. ; franc, frank, P.

LIBESTICA, *s.*   (Herb).   Gwylés, B.

LIBRARY, *s.*   Levarva, P.

LICENSE or LEAVE, *s.*   Cummeas, cummyas, kym-myas cymmyas, cummyes, w. ; uary, B. See LEAVE.

LICENTIOUSNESS, *s.*   Wary, w. ; uary, P.

LICK or SLAP, *v.*   Lacé, w.   *Me a'th lak,* I will lace (lick) thee.

LIE, *s.*   (Falsehood)   Gow, gou, w. ; gowe, c.w. 65 ; wow, ow, w.   *Pl.* Gewan, w. ; geuan, P.

LYING or IDLE TALES.   Whetlow, P.   They still call such tales *whiddles.*

LIE, *v.*   Karwedha, B.   *Ma'n lada y karwedha,* the thief lies (lie down`.   Gowhelés, wowhelés, w. ; dho laol gou, P., to tell a lie.

TO LIE ALONG, *v.*   Wrowethé, killin, B.

TO LIE DOWN, *v,*   Growedhé, crowedhé, wrowedhé, growetha, M. 3569.   *In preson the growetha,* in prison to lie, M. 3569 ; groweth, P. ; gorwedha, corwedha, gurwedha, w. ; gurvedhu, karwedha, B. ; koruedha, P. ; goruedh, cowethas, B.

TO LIE HID, *v.*   Gova, gowea, w. ; gouea B.

TO LIE QUIET, *v.*   Cescy, kesky, coscé, euscé, cuské, cusga, cysga, w.

TO LIE SHELVING or SLANTING, *v.*   Killynia, B.

TO LIE WITH, *v.*   Gorwedha, corwedha, growedhé, w. ; gorued, groweth, wrowethé, P.

LIEGE, *s.*   Lych, M. 271 ; lich, M. 278.

LIFE, *s.*   (The living principle).   Bew, biu, w.

LIFE, *s.*   (Existence, state of being).   Bewnans, vew-nans, w. ; beunans, B. ; bewnens, N. ; bewnas, c.w. 349 ; vewnas, B. ; bownas, w. ; bounaz, B. ; bounas, *Capt Hitchens' Cornish epitaph in Paul churchyard.*

LIFE, AGE, *s.*   Hoedel, B. (*sic.*)

LIFELESS, *adj.*   Marow, maro, w.

LIFT UP, *v.*   (To lift up.)   Cosowa, cosoua, kosoua, B. ; drehevel, dereval, w. ; derebal, dreval, gorren, hwedhy, hudhy, huthy, P.

LIFTED UP.   Derevas, deraffas, B.

LIGHT or KINDLE, *v.*   Tehen, tewyn, B. ; tine, D.

LIGHT, TO GIVE LIGHT, *v.*   Golowa, colowa, gouloua, gylywi, w. ; gylyua, goloua, kylyui. P.

LIGHT, *s.*   (The light, as of the sun, &c.)   Golow, golou, P. ; golowe, c.w. 45 ; gollow, B. ; gulow, gulu, golowder. uolou, wolow, P.   *Y wéth lanters gans golow,* also lanterns with light, P.c. 609.   *Rák golowder ny'mbús gráth,* for the light there is not grace to me, O.M. 1413.   *Y wolow o múr a splan.* his light was very brilliant, R.D. 535.

LIGHTS, *s.*   (As of sun, stars, &c.)   Golowys, wolowys, w. ; wullowys. c.w. 736 ; golow, O.M. 40 ; golou, uolou, B.   *Bestés, puskés, golowys,* beasts, fishes, lights, O.M. 52.   *May rollons y golow splan,* that they may give their shining lights, O.M. 40.

LIGHT, *s.*   (A light, lamp, or candle).   Lugarn, w. ; lygarn, cantyl, P.

LIGHT, *adj.*   (Bright, shining).   Golow, w.

LIGHT, *adj.*   (Easy).   Glew, gleu, P. ; glev, P.c. 2088.   *Ow bommyn yv marthys glev,* my blows are wondrous light, P.c. 2088.

LIGHT, *adj.*   (In weight).   Laha, lagha, P. ; scâf, scâff, scâv, sgâv, w. ; skave, c.w. 1198 ; sgau, B.

LIGHTNESS, *s.*   (In weight).   Scâvder, w. ; skâv-der, P. ; sgâvder, B.

LIGHTNESS, *s.*   (Brilliancy).   Golowder, N.

LIGHTEN, *v.*   (To ease).   Cosowa, w. ; kosoua, dho aizia, P.

LIGHTEN, v. (Lightning). Cylywi, w.; kylyui, kuluwi, P. *Idzhi kuluwi ha tredna*, it lightens and thunders, P.

LIGHTNING, s. Côlbran, B.; golowas, w.; golouas, P.; goleuas, B.; luhás, luchas, lowas, luhés, w.; louas. B.; luehés, M.; 2149; luhet, w.; luwet, B.; collybran, D. *Collybran* is used for summer lightning, and also for the smut in corn.

A FLASH OF LIGHTNING. Luhesen. w. *Th'y lesky vn luhes n*, a flash of lightning to burn him, R.D 294. *Pl.* Luhes, N.

LIGHT-VESSEL, s (Vessel with a light). Golowlester, w

LIGHTS, s. (The lungs). Scevens, skephans, sceuens, w.; broden. B.

LIKE. Avel, hevel, haval, havel, cehafal, kehaval, w.; keif, kief, kev, kevelep. P.; cevelep, hevelep, hyvelep, w.; pocar, pokar, w.; pycar, B.; pekar, pokara, P.; del, pâr, w.; kepar, N.

LIKE AS. Câr, pocar, pecar, cara, w.; kara, P.; avel, mal, tro, tra, try, tre, dre.

LIKENESS, s. Havalder, hevelés, w.; haval, aval, avell. B.; hevelepter, hyvelep, hevelep, w.; kyffris, P. *Hevelep tho'm face vy*, the likeness to my face, O.M. 233?.

LIKING, s. Gre, w. *Arluth why yv a thy gre an bous*, Lord to your liking is the robe? R D. 1923-4

LIKE TO. Avel, cepar, kepar, w.

LIKEWISE, adv. Ynwedh, w.; ynweth, B.; yn weth, iu weth, P.; inweth, M. 293; weth, P.; weyth, weydh, w.; ceceffrys, kekeffrys, B.; kekyfrys, O.M. 464; ceverys, keverys, keverys, cefrys, keffrvz, cyfreys. cyffrys, P.; kyfrys, O.M. 463; cetella, ketella, kettermen, cettermyn, del, della, an della, andellan, parthy, P.; hagenzol, B.

LILY, s. Lilie, w.; lili, B.

LIMB, s. (Of the body). Asel, esel, w.; ysel, P.; leyth, lyth, mell, cefals, ehefals, w.

LIMBS, s. (Of the body). Esely. esyly, ysyly, yssilli, w.; yshili, B.; yssyly, O.M. 1012. *Mar vrew ov yssyly*, so bruised are my limbs, O.M. 1012.

LIME, s. Calch, w.; calk, P.; kalch, kaik, B.

LIMIT or BOUNDARY, s. Diwedh, dywedh, dewedh, duadh, dyweth, w.; diuadh, P.; diuath, B.; diua, P.; fen, fin, w.; geyth, gyst, P.

LIMIT or BOUNDARY OF A COUNTRY. Urrian, yrrian, w.

LIMPET, s. Brenigen, brennigen, bernigan, w.; brenigan, P. *Pl.* Brennic, w.; brennik, P.

LIMPET-SHELL, s. Croggan, B.V.

LINE, s. (Cord). Lovan, louan, P.

LINE, s. (A row). Rew, w.

LINE or LINEAGE, A RACE, s. Linieth, lynnyeth, lynneth, w.; lydnyathe, c.w. 2097.

LINEN, s. Lin, lien, lyen, w.; lian, B.

A LINEN CLOTH. Lien, lyen, w.

FINE LINEN. Sendal, sendall, cendel, cendal, w. *Yn cendel hag yn ourlyn*, in fine linen and in silk, O.M. 1752.

LING or HEATH s. Grig. griglans, w.; gryglans, P. The word *griglans*, for heath, is still in use in Cornwall.

LING, s. (Fish). Lên, w.; lenez, B. *Pl.* Lenesow, w.

LINGER, v. Hethy, P.

LINGER NOT. Na streth, na streché, na strelha, P.

LINGERING. Kurtaz, B.

LINK, s. (Of a chain). Merle, D.

LION, s. Leu, w.; lew, lheu, withell, withellonack, B.; onak, P.

LIONESS, s. Leués, P.

LIP. s. Gwelv, w.; guelv, P.; guelu, B.; gueus, gweus, mein, min, meyn, myyn, w.; vyn, M. 1450. *Myr warvan drefe the vyn*, look up, raise up thy lip, M. 1450.

LIPS, s. Gwelvans, w.; guelvanz, vlawmennow, P.; welv, P.C. 2085. *May fo gós y vlawmennow*, that there be gore on his lips, P. *My an knouk ef er y welv*, I will beat him on his lips, P.C. 2085.

LIQUIFY, v. Tedha, w.

LIQUOR, s. Lâd (compare this with the English word ladle), w.; cad, P.; lyn, lin, w.; lywar, B.

LIQUOR, DRINK, s. Gwiras, gwyras, wyras, w.; eveugh, methow, P.; pymeth, pyment, w. *Rág hemma yv pyment fyn*, for this is a fine liquor, O.M. 1915.

LIQUORICE, s. Gouilés, guylys. w.; guylés, P.

LISTEN, v. Golé, gola, colé, cola, golsowas, wolsowas, w.

LISTEN THOU. Cool, w.; coyl, M. 407.

THOU WILT LISTEN. Colyth, w.

LISTENED or DID LISTEN. Gyzyuaz, B.

LITERATURE, s. Lyen. w.

LITTER, s. (Straw, &c.) Gwells, gwels, gwelz, guelz, w.; gwyls, P.

LITTLE, adj. Bean, behan, bian, bihan, byan, byhan, bechan, bichan, w.; biggan, bighan, P.; beghan, B.; bychan, bochan, w.; boghan, B.; bohan, w.; wiggan, P.; also the mutations by changing *b* to *v* as in the following, *viz.*: vean, vian, B; vyan, vychan, w.; vichan, vighan, B., &c.; menow, minow, minis, w.; minnis, B.; minys, menys, munys, venys, w.; go, P. *Go dol*, a little valley, P.

A LITTLE BIT, SOME. Nebés, w.; nebaz, P.

A LITTLE or SMALL MATTER. Bochés, bohés, bochod, boghés, w. *Bohés ov henna thy'nny*, little is this for us, O.M. 381. *Merebae boghés coynt*, I was too little sharp, P.

A LITTLE DISTANCE. Pols, R.D. 1610. *Pols a lemvia* a little (distance) from here, R.D. 1610.

A LITTLE WHILE. Pols vian, P.; teken, B.

LIVE, *v.* Bewé, bewa, pewé, pewa, bew, pew, vewé, vewa vew, vewé. *Nynsus bewé na fella*, there is no living any longer, O.M. 1703.

LIVING, *part.* Bew, biu, w.; bêu, P.; byw, vew, W.; veu, P.

HE HAS LIVED. Vewas, a mutation of *bewas*, 3 pers. s. preter. of *bewé*, to live, w.

HE HAD LIVED. Vewsé, a mutation of *bewsé*, 3 pers. s. pluperf. of *bewé*, to live, w.

HE WILL LIVE. Vew, a mutation of *bew*, 3 pers. s. fut. of *bewé*, to live, w.

HE SHALL HAVE LIVED. Vewo, a mutation of *bewo*, 3 pers. s. 2 fut. of *bewo*, to live, w.

LET THEM LIVE. Bewens, w.

THOU MAYEST LIVE. Vywy, a mutation of *bywy*, 2 pers. s. subj. of *bywé* or *bewé*, to live, w.

HE MAY LIVE. Vewhé, veuché, mutations of bewhé and beuché, 3 pers. s. subj. of *bewé*, to live, w.

LIVING, *s.* (A living, a livelihood). Bewnans, bownas, w.

TO LIVE WITH, *v.* Cesvowa, kesvowa, w.

TO LIVE AGAIN, *v.* Gorthewy, P.

LIVE or RESIDE, *v.* See DWELL.

LIVELIHOOD, *s.* Bewnans, bownas, w.

LIVER, THE LIVER, *s.* Avy, w.; avi, avey, P.; aui, w.

LIVING, ALIVE. Yn few, R.D. 1442; yn beu, P. *Yn few aban dassorghas*, living when rising again, R.D. 1402.

LIZARD, *s.* Pedrevan, pedrevor, w.; pedreriff, P.; pedresif, w.; pedresiv, B.; croinoc (?), P. See also NEWT.

LO! At! M. 599. *At eve fast bys in top*, lo! it is quite up to the top, M. 599. For the other forms see BEHOLD!

LOAD, *v.* Argha, P.

LOAD or BURDEN, *s.* Be, ve, w.; bedh, P.; carg, w.; karg, P.; sam, saw, w. *Ota saw bós war ov kyn*, see the load of food on my back, O.M. 1053.

LOAF, *s.* Torth, w.; nugan, nogen, hogan, B. Borlase uses these words for pie-crust also. *Hogan*, is still in common use among miners for a dinner-cake; also for a tinner's pasty; also called *fuggan*, *hobbin*, and *hobban*, D.

THE SOFT PART OF A LOAF OF BREAD. Wigan, B. Compare this word with the Cornish for "pudding," *q.v.*

LOATHING, *s.* Bisné, bysné, P.

LOATHSOME, *adj.* Mousegy, P.; anhethek, M. 1853. *Kynthesté claff anhethek*, though thou wert a loathsome leper, M. 1853.

TO BE LOATHSOME. Mousegy, w.

LOBSTER, *s.* Legast, gavar-môr, w. Borlase calls a polypus, *legesti*, but legesti is also a plural for lobsters.

LOBSTER or CRAB POT, *s.* (A floating one). Weely, D.

LOCK, *s.* Flyran, hesp, w.; sera, P.

LOCK, *s.* (A lock of hair). Cudin, P.

LOCK, *v.* Sera, P.; serra, B.; alwedha, lyhwedha, w.; lyhuetha, P.

LOCKED, *part.* Alwethys, M. 3644. *Oma alwethys certeyn*, here locked certainly, M. 3644.

LOCUST, *s.* Cafor, w.

LODE, *s.* (Of mine ore). Meine, D., a form of *mên*, a stone. There is a word used, says Dr. Paris, for the centre of a lode—" In most veins (lodes) there is a central line or fissure. . . . . . formed by the close apposition and occasional union of two crystallized, or as they may be called *drusy* surfaces."

LODGE, TO LODGE AT AN INN, *v.* Ostia, w.

LODGING, *s.* (A place to live in). Cylden, kylden, w.

LOFTY, *adj.* Huhel, euhel, w.; euhell, P.; uhel, w.; uhal, P.; ewhal, w.; euhal, B.; yuhal, uchel, w.; ughal, B.; uhan, P.; huch, ard, arth, earth, w.

LOFTINESS, *s.* Uchelder, w.; ughelder, B.; uhelder, huhelder, w.; huheldar, P.

LOGGING, *adj.* Logan, B.

LOIN, *s.* Tenewen, tanewhon, w.; tarneuhon, B.; loin, w.

LOINS, THE LOINS, *s.* Diuglun, lonath, efer (?), w. *Diuglun* is an example of the dual number. See also HANDS and FEET.

LOITERER, *s.* Sevylliac, sevyllyak, w.; sevyllyake, C.W. 458.

LONDON, *s.* Loundrez, w.

LONELY, *adj.* Jowan, P.; wisht, whisht, D.

LONG, *adj.* Hir, hyr, w.; here, heer, heere, P.

LONG, FAR, *adj.* and *adv.* (Also as to time). Pell, pel, bell, w.; bel, O.M. 467. *Ha ny vynnys lettya pel*, and I would not hinder long, M. 3996. *Abel pe feste mar bel*, Abel, where hast thou been so long? O.M. 467.

LONG-BOAT, A LONG-BOAT, *s.* Scâth hîr, w.; skâth hyr, P.

LONG-HOSE or STOCKINGS, *s.* Tosanea, P.

LONG-OYSTER, *s.* Gavar môr, P. Also called *segar* (Eng.), perhaps from its resemblance in form to a cigar.

LONG SINCE. Pel, pel dhan urma, poagan, P.; polta, c.w. 2403. *Nysyv na pel*, it is not long since, M. 2220; sol a breys, P.

LONG TIME, A LONG TIME. Hirenath, w.; hyrenath, sol, P.

LONGER, FARTHER, *adj.* Pella, pellach, w.; pellaf, P.; fella, o.m. 1604.

LONGING, A LONGING, *s.* Hireth, hyreth, w. *Yma thy'mmo hyreth tyn*, there is to me a sharp longing, R.D. 747; hirath, B.; hyrathe, c.w. 590; herath, w.

LONGITUDE, LENGTH, *s.* Hêd, hês, heys, hys, w.; hâz, P.

LOOK, *s.* (Aspect, view, appearance). Goloc, golok, woloc, tremyn, w.

LOOK, *s.* (The look, mien, visage). Miras, w.; miraz, B.

TO LOOK AT, *v.* Miras, w.; miraz, B.; myras, meras, w.; viraz, viroz, P.; sul, the sul, R.D. 1833. *Na nyl the wyth na the sul*, nothing to do nor to took at, R.D. 2250.

TO LOOK FOR, *v.* Whelas, welas, w.; wellas, P.; whyles, whelé, w.; whela, P.; whythré, w.

TO LOOK OUT, *v.* Aspyé, w.; sul, the sul, P.

TO LOOK UPON, *v.* Gwelas, w.; guelaz, P.; gwelés, welés, w.; wellas, guella, P.

LOOK, LOOK. (See, see). Mere, mere; meir, meir, P.; forms of *wêr*, 2 pers. s. imp. of *miras*, to look at, w.

LOOK YE. Mira, B.; meero, w.; forms of *mirouch*, 2 pers. pl. imp. of *miras*, to look at, w.

LOOKED. Miraz, viraz, veraz, B.

HE LOOKED AT. Wetras, another form of *whythras*, 3 pers. s. preter. of *whythré*, to look at (or for), w.

LOOSE, *adj.* (Slack). Lausq, B.

LOOSE, *adj.* (Remiss, lax). Lac, w.

LOOSE or UNFASTEN, *v.* Louzall, P.; sewillaf, B.

LOOSE or SHELFY GROUND. Kivully, D.

LORD, *s.* Arluidh, arludh, w.; arlud, M. 142; arluth, w.

A LORD OVER A TRIBE. Arlywith, P.

LORD OR SUPERIOR. Glyd, maer, mester, B.; somot, P.

LORDS, *s.* Arlythy, M. 2278. *Leferugh ov arlythy*, say, my *lords*, M. 2278; arlyzy, M. 172; aylydhy (? arlydhy), bryntyn, P.

LORD-LIEUTENANT, *s.* Brodit, luder, w.; lyder, B.

LORD'S-PRAYER. Padar an Arluth, w.; padar, P.

LORDSHIP, *s.* (Dominion). Arthelath, P.; vryans, M. 3959; wryens. M. 3963. *Y vryans eff yv helma*, his lordship is this, M. 3959.

LORDSHIP, *s.* (A lordship). Arlottés, w.; pill, P.

LOSE, *v.* Celly, kelly, gelly, celli, w.; kelli, geli, P.; cylly, gylly, w.; gyll, P.; goll, B.; colli, golli, colly, w.; gollas, dho gollas, regolli, rygolly, golsé, gulsé, P.

HE LOST. Gollas, a mutation of *collas*, 3 pers, s. preter. of *colly*, to lose, w.

WE LOST. Gylsen, a mutation of *cylsen*, 1 pers. pl. preter. of *cylly*, to lose, w.

HE HAD LOST. Golsé, a mutation of *colsé*, 3 pers. s. plup. of *colly*, to lose, w.

THOU SHALT LOSE. Cylly, kylly, w.

HE WILL LOSE. Ceyl, cyll, kyll, and the mutations geyl, gyll, 3 pers. s. fut. of *celly* and *cylly*, to lose, w.

LOSS OR DAMAGE, *s.* Coll, goll, collet, w.; kollet, B.; cellad, w.; câs, gâs, P.; col, M. 479. *Gallus the col*, to go to loss, M. 479.

A LOSS. Veyns, P.

LOST, *part.* Cillis, cellys, w.; kellys, R.D. 11; cyllys, kyllys, gillis, w.; gilliz, B.; gyllis, gellis, gellas, gallus, P.; gollas, gulsé, galsé, galso, gyld, vêz, B.

LOSTWITHIEL, *s.* Lostuythyel, o.m. 2400.

LOT or CHANCE, *s.* Pren, predn. w.; pran, P. This means a stick, but *pren, predn*, or *pran*, " because by sticks the Druids divined," w.

LOT, *s.* (Condition). Bys, P.C. 3193. *A thu guyn ov bys neffre*, Oh God! happy my lot ever, P.C. 3193.

LOT, *s.* (Quantity of anything). Tomals, w. The Cornish still use this word, pronouncing it *tummals*, as " tummals of meat," *i.e.*, lots of meat.

LOUD, *adj.* Huth, cuth, P.; vth (*uth*), R.D. 2244. *Púr vth o clewas an cry*, very loud was heard the cry, R.D. 2244.

LOUDLY, *adv.* Huthick, P.; huthyk, R.D. 2304.

LOUSE, *s.* Lewen, louen, luan, w.; loyen, trûz, booey, kynak, B. I have often, when a boy, heard *boo* and *booey* used for *louse*. *Pl.* Loow, lou, w.

LOUT, *s.* Jannak, D.

LOUSY, *adj.* Lestezius, w.; myllusyon, M. 3805. *Agis pennov myllusyon*, your lousy heads, M. 3805.

LUBBER, *s.* Gossawk, D.

LOVE, *s.* Carensé, cerensé, w.; kerenzé, karens, P; cerengé, kerengé, w. *The dreys râk evn kerengé*, thy feet, for true love, P C 483; carengé, carenga, w.; karenga, P.; gerensé, w. *Marow râg the gerensé*, dead for thy love, o.m. 2138; garensa, w.; garenga, P.; harenga, herensé, w. *Ty a kyl ow herensé*, thou shalt lose my love, o.m. 242; kêr, ceer, kerd, carer, B.; tregereth, w.; dregereth, P.; yeués, o.m. 2135. *Râg ól ov yeués pup prys*, for all my love always, o.m. 2125.

LOVE, *v.* Caré, w.; charé, charer, P.; cara, w.; kara, cary, kerry, kyry, câr, kear, caruyth, P.; garé, gara, w. ; gary. gery, garthy, carsé. garsé, razé, P. rasé, P *Me an raxe*, I him love, P.

I HAD LOVED or WOULD HAVE LOVED. Carsen, garsen, w.

THOU HADST LOVED or WOULD HAVE LOVED. Carsesta, garsesta, w.

HE HAD LOVED or WOULD HAVE LOVED. Carsé, garsé, w.

I SHALL or WILL LOVE. Caraf, garaf w.

THOU SHALT or WILT LOVE. Cerry, kerry, cyrry, kyrry, ceryth, geryth, w.

HE SHALL or WILL LOVE. Car, gar, carvyth, w.

WE SHALL or WILL LOVE. Ceryn, geryn, w.

YE SHALL or WILL LOVE. Cyrreuch, kyrreuch, w.

THOU MAYEST LOVE. Kyrry, kyry, kerry, N.

HE MAY LOVE. Carro, carra, w.

LOVEABLE, *adj.* Caradow, w. ; karadow, M. 74 ; garadow. c.w. 189 ; cûf, w.

LOVEABLENESS, *s.* Caradevder, M. 1309, 3668.

LOVED. *part.* Cerys, kerys, cyrys, kyrys, w.

LOVING or AFFECTIONATE, *adj.* Cescer, serchog, w.

LOVELY, *adj.* Hegar, from *hedh* and *gare,* easy to be loved, B.

LOW, *adj.* Isal, w. ; isall, B. ; izal, P. ; esal, isel, w. ; yssel, ysel, P. *War pen the thew glyn ysel,* low on thy two knees, P.C. 136 ; iza, P. ; is, jack, B. ; down, town. w. ; doun, vown, P.

LOW-FELLOW or SCAMP, *s* See SCOUNDREL.

LOW WATER. Bas dhour, P.

LOWER, *adj.* Isala, isa, iza, w. ; izala, gullo, gollas, P. ; gullas, B. *Gueal gullas,* the lower field, B. ; wolla, wollas, lour, P.

LOWER, *v* Bassé, bashé, w.

TO LOWER DOWN, *v.* Cyldené, w.

LOWER ORDERS, THE COMMONALITY, *s.* Lu, megganu, B.

LOWEST, *adj.* Isella, w. ; ceriss, keriss, B.

LOWEST, LOWEST PART, BOTTOM, *s* Golés, wolés, golas, wolas, w. ; golaz, B. ; gollas, P. ; iseldor, w.

LOWLIEST, *adj.* (Most humble). Isella, w.

LOWLY, *adj.* Deboner, dyboner. w. ; dybour (? dybonr). B. ; huvel, evall, isel. ysel, w. ; izal, iza, P.

LOWNESS, *s.* Yseldar, c.w. 447 ; iseldor, w.

LOYAL, *adj.* Laian, leal, B. ; leel, c.w. 893 ; lêl, P. ; leyn, c.w. 2496.

LOYALLY, *adv.* Lell, M. 392 ; lên, M. 824.

LOYALTY. *s.* Lauté, louté. leuté. leauté, lewté, w. ; lowta, c.w. 267 ; lendury, M. 3490 *Me a ra gahs lendury.* I will with loyalty, M. 3490.

LUCID. *adj.* Splan. spladn, w. ; splên, P.

LUKEWARM, *adj.* Tabm. See HEATED.

LUMP, *s.* Pêth, peyth, pêz, B. ; lam, P.

A LUMP OF CLAY or EARTH. Clob, D.

LUNATIC, *s.* Badus, w.

LUNCHEON, *s* Croust, kroust, P. ; crûst, crowst, w. ; crwst, B. ; tam, tabm, P. These words are still used in Cornwall. They call a bit of bread and butter. a *tam* or *tabm.*

LUNGS, THE LUNGS, *s.* Scevens, skephens, sceuens, w. ; broden, B.

LURDANE, A LURDANE, *s.* Lorden, w.

LURK, *v.* Gouea. P.

LURKING-PLACE, *s.* (For wild beasts). Fow, w. ; fou, B.

LUST, *s.* Whans, w. ; whanz, P. ; hwans, w. ; gwenar, guenar, P.

LUSTY, *adj.* Stric, strik, B.

LUTES, *s.* (The musical instruments). Gyttrens, O.M. 1998.

LYING, *adj.* Gowec, gouhoc, gauhoc, guac, gôc, gow, w. ; fykyl. *Fikyl lavarou,* lying words, B.

LYING, *s.* (A telling of lies). Gowegneth, gouegnêth, gouegueth, P.

LYNX, *s.* Hachs, bleit hahchs, bleit hachs, *i.e.,* a cruel wolf, P ; hanehi, hanchi, kymmisk-bleid, *i.e.,* a spotted beast, B.

M.

" This letter, sounded as in English. is a mutable radical initial in the six Celtic dialects, and changes into *mh* or *v.* Thus in Cornish, *mam,* a mother ; *y vam,* his mother. The changes into *mh* in Irish and Gaelic, are pronounced as *v.*" w. *Lex. Corn. Brit.*

MACKEREL, A MACKEREL, *s.* Brethil, brethal, brithel, brethyl, breithil. *Pl.* Brilli, brithelli, w. The Cornish still call a mackerel, *breal, breel.*

MAD, *adj.* Mûs, muscoc, w. ; muscok, muskegvi, P. ; muskegy, R.D. 1466 ; mustok, P. ; mescat, w.; meskat, B. ; conerioc, w. ; koneriok, B. ; conerive, P. ; gurbulloc, B. ; gurbullog. w. ; fol, M. 3210. *Pan veua fol ha garov,* though he be mad and rough, M. 3210 ; wôd, R.D 544. *Kyn fo an harlot mar wôd,* though the rogue be ever s omad, R.D. 544.

MADAM, *s.* Bednuaaz, for benen-vaz, B.

MADDER, *s.* (The plant). Madere, w.

MADEFY or MOISTEN, *v.* Glibbie, glýbyé, w. ; glibié, P.

MADE KNOWN. Gôthfethys, p.

MADE READY. Kerghys, b.

MADMAN, *s.* Badus, w.

MADNESS, *s.* Mescatter, muscochneth, w.; muscoghneth, n.; muscokneth, R.D. 1127; mustoghneth, p.; discoruunait, w.; discorvanait, diskians, buanegez, b.; conner, connor, p.

MAGIC, *s.* Pystry, pystic, pystyk, w.; hûs. m. 3376 *Der the ingynnys hath hûs,* through thy engines and thy magic, m. 3376.

MAGICIAN. *s.* Pystryor, pystryour, w.; huder, hudol, nudol, b.

MAGISTRATE, *s.* Gueshevin, guashevyn, gueskeuyn, b.

MAGNIFICENT, *adj.* Mourobrur, brâsoberys, w.

MAGNITUDE, *s.* Myns, mêns, w.

MAGPIE, *s.* Berthuan, b.

MAID or GIRL, *s.* Môs, môz, w.; moaz, maoz, mauz, mowés, myrgh, moid, p.; moren, moroin, w.; morain, p.; voren, w.; voran, p. *Pl.* Musy, w.; mowyssye, c.w. 1455; mozi, muzi, b.; mowysy, n.

MAID, THE MAID, THE SERVANT-GIRL, *s.* Môz, an voze, voos, c.w. 1390; mayteth, maythys, maithee, p.; maithez, b.; mounz, d. *Pl.* Muzy, p.; muzi, mozi, b.

MAID or VIRGIN, *s.* See VIRGIN.

MAIMED. *adj.* Evredhec, effredh, w.; efrethek, m; 540; mans, m. 695; moign, b.

MAIN, THE MAIN, *s.* (Sea). Môr difeid, p.

MAJESTY, *s.* Braster, broster, w.

MAKE, *v.* Formyé, obery, w.; huarfo, nova, p.

MAKE or DO, *v.* Gil, cil il, w.; geil, p.; gûl, cûl, kûl, wûl, gwil, w; guil, b.; hwil, w.; huil. b.; gweyl, gwyll, whûl, w.; dho gurel, b.; gwrey, w.; gurei, gurey, p.; gura, ara, b.; gwrellé, w.; gurellé, whrylly, p.; grugé, crugé, krugé, gwrugé, gwregé, gwethé, gwethyl, wethyl, w.; wathyll, wythyl, p.; wythell, c.w. 2310; guthyl, cuthyl, wuthyl, w.; wuthell, b; gurythyl, p.; gruthyl, gwruthyl, wruthyl, w.; cra, cruf, p. *Cra is gura* abbreviated, p.

MADE or DONE. Gwrys, gurys, wrys, gwreys, wreys, w.; rûg, ryg, arûg, p. See also TO DO.

THOU MADEST or DIDST. Grussys, 2 pers. s. preter. of *gwrey,* to make or do, w.

HE MADE or DID. Wrûg, rûg, rûc, ruk, 3 pers. s. pret, of *gwrey,* to make or do, w.

THEY MADE or DID. Gwrussons, grussons, wiussons, w.; wressons, wryssens, p.

YE MADE or DID. Grussouch, 2 pers. pl. preter. of *gwrey,* to make or do. w.

WE HAD MADE or DONE. Grussyn, 1 pers. pl. pluperf. of *gwrey,* to make or do, w.

THOU DIDST MAKE. Grûsté, crûsté. *Crûsté* is a mutation of *grûsté,* compounded of *grûst,* the 2 pers. s. pret. of *gwrey,* and *te,* thou, w.

MAKE YE. Gwreuch, greuch, grew, w.

LET US MAKE. Gero in guil, p.

MAKE HASTE. Festyn, ffystyn, ffystyne, b.

TO MAKE ACCOUNT OF or APPROVE, *v.* Lymery, p.

TO MAKE ANGRY, TO ANGER, *v.* Provycha, b.

TO MAKE BETTER, *v.* Gwella, w.; guella, ewna, owna, ouna, p.

TO MAKE BLIND, *v.* Dalla, w.; dallu, b.

TO MAKE BROAD, *v.* Lesé, w.

TO MAKE CLEAN, *v.* Ystynny, p.

TO MAKE CROOKED, *v.* Camma, gamma, w.; cabmy, p.

TO MAKE EXCUSE, *v.* Cavanscusé, w.; kaunscusé, p.

TO MAKE A FACE, *v.* Facyé, w.

TO MAKE FALSE, *v.* Gova, gowea, w.; gouea, b.

TO MAKE FAST, *v.* Fastyê, fasté, w.

TO MAKE FRIENDS, TO RECONCILE, *v.* Cysolatha, dho kysalatha, w.

TO MAKE GLAD, *v.* Lowenhé, lowenny, dydhané, dhydhané, w.

TO MAKE GREATER, *v.* Mochahé, w.

TO MAKE HASTE, *s.* Fysteny, fystynny, festynna, w.; dho festinna, p.

TO MAKE HIGH, *v.* Uchellé, uhellé, ychellas, w.

TO MAKE A HOLE, *v.* Tulla, b.

TO MAKE HOT, *v.* Tumma, tomma, p.; tubma, tubmy, b.

TO MAKE KNOWN, *v.* Daryvas, dharyvas, dyryvas, dascudhé, dyscudhé, dyswedhy, disquedha, dyswedha, dysquedhas, desmygy, dysmegy, notyé, w.

TO MAKE LESS, *v.* Lehé, leyhé, leyhy, lyha, lyhy, w.

TO MAKE MOIST, *v.* Glibbié, w.; glibie, p.; glybyé, w. They still use the words *glibby* and *clibby,* for anything wet, or moist and sticky.

TO MAKE A NEST, *v.* Nyethy, w.

TO MAKE A NET, *v.* Lreedy, p. This is still a common word among fishermen.

TO MAKE A NOISE, *v.* Kanvas, b.

TO MAKE ONE'S SELF, *v.* Omwrellé, omwrey, ymwrey, ymwryl, w.

TO MAKE PEACE, *v.* Hêdhy, w.

TO MAKE PLAINT, *v.* Plêntyé, w.; pleyntyé, b.

TO MAKE READY, *v.* Darbary, parusy, w.

TO MAKE RIGHT, *v.* Ewné, ewnné, w.; euna, b.

TO MAKE SMALLER, *v.* Lehé leyhé, leyhy, lyhy, lyha, w.

TO MAKE A SMELL, *v.* Gwell bremmyn, brâs dyllo, w.

TO MAKE A BAD SMELL, *v.* Fleryé, fleyryé, w.

TO MAKE STRAIGHT, *v.* Ewné, ewnné, w.; euna, P.

TO MAKE (er PAY) TITHE, *v.* Degevy, P.

TO MAKE UGLY, *v.* Hagry, w.

TO MAKE USE OF, *v.* Wyny, P.

TO MAKE WATER, TO URINATE, *v.* Pisa, w.; troaza, B.

TO MAKE WELL or WHOLE, *v.* Iaché, w.

TO MAKE WHITE, *v.* Gwynna, w.

TO MAKE WORSE, *v.* Gwaythy, w.; gwaythé, B.; gwethé, w.; guethé, P. The verbal form is *jethy*, w.

TO MAKE WRY, *v.* Camma, gamma, omgamma, w.

MAKER or CONTRIVER, *s.* Formyer, formyas, P.; gwrear, wrear, w.; gylwyr, B.

MALADY, *s.* Clevés, clevas, w; klevas, B.; klevaz, clewet, P.; clevel, cluyan, w.

MALE, A MALE, *s.* (Man). Gour, gûr, gôr, mâb, mâp, w. *Mâp lyen*, a clergy-man, w.

MALE, MALE-KIND, *s.* Gurriw, w.; gurow, gorawe, gorryth, gurriud, uraid, ti uraid, P.

MALES, *s.* Gorow, O.M. 1022; gorrow, C.W. 2271. *Gorow ha benow*, males and females, O M. 1022; mebion, mebbion, meyb, mybyon, w.

MALE, *adj.* Gour. *Ol ow tûs gour ha benen*, all my people male and female, P.C. 768.

MALE CHILD, *s.* Mâb. *Pl.* Mebion, mebbion, meyb, mybyon, w.

MALEFACTOR, *s.* Drôgoberor, drôchoberor, w.

MALEDICTION, *s.* Molleth, molloth, mollath, w.; molath, P. *Pl.* Mollethow, mollothow, mollathow, w.; molathow, P.

MALICE, *s.* Avey, avy, aui, P.; belyny, velyny, vylyny, w.

MALICIOUS, *adj.* Drôgbrederys, w.; pedn-drôg, P.

MALLARD or DRAKE, *s.* Kiliagaws, w.; kulliages, P.; kulliaghaz, kuliagaz, B.

MALLET, *s.* Malou, morthol, morben, w. *Gans morben bom trewysy*, with a mallet a terrible blow, O.M. 2704.

MALT, *s.* Brâg, w.; vrâc, B.

MALT-DUST, *s.* Skyl brâg, P.

MALT-LIQUOR, *s.* Brihi, B.

MALT-LIQUOR or DRINK, *s.* Diautvrâs, B.

MAN, *s.* Dèn, dhèn, dean, w.; deen, dien, dyn, teen, B.; thean, C.W. 2121; tyn, dûs, tûs, B.; gûr, w.; guyr, B.; gôr, gour, wour, w.; gerut, P.; gurraid, B.; gorryth, R.D. 420; mâb. w. *Nysus gorryth na benen,* there is no man or woman, R.D. 420. See MEN.

A FAMOUS MAN. Gerut da, P.

A GREAT MAN. Dèn brâs, w.

A CHILDLESS MAN. Gale, D. (impotent).

THE MAN OF THE HOUSE. Worty, P.; guyr an chy, B.

AN HONEST MAN. Dremas, M. 1103; dremays, M. 1112. *Dremas beth war pythylly*, honest man be wary where thou mayest go, M. 1103.

A JUST MAN. Cûnhinsik, B.

A MARRIED MAN. Gûr priot, w.

AN OLD MAN. Dèn côth, B.

A POOR MAN. Bochodoc, bohodzak, P.

A RICH MAN. Pwludoc, P.

A TRUE MAN. Gueryion, P.; guirion, B.

A TRUTHFUL MAN. Guirla veriat, P.

TRUE MEN. Gwyryon, N.

A WORTHY MAN. Thermas, M. 3043. *A thermas cry war the gam*, oh worthy man, cry on thy way, M. 3043.

A WITHERED LOOKING MAN. Kiskey, D.

A MAN'S YARD. (*Penis*). Gwelen, gwelan, w.; guelan, P.

A YOUNG MAN. Dèn iunc, w.; dèn junk, P.; dèn yynk, w.

MANCIPLE, *s.* Menistror, w.

MANE, *s.* Rên. *Rên verh*, a horse's mane, w.

MANIFEST, EVIDENT, *adj.* Dilus, B.; uredy, P.

MANHOOD, *s.* Densés, densys, w.

MANKIND, *s.* Mâp dèn. *Mâp dèn my re wruk prenné*, mankind I have redeemed, R.D. 2622.

MANNER, *s.* (Occasion, sort). Tro, w.

MANNER, *s.* (Semblance, form). Del, w. *Yn-delma*, in this manner, w.; côr, kôr, B. *War nep côr*, in any manner; fest, wôs, wose, P.

IN WHAT MANNER. Pattel, patel, patla, fattel, fatel, fatla, fatl, fettyl, fetyl, fettel, P.

IN SUCH A MANNER. Cetella, ketella, kettermen, cettermyn, ceverys, keverys, kevrys, cefrys, P.

IN THE MANNER THAT. Cetel, kettel, kettyl, w.

IN THE SAME MANNER. Cepar, kepar, w.

IN THIS MANNER. Cetelma, ketelma, w.

IN THIS SAME MANNER. Yn ketel-ma (*kéth-del-ma*), w.

IN THAT SAME MANNER. Yn ketella (*kéth-del-na*), w.

IN THAT MANNER. Del, della, an della, andellan, yn della (*del-na*), P.

IN LIKE MANNER. Awedh, yn wedh, w.; parthy, P.

IN WHICH MANNER. Fatel (*pa-del*), w.

MANNERS, BEHAVIOUR, *s.* Arweddiad, B.

MANOR, A MANOR, *s.* Arlottés, w.; gweal, gwêl. gueal, têr (*terra*, Lat.), B.; pil, P.

MANOR-HOUSE, *s.* Llys, B.

MAN-SERVANT, *s.* Kaith, B.

MANSION, *s.* Plâs, ostel, w. *Ha drehevel thy'm ostel,* and build myself a mansion, o.m. 1710.

MANSLAUGHTER, *s.* Calanedh, w.; kalanedh, P.; dên lâdh, dênladh, w.; lâthdên, latha, P.

MAINTAIN, *v.* (Support, uphold). Succra, c.w. 1949; venteyné, P.; vayntaynya, c.w. 1950.

MANTLE, *s.* Mantel, w.

A WOMAN'S MANTLE. Ulair, w.

MANUAL, A MANUAL or HAND-BOOK, *s.* Coweid-liver. cowaithliver, w.; kouaith-liver, B.; stollof, P.; manule, w.

MANURE, *s.* Teil, w.; tyle, w.; câc, cauch, cau, cauh, gau, w.

MANY. Luas, lués, w.; luyés, M. 4401; leas, lias, w. *Yn lias lé*, in many places; lyys, lyés, lys, liaz, w.; lius, M 397; luhas, luhés, w.; lower, B. *Lower le*, many places, B.; fire, P. *Nangew fire by as bleth-hon*, not these many years past, P.; meur, mûr, maur, mear, mêr, w.; menough, minough, B.; morhaus, P.

AS MANY. Maga lias, w.

MANY A ONE. Lias onon, w.; liaz onon, P.

AS MANY AS. Suel. sûl, w.

SO MANY AS. Pezealla. w.

MANY TIMES. Lias termen, w.; liaz termyn, R.; lyés trefeth, P.; manno. B.; menouch. minouch, w.; menough, minough, mennough, P.

MARCH, *s.* (The month). Merh, Meurz, B. Lide, D.

MARCH MONTH. Mîs Merh, P.; Mîs Meurz, B. *Mîz Merh. Lit.* The horse month " when the Gauls began to set forth with horses to war," P.

MARE, *s.* Casec, casac. w.; kasak, kazak, kasseg, P.; casak, c.w. 406; cazak, P.; cossec, cazau. B.; gasac, w. *Pl.* Cassiggy, P.

MARGIN, *s.* Mein, mîn, urrian, yrhian, w.

MARINER. *s.* Dên mor, w.

MARINERS, *s.* Marners, M. 587.

MARITIME, *adj.* Morec, w.

MARK. *s.* (As of a hurt. &c.) Goly, w.; golu, B.; ôl, ool, nôd. nôs, nôz, w.

MARKS, *s.* (Traces). Goleow, P.; goleou, B.; goly, oleow, owleow, P.; owleou, B.

FRESH MARKS. Goleou pals, B.

MARK or BRAND, *s.* Arwydd, B.

MARK, *s.* (Note. dignity). Aynôs, P.

MARKET, *s.* Marchas, w.; marghas, P.; marhas, w.; marhaz, B.; maraz, P. *Yn chy dev mar sues marghas*, if there is a market in God's house, P.C. 316; varhas, varha, w. *Pl.* Marchasow, marhasow, w.; marhasion. Hence most probably the name of present town, *viz.*: Marazion.

MARKET-HOUSE, *s.* Tshy-marhazno, B.

MARKET-PLACE, *s.* Telhar marhas, w.; telhar marhaz, B.

MARKET-JEW. *s.* (Marazion). Varha Dzhou, w. See MARKET.

MARIGOLD, *s.* Lêsengoc, w.

MARRIAGE, *s.* Dimedha, B.; maryach, M. 332.

MARRIED, *adj.* Priot, w.

MARRIED PERSON. Cespar, w.; chaspar, kaspar, P.

MARRY, *v.* Demidhy, dimedha, w.; dimedho, P.; demytho, B.; domethy, M. 327.

MARROW, *s.* Muydion, B.; maru, w.

MARS, *s.* (The heathen god of war). Merh.

MARSH, *s.* Winnick, whynick, P.; tir devrak, w.; devrak, P.

A MARSH NEAR THE SEA. Morva, w.

MARSHES, *s.* Hellov (*hellou*), M. 3411. *War geyn margh mês an hellov*, on a horse's back out of the marshes. M 3411.

MARSH IRIS, *s.* (Plant). Laver, leaver, D.

MARSHY. *adj.* Gwernic, w; guernick, P; gwinic, winnic, w.; winny, P.; helek, B. *Helek* from *hêl* a river.

MARSHY LAND. Tir devrak, B.

MART or FAIR, Fêr, w.; feur, B.

MARTYR, *v.* Merthuryé, verthuryé. w.

MARVEL, *s.* Marth, marthus, varth, varthus, w.

MARVELS, *s.* Marogyan, c.w. 1874; marodgyan, c.w. 1804; marudgyan, c.w. 1765. See WONDERS.

MARVELLOUS, *adj.* Marthusec, varthusec, marthys, varthys, w.; marthusy, P.; merthusy, B.; marthas, P.

MARY, *s,* Maria, Varia, Faria, w.; Marya, M. 154; Varya, M. 62.

BY ST. MARY! Re-Faria, Refaria, Re-Varia, Re-varia, w.

MASON, *s.* Mysterdên. *Pl.* Mysterdys, P.

MASS, A MASS or LUMP, *s.* Pêth, peyth, pêz, w.

MASS or MORSEL, *s.* Suben, w. It was also used as the name of a kind of pudding.

MASS, *s.* (In the church service). Oferen, w.; offren, B.; offeren, M. 4419. *Y leferys offeren,* he said mass, M. 4419.

MAST, *s.* (Of a ship). Guern, gwern, vern, w.

MASTER, *s.* Maister, mêster, vêster, w. · *Pl.* Mestresy, M. 3313; mestrygy, mestrigi. N.; mestrizi, P. *Hov mestresy ús lemyk,* how, masters, is there a sup? M. 3313.

MASTER, MASTER OF THE HOUSE, *s.* Penteilu, w.; pennou-ties, B.

MASTER, MASTER OF A SHIP. *s.* Leuuit, w.; leuiut, leuyidh, B.; lewyidh, w.; leuiader, P

MASTERY, POWER. *s.* Mestry, maystry, meystry, w., maistry, maistrizi, P.; vestry, B.

MASTIFF, *s.* Meslan, w.; guilter, brath. brathky, bratchy, B.; brathye, brakgye, B.

MAT, *s.* Strail, P. *Pl.* Strail elestr, B.

MATE or COMPANION, *s.* Cothman, cydhman, w.; kydhman, B.

MATE or FELLOW, *s* Kyvadhas, kyuedh, B.

MATCH or EQUAL, *s.* Pâr, w.

MATCHLESS, *adj.* Hepparow, hepparou. hepar, B.

MATRIX, THE MATRIX, THE WOMB, *s.* Brys, w.

MATRIX, *s.* (*Vulva, Lat.*) Ceber, w.

MATRON, *s.* Benen-vat, B.

MATTER, *s.* Defnydh, w. (The word means as to use of a thing.) *War Cedron ow cowedhé yma prén da, ha hen yw emskemunys, râk ny allas dén yn beys anodho gûl* defnydh *uds,* on Kedron there is lying a good tree, and this is accursed, for no man in the world has been able to make a good use (or matter) of it, P.C. 2548 (w. as quoted).

MATTER. A SMALL MATTER, A LITTLE, *s.* Bochés, bohés, bochod, w.

MATTER, MATERIAL or STUFF, *s.* Gwyrras, P.; wyras, P.C. 2975.

MATTOCK, *s.* Pigol, pâl, w.; paal, B.; bâl, fâl, w.; visgy, visgie, visgay, D.

MATTRASS, *s.* (Of straw). Cala gueli, w.; kala gueli, P.

MATURE or RIPE, *adj.* Ao, w.

MAUL or HAMMER, *s.* Morthol, morben, w.

MAUNDAY THURSDAY. Deyow hablys, duyow hamlos, w.

MAW, *s* Glâs, w.; glayis, B. *An jawl re'th ewno th'y glâs,* the devil may adjust thee to his maw, O.M. 2527.

MAY, *s.* Mê. *Mis Mê,* w. *Mis Mê,* P.; the month of May, *i.e.,* "the flowing month, P."

MAY. Yll, yl. *Yll gwellas,* may see, B.

WE MAY. Hellyn, a mutation of *gellyn,* 1 pers. pl. subj. of *gally,* to be able, may or can, w.

I MAY or CAN. Hyllyf, B.

IT MAY or CAN. Kôr, P.

IF HE CAN. Mara kôr, P.

ME, *pron.* Me, mi, my, ma, ve, w.; vee, C.W. 82; vi, w.; vy, N.; am, fe, P. *Ma* is a form which occurs only in composition.

LET ME. Gas vy, N.

AT ME. Hanaf, P.

BEFORE ME. Ragof, ragoff, w.

BY ME. Dred hev, B; drethof. N.; dresof, genef, w.; rûm, rôm, P.

FOR ME. Ragof, ragoff, w.; thymmo, B.; thymo, C.W. 1035.

FROM ME. Ahané, ahanaf, deworthyf, dyworthyf, dheworthyf, deworthef, w.; dhortum, B.; ragof, ragoff. w.

IN ME. Ynnof, yn-mi, w.

OF ME. Ahané, w.; hanaf, P.; ow, vi, evi. B.; evy, w. *Ow map evy,* my son mine; the orthoff vy, M. 2577; orthav ve, C.W. 1430.

ON or UPON ME. Warnaf, C.W. 1530.

TO ME. Thym, N.; tym, C.W. 2412; them, thum, thebm, thymmo, P.; thymo, C.W. 844; thema, C.W. 801; thymmo vi, P.; thymmo vy, N.; dhym, P.; dym. dheym, dem. w.; dhem, P.; debm. B.; dhebm, dhymmo, dhov, dhovi, P.; thyso, dyso, M.; worthyf, orthyf. w.; vi, si, sy, B. *Sy glewyough,* hearken ye to me, B.; aga, P.; a'm, w.

WITH ME. Genef, ghenev, genaf, gené, gyné. genefvy, gynefy, genama, P. *Genama* is a poetic form of *genefvy.*

MEAD or METHEGLIN, *s.* Mêdh, w.; medd. medhu, B.; medu, meddou, w.; bregaud, bragot, brakat, P.

MEADOW, *s.* Prâs, budin, bidin. bidhin, bidhen, w.; beidhen, bithen, B.; vidn, vethan. vythyn, tôn, tôdn, w.; rôs, guain. nain, ludin, meddou, B.; meddan, P.

MEADOWY, *adj.* Prathec, pratheck, w.

MEADOW-SAFFRON, *s.* Goitcenin, w.; goitkenin, B.; goickennin, P.

MEAL or FLOUR, *s.* Blês, blêz, blôt, P.; huigan, guthot, B.

MEAL, A MEAL, *s.* Prys, prês, preys, pres-buz, w.; biner, byner, P.

MEAL-TIME, *s.* Prys, prês, preys, pres, prez, w.; prez-buz, B.

MEALS, *s.* Preggyov (*preggyou*), M. 1972. *A veth ov bôs thúm preggyov,* and my food for my meals, M. 1972.

MEAN, v. Yflé, p.

MEAN, adj. Hogen, w. ; hogan, p. ; lôs, w.

MEAN or MEANS. s.   Mayn (mein), w. ; mayn (means), B. Mayn avé guris, means were found out, B.

MEAN PERSON. Gwâs, gnas, w. ; guaz, B.

MEAN FELLOWS. Gwesion, gwesyon, wesyon, w.

MEANS. BY MY MEANS. Dresof, p.

MEANS. BY WHAT MEANS, HOW, Pattel, patla, fattel. fatla, w.

MEANING. s. Daryvas, B.

MEANWHILE. Hedré, heddré, p

MEASLES, s. Poccys minis, w.

MEASURE, v. Musuré, vusuré, w.

MEASURE, s. (For measuring with). Scanntlyn. w. From the Old English scantelvun, a carpenter's measure.

MEASURE, SIZE, PROPORTION, s Gûr, p. Ny thue the gûr, it will not come to measure, p.c. 2730 ; fest, B. Fest cress, abundant measure, B.

MEAT or FOOD, s. Buit, w. ; buyd, p. ; boys, bôs, bûs, bûz, boos, w. ; bôz, p. ; ferclin, crâg, saut, sant, B.

A SCRAP OF MEAT or FLESH, Slam, scram, D.

MEAT-SPIT or FLESH-SPIT, s. Kigvêr, w.

MEDDLE, TO MEDDLE WITH, v. Mellya, w.

MEDICINE, s. Medhecnaid, mydhygyeth, w.

MEDITATE, v. Predery, w. ; prediri, prederi, p. ; predyry, prydery, prydyry, w. ; thugy, p.

MEDIUM, s. Mayn, w. See also MEAN and MEANS.

MEEK, adj. Deboner, dyboner, w. ; triwardhec, triaudhek, p. ; triuadhek, B.

MEET, v. Dyerbyné, dyerbin. dhyerbin. dierbyn, w. ; metyé, vetyé, B.

MEET or PROPER, adj. Ewn, ewen, w. ; eun, ewhinsic, p. ; pâr, w.

MELANCHOLY, DISMAL, SAD, adj. Morethek, B. Wisht, whisht, D.

MELLOW or RIPE, adj. Arvez, w.

MELT, TO MELT, TO BECOME MELTED, v. Tedha, w.

MEMBER, s. (Of the body). Esel, w. Pl. Esely, esyly, ysyly, yssili, w ; yshili, B.

MEMBRANE, s. Vellum, D. A person who is suffering from rupture (hernia), or from hydrocele, is said to be vellum-broken.

MEMORY, s. Côf, côv, w. ; cûf, co, covath, p.

MEMORIAL, s. Acheson, p.

MEN, s. Dees, w. ; tees, tiz, B. ; têz, B. ; dûs, w. ; dues, c.w. 1057 ; tûs, tues. w. ; dêns, p. ; denes, denses, w. ; dyn, B. ; dynion, w.

SICK MEN. Dynion clevion, w.

WICKED MEN. Scherewys, D.

TRUE MEN. Gueryon, N.

MEND, v. (To improve, to get better). Gwella, w. ; guella, B. ; palch p. The Cornish often say of a person who has improved a little in health that he has been "palched up."

MEND or REPAIR. v. Beety, D. This word is only used in the mending of a net. To make a net they say, breedy.

MEND ONE'S SELF, v. Ymamendyé, w.

MENDER or PATCHER, s. (Of clothes). Seufad, B.

MENEAGE, s. (In Cornwall). Menek, M. 2467.

MENIAL, adj. Labbut, D.

MERCHANT, s. Gwiccor, gwicor, gwiccur, gwicur, w. ; gwicher, p. ; gwicgur, guicgur, w. ; guikyr, B. ; gwecor, wecor, goccor, w.

MERCHANDISE, s. Gwara, waroe, w. ; warol, B. ; ferna, p.

MERCIFUL, adj. Triwardhec, triaudhek, p. ; trucaraue, tevas, B.

MERCILESS, adj. Dibitti, p.

MERCURY, s. (The planet). Marhar, w.

MERCY, s. Kên, c.w. 886. Tulla tha bryas heb kên, deceive thy spouse without mercy, c.w. 886 ; tregereth, dregereth, w. Luen tregereth me a pys, abundant mercy I pray, R.D. 1148 ; trugarez, B. ; trueth, treweth, triwath, trumyth. p. ; trumeth, w. Nysus trumeth vyth thy'nny, there is not any mercy for us, o m. 1650.

MERE, adj. Menas. Menas belyny, mere reproach, B.

MERIT, v. Rethy, p.

MERIT, s. Reth, p.

MERMAID, s. Morvoron, morvoren, vorvoron, vorvoren, w. Dên yv hanter morvoron, human is half the mermaid, p.c. 1742 ; moruerchés, B.

MERRILY, adv. Lowan, B.

MORE MERRILY. Lowené, w.

MERRIMENT, A MERRIMENT, A FEAST, s. Lit, B.

MERRY, adj. Lowen, louan. lawen, B. ; leunik, leunek, p. ; leuenik, louenak, lauenik, lowenic, lawenic, lewenic, lawennek, B. ; lowenec, lowenek, luan, sceans, w. ; skeans, p.

MESH, s. (?). A broken mesh in a net. Shong, B.v. Large meshes in a trammel net. Capis, B.v.

MESS, s. Caugh, cauch, D. (See m. 3255 ; caugyan). A mess of ill made liquid food is called a lauch, looch or loach. These are still commonly used in Cornwall.

A MESS OF FOOD. (Solid food). Scub-maw, D.

A MESS OF MEAT. Lommen, w.

A DIRTY MESS. Slotter, D.

MESSAGE, s. Neges, negys, negis, w.; nagys, nygys, thanwell, P.; danvonad, w. See COMMAND or COMMANDMENT, for other forms of *danvonad*.

MESSENGER, s. Cannas, w. *Pan danfenys the cannas*, since thou has sent thy messenger, O.M. 1670; gannas, M. 1433. *Gans an gannas*, with the messenger, M. 1433; maseger, M. 1378; messeger, P.C 1956; messyger, P.

MESSENGERS, s. Canasow, B.; cannasow, w.; canhasowe, C.W. 29; canhagowe, C.W. 66.

MESSER or MESS-MAKER, s. Caughyan, M. 3255. *Agan mav plosek caughyan*, our boy, dirty mess-maker, M. 3255.

METAL, s. Muyn, môn, mûn B,

INFERIOR METAL. Manillion, D.

METHEGLIN, s. See MEAD or METHEGLIN.

MEW, SEA MEW, COB or GULL, s. Seithor, zethar, w

METHUSELAH, s. Vantusalé, 1435.

MICHAEL, s. Mihal, w.

MID-DAY, s. Hanter dydh, w.; hanter dêth, P.

MID or MIDDLE, adj. Hanter, B. *Kyns avorow hanter dêth*, before to morrow mid-day, P.C. 722.

MIDDLE, THE MIDDLE, s. Crês, w.; krês, N.; crêz, krêz, B.; creis, creiz, P.; creys, greys, crêd, mêsc, mêsk, mysc, mysk, w.; misk, hyll, P.

IN THE MIDDLE. Yn mêsc, w.; yn mêsk, yn mysk, P.; ynmés, B.; aberveth, M. 284. *Rân arâk rân abervêth*, part before, part in the middle, M. 284.

MIDDLE-FINGER, s. Ber-kréz, B.

MIDNIGHT, s. Hanternôs, anternôs, P.

MIDST, THE CENTRE, THE HEART OF, s. The same words are used as for MIDDLE, q.v. *Yn crês a'n ebron avan*, in the midst of the sky above, O.M. 38. *Senseugh ef yn agan mysk*, hold him in our midst, P.C. 1374. *In krês an dre*, in the midst of the town, N.

MIDSUMMER, s. Goluan, B. That is, the time of lights or bonfires.

MIDWIFE, s. Benen glyvedhaz, w.; bennen glyvedhez, P.; glavethas, lavethas, B.

MIDWIFERY, s. Glyvedhas, w. Perhaps a mutation of *clyvedhas*.

MIEN, s. Miras, miraz, P.

MIGHT, POWER, STRENGTH, s. Gallos, gallas, galloys, nell, nel, nerth, w.; nerh, nerg, B. *Mûr y nel*, great his might, M. 3933.

MIGHT, COULD, WOULD. Hylly, ylly, callo, callé, B.; têth, P.

THAT HE MIGHT BE. *May ef têth bo*, P.

I MIGHT. Galsen, w.

THOU MIGHTEST. Galsest, galsesta, w.

HE MIGHT. Galsé, w.

WE MIGHT. Ni a elsin, w.

MIGHTY, adj. Crêf, crêv, w.; krêv, B.; crif, cryf, cryff, w.; galluidoc, B.; galhydock, P.; gallydhog, gallosec, galluzack, B.; gallusec, w.; gallogek, gallogec, galluster, B.; gallas, P.; tryher, w. *Amboso-worth tryher gureys*, promises by the mighty made, w.; vote, M. 3089. *The vote sûr in bysma*, so mighty surely in this world. M. 3089.

MILD, GENTLE, adj. Medhal, medhel, meddal, hynwys, triwardhec, w.; triaudhek, P.; triuadhek, w.

MILDEWED, adj. Cuny, D.

MILDLY, adv. Pardec, B. As if *pûr dék*, very good.

MILDNESS, s. (Gentleness). Medhalder, medalder, w.

MILE, s. Mildir, w.

MILFOIL, s. (Herb). Minfel, milfel, nintell, B.

MILK, v. Gudra, w.

MILK, s. Lait, leyth, lêth, leath, lâth, w.

THE FIRST MILK OF THE COW AFTER CALVING. Gudrak, guedrak, B. In the dialect called buzza-milk.

RAW MILK. Leath creve. *Raw milk* is a provincial term for milk which has not been "scalded," or heated so as to separate the cream; the clotted or clouted cream of Cornwall and Devon. The milk after being scalded, is called "scald-milk."

SOUR MILK. Buchar, w.

SWEET MILK Leuend-lac, leuerith, B.

MILK-HOUSE or DAIRY, s. Laitty, w.

MILK-PAIL or MILK-BUCKET, s. Buket gudra, P.; stén, B; lattis, D.

MILK-PAN, s. Panshion, D.

MILL, s. Melin, mellin, mellyn, belin, velin, vellin, vellyn, brou, w.; tshyi pobaz, P. *Tshyi pabas*, is more correctly *bakehouse*.

MILLER, s. Belender, w.

MILLION, s. Milvil, mylvyl, w.; myl vyl, N. *Lit.* A thousand thousands. Also, mylyon, N.

MILL-POOL, s. Polvellan, B.

MILLSTONE, s. Brôn, brûn, brodn, B.

MILT, s. (The roe of fishes). Leuilloit, vabm, B.

MIMIC. A MIMIC, s. Bardh, barth, w.

MINCED, part. Dufunys, M. 3224. *V lôn bowyn dufunys*, five loins of beef minced, M. 3224.

MINCING, AFFECTED, adj. Foo-ty, D.

MIND, THE MIND, *s.* Breys, w. ; breis, c.w. 106 ; brêz, P. ; brys, brûs, breus, w. ; brues, P. ; vrês, vrys, &c., w.

IT COMES IN MIND. Govenek, P.

NOT OF ONE MIND. Ancombrys, w.

OF ONE MIND. Unver, w.

MINDFUL, *adj.* Covys, w. ; kovys, B. ; kovyz, P.

MINE, A MINE, *s.* Whêl, hwêl, huel, &c., used in naming mines, but properly mean a "work." Underground evcavations are called "the workings," and an open excavation, as in streaming for tin, is always called a stream-*work*. Pryce calls tin *mines* (*i.e.*, mines with shafts, and levels or adits), *moina* stean. For instance, Wheal Alfred (the name of a mine) is simply Alfred's work. For the various forms of *whêl*, see A WORK. The Cornish miners call a mine, a *bal*. For this see DIG, *v.*

AN OLD, BUT OPEN, MINE EXCAVATION. Koffen, P.

A LARGE AND OPEN MINE WORK. Lawn, lawen, D.

MINES, *s.* Moina, P. *Moina stean*, tin mines, P.

MINE-PUMP, *s.* Skit, D.

MINE-SHAFT, *s.* Paladôr. *Lit.* A cast of earth, P.

MINE-SPIRIT or PHANTOM, *s.* Gathorn, D.

MINE-WINCH, *s.* Whinz, B.v.

MINE-WORK, *s.* See WORK.

MINE, *pron. poss.* Am, evy. *Ow map evy*, my son of me ; thum, P.

MINE, *pron. adj.* My, mo, ow, ˅ ; oɪ. ɽ.

BY MINE. Rum, rom, P.

MINER or DIGGER, *s.* Derrick, D.

MINER'S CAKE. Fogans, foogons, fuggan. Plain or not, unleavened, and eaten as a dinner. The same name is also used for a pork pasty.

MINER'S DINNER. Hogan, hoggan, hobbin. This is just the same as what some call the miner's cake, *q v.*

MINGLE, *v.* Cemyscy, kemysky, cymyscy, cymmyscy, w.

MINNOW, *s.* Mimsy, D.

MINSTRELS, *s.* Menestrouthy, w.

MINT, *s.* (The herb). Menté, w. ; mentula, B.

MIRACLE, *s.* Marth, marthus, varth, varthus, w. ; merkyl, P.

A MIRACLE! BY ST. MARY! Rafaria! B.

MIRACLES, *s.* Marthegion, maradgion, marthys, P. ; merclys, M. 688 ; verclys, M. 2527. *Y vose in y verclys*, is mighty in his miracles, M. 2527.

MIRACULOUS, *adj.* Marthusec, w. ; marthusy, P. ; merthusy, P. ; marthys, w. ; marthas, P. ; varthusec, varthys, w.

MIRE, *s.* Pol, poll, w. ; bol, bowl, P. ; pul, caillar, w. ; casa, gasa, gasow, P. ; teil, tyle, B. ; lued, luth, lys, lyys, w. *A bol hag a lyys formys*, made of clay and mire, o.M. 1070.

A MIRY PLACE. Pol, w.

MIRTH. *s.* Lowender, lowenna, lowyné, w. ; lowené, lauen, lowenés, lauenez, P. *Râg ioy ha râg lowené*, for joy and for mirth, o.M. 154.

MIRY, *adj.* Luedic, w. ; luedik, P.

MISCHIEF, *s.* Anfugy, w. ; anfugye, c.w. 1057 ; enfugy, P. *Me a wra neb enfugy*, I will do some mischief, ɪ̶ ; anfus, N. ; dregyn, M. 1110. *Thymmo na rylly dregyn*, that to me thou do no mischief, M. 1110 ; meul, meawl, w. ; myshyf, w. ; vyshew, c.w, 789 ; vyshow, c.w. 1484.

WITH A MISCHIEF. Meaul, B.

MISCHIEF-MAKER, *s.* Strifor, w.

MISCHIEVOUS, *adj.* Anfugyc, w. ; anfusyk, N. ; enfugyk, P. ; anfusyg, enfugyc, w. *Pûr wyr ha mûr anfusyk*, most truly, and very mischievous, R.D. 1520 ; purcheniat, purkeniat, purceniat, B. ; drôc, drôk, drôg. w.

MISERABLE, *adj.* Difrêth, dyfrêth, dyffryth, deffryth, aflydhys, w. ; goef, gweve, P. ; goy, R.D. 1187 ; morethec, morethek, w. ; trot, troth, B. ; wisht, whisht, D.

MISERABLE I. Govy, w.

MISERABLE HE. Goef, w.

TO BECOME MISERABLE, TO RENDER MISERABLE. Treynyé, trynyê, w.

MISERY, *s.* Gû, gew, wew, gwae, w. ; gweve, c.w. 2137 ; govid, myshew, vyshew, w. ; vyssow, vystow, P. ; dysés, o.M. 1432. *Na pel ena yn dysés*, any longer there is misery, o.M. 1432. *Pl.* Govis, govys, govidion, govigion, govegion, govîdzhion, w. ; worthenys, B.

MISFORTUNE, *s.* Câs, gâs, w. *Yma câs brâs warfethys*, a great misfortune has occured, o.M. 1542.

MISLEAD, *v.* Sawtheny, w ; sawthenas, P. *Ma na veny sawthenys*, that we be not misled, P.C. 610.

MISPRIZE, *v.* Dispresy, dyspresy, w.

MISSION, *s.* Danvonad, w.

MIST, *s.* Niul, w. ; niull, huibren, uibren, B.

A DRIVING MIST or DRIZZLE. Skew, D.

A THICK MIST. Gorthuer, goruer, w.

MISTY RAIN or SLEET. Slag, D.

MISTAKE, *v.* Miscemeras, w. ; miskymeraz, P. ; meskymera, B.

MISTAKE, *s.* Miscymerians, w. ; myskymerians, P. ; mystite, B.

MISTAKEN, *adj.* Fellyon, B.

MISTAKEN YOUR WAY. Gyz vôrdh, B.

MISTLETOE, *s.* Guthyl, B.

MISTRESS, *s.* Mestrés, vestrés. *A vestris,* my mistress, w.

THE MISTRESS OF THE HOUSE. Mam-teilu, P.

MISTRUST, *v.* Dismigo, dysmegy, w.

MITE, *s.* Mân, R.D. 1437. *Ny dalons mân,* they are not worth a mite, R.D. 1437.

MITTEN, *s.* Manak, P.

MITRE, *s.* Vytour, P; muter, M. 3010.

MIX, *v.* Cemyscy, kemysky, cymyscy, cymmyscy, w.

MIXING, A MIXING, *s* See MIXTURE.

MIXTURE, *s.* Commysc, cymmysc, cymmysk, cemescys, kemeskys, w.; kemskys, B.; comiska, P.

A NAUSEOUS MIXTURE or MESS. Cauch, caugh, D.

MIZEN-SAIL, *s.* (Of a fishing boat). Kicker, B.V.

MOAN, *v.* Ega, w.

MOAT, *s.* Fôs. w.; vozé, fossa, foza, voza, P.; pullan troillia, w.

MOB or RABBLE, *s.* See COMMON PEOPLE.

MOCK, *v.* Dafolé, w.; daffolé, P.C. 1398. *Ha daffolé fâst an guas,* and mock the fellow much, P.C. 1398. dvalé, w.; dyalas, dhyallas, gesky, P.; gescy, w.; cuthil gês, kuthil gês, P.; moccio, B.

MOCKERY, *s.* Flous, geyll, gês, w.; mogh, M. 955. *Pan yv mogh ol ov duwon,* since all my grief is a mockery, M. 955.

MODESTY, *s.* Mêz, B.; serfans, P. *Ow setha in pûre serfuns,* sitting in great modesty, P.

MOIETY, *s* Hanter, w.

MOIST, *adj.* Glêb. gleab, glib, lêb, gleu, glew, B.; lynnic. w.; lynnek, P.; sôg, sûg, w.

MOISTEN, *v.* Glybyé, glibbie, w.; glibie, P.; clybyé, klybbyé, w.

MOISTURE, *s.* Glibor, glybor, w.; glibbor, lyn, P.; sygan, w.

MOLE, *s.* (Spot or freckle). Taish, w.

MOLE, *s.* (The animal, in Cornwall, called a *want*). Gôdh, gôd, gûdh-dhar, w.; gudh-dhaor, gudh-doar, gudhor. B.; godh-dhar, P.; gudhthaur, B.

MOLE-HILL, *s.* Pil gudhar, w.; turumel, B.

MOLEST, *v.* Dygnas, w.

MOLLIENT, *adj.* Medhal, medhel, meddal, w.; medal, B.; methel, P.

MOLLIFY, *v.* Tempré, B.

MOMENT, *s.* Tûch, w. *Na wreugh vn tûch vyth letyé,* do not any one moment delay, P.C. 1714. See TIME.

MONDAY, *s.* De lûn, w.; de lîn, P.; dillûn, B.

MONEY, *s.* Bat, w.; bath, P.; moné, mona, monnah, w.; voné, B.; vona, M. 1917; vonés, sols, diriair, B.

MONEY, BELONGINGS, NECESSARIES, *s.* Pegans, w.; peganz, P.; fegans, w. In the Cornish dialect they use the words *fangings, vangings.* (The *g* hard).

MONEY or SAVINGS, *s.* Cobshans, D.

MONEY. (A small piece or coin of it). Scût. B. "I havn't a scute" is still a phrase of the Cornish dialect. They say of a man who is bankrupt that he is *scat.* Does the expression "scot free" mean *scût* free, *i.e.,* to be free of costs or liability ?.

MONEY-CHANGER, *s.* Bathor, w.; bather, w.

MONK, *s.* Manach, manah, vanah, w. *Pl.* Menech, w.

MONK'S-HOOD, *s.* (The plant *Aconitum napellus*). Cugol, w.; kugol, B.

MONKEY, *s.* Sim, w.

MONMOUTHSHIRE, *s.* Guent, B.

MONTH, *s.* Mîs, w.; mîz, B.; mys, N.; meys, M. 2200; vîs, w.; vîz, B.; vys, N.; vyz, P. *Pl.* Mysyov (*mysyou*), M. 803. *Sûr kyns pen vys,* surely before the end of the month, P.C. 1646.

MOON, *s.* Loer, lôr, loor, lour, lûr, w.; laur, B.; ler, P.; lin, w. *An houl ha'n lôr ha'n stergan,* the sun, the moon, and the stars, O.M. 36.

FULL MOON. Cann, B.

THE MOON'S COURSE. Redegva, P.

MOOR, *s.* (Moor-land). Cors, hâl (*Pl.* Hallow), w.; hêl, hêll, B.; rôs, w.

MOORS, *s.* Gwinnow, winnow, w.; winny, P.

MOORISH, *adj.* Gwinic, winnic, w.; winny, P.; gwernic, w.; guernik P.; helek (from *hêl*), B.

MOORY LAND. Tir devrak, B.

MOORY PLACE. (Near the sea). Morva, w.

MORE. Moy, moi, mui, w.; muy, B.; voy, brâf, w.; fire, P.; mogha, moghya, moghye, N. The three last words also mean *most, q. v.*

MORE ADO. Ken scyle, B.

MORE LIKE. Havalla, w.

MORE THAN. Moy vel, moys (*moy-ys*), w.

MORE THAN USUAL. Nauy (? Mauy), B.

MOREOVER, *adv.* Hagenzol, nena, nenna, w.; awedh, auedh, aweeth, awyetha, P.; três, B.

MORNING, *s.* Metin, mettyn, vettyn, w.; myttyn, vyttyn, B.; meten, M. 2378; vetten, M. 4420; boré, borégweth, cenzhoha, kenzhoha, w.

THE MORNING TIME. Borégworth, w.

ON A MORNING. Borégeth, B.

ON THE MORNING. Boréqueth, P.

IN THE MORNING. Arvis, w.; metui, mintin, B.

MORNING STAR. Byr luan, B.

MORRHUA MINUTA. (The   ). Glawer, D.

MORROW, *s.* Avorow, vuru. w.

TO-MORROW. Y vuru, w.

MORSEL. *s.* Mican, w.; mikan, P.; genawed, suben, tâbm, tâm, P. *Suben* was also used as the name of a kind of pudding. w. See BIT, JOT, PIECE.

MORTAL, *adj.* Hogen, w.; hogan, P.

MORTICE, *s.* Morter, P.C. 2816. *Yn morter skuat the gothé*, into the mortice, crack, to fall. P.C. 2816.

MOSS, *s.* Best, neag, B.; neage, rôs, P.; mews, moth, D.

MOSSY, *adj.* Neag, B. *Mean neag.* a mossy stone. *Ké neag*, a mossy hedge, B.

MOST, *adj.* Mochya, w.; moghya. M. 1544. *Neb may fe moghya geffys.* he who is forgiven most, P.C. 513; moygha, B.; mocha, w.; moghye, moghya, moghe, N.; moycha, moicha, moya, w.

MOST OF ALL. Ithik tra, w.; ithick tra, uthick, P.

MOTH, *s.* Goudhan, w.; gouwan, B.; gouyan, P.; pisky, D.

MOTH-WORM, *s.* Gonyaz (? gouyaz), prevan, B. Lhuyd gives *prevan* for cheese-worm, or any other worm.

MOTHER, *s.* Mam, vam. mabm, vabm, dama, w.; damma, B.; dâm, P.

HIS MOTHER. Y vam, N.

MOTHER'S-MILK, *s.* Dripshan, D. "A drop of dripshan" This word is also used for a draught or drink of spirit, &c.

MOTHER-IN LAW, *s.* Hweger, w.; hueger, B.; huweger, P.

MOTHERLY WOMAN. Benen vât, P.

MOTION or ACT, *s.* Gwyth, gueid, w.

MOTLEY, *adj.* Brith, bryth, bruit, B

MOTTLED, *adj.* The same as for *motley, q.v.*

MOULD or EARTH, *s.* Pri, pry, bry, vri, vry, w.

MOULD, *s.* (As on a liquid). Keam, D.

MOUND, *s.* Pil, w. See HILLOCK.

MOUNT, *s.* Din, w. See HILL and MOUNTAIN.

A HIGH MOUNT. Guydh-grûg, B.

MOUNT, *v.* Yskynné, O.M. 1976. See ASCEND.

LET HIM MOUNT. Yskunnés, B.

MOUNTAIN, *s.* Menedh, menydh, mynydh, w.; meneth, menyth, P.; menythe. c.w. 1082; menit, monedh, w.; monadh, B.; venedh, w.; veneth, O.M. 1281; mener, P.; menar, B.; menés, P.; brê, brea, w.; bray, P.; vrê, bryn, ban, pan, van, tor, torr, w.

ON THE MOUNTAIN. Uar an venedh, P.

A GREAT MOUNTAIN. Monedh brâs, w.

THE SWELL OF A MOUNTAIN. Tor, torr, w.

A MOUNTAIN MEADOW. Rôs, w.

MOUNTAIN-ASH, *s.* Cerden, w.; kerden, P.

MOURN, *v.* Cyny, kyny, w.

MOURNFUL. *s.* Morethack, c.w. 381; morethec, w.; morethek. P. *My a yl bós morethek*, I may be mournful. P.C. 3187; trawethac, w.; trauethak, P.; travethak. B.; trawedhak, w.; trauedhak, B.; trewesy, drewesy. trewysy, w.; trewisy, trawesy, P.; trewath, c w. 837; trest, trist, w.; trûs, trys, P.; wisht, whisht, D.

MOURNFULNESS, *s.* See SORROW.

MOUSE, *s.* Logoden, logosan, lygodzhan, w. *Pl.* (mice). Logaz, loggas, B. *Treloggas*, the town of mice, or mice-town; legessa, M. 3414. *Ny yl boys guel legessa*, there cannot be better to catch mice, M. 3414; murs *(Pl.)*, *Polwhele*.

MOUTH, *s.* Ganow, w.; ganou, B.; genow, anow, w. *An try spûs yn y anow*, the three grains into his mouth, O.M. 870; mein, min, meyn, w.

MOUTHS, *s.* Mowys, B.

A LITTLE MOUTH. (*i.e.*, a pursed up mouth). Pokkail, B. See KISS.

MOUTHFUL, *s.* Genawed. w.

MOVE, *v.* Gwayah, w.; gwayath, P.; guaya, B.; gueny, P.

TO BE MOVED. Meviy, P.

TO MOVE AGAIN. Remufé, P.

TO MOVE ONE'S SELF. Ymguen, w.

HE MOVED. Remufé, w From the English.

MOVED, *part.* Mevys, P.; meviys, w.; gozez, P.

MOW, *v.* Medé w.; medi, B.; midi, medgé, w.

MOW, *s.* (As of corn). Dise, B.

MOWER, *s.* Meder, meter, meader, w.; mediur, midar, midzhar, midil, B.; midhil, P.; medwas, w.

MOWING, *s.* Mediud, B.

MUCH. Meur, mûr, vûr, fûr, maur, mear, mêr, meyr, w.; maer, mâr, mu, mych, P.; lower, loer, lawer, luas, lues, luhas, luhés, leas, lias, w.; liaz, P.; lyés, lyys, lys, w *An awayl-ma taveth lys*, this tragedy much talked of, P.C. 551. Pylta, pôs, P.; yn frâs, R.D. 1098. *A peghas marthys yn frâs*, I have sinned wondrous much, R.D. 1098.

MUCH ADO. Nêb-mêr, B.

MUCH BETTER. Pylta gwêl, w.

MUCH LESS. Mêr lê, P.; mêrlé, B.

SO MUCH. Gemmys, a gymmys, P.

TOO MUCH. Re, R.D. 2056. *Thotho byny vye re,* for him never would it be too much, R.B. 2056.

VERY MUCH. Ithik tra, w.; ithick tra, uthick, P.

MUCK, *s.* Teil, w.; tyle, B. See DUNG.

MUD, *s.* Lued, lys, lyys, w. *Kepar ha seym py lyys haal,* like train-oil or salt-marsh mud, o.m. 2708; pol, poll, w.; pul, p.; pal, d.

MUD-POOL, *s.* Pol-pry, b.

MUGGY, *adj.* Looby, d.

MUGWORT, *s.* Lêsluit, luitlês, lotlês, p.

MULBERRY, *s.* Moyr, w.; mouar, b.

MULBERRY-TREE, *s.* Moyr-bren, w.

MULLET, *s.* Mehil, mehal, w.; meill, brerthil, b.

MULTITUDE, *s.* (Number, quantity). Myns, mens, lias, w.

MULTITUDE, *s.* (Congregation, assembly). Bagat, w.

MULTITUDE or CROWD, *s.* Rûth, w.

A GREAT MULTITUDE, A HOST. Lû, luu, llû, w.

MURDER, *s.* Ladhva, dên ladh, w.; latha, lathdên, p.; calanedh, w.; kalanedh, p.; hâr, b.

MURDERING, *part.* Moldra, m. 1189. *Heb moldra an crustunyon,* without murdering the Christians, m. 1189.

MURMUR or HUM, *s.* Drilsy, drulgy, d. See HUM.

MURMUR or GRUMBLE, *v.* Ascably, p.

MUSCLE, *s.* (Shell fish). Mesclen, bezlen, w.; mesilen, beslen, besl, p.; treage, b.

MUSICAL PIPE, *s.* Pib, w.

A SMALL MUSICAL PIPE. Piban, peban, w.

MUSICIANS, *s.* Menestrouthy, w.

MUST or OUGHT. Gorthyn, gorweythy, b.

YOU MUST Reys yu dheuh, p.

MUSTY, *adj.* Lous, p.; pindy, b.; peendy, d. This word is often used as "the flour is peendy," also vady, d.

MUTE or DUMB. *adj.* Avlavar, a flavar, w.; anlavar, b.

MY, *pron.* Ow, w.; owe, c.w. 4; ou, ew, p.,; a, am, om, y'm, mo, my, w.

BY MY. Râm (*re-am*), rôm, rûm (*re-'m*), w.

FOR MY. Thom, c.w. 1035. *Thymo ve ha thom fle-hys,* for me and for my children, c.w. 1035.

IN MY. Ym (*y-am*), i'm, w.

OF MY. Am, w.

TO MY. Dom, dhom, w.; thom, c.w. 896; dum, dhum, thum, w.; am, p.

WITH MY. Am, w.

MYSELF, *pron.* Ow honan, ow honyn, ma honan, p.

N.

" This letter is a primary initial and immutable, in Cornish," w. *Lex. Corn. Brit.*

NAIL, *v.* (Or fasten with nails). Centré, kentrê, w.; warré, p.

TO NAIL TOGETHER. The warré yn ten, p.

NAIL, *s.* Center, kenter, genter, w.; kentar, p. *Pl.* Centrow, kentrow, w.; kentron, p. Also a *pin* or *peg,* q. v.

A LITTLE NAIL. Tach, p.

AN IRON NAIL or SPIKE. Ebil hoern, w.; ebal hoarn, p.

NAIL, *s.* (As of the finger or toe). Ewin, p.; juin, b.

NAILS, *s.* (As of the fingers or toes). Ewinas, euinaz, winas, winaz, p.; juinaz, b.

NAILED, *adj.* (Having nails or claws). Ewinog, w.

NAILED, *part.* (Nailed or spiked). Kentrewys, m, 2603. *Kentrewys treys ha dula,* nailed feet and two hands, m. 2603.

NAKED, *adj.* Nôth, noath, noeth, noyth, p.; nooth, c.w. 856; ernoyth, w.; fernoyth, fernêth, b. *Dyragough nôth y fyen,* before you naked I should be, r.d. 1942.

NAKEDNESS, *s.* Noatha, notha, w.; nootha, c.w. 969.

NAKEDLY, *adv.* Inhoth, m. 3064. *Kynthellen vy prest inhoth,* though I (myself) should go nakedly, m. 3064.

NAME, *v.* Henwel, honwa, w.; honua, p.; gelwel, celwel, w.; gulwel, p.; gylwel, cria, w.; kriha, b.; creia, w.; kreia, p.

I NAME. Ydhanwaf, a contracted form of *ydh* and *hanwaf.* 1 pers. s. fut. of *henwel,* to name, w.

I WILL NAME. Hanwaf, 1 pers. s. fut. of *henwel,* to name, w.

NAME, *s.* Hanow, w.; hanou, hanno, b.; hanowe, c.w. 119; anow, w.; henwel, henual, henwyn, henwys, hynwys, p. *Ry hanow thethy hy gvra,* do thou give a name to her, o.m. 103.

NAMES, *s.* Hynwyn, the plural of *hanow.* *H'aga hynwyn y a vyth,* and their names they shall be, o.m. 35.

NAMED, *part.* Hinwys, hynwys, w.; henwys, b.; henwis, c.w. 12; honwys, honys, w.; henuelez, b.; henuelés, hylwys, p.

NAP or DOZE, *s.* Sog, b.; zog, d. This word is still used.

NAPE, *s.* Kyl, o.m. 1781. *Lyskys of a'n kyl the'n tâl,* I am burned from the nape to the forehead, o.m. 1781.

NAPKIN, *s.* Lysten, w.; lian-duylou, stollowfet, b.; hynelep, mantel, p.

NARRATION, *s.* Daralla, b.

NARROW, *adj.* Cûl, edn, w.; ydn, yn, p.; idne, b.

NASTINESS, *s.* Lâst, w.

NATION, *s.* Tûs, tues, w. ; tis, tiz, p. ; teuth, b. See PEOPLE.

NATIVE, *s.* Genesek, m. 2287. *Us then tebel genesek*, the evil native has, m. 2287.

NATIVITY, *s.* Genedigveth, b.

NATIVITY, THE NATIVITY, *s.* Nadelic, Nadelik, Nadelic, w. ; Nedelek, b. (*i.e.*, Christmas).

NATURE, *s.* Nater, natyr, w. *Ha'n enef del dascorsé erbyn nater gons un cry*, and how he gave up the soul against nature with a cry, m.c 208. (w.) (From the English) Cendé, kendé, w *Pûr contraryus yn kendé*, quite contary to nature ; cunda, kunda, w. *Râg henna warbyn cunda*, therefore against nature, c.w. 1302.

NATURE, BEING, PROFESSION, *s*, Drés, b. *Ladron drés*, thieves by profession, b.

NATURAL AFFECTION. Natureth, w.

NAUGHT. Mân, w. ; lâk, aeke, aege, p.

NAUGHTY, *adj.* Hager, w. ; hagar, p. ; lâc, w.

NAVEL, *s.* Begel, bigel, w.

NAY, *adj.* Nag, nagg, ny, na, p.

NEAR. Nes, nez, nees, p. ; nessé, p.c. 1096. *Ov nessé yma an preys*, drawing near is the time, p.c. 1096 ; neese, c.w. 727 ; nur, ny, p. ; ryb, w. ; ryp, n. ; reb, rebbon, rybbon, w. ; rybon, p.c. 460. *Yn plas vs omma rybon*, in a place which is here near, p.c. 460 ; agos, ogas, w. *Ogas yma*, is near, p.c. 1102 ; óges, m. 1013. *Oges yma ov envy*, near is my enemy, m. 1013. *Na nyl oges nag yn pel*, not one near, nor at a distance, o.m. 1141.

NEAR, NEARLY, *adv.* Enagos, w. ; enagoz, p.

NEAR US Rybbon, rybon, rebbon, b.

NEAR TO HIM or HER. Aytu (*a y tu*), p.

NEAR TO HIM. Orta eff, b.

NEAR TO Ordan, orta, b.

NEAR, AT HAND. Whêth, p.

NEARER, *adj.* Nessa. b. ; in neys, m. 3470. *Saff in neys*, stand nearer, m. 3470 ; nêz, p.

NEAREST, *adj.* Nessav, p. ; nessé, m. 239 ; nessa, m. 263.

NEAT, *adj.* Gulan, p. ; feyn, fein, b.

NEATLY, *adv.* Yn clôr, b

NEATNESS, *s.* Glannithder, w. ; glannuthder, p. ; clôr, b

NECESSARY, *adj.* Reys, r.d. 639 ; reyse, c.w. 170. *Dy'nny yv reys*, to us is necessary, r.d. 369 ; yn otham, b.

VERY NECESSARY. Porrés, porris, porrys, purryés, w.

NECESSARIES, *s.* (Belongings, necessaries of life). Pegans, w. ; peganz p. ; fegans, w. The Cornish use the words *fangings*, and *vangings* (*g* hard).

NECESSITOUS, NEEDY, *adj.* Ethomog, w. ; orthommek, p.c. 2639.

NECESSITOUS, *s.* (The needy). Othomegyon, p.

NECESSITY, *s.* Edhomeg, odhomec, w. ; ethom, othom, p. ; otham, b. ; othem, m. 356 ; reys, reis, rês, w. ; rêz, p. ; rys, w.

OF NECESSITY. Porris, b.

NECK, *s.* Codna, w. ; kodna, b. ; conna, cona, w. ; kona, godna, b. ; hodna, w. ; kil, b. *Polkil*, the top of the neck, b. ; gwar, guar, w. ; brandzha, b. *Gebal the conna a greg*, Gebal, thy neck be hanged, o.m. 2813.

THE NAPE OF THE NECK. Cyl, kyl, kyll, cil kil, chil, w. ; col, p. ; hyll, b. ; pol kil, w.

NECK-CLOTHS, *s.* Kuethiou, ked penna, b.

NECKERCHIEF, *s.* Follat, w.

NECK-JEWEL, *s.* Deek, b.

NECKLACE, *s.* Delc, w ; deek, b.

NEED, *s.* Edhomog, odhomec, w. ; ethom, othom, p. ; otham, b. ; othem, m. 356. *Thymo othem o hena*, need to me was that, m. 4109. *Y feth othom annethé*, there will be need of them, o.m. 1949 ; reys, reis, reys, w. ; rez, p. ; rys, w. *Reys yv thy's ynno crysy.* need it is that thou believe in him, o.m. 1508.

FOR VERY NEED. Purryés, p. ; porris, b. ; rêz, reys, p.

NEEDMENTS, *s.* See NECESSARIES.

NEEDS, *s.* See NECESSARIES.

NEEDS BE, NEEDS IT IS. Reys yw, w. ; reys yv, o.m. 1508.

NEEDS MUST. Porris, b. ; purryes, rêz, reys, p.

IT MUST NEEDS. Dâl e dâl, p.

NEEDLE, *s.* Nadedh, nadzhedh, w. ; nasweth, m. 468. *Der trov nasweth*, to go through a needle's eye, m. 468 ; notusdh, b. ; girak, p.

NEEDLE-FISH, *s.* Girac, girak, p.

NEEDFUL, *adj.* (Need is). Besy, bysy, w. *Besy yv cafus cusul*, need is to take counsel, m. 2369 ; reys, r.d. 369 ; reyse, c.w. 170 ; porrys, o.m. 683. *Rys yw porrys laffuryé*, to labour is needful, m. 683.

NEEDY, *adj.* See NECESSITOUS, *adj.*

NEEDY ONES, THE NEEDY. See NECESSITOUS, *s.*

NEIGH, *v.* Cryhias, cryhiaz, w. ; kryhiaz, p.

NEIGHBOUR, *s.* Centrevec, centrevek, centrevac, cyntrevac, w. ; kyntrevak, p. ; contrevac, w. ; kontrevak, contrevak, contreva, p. ; neshevin, w. ; nesheuin, b. ; ages, agos, oges, ogos, ogas, ogaz, p.

A DEAR NEIGHBOUR. Câr, w. ; kâr, b.

NEIGHBOURS, *s.* Controvagion, p.

NEIGHBOURHOOD, *s.* Ogés, M. 2246. *In y ogés púr eerten,* in his neighbourhood right certainly, M. 2246.

NEIGHBOURING, *adj.* Ogas, ogés, ogos, agos, w.

NEIGHING, *s.* (A neighing). Cynihas, kynihias, cryhias, w.; kynihas, P.

NEITHER. Na (before consonants); nag (before vowels), w.; bythny, P.

NEITHER OF THE TWO. Na neite, w.

NEGLECT, *v.* Ascongo, P.

NEPHEW, *s.* Noi. (*Lhuyd,* Nepos, *Lat.*) Borlase gives *noi* for grandchild; also for a prodigal.

NERVE, *s.* (Meaning a sinew or tendon). Geyen, geien, w.; goiuen, P.; goucen, B.

NERVES, *s.* Geiow, eiow, ieyw. w.

NEST, *s.* Neith, neid, w.; nied, B.; nid, nyth, w.

NESTLE, *v.* Nyethy, w.

NET, *s.* Rôs, rûz, rethe, w.; ruyd, B. *Pl.* Rethys, M. 3166.

A NET FOR VEGETABLES TO HANG IN. Kip, D.

THE LARGE MESHES OF A TRAMMEL FISHING NET. Capis, B.V.

NETTLE or VEX, *v.* Tardha, B.

NETTLE, *s.* (The plant). Linaden, linaz, w.; linachs, P.; brouda, B.

NETTLE HEDGE. Linar, ke linachs, P.

NEVER, *adv.* Byner, vyner, w; bener, M. 1020; bydnarre, c.w. 1161; bythni, bithqueth. bythqueth, bysqueth, besga. bysgueth. vythgueth, ny vythyth, P.; venestre, neffre, B. *Neffre trystyns ny gen byth,* never is sorrow with us, P.C. 731; na nefre, w; nefra, nevra. P.; na nevra, navyth (*na-byth*), w.; nywra, nyver, P.

NEVER MORE. Bynytha, N. *My ny vennaf growethé bynytha,* I will never more lie down, O.M. 625.

NEVERTHELESS, *adv.* Betegyns, bytegyns, bytygyns, w.; betygons, P. *Saw betygyns cresough why,* but nevertheless believe ye, R.D. 1300; awos, auoz, P.

NEW, FRESH, LATE, RECENT, *adj.* Newydh, newedh, nowydh, w.; noweth, nouedzha, nooth, êr, P.

NEW THING, THAT WHICH IS NEW. Newydh, newedh, nowydh, w.

NEWS, *s.* Nowedhow, noadho, w.; noaudho, B.; neuydho, P.; newydhow, nedhow, w.; nethow, newethow, P.; nawothow, c.w. 724; nowothov, M. 3315; nowethis, c.w. 1886; nowethys, c.w. 1136.

NEWT, *s.* Anaf, w.; anau, B.; pedrevan, pedrevor, pedresif, w.; pedreriff, P.; wedresif, w.; padgy-paw,

pagety-paw, paget-e-poo, padzher-pou, D. *Lit.* Four footed.

NEXT, *adj.* Nessa, nesav, w.; nesa, P.

NIECE, *s.* Noit, w.; noith, nith, B.

NIGH, *adj.* See NEAR.

NIGHT, *s.* Nôs, nôz, w.; nooz, c.w. 85; noys, nei, w.

LAST NIGHT. Nehuer, neihûr, w.

TO-NIGHT. Haneth, w.

THIS NIGHT. Ha neth, P.; haneth, P.C. 719; nosma, noysma, P.

NIGHTINGALE, *s.* Eus, B.

NIGHTMARE, *s.* Hillab, B.

NIGHTSHADE, *s.* (*Atropa Belladonna*). Scaw-coo, D.

NIMBLE, *adj.* Scâf, scaff, scâv, sgâv, schâf, stric, strick, w.

NIMBLY, *adv.* Scafe, P.; scaff, B. *Mar scaff,* so nimbly, B. *Ha the scafe súr ytheth,* and thou more nimbly sure will go, O.M. 2295.

NINE. Naw, w.; nawe, nau, P.; naou, B.

NINE HUNDRED. Naw cans, w.; nau kanz, P.

NINETEEN. Nawnzac, w.; nawnzack, P.; nownsec, nowndzhak, w.; naunjak, D.; naunthek, N.

NINETEENTH. Naw dêgves, w.; naw dêgvas, P.

NINETY. Padzhar iganz ha dêg, padgwar igans ha dêk, P.; padgwar iganz ha dêk (peswar ugens ha dêk), N. *Lit.* Four twenties and ten.

NINTH. Nawas, nauhuas, nahuaz, P.

NIP or DRAM, *s.* (Of spirit). Tot, D.

NITS, *s.* (Eggs of lice). Nedh.

A NIT. Nedhan, w.

NOAH, *s.* Noy, O.M. 1017. *Lemyn noy y'th worhel ke,* now, Noah, go into thy ark, O.M. 1017.

NO. Na, ny, nag, nagg. *Na* is used before a consonant, and *nag* before words beginning with a vowel.

NO HOW. Malbew, P.

NO MATTER, NO ODDS. Na fors, P.

NO ONE. Nagonen, nagonan, P.

NOBILITY, *s.* Pednzhivikianz, P.

NOBLE, *adj.* Pednzhivik, P.; hyuelar, B.; brentyn, bryntyn, w. *The wûl fôs a vyn bryntyn,* to make a wall of noble stones, O.M. 2281.

NOBLE or NOBLEMAN, *s.* Pendevig, pensevic, penzivik, w.; penzhivik, pendefig, P.; pednzhivig, w.

NOBLES or NOBLEMEN, *s.* Bryntyn, P.

NOD, *v.* Pendruppia, w.; pendruphia, P.; gogwyddo, gogwyddo pen, B.

NOD or BECK, *s.* Amnuid, B.

NOISE, *s.* (As to sound). Gyc, w.; guith, ow. *Heb iw*, without noise, B.; sôn, w. *A són a'n debel bobel*, at the noise of the wicked people. O.M. 1815; trôs, w.; trôz, P.; troes, c.w. 549. *Gans golov ha mûr a trôs*, with light, and much noise. *Then keth dev-na gans mûr trôs*, to that same God with much noise, O.M. 1558.

A NOISE. Now (*an ow*), P.

A MONOTONOUS NOISE or SOUND. Drilgy, B. The *g* soft. This word is still used in the Cornish dialect. Also *drilsy, drulgy*, D.

NOISE, CLAMOUR, *s.* Crei, krei, cri, cry, gri, gry, w.; tousse, D.; randigal, B. *Tousse* is still in frequent use. The word *randigal* is also often used, but the meaning given to it is "a rambling tale," or story. Borlase gives *saunt* for a noise or *dispute.* " What a saunt is here ?"

NOISELESS, *adj.* Dysôn, w.

NOISOME THING. Plôs, w.

NOMINATE, *v.* Henwel, honwa, w.; honua, P.

NONE. Gonon, vyth, nagonen, nagonnon, B.

NOOK or CORNER, *s.* Côr, corn, cornat, cornel, cornal, w.; kornal, elin, elyn, P.

NOON, NOON-DAY, *s.* Hanter dydh, hanter dêth, P.

NOOSE, *s.* Colm, P.C. 1525. *Colm re*, a running noose.

NOR. Na, ny, nag, w.; nagg, P.; nan, P.C. 1578. *Na* is used before a consonant, and *nag* before words beginning with a vowel.

NORTH, THE NORTH, *s.* Gogleth, B.

NOSE, *s.* Trein, trôn, w.; frigau, fron, frûc, B. (? früc).

NOSE, *s.* (Of land). Ryn. *Polwhele.*

NOSTRIL, *s.* Frig, w.; fridg, c.w. 1854; frygov, c.w. 1933 (? *Pl.*); früc, P.

NOSTRILS, *s.* Freygow, frygow, w.; frygov, M. 1454.

NOT. Na, ni, w.; nyn, P.; nan, B.; nag, nagg, P.; Also *ne* prefixed, as *nel e*, he cannot, for *ne el e*; and *neg* before a vowel. *Nyn* is used before consonants, *nyns* before vowels. *Na* is used before consonants, and *nag* before words beginning with a vowel.

NOT HIM. Nan, na'n, w.

NOT——HIM, HER, IT, THEM. Ny's (*ni-s*), w.

NOT ME. Ni'm, ny'm, w.

NOT MINE. Ni'm, nu'm, w.

NOT, THAT NOT——HIM, HER, IT, THEM. Nas (*na-as*), w.

NOT THE. Nan, na'n, w.

NOT——THEE. Nyth (*ni-ath*), w.

NOT THY. Nath (*na-ath*), w.

NOT TO ME. Nym, num, B.

NOT YET. Nawanyo, B.

NOTABLE, *adj.* Nodedec, nodzhedzhek, w.

NOTE, *s.* (Mark, dignity). Aynos, P.

NOTE, *v.* Notyé, w.

NOTED, *adj.* Nodedic, nodzhedzhek, w.

NOTHING, *s.* Laduit, ni tra vyth, w.; ni tra veth, P.; ni nêb tra, B.; ni nebtra, P.; travyth; travith, B.

NOTICE, *s.* Fara, w.; goyns, P.

NOTION, FANCY, or CONCEIT, *s.* Vang, D.

NOTWITHSTANDING. Awos, w.; auoz, P. *Awos ol ow gallos*, notwithstanding all my power, R.D. 53; hagen, w.; rynnan, P.; betegyns, bytegyns, bytygyns, w.

NOURISH, *v.* Maga, w.; methia, P.

NOURISHED, *part.* Megys, migys, mygys, w.; mygyz, P.

NOURISHER, *s.* (Or bringer up of any one). Deriaeth, P.

NOUSE, GUMPTION, SENSE, *s.* Rode, D.

NOVELTY, *s.* Nowedhans, nouedzhans, nouedzhanz, P.

NOVEMBER, *s.* Mis du, Mis diu, w.; Miz-diu, P. *Lit.* The black month.

NOW. Leman, lemen, lemmen, lemman, w. *Lemman warbarth ow fleghys*, now together, my children, P.C. 307; lemyn, w. *Lemyn súr yth yu ewn hys*, now surely it is the right length, O.M. 2325; lemmyn, w. *Lemmyn a abrsteleth*, now, O apostles, R.D. 893; luman, B.; lymmyn, lebmen, lebmyn, w.; lebben, P.; nena, nenna, w,; nawnj, nam, nan, nans, prest, ys, P.; ytho. w. *Ytho thym lavar*, now tell me, R.D. 787; ythew, hetheu, w.; whet, P.C. 696. *Whet avar prys soper yv*, it is now late (? early) time for supper, P.C. 696; breman, w.; cumah, B.; ûrma, enûrma (*en-ur-ma*, in this hour), in nanz, P.; innanz, B.; yn tor-ma, N. *Na vo marow yn tor-ma*, that he be not killed now, P.C. 2446.

NOW IS. Nansyw, B.; nangew, c.w. 1914. *Nangew termyn tremenys*, now is passed a time, c.w. 1914.

NOW WAS. Newngo, w.

NUMBER, *s.* Niver, nyver, w.; never, B. *Heb never*, without number, B.; nyuer, O.M. 569. *Ha dewolow hep nyuer*, and devils without number, O.M. 569.

NUMBER, MULTITUDE, *s.* Mens, myns, w.

NUMBER, *v.* Nivera, nevera, w.; nyfyra, R.D. 558. *Ny yllons bós nyfyrys*, they could not be numbered, R.D. 558.

NUMBNESS, *s.* (As from cold). Ewinrew. windraw, w.; uindrau, vindrau, w. In Cornwall now called *wonders* and *gwenders.*

NUMBNESS, *s.* (As from drowsiness). Sog, B.

NUN, *s.* Manaes, lainés, w. ; cainés, B.

NURSE, *v.* Methia, B.

NURSING, *s.* Methia, B.

NURSE, *s.* Mamaid, mammaith, w. ; mammath, P.

NURSER, *s.* Tadvath, tatvat, w.

NURSE-HOUND. *s.* (*Squalis canicula*). Delbord, D.

NURTURE, FOSTERAGE, *s.* Meidrin, meithrin, w.

NURTURED, *part.* Megys, mygys, w.

NUT, *s.* Cnyfan, cynyfan, kynyfan, kynyphan, w.

NUTS, *s.* Craouen, B.

O.

" This letter has the same sound as in English; when short as in *for, pot, sort,* and when long as in *bone, cone, lone.*

It is a mutable vowel changing into *e,* as *corn,* a horn ; *cerniat,* a horn-blower. *Cernow,* Cornwall." w. *Lex. Corn. Brit.*

O ! *exclam.* A. (For OH ! see further on). Used as a sign of the vocative case.

OAK, *s.* Dâr, w. ; derven, B. (*Pl.* Derow, w. ; deru, P.); dryst, B. ; glastenen, glastennen, glastanen, glastan, w.

THE SCARLET OAK. Glastenen, w.

OATH, *s.* Toan, tyan, B. ; toun, P ; ty, w.

TO TAKE AN OATH. Toy, tyé, tiah, w.

OAR, *s.* Ruif, rêv, w.

OATS, *s.* Ceirch, w. ; keirch, B. ; cêrch, kêrch, w. ; kerh, B.

OATS CLEARED OF THE HUSKS. Brynnian, brydnian, w.

OATEN BREAD. Bara kerh, bara ceirch, w. ; bara keirch, B.

OATMEAL, *s.* Brynnian, brydnian, w.

OARSMAN, *s.* Ruifadur, ruivadur, w. ; ruifa-dur, P. ; revadar, w.

OBEDIENCE, *s.* Bryge, deffry, devry, vry, P. , hyvel-dor. B.

OBEDIENT, *adj.* Huvel, hyvel, gostyth, w. ; gus-tyth, gosteyth, P. *Gosteyth thy'mo y a veth,* obedient to me they shall be, O.M. 53 ; guthoc, gwyw, guyw, gweff, P. ; vuel, w.

MOST OBEDIENT. Hyvela, w.

OBEY, *v.* Hyvla, w. ; hyvia, B. ; vry, P.

OBJECT, *s.* Vysmer, vismer, P. *Bós gurys mar ver vismer,* to be made so great an object, P.

OBJECT, *v.* Sconya. *Py penag ol a sconya,* whoever may object, N.

OBLIGED, BOUND, *part.* Sensys, sengys, syngys, w.

OBLIGED, BOUND, *adj.* Dysosy, w.

OBSCURE, *adj.* (Dark) Tewal, w. ; teual, P.

OBSCURITY, DARKNESS, *s.* Tewlder, tulder, w. ; tiulder, P. ; tiwlder, tuylder, tyuldar, tewolgow, tiwulgou, tulgu, w. ; tiuwegou, P.

OBSERVE, *v.* Notyé, sylly, w. ; whyrvyth, whow, P.

OBSTINATE, *adj.* Dynas, w. (?).

OBSTINATE FELLOW. Jaudyn, w.

OBTAIN, *v.* Cael, gael, cafos, cafus, cafes, cafel, w. ; cawas, gawas, kouaz, gouaz, P.

OBTAINED, *part.* Gallons, B.

OBTRUDE, *v.* Dho toula en, P.

OCCASION, *s.* Ahozon, treveth, trefeth, tro, w. *Ha nep na'n grûk war nep tro,* and he who has not done it on any occasion, R.D. 158 ; spâs, R D. 840. *The gafos spds,* to find occasion, R.D. 840.

OCCIPUT, *s.* Pol kil, B.

OCCUR, *v.* Wharfos, w. See HAPPEN.

OCEAN, *s.* Môr-difeid, môr-diveid, an môrbrâs, môr-tôt, B.

OCTOBER, *s.* Hedra, w. ; Hezré, B. *Mis-hezre,* October month, B. *Mis-hedra,* October month, P. It means the watery month, or else the month of courage. Pryce says, " I prefer the first."

OCTOPUS, *s.* Podlinker, D.

ODIOUS, *adj.* Cesadow, w. ; kesadow, P. ; casadow, gasadow, w. ; hakere, R.D. 350. *Ha hakere es an dalleth,* and more odious than the beginning, R.D. 350.

ODOUR, *s.* Sawor, sawarn, w. ; sauarn, P. ; savarn, B.

OF, *prep.* A. *Luen a byté,* full of pity, O.M. 2369 ; y, i. e, ha, ou, ow, P. ; de, dy, dhe, w. ; rib, ryb, worthe, B.

OF. FROM, TO, AGAINST THEE. Orthys, worthys, w.

OF, FROM, TO, AGAINST ME. Orthyf, wor-thyf, w.

OF, FROM, TO YOU. Ortheuch, worthouch, w.

OF, FROM, TO, AGAINST US. Orthyn, worthyn, w.

OF or FROM. The words *do, dy, dhe,* are late Cornish, only compounded with *worth,* as *dyworth,* from by, w.

OFFENCE, *s.* Nam, pêch, bêch, pêchas, bechas, pechad, bechad, peh. w. ; pek, B. ; pe, pêth, pehas, pehaz, pyas, P. ; peghe, beghas, B.

OFFEND, *v.* Pecha, peché, becha, beché, pehé, w. ; peghy, rebeghy, gamwuly, offendyl, P. ; serry, sorry, w. ; sorren, P. ; sclandry, w. ; scallyé, P.

TO BE OFFENDED, *v.* Serry, sorry, w. ; sorren, P.

OFFENDER, *s.* See SINNER.

A FOUL OFFENDER. Plôs, w.

OFFER, *v.* Gytheffia, offryné, w.; offryna, hyrsy, p.

OFFERED, *part.* Gyrheffias, gytheffys, b.

OFFERING, *s.* Offryn, w.

OFTEN. Mencuch, minouch, w.; mennough. p; menogh, m. 2693. *Hebogh why sur na menogh,* without you surely not often, m. 2693; venouch, envenouch, w.; envenough, b. Pryce gives *leas lues, lias,* and *liaz* but these seem to be compounded with *tre* and *termen* to form the Cornish for *oftentimes, q.v.*

OFTENTIMES. Lias-termen, w.; liaztorn, liastre, liaz-tre, b.

OFFCAST OF THE SARACENS. Atal Sarsen, atal Saracen, d. It means the rubbish of the most ancient Cornish miners. The word *atal,* pronounced *attle,* is still much used by miners for what is called the "deads," or rubbish from a mine.

OFFICE, DUTY, SERVICE, *s.* Gruyth, dodlos (?), w.

OFFSPRING, *s.* Ach, (*Pl.* Achow) w.; aho, p.; ascor, w.; ascore, c.w. 357. *Yn certen râg dry ascore,* certainly to bring offspring, c.w. 357; astor, b.; linieth, lynnyeth, lynneth, w. *Ha lynneth benen pup preys,* and the offspring of the woman always, o.m. 316.

AN OFFSPRING. Leid, leith, luyte, p.; luyth, b.

OH! *exclam.* Oh! Och! w.; Ogh! p.c. 3021; Oyech, (an outcry), w.

OH! AH! OH SAD! OH SAD, SAD! A syueth! Ogh tru, tru!

OH STRANGE! OH WONDERFUL! A rea! Rea! Suas! Sioas! Repharia! Borlase says *Repharia* was a common exclamation. He seems to mean that it was so in his time (circa 1754). *Repharia!* is *Re Varia! i.e.,* "By St. Mary!" The Virgin Mary; arear, d.

OH WOE! Eychan!, Eyhan!, w.; Eyghan!, p.c. 2599.

OIL, *s.* Oel, oleu. w.; seym, saim, b. *Seym* and *saim* are the terms used for train-oil.

OINTMENT. *s.* Onement, w. *Gans onement kêr yn certen,* with precious ointment certainly, p c. 475; oynment, unnient. w.; uncent. p.; urat, irat, w.; tairnant, untye, ylly, b.; yly, w.

ANY SWEET OINTMENT. Yrat, p.

OLD. *adj.* Côth, w.; kôth, cooth, p.; coyth, gôth, w.; goath. b.; goeth, m. 1979; côz, henn, b.; hên, w.; hean, hane, heny-wys. hennaways, p.

OLD AGE. Us côth. oge côth, w.; côzni, côthni, b.

OLD MAN. Dên côth, w.

OLD WOMAN. Gurah, p.

OLD, OF OLD. Anallod, b.

OLDER, OLDEST, *adj.* Kotha. *Kotha lavor,* oldest language, p.

OLIVE, *s.* (The berry). Olew, olewen, w.; oleu, p.

OLIVE-TREE, *s.* Gwedhan olew, oleubren, w.; guedhan oleu, p.

OMIT, *v.* Koilgim, foilligim, p.

OMNIPOTENT. *adj.* See ALMIGHTY.

ON, *prep.* A, âr, êr, w. *Er the fyth,* on thy faith, o.m. 1441; wâr, w. *Wâr beyn cregy,* on pain of hanging, o.m. 2280. *Wâr veneth (meneth),* on a mountain, o.m. 281; uâr, vâr, p.; yn, y, orth, ord, barh, barth, w.; bardh, p.; aberth, abervedh, aperfeth, w.; abervadh, aberneth, p.

ON, AWAY. Yn kergh, n.

ON HIGH. Auch, avan, aban, w.

ON HIM. Wartho, b.

ON ME. Ahanaf, w.

ON THE. A'n.

ONE. (As a card. num.) Un, udn, on, idn, ydn, w.; vdn, c.w. 11; idne, b.; onan, onen, onon, w.; uonon, p.; wonan, wonyn, w.; wynyn, wonnan, p. *Wonnan war igans,* one and twenty. p.

ONE, *s.* (An individual, single person or thing). Onan, onen, onyn, odn, w. *Nag vs dev lemyn onan,* there is not a God but one, o.m. 1760; huny, w. *Brâs ha byan pub huny,* great and small every one, m. 267; uynyn, p.

THE ONE (ONE OF TWO). Eil, eyl, w.; eyll, an eyl, b.; neil, neyl, neyll, nyl, w.; an nyl, p. *Me a teyl tol rag an nyl,* I will bore a hole for the one, p.c. 2743 (*Nyl ha'n gyle,* the one and the other); yll, w.; rld, b.; celé, gelé, w.

THE ONE AND THE OTHER, *i.e.* BOTH. Diew, an diew, dieu, an dieu, p.

ONE ANOTHER. Gilez, w.

THAT ONE. Henna, honna, w.

THE ONE THERE. Henna, w.

ONE OF YOU. Onan a hanough, p.

ONE-EYED, *adj.* Kuick, b.; ydn lagadzhac, w.; ydn lagadzhak, p.

ONE-HORN, *s.* (One horned animal). Ynikorn, b.

ONE HUNDRED. Kanz, p.; cans, w.

ONE JOT. Tâbm, tâm.

ONE BESIDE HIMSELF. Guan ascient, b.

ONE-MINDED, *adj.* Vnferheys, m. 2982. *Vnferheys kepar del ón,* one-minded as we are, m. 2982.

ONE-POSSESSED, DEMONIAC. Sach diaul, b.; sach-diavol, p.

ONE'S OWN. Eiddo, b.

ONE'S SELF. Honon, honan, honyn, w.

ONE SIDE. Nyl tenewan, p.

ONCE. Unweth, enweth, w.; unwith, p.; ynwyth; vn wyth, o.m. 685. *Uyn veys a quellen vn wyth,* gladly I would see once, o.m. 685.

AT ONCE, SOON. Wharré. waré, warré, w.; in scôn. m. 4563. *Pyboryon wethugh in scôn,* pipers blow at once, m. 4563; pûrdyson, m. 4533. *A ra oma pûrdyson,* will make here at once, m. 4533.

ONCE MORE. Arté, w.

ONLY. Ednak, ednac, en ednak, w.; nuel, b.; saw, w.'; sau, gew, gyu, b.

OPEN, *v.* Agory, agery, w.; agheri, b.; ageri, p.; egery, egyry, ygery, w.; ygory, r.d. 632; ugery, w.; egoru, agerou, b.; agory, gorow, w.; gorou, uger p.; dascudhé, dyscudhé, dyswedhy, dyswedha, disquedha, dysquedhas, dialwhedhé, dyalwhedhé, w.

OPENED, *part.* Agerys, egerys, w.; ageris, agores, p.

HE OPENED. Agorés. The preterite of *agory,* to open, w.

OPEN, *adj.* Apert, lawn, w.; leas. lees, lês, leys, p. *Aleys,* wide open, m. 1256; ryth, w.; rydh, p. *Rydh* was pronounced *reeth,* in Pryce's time (circa 1790).

AN OPEN PLACE IN A WOOD. Lanherch, w.

PARTLY OPEN. (As of a door). Asam, d.

OPENLY, *adv.* Awheyl, w.; apert, p.

OPINION, *s.* Tybyans, tybians, tibians, w.; tibianz, p.; cyhudhas, cuhudhas, gyhudhas, gyhydas, gydhas, gydhaz, b.

OPPORTUNITY, *s.* Ahozon (*Pl.* Ahozonow), w.; anzaoue, b.; daffar, (*Pl.* Daver), w.; gwyth, guyth, gwêth, b.

OPPOSE, *v.* Dygnas, w

OPPOSED, AVERSE, *adj.* Destotha, p.

OPPOSING. Dygnas. *O dygnas,* were opposing, b.

OPPOSITE, *adj.* Worth, w.

OPPRESS, *v.* Gorlené, worlené, p.

OR. Po, pe, pi, w.; py, bo, p. *Py yn sorn,* or in a corner, r.d. 539 *Pynak bo lettrys py lék,* whether he be lettered or lay, p.c. 681.

OR ELSE. Pocen, poken, w.; boken, n. *Bo ken deaul yw,* or else he is a devil, r.d. 2104.

ORATION, *s.* Areth, w.; progath, pregoth, b.

ORATOR, *s.* Dadloyer, w.; dadloyar, p.; dathluur, w.; datheluar, p ; satheluur, b.; pregowther, progowther, progouther, progathar, w.

ORCHARD, *s.* Dzharn, w.; dzarn, b. It simply means *garden.*

ORDAIN, *v.* Ordené, ordeyné. ordyné, ordné, w.; ordnés, ordnys, ordnen (?), p.

ORDAINED, *part.* Ordnys, o.m. 92; ornys, c.w. 907; ornés. c.w. 1015. *A'n ven cowethés ordnys,* of the true helpmate ordained, o.m. 92.

ORDER, *v.* Ordené, ordeyné, ordyné, ordné, w.; ordnés, ordnys, ordnen (?), p.

ORDER, RULE, *v.* Rewlé, rewlyé, rowlia, w.

ORDER, COMMAND, *v.* Ryghthé, b. See also COMMAND, *v.*

ORDER, *s.* (Form). Composter. *Ha dhera an noar heb composter,* and the earth was without form (order), w.

ORDER, *s.* (A rulé, rule, government). Rowl, reol, w.

ORDER or COMMAND, *s.* See COMMAND, *s.*

ORDERLY, *adj.* Rewlys, p.c. 2441. *Ena rewlys o an beys,* there the world was orderly, p.c. 2411.

ORDINANCE, *s.* See COMMAND, *s.*

ORDURE, *s.* See EXCREMENT, *s.*

ORE, *s.* (?). ORE OF NO WORTH or USE. Podar, p.; halvan, d.

AN ACCUMULATION OF ORE IN A LODE Carbona, carbonas, môr, morc, maur, d.

THE BEST ORE IN A MINE. Prill d.

A MACHINE FOR RAISING ORE. Whipsidery or whipsy-derry, d.

ORE-WEED, *s.* (Sea-weed). Gumman, gubman, p.

ORNAMENT, *s.* (An ornament). Casmai, b.; kasmai. *Polwhele.*

ORPHAN, *adj.* Omthevas. *Tûs omthevas,* orphan folk, m. 1827.

OSIER, *s.* Ausillen, b.

OTHER. Cên, kên, kyn, cyn, gên, w.; keen, p.; hên, arall, w.; aral, n.; kên scyle, b.; gyle, yben, ybeyn, hybeen, n. *My a dyl tol rak hybeen,* I will bore a hole for the other, n.

ONE AND THE OTHER. *Nyl ha gyle,* n.

THE OTHER ONE (OF TWO). Ybên, hybên, w.; hybeen, p.c. 2749; ybeyn, p.c. 2826.

OTHER THAN GOOD. Kên ysda, p.

THE OTHER SIDE. Parh aral, barth aral, p.

OTHERS. Erel, n.; erell, eraill, w.

OTHERWISE. Nahên, w.; nahean, c.w. 1024. *Nynsus nahên,* it is not otherwise, m. 3623; pocên, pokên, pycên. w.; bokên, gweyth, wankên, p.; kên (See OTHER) c.w. 1123. *Kên na bredar,* think not otherwise, c w. 1123.

OTTER, *s.* Dour-chi, p., dourgi, durgi, deuergy, b.; dovergi, p.; dhofergi, b.; doferghi, dofergi, devergi, w. *Lit.* Water-dog. Towan, b.

OUGHT. Couth, cothe, gothe, goth, p.; deve, ffylly, gew, gyu, gorthyn, gorweythy, b.

I OUGHT. Delev, delon, mi a dhelon, w.; gosse, gwesta, p.

THOU OUGHTEST. Deliz, ti a dheli, w.

OUGHTEST. Dayl, dalt, dolle. b.

THOU OUGHTEST NOT. Ny dayll, b

HE OUGHT. Dele, ev a dhyk, w.

SHE OUGHT. Delveth, w.

IT OUGHT. E dâl. w.; reys, rêz, rethy, p. *Re rethy seryfys*, it ought to be written, p.

OUGHT TO. Dolos, p.

OUGHT TO BE. Doleth, p.

YE OUGHT. Why dâl, w.

OUGHT NOT. Ny goth.

OUR. *pron.* An, en, gan, w.; gen, p.; ghen, b.; gyn, p.; ghyn, b.; gon, p.; gun. *Gun chaz*, our health; zen. *Zen enevou*, to our souls, b.; agen, agan, p.; agyn, w.

AND OUR. Hawé, p.

TO OUR. Dagan, p.; nei. *Epitaph in Paul Church-yard.*

OURSELVES. Agan honan, hagan honan, p; omwetha. c.w. 1047. *Fatla wren omwetha bew*, how shall we keep ourselves alive? c.w. 1047.

TO OURSELVES. Dho pyn honan, p.

OUSEL, *s.* Moleh, mola, w.

OUT. See OUTSIDE.

OUT. (As in play). The-wary, b.

OUT, OF. A, ador, w.; dort, dho ort, dhort, e, p.; mes yn mes, n.

OUTCRY. *s.* Garm, scrymba, skrymba, w.; oyech, oyez, b.

OUTLAW, *s.* Adla, w.

OUTSIDE. OUT, OUT OF DOORS. Ynmês, b.; yn meys, yn meas, yn mêz, p.; yn mês, mês, b.; amês, a vês, w.; a vease, aver, p.; vês, vez, b.; dyveas, w. *Da yu yn mês d llo brân*, it is good to send out a crow, o.m. 1099. *Tynneugh yn mês agan temple*, drag out of our temple, o.m. 2693. *Eugh yn mês a thysympys*, go outside immediately, o.m. 318. *Greugh y tenné mês a'n dour*, drag him out of the water, r d. 2232.

OUTWARD *adj.* Vêz. *Gweal an vêz*, the outward (outer) field, b.

AN OUTWARD FORM. Kairder.

OVEN, *s.* Forn, vorn, w; tern, b. (? fern).

OVER. Drês, w.; drêz, p.; dreys, w.; dreyz, p.; drys, dreia, dris, w.; driz, p. *Ow môs drês pow*, going over the country, r.d. 1511; destrias, b. *Destrias enefou*, over souls, b.; tra, w.

OVER. (Above, on high) Auch, w.; augh, p. *Augh y pen*, over his head, p.; a uch, w.; a-ugh. n.; *A-*

ugh y pen, over his head, p.c. 2808; athugh, p.; ahugh, o.m. 37. *My a set ahugh a'n gvyeth*, I place them over the trees, o.m. 37; ayuh, p.; uch, huch, w.; uge, b.; iuh, euh, yuh, ûs, yûs, w.

OVER. Tre, tra, w. A particle used in composition, as *tremenés*, to pass over. *Tra mor*, beyond the sea, w. It answers to the Latin *trans*, w.

OVER AND ABOVE. Whath, hwath, huath, wêth, w.; what, p.; worthe, b.

OVER HIM or IT. Dresto, w.

OVER ME. Dresof, warof, w.

OVER THEM. Uarnedhe, uarnydzhanz, p.

OVERCOME, *v.* Fethé, fethy, frethy, w.; wharfethy, p.; krongkia, terhi, b.

OVERCOME, *part.* Fythys, gwithys, contreweytys, w

HE WILL OVERCOME. Feeth, 3 pers. s. fut. of *fethy*, to overcome, w.

OVERFLOWING, *adj.* Gymps, gempes, gympes, gympe, p.

AN OVERFLOWING WELL. Fenton gymps, p.

OVERHANGING, *adj.* Crôc, crôk, w.

OVER-LAX, *adj.* Relogh, m. 3797. *Maria re vaff relogh*, Mary I have been overlax, m. 3797.

OVERMUCH, *adv.* Ree, m. 3328. *Ny re eves ree*, we have drunk overmuch, m. 3328.

OVER-RIPE, *adj.* Rees, reez, d.

OVERSEER, *s.* Mair, b.

OVERTHROW, *v.* Umhely, ommely, w.; dyswul, dyswel, dyswrey, dho diswrug, diswreys, dyswruthyl, dyswythyl, tystrywy, p.

OVERTURN, *v.* Umhely, ommely, w.

OWE, *v.* Dyndyly, w; dely, delly, dylly, doly, delov, delon, p.

OWL, *s.* Ula, w.; hule, stich, tyllian, b.

THE LITTLE HORNED OWL. Frao, b.

OWN, *v.* Pew, bew, w.

TO BE OWNER OF. Bywfy, w.

OWING, DUE, *adj.* Devar, p.

OWNED, *part.* Abewé, p.

OWNER, *s.* Perhen, berhen, w.; perhenek, m. 16; perhennek, p.c. 2752. *May fo perhenek (perhennek) gwlasow*, that he may be owner of countries, m. 16. *An harlot foul y berhen*, the knave, foul his owner, p.c. 2112. *Ty losel y perhen*, thou knave, foul his owner, p.c. 2752.

OX, *s.* Odion, odgan, udzheon, w.; odzhon, ohan, b.; oh, w; boen, bowen, p.; buch, biuch, byuh, bu, b.; gale, d.

A YOUNG OX. Lodn, ywegés, w.

OX-EYE, *s.* (Plant). Gadjefraus, w.f.p.

OX-SHOE, *s.* Cue, D.

OYSTER, *s.* Estren, w.

OYSTER-SPAT. Cukch D.

P.

" This letter in Cornish is both a radical initial and secondary.

When primary it changes into *b* and *ph* (generally written *f*), as in the other Celtic dialects. Thus *pen*, a head ; *y ben*, his head ; *ow fen*, my head.

When secondary. *p* in Cornish is a mutation of *b*. Thus *bewé*, to live ; *ow pewé*, living." w. *Lex. Corn. Brit.*

PACE, *s.* (In going). Cam, w. *Ma kerdho garow y cam*, that he go at a rough pace. P.C 1197.

PAGE, *s.* (Of a book). Enep. enap. w. ; eneb, tyrnehuan livan, P.

PAID. (Settled). Pês, B. ; pys, tylys, w. The *part.* of *pea* and *taly*.

PAIN, *v.* Peyné, peynyé, w. ; peyny, B.

PAIN, *s.* Angus, B. ; ancen, anken, w. *Ty a fyth cowal anken*, full pain shall be to thee, P.C. 2530 ; poan, poen, pyn, payn, peyn, beyn, w. ; byn, P. ; feyn, glous, w. ; gloys, glos, w.

A DULL HEAVY PAIN. Goal, joul, D.

PAINS, *s.* Poenow, ponow, peynys, w. ; penys, penaz, B. ; feynys, w. ; fynys, P.C 45 ; thewsys, B.

PAINS OF CHILDBIRTH. Golovas, P.

PAINED, *part.* Peynys, poenys, w. ; poenis, P.

PAINFUL. *adj.* (Keen, sharp, tight. strait). Tyn, dyn, w.

PAINFUL, *adj.* (Mentally). Tidden, D.

PAINFULLY, *adv.* Yn tyn, w. *Cryst agan prennas yn tyn*, Christ received us painfully, P.D. 1204.

PAINT, *s.* Liumelet, B.

PAINT, *v.* Liué, w.

PAINTER, *s.* (Pictor, *Lat.*) Liuor, w.

PAIR or COUPLE, *s.* Dew, dhew, dyw, dhyw. See TWO.

PALACE, *s.* Lês, lys, lis, plâs, tour, tur, w. ; telhar, tyller, P. (*Pl.* Telario, P.); thour, O.M. 2110. *Rov thy's ov thour*,'I will give thee my palace, O.M. 2110

PALATE, *s.* Stefenic, stevnig, stevaic, w. ; guarhaz ganou, P. ; guarhas ganow, w. *Lit.* The top of the mouth.

PALE, *s.* (Post or stake). Sticedn, w.

PALE, *adj.* Gwyn, gwidn, w. ; guin, guidn, P.

PALE, *v.* (To grow pale). Glasé w.

PALENESS, *s.* Gloys, P. ; gluys, B.

PALM THE PALM OF THE HAND, *s.* Palf, tor an dorn, w , torandorn, B.

PALM-SUNDAY, *s.* Dinsyl blegyow, *i.e.*, the Sunday of boughs, P.

PALMER, *s* Palmor, w.

PALPITATION, *s.* (Of the heart). Pulcolan, B.

PAN, *s.* Padel, pudal, w.

A COARSE EARTHENWARE PAN. Buesa, buzza, D.

A LARGE BROWN SALTING PAN or POT Steyn, stugg, D.

PANCAKE, *s.* Crampedhan, crampodhan, crampessan, w ; krampothan. P.

PANG, *s.* Galar, gelar, gloys, loys, glôs, w. ; glous, P. ; glovs, P.C. 1147. *Ma an glovs dre ow colon*, there is a pang through my heart, P.C. 1147.

PANNIER, *s.* Kiguer, P.

PANT, *v.* Dyené, tyené, w. *Del esof ov tyené*, I was panting, P.C 2511.

PANTRY, *s.* Talgel, w.

PAP, *s.* Bron, brodh, w. ; brun, B. ; têth, w. ; tidi, tidy, P.

A LITTLE PAP. Tethan. "Give the child some tiddy," is a phrase still used in Cornwall.

PAP, *s.* (Baby's food). Jot, P

PAPER, *s.* Papar. w.

PARADISE, *s.* Paradys, parathys, w.

PARAMOUR, *s.* Vanah, B.

PARASITE, *s.* Boawhoc, P. ; boayok, bohauok, bowhoc, bauhoc, uayvok, pilecur, vilekur, B. ; wilecur, w.

PARCHED, *part.* Sechys, seghys, sychys, syhys, sehys, zehys, sechés, sychés, P.

PARCHMENT, *s.* Parchemin, w. ; parkemmin, pairchemin, parshmennen, B.

PARCHMENT LIKE or LIKE PARCHMENT. Parkmennik, B.

PARDON, *v.* Gafé, givia, gava, w. ; gevé, prunny, P.

HE MAY PARDON. Affo, a mutation of *gaffo*, 3 pers s. subj. of *gafé*, to pardon, w.

PARDON, *s.* Gevyans, w. *Arluth gevyans thu'm ene*, Lord, pardon to my soul, O.M. 2249; gefyans, gyvyans, w ; gyffyans, R.D. 1159; gevyons, B. givians, trumeth, trumyth, P.

PARDONED, *part.* Gevys, gefys, givys, gyfys, w. ; prunnys, B.

PARE, *s.* (A gang of workmen). Pâr, w. This word is in common use among Cornish miners.

PARENTAGE, *s.* Deskés, P. ; goys, guydh, gudzh, B.

PARING, *s.* (As of an apple). Plisg, plysg, B.

PARISH, *s.* Plû, pleu, plew, blû. w. ; bleu, B.

PARISH-PRIEST, *s.* Oferiat, hebrenciat phui, B. (fui).

PARK, *s.* Parc, w.

PARLOUR, *s.* Parledh, parleth, B.

PARSNIP, *s.* Panan, w. *Pl.* Panés, w. ; panez, P.

WILD PARSNIP. Kager, kai-ger, keggas, D. See CARROT.

PARSNIP or **CARROT**, *s.* Caretys, B. (*sic.*) See CARROT.

PARSON, *s.* Prounder, pronter, praonter, proanter, w. ; praunter, P.; prontir, punder, B. See PARISH-PRIEST.

PART or **DIVIDE**, *v.* Parri, parhy, barri, barhy, w.

PART or **SHARE**, *v.* Ranné, w.

PART, SHARE or **PORTION**, *s.* Ran, radn, w. ; peth, peyth, B. ; darn, M. 2476.

PART, PIECE, or **BIT**, *s.* Drâl, w. ; tâm, tâbm, tân, P. ; pêz, piz, B.

PART, SIDE or **DIVISION**, *s.* Parth, parh, w. ; part, barth, P.

PART, PLACE, or **REGION**, *s.* Tû, tew, w. ; gwythrés, B.

PARTLY, IN PART. En rân, enrâdn, w.

ON THE PART. Abarh, abarth, w.

PARTIAL, *adj.* Pers, w. ; kamhinsek, B.

PARTICLE, *s.* (A small piece). Temmig, temig, demig, w. See BIT.

PARTI-COLOURED, *adj.* Brith, bruit, w. ; bryth, B.

PARTICULAR, *adj.* Anuesec, w.

IN PARTICULAR. En anuesek, w.

PARTICULARLY. Enwedhec, enuedzhek, w. ; demigou, yn demigou, B.

PARTRIDGE, *s.* Gregor, w. ; grigear, grygiar, B. ; grygver, P. ; grugyer, w. ; corgark, P. ; girgiric, girgirik, gyrgiric, w. ; gyrgirik, P.

PARTY, FACTION, *s.* Herwyth, P.

PASS, COURSE, PATH, WAY. Arrez, B.

PASS, *v.* Tremené, dremené, w. *Kyns ys y the tremené*, before that they pass, O.M. 1634.

TO PASS OVER. Tremené, dremené, w. *Kyns ys y tremené an mór ruyth*, before that they pass (over) the red sea, O.M. 1634.

PASS, *v.* (Go, flow, rush, run). Redec, resec, resek, w. ; rees, P.

PASS, *v.* (Go, come, proceed). Garras, B.

TO PASS SENTENCE, *v.* Brugy, brusy, vrusy, w.

PASSAGE. ROAD, WAY, *s.* Fôr, vôr, fôrdh, vôrdh, ferdh, fôrth, tremvn, tremene, tremain, P. ; trumach, M. 1075. *The welés thymmo tru-mach*, to seek for me a passage, M. 1075. *Tremyn, tremene, tremain,*

more correctly mean a crossing or passing place, and *truimach*, as in the above quotations, the journey itself over a road or way.

A PASSAGE OVER A RIVER. Tyn, B.

PASSAGE, FURROW, WRINKLE. Droke, D.

PASSING-BELL, *s.* Cnil, cnill, clil, B.

PASSOVER, EASTER, *s.* Pasc, w. ; pask, P. ; pasch, w.

THE MEAT OF THE PASSOVER. Bôs pask.

PAST. Byas, P. *Nangew re byas blethen*, not this many past years, P. ; passiez, *part.* B.

PASTE, *s.* Glut, w.

PASTE, *s.* (In mining). Toas, B. In the Armoric, language, *toasez*, a kneeding-trough, whence, says Borlase, the phrase used by miners, *to toas*, or *tose, i.e.*, to shake the tin (in the form of paste or slime) to and fro, to cleanse it of the earth.

PASTIME, *s.* Choary. *Pl.* Choarion, w.

PASTURE or **FEEDING GROUND**, *s.* Gwerwels, w. ; gueruelz, P. ; bounder, vounder, w.

PORK-PASTY, *s.* Hogen, w. ; hogan, hoggan, fuggan, P. The same is used for a flat cake ; called now a *hobbin*, when of the shape of a pasty ; when flat, a dinner-cake.

PATCH, *v.* Clouty, R.D. 1509. *Cloutys gans diuers pannow*, patched with divers cloths, R.D. 1509.

PATCHER or **MENDER OF CLOTHES**, *s.* Seufad, B.

PATENT, A PATENT, *s.* Guarac, w. ; guarack, P.

PATER or **PATERNOSTER**, *s.* Pader, w. ; padar, B.

PATHWAY, COURSE, PASS, *s.* Arrez, B. ; cammen, w. ; kammen, P. ; rût, malc, B.

PATIENCE, *s.* Perthyans, B.

PATRIARCH, *s.* Huheltat, w. ; huweltat, B. ; threodaz, P.

PATTEN or **ALTAR-PLATE**, *s.* Engurbor, w.

PAUNCH, *s.* Bôl, w. ; agan, B. (The Cornish now call the stomach of a pig, *agan*). Gasen, M. 3927. *Gvak yv thym an pengasen*, empty have I the end of the paunch, M. 3927.

PAVEMENT, A PAVEMENT, *s.* Lear, lêr, leur, luer, lûr, lôr, w.

PAVED WAY or **STREET**, *s.* Rew, ru, w.

PAVILION, *s.* Scovva, w. ; gulscouua, P.

PAW, *s.* Paw, baw, w.

PAY, *v.* Talу, dâl, w. ; pea, B.

PAY FOR, TO PAY FOR, *v.* Preuné, prynny, w. ; pryné, prenna, perné, P.

HE WILL PAY. Tâl, dalvyth,. *Dalvyth* is a mutation of *talvyth*, 3 pers. s. fut. of *taly*, to pay, w.

PAY YE. Telywch, 2 pers. pl. imp. of *taly*, to pay, w.

PAY TITHE, TO PAY or MAKE TITHE, *v.* Degevy, P.

PAYMENT, *s.* Pemet, B. (? pernet); gobyr, O.M. 2587. *Agas gobyr eredy*, your payment surely, O.M. 2587.

PEACE, *s.* Crês, creys, w.; creez, P. *Gase crês thyn yn nep tv*, allow peace to us on every side, O.M. 1598; ccsoleth, kesoleth, cysolath, cyzaleth. w.; kysalath, P.; hêdh, hêdwch, w. See TRANQUIL-ITY.

TO BE AT PEACE. Hêdhy, w.

PEACEABLENESS, *s.* Cesoleth, kesoleth, cysolath, cyzaleth, w.; kyzalath, kyzauleth, B. See TRAN-QUILITY.

PEACOCK, *s.* Paun, payon, w ; payn, P.

PEAHEN, *s.* Paynés, w.; payness, B.

PEAK or PROMONTARY, *s.* Col. w. See also CAPE.

PEAR, *s.* Peran. *Pl.* Per, w.

PEAR-TREE, *s.* Perbren, gwedhan peran, w.

PEAS, PULSE, *s.* Pês, pêz, w. (*Sicer*, Cott. Ms.)

PEA CODS, *s.* Cuthu pês, cuthu pêz, w.; kuthu pez, B.

PEAT-LAND, *s.* Rôs, w.

PEBBLE, *s.* Bilien, P.; cellester (? a flint), w.; grouanen, P.; mean byan (*Lit.* A small stone), B.; totty, D.

PEBBLE, *s.* (A mass of pebbles). Treas, P.

PEDAGOGUE, *s.* Maister mebion, w.

PEDESTAL, *s.* Dulw, B.

PEDIGREE, *s.* Aho, P.

PEDIGREES, *s.* Aho, w.; more correctly *ahow*, the pl. of *ach*, w.

PEDLER or PEDDLER, *s.* Goccor, gwicur, w. See MERCHANT.

PEEL, *v.* Pylsé, O.M. 2704. *Me a pylsé the pen blogh*, I would peel thy blockhead, O.M. 2704.

PEEL or SKIN, *s.* Cen, w.

PEER, A PEER, *s.* (Nobleman). Brodit, guahalech, w.; guahalegh, P.; guahalegeh, B.; luder, P.; lyder, B.

PEER, *v.* (To stare about). Gaké, geké, D.

PEER, *s.* (Match, fellow, equal). Par, w.

PEER or PEEP, *s.* Geek, D.

PEG, *s.* Ebil, obil. *Pl.* Ebyl (?), w. *Ha'y fastie gans ebyl pren*, and fasten it with pegs of wood, P.C. 1563; pidn, w.; spillan, P.

PELISSE, *s.* Pellist, w.

PEN, *s.* Pluven, plyven, blyven, w.; pluuen, B. *Pl.* Plûv, w.; pliv, plyv, P.

PENANCE, *s.* Penys, w.; penaz, B.; pynys, M. 164. *Penys a reys* penance is necessary, P.C. 43.

TO DO PENANCE, *v.* Penys, w.

PENCE, *s.* Dyenar, B.

PENETRATE, *v.* Gwané, w.; tardhe, croppyé.

PENETRATING, *adj.* Glew, w.

PENETRATING, A PENETRATING, *s.* Gwân, w.

PENINSULA, *s.* Enys, enés, ynés, w.; ynez, P.; ennis, ince, w.

PENIS, *s.* Cal, w.; kal, P. (*Sanscrit*, Cal. Penetrare, *Lat.*) tus, P.

PENITENTIAL HYMN. Ancenec, ankenek, w. *Dysk thy'mmo vn ankenek*, teach me a penitential hymn, O.M. 2256.

PENKNIFE, *s.* Cellilic, w.; kellilic, collel, P.; coltel, B.

PENNY, *s.* Dinair, dinar, dynar, dynnar, diner, dyner, w. *Pl.* Dyenar, B.

PENNYLESS, *adj.* Ligan, B. The Cornish use the word *penny-liggan*, meaning one who is pennyless.

THE LAST PENNY, THE LAST STAKE. Ligan, B.

PENNY-ROYAL, *s.* (*Mentha pulegium. Lat.*) Orgal, D.

PENRYN, *s.* Preen, D.

PENSION, *s.* Pencion, B.

PENSIVE, *adj.* Prederys, priderys, pryderys, w.

PENTICOST, *s.* Pencast, w.; penkast, P.

PENURY, *s.* See POVERTY.

PEOPLE, *s.* Popel, pobel, w.; pobl, *On an epitaph in Paul Churchyard*; poble, P.; pobyl, bobyl, w.; bo-bl, P·; bobel, O.M. 1815. *A són a'n debel bobel*, at the noise of the wicked people, O.M. 1815; tûs, P.; tûz, B.; tues, tis, w.; tiz, ties, tees, this, P.; dûs, w.; dûz, B.; dues, C.W. 1499; dis. *An dis*, the people. *An díz*, the people, w.; dêz, dees, B.

THE PEOPLE THERE, THOSE THERE. Rêna (rê-na), w. *En rê-na a worthebys, Ihesus yw a'n caffans ny*, those there answered, it is Jesus whom we would take, M.C. 67 (w). *Tús, tues*, &c., were used for the plural of *dén*, a man, w.

OBSTINATE or NOISY PEOPLE. Meara-geeks, moragiks, merasicks, D.

PERCEIVE, *v.* Adzhan, whow, whyrvyth, P.; ervyr, B.; clewas, clowas, clewés, aswon, w.

I PERCEIVE. Adzhan, azwen. These are corruptions of *aswon*, to perceive, w.

PERFECT, *adj.* (In perfection). Perfyth, perfêth, perfeyth, pyerfyth, w.

PERFECT, *adj.* (Entire, complete, full). Cowal, gowal, coul, w.; coual, coule, trom. *Trom dyal*, a perfect deluge, P.

PERFECT, *adj.* (Whole, sound). Dyen, tyen, w.; tyan, P.

PERFECT, *adj.* (Fine). Fyn, w.

PERFECT, *adj.* (Open, unconcealed). Apert, w. *Dên apert ha mear y ras*, a man perfect, and much his grace, M.C. 243, (w.)

PERFECTION, *s.* (The fulfilment, the accomplishment). Coweras, w.

PERFORATE. *s.* (Or bore through). Telly, tolly, tulla, tylly, w.

PERFORATED, *adj.* (Holed). Tollec, w.; tollek, B.

PERFORATION, *s.* Toll, tol, towl, teul, w. See HOLE.

PERFORM, *v.* (In a play). Gwaré, gwary, w.; guaré, P.; huaré, B.

PERHAPS, *adv.* Martesen, w. *In ur-na martesen*, in that hour perhaps, P.C. 2870; tezen, P.; mar tesen, P.C. 2451. *Mar tesen vyth yn y vrys*, if perhaps any, in his judgment, P.C. 2541.

PERIL, *s.* Antell, P.; perill, peryl, feryl, w.

PERIOD, TIME, SEASON, *s.* See TIME.

PERIOD OF TIME. Uz, w.; uze, oze, P.; ooz, oys, huis, oge, oydge, w.

PERIWINKLE, *s.* Gwihan, w.; guihan, guihian, P.; gwean, quean, D. See SCALLOP.

PERIWINKLE SHELL. Guihan, P.; gwean, quean, D. See SCALLOP.

PERMISSION or CONSENT, *s.* Cesenyans, w.; kesenyanz, P.; cummeas, cummyas, gummyas, w. *Luen gummyas yma thy'mmo*, there is to me full permission, O.M. 410; cemeas, kemeas, cummyés, cymmyas, kymmyas, w.; evodh, P.

PERMIT, *v.* Gasa, gasé, w.; gesy, gyssy. gosheny, P.; rhei an guella, B.

PERMITTED, *part.* Gesys, w.

PERPLEXITY, *s.* Fyenas, w.; crum a grakl, goss, D.

PERSECUTE, *v.* Hella, helhia, hellyrchy, w.

PERSECUTOR, *s.* Helhiat, w.; helyiat, helyad, helyur, B.; helhwar, hellier, P.

PERSON, *s.* (?). A BUSY or RESTLESS PERSON. Staver, D.

A FUSSY PERSON. Whiz, D.

A STUPID PERSON. Tut. This really means a foot-stool.

WISE PERSONS. Kefyon, cufyon, N.

PERSONS or THINGS. The word *re*, so often used in Cornish, means persons or things, thus:—*An rema yu oberys*, these (things) are made. *Cafus re me*

a vyn, take those (persons) I will. *An keth re-na*, these same (men). *The wruthyl gans an re-na*, to do with them, N.

PERSPIRE, *v.* Hwesa, hwesy, wesé, wesy, wheys, w.

PERSPIRATION, *s.* Wheys. whys, hwês, hués, w.; huez, P.; hallus, B.

PERSUADE, *v.* (Draw, induce). Tenné. *Mar a canaf y tenné*, if I can him persuade; daryvas, dharyvas, P.

PERSUADED, *part.* Gallons, B.; gellés. *Ham gellés*, I am persuaded; lauasos. *Me a pyth a lauasos*, I thee pray be persuaded, P.

PERT, *adj.* Corrat, D. "As corrat as Crocker's mare." *Prov. Saying.* Toit, D.

PERVADE, *v.* Tardhé, w.

WHAT PERVADETH. Tarad, w.

PERVERSE, *adj.* Cam, cham, cabm, gam, ham, w.

PEST, PESTILENCE or PLAGUE, *s.* Bâl, w.; vâl, P.; pla, w.

PETER, *s.* Pedyr, Peder, w.

PETITION, *s.* Desif, P.; desyf, B.; orphenniaz, P.

PETTICOAT, *s.* Peis, peus, w.; kota, B.

PEWTERER, *s.* Stynnar, P.

PHALLUS, *s.* Câl, kâl, B.

PHANTOM, *s.* Tarofan, tarosfan, tarnytuan, w.; tarnutuan, P.; tarosvan, M. 2566. *Rdg nysyv más tarosvan*, for it is nothing but a phantom, M. 2566.

A MINE SPIRIT or PHANTOM. Gathorn, D.

PHEASANT, *s.* Feesont, P.; ffesont, B.

PHLEBOTOMY, *s.* Dilla gudzh, w.; dylla guyzh, B.

PHOSPHORESENCE, *s.* (Of the sea). Brime, breem, D.

PHYSIC, *s.* Medhecnaid, mydhygyeth, w.

PHYSICIAN, *s.* Medhec, medhek, methec, w.; vethek, M. 4245; methik, medhik, P. *Eff yv the vethek certen*, he is thy physician certainly, M. 4245.

PICK. Pigol, w.; piggal, D.

A DOUBLE MINE PICK. Tubbal, B.V.

PICKMAN, *s.* (In a mine). Spaliard, spadiard, spallier, D.

PICTURE or PRETENCE, *s.* Kairder, B.

PIE, *s.* Krampez. *Gil krampez l'avalou*, to make an apple pie, B.

PIE-CRUST, *s.* Nugan, nogen, hogan, B. Borlase also uses these terms for a loaf of bread.

PIECE, MORSEL or BIT, *s.* Brewyonen, w.; brouian, B.; darn. *Mil darn*, a thousand pieces; drâl, tâm, tâbm, pêg, w.; piz, P. See also BIT and PIECES.

A SMALL PIECE. Frôth, mican, mikan, B.; pêg, w.; didjan, midjan, mijum, D.

PIECES, s. Brewyon, R.P. 126. *Ol the brewyon*, all to pieces, R.D. 1893; tharnou. *Ol the tharnou*, all to pieces, B.; tymmyn (the pl. of *tâm*), dymmyn, w. *Ov holan ol the dymmyn*, my heart all to pieces, O.M. 357; jowds, jowders, D.

ALL TO PIECES. Dowstoll, dewscol (?), w.; jowds, jowders, D.

A PIECE OF WOOD. Prennyer, prenyer, P.

PIECES OF WOOD. Prynner, prynnyer, w.

PIECEMEAL, *adj*, Anuezek, en anuezek, demigou, en demigou, P.

PIECE BY PIECE. Drâl ha drâl, O.M. 2782. *Ha teuleugh e drâl ha drâl*, and cast it piece by piece, O.M. 2782.

PIED or SPECKLED, *adj*. Brith, w.; bryth, B.; bruit, w.

PIERCE, v. Gwané, wané, w. *Pan wylys vy y wané*, when I saw them pierce him, R.D. 431; gwana, C.W. 1971; wana, C.W. 1997; tardhé, w.; tardha, P.; grupyé, telly, tolly, tulla, tylly, w.; sanqua, B.

TO PIERCE WITH A SPEAR or LANCE. Gyé, w.

HE WILL PIERCE. Wân, a mutation of *gwan*, 3 pers. s. fut. of *gwané*, to pierce, w.

HE SHOULD PIERCE. Whané, a mutation of *gwané*, 3 pers. s. subj. of *gwané*, to pierce, w.

PIERCED, *part*. Gwenys, gwynys, w.; guenys, guenyz, B.

PIERCER, s. Tarad, tardar, w.

PIG, s. Hôch, hôh, w.; môch, yerrés, B.

A LITTLE PIG. Porchel, w.; porhal, B.; slip, D.

A YOUNG or SUCKING PIG. Veer, D.

A MALE PIG. Baedh, bahet, w.; baeth, B. See BOAR.

PIGS, s. Môch, môh, w.; môgh, O.M. 1065. *Mergh guarthek môgh ha devés*, horses, cattle, pigs, and sheep, O.M. 1065; porelli, P.

PIGS' KIDNEY FAT. Flair, D.

PIGEON, s. Colom, w.; kolom, P.; golom, B.; colommen, cylobman, w.; kylomman, kylobman, P.; kydhon, B. *An golom*, the pigeon, P.

PIGEON-HOUSE, s. Clomiar, w.; klomiar, P.; clymiar, w.; klymiar, klymmiar, P.

PIG-STY, s, Crow-môh, w.; krow mow, P.; krou môh, B.

PIKE or JACK, s. (Fish). Denshoc dour, B. Williams applies this name to a hake, which Pryce and Borlase call a *denjack*. See HAKE.

PILCH or PELISSE, s. Pellist, w.

A LEATHER PILCH. Pellistgûr, B.

PILCHARD, s. Hêrnan, w.; lean, llean, B.

PILCHARDS, s. Hêrn. *Pan a priz râg hêrn?* What price for pilchards?; allec, B. *Allec* is a general term also for herrings, B.

PILCHARD WITH A BROKEN BACK, Pezac. D. *Lit. Pesach*, rotten.

PILGRIM, s. Palmor. *Pl.* Palmoryion, P.

PILOT, s. Leuuit, lewyidh, lewiader, w.; leuiader, P.; leuiût, leuyidh, brenniat, brennyat, B.

PILLAGE, v. Ladra, laddré, w.; lyttry, P.

PILLAGER, s. Lader, w.; ladar, P.

PILLAGERS, s. Ladron, laddron, w.; ladran, ladhran, laddarn, P.

PILLAR, s. Post, pos, poz, w.

PILLIS, s. Whiggian, B. This appears to be the name of the seed of the *avena nuda*, or naked oat, also called the bald oat. The Cornish still use the word *pillis*.

PILLOW or BOLSTER CASE, s. Slip, D. (?)

PIMPLE, s. Cyriac, kyriak, w.; gwenan, guenan, B.

PIN or PEG, s. See PEG and NAIL.

PIN, s. Skinan, P. scinan, scinen, w.

PIN-BONES, THE HIP BONES, s. Gulbredengu, B.

PINCERS, s. Gevel, w.; turques, B.

PINE, v. Ymwedhé, w.

PINE, s. (Tree). Sibuit, saban, zaban, pìn, pînbren, gwedhan pîn, w.

PINE-CONE, s. Aval saban, aval zaban, w.; avelzaban, B. *Lit.* Pine *apple*; guedhan peran, P. *Lit.* Tree pear.

PINNACLE, s. Penakyl, B.

PIPE, s. (Tube). Pîb, canel, B. *Tâp an canel*, the pipe and its peg, B.; wib, w.; piban, B.; peban, w.; pibonoul, B.; biban, w.; lituen, cornbrican, B.

A LITTLE PIPE. Piben, peban, w.

PIPE, s. (A musicial pipe). Pîb, wibonoul; tolcorn (*Lit.* A holed pipe), kernat, piban, biban, w. *An biban*, the pipe, P.

PIPE or BARREL, s. Ceroin, keroin, w.; kerrin, P.

PIPE, s. (A kind of cord or cording). Corden, B. This word is the Cornish for a cord or string. It does not mean a tube. It is a kind of cord used by milliners, and by them called *piping*, of which a *pipe* is a course or seam.

PIPE, v. (To play a tune). Piba, peba, w.

PIPER, s. Cerniat, cherniat, cernias, w.; kernias, kerniat, B. (Borlase uses the word *harfellor*, but Williams applies this term to a fiddler); pibydh, w.; pibidh, B.; piphit, wiphit, w.; pybor, M. 4563.

PIPERS, s. Pyboryon, M. 4563. *Pyboryon wethugh in scôn*, pipers blow at once, M. 4563.

A SHE PIPER. Fiala, harfel, B.

PIPER-FISH or ELLICK, *s.* Denneck, redanneck, B.

PIPE-MAKER, *s.* Pipidh, pibydh, B.

PIPPIN, *s.* (The fruit). Splusen, B.

PIQUE, *s.* Mican, mikan, B.

PIRATE, *s.* Ancredvur môr. w.; ancred vûr môr, angredar, B.; ancredcur. P.

PISMIRE, ANT, or EMMET, *s.* Meuwionen, w.; mevionen, murianean, meuionen, B. Menwionen is an error. *Pl.* Murrian, B.

PISS, *s.* Pizaz, P.

PISS, *v.* Troaza, B.

PIT, *s.* Pul, pol, bol, w.; bowl, P.; lacca, w.; lakka, B.; dippa, B. and D. *Dippa* is still used by miners.

A DEEP PIT. Pol doun, B.; pol down, w.

PITCH, *s.* Pêg, pêk, peyk, w.; peyke, c.w. 2259.

PITCH, *v.* (To pitch or put). Goer, P. *Lemyn me as goer ynbadn*, now I will pitch them upright, P.

PITCHER, *s.* Pitshar, P.; pycher, P.C. 629; fycher, P.C. 656.

A LITTLE PITCHER. Paddick, pattick, D.

PITCHFORK, *s.* Fôrh, vôrh, P.

PITCH AND TOSS, *s.* (Boys' game). Feeps, feebs, D.

PITH, *s.* (?). THE PITH OF A RUSH. Purvan, D. This word is still used in Cornwall for the wick made of the pith of the rush.

PITEOUSLY, *adv.* Truethek, M. 2152. *Me a greys truethek*, I cried out piteously, M. 2152.

PITIABLE, *adj.* Trewyth, trewath, w.

PITIFUL, *adj.* (Compassionate). Trewardhec, triaudhek, P.; pytehays, M. 1678.

PITIFUL, *adj.* (Sad, sorrowful). Trewysy, trowesy. trauethak, P.; trueth R.D. 899. *Aga guelas o trueth,* it was pitiful to see him, R.D. 889; wisht, whisht, D.

PITILESS, *adj.* Dybyté, w.; debyta, M. 1591.

PITTANCE, *s.* Pegans, M. 4292. *Ha lôr pegans the vewa,* and enough pittance for living, M. 4292.

PITY, *s.* Pyté, byté, vyté, B.; cên, kên, chên, w.; kene, c.w. 855 (*Hebkén,* without pity, w.; heb kên, o.M. 252); dyeth, dycheth, w.; dygeth, digheth, P, *Ha henna dyeth vye,* and that would be a pity, o.M. 1804; pyteth, B.; treweth, triwath, trueth, w.; truath, P.; triuath, truez, B.; tregereth, dregereth, yttern, yntên, w.

PITY! SAD! *exclam.* Trew! Tru!

MORE THE PITY. Soweth, syweth, w.; syuedh, P.

PITY 'TIS. Trueth, truath, P.

PLACE, *v.* Gora, gorré, corré, worré, w.; woré, P.; gurra, gôr, wôr, lathyé, settya, syttya, w.

PLACED, *part.* Settyas, B.

YE HAVE PLACED. Worseuch, a mutation of *gorseuch,* 2 pers. s. preter. of *gora,* to place, w.

PLACE, *s.* Teller, tiller, tyller, telhar, w.; tellar, c.w. 866; tylhar, dyller, B. *Moys then teller may meve,* go to the place where he is, M. 2922; plâs, w.; plâth, M. 946. *Marov off in krês an plâth,* dead am I in the midst of the place, M. 946; plaeth, M. 4562; plên, o.M. 2151; lea, c.w. 337; le, w. *Orth the werés yn pup le,* to help thee in every place, o.M. 1469; li, leh, lû, P.; menn, mann, B.; hês, hêz, P.; va, w. *Va* is a mutation of *ma,* as *môr va,* a sea place, or place by the sea.

IN PLACE. En le, P.

THIS PLACE. Helma, P.

IN THIS PLACE, HERE. Ymma, ybma, w.; ybba, yma, P.; ubba, hubba, obba, B. For other forms see HERE.

IN THAT PLACE, THERE. Ena, unna, yna. For other forms see THERE.

IN WHAT PLACE. Pylêch, plêch, plé, pelé. For other forms see WHERE.

FROM THIS PLACE. Alemma, w.

A PLACE OF BATTLE. Heirva, heirua, P.

A DEFENSIBLE PLACE. Mechain, machno, B.

A PLACE FULL OF SMALL WOODS. Cors, B.

A PLEADING PLACE. Pyrcat, w.; pyrkat, P.

A PLACE OF REST. Powesva, w.

A PLACE OF SAFETY. Guarth, B.

A PLACE BY THE SEA. Môr va, w.; mor-vah, B.

A CROWDED PLACE. (A crush). Dring, D.

A PLACE. PART, or QUARTER. Gwythrés, B.

A NARROW or CONFINED PLACE. Drang, D.

PLACE, POSITION, or STANDING, *s.* Trig, D.

PLACID, *adj.* Hynwys, w.

PLAGUE, THE PLAGUE, *s.* Bâl, vâl, P. *An vâl,* the plague, w.

PLAGUE, A PLAGUE. Pla, w.

PLAICE, *s.* (Fish). Perpoz, B.

PLAIN, *s.* (A plain). Gôn, w. *Gôn dansetha ha crûk heyth,* the plain of Dansetha and Barrow heath, R.D. 377; goon, gûn, gwon, gwen, guen, wôn, woon, plên, w.; gumpas, meath, dole, B.; tôn, o.M. 1164. *Ough the wonys guel ha tón,* go and till field and plain, o.M. 1164.

PLAIN, EVIDENT, *adj.* Efan, effan, w.; evan, da, dah, P.

PLAIN, OPEN, *adj.* Ryth, reeth, w.; rydh, P. *Goon reeth,* the plain or open downs.

PLAINNESS, *s.* Dole, B.

PLAINLY, *adv.* (Evidently). Apert, lûr, scyle, P.

PLAINLY AND FULLY, *adv.* Whêt, whêth, P.; warre, P.C. 445. *Me a leuer though warre*, I tell you plainly, P.C. 445; dyougel, P.C. 1307. *Me an glewas dyougel*, I heard him plainly, P.C. 1307. For various forms of *dyougel*. See CERTAIN and CERTAINLY.

PLAIT, *v.* Plyé, P.; plethan. *Polwhele.*

PLAIT or FOLD, *s.* Plêg, w.; plêk, P.; pléth, w.

PLAN, *v.* Arveth, w.; leustré, D.

PLANCHER or PLANCHING, *s.* (Wooden floor). Plynch (*ch* soft), P.

PLANET, *s.* Plannanth, P.; sterran guandré, B. *Lit.* A wandering star.

PLANK or BOARD, *s.* Astel, w.; astell, B.; astull, w.; astyllen, B.; plancen, planken, plyncen, plynken, w.; plankan, P.; plyenkyn, C.W. 2285. *Pl.* Planckés, C.W. 2284; plenkos, *Polwhele*; plankyz, plankoz, plankez, P.

PLANT, *v.* Plansy, plansé, blansé, w.; plensy, P.; plontyé, gonys, gynés, w.; gynez, B.; geso, P.; gonedhy, w.; gonethy, P.; wonedhy, w.; ureha, B.

PLANTED, *part.* Plausys, plynsys, w.

PLANT, *s.* Lushan, lyzuan, lysuan, B.; plans, w.; planz, P.

PLANTS, *s.* Losow, lusow, lusu, losowés, lyswys, losowys, w. *May tefo gveyth ha losow*, that trees and plants grow, O.M. 28.

PLANTAIN, *s.* Enlidan, w.; ledan-en, B.; ledanlés, w.

PLANTATION, *s.* (Of wood). Cotelle, w.

PLATTER or DISH, *s.* Podzhar, podzher, P.

PLATTER or BROAD PLATE, *s.* Scudel, w.; scudell, skydel, skudel, B.; tallyour, w.; talhiar, B.; tolyer, D. *Tolyer pren* or *tolyer predn*, a wooden platter D. See DISH.

PLAY or ACT, *v.* Gwaré, w.; guaré, huari, P.; huaré, B.; hwary, w.; gwarry, C.W. 2534.

PLAY, *v.* Huerthin, P.; huerthyn, hwerwin, B.; higa, w.

TO PLAY THE FIDDLE. Crowdy, D.

TO PLAY THE FOOL. Folié, w.

PLAY or PASTIME, *s.* Choary. *Pl.* Choarion, w. *Choary* seems to be only a form of *gwary*, a play or performance.

PLAY or PERFORMANCE, *s.* Gwaré, gwary, w.; wary, B.; guaré, guary, P.; uary, B. *An guary yw dywythys*, the play is ended, P.C. 3238.

PLAY, COMEDY, AN INTERLUDE. Rocca, w.; antarlick, B.

A MIRACLE PLAY. Gwaré-mirkl, w.; guarémirkl, P.

GREAT PLAYS. Gwary-meers, guary meers, w.

PLAY-HOUSE, *s.* Gwardy, w.; guardy, guar-ty, P. *Pl.* Guarimou, B.

PLAYING-PLACE, *s.* Plaen an gwaré, plainen guaré, P.

PLEA, *s.* Breuth, P.

PLEASANT, *adj.* Gwyn, w.; guyn, guydn, P.; gluys, B.; whêc, whêk, hwêc, whêg, hwêg, whegol, hwegol, têc, têk, w.; teek, thêk, P.; têg, w.; teage, blêk, P.

PLEASANTNESS, *s.* Huekter, P.

PLEASANTLY, *adv.* Pleag, P.

PLEASANT, WITTY, MERRY, *adj.* Sceans, w.; skeans, P.

PLEASE, *v.* Plecyé, plegyé, w.; plezia, P.; pleycya, C.W. 728.

HE WILL PLEASE. Plêk, blêk, w.

PLEASE, IF YOU PLEASE. Pag-ae, B.V.

PLEASETH. Amplêk, w. (*am plêk*). *Mar thym amplêk*, it much pleaseth me, w.

PLEASING, *adj.* Hegar, w.; lués, luhés, P.; plêk, M. 3874. *Y oberov dym a plêk*, his works are pleasing to me, M. 3874.

PLEASINGLY, *adv.* Pleag, P.

PLEASURE, *s.* Tekter, R.D. 186. *Yn tekter hág yn múr ioy*, in pleasure and in much joy, R.D. 1861; paravü B. *Paravü gwaynten*, pleasure of the spring. B; plegadow, C.W. 735; plygadow, O.M. 2115. *Assevye plygadow*, it would be a pleasure, O.M. 2115.

THE GOOD PLEASURE or WILL. Bôdh, vôdh, w.; vôth, O.M. 1153. *Gurens dev y vóth*, let God do his will, O.M. 1153; vynnas, O.M. 1153. *Gurens dev y vóth ha'y vynnas*, let God do his will and his pleasure, O.M. 1153.

PLEDGE, *s.* Guistel, w.; gage, P.C. 1186.

PLEDGE, *v.* (To pledge one's faith). Thethywy, P.

PLENTEOUS, *adj.* Pals, w.

PLENTY, *s.* Liasder, w.; liastre, leasder, amul, pith, pêz, P.; pêth, B.

PLIANT, *adj.* Hibblyth, B.; hyblyth, hablyth, P.

PLIGHT, *s.* Scûth, w. *A tebel scûth*, in evil plight, R.D. 2519; plêt, M. 610. *Doys then plêt ma*, to come in this plight, M. 610.

PLOT, *v.* (To plot against). Arveth, w.

PLOT or GREEN, A GREEN PLOT, *s.* Glassygyon, w.

PLOUGH, *v.* Aras, w.; dho araz, P.

TO PLOUGH LAND. Dho aras tîr, w.

PLOUGH, *s.* Arad, arat, ardar, B.; aradar, w.; carru. *Carew.*

PLOUGHMAN, *s.* Ardur, B.; dên aradar, araderuur, w.; dean ardar, P.; tiak, tyac, dyac, tioc, tyoc, w.

PLOUGHSHARE, *s.* Sôch, zôh, w.; zoha, B.

PLOUGH-TAIL or HANDLE, *s.* Dorn ardar.

PLUCK or PULL, *s.* Tên, tyn, w.

PLUCK or TWITCH, *s.* Pyn, p.

PLUCK, *v.* Scuattya, skuattia, squattya, sguattia, w.

PLUCK OFF, *v.* Terry, terhi, tyrry, torry, w.; torri, dyrry, p.; derry, c.w. 770.

PLUM, *s.* Eirinen, b.; pluman, w.; plymon, p.

PLUMS, *s.* Aeran, w.

PLUM-STONE, *s.* Mean plymon, p.

PLUM-TREE, *s.* Gwedhan plumen, plumbren, w.; plymbren, p.

PLUME or TUFT, *s.* Criban, kriban, b.

PLUNDER, *v.* Laddré, ladra, w.; laddra, m. 2148; lyttry, p.; robbia, b.

PLUNDERER, *s.* Lader, w.; ladar, p.

PLUNDERERS, *s.* Ladron, laddron, w.; ladhron, ladran, laddarn, p.

POCKET, *s.* Logel, logell, w.; loghel, b.; logol, w.; phokkat, p.

POD, *s.* Gwisc, guisc, gwesc, w.; guesk, p.; cuth, w.; kuth, b *Pl.* Cuthow, cuthu, w.

POEM, *s.* Kân. b.

POET, *s.* Bardh, barth, pridit, w.; prydyth. b.

POINT or EXTREMITY, *s.* Blyn, mîn, meen, veen poynt, w.

POINT, *s.* (Of a sharp instrument). Brôs, w.

POINT, *s.* (Of land). Rhyn (pronounced *reen*), rûn, w.

POINTED, *adj.* Lym, w.

POINTER, *s.* (As used by schoolmasters, &c., in teaching). Fescue, vester, d.

POISON, *s.* Guenoin, gueinoin, w.; guenuyn, b.

POISONER, *s.* Guenoin riat, w.; guenoin rejat, p.

POKE or PUSH, *v.* Pokkia, b.

POLE, *s.* Bâz, b.

POLE, *s.* (Of an ox wagon). Tuntry, d.

POLL, *s.* (Of the head). Pôl, w.

POLLUTE. *v.* Schyndy, p. *Aga ffleyr a yl schyndyé,* their smell may pollute, p.c. 1547.

POLYPUS, *s.* (Fish). Legesti, b.

POND, *s.* Lo, w.; loe, p.; lyn, lin, lagen, pul, pol, w.

PONDEROSITY, *s.* Pysder, b.

POOL, *s.* Lo, w.; loe, p.; lyn, lin, lagen, pul, pol, w.; bowl, p.; pludn, b.; plodden, lodden, d.; stagen, w.; stanc, b.

A SMALL POOL or POND. Pullan, polan, w.

A STAGNANT POOL. Porf, d.

A POOL OF STANDING WATER. Stanc, b.

POOL or BULL TOAD, *s.* (In the sea rock pools). Bulgrannack, bulgranade, d.

POOP, *s.* (Of a ship). Airos, pûppis, w.

POOR, *adj.* Bochesog, bochodog, bochodoc, bohosog, w.; bohosak, b.; bohosek, m. 450; bohodzhak, vohodzhak, w.; didra, b.; kesc r, r.d. 910. *Ha me an p,éf kyn kescar,* and I will prove it though poor, r.d 910.

POOR, WEAK, FEEBLE. INFIRM, *adj.* Gwan, w.; guan, guadn, p.; wan, w.

POOR, ABJECT, *adj.* Trôt, trôth, b.

POOR AND THIN. (As of silk, stuffs, &c.) Scoy, d.

POOR, THE POOR, POOR PEOPLE, *s.* Bokesegyon; bohusugion, bohosgyon, bohowgyon, bosogyon, b.; bohasaghiam, vehosugyon, p.; vosogyon, vohosugion, b.; vohosogyen, m. 4261. *Ha vohosogyen pub vr,* and the poor people always, m. 4261.

POORLY, *adj.* Palch, w. This word is still used in the dialect. It is also used now as a verb, thus, "he is only palched up." There is another form for *palch,* viz., *palchy.* A weakly person is said to be "very palchy."

POPLAR, *s.* Bedewen, bezo, bedho, w.

POPPY, *s.* Mill, w.

PORCH, *s.* Portal, w.

PORKER, *s.* Porhel, m. 1557.

PORPOISE, *s.* Porpos, w.; porpez, p; môrhoch, w.; môrhuch, môruch, b. *Lit.* A sea hog.

PORRIDGE, *s.* Iskal, isgal, p.; coul, cowl, caul, w.; joul, p.

PORRINGER, *s.* Podzher, w.; podzhar, p.; scudel, scudell, skydel, skival, b.

PORT or HAVEN, *s.* Porth, w.; porh, por, haun, b.; hean, p.

PORTER, *s.* Porther, w.; portherer, p.

PORTERESS, *s.* Portherés, w.

PORTION, *s.* Rân, râdn, temmig, w.; temig, demig, pêth. peyth, pêz, b.; êr, o.m. 354. *Ov êr tech grûk the gylly,* I lost my fair portion, o.m. 354.

POSE or PUZZLE, *v.* Puza, p.

POSITION, PLACE, or STANDING, *s.* Trig, d.

POSSESS, *v.* Abewhy, p.; bywfy, pew, bew, w.

THOU MAYEST POSSESS. Bewhy, a mutation of *pewy,* 2 pers. s. subj. of *pew,* to possess, w.

POSSESSED, *part.* (One beside one's self). Guan, ascient, b.

POSSESSION, A POSSESSION, *s.* Achta, ehtas, b.

POSSESSOR, *s.* Perhen, berhen, w.; perhennek, perhenek, m. 16.

POSSIBLY, *adv.* Martesen, w.

IT IS POSSIBLE. Geller, celler, heller, galler, cal- ler, haller, gyller, gyllyr, cyllyr, hyllyr, yllyr, w.

IT WOULD HAVE BEEN POSSIBLE. Galser, w.

POST, s. Pôs, pòz, post, w.

POST or STAKE, s. Kundura, B.

POSTERIOR, adj. Direttha. B.

POSTERIOR TO. Wosé, udzhé, w.

POT or CROCK, s. Crochan, crochadn, seth, zeth, seith, B.; zcath, seit, w.

POTENT, POWERFUL, ABLE, adj. Cyvethidog, w.; kyvethidog, B.; covaithac, cefuidoc, w.; gal- luidoc, B.; galhydock, P.; galhydhog, gallosec, gallosek, galluzack, gallogek, gallogec, galluster, gallas, dich, B.; taer, mên, vên, fên, w. Taer is a common word in Cornwall for hurry, excitement, fuss.

POT-HERBS, s. (Generally). Caul, caol, cowl, cawl, P.; kaul, B.

POTTAGE, s. The same as for PORRIDGE, q. v.

A MESS OF POTTAGE. Lommen cowl, w.

POTTER, v. Kouaz, B.

POUCH, s. Daver, w.

POULTICE, s. Tairnant, w.

POUND, s. (Money or weight). Puns, pons, pens, w.; penz, poyns, P.; pynz, B. Pl. Punsov, M. 2579; bynsow, c.w. 740.

POUR, v. Denewy, dhenewy, w.; thenewy, P.C. 487. War the pen y thenewy, upon thy head I will pour it, P.C. 487; scollyé, scullyé, w. See SHED and SPILL.

POUR OUT, v. Toula, P.

POUR OUT. Toula emeas, B.

POVERTY, s. Pethkester, P.; keskar, guag, B. Res ov keskar dre terros, I must go in poverty through the land, O.M. 360; bohogogneth, M. 2010. Bohogogneth abreth du, poverty on behalf of God, M. 2010.

POWDER, s. (Dust). Treust, B. See DUST.

POWER, s. Crêvder, w.; krêvder, P.; creys, greys, gallos. gallus, w. Púr wyr y gallus yv brás, very truly his power is great, O.M. 1155; galloys, w.; allus, R.D. 426. Hag a allus kekeffrys, and of power likewise. R.D. 426; gel, herwydh, w.; herwyth, O.M. 1464 Hedré vo yn the herwyth, as long as it is in thy power. O.M. 1464; mestry, vestry, w.; meistry, P.; meystry, maistry, maystry, maistrizi, nell, nel, w. May fo formys dre ov nel, that he made by my power, O.M. 42; nerth, w.; nerh, nerg, B.

POWERFUL, adj. See POTENT.

TO BE POWERFUL. Dichon, B.

POWERLESS, adj. Dyspusant, M. 2284. Erbyn fay crist dyspusant, powerless against the faith of Christ, M. 2284; antythy, M. 3052. Ov corff vy yv antythy, my body is powerless, M. 3052.

POX, s. (Disease). Pocvan, w.

PRAISE, s. Gormola, golochas, gollohas, w.; golog- has, P.C. 116. Gans penys ha gologhas, with penance and praise, P.C. 116; lawe, w.; lau, P.

PRAISE, v. Eysyé, w.; eysya, rysyé, P.; lawyé, w.; moli, mawl, B.

PRATE or PRATING, s. Clâp, w. Sens the clâp, hold thy prate, R.D. 1113; tavasec, w.; tavazek, P.

PRAY, v. Pesy, w.; pesa, B.; pysy, pisy, w.; pys, pîs, pidzha, B.; pidzhi, pegy, w.; peidgy, B.; pygy, pigy, w.; pidgy, B.; besy, bysy, w.; bisy, P.; bys, abys, B.; plygyé, blygyé, w.

I SHALL or WILL PRAY. Pysaf, 1 pers. s. fut. of pysy, to pray, w.

HE WILL PRAY. Peys, pys, bys, 3 pers. s. fut. of pesy, pysy, and bysy, to pray, w.

HE WOULD PRAY. Pysse, 3 pers. s. subj. of pysy, to pray, w.

LET US PRAY. Agan bys, B.; agan byz, P.

PRAYER, s. Pesad, pysad, pydzhad, pidzhad, pyjad, w.; pidzhi, P.

PRAYERS, s. Pesadow, pysadow, pydzhadow, pidz- hadow, pijadow, pyiadow, w.; peiadow, M. 132; peyadow, M. 143; besadow, bysadow, w.; bederow, B.; fesadow, fysadow, w.; fysadou, B. Ou fysadou, my prayers, P.

PREACH, v. Progowthy, pregowthy, pregewthy, bregewthy, bregowthy, w.; bregethwy, P.

PREACHED. Bregeth, B.

THOU PREACHEST. Bregowthys, B.

PREACHER, s. Progowther, progouther, w.; progathar, B.; pregowther, w.

PREACHING, A PREACHING, s. Progath, pre- goth, w.

PRECINCT, s. Luid, B.

PRECIPICE, s. Clegar, cleghar, clicker, cligga, ledra, ledr, w.

PREPARE, v. Parusy, dugtyé, dychtyé, dychyé, dhychyé, dychthyé, dygthyé, dygtyé, dhygtyé, dythgthtya, w.; thyghyé, P.C. 651. The thyghyé bós, to prepare food, P.C. 651.

TO PREPARE ONE'S SELF. Omdhychtyé, w.

PREPARED. adj. Parot, parys, parez, w.

PREPARED, part. Parusys, w.; hamblys, hablys, B.

PREPARATION, s. Paravü, hamlos, hamlus, ham- blys, hablys, B.

PRESBYTER, s. Hebrenciat, hebrenchiat, hebryng- kiad, B.

PRESENCE, s Lôc, w.; lôk. Drough an prysners ól y'm lôk, bring all the prisoners to my presence.

IN PRESENCE OF. Dirâg, dyrâg, w.; athyrâg, a râk, N.; a râg, râc, yn râk, w.

PRESENT or GIFT, *s*.   Ro, w.; roth, p.; rew, c.w.
2145. *Pl.* Roow, rohow, w.

PRESENT, *v.* See GIVE, v.

PRESENTLY, *adv.* Fastsens, B.; warre, P.C. 781.

AT PRESENT. Breman, luman, leman, lemen,
lemman, lemmen, lemyn, lemmyn, lymmyn, w.

PRESERVE or SECURE, *v.*   Anysya, sawyé, w.;
rensawy, p.

PRESERVE or KEEP, *v.*   Gwethé, gwithé, gwythé,
w.; guitha, B.; gorwith, gorquith, P.; gorwythy,
cuitha, cwitha, w.; kuitha, P.; anquathy, wetha,
P.; wethé, w.

TO PRESERVE or KEEP ONE'S SELF. Omwethé,
ymwythé, w.

PRESERVATION, KEEPING, *s* Sawment, w.

PRESIDENT or GOVERNOR, *s.*   Guahalgeh, B.;
guahalech, gualegh, P.

PRESIDENT OF A COUNTY. Brodit, B.

PRESS, *v.* (Or squeeze). Guasga, puza, P.; guryn, w.

PRESS or URGE, *v.* Ynnya, w.

PRESSED or SQUEEZED, *part.* Gwridnias, w.;
guridnias, P.

PRETENCE, *s.* Kairder, B.; kauanskis, P.; fooch, D.

PRETEND, *v.* Facyé, omwrey, ymwrey, ymwryl,
omwrellê, w.

PRETTY, *adj.* Louan, skeans, B.; têc, têk, têg, w.;
teage, teek, thêk, P.

PREVENT, *v.* Lettya, w.

TO PREVENT ONE. Omweras, P.

PREY, *s.* Praed, B.

PRICE, *s.* Pris, priz, prys, brys, w.; brez, P ; bry,
vry, w.

PRICK, *v.* Piga, w.; sanqua, tardha, B.

PRICK, *s.* Arho, garthou, w.

THE PRICK OF A GOAD. Brôs, P.

PRICK, *s.* (As with a pin). Pêg, gwân, w.

PRICKLE, *s.* Draen, drain, drên, w.; brôs, B.

PRICKLES, *s.* Drein, w.; dreyn, B.

PRIDE, *s.* Gôth, wôth, P. *Dre góth y wrúk leuerel*,
through pride he did say, P.C. 381 ; comer, brâsder,
vrâsder, w.; vrâster, scherewneth, B.

PRIEST, *s.* Pronter, praonter, proanter, w.; praunter. P.; prontir, B.; prounder, w.; punder (?), bron-
ter, B.; hebrenchiat, coggaz, P.; mâb lyen, w.;
oferiat, w.

PRIESTS, *s.* Pronteryon, bronteryon, w.

PRIMATE, A PRIMATE, *s.* Guesbeuin, gueshevin,
w ; guashevyn, gueskeun, B.

PRIMROSE, *s.* Breilu, B. See also ROSE.

PRINCE, *s.* Pensevic, penzivik, w.; pensevyk, M.
3022; pensevicke, c.w. 120; penzhivig, P.; pendevig, w.; pendefig, P.; prins, fryns, B.; fâl, w.;
rueik, ruy, B.

PRINCES, *s.* Prinnis, B.

PRINT or MARK, *s* Ooll, c.w. 1763. *Me a weall
ooll tryes ow thas*, I see a print of my father's feet,
c.w. 1763. *Pl.* Olow, O.M. 711. *Sew olow ov thryys
hyskys*, follow the marks of my feet, burnt, O.M. 711.

PRISON, *s.* Carhar, karhar, B.; clochprednier, w.;
cloghprennyer, M. 923. *Ty a crêk in cloghprennyer*,
thou shalt hang in prison, M. 923.

PRISONER, *s.* Gûr-caeth, w.; gûrkaeth, B.

A PRISONER OF WAR. Gûrkaeth, B.

PRIVATE, *adj.* Pryvé, pryvy, pryveth, priveth, P.

PRIVATELY *adv.* Yn priveth, brevath. P.; ledradeth. B.

PRIVATION, *s.* Brevath, P.

PRIVET, *s.* Scedgwith, B.; skerrish, D.

PRIVILEGED, *adj.* Brentyn, bryntyn, w.

PRIVY, SECRET, *adj.* Guythysy, P

PRIVY-COUNSELLORS, *s.* Guythysy, P.

PRIVY-PART OF A WOMAN, *s.*   Cheber (*pron.*
keber), P.; kypher, D.

PRIZE, *v.* Rên, P.

PROCEED or ISSUE, *s.* Henath, w.

PROCEED, *v.* Cerdhés, kerdhés, w.; kerdhez, r.;
cerras, kerras, garras, monas, monés, w.; monez, P.;
mynés, môs, finney, w.

PROCEEDED, *part.* Drevethys, B.

PROCESS or PERIOD, *s.* (Of time). Uz, ooz, w.;
ûze, oze, P.; oys, huis, oge, oydge, w.

PROCLAIM or PUBLISH, *v.* Dolos, w.

PROCURE, *v.* Dhrchyé, dychyé, dychthyé, dygthyé,
dhygtré, w.; dyghthy. P.; gwaynia, w.; guaynia,
B.; cafés, cafos, cafus, cowas, w.; kouaz, cawas, P.;
gowas, w.; gouaz, gaval, athytta, P.; pryvia, B.

PRODIGAL, *s.* Noi, B.

PRODIGY, *s.* Marth, varth, marthus, varthus, w.

PRODUCE, *v.* (Bring, bear). Doen, dôn, doyn,
doga, degy, w.; degyn, thegyn, thogga, tocka,
rethokko, teigé, P.

PRODUCE, *v.* (Give birth to). Denethy, denythy,
dynythy, w.

PRODUCE, TO RAISE, *v.* Fysel, P. *Ráq esow
galso fysel*, that I might raise grain. P.

PROFESSION, BEING, NATURE, *s.* Drês.
Ladrón drès, thieves by profession, B.

PROFFERED, *part.* Gyrheffias, gytheffys, B.

PROFIT, *v.* Gwaynia, guaynia, B.

PROFIT, *s.* Lês, leas, P.

PROFITABLE, *adj* Kyvadhas, B.

PROFOUND, *adj.* Down, town, w.

PROFUNDITY, *s.* Downder, w.; dounder, B.

PROGENITOR, *s.* Hendas, hengyke, P.

PROGENY, *s.* Ach (*Pl.* Achow), linieth, lynnyeth, lynneth, w.

PROHIBIT, *v.* Defen, dhefen, dyfen, dhyfen, defenny, w.

PROHIBITION, *s.* Defen, w.; deffen, c.w. 853; deffan, dyfen, defennad, w. *Drês dyfen ou arluth kêr,* beyond the prohibition of our dear Lord, o.m. 172.

PROJECTION, *s.* Trein, trôn, corn, w.

PROLIX, *adj.* Hîr, hyr, w.

PROMINENCE, *s.* Tor, torr, w.

PROMINENT, *adj.* Herdya, B.

PROMISE, *v.* Ambosé, dedhewy, dedhywy, dydhywy, dhedhywy, w.; didhywy, didhiwy, dythywy, P.; dethewy, w.

PROMISE, *s.* Rôs (from *ro*, to give); ambôs, w. *My a wra thy's ambôs da,* I will make a good promise, o.m. 1232.

PROMISED, *part.* Ambosas, dythywys, w.

PROMONTORY, *s.* Rhyn (pron. *reen*), rûn, trein, tron, col, w.; antron. *Polwhele.*

PROMPTLY, *adv.* Snell, m. 4342. *Ny a ra snell,* we will do promptly, m. 4342.

PRONOUNCE, *v.* (Affirm). Lavary, leverel, w.

PROOF, *s.* Prêf (*Pl.* Prevas); prôf, w.; scyle, B. *Scyle vâs,* good proof, B.

PROP, *s.* Horven, w.; trig, D.

PROP, *s.* (To a lever). Colpas, D.

PROPS or STAYS, *s.* Stanconnou, B.

PROP, *v.* Stanconni, B.

PROPER, *adj.* Gwyw, w.; eiddo, B.; eiddio, *Polwhele;* kyvadhas, B.

IT IS PROPER. Teleth, P.C. 2553.

PROPERTY, *s.* Eythe, c.w. 1133.

PROPHET, *s.* Profuit, B.; prufuit, w.; profuut, P.; profés, P.C. 562; profos, P.C. 2367; profus.

PROPHETS, *s.* Brefusy, B.; profugy, N.

PROPORTION, *s.* Gûr, P.

PROPORTIONABLE, *adj.* Dibblans, dyblans, dhyblans, w.

PROPOSE, *v.* Gytheffia, w.

PROPRIETOR, *s.* Perhen, berhen, w.

PROSPECT or VIEW, *s.* Sell, syll, sîl, sûll, w.; sôl, P.

PROSPER, *v.* Sowené, sowynny, w.; sowyny, sowyn, P.; fynny, B.

PROSPERITY, *s.* Anzaoue, B.

PROSPERITY TO YOU, HEALTH TO YOU. Sewena, sowena, P.

PROTECT, *v.* Dyffrés, dbyffrés, w.

PROTECTION, *s.* Achless, B.; gwîth, guyth, wîth, wyth, w.

PROTRACTED, *part.* Dhelledzhaz, B.

PROUD, *adj.* Gothus, gothys, othys, w. *Râg ef o stout ha gothys,* for he was stout and proud, o.m. 2221; sherewys, P.; stowte, c.w. 213; trahaut (*três hâut,* French).

A PROUD MAN. Gochus, B.

PRUDENCE, *s.* Furnés, w.; furnez, B.; sciantuleth, scentuleth, w.; skiantoleth, P.

PRUDENT, *adj.* Fûr, fîr, feer, w.; fyr, P. *Lemyn byth fûr,* now be prudent, o.m. 1638.

PRUNES *s.* Aeran, w.

PROVE, *v.* Scylé, P.; tria, B.; preva, provi, provy, w.; dho prêf, P.

PROVED, *part.* Prêfyas, brêvyas, w.

THOU HAST PROVED. Prêfsys, brêfsys, w.

HE WILL PROVE. Prêf, brêf. From *preva,* to prove, w.

TO PROVE ONE'S SELF. Ombroy (*om-provy*), w.

PROVERB, *s.* Lavar, w.

PROVIDE, *v.* Darbary, dugtyè, dychtyé, w.; dyghthy, P.; dythgthtya, w.; cawas, asthytta, P.

PROVIDED, *part.* Thytryas, P.

DID PROVIDE. Digthyas, B.

PROVIDENT, *adj.* Fin, w. See also PRUDENT.

PROVINCE, REGION, *s.* Pow, w.; pou, P.; poli, B.; woli, w.

PROVISION, MEAT, *s.* Krâg, B.

PROVOKE, *v.* Serry, sorry, provyeha, w.; tosoanna, B.; iskinat, P.

PROW, *s.* (Of a ship). Flurr, flurrag, P.

PSALTERY, *s.* Savtry, o.m. 1997.

PUBLIC AFFAIRS. Yeveren, B.

PUBLIC STOCK or BANK, *s.* Tryssor, B.

PUBLISH, *v.* Dolos, derevas, dherevas, deryfas, w.; asderua, P.

PUDDING, *s.* Pot, w.; hygan, higan, B.; hogan, hoggan, D.

A BLACK PUDDING. Gudzhygan, w.; gudzhigan, B. *Lit.* A blood or bloody pudding.

A HARD (HEAVY) PUDDING. Pellen, B. Its proper meaning is a round body or ball, but used derisively for a very solid pudding.

A WHITE PUDDING. Pot gwidn. The Cornish still say white *pot* for a white pudding.

PUFF, FART, SMELL, s. Bram. *Pl.* Bremmyn, w.

PUFF, s. (Of wind). Whêth, hwêth, êth, w.; whâth, c.w. 2299.

PUFF UP, TO PUFF UP, TO BE PUFFED UP, v. Hwêdhy, hudhy, w.; huêdhi, p.

PUFFIN, s. Pope. d.

PUFFING, A PUFFING UP, s. Hwêdh, huêdh, w.

PULL or HAUL, s. Tên, tyn, w.

PULL, v. Tenna, tedna, tynné, w.

TO PULL THE HAIR. Weet, wheet, d. I have often heard the latter (*wheet)* used.

PULLET, s. Mabyer, w.

PULLING or HAULING, *part.* Hallyah, b.; tynnys, p.

PULPIT, s. Pyrcat, w.; pyrkat, p.; ogal, b.

PULSE, s. (As peas, &c.) Jot, b.

PULSE or PEAS, s. Pês, pêz, w.

PULSE, s. (Of an artery). Gloys, b. *Gloys créf,* a strong pulse; polge, m.

PUMP. (?) The lowest of the tier of pumps in a mine water-engine is called *driggoe* or *drigger,* p.

A SMALL MINE PUMP. Skit, skeet, d. See SYRINGE and SQUIRT.

PUNISH, v. Cyssythy, punsyé, w.; punsuié, curo, p.; peyné, peynyé, peyny, b.; penya, c.w. 1259; ymskemyny, p.

PUNISHMENT, s. Cossythyans, gossythyans, dial, dyal, dyhal. anfus, enfugy, anfugy. *Y a's tevyl anfugy,* punishment shall come to them, o.m. 2328; penys, penaz, b.

PUNY, adj. Pinnikin, d.

PUPIL, s. Diolacht, dileakta, p.

A PUPIL UNDER WARD. Eisreacht, p.

PUPIL, s. (Of the eye). See APPLE OF THE EYE.

PUPPY or YOUNG DOG, s. Coloin, w.

PURBLIND, adj. Coegdale, b.

PURE, adj. Glân, lân, w.; glane, p.; gulan, w.; glannith, p. *Trueth vye dén yw gulan,* it were pity that a man who is pure, p c. 2437; pûr, w.; clour, m. 151.

PURE AND CLEAN. Skove, d. The Cornish miners say of a rich lode " 'tis all skove," that is all ore, " pure and clean."

PURCHASE, v. Prenny, prynny, w.; prenna, p.; perna, berna, w.; perhen, p.

PURCHASE, A PURCHASE, s. Purvers, w.

PURCHASER, s. Pernar, w.

PURGE, v. Carthu, b.; pyrdzha, p.

PURITY, s. Glander, m. 533. *Omguythé prest in glander,* to keep thyself ever in purity, m. 533.

PURPLE, adj. Coch, b.; pu pur, w.

PURPOSE, v. Tewlel, w.; teulel, tiulel, p.; tywlel, tyulel, b.; tow.al. teuly, p.; towla, toula, w.

PURPOSE, A PURPOSE, s. Toul, teul, tewl, w.; doul dowle, p.; mynnas, vynnas, w.; dryff, b.

ON PURPOSE. Adriff, w.; adryff, b.

FOR THE PURPOSE OF. Râg, râc, râk, w.

PURSUE, v. Sewyé, sewé, sywé, w.; sewya, sewsya, p.; hella, helhia, w.; helfia, p.; hellyrchy, w.; hellyrghy, p.

PURSUER, s. Helhiat, w.; helyiat, helyad, helyur, b.; helhwar, hellier, p.

PURSUIT or FOLLOWING, s. Helhiat, p.

PUSH, v. Herdhya, herdhyé, w.; herthy, p.

PUSH, s. Pôc, w. The word is still used for *shove* or *thump.*

PUT, v. Gora, w.; goira, b.; worra, n.; woré, p.; corré, w.; fytsé, p.

HE WILL PUT. Wor, a mutation of *gor,* 3 pers. s. fut. of *gora,* to put, w.

TO PUT ASIDE, v. Dyscy, w.

TO PUT TO FLIGHT, v. Fyé, w.; fué, p.

TO PUT ON. v. Gwiscy, gwiscé, gwesca, gwesga, w.; guesga, p.; wyscé, w.

TO PUT or TURN OUT, v. Asgor, p.

TO PUT ON A CROWN. Curuné, w.

TO PUT TO DEATH. 'Uras the mernans, b.

PUT, *part.* Gurys, gora, woras, b.

PUT FORTH. Raggorys, w.

PUT OUT. Vês guris, b.

PUT THOU. Tommans, tommés, p. *Tommans onan dour wár lán,* put someone water over the fire, p.

PUT YE. Gorreugh, p.

PUTREFY, v. Pedry, peddry, dho peddry, podré, w.; potré, p.

PUTRID, adj. Pedrys, m. 3066; podrek, m. 3048. *Moy podrek ay esely,* more putrid in his hands, m. 3084.

PUTTOCK or KITE, s. Bargés. w.; bargez, p.; bargos, w.

PUZZLE, v. Puza p.

Q.

" This letter is not a regular member of the British alphabet, but it is used in a few Cornish words with *u* following to express the sound of *cw,* as *quellen, qura, quréth, bysqueth,* for *cwellen, cwra, cwréth, byscweth,* &c.

That it was in early use is proved by an inscription on a tone in Gulval, near Penzance, where the British name Cynedhav is written Quenetav," w. *Lex. Corn. Brit.*

QUACKERY, *s.* Ponster, w. The word *pomster*, a corruption of *ponster*, is still used for a quack-doctor. A so as a verb, *to pomster* i.e., to heal, or rather, "quack."

QUAGMIRE, *s.* Plashet, ploshet, D.

QUAIL, *s.* (Bird). Rinc. w.

QUAKE, *v.* Cerna, kerna, crenné, krenné, w.; krenna, P.; crenna, krena, B.; kerniah, P.; crys, grys, w.; vrama, P.

QUAKING, A QUAKING, *s* Vrama, P.

QUANTITY, *s.* Myns, mêns, tomals, w. *Tummals*, for lots or quantities of anything is still often used.

QUARREL, *v.* Omdhal, cably, w.; kennkia, gueskal, B.; garey, D.

AN OLD FAMILY QUARREL. Corrosy, correesy, corrizeé, D.

QUARRELED, *part.* Cablas, cublas, scablé, B.

QUARRELSOME, *adj.* Garey, D.

QUARRELSOME PERSON. Strifor, w.

QUARRY, *s.* (As of stone, &c.) Cuaré, P.; kuarré, B.

QUARTER or FOURTH PART, *s.* Kuartan, P.

QUARTER, PART, or LOCALITY, *s.* Gwythrés, B.

QUARTZ, *s.* Cam, cand, carn-tyer, D.

QUASH, *v.* Gwaythy, gwethé, fethy, w.; guethé, P.

QUEEN, *s.* Michtcrnés, mychternés, w.; migternés, P.; myternés, maternas, ruifanés, ruivanés, w.; rhuyfanés, B.

QUELL, *v.* Gorlené, worlené, w. *Ny wra bom y worlené*, a blow will not quell him, P.C. 2111.

QUENCH, *v.* Defydh, w.; defyth, deveth, P.; dufydh, dufydhy, difydhy, defydhy, w.; difythi, P.

TO QUENCH THIRST. Dysehy, w.

QUENCHED, *part.* Devidhyz, B,

QUESTIONED, *part.* Bressys, B. See JUDGE, *v.*

QUICK, *adj.* (Soon). Dyhons, dhyhons, dhydhuans, w.; dyhuanz, B.; dywhans, defry, dheffry, deffry, devry, w.

QUICK, *adj.* (Speedy). Cut, cot, w.; got, P. *Ha the'n mernans cot gorrys*, and to death quick put, O.M. 1522; fast, w.; fastsens, B.; snel, R.D. 2144; stric, strik. The Cornish miners say *stric* when they wish to lower the *kibble* or mine bucket with greater speed.

QUICK, *adj.* (Alive). Bew, biu, byw, vew, w.; buhan, B.

QUICKLY, *adv.* Fest, prest, dewhans, duwhans, dyw-hans, w.; dyhuanz, P. *Ffystyn alemma duwhans,*

hasten hence quickly, O.M. 169; meugh, P.C. 1118. *Ny'n geuyth meugh*, we will find him quickly, P.C. 1118; snel, M. 3368. *Alemma then guelfos snel*, hence to the wilderness quickly, M. 3368; tythy, w.; toothda, tothda, tuthta, P.; tothta, c.w. 850; totta, tothetta, P.; touth-da, N.; toyth ta, O.M. 1001; warnot, P.; uscrys, w.; uskys, P.; yskys, w.; uskis, M. 2733; uth, P. *Uskis ha schaff*, quickly and rapidly, M. 2733.

QUICKSAND, *s.* Dreath lenky, w.

QUICK-SIGHTED, *adj.* Lagadec, lagadzhak, w.; lagadzhek, B.; lagasek, M. 1018.

QUICKEN-TREE, *s.* Cerden, w.; kerden, P.

QUIET, *adj.* Cosel, kozal, cusal, kuzal, crês, creys, w.; creez, P.; dyson, w.

QUIET, REST, *s.* Cosoleth, gosoleth, powés,

A PLACE OF REST. Powesva.

QUIETLY, *adv.* Cosel, P.; cusual, w.; yn kesoleth, P.C. 715. *Ysetheugh yn kesoleth*, sit down quietly, P.C. 715.

QUIETNESS, *s.* Callamingi w.; kallamingi, kallaminghi, B.; hêdh, hedwch, w.

IN A STATE OF QUIETNESS, REPOSE, or SLEEP. Cûsc, kûsg, w.

QUILL, *s.* Coilen, w.; koilen, P.; kuillan, B.; kuilan, P.; korsen, B.

QUILT, *s.* (For a bed). Pengughret, B. See also FUR COAT.

QUIT, *v.* Gara, garera, gasé, w.

QUITE, *adv.* Whâth, whêth, w.; methen, pûr, pôr, pyr, pre, P.; fest, M. 107; coul, O.M. 2581; cowle, c.w. 794; cowal, O.M. 2702. *Bonés an temple coul wrys*, the temple to be quite done, O.M. 2581. *Marrow cowal ty a vyth*, killed quite thou shalt be, O.M. 2702.

QUOIST or RING-DOVE, *s.* See RING-DOVE.

QUOIT, *s.* Scudell, B.; koeten, P.

R.

"This letter is an immutable radical in all the Celtic languages except the Welsh," w. *Lex. Corn. Brit.*

RABBIT, *s.* Cynin, w.; kynin, P.; couniel, B.; cyningen, w.; kyningen, P.

RABBLE, MOB, *s.* Tiogou, pobel tiogou, tuogu, w.; mogyon, B.; meggany, P.

RABID, *adj.* Conerioc, w.; koneriok, B.; conerive, P.

RACE, LINEAGE, *s.* Linieth, lynnyeth, lynneth, w. *Rák sawyé lynnyeth máp dên*, to save the race of sons of men, R.D. 1810; devethyans, M. 1830. *Hath devethyans*, and thy race, M. 830; ehen, M. 2913. *Ha lés the ôl y ehen*, and benefit all his race, M. 2913.

RADIANCE, *s.* Golevder, M. 3669; golvygyen, M. 3681. *Pendra yv an golevder*, what is the radiance, M. 3669

RADISH, *s.* Redic, rhedic, w.

RAFTER, *s.* (Beam). Keber (pron. *tcheber*), P.; ceber, P.; cledr, B.; troster, trester, stîl, styl, stull, w.

RAGE, *s.* Gewar, B.; conner, connor. P.

RAGING, RABID. MAD, *adj.* Conerioc, w, ; koneriok, B.; conerive, P.

RAIMENT, *s.* Gwisc, guisc, w.; guisk, P.; gwesc, w.; guesk, P.; dellés M. 3063; dillas, c.w. 1037; thyllas, c.w. 1036.

RAIN, *s.* Glaw, w.; glawe, P.; glau, w. *Glaw the gothé awartha*, rain to fall from above, O.M. 1028.

A DRIVING SHOWER OF RAIN. Skiff, D.

THICK DRIZZLING RAIN. Skew, D.

RAINBOW, *s.* Camdhavas, w.; cabmthavas, P.; gabm-thavas, c.w. 2501; kamdhavas, camniuet, B, ; cam, P.

RAINY, *adj.* (Muggy, dirty weather). Slotteree, w. This is a word in very common use in Cornwall.

RAKE, *s.* Rakkan, B.

RAISE or PRODUCE, *v.* Fysel. *Rág esow galso fysel*, that I might raise corn, P.

RAISE, TO RAISE UP, *v.* Drehevel, w.; dreheuel, trehevel, dhrewel, P.; dereval, dreval, w.; derebal, P.; therevel, B.; sevel, syvel, w.; syuel, sewel, seval, sef, P.

RAISE, *v.* Gorren, P.

RAISE, TO BE RAISED, *v.* Sordya, w. *Ternoys y sordyas bresel gans an Edhewon goky*, the day after there arose a contest among the foolish Jews, M.C. 238 (w.).

RAISE UP or EXCITE, *v.* Amsevy, w.

TO RAISE ONE'S SELF. Ymdhreshevel, w.

TO RAISE A SHOUT. Garmé, w.; garmi, karmé, P.; carmé, w.

RAISED UP, *part.* Sordys, P.; sordyys, w. From *sordya*, to arise.

RAISED UP or EXCITED, *part.* Ansueth, P.

RAISED or ELEVATED, *part.* Drehevys, trehevys, w.

HE WOULD RAISE. Drehefsé, dreafsé, w.

RAISINS, *s.* Figés an houl. *Lit.* Figs of the sun.

RAM, *s.* Hôrdh, w.; hôrth, P.; hôr, w.

A BLACK RAM. Hôr diu. *Pl.* Hyrroz dyon, w.

RAMBLE or STAGGER, *v.* Rambla, P.

RAM-CAT. TOM-CAT, *s.* Gûrcâth, w.; gûrkâth, P.; kûrkâth, B.

RAMPART, *s.* Tuban, w.; tuban agger, P. This must mean a rampart of turf. The Cornish at this time call a bit of turf a *tab*.

RANK or DEGREE, *s.* Pryckna, pruckna, P.

RANSOM or REDEEM, *v.* Prenna, P.

RAPID or SWIFT, *adj.* Cywlym, B.; schâf, scâf, scâff, scâv, sgâv, P.

RAPIDLY, *adv.* Schâff, M. 2733. Also the other forms of this word as given for *rapid. q.v.*; schâf, in R.D. 1731.

RARE, *adj.* (Scarce). Trawythés, w.; trauythés, P.

RASCAL, *s.* Lorel, w. *Rág nyns ouch más dewlorel*, for ye are naught but two rascals, O.M. 1504; losel, w. *Lavar lemyn mars yw prys danvon genés tús ervys dhe gerchés an vyl losel*, say now if it is time to send armed men with thee to bring the vile rascal, P.C. 940; iouden (*iovden*), M. 778; jaudyn, w. *Nyns yw saw un plos iaudyn*, he is not but a foul rascal, P.C. 1894; gwâs, guâs, wâs, w. *Ér na'n prenné an guâs-na*, until that rascal catches it, O.M. 2152. *Tebel wâs woteweth lader vyé*, a wicked rascal, at last a thief he was, M.C. 38; gâl, M. 1528. *Kekefrys gâl ha brentyn*, as well rascal as noble, M. 1528; gadlyng, P. *A vyl gadlyng dues yn rág*, Oh vile rascal, come forth, P.C. 1817; harlot, P.C. 2751. *Rág tempré an harlot fól*, to tame the mad rascal, P.C. 2751; negethys, M. 777. *Ty falge negethys*, thou false rascal, M. 777; piliack, culiak, D.; voran voren, P.; drôcgerut, drôkgeryt, B.

RASCALLY, MOST RASCALLY. Scherevwa, M. 3269. *Ty vav scherevwa del oys*, thou boy, most rascally as thou art, M. 3269. The Cornish use the word *skerry-werry*, for an active young rascal, D.

RASPBERRY, *s.* (The bush). Dreisan, dreizan, w.

RAT, *s.* Logosan vrâs. w.; lygodzhan vrase, lygvraoz. logoden, P.; yermis-priv. B.

RATHER, *adv.* Cens, kens, w.; kenz, P.; gens, hens, w.; kynz, P ; cyns, kyns, w.; kins, P.; ja, B.

RATHER THAN. Kens vel, w.; kenz vel, P.

HE HAD RATHER. Vendzha, a mutation of *mendzha*, a corrupt form of *mensé*, 3 pers. s. plup. of *menny*, to will, to wish, w.

RATTLE, *v.* Crehylly, w.; kanvas, B.

RAVEN, *s.* Brân vrês, w.; brane vrase, c.w. 2450; vrane vrâs. c.w. 2464; marchvrân, w.; marvrân, P.; varchvrân, w.; vargh-vrân, O.M. 1106. *Lit.* *Brân vrân*, a great crow, and *marchvrân*, a horse crow.

RAVENS, *s.* Lugu, B.

RAVINE, *s.* Nans, w.; nance, nantz, P.

RAVISH or DEFLOUR, *v.* Guasga, B.

RAVISHED, *part.* Rassys, B.

RAW, CRUDE, *adj.* Criv, w.; kriv, B.; êr, crêv, w.

RAW-MILK, *s.*   Leath crêv, w.

RAY or SKATE, *s.*   (Fish). Carcath, karcath, w. ; karlath (?), p.; môrcáth, w.; môr-cath, p. *Lit.* Sea cat.

RAZOR-FISH.   See SHEATH-FISH.

REACH, TO REACH AT or TO, *v.*   Hedhés, hedhy, w.; hedha hethé, p.; ystyné, w.; ysten, p.; ystyn, B. *Ystym thym*, reach to me, B.   Drehedhy, w.; thehesy, p.

REACH IT ME.   Ystym e dhym, p.

REACHING, *s.* (A reaching of the body). Cehedzhé, w.; kehedzhé, p.

READ, *v.*   Lenn, redyé, redi, w.; rhedi, p.; redyn, B.; porogga, legria, p

READER, *s.*   Lenner, B.; redior, w.; ledior, B.

A FEMALE READER.   Rediorés, w.; lediorés, B.

READILY, *adv.*   Eredy, w.; aredy, c.w. 341 ; yredy prest, w.; paris, baris. B.

RIGHT READILY.   Pûr eredy, B.

READINESS, *s.*   Adoth, B.

READING, *s.*   (A reading or version). Legradz, p.

READY, *adj.*   Parot, parez, parys, w.; ven, B.; pront, o.m. 2669. *Kyn fy mar pront ty a'n pren*, since thou art so ready for the tree, o.m. 2669.

REAL, *adj.*   Defry, deffry, dheffry, devry, w.; teffry, N.

REALLY, *adv.*   Yn teffry, N.; defry, m. 4387.

VERY REALLY.   Yn pûr deffry, N.

REAP, *v.*   Medé, midi, medgé, w.; midzhi, p.; cynivias, kynivias, B.

REAPER, *s.*   Meder, meader, meter, midzhar, midil, w.; midhil, p.; medwas, w.

REAPERS, *s.*   Medweision, megousion, w.; megouzian, B.

REAPING-HOOK, *s.*   Cromman, crobman, fils, fowls, voulz, w.; vaulz, B.

REARED or BRED, *part.*   Megys, mygys, w.; mygyz, p.

REASON or CAUSE, *s.*   Ceson, cheson, ceyson, keyson, w.; cheyson, câs, p.; kâz, B.; kauanskis, p.

REBOUND, *v.*   Argila, p.

REBUILD, *v.*   Therevel, B.   See TO RAISE UP.

REBUKE, *v.*   Omdhal, B.

REBUKED, *part.*   Rebecis, w.

RECEIVE, *v.*   Cemerés, kemerés, gemerés, cymerés, kymerés, w.; kymeraz, astel, resevé, p.

RECEIVED, *part.*   Rysevé, B.

RECENT, NEW, FRESH, LATE, *adj.*   Newedh, newydh, nowydh, w.; noweth, nooth, nouedzha, p.; pals, p.

RECENTLY, *adv.*   Agensow, agynsow. N. *Agensow my a'n guelas*, I saw him recently, R.D. 911.

RECESS, *s.*   Cil, kil, chil, kyl, kyll, hÿll, w.

RECKON, *v.*   (To count or number). Nivera, nevera, w., ; amontyé, B.

RECLINE, *s.*   Gorwedha, corwedha, gurwedha, w.; gurvedhu, B.; growedhé, w.; groweth, p.; growedh, B.; goruedh, p.

RECLUSE, *s.*   (Female). Manaes, w.

RECOGNIZE, *v.*   Aswon, aswony, aswonyn, aswonvos, p.

I RECOGNIZE.   Adzhan, azwen. These are late corruptions of *aswon*, to recognize, w.

RECOIL, *v.*   Argila, w.

RECOLLECT, *v.*   Covio, w.

RECOLLECTION, *s.*   Adof, covath, côv, côf, kôf, co, w.; kôf, govenek, p.

RECOMPENCE, *s.*   Gober, gobar, gobyr, w.; gobr, gubar, gu, guu, p.; pewas, w.

RECONCILE, *s.*   Cysolatha, dho kysalatha, w.

RECOVER, *v.*   Cevarvos, w.; kevarvoz, p.

RECOVER, *v.*   (To get or take back again). Dascemeras, dazkemeraz, p.

RECOVER, *s.*   (As from sickness). Dasvewé, hethy, p.

RECTIFY or MAKE RIGHT, *v.*   Ewné, ewnné, ewna, w.; dha euna, p.; euna, B.; ouna, rethewno, reth ewno, p.

RED or RED-COLOURED, *adj.*   Ridh, w.; rydh, rûd, rudh, ruth, ruydh, p.; ruÿth, N.; côch, couch, oyrec, w.; oyrek, p.

REDDISH, *adj.*   Rydhic, w ; rydhik, B.; rydik, p.

REDEEM, *v.*   Disprenna, dasprenna, dysprenna, w.; dyprena, p.; dysprenné, dysprené, w.; thyspreen, o.m. 1935. *Genys a thyspreen an bys*, born to redeem the world, o.m. 1935 ; prenna, p.; prenné, prynny, w.; pryné, p,; perna, attamyé, w.; attamy, p.

REDEEMER, *s.*   Dysprynniar, dysprynias, dysprynnyas, w. *Mâp dev agan dysprynnyas*, Son of God our Redeemer, p.c. 404 ; pernar, w.   See also SAVIOUR.

RED-FERN, *s.*   Reden rydh, w.

RED-HAIRED, *adj.*   Pedn-ryth, p.; pedn rydh, B.; pedn rooz, w.

RED-HEADED, *adj.*   The same as for *red-haired*, q.v.

A RED HEAD.   The same as for red-haired.

RED-HOT, *adj.*   Oyrec, oyrek, oyrech, B. *Lit.* Gold colour.

RED-LEAD, *s.*   Melet, liu melet, w.; plobm rydh, B.

REDUCE TO POWDER, TO GRIND, *v.*   Melias, w.

REDWING or WHINNARD, *s.* Suellak, P. This name now spelt *swellack*, is still used in Cornwall.

REED, *s.* (A reed). Pendiwen, w.; pendiuen, B.; hescen, heschen, coilen, w.; koilen, kuilan, corsen, korsen, gorsen, P.; kuillan, B.; brunnen, bronnen, w.

A REED OF STRAW. Gwadégala (gwadé gala), P.

REED, *s.* (To thatch with). Soul, zoul, w.

REEL or STAGGER, *v.* Thysplevya, thysplevyas, P.

REFECTORY, *s.* Bindorn (?), P. (Perhaps *buidorn*).

REFRAIN, *v.* Ymdenné, w.

REFRESH, *v.* Dysehy, w.

REFUGE, A REFUGE, *s.* Guest, P.

REFUGEE, *s.* Fadic, P.

REFUSE, *v.* Naché, nahé, nacha, naha, nea, w.; naghé, nagha, P.; naugha, reneag, B.; ynnya, sconya, sconyé, w.; asconya, P.

REFUSE or RUBBISH, *s.* Atal, attle, w.; henyways, hennaways, P.; caff, guff, gard, D. These words are still used by Cornish miners.

REFUSE or RUBBISH OF A SLATE QUARRY. Scolluck, D.

REFUSE OF COPPER or LEAD ORE AFTER SPALLING. Halvan, D.

REFUSAL, *s.* Ynny, ynnyas, w. *My a wra prest hep ynny*, I will do at once without refusal, O.M. 2148.

REGARD, ESTEEM, *s.* Gré, w.; govys, wow, woolack, vry, P.

REGARD, NOTICE, *s.* Fara, w.

REGARD, *s.* (With respect to, in that case). Areth, dyweth, dywyth, kèn, P.

REGARD or ESTEEM, *v.* Gorneal, govys, w.

REGION, PART, DISTRICT, *s.* Tu, w.; tew, P.

REGION, *s.* (A region, a country). Bro, vro, gwlàd, w.; gulad, B.; glàs, gwlâs, w.; ulas, P.; ulaz, B. For more forms see COUNTRY.

THE MIDDLE REGION. Pervedh (*a bervedh*, within), w.

REGRATOR, *s.* (Trader). Gwicher (coynt). *Pl.* Gnyckoryon, P. See also MERCHANT.

REGRET, *s.* Bearn, bêrn, vêrn, hireth, hyreth, w.

REGRETTING, *s.* Hireth, hyreth, w.

REINS or LOINS, *s.* Mellow, P. *Re dorrow mellow y gyn.* the reins of his back may break, P.C. 1619; duiglun (*Lit.* The two hips); lonath, B.

REJECT, *v.* Dynaché, sconya, sconyé, w.; hepcor, R.D. 1433. *Monés the hepcor an ioy*, to go to reject the joy, R.D. 1433.

REJOICE, *i.e.*, TO CAUSE TO REJOICE, *v.* Lowenhé, lowenny, w.

REJOICING, *s.* Goluan, *i.e.*, the time of lights or bonfires, B.

RELATE, *v.* Cewsel, kewsel, w.; keusel, P.; gewsel, geusel, daryvas, dyryvas, w.

RELATION, A RELATING. A TALE, *s.* Daralla, w.

RELATIVENESS, A RELATIVE POSITION, *s.* Cever, gever. *Yn y gever*, in relation to him, w.

RELIABLE, *adj.* Ven, P.

RELIEF, SUPPORT, *s.* Gew. On many estates in the west, one of the best fields is called the *gews*, probably from hence as being the stay and support, P.

RELIEVE, *v.* Dyffrés, dhyffrés, w.

RELINQUISH, *v.* Esgara, gasa, gasé, w.

REMAIN, *v.* Cyrtas, w.; kyrtaz, B; trigé, drigé, trega, drega, tregé, dregé, w.

HE REMAINED. Drigas, a mutation of *trigas*, 3 pers. s. preterite of *triga*, to remain, w.

HE WILL REMAIN. Dric, a mutation of *tric*, also written *trig*, 3 pers. s. fut. of *triga*, to remain, w.

REMAINDER, *s.* Remenat, w.

REMARKABLE, *adj.* Sellic, w.

REMEDY, *s.* Mydhygyeth, w.; mythygyeth, R.D. 1670.

REMEMBER, *v.* Covio, govys, w.; perko, perkou, P.

REMEMBER. Côf, P.; percou, w.; perko, pergho, B.

SHALL REMEMBER. Cofua (cové ?), w.

REMEMBERED, *adj.* Covenec, govenec, w.

REMEMBERING. *adj.* Covys, w.; kovys, P.; kovyz, B.

REMEMBRANCE, *s.* Côf, côv, co, w.; cove, C.W. 2233; kôf, ko, B.; kûf, P.; covath, w.; cofua, P.C. 227; cofva, N.; govenek, B.

REMEDY or CURE, *s.* Iag, yly, w.

REMISS, *adj.* Lac, w.

REMISSION, *s.* Dewellens, dewyllyens, dewhyllyans, w.; dywlly, P.

REMIT or FORGIVE, *v.* Wâs. *Da Dew thothef a wâs*, and God to him did remit, P.

REMNANT or REMAINDER, *s.* Remenat, B.

REMOTE, *adj.* Pel, pell, bell, w.

REMOTENESS, *s.* Pelder, pellder, w.

REMOVE, *v.* Mosé, vosé, ommely, umhelys, w.; heny, P.

TO REMOVE FAR OFF. Pelly, w.

REMOVAL, *s.* Remoccon, M. 2011· *Remoccon then cúr ythys*, is removal to the court (of heaven), M. 2011.

REND, *v.* Squardyé, squerdyé, w.; squerdya, P.; terry, terhi, tyrry, torri, torry, B.

RENDER ANGRY, TO ANGER, *v.* Serry, sorry, w.; sorren, P.

TO RENDER DISTANT. Pelly, w.

TO RENDER SOUND, TO HEAL. Iaché, w.

RENOUNCE, *v.* Hepcor, w.

RENOWN, *s.* Clôr, gerda (*ger da*, a good word), gordhyans, gworyans, w.; guorhyans, P.

RENOWNED, *adj.* Gerûtda, w.

RENT, TO BE RENT. See REND.

RENT or TEAR, *s.* Squerd, squard, w. Still used in Cornwall.

REPAIR, *v.* Therevel, B. For other forms see RAISE UP.

REPAST, *s.* Prys, preys, prés, près-buz, w.; guledh, B.

REPENTANCE, *s.* Edrec, eddrek, edrek, w.; edrak, P.; eddrak, B.; eddrag, c.w. 2339; yddrag, c.w. 1141; edrege, P.; edrega, M. 2175. *Pan ús dywhy edrega*, since you have repentance, M. 2175.

REPENTANT, *adj.* Eddrak, c.w. 717. *An bargayne ny vyth eddrak*, of the bargain he will not be repentant, c.w. 717.

REPLENISH, *v.* Cowlenwel, gowlenwel, w.; goullenwell, P.; lenwel, w.

REPLY, *v.* Worthyby, P.C. 2493. *Geseugh vy the worthyby*, allow me to reply, P.C. 2493. For other forms see ANSWER, *v.*

REPORT, *s.* (Statement, rumour). Ger, gês, sôn, w. *Pyth yw an whethlow ha'n són*, what are the tales and the report? R.D. 608.

REPORT, NOISE, SOUND, *s.* See SOUND and NOISE.

REPOSE, *v.* Powés, powesy, w.; rebowés, P.; sypposia, w.; syppozia, P.

REPOSE, *s.* Powés, w.; ehan, P.

A PLACE OF REPOSE or REST. Powesva, w.

REPRESS, *v.* Omdhal, w.

RE-PRINT, *v.* Dasargraphia, w.; dazargrafa, P.

REPROACH, *s.* Belyny, velyny, drôcger, drôgger, w.

REPROACH, *v.* Flamya, w.; slumyas, B.

REPROACHED, *part.* Rebecis, drôcgerüt, drôg gerüt, w.; drôg-gerat, P.

REPROBATE, *s.* Drôcgerut, drôkgeryt, B. See also RASCAL.

REPROOF, *s.* Molath, P.; mollath, molleth, molloth, w. *Pl.* Molathow, mollathow, mollethow, mollothow, w.

REPTILE, *s.* Prif, prêf, prêv, pryf, w. *Pl.* Pryvés, w.; prevyon, N.

REPUGN, *v.* Omdhal, w.

REPULSE, *s.* Innias, w. *Pl.* Inniadow, w.; inniadou, P.

REQUEST, *s* Govynnad, govenec, w.; govenek, O.M. 453. *Rág thym yma govenek*, for my request is, O.M. 453, lawe, w.; orphenniaz, P.

REQUIRE, *v.* Gulen, cria, creia, greia, greiah, P. *Dho greiah rág*, to require or call for.

REQUIREMENTS, *s.* See NECESSARIES.

REQUITAL, *s.* Dalasias, drôggrâs, dròg-grâs, w. *Yn drôg-grás th'y das Adam*, in requital to his father Adam, O.M. 550.

REQUITE, *v.* Taly, w.; tyly, P.; dalvith, B.

REQUITED, *part.* Tylys, w.

RESEMBLANCE, *s.* Havalder, w.; aval, haval, avell, B.

RESEMBLING, *part.* Haval, havel, w.

MOST RESEMBLING. Havalla, w.

RESENTMENT, *s.* Sôr, sorras, fôr (?), P.

RESERVE, *v.* Reordiny, P.

RESIDE, *v.* See DWELL, *v.*

RESIGN, *v.* Dascor, w.; cummyn, gemyn, gymyn, P.

RESIST, *v.* Omdhal, w.

RESOLUTE, *adj.* Glew, w.

RESOLUTION, *s.* Doul, dowle, P.

RESPECT, *v.* Gorneal, parthy, perthy, w.; pertha, B.; perchy, w.

RESPECT, IN THAT RESPECT. Areth, P.

RESPECT, REGARD, *s.* Govys, vry, wow, woolack, P.; woolac, B.

GOOD RESPECT. Woolac da, B.

IN RESPECT OF. Herwyth, heruyth, P.; heruedh, kyffris, B.

WITHOUT RESPECT OF WHOM. Heruedh nep, B.

RESPITE, *s.* Symueth, P.

RESPLENDENT, *adj.* Splân, splâdn, w.

RESPOND, *v.* Goriby, gorryby, gortheby, gorthyby, worthyby, w.

RESPONSE, *s.* Gorib, gorryb, gortheb, gorthyp, w.

REST or PEACE, *s.* Cesoleth, kesoleth, cysolath, cyzaleth, w.; kysoleth, kysalath, P.; cosoleth, gosoleth, w. *Yn ov qulas ha cosoleth*, in my land and rest, O.M. 518; crês, creys, creez, P. *Nyn geuyth crês*, takes no rest, P.C. 1882; powés, w.; powas, c.w. 1515; ehan, P.; powesva, bowesva, w. *Hen yw dyth a bowesva*, this is a day of rest, O M. 145.

REST or REMAINDER, *s.* Remenat, w.

REST, *v.* Hedhy, powés, powesy, w. *Cosk wâr the tôr ha powés*, sleep on thy belly and rest, O.M. 2070; bowés, rebowés, P.

TO BE AT REST. Cescé, kesky, cuscê, cuskê, coscé, cusga, cysga, kusga, kysga, B.

TO REST ON, TO REST ONE'S WEIGHT UPON. Powesy, posê, w.; possé, bossé, P.; restoua, B.

HE RESTED. Bowesas, a mutation of *powesas*, w.

HE WILL REST. Bowês, a mutation of *powés*, w.

RESTORED, *part.* Dighthtyas, B.

RESURRECTION, *s.* Dedhoryans, dasserchyans, dhasserghyans, dhasserchyans, w.; thasserghyens, R.D. 2632; taserghys, B.; deraffa, w.; tery-fas, theryvas, B.

RETAIN, *v.* Duethy, P.

RETAINED, *part.* Duedhaz, P.

RETINUE, *s.* Cosgor. kosgar, w.

RETIRE, *v.* Anneyley, w.

RETIREMENT, *s.* Kil, B.

RETRACT, *v.* Dynaché, fyé, w; fué, P.

RETREAT or FLIGHT, *s.* Fo, w.; ffo, B.

RETRIBUTION, *s.* Dyal, R.D. 723.

RETURN, *v.* Thewhylly, O.M. 2196. *Sav vynerre thewhylly*, but always that thou return, O.M. 2196.

TO RETURN or COME HOME. Maoz dan dre, P.

I MAY RETURN. Tewhyllyf, a mutation of *dewhyllyf*, 1 pers. s. subj. of *dewhel*, to return, w.

REVELATION, *s.* Discwedhyans, dysquedhyens, w; disquethians, P.

REVENGE, *v.* Dyliê, P.

REVENGE, *s.* Dial, dyal, dyhal, drôggrâs, drôggrâs, w.

REVENGED, *part.* Dyliez, B.

REVERENCE, *s.* Kadar, B.

REVEREND, *adj.* Dyhogall, w.; dyogall, P. *Arluth dyhogall*, reverend Lord, w.

REVILING, *adj.* Drogdavasec, w.; drokdavazek. B.; mollethians, w.

REVIVE, *v.* (To live again). Dasvewé, dhasvewé, w.; dyerbeué, P.; dyerbine (?), B.; rewesé, P.

REWARD, *v.* Dalheugh, tyly, P.; talvega, B.; taluyth. P. *Me an taluyth thugh*, I will reward you, P.

REWARD, *s.* Gober gobar, gobyr, w.; goober, guber, B.; gubar, gobr, gu, guu, P.; pewas, gweryson, weryson, w.

RIB. *s.* Asen, w.; asan, c.w. 395; ason, c.w. 450; azan. B. *Pl.* Asow, w.; assow, c.w. 1572.

RIBBAND, *s.* Funen, snôd, w.

RICH. *adj.* Berthog, B.; cefuidoc, covaithak, w.; kovaithak, P.; wuludoc, w.; puludoc, B.; pêth, pith. P.

RICH or FRUITFUL, *adj.* Voeth, veath, P.

RICH AND PURE. (As of tin ore). Scove, D.

RICHARD, DICK, *s.* Hecca, w.; Hecka, P.

RICHES, *s.* Covaith, w.; kovaith, pethou, pythou. P.

RICK, *s.* Dise, B.

A RICK OF HAY. Bern, w.

RIDDLE or SIEVE, *s.* Ridar, w.; ridara kazher, P.

RIDDLE or SIFT, *v.* Croddré, kroddré, w.

RIDE. *v.* Morogeth, marogeth, varogeth, w; guarthek. P.

RIDGE, CREST, SUMMIT, *s.* Crib, w.; krib, B.; greab. grib, w.

THE RIDGE OF A HOUSE. Crib an ty, crib an tshyi, krib an chi, B.

RIDGE OF A HILL. Mydzhovan, B.; crib, greab, grib, cein, cyn, gein, hein, w.; jên, B. For other forms of *cein*, see BACK.

RIDGE or DAM, *s.* Astyllen, D. A mining term still used.

RIDGE OF ROCKS. (When bare at half tide). Rany, D.

RIDICULE, *v.* Cuthil-ges, kuthil-gês, P.

RIGHT, *adj.* (Correct). Ewn, ewen, eon, w.; ynion, B.; eun, P.; evn, O.M. 2525. *Lemyn sûr ythyv evu hys.* now certainly it is the right length, O.M. 2525.

RIGHT, *adj.* (Proper). Poran, F. (Exact, B.)

RIGHT, STRAIGHT, EVEN, *adj.* Compos, compés, compys, cympés, kympez, w.; compez, B.; thyggyow, P.; poran, w.

RIGHT, THE RIGHT AS OPPOSED TO LEFT. Dychow, dhychow, w.; dyghou, P.; dygow, thyghou, B. *Leffe thyghou*, the right hand, B.; thyggyow, dythyow, P.; dyhow, dyow, w.; dyhou, thyow. P. *Yn nêf a thyow thu'm tâs*, in heaven at the right of my father, R.D. 1582; dehou, hâs, P. *A hâs a glû*, from right to left, P.

RIGHT. *adj.* Pûr. w. *Pûr wyre me ew*, right truly I am, c.w. 3.

RIGHTLY, *adv.* Poran, w.; dyg, euné, ewné, lel, leal, P.

RIGHT OVER. Poran wâr, B.

RIGHTEOUS, *adj.* Guyryon, M. 2147. *Tús pûr guyryon*, very righteous people, M. 2147.

RIGHTNESS, *s.* (Exactness). Combrynsy, w.; combrinsy, P.

RIGOUR, *s.* Echen, hechen, ehen, hehen, w.; rigol, B.

RIME, *s.* (Hoar frost), Glit, w.

RIND, *s.* (As of a tree, &c.) Risk, P.; risc, rusc, ruscen, w.

RING, *s.* Bisaw, besaw, w.; besau, P.; bezau, B. bisou, w.

A GOLD RING. Besaw our, w.; bezau our, P.

A RING (or RINGS) FOR THE FINGER. Mode-ruy, modereuy, B. The same term is also used for a bracelet.

RING, *s.* (To play in). Clôs, P.

RING-DOVE, *s.* Kydhon, B.; kylobman kûz, (*Wood-dove*), P.

RIPE, *adj,* ' Ao, arvez, w.

RISE, *v.* Drehevel, w.; trehevel, P.; dereval, w.; derebal, P.; dreval, w.; dhrehuel, dreheuel, P.; sevel, syvel, w.; seval, sewel, syuel, sef, P.; surgya, dho surgya, w.; thethoras, B.

TO RISE AGAIN, *v.* Dasserchy, dhasserchy, w.; dasserghy, dathergy, thaserhy, P.; dasserhy, tas-serhy, tasserchy, w.; thasserghy, R.D. 1081; ded-hory, dethory, w.

SHALL RISE AGAIN. Trehavo, trehavo; P.

RISE UP, STAND UP. Sav, soth, B.

RISEN UP. Dyenkys, B.

RISING AGAIN. See RESURRECTION.

RISK, *s.* Perill, peryl, feryl, w.

RIVE, *v.* Fallia, w.; fellia, B.; feldzha, w. See REND. *v*

RIVER, *s.* Avon, aun, awan, gy, w.; gwy, P.; wy, w.; vy, P.; guher, hêl, hêll. heil, hail, heyle, B.; thour, P.; dour, N. *Dreys dour tyber,* through the river Tyber, R.D. 2214; tâm, *Polwhele*; ruan, w. *Polruan,* the pool of the river, w.; karrag, B. This (*karrag*) is a doubtful word; but Pryce applies the term *carrog* to a brook.

A GREAT RIVER or FLOOD. Auan brâs, P.

A RIVER THAT ENDS WITH A CREEK. Haile, hayle, P.

RIVER-BANK, *s.* Torlan, torneuan an avon, B.

RIVER-BED or CHANNEL, *s* Trôt, P.

RIVULET, *s.* Gover, guuer, w.; guver, guner, B.; ick, P., lacca, w. A water-course is still called a lake at Lostwithiel.

ROACH, *s.* (Fish). Rocca, tallok, talhoc, B.

ROAD, *s.* Fôrdh, w.; fôrd, fôr, w.; fôrth, ferth, P.; vôrdh, vôr, w. *Ha war forth ny a gafas,* and on the road we met, R.D. 1474. *Pl.* Furu, vuru, w.

ROAD or JOURNEY, *s.* (*Iter,* Lat.) Cerdh, kerdh, kerd, cerch, kerch, w.

ROAR, *v.* (As a lion). Pedhigla, w.

ROARING, *part.* A pedhigla, w.

ROAST, *v.* Rostia, w.

ROAST MEAT, *s.* Guleit, w.

ROB, *v.* Ladra, laddré, w.; lyttry. robbia, P.; raffna, M. 2144.

ROBBING, *part.* Raffna. M. 2091. *Nêb a cove erbyn raffna,* who speaks against robbing, M. 2091.

ROBE, *s.* Pows, bows, fows, w.; pous, P.; bous, N.; dyllés, M. 3003. *Guyske the dyllés yth kerhyn,* put on thy robe around thee, M. 3003.

A PURPLE ROBE. Purpur, w.

ROBBER. *s.* Lader, w.; ladar, P.; ferhiat, B.; rob-bior, P.

ROBBERS, *s.* Ladron, laddron, w.; ladhron, ladran, laddarn, P.

ROBIN, *s.* Ruddoc, w.; ruddock, P. Still used in Cornwall.

ROCK, *s.* Carrag, carrac, carak, P.; karrak, karak, kraig, carreg, B.; carrick, garrik, garrac, garag, P.

ROCKS, *s.* Kerrig, &c.

A RIDGE OF ROCKS BARE AT HALF-TIDE. Rany, D.

ROCK or CLIFF, *s.* Clegar, cleghar, clicker, cligga, w.

A STEEP ROCK. Clôg, w.; clôgwyn, P.

A HIGH ROCK. Carn, w.; kearne, P.

A HIGH PLACED ROCK. Tor. torr, B.

A FLAT ROCK or LARGE FLAT STONE. Lêch, lêh, P.

A CROOKED FLAT ROCK or STONE. Crumlêch, krumlêh, P.

A ROCKY PLACE. Carn, w.; kearne, P.

ROCKING, *adj.* Logan. Hence " Logan Rock," the rocking rock.

ROCKY, *adj.* Cernic, w; kernick, P.

ROCK-FISH, *s.* Talhac, w.; talhoc P.

ROD, *s.* Gwelen. w; guelen, welen, B. *Wele dyn pob y welen,* see for us every one his rod, M. 3294; guailen, guaylen, gwelan. w; guelan, guailan, P.

A ROD or TWIG. Guaglen, B.

RODS, *s.* Gweel, gwêl, w.; gueel, B.; gwelynny, w.; geulinny, P.; guelynny. M. 3298; guellynni, P.

ROE. *s.* (The female of the hart). Iorchés, w.; yorch, P.

ROE-BUCK, *s.* Iorch, yorch, w.; yorkh, kytiorch, kydiorch, P.; kidiorch, P.

ROGUE, *s.* Gwâs, guâs, harlot, w.; losel, P.C. 2589; dicreft, B.; cam, P.C. 1126. *Syttyough dalhennow yn cam,* set hands on the rogue, P.C. 1126. For other names see RASCAL.

ROLL, *v.* Rgruatt, ruilla, B. (*Voluto,* Lat.)

ROLL or WALLOW, *v.* Egruath, w.

ROME, *s.* (The city). Reven, w.; Reve, P.; Ruan, B.

ROMAN, *adj.* Rouan. *Pol rouan,* the Roman pool, B. A different meaning is given under RIVER, *q.v.*

ROMAN, *s.* (A Roman). Revenuer (*Reven-gour*), w.

ROMANS, *s.* Tiz-Rûm, *i.e.*, Rome folks, or men of Rome, B.

ROMP or HOIDEN, *s.* Hoeden, w.

ROOK, *s.* Brândré. *Lit.* Town crow, B.

ROOF, *v.* Ty, w.

ROOF, *s.* To, w.; nenbren, B. Pryce calls the roof (ceiling ?) of a chamber *nenbren.*

ROOFER, *s.* Tyor, w.

ROOM, *s.* (*i.e.*, a large room, also a barn). Sciber, scibor scaber, skibor, skyber, w. *Vn skyber efan yn scón,* a large room soon, P.C. 638. From this quotation it appears that *skyber,* &c., apply to a room of any size.

A GROUND ROOM. Soller, saller, D.

ROOT, *s.* Gwredh. gwreydh, gwredhan, w.; guredhan, P.; gwrydhen, grueiten, w.; gureitan, P.; grueirten, B.

THE ROOT OF A TREE. Ach, B.

ROOTS, *s.* Gwrydhyow, w.; gwrethow, C.W. 1828; gurethow, c w. 1902; guredhiou, P.

TO ROOT UP, *v.* Clowté, P.

TO ROOT UP GROUND. Gwaythy, gwethé, guethé, fethy, P.

TO TAKE ROOT, *v.* Gwrydhyé, w.

ROOTED, *part.* Gurythvys, P.

ROPE, *s.* Guzen, B.; lovan, w.; louan, P. *Gans louan ha chaynys yen,* with a rope and cold chains, P.C. 2060.

ROPES, *s.* Lavonowe, C.W. 2291.

A SMALL ROPE. Lovannan, w.

ROSE, *s.* Breilu, w.; breily, B. (Borlase calls a primrose *breilu*) ; rosen, B.

ROT, *s.* Pôth, M. 3066. *Pedry ye kyk avel póth,* thy flesh putrid like rot, M. 3066.

ROT, *v.* Pedré, pedry, peddry, podré, w.; potré, P.; centreyny, kentreyny, w.

HE MAY ROT Potro, 3 pers. s. subj. of *pedré,* to rot, w.

ROTTEN, *adj.* Pesach, w.; podrethek, M. 541; peydrennow, P.; casadow, w.; kesadow, P.; gasadow, w.

A ROTTEN THING. Podar, P.

ROTTENNESS, *s.* Podreth, harlutry, w.

ROUGH, *adj.* Garow, w. *Yma dour ow môs garow,* the water is going rough, R.D. 2298; garou, B.; garo, gara, guariow, P.; garov, M. 3210. *Pan veua fól ha garov,* though he be mad and rough, M. 3210; harow, w.; haro, haru, P.; huero, B.; hager, anwhec, difeid, w.; roche, reuch, D.

ROUGH or RUDE, *adj.* Coynt, w.

A ROUGH DEALER. Gwicker coynt, P.

ROUGHNESS, *s* Yeinder, B.

ROUND, CIRCULAR, *adj.* Cren, w.; kren, kern, pyr, P.

ROUND or CIRCLE, *s.* Bondhat, w.

ROUND or CIRCLE, *s.* (To play in). Clôs, P.

A ROUND BODY or BALL. Pellen, w.

A ROUND HEAP OF STONES. Crûg, crig, D.

A ROUND PROTUBERANCE. Bron, w.

ROUND ABOUT. Adro, edré, edré dro, w.; a der dro c.w. 1431 ; am, P.

ROUNDED, *adj.* Crûm, crôm, w.; krôm, croum, crobm, B. *Brás ha crôm y ben golés,* large and rounded its lower end, O.M. 2443.

ROUT, TUMULT, *s.* Randigal, B. This is now a provincial word for a rambling tale.

ROW, *s.* (Quarrel among miners). Bal por, D. See UPROAR.

ROW or LINE, *s.* Rew, w.

A SHORT ROW ON THE SEA. Troil, D.

ROWER, *s.* Ruivadur, ruifadur, revadar, w.; ruivadar, B.; reuadar. P.

ROYAL, *adj.* Ryal, w.; ryel, P.; real, bryntyn, brentyn, w.; ruif, B.

A ROYAL LAW or PROCLAMATION. Gurthemin ruif, B.; gurhemin ruif. P.

ROYALTY, *s.* Mychternés, myhterneth, myterneth, mychterneth, vychterneth, w.; myghterneth, vyghterneth, N.; reelder, M. 2942. *Exaltys te reelder,* exalted to royalty, M. 2942.

RUB, *v.* Gueska, guesga, B.; rhyttia, w.; rhittia, rhuttia, B. *Rhytti marh na,* rub that horse, B. *Dho rhittia'n dha,* to rub well, w.

RUBBISH, *s.* Cagal, B. The rubbish or rubble from the shoad pits is called *guag,* D. The name *rabban,* is, says Borlase, "that mixture of clay and stone which has not been moved since the flood, and generally lies over the *kam,* the head or rocky ground below the *rabban,*" *i.e.,* the rubbish or rubble above. Rubbish or stuff is also called caff, guff, D.

THE RUBBLE OF GRANITE. Rab, D. See also REFUSE or RUBBISH.

RUBBISH or RUBBLE OF A STREAM or TINWORK. Stent, D.

RUDDER, *s.* Leu; *Lew gurhal, Leu gurhal,* the ship's rudder; lahvelet, leu pi obil, P.

RUDDY, *adj.* Oyrec, w.; oyrek, P. (*Lit.* Golden); ridh, rudh, ruydh, ruth, rooz, P.

RUDE or ROUGH, *adj.* Coynt, w.

RUDE, *adj.* (Churlish). Gocy, wocy, w.; goky, woky, P.

RUDE, RAW, NEWLY MADE, *adj.* Criv, w.; kriv, B.

RUE, *s.* (The plant). Rute, ryte, w.

RUE, *v.* Pea, B.

RUFFLE, *v.* Dystempra, M. 2937. *Truethyv y dystempra*, a pity it is to ruffle him, M. 2937.

RUG, *s.* Pengughret, B. See also FUR COAT.

RUGGED, *adj.* Garow, harow, w.; garo, haro, hara P.

RUIN. *s.* Dâr, M. 953. *Dâr ny regh vry*, ruin you don't regard, M. 953.

RUIN, *v.* Destrewy, dhestrewy, w.; dystrewy, trystrywy, P.; diswruthyl, w.; dyswruthyl, dyswythyl, dizurythyl, P.; disil, w.; dizil, diswel, P.; dyswel, dhyswul, w.; dyswul, P.; diswul, diswrey, w.; dyswrey, dizurey, diswreys, P.; destria, w.; dho diswrug, P.

RUINED, *part.* Dizureys, &c. See RUIN, *v.*

RULE or REGULATION, *s.* Loe, rowl, reol, w.

RULE, *v.* (Guide or govern). Rewlé, rewlyé, rowlia, w.; roula, P.; roulla, R.

RULE, *s.* (A nine foot rule to measure land). Gord, B.V.

RULER or GOVERNOR, *s.* Rowler, w.; rouler, B.; ruif, rêv, arluth, arludh, arluidh, w.; luder, B.

A FEMALE RULER. Luifanés, ruivanés, w.

RUM, *s.* Dour tabm Lollas. *Lit.* The American or West Indian hot-water.

RUMP or BUTTOCK, *s.* Cylbah, kylbah, lôst, w.

RUN, *v.* Ponyé, w.; ponya, P.; punnia, w.; punnio, B; punnya, poynyé, w. *Vskys na yllyn ponyé*, I could not run immediately, P.C. 2510.

RUN or FLOW, *v.* Redec, resec, resek, w.; rees, P.

HE WILL RUN. Reys, rês, 3 pers. s. fut. of *resec*, to run, w.

TO RUN AWAY, *v.* Fyé, fué, w.; punnya ker, ehed, P.; skesy, scusy, skusy, B.; fadé, D.

RUNAWAY, *s.* Fadic, B.

RUNNING, *adj.* Re, w.

A RUNNING NOOSE. Colm re, w.

RUPTURE, *v.* Terry, terhi, tyrry, torry, w.; torri, P.

RUSH, *s.* (The plant). Bronnen, brunnen, w.; brydnan, brydn, B.; gweth, gueth, P.; purvan, B.

THE SEA RUSH. (*Arundo arenaria*). Starr, D.

RUSH-HEAD, *s.* (A term of contempt). Pen bronnen, R.D. 2096.

RUSH PLACE or A PLACE OF RUSHES. Brennick, P.

RUSH MAT, *s.* Strail elester, w.; strail-lestre, B.

TO RUSH OUT, *v.* Redec, resec, resek, w.; rees, P.

RUSHY, *adj.* (Of the plant). Bruinic, w.

RUST, *s.* Gal, gossan, gozan, w.; marg, merel, B.

RUST. *s.* (Of corn). Cankar, P.; kankar, P.; colbran, colibran, D.

RUSTY, *adj.* Gal, w.

RUSTIC, *s.* (One from the country). Tioc, tyoc, tiak, tyac, dyac, trevedic, w.

RYE, *s.* Sogal, B.; sugall, sygal, w.

RYE BREAD. Bara sogal, w.

A FIELD OF RYE. Sygalek, w.

S.

"This letter in Cornish and Welsh is an immutable radical. In Armoric it is mutable, changing in construction into z, as *seched*, thirst, *ar zeched*, the thirst," w. *Lex. Corn. Brit.*

SABBATH, *s.* Sabot, P.C. 1504.

SABLE, *adj.* Du, diu, dhiu, w. See also BLACK.

SACK, *s.* Sach, zâh, w.

A LARGE SACK. Tigan, B.

SACRED, *adj.* Sant, P.; sanct, sans, san, w.

SAD, *adj.* Trest, trist, trewesy, trewysy, w.; trewisy, trowesy, P.; drewesy, w.; trauethak, P.; trom, w.; gwef, gwelh, B.; morethec, morethek, w.; wisht, whisht, D.

SAD! *exclam.* Trew!, tru!; govy!, gony!, harow!, harrow!, P. See also ALAS!

SAD IT WILL BE. Gony vyth, P.

SADDLE, *s.* Diber, debr, w.

SADDLE-GIRTH, *s.* Gees, geez, giss, geis, D. See GIRDLE.

SADLY, *adv.* Soweth, syweth, w.; seweth, B.; syuedh, w.; trys, trûs, P.

SADNESS, *s.* Awher, tristans, trietyns, trystyns, tristys, trystys, tristyys, w.; trewath, c.w. 1006; dâr, P.

SAFE, *adj.* Diogel, dyogel, dyougel, dyowgel, dyhogel, diougel, P.; jach, B.; saw, N.; sau, P.

SAFETY, *s.* Diahé, dyaha, w.; cosel, ehaz, gwyth, P.

SAFFRON, *s.* (The wild or meadow saffron). Goitcenin, w.; goitkenin, goickennin, B.

SAGACIOUS, *adj.* Guenuuit, gwenwit, guenwuit, w.

SAGE, WISE, PRUDENT, *adj.* Fûr, feer, fîr, fyr, w.

SAIL, *s.* Guil, gôl, goil, goyl, w. *Y goyl yn ban*, her sail up, R.D. 2291.

SAIL-YARD, *s.* Gwelan gôl, w.; guelan gôl, guelan goil, B.

SAKE, FOR THE SAKE OF. Awoys, M. 1043.
Awoys dyv rân, for the sake of two parts, M. 1043.

FOR THY SAKE. Gothaf, P.

SAINT, *s.* Sans, W.; sanz, zanz, P.; zans, synt, B.; sant, P.

A FEMALE SAINT. Sansés. See M. 579.

SAINTS, *s.* Sansow, syns, seins, W.; seinz, P.

FEMALE SAINTS. Sansesov (*sansesow*), M. 579.

ST. JOHN'S FIRES. Tantat St. Jan, *i.e.*, good or holy fires of St. John, B.

SALARY, *s.* Gober, gobar, gobyr, gobr, gubar, guu, gu, P.

SALIVA, *s.* Trifias, W.; trifiaz, B.

SALMON, *s.* Ehôc, W.; ehuac, ehôg, eaug, P. As a plural Borlase gives *sowmens*.

SALT, *s.* Sâl, zâl, haloin, W.; holoine, B.; holan, halan, W.; halen, B.; halein, W.

SALT, *v.* Salla, zalla, W.

SALTED, *adj.* Sâl, zâl, W.

SALTED, *part.* Sellys, W.; selliz, B.

SALTER, *s.* Haloiner, W.

SALT-MAKER, *s.* Haloiner, W.

SALT-MARSH, *s.* Hâl, W.; haal, O.M. 2708. *Pl.* Hallow, W. *Kepar ha seym py lyys haal*, like train-oil or salt-marsh mud, O.M. 2708.

SALT FISH. Pesk zâl, W.

SALT-WATER. Hyly, W.

SALTING-PAN, *s.* Stên, B. This word, also spelt *steyne*, is in common use in Cornwall. The same word (*stên*) is Cornish also for a milk-pail. A coarse brown earthenware pan of an oval form is called a *stugg*. This last word is also commonly used.

SALUTE, *v.* Dynerchy, dinerchy. W.; dinyrghy, P.; dynerhy, W.; dynerhi, B.; salugy, P.C. 972; sallugy, P.C. 2126.

SALUTATION, *s.* Dynnarch, dhynnarch, W.

SALVATION, *s.* Sylwans, sylwyans, W.; selwyans, M. 3077; selwans, M. 2026; sylvans, sylwyas, P.

SALVE, *s.* Urat, yly, W.; ylly, B.; ely, M. 1007, 3079; savment, M. 1376. *Marsus savment in bysma*, if there be salve in this world, M. 1375.

SAME, THE SAME. Rên, rêth, B.; honys, P.; cêth, kêth, W. *A'n kêth renna the'n tyr sans*, of these same to the holy land, O.M. 1879.

SANCTIFIED, *adj.* Sanct, W.; sant, P.; sans, W.; zanz, P.; san, W.

SANCTIFY, *v.* Soné, sona, zona, uchellé, uhellé, ychellas, W.

SAND, *s.* Grouan, grean, grow, grou, grouder, W.

COARSE SAND. Trêas, B.

GRAINS OF SAND. Treysy, M. 2399.

SAND, A SAND, A SAND-BED *s.* Trêath, traith, dreath, drêth, draith, drethan Commonly if not always used of sea-shore sand, as a sandy beach, a sandy shore-bank. A hillocky accumulation of sand, just beyond the tide, and sometimes inland from the the coast, is called a *towan*. There are various forms of *towan*, viz., towan, W.; towin, towyn, tewen, tuan, P.; tuen, tuyn, W. These *towans* (a name still in common use) become covered with a fine grass of which sheep are very fond. The term "towan mutton" is given to sheep which are fed on the towans. The flesh is much esteemed. See DUNE.

A SAND AREA or SPOT OF SAND. Drethan, D.

SAND-ELL, *s.* Visnan, vidnan, D.

SAND-LANCE, *s.* See SAND-EEL.

SANDERLING, *s.* (Bird). Towillee, D.

SAND-SMELT, *s.* Guid, D.

SANDYX, *s.* (Herb). Glesin, B.

SANITY, *s.* (Sound health). Iachês, iechés, W.

SAP, *s.* Sygan, W.

FULL OF SAP. Êr, W.

SARACEN, *s.* Sarsyn, P. The Cornish also used this name for a heathen. See also SAXON and SAXONS.

SASH or BELT, *s.* Grugis, grigis, grigiz, grygis, W.; grygys, gwregus, grwegus. B.; guris, W.; gouris, grûg, cleddif, clediff, B.

SATAN, *s.* Satnas, B.; Sowthanas, P C. 2417.

SATIETY, *s.* Lanwés, W.

SATIN, *s.* Paly, baly, W. *Hethough cercot a baly*, reach a surcoat of satin, P.C. 1784.

SATRAP, *s.* Guahalech, W.; guahlegh, P.; guahalgeh, B.

SATURDAY, *s.* De Sadarn, W.; De Zadarn, P. *Lit.* Saturn's day.

SATURN, *s.* Sadarn. W.; Zadarn, B.

SAUCY or PERT, *adj.* Corrat, toit, D.

SAVAGE, *adj.* Gwylls, W.; guellz. P.; guit, W.

SAVE, *v.* Sawyé, W.; sawya, C.W. 2311; selwel, sylwel, W.; rensawy, P.

TO BE SAVED. Selwel, sylwel, W.

TO SAVE ONE'S SELF. Omsawya, ymsawyé, W.

SAVINGS or MONEY, *s.* Cobshans, D.

SAVIOUR, THE SAVIOUR, *s.* Sylwadur, sylwador, sylwader, W.; selwadour, M. 536; salvador, C.W. 1865; sylvias, P.; sylwyas, salver, W.; sawya, an sawya, P.

SAW, *v.* Terry, terhi, tyrry, torri, torry, B.

SAXON, *adj.* Saesnek, B.; Sasnec, Zaznak, Sowsnac, W.

SAXONS, *s.* Zouzn, B.

SAY, *v.* Cewsel, kewsel, W.; keusel P.; gewsel, geusel, gwesys, cows, W.; cous, tho cous, P.; dho kouz, B.; caws, W.; kauz, B.; dhe cousa, mêdh, mêth, P.; lavary, leverel, laol, laul, W.

SAID, *part.* Cewsys, cawsys, W.; cawsés, P.; cowsys, W.; leverys, meth, B.

SAID HE. Mêdh e, fettow, W.

I SAY. Lavaraf, levaraf, N.

THEY SAID. Methens, B.

SAYING, *s.* (A saying). Ger, lavar, W.

SAYINGS, *s.* Diskus, P.

SCAB, *s.* (As of a sore). Crevan, W.; debarn, rougn, B.; hud, scud, D.

SCABBARD, *s.* Gôn, gûn, W.; gwân, P.; gwein, guein, guain, goyn, W.

SCABBY, *adj.* Rougnus, B.

SCAFFOLDING, *s.* Horvenow, O.M. 2322.

SCALD-MILK, *s.* Leath kither, B.

SCALDING, *adj.* (Very hot). Wylast, P.; ylast, B.

SCALES, *s.* (For weighing). Clorian, mântôl, B.

SCALLOP, *s.* (Shell-fish). Gwean, quean, D. This is also used for PERRIWINKLE, *q.v.*

SCAMP. *s.* See RASCAL.

SCANDAL, *s.* Drôcger. *Lit.* Evil word or saying.

SCANT, SPARING, *adj.* Scent, skent, W.; scant, P.

SCANTY, *adj.* Ascant, M. 658.

SCARCE, *adj.* (Few). Tanow, tanaw, W.; tanau, P.

SCARCE, *adj.* (Rare). Trawythés, W.; trauythés, P.

SCARCE or SCARCELY, *adv.* Schan, M. 543. *Schanlour y halla kerthés,* scarce enough can I walk, M. 543.

SCARCITY, *s.* Tanowder, tanauder, W.

SCARECROW, *s.* Bucca, W.; bucha, P.

SCARF, *s.* Stôl, W.

SCATTER, *v.* Scollyé, scullyé, W.; skulyé, P.C. 260; fyé, B. For more see SPILL, SHED, POUR.

WHAT IS SCATTERED. Scyl, skyl, scûl, skûl, W.

SCENE, *s.* (Of a play). Gwardy, W.; guardy, P.

SCEPTRE, *s.* Guailen, B.

A ROYAL SCEPTRE. Ruyvanadh, B.; ruyfanaid, P.

SCHEDULE, *s.* Ymbithionen, W.

SCHIST, *s.* (Clay slate). Killas, callys, cals, D.

SCHOLAR, *s.* (One who is learned). Scôlheic, W.; scôl heick, P.; scylur, W.; skylur, B. *Pl.* Skylurion, P.

SCHOLAR or DISCIPLE, *s.* Desgibl, dyscybel, discybel, W. *Pl.* Dyskyblion, P.

SCHOLARSHIP, *s.* Lyen, W.; litherau, B.

SCHOLASTIC, *s.* See SCHOLAR (one who is learned).

SCHOOL, *s.* Scôl, W.

SCHOOLING, *s.* Vestrigy, M. 198. *Am vestrigy* for my schooling, M. 198.

SCHOOLMASTER, *s.* Maister mcbion, W.

SCIENCE, *s.* Scient, sceans, skeans, scians, skyans, skyens, skeyens, W.; askenteleth, P.

SCILLY ISLANDS. Zillan, B.

SCOFF, TO SCOFF AT, *v.* Dyalé, dyalas, dhyllas, P.

SCOFF, A SCOFF, *s.* Gês, geys, P.; geyll, B.; scoff, P.

SCOFFER, *s.* Barth, B.

SCOFFING, *s.* See SCOFF.

SCOLD, *v.* Deragla, P.; ymerio, B.

SCOLDED. *adj.* Huscen. D. In Armoric *hesken,* an instrument of torture.

SCONCE, *s.* Spâl. (That used for a candle).

SCORE, *s.* Ugans, igans, W.; iganz, B. See TWENTY.

SCORNFUL, *adj.* Dyveth, B.; scherewys, P.

SCOUNDREL, *s.* See RASCAL.

SCOUR, *v.* Seha, dho seha, skibia, P.

SCOURGE, *v.* Scorgyas, B.

SCOURGE or WHIP, *s.* Scubilen, W. Borlase gives this word for a broom. The scourge used at a classical school where I was a scholar, was indeed no other than a very small broom, so *scubilen* is correct for both a scourge and a broom, and doubtless, of ancient use.

SCOURGES, *s.* Skorgys, N. From the English.

SCOURING-SAND, *s.* Grouder, D.

SCOWL, *v.* Scrynkyé, O.M. 570. *Pup vr orthys ov scrynkyé,* always scowling at thee, O.M. 570. The word *skrinking* is still used in the Cornish dialect. It refers to one who has a trick of "screwing" up his face and eyes as if he were scowling.

SCRAMBLE, *v.* Grambla, dho grambla, P. In the Cornish dialect a rough or stony place is called a *grambler.* To scramble, *scranny,* D.

SCRAP, *s.* See BIT.

A SCRAP of MEAT. Slam, scram, D.

SCRATCH, *v.* Scrivinas, W.; skrivinas, B.; sclum, sclow, scrow, D.

SCREECH, *v.* Scrygé, P.; skryga, B. *Na skrig,* don't screech.

SCREECH-OWL, *s.* Berthuan, W.; stix, P.

SCRIBE, *s.*   Scherewys, P.

THE SCRIBES.   Scherewys, B.   See WICKED MEN.

SCRIP, *s.*   Daver, W.

SCRIP, *s.*   (A very small bit of anything).   Screed, skerrick, D.

SCRIPTURE.   Screft. W.; scrividh, P.

THE SCRIPTURE, *s.*   Scriptir, scriptyr, P.

SCRIPTURES, *s.*   Scryptours, N.   From the English.

SCRIVENER, *s.*   Scriviniat, P.

SCROLL, *s.*   (Of paper or parchment).   Ymbithionen, B.

SCULL, *s*   Grogen, P.C. 2141.

SCULLION, *s.*   Guaz hegin, B.   This is a misprint. It should be *guaz kegin*, (or *keghin*).   *Lit.* The kitchen man, or kitchen servant.

SCULPTOR, *s.*   Gravior, B.

SCUM, *s.*   Spoum. B.   This word is still used.   It is pronounced *spoom*.

SCUM, *v.*   Spouma, B.

SCYTHE, *s.*   Filh. voulz.   Williams calls these corrupt forms.

SEA, *s.*   Môr, w.; moar, c.w. 88; moer, c.w. 355; moyr, M. 2538; vylgy, w.; weilgi, B.   *Moyr ha tyr*, sea and land, M. 2538.   *Môr difeid, môr diveid*, the rough or wild sea.   *Spaven môr*, a smooth sea, w.   *Tra môr*, w.; *tre môr*, B.; beyond sea.

SEA CALF, *s.*   Tahua, w.

SEA CARP, *s.*   Cunner, D.

SEA-CAT, *s.*   (Skate) Môrcath, w.

SEA COVE or INLET, *s.*   Gwic.   Not *cave*.   See CAVE and the *Lex. Corn. Brit.*

SEA-COAST, *s.*   Brou an môr, P.; brouan môr, P.

SEA CRAY-FISH, *s.*   Gaver *môr*, w.

SEA DITCH.   (*sic.*)   Pill, P.

SEA DOG, *s.*   Môrgi, w.

SEAMAN, *s.*   Dên môr, w.

SEA-MEW, *s.*   Saithor, sethar, zethar, w.

SEA-NEEDLE or GAR-FISH, *s.*   Girac, w.; girak, girrock, gerrick, D.

SEA-PORT, *s.*   Porth, w.; porh, pôr, B.   See HAVEN.

SEA-EBB or REFLUX OF THE SEA.   Trig, drig. w.

SEA RUSH, *s.*   (Plant).   (*Arundo arenaria, Lat.*)   Starr, D.

SEA-SHORE, *s.*   Als, w.; aut, P.; arvor, B.; sian, zian, w.; torneuan, traeth, B.

SEA-STRAND, *s.*   See SEA-SHORE.   Pryce gives as an example, Marazion, "the market on the strand."   Borlase says "the market by the sea side."   The word *traeth* properly means a sea-shore of sand, a sand, or sandbank.

NEAR THE SEA, OF THE SEA.   Môresk, môrick, P.

SEA-ROBBER, *s.*   Ancredvur môr, ancredour, w.

SEA-WATER, *s.*   Hyly, w.; dour an môr.

SEA-TANG or WRACK, *s.*   Gumman, gubman, w.

SEA-WEED, *s.*   Gumman, gubman, w.

SEAL, *s.*   (Animal).   Tahua, w.; talgel, P.; leuirgo, B.; groyne, D.

SEAM or JOINING, *s.*   Enniou, gwry, w.

SEAM, *s.*   Sawe, B.   *War an sawe*, by the seam, B.

TO SEARCH FOR, *v.*   Whela, w.; huila, P.; hwila, chwila, whelê, whelas, hwilas, whylas, whythre, w.

THEY SEARCHED.   Hwalsons, more correctly *hwilsons* or *hwelsons*, being the 3 pers. pl. preterite of *hwila* or *whela*, w.

TO SEARCH INTO, *v.*   Croppye, croppy, P.

TO SEARCH OUT, *v.*   Guydher, P.

SEARCHER, *s.*   Hwiliog, w.; huiliog, P.

SEARING, *s.*   (A searing or singing).   Losc, losk, w.

SEASON, TIME, or PERIOD, *s.*   Prys, preys, prês, prez, prit, termyn, dermyn, termen, w.; tervyn (?), P.

A BAD SEASON.   Hagar auel.

SEASON, TO SEASON WITH SALT, *v.*   Salla, zalla, w.

SEAT or HABITATION, *s.*   Asedh, w.

SEAT, *s.*   (To sit on).   Se, sedhec, sedhva. w.; sethe, P.; setha, c.w. 16; sichen, B.

SEAT or CHAIR, *s.*   Tutton, B.

A HIGH SEAT or BENCH.   Soler, B.

TO BE SEATED.   Esedhé, ysedhé, w.; ysethé, P.

IN THY SEAT.   Yssé, a contraction of *yn dhe se*, w.

SECOND or NEXT, *adj.*   Nessa, P.; secund, N.

SECRESY, *s.*   Ledradeth, B.

SECRET PLACES.   Wrunch, P.

SECRETLY, *adv.*   Pryveth, P.C. 598.   *Yn nôs pryveth*, at night secretly, P.C. 598.

SECURE or PRESERVE, *v.*   Anysya, w.

SECURE, *adj.*   Diogel, dyogel, dhyogel, w.; diougel, P.; dyougel, dyowgel, prive, w.

VERY SECURE.   Per thewans, per tewans, B.

SECURITY, *s.*   Diahé, dyaha, w.   *Coskyn ny gans dyaha*, let us sleep with security, R.D. 402; secerder, w.; sekerder, P.; sekerden, B.

SECURITY, STRENGTH, *s.*   Crêvder, w.; krêvder, P.

SEDGE or FLAG, ₰ Elestren, w.; elesbren (?), P.

A MAT OF SEDGES. Strail elester, w.

SEDGE, s. (A sedge). Hescen, heschen, w.; pendiuen, B.

SEDIMENT, s. Godhas, godho, w.; grooshans, growshans, grushans, grudgens. grudglins, grishens, D. These dialectic words are still used for the sediment or grounds of tea, coffee, &c.

SEDITIOUS, adj. Dislaian, B.

SEDUCER, s. Lafurye, P.

SEE, v. Gwelés, gwelas, w.; gwel, N.; guelaz, guella, gweall, gwortheuy, P.; welés, w.; wellas, whylly, rewelas, wylfys, wylfyth, wylfyeth, P.; meras, miras, w.; mirés, N.; miraz, P.; myras, w.; miroz, veras, P.; verays, M. 733; viraz, viroz, dho viroz, P.

TO BE SEEN. Silly, sylly.

I SEE. Oyv a guelez, B.

I SAW. 1 Verys, a mutation of merys, 1 pers. s. preter. of meras, to see, w.

　　2. Welys, a mutation of gwelys, 1 pers. s. preter. of gwelés, to see, w.

HE SAW. Welas, a mutation of gwelas, 3 pers. s. preter. of gwelés, to see, w.

WE SAW. 1. Gwylsyn, 1 pers. pl. preter. of gwelés, to see, w.

I DID SEE. Wylyn, a mutation of gwylyn, id.qd. gwelyn, 1 pers. s. imperf. of gwelés, to see, w.

I HAVE SEEN. Wylys, a mutation of gwylys, id.qd. gwelys, 1 pers. s. preter. of gwelés, to see, w.

THOU HAST SEEN. 1. Guelyst, B.

　　2. Wylsta, a mutation of gwylsta, a compound form of gwylsys, 2 pers. s. preter. of gwelés, to see, and te, thou, w.

　　3. Wylsys, a mutation of gwylsys, id.qd. gwelsys, 2 pers. s. preter. of gwelés, to see, w.

WE HAVE SEEN. Wylsyn, a mutation of gwylsyn, id.qd. gwelsyn, 1 pers. pl. preter. of gwelés, to see, w.

I HAD SEEN. Welsen, a mutation of gwelsen (guelzen, B.), 1 pers. s. plup. of gwelés, to see, w.

HE HAD SEEN. Quelsé, a mutation of gwelsé, 3 pers. s. plup. of gwelés, see, w.

I SHALL SEE. 1. Gwylfym, w.; guylfym, B.

　　2. Welaf, a mutation of gwelaf, 1 pers. s. fut. of gwelés, to see, w.

　　3. Whelaf. The aspirate mutation of gwelaf, w.

THOU SHALT SEE. 1. Gwylly, 2 pers. s. fut. of gwelés, to see, w.

　　2. Welfyth, a mutation of gwelfyth, 2 pers. s. fut. of gwelés, to see, w.

　　3. Welté. Composed of wél, a mutation of gwél, 3 pers. s. fut. of gwelés, to see, and te, thou, w

　　4. Ti a ueli, ti a vyl, B.

HE SHALL SEE. 1. Vîr, a mutation of mîr, 3 pers. s. fut. of miras, to see, w.

　　2. Gwêl, gweal, 3 pers. s. fut. of gwelés, to see, w.

　　3. Wêl. a mutation of gwel, 3 pers. s. fut. of gwelés, to see, w.

　　4. Wêyl. The same as wél, q.v.

　　5. Wyl. Another form of wél, a mutation of gwêl, 3 pers. s. fut. of gwelés, to see, w.

　　6. Whylfyth. The aspirate mutation of gwylfyth, 3 pers. s. fut. of gwelés, to see, w.

WE SHALL SEE. 1. Welon. A late form of welyn, a mutation of gwelyn, 1 pers. pl. fut. of gwelés, to see, w.

　　2. Whyllyn. The aspirate mutation of gwyllyn, 1 pers. pl. fut. (and subj.) of gwelés, to see, w.

　　3. Quelyn, a mutation of gwelyn, 1 pers. pl. fut. of gwelés, to see, w.

YE SHALL SEE. 1. Gwyllouch, 2 pers. pl. fut. of gwelés, to see, w.

　　2. Welouch, a mutation of gwelouch, another form of the 2 pers. pl. fut. of gwelés, to see, w.

　　3. Weloh, a late form of welouch, q.v., w.

THEY SHALL SEE. Whyrvyth, B.

I MAY SEE. Hwellam, w.; huellam, B.

THOU MAYEST SEE. 1. Wylly, a mutation of gwylly, 2 pers. s. subj. of gwelés, to see, w.

　　2. Whylly. The aspirate mutation of gwyly, 2 pers. s. subj. of gwelés, to see, w.

HE MAY SEE. 1. Wella, a mutation of gwella, id.qd. gwello, 3 pers. s. subj. of gwelés, to see, w.

　　2. Whello. The aspirate mutation of gwello or gwelo, 2 pers. s. sub. of gwelés, to see, w.

I SHOULD SEE. Quellen, a mutation of gwelen, 1 pers. s. subj. of gwelés, to see, w.

SEE, SEE THOU. Gwothemys, B.

SEE, SEE YE. Mirouch, mirough, merrow, B.

SEE, SEE, LOOK, LOOK. Mere, mere, meir, meir, P.

SEE, BEHOLD. Otté, wetté, w.; wetta, welte, N.; ota, oté, ottensa, ottensy, P.; yta, w. See BEHOLD.

SEE HERE. Awatta, awot, awottué, awetté, attoma, P.; ottoma, w.

DO YOU SEE? Gwelta? (gwellés ta?), w.

SEEING THAT. Wôs, pa, B.

SEEN, part. Gwylys, w.; guellys, huellaz, B.

HAVE SEEN. Gwylvyth, B.

SEED, s. Hâs, hâz, hays, w.

SEEDSMAN, s. Gynnadar, w.; gynnadwur, P.; gynnodur, B.

SEEDY, *adj.* Hâzick, P.

SEEM, *v.* Silly, sylly. *My a sylly in úrna,* to me it seemed in that hour, P.

IT SEEMS. Ythvy, P.; falsé, valsé, w.; valsa, haval, y thewel, P.

SEEK, *v.* Whela, hwila, w.; huila, P.; chwila, whelé, welas, whelas, whylas, hwilas, whythré, w.; thenwell. P.

TO SEEK FOR, *v.* Thymwethé, P.

SEEK THOU. Wyla, 2 pers. s. imp. of *whylas,* to seek, w.

SEEK YE. Whelough, B.

SEEKS HIM. Omwrello, B.

SEEKER, *s.* Hwiliog, w.; huiliog, P.

SEINE-BOAT, *s.* Skâth rûz, P

SEISURE, *s.* Brêg, B.

SEIZE, *v.* Cemerés, kemerés, kymerés, cymerês, chymerés, gemerés, gymerés, dalhenné, w.; dicemmer, prenny, P.; sensy, synsy, sengé, sendzha, dho sendzhé, sinsy, w.; sindzhy, B.; sindzya, P.; syngy, w.

TO SEIZE ON, *v.* Askemery, P.; gathya, B.

SEIZED, *part.* Gachyas, gathyas, agathyas, B.

SEIZING, A TAKING HOLD OF, *s.* Dalhen, w.

SELECT, *v.* Diwys, dywys, dewesy, w.

SELF, ONE'S SELF, *s.* Honon, honan, honyn, w.; hwnyth, P.; ynan, w.

SELL, *v.* Gwerthy, gwyithy, gwerthé, w.; guerthé, B.; gwertha, gwetha, guerha, P.; gwerra, gwerhy, querthé, werthé, w. *Râg ow guerthé the'n traytors púr,* to sell me to very traitors, P.C. 1108.

SELLING, *part.* Ow querthé, N.

SEMBLANCE, *s.* Semlant, w. *Ha pan semlant vs ganso,* and what semblance is to him? R.D. 2060.

SEMBLANCE, FORM, or MANNER. Del. *Yn del ma,* in this manner, w.

SEMPSTRESS, *s.* Seuyadês, w.; seudés, P.

SEND, *v.* Danfon, dhanfon, danvon, dhanvon, w.; thanfonno, danfen, thanson (? thanfon), P.; danin, danyn, w.

TO SEND FOR, *s.* Dinerchy, dynerchy, dynerghy, P.

TO SEND FORTH, *v.* Dyllo, w.

SENSE, NOUSE, GUMPTION, *s.* Rode, ᴅ.

SENT, *part.* Danfenys, danvenys, w.; danvonys, damenys, tevenés, woromynys, B.

HE SENT. Tanfonas, a mutation of *danfonas,* 3 pers. s. pret. of *danfon* or *danvon,* to send, w.

I HAVE SENT. Mi rig dain. *Mi rig dain dythi,* I have sent unto him, B.

THOU SHALT SEND. Tanfenny, a mutation of *danfenny,* 2 pers. s. fut. of *danfon* or *danvon,* to send, w.

HE MAY SEND. Tanfonno, a mutation of *danvonno,* 3 pers. s. subj. of *danfon* or *danvon,* to send, w.

TO SEND AWAY, *v.* Mosé, vosé, w.

I WILL SEND AWAY Vossav. a mutation of *mossaf,* 1 pers. s. fut. of *mosé,* to send away, w.

SENDING OUT, A SENDING OUT, *s.* Dilla, dyllo, w.

SENSELESS, *adj.* Discient, diskient, w.; dikref, B.

SENSITIVE, *adj* Tidden, D.

SENTENCE, *s.* See JUDGMENT.

SEPARATE, *v.* Deberthy, dybarthy, deberhy, dhebery, w.; deberhée, deberhé, dyberhée, deberh, P.; debarra, B.

SEPARATE or DISPERSE, *v.* Cescar, keskar, w.

SEPARATED, *part.* Debarris, B.

SEPARATION, *s.* Deberth, dybarth, deberthva, w. *Yn tressé dyth dybarth, gyraf,* on the third day I made a separation, O.M. 25.

SEPARATION or BREACH, *s.* Tolva, dolva, w.; gwyth, with, P.

SEPTEMBER, *s.* Gwengala, w.; Guedn-gala, P.; Guengolo, B.; Gvyn-gala, M. 2076.

THE MONTH OF SEPTEMBER. Mis gwen-gala, Miz gwedn gala, w.; Miz-Guedn-Gala, *i.e.* the white straw month, P.; Mis guengolo, B.

SERENADE, *s.* (One of kettles and pans). Shallal, D.

SERENE, *adj.* Cosel, cusal, w.; kuzal, cuzal, P.

SERIOUS, *adj.* Defry, deffry, dheffry, devry, w.

SERIOUSLY, *adv.* Deffry, devry, teffry, theffry, P.; thevrey, M. 2359; trewysy, O.M. 511. *Ym colon púr trewysy,* in my heart very seriously, O.M. 511.

VERY SERIOUSLY. Púr theffry, P.; púr thevrey, M. 2359. *Púr thevrey orth y sewa,* very seriously following him, M. 2359; púr trewysy, O.M. 511.

SERMON, *s.* Pregoth, progath, w.

SERPENT, *s.* Sarf, w.; nader, P.; nadar, naddyr, pref, bref, B.

SERVANT, *s.* Gwâs, gnâs, w.; guâz, B.; wâs, servis, aber, w.; gonidoc, gonidog, goneseg, têz, tîz, thîs, B.; teithioc, mâb, maw, w.; menistror, B. *Menistror* was also used for a butler.

SERVANT BOY. Maw, mau, vau, P.

SERVANT MAID. Caités, P.; caithês, kaithés, B.

SERVANTS, *s.* Gwêsion, gwêsyon, wêsyon, w.; cosgar, P.; servisi, w.; servysy, P.; servidzhi, w.; servidzhy, P.; servygy, w.

SERVE, *v.* Servyé, w.

SERVICE, *s.* Gwryth, gruyth, w.; guryth, P.C. 2023. *Râg dón dustiny ha guryth,* to bear testimony and service, P.C. 2023; gwasanaeth, w.; guasanaeth, P.; lês, w.; wonys, M. 3891. *In bysma ath kel wonys,* in this world from thy loyal service, M. 3891.

SET, *v.* Gonedhy, w.; gonethy, p.; wonethy, gurra, gora, gorré, worré, settya, syttya, w.

TO SET BY, *v.* Settya, w.

TO SET ON FIRE, *v.* Dewy, dywy, w.; diwy, p.; tewyn, tchen, b.

TO SET FREE, *v.* Dylyr, p.; dilvar, b.

TO SET ON, *v.* Dylla, p.

SETTLE, *v.* Feeth, p.

SETTLED, *part.* Regeth, p.; rogeth, thyasseth, b.

IS SETTLED. Regeth, b.

SEVEN. Seith, seyth, syth, w.; zeath, p.

SEVEN HUNDRED. Syth cans, n.

SEVENTEEN. Seitag. More correctly *seitek*, w.; *seytek*, n.; seithack, d.

SEVENTEENTH. Seith dêgvas, p.

SEVENTH. Seithas, w.; seithaz, seythaz, p.; seithves, w.; seythvez, b; seythves, sythvas, w.

THE SEVENTH DAY. Seithves dyth, p.

SEVENTY. Trei igans ha dêg, w.; try ugens ha dêk, n. *Lit.* Three twenties and ten.

SEVERAL, *adj.* Lawer. For the other forms of this word see MANY.

SEVERE, *adj.* Garow, w.; garou, b.; harow, w.; guariow, garo, p; tin, tyn, dyn, b. *Ty a vyth punsys púr tyn*, thou shalt be punished very severe (*sic.*), o.m. 1600.

SEVERITY, *s.* Sevureth, m. 933. *Oma súr in sevureth*, here surely in severity, m. 933.

SEX, SORT, KIND, *s.* Riw, riu, w. *Beninriw*, woman or female kind.

SEX, *s.* Hynsé, w. *Dew ryth rós flour hy hynsé*, God made a rose flower of her sex, o.m. 2136.

THE SEX, *s.* Antromet, w.

SEXTON, *s* Derric w.; derrick, p.; dên an cloc, b.

SHACKLE, *s.* Fuai, fu, hual, w.; ettaw, w.f.p. Pryce gives *fual* for shackles.

SHAD, *s.* (Fish). Lobmas, ceinac, w.; keinak, p.

SHADE, *v.* Coscasa, kosgaza, w.; kosgazo, p.; kosgezys, w.

SHADE or SHADOW, *s* Scôd, scês, skêz, w.; yscôd, b.

SHADY, *adj.* Scodec, w.; guaskettek, b.

SHAFT or DART, *s* Gew, w.; geu, gu, guu, p.; guw, giw, gwayw w. Also names for a spear or javelin.

SHAFT, *s.* (Of a mine). Palador, w.

A SHORT UNDERGROUND MINE SHAFT. Winz. It is a shaft from one adit to another below it, often made for ventilation. Perhaps from *gwynys*, pierced, d.

THE BOTTOM OF A MINE SHAFT. Sump, d.; sumph, p.

SHAFT, *s.* (Of a pillar). Strest, w.

SHAG, *s.* (Cormorant or sea raven). Shagga, saithor, w.; sarthor, b. *Farthor* is a mistake.

SHAGGY, *adj.* Blewac, w. See HAIRY.

SHAKE or QUAKE, *v.* Crys, grys, w.

SHAKE, *v.* (As to shake the head). Pendruppia, w.; pendruphia, p.; gogwyddo, b.

SHAKING or ROCKING, *adj.* Logan, ambreth, b.

SHALLOT *s.* Cenin, cinin, w.; kinin, p.

SHALLOW, *adj.* (In depth). Bâs, w.

SHALL NOT. Bythny, p.

SHAME, *s.* (Infamy). Belyny, velyny, vylyny, basnet (?) w.; quêth, p.; guêth, p.c. 2606. *A váp the guêth ru'm lathas*, Oh! son, thy shame hath killed me, p.c. 2606.

SHAME, *s.* (Bashfulness). Mêdh, w.; mêth, moth, mulder, b. *Ty a fêth méth* thou shalt have shame, m. 2442.

SHAMEFUL, *adj.* (Disgraceful). Dyflas, dhyfflas, thyfflas, p.c. 1418.

SHAMELESS, *adj.* Deveth, diveth, dyveth, w.

SHANK, *s.* (Shank or leg). Gar, esgar, ber, ver, w.

THE SHANKS. Garrow, w.; garrou, b.

SHANK or SHINBONE, *s.* Elesker, b.; elescer, elescher, w.; elesfer, p.

SHANNY, *s.* (Fish). Gur, male, pullcronack, bulgranak, d.

SHAPE or FASHION, *v.* Schapy, p.

SHAPE or FORM, *s.* Furf, fu, fuw, gwedh, w.; kairder, b.; lyu, p.

SHARE or PORTION, *s.* Rân, râdn, w.; dôl, p. *Dôl* is given by Pryce for a share, a part, one eighth.

SHARE, *v.* Ranné, w.; radna, b.; ranna, p.

SHARED, *part.* Rynnys. From *ranné*, to share, w.

SHARER, *s.* Renniat, w.

SHARK, *s.* Scarceas, w.; skarkeas, b.

SHARP, *adj.* Grisyl, w. *Otté spern grisyl gyné*, see sharp thorns with me, p.c. 2118; lym. *Gans gu lym*, with a sharp spear, w.; leym, r.d. 1117. *Gans gu leym y u'n guanas*, with a sharp spear they pierced him, r.d. 1117; tin, tyn, dyn. *Pen tyn*, a sharp point, w.; lemmys, b.

SHARP, *adj.* (Severe). Garow, w.; garou, b.; garo, guariow, p.; harow, w.

SHARP, *adj.* (Cunning). Coynt, w.

SHARP, *adj.* (As a sharp blow). Glew, w.

SHARPEN, *v.* Lemma, lebma, w.

SHARPENED, *part.* Lemmys, lebmys, p.

SHARP-SIGHTED, *adj.* Lagadec, lagadzhak, P.

SHATTER, *v.* Crebylly, w.

SHAVE, *v.* Cynivias, kyniviaz, P.

SHAVED, *part.* Thyguethys, trysyvethés, P.

SHAWMS or SHALMS, *s.* Psalmus, o.m. 1998.

SHE, *pron.* Hi, w.; hy, hye, i, P.; y, B.; se, P.; 's, 'y, N.; hai, w.

AND SHE. Hai, P.; hay (*ha y*), B.

SHE HERSELF. Hyhy, w.

SHE-DEVIL, *s.* Diowlés, dzhowlés, w.; dzhoulés, P.

SHEAF, *s.* (As of corn, &c.) Attock, manal.

A SHEAF OF CORN. Manal ys, w.; manal yz, P.

A THRESHED SHEAF OF CORN. Liner, D.

A SMALL SHEAF OF GLEANED CORN. Sang, zang, D.

SHEAR or CLIP, *v* Cynivias, w.; kynivias, P.

SHEARS. A PAIR OF SHEARS. *s.* Gweldzhow, w.; gueldzhou, P.; gueldzha, B.

SHEARWATER, *s.* (Bird). Crew, cockathodon, P. The *Puffinus anglorum.*

SHEATH, *s.* Gôn, gûn, goyn, gwein, guain, guein, w.; gwân, P.; wôn, w. *Gorré yn y wôn arté,* put it into its sheath again. P.C. 1156.

SHEATH or RAZOR FISH, *s.* Cilygan, w.; kilygan, P.; keligan, capa-longa, D.

SHED, *v.* (Pour or effuse). Denewy, dhenewy, w. For more see SPILL.

SHED, SPILL, POUR, or SCATTER, *v.* Scollyé, scullyé, w.

SHED, DROP, or TRICKLE DOWN, *v.* Devery, dyvery, dyveré, w.

TO SHED TEARS. Diveré, P.

SHED, *s.* (For cattle). Bowgie, bougie, D.   See COWHOUSE.

SHE-GOAT, *s.* Gever, B.

SHEEP, *s.* (A sheep). Davas, w.; daves, N.; davaz, dhavaz, P.; davat, w.; devet, B.; devas, w.; mols, o.m. 1384.

SHEEP, *s.* (*Pl.*) Devés, w.; devez, B.; devidgyow, w.; dewysyov, M. 2981 ; eunow, P.

A BLACK SHEEP. Davas dhiu, w.

A LEAN SHEEP. Davas tanow, davaz tanaw, w.

SHEEP-COTE. *s.* Corlan, w. See SHEEP-FOLD.

SHEEP-DUNG, *s.* Cagal, B.

SHEEP-FOLD, *s.* Corlan, gorlan, w.; crou an devet, B.; boudzhé devas, boudzhi devés, w.; boudzhi devez, P.

SHEEP'S-HOLE, *s.* Sawan davis, w.

SHEEP'S-SKIN, *s.* Crawn, D.

SHEER-GRASS, *s.* Elestren, B.

SHEET, *s.* (Of paper or parchment). Ymbithionen, B.

SHEETS, *s.* (For a bed). Lennow, P.

SHELF, *s.* (In the sea). Cârn, w.; kearne, P.

SHELFY GROUND or LOOSE GROUND. Kivully, D.

SHELL, *s.* (As of a nut). Plisg, plysg, B.; hud, hull, D.

SHELL, *s.* Cib, B. Borlase also gives this name for a *cabinet.*

SHELL, *s.* (As of shell-fish). Crogen, w.; krogen, B.; crogan, w.; krogan, w. *Pl.* Kregyn, P.

SHELL-FISH, *s.* Besl, B.; trig, D.

TO GATHER SHELL-FISH. Trig, D.

A SHELL-FISH, *s.* Askal, B

SHELL-DRAKE, *s.* Burranet, D.

SHELTER, *v.* Coscasa, kosgaza, w.; kosgazo, P.; kosgezys, w.; goskesy, P.

SHELTER, *s.* Guscys, guskys, w.; guest, P.; gostotter, o.m. 361 ; goscotter N. *Rág fout gvest ha gostotter,* for want of clothing and shelter, o.m. 361.

A SHELTERED AREA. Lanherch, w.

SHEPHERD, *s.* Bugel, begel, w.; bygel, P.; bigel, w.; begol, byzel, B.

SHERIFF, *s.* Huwelwair, hyuelvair, B

SHEW, ARRAY, *s.* Atheray, P.

SHEW, *v.* Gwelhé, w.; guelhée, P ; dascudhé, discudhé, w.; discuthé, P ; dyscudhé, dhyscudhe, disquedha, dysquedhas, w.; dysquethas, thyswethas, B.; dyswedhy, w.; dyswethy, P.; dyswithy, B.; dyswedha, diswedha, discwedha, w.; dyscus, P.; daryvas, dharyvas, dyryvas, w.

HE SHEWED. Dysquedhas, tysquedhas, w.

TO SHEW ONE'S SELF. Ymdhysquedhas, w.

SHEWED. Fekyl, B.

SHEWING, *s.* (A shewing). Dysquydhyans, w.

SHIELD or BUCKLER, *s.* Costan w ; kostan, B.; gostan, w.; ysguydh, B.

SHIFT, CHEMISE or SMOCK, *s.* Creis, crys, w.; hevis, hevez, heuis, B.

SHILLING, *s.* Sôl, B.; sôls, sowls, zoulz, zowlz, w.

SHIN-BONE or SHANK, *s.* Elescer, w.; elesker, B.; elescher, w.; elesfer, P.

SHINE, *v.* Golowa, w.; goloua, P.; gouloua, gollowy, gylywa, gylywi, colowa, collowy, terlentry, w.; splanna, thywhyn, P. *An houl pan thywhyn,* the sun when it shineth, P.; dywhyny, dywhynny, dewynnyé, tewynnyé, w.

SHINING, *adj* Splan, w. *May rollons y golow splan,* that they may give their shining lights, o.m. 40.

SHINING LIKE GOLD. Oyrec, w.; oyrek, p.

SHINING, *part.* Ow collowye, c.w. 125. *Avell tane ow collowye*, like a fire shining, c.w. 125.

SHIP, *s.* Gurhal, gorhel, w.; gorhall, p.; gurchel, worhel, w. (*Pl.* Gurhaliou, w.) lester, w.; lysster, c.w. 2261; lesster, c.w. 2310; scharron, p.

A LITTLE SHIP. Gurhal bien, p.

SHIP'S BOAT, *s.* Lestercoc, w.; lester côk. p.

SHIP'S MAST. Warne, wern, p.

SHIRT, *s.* Hevis, hevez, w.; heuis, b.; hevys, m. 1938. *In y nessé hevys ruen*, next him a shirt of hair, m. 4443; rochet, b.; creis, crys, w.; kreis, krys, p.

SHITE, *v.* Kakan. *Kaka angwillé*, to shite a bed, p.

SHIVE or SHALLOT, *s.* Cenin, cinen, w.

SHIVER, *s.* Scruth, w. (*Pl.* Schorys, m. 681). shrim, d.

SHIVERING, *s.* (A shivering). Rynny, w.

SHOCK or SHEAF, *s.* (As of corn). Attock, manal, w.

SHOE, *s.* Escid, esgid, eskis. esgis. w.; esgiz, b.; eskas, w.; eskaz, ergiz, egiz, fosaneu, p.; orchinat, w.

SHOES, *s.* Eskidieu, esgidiow, eskygyow, eskyggyow, esgisow, w.; skyggyow, p.; sgyggyow, eskittias, w.

SHOE. TO SHOE HORSES, *v.* Hernia, w.; herniah, b.; wrennyé, w.

SHOELESS, *adj.* Diesgis, w.; diesgiz, p.

SHOEMAKER, *s.* Cereor, w.; kereor, chereor, b.; cherior, p.

SHOOT, *v.* Tynné, tenna, tedna, w.; sethy, b.

TO SHOOT OFF, *v.* Duello, thello, thelly, p.

SHOOTER, *s.* Saithor, sethar, zethar, w.

SHOOTS or SPROUTS, *s.* (Or suckers of trees). Lyuorch-guydh, p.

SHORT, *adj.* Ber, ver, w. *A ver termyn*, in a short time, o.m 1362; byr, b; cut, cot, w. *Cot yv the thythyow*, short are thy days, r.d. 2037; cutt. c.w. 88; cuttu, cueth, b.; got, p. *Re got o a gevelyn*, too short it is by a cubit, o.m. 2520; tâm, tame, d.

SHORTER, *adj.* Cotta, gotta, p.

SHORTLY, *adv.* Crac, w.

A SHORT TIME. Cut termyn, p.; cutt termyn, c.w. 88.

A SHORT SPACE OF TIME. Tuch, w. See TIME.

SHORTNESS, *s.* Berder, breder, vreder, w.

SHORT BREATH or SHORTNESS OF BREATH. Beranal, w.; cueth anall, b.

SHOULD. Teffa, thyvas, b.

SHOULD I. Veam, b.

IF I SHOULD. Mar sellen, p.

IT SHOULD or OUGHT. Dâl e dâl, p.

SHOULDER, *s.* Scûid, scûdh, w.; skûd, b.; scûth, skûth, skudh. scouth, p.; scodh, scoudh, w.; scoth, scooth, b. *Dro hy thy'mmo wâr ow scouth*, put it to me on my shoulder, p.c. 2623.

SHOULDERS, *s.* (*i.e.*, the two shoulders). Discodh, dywscodh, w; dywscoth, n.; duscodh, duscoudh, w.; duscoth, n.; duscouth, p.

SHOULDER-BLADE, *s.* Scuid, p.; Sguth, b.

SHOUT, *s.* Garm, w.

SHOUT, *v.* Garmé, w.; garmi, p.; carmé, w.; karmi, p.; gwaeddi. b.; helwy, hilwy, hylwy, lefa, w.

THEY SHOUTED. Hawlsons. The 3 pers. pl. preterite of *helwy*, w.

SHOUTING, *s.* Trôs, w.; trôz, p.

SHOVE. *s.* Pôc, w.; fooch, d. These words are still in use.

SHOVEL, *s.* Pâl, w.; paal, b.; bâl, baal, fâl, rêv, w. *Héz ou fâl*, the length of my shovel, p.

SHOWER, *s.* (Of rain). Cowés, w.; cwas, kuas, kuaz, b.; cuas, cowat, w.; couat, b.; gowés, w.; glau, gleau, b.; skew, skud, d. *Hagar gowés war ov jêth*, a fierce shower, on my faith, o.m. 1080. *Ota cowés pûr ahas*, see a shower very disagreeable, o.m. 1081.

A HEAVY SHOWER. Koust, b.

SHRED or TATTER, *s.* Midjan, jowd, d. See PIECE and BIT.

SHRED OF CLOTH. Purvan, porvan, d. This is also the name for the wick of a lamp called a *chill*. This wick is made from the pith of a rush, or a rag.

SHREWD, *adj.* Queedy, d.

SHRIEK, *v.* Scrygé, w.; skriga, b.

SHROVE-TIDE, *s.* Enés, Enez, w.

SHRUB, *s.* Luworch-guit, lyuorch guydh, seruic, b.; servic, p.

SHRUBS, *s.* Guit, gwydh, w.

SHUDDER, *v.* Owerené, p.

SHUT or CLOSE, *v.* Alwedha, lyhwedha, w.; lyhuetha, p.; ceas, keaz, b.; degy, w.; dygy, sera, p.; serra, b.

SHUT, *part.* Degés, degees, degeys, dygés, w. *Ha'n durasow ól degés*, and the doors all shut, p.

SHY, *adj.* Mul, b.

SHY, *s.* (As of a horse). Bawk, d.

SHYNESS, *s.* Mulder, mêth, moth, b.

SICK or ILL, *adj.* Clâf, w.; claff, b.; clâv, w.; klâv, clêf, clevas, clevys, b. *Dén clâv*, a sick man, w. *May thyw pûr clâf*, so that it is very sick, r.d. 1377. Wingarly, b. A word still used.

SICK, *s.* (Sick people, the sick). Clefyon, clevyon, w.; glevyon, b.; klevion, p.

SICKLE, *s.* Cromman. crobman, filh, voulz, w. The last two words, says Williams, are corrupt forms.

SICKLY, *adj.* Palch, w. A word still often used.

SICKNESS or MALADY, *s.* Clevés, clevas, w.; klevas, B.; klevaz, P.; clevel, w.; clewet, P.; cluyan, gluyan, w.; galer, M. 566; pocvan, w. *Tán ha môk ha pocvan brâs,* fire and smoke and great sickness, R.D. 2341.

SIDE, *s.* Tenewen, denewen, tenewan, denewan, ternewan, tyrnewan, w.; ternehuan, P.; tenewon, M. 2604. *Gans gu lym in tenewon,* with a sharp spear in the side. M. 2604; denewhan, c.w. 1553; tornewan, tu, du, w.; teu, tew, P.; thew (*Pl.* Thewen), B. *Pup tu,* each side, w.; *pub tu,* every side, B *A y du,* on his side, w. *Avertu (a ver tu),* on either side, P. *Pop ay du,* on every side, P.

SIDE or PART, *s.* Parh, parth, w.; part, barth, P.

ON EVERY SIDE. Warbarth, warbarh, B.

ON THE SIDE. Abarth, abarh, w.

ON THE SIDE OF. Barth, w.; bardh, P.; barh, w.

ON ALL SIDES. Tro, dro.

ON THE OTHER SIDE. Trez, P.

ON THIS SIDE. Antyman, w.

SIDES, *s.* Tênewennow, tênwennow, dênwennow, tynwennow, w.

SIDE, BANK, or BRINK OF A RIVER. Glân, glând. Also meaning the side of anything. *Glân* and *gland* are still much used among miners, &c.

SIDEWAYS, *adv.* A denewen, o.m. 2063. *A râg ha a denewen,* forewards and sideways, o.m. 2063.

SIEVE, *s.* Croider, crodar, w.; krodar, B.; ridar, ridar a kazher, w.; ridara kazher (*ridar a kazher*), P.; casier, D.

A COARSE SIEVE. Kayer. D.

A STRAINING SIEVE. Tammy, D.

A HORSE HAIR SIEVE. Dilluer. D. It is used in washing fine ore. From *dilleugh,* or *dylyer,* to let go, to send away, P

AN IRON SIEVE Searce, searge. D.

SIFT, *v.* Croddré, kroddré, w.; kayze, D.

SIGH, *v.* Hynadzha, w.

SIGH, *s.* Hanadzhan, w.; hanadzhans, hynadzhan, B.; hynadzhas. w.

SIGN or TOKEN. *s.* Peynye, poenis, thavaz, B.; thavas, P.

SIGHT, *s.* Goloc. w. *Pan dyffu yn ow goloc,* when he comes into my sight, P.C. 964; golok, woloc. golos, wolos, wlos. w.; ulos, B.; gwêl. wêl. w.; guêl, R.D. 842. *Ha guêl a'th fâs,* and sight of thy face, R.D. 842; gweyl, w.; gweall, c w 1209; weyl, P. *A weyl ól then arlythy,* in the sight of all the lords, P.; gwelas, w.; guelaz, welas, P.

SILENCE, *s.* Dava, P.C. 1002. *Scolkyough th'y an dan dava,* lurk after him under silence, P.C. 1002.

SILENCE! *exclam.* Huist! B.; stash, D.

SILENT, *adj.* Dysôn, w.; sioul, B.; tewel, P.C. 1320; *Gynés pan wreta tewel,* in thee since thou wilt be silent, P.C. 1320.

TO BE SILENT, *v.* Tewel w.; teuel, P.; taw, N.

WE ARE SILENT. Tywyn, N.

I WILL BE SILENT. Tawaf, 1 pers. s. fut. of *tewel,* to be silent, w.

WE WILL BE SILENT. Tewyn, 1 pers. pl. fut. of *tewel,* to be silent, w.

BE THOU SILENT. Taw, 2 pers. s. imp. of *tewel,* to be silent, w.; tau, tausy, P.

HE MAY BE SILENT. Tawo, 3 pers. s. subj. of *tewel,* to be silent, w.

BE YE SILENT. Teweugh, N.

SILK, *s.* Ourlen, B.; ourlyn, w. *Yn cendel hâg yn ourlyn,* in fine linen and in silk, O.M. 1752; sirig, B.; syrig, *Polwhele.*

SILL, *s.* (As of a window). Stull, B.

SILLY, *adj.* Discient, diskient, dikref, B.; fôl (fellyon, *Pl.* of *fôl*). gocy, gokr, gokky, wocy, woky, uccy, ucky, w.

SILVER, *s.* Archans. w.; arghans, P.; arhans, arrans, w.; arans, O.M. 2100. *Fenten bryght aval arhans,* a fountain bright as silver. O.M. 771.

SILVERSMITH, *s.* Gueid-uur argans, B.

SIMILAR. *adj* Keif, kief. kêv, kevelep, P.; cevelep, hevelep, hyvelep, avel, bavel, haval, hevel, cehafal, kehaval, w

MOST SIMILAR   Havalla. w.

VERY SIMILAR.   Pûr havel, w.

SIMILITUDE, *s.* Havalder, hevelepter, hevelep, hyvelep, hevelés. w.; haval, aval, avell, B.

SIMPLE, FOOLISH, *adj.* See SILLY.

SIMPLETON, *s.* Edyack, P.; cobba, bucca-gwidn, gaupus, gommok, D. For more see FOOL.

SIMPLY, FOOLISHLY, *adv.* Sempel, M. 1994. *Ty the rynnés mar sempel,* that thou wishest so simply, M. 1994.

SIN, *s.* Pêch. w.; pêk, B.; pêgh. M. 883, peghe, B.; peyghe, c.w. 875; pêh, w.; pê. pêth, P.; bêch, fêch. pechas. w.; peghas. B.; bechas, w.; beghas, B.; fechas, pehas. w.; pehaz, pyas, P.; feas, fehas, pehad, pechad. pechat. P.; bechad, w.; thrôk, M. 1898. *Ov repentya râg y thrôk,* repenting for her sin, M. 1898; anfus, N. *Pl.* Anfusy. N.

SIN, *v.* Pecha, becha, peché, beché, pehé, behé, w.; peghy, rebeghy, P.

HE SINNED. Pechas, pehas. Also their mutations, viz, bechas, behas. w.

HE HAD SINNED. Rebechsé. The particle *re* and *bechsé*, a mutation of *pechsé*, 3 pers. s. plup. of *pechy*, to sin, w.

HE WOULD SIN. Peha, pea, fea, w.

SINCE. Aban, w. *Aban ywe in della*, since it is so P.C. 1953 ; apé, P. ; ceth, keth, w. ; kyn, P. *Kyn thaw*, since that it is. P. ; hane, pam, pan, pahan, sol, P. *Sol a theth*, since I came to thee, P. ; wôs, B.

SINCERE, *adj.* Cylednac, w. ; kylednak, B. ; colenec, colanec, colannec, w.

SINCERITY, *s.* Leauté, P.c 760. See LOYALTY for other forms of this word.

SINEW, *s.* Gcien, geyen, goiuen, w. ; gelen, gelyn, P.

SINEWS, *s.* Geiow, geyow, eiow, ieyw, w. *Certan yagh ens aga ieyw*, certainly sound were their sinews, P.C. 2681 ; scenys, w. ; skenys, P. ; skennys, w.

SING, *v.* Cané, gané, cana, w. ; kana, B. ; gana P.

HE SHALL SING. Cân. Also *gán*, a mutation of *cán*, 3 pers. s fut. of *cané*, to sing, w.

LET IT BE SUNG TO EACH OTHER. Ymcener, 3 pers. s. imp. pass. of *ymcana*, comp. of refl. part. *ym*, and *cané*, to sing, w.

SING YE. Cenouch, kenouch, w.

I WOULD HAVE SUNG. Gansen, a mutation of *cansen*, 1 pers. s. plup. of *cané*, to sing, w.

HE MAY SING. Ganno, a mutation of *canno*, 3 pers. s. subj. of *cané*, to sing, w.

TO SING AFTER OTHERS. Bozzorés, bozzorrés, B.

SINGER, *s.* Ceniat, keniat, cheniat, w. ; chennicat, P.

A FEMALE SINGER. Canorés, w.

SINGLE PERSON or THING. (*i.e.*, one). Onan, onen, onon, w. ; onyn, odn, P.

SINGLE, *adj.* (Alone). Jowan, P.

SINLESS, *adj.* Dipeh, dibeh, w.

SINNER, *s.* Pechadyr, P. ; pechadur, pehadur, w.

A FEMALE SINNER. Pechadyrés P. ; peghadurés, P.c. 491 ; peghadoras, R.D. 1097 ; pechadurés, pehadurés, w. ; pehadorion, B.

SIP. See SUP.

SIR, *s.* Sera, seera, sira, sarra, P. *Pl.* Serys, M. 456; syres, N., but this is from the English.

SIRE, A SIRE, *s.* The same as for SIR.

SISTER, *s.* Hôr, hoar, hoer, w. ; hora, P. ; huir, wuir, w. ; huyr, puir (? *huir*), choar, soster, B.

SIT or SIT DOWN, *v.* Esedhé, asedhé, ysedhé, w. ; ysethé, reysetha, P. ; sedhé, w. ; sethé, seadha, P.

TO SIT ONE'S SELF. Omsettya, w.

SITTING-PLACE, *s.* Asedhva, w.

SITUATION or PLACE, *s.* Lê, lêh, ly, li, lu, w.

SIX. Whêh, hwêh, huih, w. ; hué, B. ; whe, N. ; whea, c.w. 42 ; whed, O.M. 142 ; whad, huik (?), P. ; wheth, D.

SIXPENCE, *s.* Hwêh dinar, w. ; hui dinair, P. *Lit.* Six pennies.

A SIXPENCE. Hanter sôl, B. *Lit.* Half a shilling.

SIXTEEN Whedhec, hwedhec, wedhec, hwettag, whettac, w. ; whettak, huettag, P. ; huehag, B. ; whethack, D. ; whethek, N.

SIXTH. Wheffés, hweffas, w. ; wheffas, P. ; hueffas, whefés, B. ; hueffaz, huefas, P. ; wehés, M. 2069; wheythaz, P.

SIXTEENTH. Whêhdêgvas, w. ; whêh dêgvas, P.

SIXTY. Tri-ugans, w ; tri igans (try ugens), N. ; tri iganz, P. ; trei-igans, tryygans, tryngens (? tryugens), B.

SIZE, *s.* Myns, mêns, w. ; gûr, P.

SKATE, *s.* (Fish). Carcath, karcath, môrcath, w.

SKELETON, *s.* Ramcs, D.

SKILFUL, *adj.* Guenuuit, gwenwit, w. ; guenwuit, skientik, P. ; skientic, slêv, w.

SKILFULNESS, *s.* See SKILL.

SKILL, *s.* Sleyveth, scient, skyens, skyans, scians, sceans, skeans, skeyens, w. ; deskans, P. ; descans, w. ; crêft, krêft, B.

SKIN or THE SKIN, *s* (As of an animal). Cen, w. *Dre an cen yn y grogen*, through the skin to his skull, P.C. 2141 (*Cen* also means the skin or *peel*, as of an orange); he, w. ; knezen. M. 3144 ; kneys, M. 4054 *Cler ha têk knezen ha fays*, clear and fair skin and face, M. 3144 ; crohen, croen, P. ; krohan, B. ; grohan, c.w. 1584 ; crehan, grehan, w. ; croin, crochen, groghen, P. ; gronen (? grohen), lezr, B. *Nynsus warnethe croghen*, there is no skin upon them, P.C. 2686.

THE SKIN OF THE LEG. Cleskber, B.

SKINNED, *adj.* Pelys, M. 3418. *Gavcr pelys*, a skinned goat, M. 3418.

SKIP or JUMP, *s.* Lanherch, B.

SKIP, TO SKIP ABOUT, *v.* Lemal, B. ; lemmel, lebmel, P.

SKIPPER FISH. Hallyhoc, D.

SKIPPING, *s.* Terlemel, M. 2100. *Us genés han terlemel*, that is with thee and the skipping, M. 2100.

SKIRT (or fringe of a garment), *s.* Pillen.

SKULKING, *s.* Scolchyé, w.

SKULL, *s* Penpral, w. ; pedn-pral, P. ; pral, crogen, grogen, w. ; croghen, groghen, P. ; grogon, M. 2994. *Yn y grogen*, into his skull, w.

THE SKULL OF A HORSE. Pen pral march, pedn pral marh, w.

SKY, *s.* Ayr, awyr, yêr, ebron, ybron, ebarn, ebbarn, ybbern, w.; yborn, néf. nêv, neve, P. *Yn ayr deth brús pup huny*, in the sky, at the judgment day, every one, P C. 1669. *Yn yêr wvrth agos yuggé*, in the sky, to judge you, P.C. 1333. *Yn creys a'n ebron avan*, in the midst of the sky above, O M. 38.

SKY-COLOURED, *adj.* Glâs, w.; glase, glaze, P.; glayis, lays, B.

SLAB or FLAT STONE, *s.* Lêch, lêh, w.

SLACK or SLOW, *adj.* Hêl, P.; lent, M. 3245. *Cowethe na vethen lent*, comrades let us not be slack, M. 245.

SLACK or LOOSE, *adj.* Lausq, P.

SLACKING, *s.* Dylly, P.

SLAG TIN, *s.* See TIN SLAG.

TO BE SLAIN, *v.* Cumma, cubma, w.; kubma, P. See SLAY.

SLAIN, *part.* Ledhys, w.; ledhaz, B.; lethys, lehys, P.

SLANDER, *v.* Sclandry, w.; scallyé, P.

SLANDERING, *s.* Mollethians, w.

SLAP, *s.* Stiran, stlap, w.; clout, R.D. 384. *Na'n geffo elout*, for getting a slap, R.D. 384. *Clout* and *scat*, for a slap or thump, are still in very frequent use.

SLAP, *v.* Lacé. w.; lâk, P. *Me a'th lâk*, I will lace (or slap) thee, w.

SLATE, *s.* (A slate or tile). Lehan, w.; lean, B.

SLATE-STONE. *s.* Mên-glâs, B.

SLATER, *s.* Tyor, w.; hellier, D.

SLATTERN, *s.* Slotteree, w. (*Slottery*, meaning dirty and sloppy, is a word in frequent use.) Tulky, tulgy, slummock, D.

SLAUGHTER, *s.* Ar, hâr, lâdh, lâdhva, w.

SLAVE, *s.* Caid, caeth, w.; caith, caid pinid, B.; vau, M. 3334. *Ty vav* (vau) *prag na ruste dre*, thou slave, why didst thou not, M. 3334.

SLAVERY, *s.* Caethiwed, B.; gwasanaeth. w.; guasanaeth, P.; habadin, w.

SLAY, *v.* Ladhé, w.; ladh, dho ladh, dho latha, P.

SLEDGES or TRUCKS, *s.* Slodys, w.

SLEDGE-HAMMER, *s.* Bôm, w.

SLEEP, *v.* Cescy, kesky, cysga, w.; kysga, B.; coscé, cuscé, w.; kusgé, cusgy, gusgy, P.; cusga, w.; kusga, goskaz, B. *Me ry goskaz*, I have slept, B.; sypposia, w., syppozia, P.

SLEEP, *s.* Cûsc, kûsg, w.; coske, B.; hûn, huyn, w.; wuin, P. *Yma hûn orth yv gryvye*, sleep is heavy on me, O.M. 1921.

A SHORT SLEEP or NAP. Sog, D.

SLEEPER, *s.* Cuscadur, w. *Cuscadur desimpit*, a continual sleeper, P.

SLEEPINESS, *s.* Entredés, P.; sog, B. *Sog* is often used for a nap or short sleep, D.

SLEEPING, *part.* Coské, B.

SLEEPLESS, *adj.* Difun, dyfun, dhyfun, dufun, w.

SLEEPY. *adj.* Heen, r; heene, B.

SLEPT AND SLEEP.

HE SLEPT. Goscés, a mutation of *cosgés*, 3 pers. s. pret. of *coscé*, to sleep, w.

THEY SLEPT. Guscens, a mutation of *cuscens*, 1 pers. pl. imperf. of *cuscy*, to sleep, w.

HE WILL SLEEP. Gosc, a mutation of *cosc*, 3 pers. s fut. of *coscé*, to sleep, w.

SLEEPING-ROOM, *s.* Cuscti, w.; cuscki, P.

SLEET, *s* Slag, D. The same word is used for misty rain.

SLEEVE, *s.* Stollof, brêchol, w.; brohal, B.

SLEEVED or HAVING SLEEVES. Brohalec, w.

SLENDER, *adj.* Edn, cûl, tanow, tanaw, w.; tanau, P.; muin, moin, moyn, môn, w. *Ha'y veen môn ha'y scorennow*, out of its slender top, and its branches, O M. 2444.

SLIDE, *v.* Slyntya, slyncya, w.; slyncha, P.

TO SLIDE AWAY, *v.* Redee, resec, resek, w.; rees, P.

SLIDING or A SLIPPING, *s.* Lam, w.

SLIGHT, *adj.* Iscawn. *Treviscaun*, a slight dwelling, B.

SLIM, *adj.* See SLENDER.

SLIME, *s* Loob, pol, poll, w.; pul, P.; teil tcyle, B.

TO STIR SLIME, *v.* Treloob, D. The tin dressers use the word *treloobing*, *i.e.*, stirring and washing the "slime tin," the ore being very fine like mud. This fine stuff the miners call *loobs*. See SLIME and SLUDGE.

SLINK, *v.* Slyncya, w.; slyncha, P.; slynckya, c.w. 913; slyntya, c.w. 924. *Hy slynckya war doer a heys*, and slink on (the) ground along, c.w. 913.

SLIP or STUMBLE, *v.* Sleppia, B.

SLIP or A SLIDE, *s.* Lam, w.

SLIP, *s.* (A slip of land). Kinin, B.

SLIPPER, *s.* Fosaneu, B.; wibanor, w. See SHOE.

SLIPPERS, *s.* Eskidieu, B. See SHOES.

SLIPPERY, *adj.* Glib, B.

SLOPE or INCLINE, *s.* Slintrim, D. From *slyntya*, to slide or glide along.

THE SLOPE OF A HILL. Bron, w.

SLOTHFUL, *adj.* Dioc, w.; diog, B.

SLOVEN, *s.* Casadow, R.D. 1781. *Plos casadow*, a dirty sloven, R.D. 1781; murrick, sproosen, D.

SLOVENLY, DIRTY, *adj.* Slotteré, B. A word still used.

SLOW, *adj.* Cosel, kozal, kazal, w.; ara, B.; sigyr, zigyr, w.; zighir, zigur, B.; hêl, w. *Ny gothe thy's bonès hêl*, thou oughtest not to be slow, O.M. 468.

SLOW, LAZY, *adj.* Dioc, w.; diog, B.

SLUDGE, *s.* Loob, w. See TO STIR SLIME, and SLIME.

SLUG or NAKED SNAIL, *s.* Melyen, molhuidhan, molhuidzhon, w.

SLUGGARD, *s.* Dioc, P.; dicreft, lodn, B. *Lodn an parnu*, such a sluggard, B.

SLUGGISH, *adj.* Cosel, kozal, dicreft, lôs, sigyr, zigyr, w.; zighir, zigur, B.; dioc, w.; thyek, M. 3360. *Boys mar thyek yth keuer*, for being so sluggish as regards thee, M. 3360.

SLUMBER, *s.* Glôs, P.; hûn, huyn, w.; huenneys, M. 4448. *Hyr ny vethe y huenneys*, long used not to be his slumber, M. 448.

SLUT, *s.* See SLOVEN.

SLY, *adj.* Câl, P.; kâl, B.

SMALL, *adj.* Bean, behan, byan, byhan, bian, bihan, bechan, beechan w.; beghan, B.; bichan, bychan, w.; bighan, biggan, P.; bochan, w.; boghan, B. Also their mutations into vean, vehan, vyan, vyhan, vian, &c. Menou, minow, menys, minis, minys, w.; minnis, venys, B.; munys, w.; grisill, B.

SMALLER, *adj.* Lê, w.; lea, P.; benna, bohatna, bohadna, B.

A SMALL PIECE or BIT. Temig, demig, temmig, w.; didgen, B.V. See BIT and PARTICLE.

A SMALL POCK. Gwenan, w.; guenan, P.

SMALL-POX, *s.* (The disease). Poccys minis, w.; pokkys miniz, B. Borlase also uses this term for measles.

SMART, *v.* Tegleué, tyn, prenna, P. *Pan clewyf vy an tán tyn*, when I shall feel the fire to smart, P. zukky, D.

SMART or SMARTING, *s.* Pêg, w.; peyn, beyn, feyn, B.

SMARTLY, *adv.* Yn tyn, P.

SMASH, *v.* Squardyé, squerdyé, w.; squerdya, P.

SMEAR or ANOINT, *v.* Uré, untyé, w. See ANOINT, *v.*

SMELL, *s.* (A smell). Flair, fleyr, w.; ffleyr, P.C. 1547; fleyryngy, sawor, sawarn, w.; savarn, B.; sauarn, P.

A BAD SMELL. Drôgsawarn, w.; drôg savarn, P.

SMELL, *v.* Clewas, clowas, clewés, w.; glewsyny, P.

TO SMELL STRONGLY. Flacraf, mâd, B.

SMELLING, *part.* Ow flerye, R.D. 171-2. *Ow flerye ov mousegy kepar ha kuen*, smelling, stinking, like to dogs, R.D. 171-2

SMELT, *s.* (A sand smelt). Guid, D.

SMITE or SMASH, *v.* Squattya, skuattia, scuattya, skuattya, sguattia, w.

SMITE or STRIKE, *v.* Gwyscy, gwyscel, gwescel, w.; guisky, guesga, P.

SMITH, *s.* Ferror, P.C. 2669; gôf, goff, w.; gofe, goffe. goyff, B.; gôv, gove, P. *Máp iosep an côth wás gôf*, son of Joseph the old smith fellow, P.C. 1695.

THE SMITH. Angove (*an gove*), P.

SMITHY, *s.* Gofail, govail, w.; gofadl, P.

SMOCK, *s.* Creis, crys, w.; kreis, krys, P.; hevis, hevez, w.; heuis, B.

SMOOTH, *adj.* Leven. *Pôr leven*, the smooth port, B.; spaven, B. *Spaven môr*, smooth sea, w.

SMOOTH or SLIPPERY, *adj.* Glib, B.

SMOOTH, *v.* Playnyé, O.M. 950. *Gorhel a blankos playnyys*, a ship of smoothed planks, O.M. 950.

SMOOTHNESS, *s.* Spaven, w.; spaueu, B.

SMOKE, *s.* Môc, môk, w.; môg, P.; moog, w.; woge, P.; voog, w.; veoge, C.W. 1093. *Yn tán yn môk*, in fire, in smoke, R.D. 1458.

SMOKE, TO MAKE SMOKE, *v.* Megi, w.; megy, P.

SMOTHER, *v.* Megi, w.; megy, P.

SMUDGE, STREAK, or BLURR, *s.* Strôm, D.

SMUT, THE SMUT IN CORN, *s.* Losc, losk, w.; collybran, colbran, D.

SNAIL, *s.* (The shell snail). Bulhorn, P. This word is still used. Also called *dodman* and *jan-jeak*, D.

A SMALL SNAIL. Sneg, D.

SNAIL or SLUG, *s.* See SLUG.

SNAKE, *s.* Aer, B.; gorthfel, w.; gorwfel, B.; nader, w.; nadar, naddyr, B.

SNAP. Knak, M. 1644. *Ha ny as láth knak oma*, and we will slay them here, snap, M. 1644.

SNAPPISH, *adj.* Toit, D.

SNARE, *s.* (Gin or springe). Maglen, w.

SNARE, *v.* Baghé, R.D. 1150. *Omma worth agan baghé*, here snaring (or trapping) for us, R.D. 1150.

SNARL, *v.* Scryncyé, skrynkyé, w. See also SCOWL, *v.*

SNEAK, *s.* (A sneak). Sevylliac, sevyllyak, w.

SNEER, TO SNEER AT, *v.* Dyalé, dyalas, dhyallas, P.

SNEEZE, *v.* Strihui, rahaya, B.

SNEEZING, *part.* Strihue, B.

SNIPE, *s.* Cio, w.; kio, P.; snît, w. *Snite* is still used.

JACK-SNIPE. Dame ku, D. Now called *hatter-flitter*.

SNIVEL or SNOT, *s.* Pûr, w.

SNIVELLY or SNOTTY, *adj.* Pûrica, P.

SNOOD, *s.* Snôd, w; nessel, D.

SNORE, *v.* Rencia, dho renkia, w.; renki, B.

SNORING, *s.* (A snoring). Rencias, w.

SNORING, *part.* Ronkye, renky, B.

SNORT, *v.* The same words as for SNORE, *q.v.*

SNORTING. *s.* and *part.* The same as for SNORING, *q.v.*

SNOT or SNIVEL, *s.* Pûr, w.

SNOTTY or SNIVELLY, *adj.* Pûrica, P.

SNOTTY-NOSED, *adj.* Goveric, w.

SNOTTY-NOSED FELLOW. Gûr-vurik, w.; goverick, P.

SNOW, *s.* Iach, w.; er, P.; err, irk, irch, B.; yrgh, M. 3055.

SNUFFERS, *s.* Gevel hoern, w.; guel hoern, P.

SNUFFER-PAN, *s.* Escop, w.

SO, *adv.* Andella, yn della, caman, camen, cammen, cetella, ketella. P.; kettella, N.; kettermen, cettermyn, ceverys. keverys, cefrys, kefrys. P. *Nep a wrella in ketella*, whoever has done so, O.M. 2240. *Yn ketella ny a vyn*, so we will, P.C. 213; mar, mor, w. *Mar da*, so good. Del, dell, tell, della, an della, andellan, ha, P.; tra, try, tro, w.

SO, AS. Ceceffrys, cefrys, cyffrys, cyfreys, keffryz, keheffrys, kevery, keverys, P.; cy, ky, w. *Ky gwêr vel an gwels*, as green as grass; maga, mal, avel, par, w.; perdel, pardel, pokara, pekar, P.; pycar, pykar, B.; pocar, pokar, w.; kara, P.; cara, w.

SO BE IT. Andella re bo, yn della re bo, w.; andel na re bo, andellarbo, P.

SO BIG. Maruthick (*mar uthick*), P.

SO FAR. Marbel, P.

SO GREAT. Cemmys, kemys, w.; kemyz, P.; kemmys, kymmis. kynnis (?), B.; cymmys, kymmys, cybmys. gemmys, gymmys, w.

SO HIGH. Mar uhel, w.

SO HUGE. Mar-uthick, P.

SO LONG. Marbel, P.

SO MANY. Cemys, kemys, w.; kemyz, P.; kemmys, kymmis, kynnis (?). B.; cymmys, kymmys, cybmys, gemmys, gymmys, cenefra. ceniver. keniver, cenifer, w.; kenifer, P.; kanifer, B.; cenyver, kenyver, kynyver, cenever, cyniver, w.

SO MUCH. Maga. cemmys, kemys, w.; kemyz, P.; kemmys, kymmis, kynnis (?), B.; cymmys, kymmys, cybmys, gemmys, gymmys, w.; kynnys (?), P.

SO MUCH AS. Mar, w.; mor, P.

SO THAT. Avel, mal, w.; awos, auoz, P.; caman, camen, cammen, ma, man (*ma-yn*), tra, tro, try, tre, dre, w

SOAK, *v.* Tempré, P.

SOAKING, *adj.* (With moisture). Sygan, B.

SOAP, *s.* Seban, tairnant, B.; seben, *Polwhele.*

SOCIETY, COMPANY, *s.* Cowethas, cowethe, w.; tyrguas, P.

SOCK, *s.* Paugen, wibanor, w.; vamp, D.

SOD, *s.* (A sod or turf). Cesan, w.; kezan, B.; *Pl.* Cesow kesow, w.

SOEVER. Penag, pynag, pennag, w.; ponag, P.; bennak, B.; bennag. w.

SOFT, *adj.* (Quiet, gentle). Cosel, kozal, w.; kuzal, cusual, B.

SOFT, *adj.* (Mollient. tender). Medhal, w ; medal, B.; meddal, medhel, w.; medel, M. 2979; methel, P.

SOFT AND SPRINGY, *adj.* (Like a pillow). Plum, D

SOFTEN, *v.* Plekgyé, R.D. 1849.

SOFTNESS, *s.* (Tenderness, mildness, gentleness). Medhalder, medalder, w.

SOFTLY, *adv.* (Quietly, gently). Cusual, P.

SOIL, *s.* (Ground). Doer, doar, dôr, oar (an oar), w.; dodnan, B.; tîr, tyr, w.

SOIL or EARTH, *s.* Pri, pry, bry, vry, w.; soul, P.

SOJOURNER, *s.* Travedig-doer, B.

SOLD, *part.* Caeth. kaeth, B.

SOLDIER, *s.* Cadwur. w.; cadwyr, B.; cadgur, P.; caduit, adletha, B.; smat, w.

SOLDIERS, *s.* Marogyon, maregyon, varogyon, w. These are the plurals of the Cornish for horsemen rather than of foot soldiers.

SOLE. ALONE, *adj.* Ednac, w.

SOLE. *s.* (Of the foot). Plans, B.; goden, golas trûs. w.; golaz truz. goden truit, B.; goden trût, P.

SOLICIT, DO, or PROCURE, *v.* Pryvia, w.

SOLICITOUS, *adj.* Prederys pryderys, priderys, w.; brederys, brederez, P

SOLICITUDE, *s.* Preder, pryder, w.; pridar, P.

SOLITARY, *adj.* Gwedho, w.; guedho, P.; guedeu, w.

SOME, *adj.* Nêp, nêp, re. *Re erell*, some others, w.; towl, B

SOME ONE. Nebyn, w.; gonon, dag, P.

SOME PORTION. Nebés, w.; nebaz, P.

SOMETHING, *s.* Neppêth, nep-peyth. w.; nepith, R.D. 769; nepyth, nebas, B.; nebtra (*neb-tra*). w.

A SOMETHING. Pêth, peyth, pyth, w. *Pl.* Pêthow.

SOME TIME AGO. Solathêth, R.D. 1929; solathyth, O.M. 2612; sollathyth, R.D. 2380; solabrys, O.M. 2322; solabreys, O.M. 2747; sollabreys, P.C. 746; sollebreys, M. 1845.

SOMETIMES. Arurou. w. ; neppêth. nepyth, nebas, B. ; trefêth. trevyth, P.

SOMEWHAT, *s.* Nep-peyth, nebés, w. ; nabaz, P.

SOMEWHAT, *adv.* Re. P.

SOMNOLENCE, *s.* Huenneys. M. 4448. *Hyr ny vethe huenneys,* long used not to be his somnolence, M. 4448.

SON, *s.* Mâb, w. ; mabe, c.w. 9; mâp, vâb, vâp, maw, vâw, w. ; vaow, P. *Pl.* Meyb, meib, mebion, mebyon, mebbion, mybion. w. ; vybbyan, c.w. 1982.

THE ELDEST SON. Mâb cotha, P.

MY DEAREST SON. Ow mâp kevarwouth, P.

A FOSTER SON. Mâb meidrin, w.

A LITTLE SON. Meppig, w.

A SON-IN-LAW. Dôf, w. ; dor, P. ; els, B.

A SON-IN-LAW BY A FORMER WIFE or HUSBAND. Elsés, B.

THE SON OF EVIL Mâp gâl, P.

THE SON OF GOD. Map deu, N.

SONG, *s.* Cân, chân, gân, hân, w. ; cans, kans, karol, pîp, B. ; pusorn, R.D. 2353. *Aga hân kepar ha my,* their song like as mine, o.M. 310. *Ha ty tulfryk pen pusorn,* and thou Tulfric, the end of a song, R.D. 2353.

SONGSTER, *s.* Piphit, pibit, B.

SONGSTRESS, *s.* Canorés, w.

SOON, *adv.* Waré, warré, w. ; wharé, N. ; wharré, w. *Mey tewe an tán wharré,* that the fire may light soon. P.C. 1221; useys, w. ; uskys, P. ; yscys, w. ; yskys, B. ; uth, P. ; prest, scôn, w *Scôn allema,* soon from hence, P.C. 1100 ; skân, P. ; defry, deffry, dheffry, devry, dewhans, duwhans, dywhans, dyhons, dhyhons, dhydhuans, w. ; dyhuanz, in nanz, P. ; innanz, B.

SO SOON. Mar scôn, P.

SOOT, *s.* Filgedh, filgeth, w.

SOOTHSAYER, *s.* Cuillioc, w. ; chuilliog, P.

A FEMALE SOOTHSAYER Cuilliogés, w ; chuilliogés, P. ; kuiogés (?), B.

SORCERER, *s.* Hudor, R.D. 1854; huder, w. *Lauar thy'n marsos huder,* tell us if thou art a sorcerer, R.D. 1831 ; hudol, nudol, B. ; purceniat, purkeniat, purcheniat, pystryor, pystryour, w. ; pystrior, pestrior, P.

SORCERER or SORCERESS, *s.* Poddrac, w. ; podrak, B.

SORCERESS, *s.* Pystriorés, pestryorés, pestriorés, poddrac, w. ; podrak, B.

SORCERY, *s.* Pystry, pystyc, pystyk, w. *Dén fyth ol murs dre pystry,* any man, unless through sorcery, P.C 1765.

SORE, *s.* Podreth, w. ; plûs, P.

SORES, *s.* Potredhés. bodredhés, w. ; bodrethés, P.

SORE or PAINFUL, *adj* Clâf, clâv, w. ; klâf, clêf, clevas, clevys, B.

SORROW, *s.* Ancen, anken, ancow, w. ; ankow, ancou, ancouyns, B ; ancrés, P. ; awher, w. ; awer, M. 195; bearn, bern, vern, cothys, cûth, cueth, kueth, gueth, w. ; cavow, cafow, (? if plural) w. It is *cavow,* as a plural c.w. 1243 *Ha gas cavow tha wandra,* and leave sorrows to wander. Dhôg, dar, P. ; edrec, edrek, w ; edrak, P. ; eddreck, w. ; eddrak, B. ; edrege, P. ; yddrac, w ; yddrage, yddraga, P. *Cothys of yn edrek brâs,* fallen I am into great sorrow, P.C. 1440 ; dewon, w. *Awos lavur na d.won,* because of labour nor sorrow o.M. 2405 ; duon, dowon, P. ; duwon, dewan, dewhan duwhan, w. ; duan, P. ; dhuan, duchan, w. ; thwan, P. ; galar, w *Ov eothaf lues galar,* suffering much sorrow, o.M. 633 ; gew, wew, wêr, P. *A vam whek na porth a wér,* oh mother sweet, bear not sorrow, P ; govid, govis, govys, layne, P. ; mêth, B ; moreth, w. *Gans moreth ythof lynwys,* with sorrow I am filled, o.M. 2194 ; morath, c.w. 177 ; panveter, panvotter, poan, B ; tristys, trystys, tristyys, tristans, tristyns, trystyns w. *Neffre trystyns ny gen byth,* never is sorrow with us, P.C. 731 ; vêth, vidn, vorêth, B. ; wryth, whêr, w. ; whear, P.

SORROW! SAD! SAD! Govy, tru, tru!, *or,* Gony, tru, tru !

SORROWFUL, *adj.* Cuthys, w. ; kuef, gweff, P. ; morethek, morethec, vorethec, ryth, trest, trist, w. ; trewesy, trewisy, trewysy, trowesy, trauethak, trys, trûs, P.

SORROWS, *s.* Govidzion, B. ; govegyon, N. : govygyon, R.D. 1154. *Râk mur yv ow govygyon,* for great are my sorrows, R D. 1154. See SORROW, to guide in forming other plurals

SORRY, *adj.* Edrak, P. ; drôk, M. 909. *D.ôk yv gena,* sorry am I. M. 909 ; kneff, B. ; drewyth, o.M. 256. *Re sorras drewyth benen,* a sorry woman hath angered, o.M. 256.

A SORRY or MEAN FELLOW. Guaeldgu, boudhyn. See RASCAL.

SORT, MANNER or WAY, *s.* Côr, w

SORT or KIND, *s.* Echen, ehen, hechen, hehen, w. ; ehin, P. ; ehan, eghen, B. ; pâr, riw, riu, w. *Nem riu guerras,* some sort of help w. ; tro, w.

SORTS, *s.* Sortowe. *Gans prevas a bub sortowe,* with worms of all sorts, c.w. 111. This is an instance of a Celtic Cornish plural for an English word.

SOUL, *s.* Enef, enav, w. ; enaff, B. ; ené. w. ; ena, P. *Rum ené,* by my soul, M. 3262. *Kymmer,* mercy, *a'm enef,* have mercy on my soul, o.M. 3722.

SOULS, *s.* Enefow, w. ; enevou, B. ; enevow, N. ; anevou, P. (enaff, M. 4164). *Lues enaff,* many souls (*sic.* Stokes). Enaff is properly singular, and the idiomatic form would seem to be "many a soul" and not "many souls."

SOUND, HEALTHY, *adj.* Iach, yach, w.; yagh, P.; yakh, B. *Certan yagh ens aga ieyw*, certainly sound were their sinews, P.C. 2681; saw. w.; sau, zehés. P.

TO MAKE SOUND, TO HEAL, *v.* Iaché, yaché, w.; yaghy. yehés, P.; sawyé, w.

SOUND, *s.* (A sound or noise). Lêf, sôn, w. *The wruthyl crothval na sôn*, to make a complaint nor a sound, O.M 1836.

A LOW SOUND. Hanas, w.

A LOW, MONOTONOUS SOUND or HUM. Drilsy, drilgy, D.

SOUNDING, *s.* (Hooting). Idzhek, P.

SOUNDNESS, *s.* As of health). Iachés, iechés, w.

SOUP, *s.* Ligge, B.V. See also BROTH.

SOUR, *adj.* Trenc, w.

SOUR MILK. Leath cowlés, w.

SOURCE, *s.* Krên, B.

SOURCE or HEAD, *s.* Mannen, B.

THE SOUTH, *s.* Dychow, dyhow, dyow, w.; dyhou, dyghou, P.; dehou, w.

SOUTHERNWOOD, *s.* (Herb). Dehoulés, w.

SOVEREIGN, *s.* (Ruler, king). Mychtern, w.; migterne, P.; megtern, mighterne, myhtern, B.; mytern. materyn, matern, ruif, rêv, ruy, brentyn, bryntyn, w.; vicker, P.; sefryn, O.M. 2189.

SOVEREIGNTY, *s.* Mychternés, mychterneth, myhterneth, w.; myghterneth, R.D. 712; myterneth, vychterneth, w.

SOW, *s.* Baneu, w.; haneu, B.; guyz, wys, B.; guis, guys, w.; hôch, bôh, plôs. *Plôs* is rather the name of a dirty person. *Guis*, for a old sow which has had a large family, is a word still in use.

SOW, *v.* Gonys, gynés, w.; gynez, gunio, B. *Gunnés ház*, to sow seed, B.; wonys, O.M. 414. *The balés ha the wonys*, to dig and to sow, O.M. 414; wreha, w.; ureha, uteha, B.

SOWER, *s.* Gynnadar, w.; gynnodar, B.; gynnadwar, P.

SPACE, SPOT, PLACE, SITUATION, *s.* Le, w.; li, lu, leh, ley, P.; mân, w.

A SPACE, *s.* Spâs, speyes, spys, speys, P. *Guragueres thy'm a ver spás*, do help to me in a short space. R.D. 1721; lâm, w. *Caym ny lettys saw vn lâm*, Cain, I stopped only a space, O.M. 470; pols, prys, preys, prês, prez, pryweth, tranc, trank. These words refer to a space of time. Perhaps some of them had a more extended meaning.

A SMALL SPACE or CORNER, *s.* Sorn, w.

SPACIOUS, *adj.* Ledan, w.

SPADE, *s.* Pâl, w.; paal, B.; bâl, w.; baal, B.; fâl, w.; faal, B.; rêv, w.

SPARE, *v.* Sparria, dho, sparria, P.

SPARE or FORBEAR, *v.* Spiena, P.

SPARING, *adj.* (Frugal). Henbidiat, henbidhiat, w.

SPARING, *adj.* (Scant). Scent, skent, w.; scant, B.

SPARK, *s.* Elven, B; gurychonen, grychonen, w.; gryghonen, P.C. 2717.

SPARKS, *s.* Gwrychon, grychon, w.; guryghon, P.C. 2101.

SPARROW, *s.* Golvan, gulvan, gylvan, w.; guennol, guenbol, P.

SPAR-THATCHED, *adj.* Eage, B. This is a rough mode of thatching stacks of corn, hay, firewood, &c., and also outhouses. A *spar* or *sparrow* is a wooden pin or peg used to fix the straw ropes to the thatch.

SPATTERDASHES, *s.* Poltrigas, B.

SPATTLE, *s.* Lo. *Pl.* Lew. Also SPOON, *q.v.*

SPEAK, *v.* Cows, w.; cous, tho cous, P.; dho kowz, B; dhe cousa, P.; caws, gows, cewsel, kewsel, cusel, w.; keusel, P.; cousall, C.W. 557; gewsel, geusel, w.; gewsy, gowsy, P.; gwesys, clapier. *Elo why clapier Kernuok?* Can you speak Cornish?; laol, lavary, leverel, dysmegy, dysmygy, desmygy, w.

SPOKEN, *part.* Cowsys, cawsys, cewsys, gewsys, w.

I SPAKE. Gowsyn, B.

YE HAVE SPOKEN. Laversough, B.

THOU WILT SPEAK. Gewsyth, gewsy. Mutations of *cewsyth* and *cewsy*, 2 pers. s. fut. of *cewsel*, to speak, w.

HE WILL SPEAK. Gews, a mutation of *cews*, 3 pers. s. fut. of *cewsel*, to speak, w.

YE WILL SPEAK. Gewseuch, a mutation of *cewseuch*, 2 pers. pl. fut. of *cewsel*, to speak, w.

THEY SHALL SPEAK. Gewsons, a mutation of *cewsons*, 3 pers. pl. fut. of *cewsel*, to speak, w.

SPEAK, SPEAK THOU. Couz, leverell, B.

HE MAY SPEAK. Gowsé, a mutation of *cowsé*, 3 pers. s. fut. of *cows*, to speak, w. Also written *gowso*, w.

SPEAKER, *s.* Leveriat, dadloyer, dathluur, w.; dadloyar, datheluur, P.; satheluar, B.; pregowther, progouther, progowther, progathar, P.

A SPEAKER OF TRUTH. Guirleveriat, w.

SPEAR, *s.* Giu, P.C. 3010; gyw, giw, gew, guw, w.; geu, gu, P.; gwayw, w.; ynn, onn, B. (? *yuu, ouu*); ber, ver, w.

A THREE PRONGED FISH SPEAR. Grail, D.

SPECIAL. Speal. *Ha speal brás*, and special great, or intimate.

SPECIES, *s.* Kunda, o.m. 989. *A bub eghen a kunda*, of all sorts of species, o.m. 989. See KIND.

SPECKLE or PIMPLE, *s.* Cyriac, kyriak, w.

SPECKLED or PIED, *adj.* Brith, w. ; bryth, b. ; bruit, specciar, w. ; spekkiar, p.

SPEECH or DISCOURSE, *s.* Cows, w. ; couz, kouz, b. ; cous, p.c. 1345. *Ru'm fay guyn yv agas cous*, by my faith, true is your speech, p.c. 1345 ; cews, gows, w. ; gowz, b. ; gews, cowms, w. ; koums, b. ; cowsys, cowsés, gowsys, w. ; gonsa (? gousa), ganso (? gauso), p. ; lavar, w.

A SPEECH, *s.* Areth, w. *Uthyk mar yv the areth*, very loud is thy speech, p.c. 954 ; leverel, w. ; progath, pregoth, b.

SPEECH, TALK, REPORT, *s.* Sôn, w.

SPEECHES, *s.* Cowsesow, gowsesow, w.

SPEECHLESS, *adj.* Avlavar, a flavar, w. ; anlavar, b.

TO SPEED WELL, *v.* Spedyé, b.

SPEED, *v.* Tewyé, p.

WITH SPEED. Mathen, p.

GREAT SPEED. Touth brâs, p.c. 660.

SPEEDILY, *adv.* Uscys, yscys, fâst, w. ; fastsens, b. ; warnot, p. *Dun ganso the dre warnot*, come with him home speedily, o.m. 559 ; toth-da, touthda, n.

SPENT or WASTED, *part.* Spendys, spengas, b.

SPENT or JADED, *adj.* Squyth, scith, b. ; skith, b.

SPEW, *v.* Hweda, hwedzha, w. ; huedzha, p.

SPHERE, *s.* (Orb). Pêl, pellan, w.

SPICED, *adj.* Pymeth, o.m. 2294. *Kens môs eyf ten guyn pymeth*, before going drink a draught of spiced wine, o.m. 2294.

SPIDER, *s.* Huilan, b. Borlase also gives this name for a beetle.

SPIKE, *s.* Ebil. b. ; center, kenter, w. ; kentar, p. ; genter, w. *Pl.* Centrow, kentrow, w.

SPIKED or TUFTED, *adj.* Tushoc, dushoc, w.

SPILL, *v.* Colli, celli, scollyé, scullyé, w. ; scullya, c.w. 2522 ; scoad, scud, d.

SPILT. Venons, b.

SPIN, *v.* Nedhé, w. ; nethé, nedha, p. ; netha, c.w. 975 ; nyddu, *Polwhele*. *The wrek genés the nethé*, thy wife with thee to spin, o.m. 346.

SPINDLE, *s.* Guerfyn, gurthyl, guerzit, kerdhit, b. ; gurthit, p. ; kiggal, d.

SPINDLE-WHEEL, *s.* Rozellen, w.

SPINES, *s.* Dreyn, p.c. 2119.

SPIRE or STEEPLE, *s.* Pele, p. ; peal, b.

SPIRIT, *s.* (*L'esprit*). Gwyns, gwens, gwins, guenz, guinz, b.

SPIRIT, *s.* (Ghost), Speris, spyrys, w. ; spiriz, p. ; sprite, spyr, b.

A MINE SPIRIT or PHANTOM, *s.* Gathorn, d.

SPIT, *s.* (For roasting). Ber, ver, w.

SPIT, *v.* Trewy, trewé, trué, treffia, w. ; shyndyz, p. *Shyndys of gans eornek du*, I am spit upon by a black toad, o.m. 1778.

SPITE, *v.* Dystpyté, dhyspptyé, w. ; speitia, dho speitia, p.

SPITE, *s.* Ate, b. *Mar ate*, so much spite, b. ; aui, avey, w. ; avey, p. ; despyth, dyspyth, w. ; dyspyt, p. ; drôgbres, mican, mikan, w.

SPITTED ON, *part.* Trewé, treefa's, drewys, b.

SPITTING, *part.* Trifiaz, b.

SPITTLE, *s.* Trifias, w. ; trifiaz, b.

SPLASH, *v.* Laggen, b.v. It refers to splashing the water in sea-fishing.

SPLAY, *adj.* Splat, plat, blat, w.

SPLAY-FOOTED, *adj.* Trûz blat, trûz splat, w.

SPLEEN, *s.* (Splen, *Lat.*) Lewilloit, leuilloit, b. ; vam, vabm, w. ; yvabm, b.

SPLENDID, *adj.* Splan, spladn, w.

SPLENDOUR, *s.* Splander, w. ; splandor, p. ; golowder, goleuder, b.

SPLIT, *v.* Fallia, w. ; fellia, feldzha, b.

SPOIL, *v.* Anglod, b.

SPOIL, *v.* (Rob). Robbia, p.

SPOILED, *part.* Distryppas, b.

SPOKEN OF, SPREAD ABROAD. Travethlys, w.

SPONGE, *s.* Spong, b.

SPOON, *s.* Lo, w. ; loe, b.

SPOONS. Lew, w. ; leu, p.

SPORT, *v.* (To play). Gwary, gwaré, guaré, huaré, b.

SPORT or PLAY, *s.* Choary. *Pl.* Choarion, w.

IN SPORT or IN FUN. Yn gês, b.

SPOT, *v.* Anglod, b.

SPOT or BLEMISH, *s.* Anav, b.

SPOT, MOLE, or FRECKLE, *s.* Taish, w.

SPOT, PLACE, or SITUATION, *s.* Le, w. ; li, ly, lêh, lu, p. ; man, w.

SPOT OF SAND. Drethan, drethen, b. See SANDS.

SPOTTED, *adj.* Specciar, w. ; spekkiar, p. See SPECKLED.

SPOTLESS, CHASTE, *adj.* Dianaff, b.

SPOUSE, *s.* (A married person). Cespar, pries, bries, fries, pryes, bryes, vryes, pryas, w. ; bryas, c.w. 886 ; freas, c.w. 1227. *Ha tollé the bryas lên*, and deceived thy faithful spouse, o.m. 294.

SPREAD, v. Lesé, w.

SPREAD ABROAD. Unlés (*un-les*), P.

SPREAD ABROAD, SPOKEN OF. Trevethlys, w.,

SPRING, *s.* (The season of spring). Guaintoin guainten, gwainten, P.

SPRING, *s.* (Of water) Fenten, funten, fvntan, krên, B.; venton.

SPRING, SOURCE, or HEAD, *s.* Mamen, B.

SPRING-WATER, *s.* Strêt, B.

A FRESH SPRING. Strêth, strêth, streyth, w.

SPRINGE or SPRINGLE, *s.* Croccan, w.; crockan, P.; maglen, w.

SPRINGY AND SOFT, *adj.* (Like a pillow). Plum, D.

SPROUTS or SUCKERS, *s.* (Of plants, &c.) Lyuorchguydh, B.

SPURIOUS, *adj.* Basa, P.

SPY, *v.* Aspyé, w.

SQUARE or CUBE, *s.* (As of granite). Kam, C. S. Gilbert.

SQUAT, *v.* Plattya, w.

SQUEEZE, *v.* Guasga, guryn, gurydn, P.

SQUEEZED, *part.* Guridnias, P.

SQUINT-EYED, *adj.* Cam, camlagadec, cabmlagadzhac, w.

SQUIRT or SYRINGE, *s.* Skit, skeet, D.

STAB, *s.* Gwân, w.

STAB, *v.* Gwané, w.; guainé, P.

TO STAB ONE'S SELF. Ymwané, w.

STABBED, *part.* Gwenys, w.; guenyz, guinys, B.; gwynys, w.

STABLE-LOFT, *s.* Tallet, D.

STACK, *s.* (Of corn). Bern, w.

STAFF or POLE, *s.* Baz, P.; fust, vust, lorch, lôr, w.; lorgh, P.C. 914.

STAG, *s.* Carow, P.; karow, O.M 126; carau, karo, caro, P. *Gaver ywegés karow*, goat, steer, stag, O.M. 126. *Pl.* Carew, P.

STAGE, STAGE OF BOARDS IN A MINE, *s.* Astull, soler. saller, w. These words are still used by miners, and also *shammel. Soller, saller* also mean an entry, a ground room, and also a gallery, D.

STAGGER or RAMBLE, *v.* Rambla, P.

STAGNANT WATER. Pol, w.; polan, as a diminutive, w.

STAGNATED, *part.* Crunnys, crummys, B.

STAIR or STEP, *s.* Grât, w.

STAKE or POST, *s.* Kundura, peul, B. (In the Armoric language. *peulia*, to round with stakes); sticedn, w.; stikedn, B.

STAKE, THE LAST STAKE, LAST PENNY, *s.* Ligan, B. In the Cornish dialect a penniless person is said to be *penniligan.*

STALK or STEM, *s.* Gwelen. gwailen (*Pl.* Gwail), w.; koilen, coilen, kuilan, korsen, corsen, gorsen, P.; iar, w.; i'ar, P.

STAMMERER, *s.* Stlaf, w.; crêg, P.; bloesy, B.

STAND. *v.* Sevel, w.; seval, zeval, B.; saval, syvel, w.; sêf. sewel, syuel, P. *Worthyn ny sef*, to stand before us. R.D. 1790.

HE HAD STOOD. Safé, saffé, 3 pers. s plup. of *sevel*, to stand, w.

HE SHALL STAND. Sêf, 3 pers. s. fut. of *sevel*, to stand. Seyf, another form of *séf*, w.

STAND THOU. Sâf, 2 pers. s. imp. of *sevel*, to stand. Also written *sâv* and *sâ*, w.

STAND UP. Sâv. B.; sâv a man, P.; sâf yn ban, P.C. 2240; ga ban, P.

STAND. Ga, P.

STAND or STANDING, *s.* Sâf, w.; saff, M. 3966; saeff, M. 4460. *Vn dên the gerthês ay saff*, one man to go from his standing, M. 3966; trig, D.

STANDING, *adj.* Saval, w.

STANDING CORN. Is saval. w.; yz saval, P Corn as it stood in the field, *i.e.*, standing corn was simply called corn or the corn, in Cornish, yd, yz. ys, iz, hit, P.

STANDING-PLACE, *s.* Stons, w.; trig (? *trigva*), D.

A STANDING POOL, *s.* Merthyn, sagen, B.

STANDING WATER. Lo, lin, lyn, w.

STAR, *s.* Steren, sterran, w.

STARS, *s.* Stêr, steyr, w.; steare, C.W. 102; steryan, w.; sterrian, P.; stergan, O M. 36. *An houl ha'n lôr ha'n stergan*, the sun, the moon, and the stars, O.M. 36.

A BLAZING STAR. Sterran leski, P.

A WANDERING STAR. Sterran gwandré, w.

STARE, TO STARE ABOUT. *v.* Gaké. geké, D.

STARLING, *s.* Troden, trodzhan. w.; stare, D.

STARLINGS, *s.* Edhnou brodzhan, B (? *trodzhan*).

START, *s.* (As from surprise). Plynch, w. *Môs the kuthé war vn plynch*, go to hide at a start, P.C. 1004.

START, *v.* Plynchyé, w.

STATE, CONDITION, *s.* Chêr, P. *May thyw lemmyn da ow chêr*, that my state now is good R.D. 501.

STATE, DEGREE, RANK, *s.* Pryckna, pruckna, P.

STAVES, *s.* Battys, w.; battyz, P.; battiz, B.; fustow, P.C. 1172. *Gans fustow ha clythythow*, with staves and swords, P.C. 1172. *Gans battys ha clythythow*, with staves and swords, P.C. 608.

STAY or GROUND, *s.* Crêvder, w.; krêvder, P.

STAY or DELAY, *v.* Hethy, P.

STAY or SUPPORT, *s.* Gew, P.

STAYS or PROPS, *s.* Stanconnou, B.

STAY or PROP, *v.* Stanconni, B.; trig, D.

STAY or TARRY, *v.* Gortés, gortez, P.; gortos, cortés, w.; kortez, B.; cortez, cortus, kortez, kyrtoz. P.; wortos, w.; wonnen, P.; streché, strechyé, w.; streuha, strelha, P. *My ny garaf streché pel,* I do not like to stay long, RD. 2249. The phrase "straking along," for sauntering, is often used in Cornwall.

STAY, ABIDE, or DWELL, *v.* Trega, tregé, triga, trigé, trigia, dregé, w.; trussen, P.

HE STAYED. Drigas, a mutation of *trigas,* 3 pers. s. preterite of *triga,* to stay, abide, or dwell, w.

HE WILL STAY. Dric, a mutation of *tric,* 3 pers. s. fut. of *triga,* to stay, abide, or dwell, w.

HE WILL STAY or TARRY. Worto, a mutation of *gorto,* 3 pers. s. fut. of *gortos,* to stay or tarry, w.

STEAD, PLACE, SITUATION, *s.* Le, w.; li, ly, leh, lu, P.

STEADFAST, *adj.* Thyasseth, B.; thyaseth, spernas, P.; spernabyll, spernafyll, B.

STEADY or STEADFAST, *adj.* See STEADFAST.

STEAL, *v.* Ladra, laddré, w.; lyttry, P.; porogga, B.; kibbin, B.V. For more see ROB, *v.* Among the miners, to steal ore, is to *kitt.*

THOU MAYEST STEAL. Lyttry, 2 pers. s. subj of *ladra,* to steal, w.

TO STEAL MARBLES. Strakye, D.

STEEL, *s.* Metol (also any metal), w.; mael (metaphorically), by mutation *vael. Tégvael,* fairly armed. *Mael,* armour, B.

STEEL-YARD, *s.* Ancell, P.

STEEPLE, *s.* See SPIRE.

STEER, *s.* Denewoit, w.; denevoit. P.; dunuvés, B.; lodn, ywegés, w. *Gaver, ywegés, karow,* goat, steer, stag, o M. 126.

STEERSMAN, *s.* Leuuit, lewyidh, lewiader, w.; leuiader, leuint, brenniat, P.; brennyat, B.

STEM, *s.* (See STALK for other forms). Sâf, w. *Pup qvethen tefyns a'n sâf,* let every tree grow from its stem, O.M. 29; boncyff, B.; blyn, O.M. 779. *Nynsese a'n blyn the'n ben,* there was none from the stem to the head, O.M. 779.

A DRIED BRITTLE STEM. Kiskey, D.

STENCH, *s.* See SMELL.

STEP, *s.* Grât, gry, P. *Dydryk gry,* nor stop a step, P.; cam, w.

STEP, *v.* Lammé, lemmel, w.; lamma, garras, P.

STEP-FATHER, *s.* Altrou, w.

STEPMOTHER, *s.* Altruan, w.

STEP-SON, *s.* Els, w. Pryce says, a son-in-law.

STEP-DAUGHTER, *s.* Elsés. Pryce says, a step-son (?).

STERILITY, *s.* (As of women). Anvabat, w.

STERN, *s.* (As of a ship). Airos, w.

STEW, *s.* (One of meat and potatoes). Scabby-gullion, scabby-gulyun, chod, D.

STEWARD, *s.* Maerbuit, w.

STEWING, *s.* Codnor, D.

STICK, *v.* (To stick to, to adhere). Glené, gleny, glyné, w.; glenaz, dho glenys, sesé, P.

STICK, *s.* (A stick). Bach, bagl, B.; polyn. B.V.

A STICK or PIECE OF WOOD. Prennyer, prenyer, P.

STICKS or PIECES OF WOOD. Prynner, prynnyer, w. *Prynnyer derow ov trehy,* cutting oak sticks, O.M. 1010.

A CROOKED or KNOBBED STICK. Pollet, polleck, W.F.P. polyn, D.

A ROTTEN STICK. Kiskey, B.V. The Cornish call a withered old man " a kiskey of a man."

STICKLEBACK, *s.* Bulgranade, bulgranack, D.

STIFF, *adj.* Glew, gleu, P.; serth, w. *May th'entre an spikys serth,* that the stiff spines may enter, P.C. 2140.

STIFFLY, *adv.* Thyfflas, P.; yeinder, B.

STIFLE, *v.* Megi, w.; megy P.; taga, w.; tagou, B.

STIFLED, *part.* Stoath, B.

STIGMATIZED, *part.* Omskemynés, P.

STILL, *adv.* Whâth, whêth, w.; whât, P. *Del vs an yethewon whêth,* as the Jews are still, R.D. 2406; prest, C.W. 1482. *Yma ef prest ow pewa,* he is still living. C.W. 1482.

STILLNESS, *s.* Callamingi, w.; kallamingi, P.; kallaminghi, B.

STING, *s.* (Of a bee). Côl, colin, conyn, B. Brôs, w. These mean the point which stings.

STING, *s.* (As by an insect). Gwân, w.; guan, B.

STING, *v.* Gueny, P.; brouda, B.; piga, w.; tardha, B.

STING-FISH, *s.* Calcar, D.

STINK, *s.* Drôgsawarn, w.; drôg-savarn, P.; flair, fleyr, fleyryngy, w

STINK, *v.* Fleryé, fleyryé, w.; flery, dho flery, P.; mousegy, w.

STINKARD, *s.* Fleryys, w.; podren, M. 3323. *Pendra leuer an podren,* what does the stinkard say? M. 3323.

STINKING, *adj.* Flerys, w.; flayrys, C.W. 2248; leudic, w.; leudik, P.; mechiec, w.; mechiek, B.;

mekiek, musac, P.; mouzak, B.; mosek, M. 2131; podrethek, M, 3061.

A STINKING FELLOW.   Plôs fleryys, P.   See STINKARD.

A STINKING WEED.   Plôs fleryys, P.

STIPEND, s.   Gober, w.; gobr, P.; gobar, gobyr, w.; gubar, gu, guu. P.

STIR or START. v.   Plynchyé, w.

STIR UP or EXCITE, v.   Desethy, w.; proyeha, P. (? proryeha).

STIRABOUT, HASTY-PUDDING, s.   Iot, (yot), w.

STIRRED or MOVED, part.   Gozez, P.

STIRRED UP, part.   Dyrguys, P.; dyrgwys, yttervis, B.

STIRRING, A STIRRING, s.   Comiska, P.

STIRRUP-CUP, s.   Dash-an-darras, D.

STOCK, s.   (Of a tree).   Stoc, w.

STOCK, s.   (Of bees).   Mam guenyn, B.; mam gwenen, P.

STOCKING, s.   Hosan.   Pl. Hosaneu, w.; lodr, B. loder. w.   Pl. Lodrow, lydrow, w.; lydrou, B.; lydraw, w.; lydrau, B.; lydru, P.

STOLE, s.   (The garment).   Stôl, w.

STOLEN, part.   Ledrys, leddrys, ledrés, w.; leddrez, B.   Po marh ledrés, when a horse is stolen, w.

STOLEN AWAY   Leddrez a kar, P.

STOMACH or MAW, s.   Glâs, w.; glayis, agan, B. The Cornish call the stomach of a pig agan.

STOMACH, APPETITE FOR FOOD, s.   Dyvotter, P.

STONE, s.   Maen, mân, mean, mên, w.; mein, vên, P.; carrag, carrac, w.; carak, carrik, garrik, P.; garrac, garag, w.   A very hard stone which will strike fire is called elvan.   Borlase says elven means a spark of fire.

STONES, s.   Meyn, w.; mein, B.; min, P.; myn, w.; myin, P.; myyn, w.; mystin, B.; vcyn, vyn, vyen, vyin, vyyn, P.

A STRATUM OF STONES CONTAINING TIN ORE.   Beuheyl, B.   Lit. A living stream.

STONE, THE STONE, s.   (The stone in the bladder). Mântedh, w.   Clevas y mantedh, the disease of the stone.

STONES, i.e., THE STONES, THE CIRCLE OF STONES, s.   Cerig, crig, crug, B.

STONE HEARTH, s.   Mênolas.   This name is still used by fishermen for a fire-place in a fishing boat. The hearth is made of clay and stones.   It is of a square form.   See HEARTH.

STONE-CUTTERS, s.   Trahesi-mein, w.; trahezimean, B.; trehesy-meyn, O.M. 2411; trahezi-mein, P.

STONE TRENCH.   Maengluadh, maengledh, B.

STONE WALL.   Fôs a vyin, w.; fôz a vyen, P.

STONY, adj.   Mansec, mansek, w.; meinek, meinig, B.; mynic, w.; meny, veney, P.

STONY PLACE.   Grambler D.   Ground or earth with many stones interspersed was called carne tyer. Hals.

STOODEST, THOU STOODEST UP.   Sefsys, 2 pers. preterite of sevel, to stand, q.v.

STOOL, s.   Scavel, scavell, w.; skaval, P.; skavall, c.w. 20; sgavel, P.

A THREE FOOTED STOOL.   Tribedh, trebath, w.

STOOP, TO STOOP DOWN, v.   Wetra, P.

STOOPED, part.   Wetras, B.

STOP, TO RETAIN, v.   Duethy, P.   Part.   Duedhaz, P.

STOP, TO STAND STILL, v.   Feeth, P.

STOP, TO HINDER, v.   Lettya, w.

STOP, TO STAY, v.   See STAY. v.

STOP, HOLD.   Sens, syns.   This exclamation is still made by the boys at Polperro in playing marbles, &c.   It is from sensy or synsy, to hold, q.v. D.

STORE or PLENTY, s.   Amal, B.

STORK, s.   Storc, w.; stork, P.

STORM, s.   Cewar, kuer, cuer, w.; keuar, aules, anauhel, P.; anavel, B.; hagar awel, haga auel, P.; hagaruel, guins a dro, B.

A HIGH STORM.   Aules ewhall, P.

A STORM OF RAIN.   Koust, B.   See SHOWER.

STORMY, adj.   Drychinog, tymbestlog, B.

STORY or TALE, s.   Daralla, whethel, whethl, hwitel, w.; huitel, B.; hwedhel, P.   The word widdles is often used, meaning whims, silly conceits, foolish tales.

A FALSE STORY.   Hwedhel gûac, w.

STOUT, VALIANT, RESOLUTE, adj.   Cadarn, w.; cadr, B.; glew, w.; barthesek, P.

STOUT, HEARTY, JOLLY, adj.   Calonec, w.; kalonek, P.; kalonnek, B.; kalonk, kelednek, kelednack, P.

STOUT AND SHORT.   (As of a man).   Durgy, dourgy, purgy, P.

STRAIT or CONFINED, adj.   Cûl, w.

STRAIT or ARM OF THE SEA, s.   Frôt, P.

STRAIGHT, adj.   Compos, w.; compas, c.w. 19; compés, w.; compez, B.; compys, cympés, kympez, w.   Ha compos y denwennow, and straight its rules, O.M. 2141.   Scôn worthe compas avith gwryés, forthwith shall be made straight, c.w. 19; ewn, ewen, w.; eun, P.; thyggyow, P.

STRAIGHT, *adv.* Sket. *Bys yn iherusalem sket*, even to Jerusalem straight, P.C. 1639.

STRAIGHT OVER. Poran wâr, B.

STRAIGHTWAY, *adv* Skòn, c w. 14.

STRAIGHTENED or MADE STRAIGHT, *part.* Ewnys, uynnas, w,

STRAIGHTER, *adj.* Compossé, w. *Compossé pren yn nep le*, a straighter tree in any place, O.M. 2577.

STRAIGHTLY, RIGHTLY, *adv.* Poran, w.

STRAIN, *v.* (As in a sieve). Sizla, B.

STRAIN or STRETCH, *v.* Dyscavylsy, dygavelsy, w.

STRAINER, *s.* Sizl, B.

STRAND, *s.* (Sea shore). Sian, zian, w. ; trig, D.

STRANGE, *adj.* Uncouth, w. ; voren, voran, P. ; shune, *Carew.*

STRANGE! *exclam.* Refaria! (*Lit.* By St. Mary). Rea! Rea, rea !, Rea suas !, Reve! (*rea reve*), w. ; Ria! A rea !, P. ; arear !, D.

STRANGER, *s.* Estren, w. ; ancouth, B. ; dên unchut, dên uncouth, pirgirin, w. ; pirgrin, P. ; pryeryn, w.

STRANGLE, *v.* Guadngyrti, B. ; taga, w. ; tagou, B.

STRANGLED, *part.* Tegés, w. ; teghez, B. ; tegez, tegys, P.

STRANGLING, *s.* Tâg, w. ; thage, P. ; ardac, w.

STRATUM, *s.* (Of alluvial tin ore). Beuheyle, P. ; benkyl, B.V.

STRATUM, *s.* (Of sandy earth and small stones). Cothan, D.

STRAW, *s.* (In the mass). Cala, w. ; kala, P. ; gala, w. *Ha cala lour war hy luer*, and straw enough on its floor, P.C. 680 ; gwells, gwels, guelz, w. ; gwyls, P. ; soul, B.

STRAW, *s.* (A single straw). Kala, B. ; cala, gala, w. ; gwehen, W.F.P.

A STRAW BED. Gwillé cala, P. ; kalagueli, B.

STRAWBERRY, *s.* Sevi, w. ; syvi, P. ; sivi, morankali, B ; moran cala, w.

A STREAK, SMUDGE, or BLURR, *s.* Strôm, D.

STREAKED, *adj.* Bryth, B. ; brith, bruit, w.

STREAM, *s.* Pûl, P. ; strêt, strêth, streyth, w. ; strêk, P. The *strake* in a china-clay work is the shallow and long pit for the *stream* of clay water passing along it. See RIVER.

A LIVING STREAM. Beuheyle, P. ; benkyl, B.V. This is a mining term and it means a rich layer of ore in a stream-work. See STRATUM.

STREET, *s.* Rew, ru, w. It also means a paved way.

STRENGTH, POWER, MIGHT, *s.* Crevder, w. ; krevder, P. ; creys, w. ; creis, creiz, P. ; crys, grys, greys, w. ; fas, fos, frêth, harth, P. ; haiarn, B. ; nell, nel, w. ; nerg, nerh, B. ; nerth, w. ; verth, P. ; sproil, sprawl, D.

STRENUOUS, *adj.* Mên, vên, fên, uthec, ithic, w. ; ithik, ithig, P

STRETCH, TO STRETCH OUT, *v.* Hedhés, hedhy, w. ; hedha, hethé, P. ; discavylsy. dyscavylsy, w. ; discavyssy, P. ; dygavelsy, ystyné, w.

STRETCHED, *adj.* Tên, tyn, w.

STRETCHED OUT, *part.* Discavylsys, w. ; stous, P.

A STRETCHED THING, WHAT IS STRETCHED. Tenewen, denewan, ternewan tornewan, tyrnewan, w. ; ternehuan, P.

STRETCHING, *s.* (Of the body). Cehedzhé, w. ; kehedzhé, P.

STRICT, *adj.* Fast, w.

STRIDE, *v.* Lamma, P. ; lammé, lemmel, w.

STRIDE or STEP, *s.* Lam, cam, w.

STRIFE, *s.* Bresel, bresell, bresul, bresyl, vresyl, strif, stryf, w. ; kynnen, B. ; errya, P.

A CAUSER OF STRIFE. Strifor, w.

STRIKE, *v.* Gwascel, guascel, gwiscel, gwescel, gwyscel, gwyskel, gwyscy, w. ; guisky, guesga, guasga, P. ; wyscel, w. ; wysk, P. ; fyscy, cnoucyé, knoukyé, cnakia, w. ; cnithio, B. ; cronkya, P. ; krongkia, gronkyé, B. ; groncyé, w. ; crunckia, B. ; dehesy, dhehesy, w. ; thehesy, P. ; terhi, caro, bluthyé, B. ; squattya, skuattia, scuattya, skuattya, sguattia, w.

THEY STRUCK. Wyskens, a mutation of *gwyscens*, 3 pers. pl. imperf. of *gwyscel*, to strike, w.

I WILL STRIKE. Wascaf, a mutation of *gwascaf*, 1 pers. s. fut. of *gwascel*, to strike, w.

HE WILL STRIKE. Wysc, a mutation of *gwysc*, 3 pers. s fut. of *gwyscel*, to strike, w.

TO STRIKE ONE'S SELF. Emwysca, w.

TO STRIKE A BLOW. Boxcusy, w.

TO STRIKE DOWN TO THE GROUND. Dho doulla a doar, P.

STRICKEN, *adj.* Guysketh, gweska, gwaska, B.

STRING or CORD, *s.* Linin, lovan, w. ; louan, P. ; corden, w. As a diminutive, Lovannan, w.

STRIP or STRIP OFF, *v.* Discy, dyscy, w, ; diski, P. ; digwisca, dygwysca, w. ; thyguisky, P.

STRIPPED, SPOILED, *part.* Distryppas, B.

STRIPT, *part.* (Script naked). Dygavelsys, w.

STRIPE, STROKE, or BLOW, *s.* Strôc, strocos, stlap, stlaf, stuan, B. See STROKE or BLOW.

STRIVE or CONTEND, *v.* Cencia, kennkia, w. ; kenkia, P. ; emdhal, omdhal, errya, w. ; gueskall, P. ; scorné, scornyé, strevyé, w. ; scranny, D.

STROIL, *s.* Pilm, B.

STROKE or BLOW, *s.* Bync, w.; bynk, p.; bank, B.; bom, bum, w.; pylt, strôc, strocos, stlap, stlaf, stuan, B. *Pl.* Strecis, strocosow, w.; strokosou, B.

STROKE BY STROKE. Tyshatas (*tys-ha-tas*), P.

STRONG, *adj.* Crêf, crêv, w.; krev, B.; crif, cryf, cryff, w.; creif, c.w. 116; creaf, c.w. 2749; greif, c.w. 423; frêth, hardh, cadarn, w.; cadr, B.; men, ven, fen, w.

STRONGER, *adj.* Creffa, M. 331.

STRONGLY, *adv.* Fest-yn-tyn, lasthe, p.; lasche, B.; in nyell, c.w. 2203.

FULL STRONGLY. Pur greyf, c.w. 720.

STRUCK or KNOCKED, *part.* Gwskys, wyskens, B.; gnacias, w. *Gnacias* is a mutation of *cnacias*, 3 pers. s. preter. of *cnacié*, id.qd. *cnoucyé*, to strike, w.

STRUGGLE, *v.* Daster, dastel, thassel, themloth, P.

STRUMPET, *s.* Druth, hora, P.

STUBBLE, *s.* Soul, zoul, w.; cala, B.

STUD or BOSS, *s.* Prumpl, B.

STUDIOUS, *adj.* Prederys, pryderys, priderys, brederys, w.; brederez, P.; ystig, B.

STUDY, *v.* Predery, predyry, prydery, prydyry, w.; prederi, pridiri, P.; madra, w.

STUDY, *s.* (A place to study in). Myfirion, B.

STUFF, MATTER, *s.* Gwyrras, P.

STUMBLE, *s.* Lam, w.

STUMBLE, *v.* Trebytchya, w.; sleppia, B. *Rdg dout why dho sleppia,* for fear you do stumble (or slip).

TO STUMBLE OVER, *v.* Treylé, trailia, P.

STUNG, *part.* Gwenys, gwynys, w.; guinys, guenyz, guenez, B.; gwenez, P.; gwinys, w. *Gwenez genadar* P.; *guenez, gen nadar,* B.; stung by an adder.

STUPID, *adj.* Talsoch, w,; talsokh, B.; taltoch, P.; pyst, bâd, w.; drazac, drazackin, droozlin, drumblin, zawkin, zawkemin, D.

A STUPID FELLOW Pen pyst, P.; droojy, D. See FOOL.

STUPIDITY, *s.* Gokyneth, N.; uindrau, P.; vindrau, B.

STUPIFIED, *part.* Omstumunys, P.

STUTTERER, *s.* Stlaf, w.; bloesy, B.; crêg, P.

STY, *s.* Crow, w.; crou, P.

STYE, *s.* (Abscess in the eyelid). Kennel, kennin, cannon, D.

STYLED or NAMED, *part.* Henyws, B.; henuelés, henuelez, P.

SUAVITY, *s.* Whecter, w.; whekter, B.

SUBDUE, *v.* Dova, w.; gorlené, worlené, P.

SUBJECT, OBEDIENT, *adj.* Gustyth, gostyth, gosteyth, w.

SUBSTANCE, *s.* Pêth, peyth, pyth w. *Pl.* Pethow.

SUBSTANCE, USE, MANNER, *s.* Defnydh, w.

SUBSTITUTE, *v.* Gorthrodhy, w.

SUBTLE, *adj.* Sotel, w.; fin, fyn, B.; fel, w.; cudnick, kydnik, P.; kudnik, B.

SUBTLE FELLOW. Guâs, gwâs, P.

SUBTLETY, *s.* Dewnos, deunos, w.; deuuos, duuos (?), deskans, P. *Dre y deunos,* by his subtlety, P.C. 20.

SUCCEED, *v.* Spedyé, B.

SUCH, *adj* Pocar, pokar, w.; pekar, P.; pycar, w.; pykar, B.; pocara, w.; pokara, P.; suel, sul, w.; pua, piua, P.

SUCHLIKE, *adj.* Parma, parna, P. See SUCH.

SUCK, *v.* Dena, dené, deny, tena, tené, w.; devona, devony, P.

SUCKED, *part.* Denys, tenys, B.

SUCKLED, *part.* Denys, M. 295.

SUCCESSFUL, *adj.* Ylwys, w.

SUCCOUR, *s.* Fors, gwerés, cyweras, w.; kyueras, P.

SUCKERS or SPROUTS, *s.* Lyuorch-guydh, P.

SUCKLING or GIVING SUCK, *part.* Ov tena, M. 1509.

SUDDEN, *adj.* Cut, cot, w.; got, P.; desempys, desympys, dysympys, w.; dhysempyys, thesempys, P.; desimpit, w.

SUDDENLY, *adv.* Adhysempyz, dhy sempys, the sempys, P. Also the other forms, cut, cot, desempys, &c., as used for *sudden* (adj.). Squat, skuat, w.

SUET, *s.* Suif, soa, w.; siuf, P.

SUFFER or PERMIT, *v.* Gasa, gasé, w.; gâs, gosheny, perthegy, P.; perthegés, porthy, perthy, prethy, w.

SUFFER or ENDURE, *v.* Godhaf, wodhaf, w.; gothef, P.; godhevel, godhewel, gothewel, w.; prenna, P.

HE SUFFERED. Wodhefys. Written also, *wodhevys,* a mutation of *godhefys,* 3 pers. s. preter. of *godhaf* or *godhevel,* to suffer or endure. w.

THOU SHALT SUFFER Wodhevyth, a mutation of *godheryth,* 2 pers s. fut. of *godhevel,* to suffer or endure. w.

HE MAY SUFFER. Wodhaffo. a mutation of *godhaffo,* 3 pers. s. subj. of *godhevel,* to suffer or endure, w.

SUFFERED or ENDURED, *part.* Galarouedgés, B.

SUFFERINGS, *s.* Thewsys, P. See PAINS.

SUFFICIENTLY, *adv.* Lour. laur, w.; lower, leas, lias. liaz, lyk, luek, luk, P.; luc, lyc, w.

SUFFOCATE, *v.* Megi, w.; megy, P.

SUFFOCATED, *part.* Stoath, B.

SUGAR-STICK, *s.* (Toffy). Clidgy, D.

SUITE, *s.* Soth, R.D. 1881. *Del farsyn ynta menough yn agas soth*, as we fared well often in your suite, R.D. 1880-1.

SUITOR, *s.* Tanter (? tauter), w. ; tymarrhar, B.

SULKY, *adj.* Nurly, D.

SULPHUR, *s.* Mygfaen, ruibht, B.

SUMMER, *s.* Hâf, hâv, w. ; hâff, P. ; have, c.w. 336; hân, P. . ephan, B. *Miz ephan*, the summer month, *i.e.*, June. B.

A DRY SUMMER. Hâv zeah, haffa zeah, P.

SUMMER LIGHTNING. Collybran, colbran. Names also for the smut in corn, D.

SUMMERLY, *adj.* Hânic, w. ; hânick, P. ; hafaid, B.

SUMMIT, *s.* Pen, pyn, w. ; pedn, pednan, P. ; pan, ban, bar, tôp, thôp, côp, w. ; coppa, B. *Esos yth cóp*, thou art on thy summit, P.C. 931 ; garras, guarhas, gwarhas, w. ; garhas, guarhaz, gwarthav, P. ; guarthav, gwarthe, B. ; crib, w. ; krib, B. *Crib or krib*, properly means the summit or crest.

SUMPTUOUS, *adj.* Mourobrur, w.

SUN, *s.* Houl, B. ; howle, c.w. 101. *An houl, ha'n lôr ha'n stergan*, the sun, the moon, and the stars, O.M. 36 ; sôl, syl, B. ; sûl, used only with *dêdh*, day, as *dêdh sûl*, sunday, w.

SUN'S COURSE or PATH. Redegva, P.

SUNDAY, *s.* De sil, w. ; De zil, P. ; Dezil, B. ; Dewsûl, w. ; Devsull, Dinsûl, B. ; Dêdh sûl, w.

SUNDAY-TIDE, THE SUNDAY, ON A SUNDAY. Silgueth, Sylgweth, Zilgueth, P. ; Zylgweth, w. ; Zylquéth, P.

SUNDER, *v.* Woslewys, P.

SUN-DIAL, *s.* Soler, B.

SUNFLOWER, *s.* Lêsengoc, w. The same for marygold, w.

SUNG. *part.* Cenys, kenys, w.

SUNRISE, *s.* Houldreval, w.

SUNSET. *s.* Houlsedhas, w. ; houl zedhaz, P. ; houlzethza, B.

SUN-TURN or TURN-SOL, *s.* Troheaul. This is a turn "such as the Druids made, and the inhabitants of the Western Isles still make (*i.e.*, A D. 1769) in salutations and worship." *Borlase's Antiq. of Cornwall, 2nd Ed. p. 459.*

SUP, *s.* Lemyk. M. 3313. *Hov mestresy ús lemyk*, how, masters, is there a sup ? M. 3313.

SUP, *v.* Ceany, cona, w.

SUPPED. *part.* Connés, connez, w.

SUPPER, *s.* Cean, côn, w. ; kone, B. ; coon, kôn, koyn, P. ; coyn, goyn, w. ; goyne, B.

SUPERSTITION, *s.* Hygoeled, B.

SUPPLE, *adj.* Hibblyth, B.

SUPPLICATE, *v.* Pesy, pysy, pisy, w. ; pesa, pidzha, B. ; pidzhi, pigy, pygy, w. ; pidgy, peidgy, pys, B.

SUPPLICATION, *s.* Pesad pysad, pydzhad, pyjad, w. ; pidzhi, P.

SUPPLICATIONS, *s.* Pesadow, pysadow, pydzhadow, pyiadow, P.

SUPPORT, AID, SUCCOUR, *s.* Fôrs, w. ; gew, P.

SUPPORT or PROP, *s.* Horven. w. ; trig, D.

SUPPOSE, *v.* Tebias, tibias, w. ; tebyaz, P. ; tebyas, w. ; tibiaz, P. ; tybias, tybyas, w. ; sybbosia, P. ; sypposia, sybottia, B.

SUPPOSED, *part.* Podeerés, a corruption of *prederys*, from *predery*, to consider. to think, P.

SUPREME. *adj.* Warrah, w. ; uthall, uhall, uhan, umhan, P.

SURCOAT, *s.* Cercot, w.

SURE, *adj.* See CERTAIN.

SURELY, *adv.* Eredy, yredy, w. ; devery, c.w. 204 ; cepar, kepar, B. ; yn sur, N. ; in suyr, M. 313; sur, B. ; suir, M. 902 ; suer, M. 4302 ; surredy, P.C. 739 ; redy, B. See also CERTAINLY.

SURETY, PLEDGE, *s.* Guistel, w.

SURGE or WAVE OF THE SEA, *s.* Armôr, w.

SUR-NAME, *s.* Leeshann, *i.e.*, a name from a place, B.

SURPLICE, *s.* Hevis, cams, w. ; kams, B. ; cercot, w.

SURROUNDING, *adj.* Cerchen, kerchen, kerchyn, gerchen, cerhyn, kerhyn, w.

SUSPECT, *v.* Dismigo, dysmegy, w.

SUSPEND. *v.* Crêgy, gregy, w.

SUSPENDED, *adj.* Crôc, crôk, crôg, w.

SUSPENSION or A HANGING, *s.* Crôc, crôk, crôg, w.

SUSPICION, *s.* Camdybians, w. ; kabmdybianz, P.

SUSTAIN, *v.* (Carry, bear, entertain). Perthy, porthy, parthy, prethy, w.

SUSTAIN, *v.* (Stay, wait for, remain). Trega, tregé, dregé, w.

SUSTENANCE, *s.* (Victuals, food). Vygyans, B. ; vygyens, w.

SUTLER, *s.* Maidor, B.

SWADDLE, *v.* Maylyé, c.w. 1909 ; malyé, maylé, vaylé, w.

SWADDLED, *part.* Malys, M. 2642. *Hâg in quethov fyn malys*, and swaddled in fine clothes, M. 2642.

SWADDLING CLOTHES. Lednow, B.

SWALLOW, *v.* Clunk, w. ; klunk, B. *Clunk*, is still in common use among the uneducated in Cornwall. Dislonka, w.

SWALLOW, s. (The bird). Tshicûc, w.; tshi-kûk. P. *Lit.* A house cuckoo. Guenol, w. Pryce gives *guenol* for a sparrow.

SWAMPY, *adj.* Gwinic, gwernic, w.; guernick, P.

SWAN, s. Elerch, w.; elerhe, elerchy, B.

SWANNERY, s. Elerchy, P.

SWARM, s. (Bees). Hês, hêz, w.; glêz (also hêz), D.; huido-wenyu, saith-beach, B.

SWATHE, v. See SWADDLE.

SWATHE, s. (As of corn). Dram, D.

SWAY, s. Moghheys, M. 313; reoute, M. 208; roweth. M. 4539. *Reoute an beys,* sway of the world, M. 208. *Kyn fo mar fur an roweth,* though so great be our sway, M. 4539.

SWEAR, v. (Or solemnly affirm). Fe, fo, vo, toy, tyé, tiah, te, de, di, P.; dye, c.w. 1629.

SWORN. Tui, tyi. *E rig tyi dho vi,* he swore to me. B.

HE SWORE. Tôs, toys, doys, w.; ef a deas, B.

I WILL SWEAR Tôf, 1 pers. s. fut. of *toy,* to swear. w.

HE WILL SWEAR. Te, de. *De,* a mutation of *te,* 2 pers. s. fut. of *toy,* to swear, w.

SWEAR, v. (To swear profanely). Methés, P.

SWEAR, v. Gele, gelle, B. (?)

SWEAT, v. Hwesa, w.; hueza, P.; hwesy, wesé, wesy, weys, w.

SWEAT, s. Whés, whese, B.; hwês, huês, w.; huez, P.; wheys, whys, w.; hallus, B. *Re hallus,* with the sweat. B.

SWEEP, v. Skibia, P.; scibia, scaberia, w.

SWEEPER, s. Scaberias, w.

SWEET, *adj.* Whêc, w.; whêk, B.; wêc, w.; week, P.; hwêc, whêg, hwêg, w; huêg, P.; wheag, c.w. 95; wheake, c.w. 537; whegol, hwegol, w.; whys, o.M. 273; melys, B.; milsey, milzey, mylgy, D.; lavur. B. Flour when damp and slightly fermented becomes sweet or mawkish, it is then called *milsey milzey,* or *mylgy* flour, D.

SWEET, AMIABLE, *adj.* Wêk, M. 527. *Ov mâp wêk,* my sweet son, M. 527.

SWEETER, *adj* Whecca, whekka, whekké, N.; huekah, P.

SWEETEST, *adj.* Wheggol, P. *Ys vam wheggol,* his most sweet mother. P.

A SWEET BREATH. Mel huêz, P.

SWEET-CANE or CALAMUS, s. Koisen, P.

SWEET-DRINK, s. Bragot, bracat, w.; brakat, B.; bregaud, w. *Braggot* in English.

SWEET-HEART, s. Shiner, D. (See also WOOER).

SWEET-HEARTS, s. Tymarrhurian, B.

SWEET MILK, s. Leverid, leverith, w.

SWEETNESS, s. Whecter, w.; whekter, B.; hwecter, w.; huekter, P.; melder, N.

SWELL, v. Hwedhy, w.; huedhi, P.; hudhy, w.

SWELLING, s. Hwedh, w; hûedh, ûth, ût, P.

SWIFT, *adj.* Stric, strik, w.; buhan, cyulym, B.

SWIFTLY, *adv.* Vskys (*uskys*), R D. 2503. *Mar vskys del thuath omma,* so swiftly as he came here, R.D. 2503.

SWIFTNESS, s. Rhedec, *Polwhele.*

SWIM, v. Nygé, nija, w.; nijah, nizhyea, P.; niedza, B.; nyidzha, nysé, w.; nys, renygia, P.

TO SWIM OVER, v. Tarneidzha, w.; tarneudzha, B.

SWITCH or TWITCH, s. Squych, skwych, scwyth, w.; skwyth, P. People in Cornwall who are troubled with twitches or "the fidgets," say they have "the squitchems."

TO BE SWOLLEN, v. Hwedhy, w.; huedhi, P.; hudhy, w.

SWOON, v. Clamderé, w.; clamdery, P.

SWOON, s. Clamder, entredés, w.

SWOONED, *part.* Clamderys, B.

SWORD, s. Cledhe, w.; kledhe, clethe, B.; gledh, gledhe, P.; glethe, o.M. 292; cledha, w; kledha, B.; cletha, c.w. 965; gletha, c.w. 317. *Cens dha gledhe,* with thy sword. w.

SWORDS, s. Clydhydhow, w.; clethethyov, M. 1266; clethythyow, c.w. 325. *Cledha bian,* a small sword, w.

SWORD-BLADE, s. Clafn, B.

SYMPHONIACA, s. (Herb) Gahen, B.

SYNAGOGUE, s. Synagys, P.C. 1255. *Lemmyn ôl yn synagys,* but all in the synagogue, P.C. 1255.

SYNOD, s. Cedva, w; chetva, ketva, P.; kedva, B.; chetua, w (properly the *place* of meeting); sened, w.; senedh, B.

SYPHILIS, s. Pocvan brâs. *Lit.* The great pox; poccys, poccys Frenc, pokkys Frenk. *Lit.* The French pox.

SYRINGE, s. Skit, skeet, D.

T.

"This letter in Cornish . . . . . . is both a primary initial, and a secondary mutation.

When a radical initial it changes into *d,* and *th,* as *tâs,* a father; *y dds,* his father; *ow thâs,* my father.

When secondary, *t,* in Cornish is the aspirate mutation of *d,* as *da,* good; *pûr dha,* very good; *maga ta,* as good; *yn ta,* well. *Dôn,* to bear; *ow tôn,* bearing; *Due, y tue,* he will come," w. *Lex. Corn. Brit.*

TABLE, *s.* Bord, moys, voys, foys, muis, w. *War an foys.*on the table, w.

TABLE-CLOTH, *s.* Lian bûz, P.

TACK (or fasten with tacks), *v.* Taccé, taccyé, takkyé, w. ; takkia, P.

TACKLE, *s.* Takel, P. ; tacel, w. *Pl.* Tacklow, P. ; taclow, O.M. 936 ; dacklow, C.W. 765.

TADPOLE, *s.* Pedn diu, w. *Lit.* Black-head.

TAIL, *s.* Lost, w.

HAVING A LARGE or LONG TAIL. Lostec. Hence this name for a fox, w.

TAIL, *s.* Guen, R.D. 2355. *Ye re gymmy tcl ow guen,* I wag my tail at ye, R.D. 2355. This seems a vulgar form.

TAILOR, *s.* Trehés, w. ; trehar, seuyad, seuadh, B.

TAILORESS, *s.* Seuyadés, w. ; seuadés, B.

TAILPIPE, *v.* Prall, D.

TAKE, BEAR, or CARRY, *v.* Perthy, porthy, berthy, prethy, w. ; aborth, P. See also BEAR and CARRY.

TAKE, HAVE, or FETCH, *v.* Fethé, fethy, w.

TAKE or HAVE, *v.* Kafus, O.M. 497. *Kafus y thege hep gréf,* to take his tenth without complaint, O.M. 497. For other forms of *kafus,* see HAVE, *v.*

TAKE, ACCEPT, TO LAY HOLD OF, *v.* Cemerés, kemerés, chymerés, kymerés, cymerés, w. ; kymeraz, P. ; kemer, B. ; gemerés, w. ; gymerés, P. ; hemerés, prenné, prynny, perna, w. *Erna'n prenné an guásna,* until I take that fellow, O.M. 2152 ; frenné, P. *Hy frenné byth nynsyw bern,* of it take never care, P.

I WILL TAKE. Gemeraf, a mutation of *cemeraf,* 1 pers. s. fut. of *cemeiés,* to take, w.

HE SHALL TAKE. Gemmer, a mutation of *cemmer,* 3 pers. s. fut. of *cemerés,* to take, w.

WE SHALL TAKE. Gemeryn, a mutation of *cemeryn,* 1 pers. pl. fut. of *cemerés,* to take, w.

TAKE THOU. Cemer, cebmer, cymmer, gymmer, gybmar, tan, w.

TAKEN, *part.* Cemerys, kemerys, w. ; hemerys, kemerag, gemerag, chechys, B. ; brys, P. *Creator a brys benen,* creature taken from woman, P. ; degys, dregy, thoké, B.

TO TAKE AWAY, *v.* Anhethy, dreval, dho dreval, kerans, kemeré kerans, kerr, rygemeraz, P.

TO TAKE VENGEANCE, *v.* Darvyngya, M. 2396.

TO TAKE IN VAIN. (*Scil.* The name of God). Towlé the skul.

TO TAKE CARE, *v.* Gwythé, w.

TAKE THOU CARE. Gwet, guet, gweyt, w. ; gueyt, queyt, P. ; gwyth, w. ; guyth, B. The 2 pers. s. imp. of *gwythé,* w.

TAKE YE CARE. Gweytyeuch, 2 pers. pl. imp. of *gwythé,* w. ; vethough, B.

TAKE CARE. Thevyth, B. This seems a rough form of cautioning. Borlase thinks it is from *theveth,* a curse.

LET THEM TAKE CARE. Gweytyens, 3 pers. pl. imp. of *gwythé,* w.

TAKEN OFF. Douthek, B.

A TAKING HOLD OF. Dalhen, w.

TALC, *s.* (The mineral). Glidder, D.

TALE or NARRATION, *s.* Daralla, w.

TALE or STORY, *s.* See STORY.

TALE-BEARER, *s.* Gowygy, whetlow. P. ; ystiferion, w.

TALE-TELLER, *s.* Gouhoc, gowec, w. ; huetlo, B.

TALK, *v.* Cows, w. ; cous, dho cous, P. ; caws, w. ; kauz, B. ; keuza, keuzel, dhe cousa, P. ; cowsy, coosy, D. See TELL or SAY.

TALK, *s.* (Discourse). Cowms, cows, w. ; kouz, B. ; cous, O.M. 1899 ; gows, w. ; kounis, B.

TALKER, A TALKATIVE MAN. Dên lavar, w.

A GREAT TALKER. Dên brâs lavar, w.

TALL, *adj.* Tal, hîr, hyr, uchel, uhel, huhel, yuhel, w.

TALLOW, *s.* Suif, soa, w. ; siuf, P. (?) ; blonec, blonit, B,

TAMBOURINE, *s.* Crowdy-crawn, D.

TAME, *adj.* Dôf, dôv, dô, w. ; doff, M. 4028. *Eff us led ón doff,* he will lead her like a tame lamb, M. 4028.

TAME, *v.* Dova, tempré, w. *Ha my a wra y tempré,* and I will tame him, P C. 1892.

TANG, *s.* See SEA TANG or WRACK.

TANKARD, *s.* Gweren, w.

TAPER, *s.* (A wax candle). Taper, w. ; tapar, P.

TAPESTRY, *s.* Strail, w. ; clestr, B. ; kyulat, P.

TARDY, *adj.* Hêl, w.

TARES, DARNEL, *s.* Ivre, w.

TARGET, *s.* Costan, w. ; kostan, B. ; gostan, w.

TARRY, *v.* Gortés, cortés, cyrtas, w. ; kyrtaz, B. ; streché, strechyé, w. ; streuha, strelha. hethy, wonnen, P. ; trega, tregé, triga. trigé, trigia, w. ; dryk, B. *Ef a dryk,* he shall tarry, B. See also STAY or TARRY.

TARRIED, *part.* Tregid, dregas, B.

TASTE, *v.* Desty, B. ; dastya, C.W. 880 ; doway, P.

TATTER, *s.* See PIECE AND BIT.

TATTLE, *v.* Canvas, dho canvas, P. ; kanvas, B. ; flout, P.

TATTLE, *s.* Wob, D.

TATTLER, s.　Cowser, D.

TAVERN, s.　Tavargn, hostleri, P.; tshyrkôg, B.; prys-ly, R.D. 2149.

TAWNY, adj.　Ridhvelyn, w.

TEACH, v.　Descy, w.; desgy, P.; desca, desga, w.; deshy, P.; dyscy, dysky, tescy, w.; teskv, B.; tysky, thysky, w.

TEACHER, s.　Descader, deskadzher, w.

TEACHING, s.　(i.e., a teaching).　Descas, dhescas, dyscas, dyskas, descés, deskés, dyscés, discans, diskans, w.

TEACHING, part.　Disky, tisky, thesky, B.

TEAR, v.　Squardyé, squerdyé, w.; squerdya, P.

TO TEAR TO PIECES, v.　Squattya, scuattya, skuattia, dho skuattya, sguattia, w.

TEAR or RENT, s.　Squerd, P.; squard, Polwhele. These words are still used.

TEAR or SMALL DROP, s.　Dagren, w.　Pl. Dagrow, w.; dacrou, Polwhele.

TEAR, s.　(In sorrow).　Dager, w.; dagar, P.　Pl. Dagrow, daggrow, w.; dagrou, B.

TEASE, v.　Tountya, M. 3300.　Râg dysky dethe tountya, for teaching them to tease, M. 3300.

TEAT, s.　Têth, w.; tidi, tidy, brodn, bron, P.

A LITTLE TEAT or PAP.　Tethan.　Tiddy is a common provincial word for mother's milk, or the breast.　"Give the child some tiddy," is a phrase often used.

TEDIOUS, adj.　Hîr, hyr, w.

TEETH, s.　Dêns, dênz, deins, dyns, dannet, P.　See TOOTH.

TELL or SAY, v.　Cows, w.; cous, tho cous, P.; dho kouz, kauz, B.; caws, w.; cousa, dhe cousa, keusel, P.; kewsel, cewsel, gewsel, geusel, gows, daryvas, dharyvas, descy, w.; desgy, P.; desca, desga, dyscy, w; deshy, P.; dysmegy, dysmygy, desmygy, w. Kyn na vynno dysmegy, although he will not tell, P.C. 1387; laol, w.; leverel, lavary, P.

I TELL YOU.　Jevody.　A Cornish form of the French phrase, je vous dis.

TELL or COUNT, v.　Nivera, nevera, P.　See NUMBER, v.

TELL-TALE, s.　Huetlo, B.

TEMPER, v.　Tempré, w.

TEMPERER, s.　(Of tools).　Minarvau, B.

TEMPEST, s.　Cewar, cuer, kuer, w.; hagarauel, anauhel, guins a dro, P.; tervyns, w.

TEMPESTUOUS, adj.　Tymbestlog, B.

TEMPLE, s.　Tempel, w.; tempell.　Pl. Templys, B.

TEMPLES, s.　(Of the head).　Erieu, B.

TEMPT, v.　Trìa, temptya, B.

TEN.　Dêc, dêk, dêg, w.; deag, P.

TEN TIMES.　Dêgwyth, w.; dêguyth, P.

TEN HUNDRED TIMES.　Dêh canquith, P.

TENACIOUS, adj.　Sinsiat, B.　From sinsy, to hold, q.v.

TENANT, s.　Dên koskor, B.

TENDER, adj.　Medal, B.; medhal, meddal, medhel, w.; methel, P.; tyner, B.; awhesyth, O.M. 1203. Grugyer têk hag awhesyth, a partridge fair and tender, O.M. 1203.

TENDER, SENSITIVE, adj.　Tidden, D.

TENDERNESS, s.　Medhalder, medalder, w.

TENDON, s.　Geyen, geien, w.; gelen, gelyn, P. See SINEW

TENDONS, s.　Scenys, w.　See SINEWS.

TENT, s.　Scovva, w.　Râg ny a yl gûl scovva, for we may make a tent, O.M. 1717; gulscouua, P.; overgugol, B.

TENTH.　Degvés.　Degvés rân, the tenth part or share, w.; dekfaz, deagvas, P.

TENTH, s.　(The tenth or tithe).　Dege, dhege, w.; thege, O.M. 497.

TERM, A TIME, A COURSE, s.　Termen, termyn, dermyn, w.; vêth, P.

TERMINUS, s.　Or, ore, B.

TERRIBLE, adj.　Uthec, uthek, uthyc, uthyk, huthyc, huthyk, w.; uter, B.; ethuc, ethec, ethyc, ythec, ithic, w.

TERRIBLE, VIOLENT, SAD, adj.　Trewysy, O.M. 2704.　Gans morben bom trewysy, with a mallet a terrible blow, o M. 2704.

TERRIFIC, adj.　See TERRIBLE.

TERRITORY, s.　Bro, vro, terros, terrus, derrus, w.; terras, P.; teroge, w.

TERROR, s.　Tarofan, tarofvan, tarosfan, tarnytuan, w.; têr, P.　Guythe ef râg tarofvan, preserve it from terror, O.M. 2364; ûth, euth, uthecter, w.

TERTIANS, s　(Agues).　Tarthennow, M. 1423.

TESTIFY, v.　Tustuné, dustuné, dustyné, w.

TESTIMONY, s.　Tistuné, testyny, tustuny, dustuny, dustyny, w.; tistum, P.

TETHER, s.　Spanjar, span, D.

THAN, SO, AS, LIKE AS, adv.　Del, mal, mel, vel, w.

THAN.　Es, eys, w.; ys, B.; agés, w.; agess, ahro, tra, try, tro, w.; to, P.　Tekké alter ês del ûs genen, a fairer altar than such as is with us, O.M. 1179. Hacré mernans eys emlathe, a more cruel death than self-killing, R.D. 2073.　Teké agés kyns, fairer than before, P.C. 348.　Ken arluth agess ef, another lord than him, O.M. 1789.　Ys kans, than before, B.　Gueth ys ky, worse than a dog, R D. 2026.

THAN THOU. Agesos, w.

THAN YE. Esouch. agesouch, w. ; agesough, N.
Ken agesough, other than you (or ye), o.m. 2357.

TO THANK, TO GIVE THANKS, v. Grassé, w. ;
carro. *Ren carro*, let us thank, P.

THANK GOD. Merastadu. *Lit.* Many thanks to
God.

I THANK. Durdalatha, B.

I THANK YOU. Durdalatha why, P.

MANY THANKS TO YOU. Merastawhy, P.

THANKS TO YOU. Durdala dho why, w.

THANKS. Durdala, P.

THANKS, GRACE, s. Grâs, râs. *Pl.* Grasow, rasow,
w. ; grassees, M. 4240. *The Ihesu rebo grassees*, to
Jesus be thanks, M. 4240 ; grassies, c.w. 2092 ;
grassyés, c.w. 2460 ; gromersy, o M. 2384 ; gromercy,
o.m. 407. *Adas a nêf gromercy*, oh father of heaven,
thanks, o.m. 407 ; zehaz, B.

THANKS. Mack, B. The Cornish used this single
word *mack*, just as we say " thanks."

I GIVE THANKS. Crasseeff, M, 3692. *Ihesu dyso
y crasseeff*, Jesu, to thee I give thanks, M. 3892.

THANKFUL, *adj.* Grassys, B.

THAT, *adj. pron.* (That there, that same). Hen, p.c.
2546. *Ha hen yv emskemunys*, and that is accursed,
P.C. 2546 ; henna, w. ; hena, P. ; hedna, c.w. 2447 ;
hed, P. ; hedda, w. ; hon, N. ; honna, hodna, hodda,
w. ; na, B. *An mawna*, that lad. *An marhna*, that
horse, B. *Yn wlâs na*, in that country, N. ; ne, N.
Yn úr-ne, in that hour, N. ; ya, i, y, B. *Y mawna*,
that boy, B.

THAT. *conj.* (So that. as). Caman, camen, cammen,
mân (*ma yn*). maga. w. ; magas, maes, may, P. *May
fo, May fe*. that there may be, P. ; ma. N. *Ma gas
bo*, that it be to you (that you may have), P.C.
226 ; suel. sûl, tre. dre, w. ; drean, P. ; tra, tro, w. ;
treu, P. ; try. w. ; taman, B. ; teffe, P. *Teffe delas
dos dêns*, so that the men come, P. ; tridzhan, par,
P. ; pan. plenys, B.

THAT NOT, Na (before consonants) ; nag (before vowels).

THAT NOT, *comp. conj.* Manno, manna, ma-na, w.

THAT WHICH. Menz, B.

TO THAT. Thyso, P.

THAT PLACE, THERE. Lena, w.

IN THAT PLACE, THERE. Dy, P.

THAT IS Us, ês, w.

THATCH, s. Teys, teyz, soul, B.

THATCH, v. Ty, w. ; tei, tey, B. ; to, P.

THATCHER, s. Tyor, w.

THATCHED HOUSE. Chy teyz, ti soul, B.

THAW. v. Tedha, w.

THE. *Definite article.* An. *An dên*. the man. Sometimes written han, en, y. yn. tha, thék, P.

AND THE. Han, ha'n (*ha an*). P.

BY THE. Ren (re-an), w. ; genas, c.w. 819.

FROM THE. A'n, w.

TO THE. Dên (*de an*). dhên, w. ; thên (*the-an*), dân,
tân, P. ; dha'n, B. ; thân (*the-an*), P. ; dhyn, dhynni,
B. ; dys, dês, w.

THEATRE, s. Gwardy. w. ; guardy, guar-ty, P.

THEATRES, s. Guarimou, B.

THEE, *pron.* Te, ti, w. ; tee, c.w. 914 ; tye, c.w.
2251 ; ty. w. ; di, dy, P. ; se, sy, w. ; she, c.w.
2296 ; chee, P. ; ge, gy (*g* soft), w. ; hauns, B.

BEFORE THEE. Ragos, w.

BY or WITH THEE. Genés, w. ; genez, genass,
P. ; genas, gynez, B.

BY or THROUGH THEE. Drethos, N.

FOR THEE. Ragos, w. ; ragas, c.w. 817 ; gothaf,
ynné, ynny, P. ; dhyso, B.

FROM THEE. Ahanés. w. ; a hanés, P. ; ahanas,
w. ; hanas, P. ; hanys, c.w. 1547 ; worthys, P. ;
dheworthys, deworthys. dyworthys, w. ; tha worthis
ge, c.w. 810 ; ragos, w.

IN THEE. Ynnos, yn-ti, w. ; yth, P.

OF THEE. Ad, a'd, a'th, w. ; dy, thesy, hanas, P. ;
ahanas, ahanés, w. ; a hanés, P.

TO THEE. Thys, B ; thyes, c.w. 698 ; theis, P. ; thyso,
M. 1120 ; thêrs, P. *Rag cvwsal thérs*, to speak to
thee, P. ; thewh, c.w. 676 ; thewhy, c.w. 702 ;
thagé, c.w. 805 ; tith, tyth, dês, deys, dheys, dys
w. ; dez, dheyz, dhiz, B. ; dhyz, P. ; deso, dheso,
w. ; dhethy, P. ; doyn, B. ; warnas, o.m. 1072 ; worthys, orthys, geta. w.

WITH THEE. Genés, w. ; genez, P. ; genas, B. ; genass,
gynez, tegen (*te-gen*), thêrs, P. *Rag cowsal thérs*, to
speak with thee, P. ; genés tha, c.w. 151 ; genas she,
c.w. 2296.

UPON THEE. Warnas, N.

THEIR, *poss. pron.* A, y, agei, aga, gei, w. ; ge, P. ;
go. w. ; dy, ella, P.

TO THEIR Thaga, c.w. 2434.

OF THEIRS. Aga, P.

THEM, *pron. pers.* An (a, anx, 'n him), a's, as, i, y,
w. ; ys, g. ge, gy, B. ; we, gzhyi, P. ; dzhei, se,
wottensé, worté, B. ; renna, renna li, ryna, rego,
ylly, dous, P.

AT THEM. Worté, orté, w.

BEFORE THEM. Raghthé, w.

BY THEM. Drethé, N. ; worté, orté, w.

FOR THEM. Raghthé, w. ; ragas, N. (*i.e.*, re agas).

FROM THEM.　Anethé, annethé, w.; annethy, annotho, anedhé, N.; anydha, annydha, w.; ahanés, N.; dyworthé, dhyworthé, w ; dhort igilez, gilez, worthys, P.; worté, orté, ragthé, w.

IN THEM.　Ynny P.; ynné (yn-ny). ythens, ettans, w.; ettanz, B.

OF THEM.　Anedhé, anethé, annethé, anydha, annydha, w.; anythy, P.; anothans, w. ; dothans, P.; dhodhans, B.; thothans, dotha, dotho, aga. P.

TO THEM.　Thethé, thêth, thothans, P.; thy, dy, N.; onethy, P.; theygh, thyugh, N.; dedhé, dhedé, w.; dethé. N.; dotho, dotha, daga, P.; dodhans, dhodhans, dodhyns, dothyns, w.; dhedhynz, B.; dothans, P.; worté, orté, w.; a wottensé, ys, B.

UPON THEM.　Warnethé, warnogh, N.; worté, orté, w.

WITH THEM.　Genaf, gynef, gynés. genogh, N.; gansé, B.; ganssé, N.; gansy, w.; gansy, c.w. 1452; gensyns, w.; genzynz, B.

THEMSELVES.　Thewna, B.

THEN, adv.　Asso, w.; agés, P.; ena, enna, henna, eno, ené, B.; nena, nenna, w.; ûrna. enûrma, theis, theys. P.; bys pan, B.; ytho, w. Ytho thy'nny yth huvel, then to us it appears, R.D. 1489.

THENCE, adv.　Alena, w.; alené, N.; anydha, annydha, anedhé, w.

FROM THENCE. Nena, nenna, tythy, B.

THERE, adv.　Ena, w. Ena in dour, there in the water, R.D. 2196; eno, w. Eno ny a'n recevas, there we received them, R.D. 2339; enna, w.; honna, hodda, B.; unna, yna, na, lena, w.; agei, gei, ge, ewe, dy, theys, theis, P.

THERE or HERE.　Dêv, dêf. Indifferently to signify, both. Dév têk a bren, here's a fair tree, or there's, &c., P.

THERE IS.　Yma, ema, w.

THEREABOUT, adv.　Tro, dro, w.

THEREFORE, adv.　Râg henna, w.; râghenna, râghhemma, P.; râg honna, w.; râg hedna, c.w. 2498.

THEREIN, adv.　Ena, enna, eno, w.; ettanz, B.

THEREOF, adv.　Anodho, an nethé, nethé, P.

THEREON, adv.　Worté, orté, w.

THEREWITH, adv.　Gans henna, w.

THEREWITHAL, adv.　Gans henna, M. 227.

THESE, pron.　Remma (re-ma), remé, w.; renna li, aure, ma, P. Gerryow ma, these words, P.

THEY, pron.　Y, i, hy. hoi. w.; eye, gi, ge, P.; gy, dzhei, dzhyi, w.; gzhyi, aga, ylly, P.; dous, B.; 'e, 's, N.

THEY BOTH.　Aga'ieyw, P.

THICK, adj.　Tew, B.; teu, P.; brâz, liaz, B.

THICKEN, v.　Tewraga, w.

THICKET, s.　Browse, bruss, D.

THICKNESS, s.　Tewder, w.; teuder, P.

THICKHEAD, s.　(Stupid fellow). Pen pyst, P.

THICKHEADED, adj.　Zawkin, zawkemin, D.

THIEF, s.　Lader, w.; ladar. P.; ferhiat, w.; forrior, B.

THIEVES, s.　Ladron, laddron, w ; ladhron, ladran, laddarn, P.

THIGH, s.　Mordoit, mordhos, morras, morraz, w.; morbots (? morboit), P.; clenniaw, B.; worthas, P.

THIGHS, s.　Worthosow, maurugo, B.

THIMBLE, s.　Besgan, biscan, w.; num, D.

THIMBLEFUL, s.　Numful, w.f.p.

THIN, adj.　Tanow, tanaw, w.; tanau, P.; trauythés, grisill, B.; muin, moin, moyn, môn, w.

THIN AND POOR.　(As of silk, stuffs, &c.) Scoy, D.

THIN, WAN, HOLLOW-EYED.　Thirl, thurl, D.

THINNESS, s.　Tanauder, P.

THINE, pron.　De, dhe, te, ty, ta, w.; tea, da, tha, P.; do, dho, dy, dhy, w.; yth, P.; ath, w.; thum, P.; thêth. c.w. 935.

THING, s.　Tra, dra, w. Orth an dra-ma the wruthyl, to do respecting this thing, p c. 1433 (Pl. Traow, trehys, w.); pêth, peyth, pyth, w. An pyth a thue yn dyweth, the thing will come at last, o.m. 936 (Pl. Pethow, w.); tacel, w.; takel, P.

A GOOD-FOR-NOTHING THING.　Podar, P.

THINGS AGREEING.　Blegadou, B.

THINGS, APPARATUS, TACKLE.　Tacklow, P.; taclow, o.m. 936; dacklow, c.w. 765. Yntrethon, taclow pryve, between ourselves, things privately, o.m. 936.

THINK, v.　Tibias, w.; tibiaz, P.; tebyas, w.; tebyaz, P.; tybias, tybyas, tybyé, w.

HE WILL THINK.　Dîp, dyp. Mutations of tip and typ, 3 pers. s. fut. of tibias and tybyé, to think, w.

TO THINK OF, TO CONSIDER, v.　Predery, predyry, prydyry, prydery, w.; prederi, pridiri, P.

TO THINK, TO CONJECTURE, v.　Kridzhi. See BELIEVE, v.

TO THINK, TO SUPPOSE, v.　Sypposia, B.; sybbosia, P.; sybottia, B.

THINKING, s.　Tybyans, R.D. 1213. Thu'm tybyans whêth ef ny grys, to my thinking he does not yet believe, R.D. 1213.

THINNESS, s.　Tanowder, tanauder, w.

THIRD, adj.　Tressa, w.; trissa, P.; tryssa, c.w. 54; trysa. P.; tryssé, tressé, w.; trissé, tredha, P.; tredzha, tridzha, tridga, trygé, tregé, w.; pregna (?), P.

THE THIRD DAY HENCE. Gudreva, B.; gydreva, P.

THIRST, s. Sichor, B.; sechés, w.; seghés, P.; sehas, zehas, zehaz, zahas, w.; zahaz, B.

THIRST, TO BE THIRSTY, v. Seché, syché, sychy, sihy, seha, zeha, w.; sehy, dho sehy, P.

THIRSTY, adj. Sechys, sychys, sehys, zehys, sihys, w.; clem, D.

THIRTEEN, adj. Tredhec, tredhek, trethek, P.; trethak, B.; tardhak, N.; tardhac, tairdhac, tairdhak, P.; torthack, D.

THIRTEENTH, adj. Par degvas, P.

THIRTY, adj. Dêgwarnygans, w.; deagwarnygans, c.w. 2265; deakwarnegans, c.w. 1977; dêk warnugens, dêk warnugans, N.; dêg war iganz, dêg uar igans, P. Lit. Ten upon twenty.

THIRTY-TWO, adj. Dewthack warnygans, c.w. 1981; dewthack warnugans, c.w. 1984.

THIS, adj. pron. Hemma, w.; hem, P.; hebma, homma, w.; omma, ymma, uppa, B.; henna, hena, hona, P.; hen, hon, w.; then, me, ma, B. Dén ma, this man, B.; elf, by, P. Bychyth, this night, P.

THIS HERE. Hemma, homma, w.; hem, P.

THIS ONE. Homma, w.

AND THIS, Hawa, P.

FOR THIS. Râgta, P.

OF THIS. H'y, P.

TO THIS. Thyso, P.; dên, M. 2619. Dén dénma, to this man, M. 2619.

THIS PLACE. Lemma, w.

FROM THIS PLACE. A lemma, w.

TO THIS PLACE. Dhybba, P.

THISTLE, s. Askellen, askallan, B.; ascallen, w. Pl. Ascall, w.

THITHER, adv. Dy, M. 58. Kezegy gans ov map dy, go thou with my son thither, M. 58.

THOMAS, s. Tummy, Tubmy, Tubby, w.

THONG, s. Crên, w.; croon, krehen, P. Pl. Cronow, P.; cronou, B.

THORNBACK, s. (A fish). Carcath, karcath, B. See RAY.

THORN, s. (A thorn bush). Spernan, draenen, w.; drachen, B.; drane, P.; drize, P. (Pl. of spernan, spern, w.; spearn, c.w. 974).

BUSH or THICKET OF THORNS. Bosnos, w.

A BLACK THORN. Spernan diu, w.

A WHITE THORN. Frith, P.

A CROWN OF THORNS. Curen spern, M. 2994.

THORN or PRICKLE, s. Draen, drain, drên, w.

THORNS or THORN-PRICKLES. Drein (Pl. of draen), w.; dryn, M. 2995; dreyn, w.

THORN-BACK, s. (A kind of crab). Crabalorgin, D. See CRAB.

THORNY, adj. (Abounding in thorns). Drenic, w.

THOSE, pron. Suel, sûl, rena (re-na), ryna, w.; hanés, B.; aure, (? anre), P.

THOSE THERE. Yn re-na, w.

THOU, pron. Te, ti, ty, w.; thu, P.; ta, di, w; 'd, 'th, ge (g soft), gy (g soft), P.; sy, w.; hês, P. Hés sogy goky, thou art a fool, P.; 's, oiz, P. Ti oiz augelez, thou seest, P.; chee (erroneusly for ge), B. See also THEE.

THOU ALSO. Tithe, w.

AND THOU. Ha'n, P.

THOUGH. Asso, bês, bys, cên, kên, w.; keen, P.; cyn, kyn, gên, ce, cy, w. Kynthoma ogas marowe, though I am nearly dead, c.w. 1690. Kyn wrello són, though he should make a noise, R.D. 2016. Ken fe terrys, though it be broken, P.C. 354.

THOUGHT, s. Preder, pryder, w.; pridar, P.; breder, tibians, tybians, tybyans, w.; tibianz, P.

THOUGHTS, s. Cowgegyow, M. 149.

THOUGHT, part. Prederys, pryderys, brederys, w.; podeerés, a corruption of prederys, from predery, to think of, w.

THEY THOUGHT. Thugsyons, B.

TO BE THOUGHTFUL. Predery, predyry, prydery, prydyry, w.; prederi, pridiri, P.

THOUGHTFUL, adj. Prederys, priderys, pryderys, brederys, w.; brederez, P.

THOUSAND. Mil, vil, myl, vyl, w.; myell, c.w. 1562. Dêk can, N., but this is lit. ten hundred.

THOUSANDS. Miliow, milliow, millyow, w.; myll, B.

A HUNDRED THOUSAND. Cans vyl, N.

A THOUSAND TIMES. Milgwêth, w.; milguêth, P.; milwêth, milwyth, w.

THREAD or FILAMENT, s. Hurle, D.

THREAD, YARN, s. Noden, w.; linyn, B.; linin, P.

THREE. Try, teir, w.; têr, P.; teyr, tair, w.; tayr, c.w. 1923; dayer, c.w. 2087; thyr, O.M. 1732; tyyr, tir, tyr, dyr, tres, w. (tresse, B. ?); trei, tre, tri, dri, w.

THREE-FOOTED, adj. Tribedh, trebath, w.

THREE-HUNDRED. Trei cans, tryhans, trihans, trehans, w.; trey hans, tri cans, N.; treykanz, P.; trychans, B.

THREE MEN. Treddên, w.

THREE-PRONGED, adj. Trivorh, w.

A THREE-PRONGED FORK, adj. Forh trivorh, w.

THREE SCORE. Tri-ugans, w.; tryngens, p. (? *try-ugens*).

THREE TIMES. Teirguêth, p.; teirgwêth, tergweyth, terguyth, tergueyth, w.; ter-gwyth, p.c. 147.

THREATEN, v. Dho thew, B.

THRESH, v. Fusta, fysta, w.; guesga, B.

THRESHER, s. Drusher, B.; drasher, D.

THRESHOLD, s. Trusû, truzu, portal, porth, w.; portal, B.; dreckstool, *Polwhele*; draxel, drexel, D.

THE THRESHOLD OF THE DOOR. Truzû an daras, w.; truzû an daraz, B.; truzuandaraz, P.

THRICE. Teirguêth, p.; teigwêth, tergweyth, tergueyth, terguyth, w.; ter-gwyth, p.c. 147.

THRIVE, v. Sowené, w.; sowcny, M. 3336. *Byth ny yllyn soweny*, never can we thrive, M. 3336; sowyny, sowyn, P.; sowynné, w.

THROAT or GULLET, s. Brangian, briangen, brandzhian, w.; brandzian, B.; bryangen, P.; bryongen, vryongen. briansen, w.; brianten, brandzhia, branzia, P.; brangain (*g* soft). In the Cornish dialect it is called the *clunker*. See SWALLOW, v.

THROATS, s. Briansen, B.; vreonsen, M. 1651. *Me a drêgh y vreonsen*, I will cut their throats, M. 1651.

THROAT, s. (Or mouth of anything). Cêg, R.

THRONE, s. Trôn, drôn, w.; trone, c.w. 201; drone, c.w. 212. *Dus genen ny quyc the trôn*, come with us quick to the throne, o.M. 2378. *Ha goryn ef yn y drôn*, and put him in his throne, o.M. 2372; soler, B.

THROTTLE, v. Taga, w.; tagou, B.

THROUGH. Tre, of which the mutation is *dre*, w. *Kentrow dre ow thrys*, nails through my feet, R.D. 25·7; tur, c.w. 2280; der, dyr, drês, dreys, N. *Dreys dour tyber*, through the river Tyber, R.D. 2214; trui, B.; troh, o.M. 342. *Fystynyugh troh an darras*, haste through the door, o.M. 349; trohan, P. *Trohan daras*, through the door, P. (this is only *troh* and *an*, joined, *trohan*, is therefore "through the"); tardha, w. *Dho gwana tardha*, to bore through, w.

THROUGH or BY. Drydh, dredh, w.; drethe, B.; re. w. *Re*, is used only in imprection, as *re Dew*, through God, w.; gan, gen, genz, P.; rib, B.

THROUGH or BY HER. Dredhy, drydhy, w.; drydhi, B.

THROUGH or BY HIM, or IT. Dredho, w.

THROUGH or BY ME. Dredhof, w.

THROUGH or BY THEE. Dredhos, w.

THROUGH or BY THEM. Dredhé, w.

THROUGH THY. Dred ha, B.

THROUGH or BY US. Dredhon, w.

THROUGH or BY YOU. Dredhouch, w.

THROW, s. (A throw). Toul, teul, tewl, w.

A THROW IN WRESTLING. Fauns, B. The obsolete name of a kind of throw or fall in Cornish wrestling.

THROW, v. Tewlel, w.; teulel, tiulel, P.; tyulel, B, ; tywlel, w.; teuly, towlal, P.; towla, toula, dowla, w.; doulla, P.

YE THREW. Dewlseuch, a mutation of *tewlseuch*, 2 pers. pl. pret. of *tewly*, to throw, w.

HE WILL THROW. 1. Tewl, 3 pers. s. fut. of *tewlel*, to throw, w.

    2. Tevyl, a form of *tewl*, 3 pers. s. fut. of *tewlel*, to throw, w.

TO THROW DOWN, v, Desevy, w.

TO THROW DOWN TO THE GROUND. Dho doulla a doar, P.

TO THROW or CAST AWAY. Redeuly, P.

TO THROW OFF, v. Dyscy, w.; thyffra, P.

TO THROW ONE ANOTHER. Ymdowla, w.

TO THROW ONE'S SELF DOWN. Omdesevy, ommely, umhely, w.

TO THROW ONE'S SELF. Ymwhelés, w.

TO THROW OUT. Toula, toleugha, P.

THROWN ASIDE, CAST AWAY. Henn. Perhaps from *hen*, old, P.

THRUST, s. (Or stab). Gwân, w.

THRUST, v. Pechyé, bechyé, herdhya, herdhyé, w.; herthy, P.; restyé, gwané, w.

THRUST or PUSH, v. Pokkia, B.

TO THRUST WITH FORCE. Dho toula en, P.

TO THRUST OUT or PROJECT, v. Herdys, P.

THRUST FORWARD. Herdya, B.

THUMB, s. Bês, P.; bés brâs, w.; pen-brâz, B. This also means the great-toe.

THUMP or BANG, v. Cronkyé, P.; croncyé, grôncyé, w.; cronkya, P.

THUMP or BLOW, s. Bynk. banc, w.; bank, P.; tummas, w.; stuan, B.; colp, coot, poot, D. See BLOW for other words.

THUNDER, s. Taran, tredna, w.; trenna, B.

A THUNDER CLAP. Crâk taran, R.D. 294.

THUNDER AND LIGHTNING. Tarednow ha golowas, w.

THUNDER, v. Tredna, trenna, P.

THUNDER-BOLT, s. Ergyd twrwf, B.

THURSDAY, s. Dê Jeu, Duyow, Du Yow, Dêyow, w.; Deth yov, M. 1472. *Lit* Jove's day.

THUS, adv. Andella, yn della, w.; an della, andellan, andellana, della, del, P.; delma, cetelma, ketelma, w.

THUS FAR. Bet an urma, w.

THWART. Adrûs, trûs, w.

THWART, *v.* Omdhal, P.

THY, *pron.* De, dhe. w. ; te, the, B. ; da, dha, w. ; ta, tha, B. ; dy, dhy, w. ; ty, thy, B. ; do, dho, w. ; thum. P. ; thêth, c.w. 955.

AND THY. Hath, P.

FROM THY. Ath, a'th, w.

IN THY. Yt. To be read y'th (*y-ath*), w. ; y'th, B. *Y'th servis*, in thy service, B.

OF THY. Ad, a'd, a'th, w.

TO THY. Dêth, dh'êth, w.

THYME, *s.* Tìm, B. The Cornish still call it *time*.

THYSELF, *pron.* Ta honan, da ynan, w.

TICK-TACK. (*e.g.*, a clock). Tys-ha-tas, w. *Ha knoukyé prest tys-ha-tas*, and strike always tick and tack, P.C. 2077.

TICKLE, *v.* Geyleisio, B. ; thythané, P.

TIDE, *s.* (Of the sea). Frôt, frôs. *An frôs*, the tide, w. ; frou, lenol. *Lenol môr*, the tide of the sea, B. ; môrlenol, P. ; thrîg, B. ; trîg ha trìg, rîg ha thrîg, drìg, P.

TIE. *v.* Celmy, kelmy, cylmy, kylmy, gylmy, colmyé, eren, B.

TIE, *s.* Colm, colmen, golmen, w.

TIE or BAND, *s.* Ere, B.

TIE or KNOT. *s.* Liam, B.

TIGHT. *adj.* Tèn, tyn, dyn, w.

TILE or SLATE, *s.* Lehan, w.

TILER, *s.* Tyor, w. *Pl.* Tyorryon, o.m. 2511.

TILL. *v.* Gonedhy, w. ; gonethy, P. ; gonés, gonys, conys, wonys, aras, w.

TILL. Bys, w. *Bys dêth fyn*, till the last day, P.C. 724 ; erna, w. See UNTIL.

TILL WHEN. Trebé, trybo, w. ; trehé, try, B.

TILLAGE, *s.* Trevas, drevas, w. *Adam a ôl the drevae*, Adam, of all thy tillage, o.m. 425.

TILLED GROUND. Drevas, B.

TIMBER, *s.* (A wood or forest). Coid, koid. coyd, coit, w., koit, B. ; coed, coet, w. ; coat, P. ; koat, B. ; cuid, cuit, w. ; cûs, kûz, P. ; cuz, cos, coys, w. ; gyth, guydh. govyth, goda, gôd, goed, gûz, gûs, gôs, gosse, wyth, P.

TIMBER, *s.* (As wood for building, &c.) Pren, predn, w. ; prin, pridn, bren, P.

TIME, *s.* Amser. Also corruptly written *anser*, w.

TIME, *s.* (A course or turn of time). Gwêth, w. *Milgwêth*, a thousand times, w. ; gweyth, gwyth, w. ; guyth, B. ; quêth, quyth, w. *Dêk can quyth thy's lowene*, ten hundred times joy to thee, P.C. 574 ; wêth, w. *Milwêth*, a thousand times, w. ; uêth, vêth, B. ; blêk, P. *Mil blêk*, a thousand times. P.

TIME, HOUR, SEASON, *s.* Prês, prêz, preys, w. ; prîs, P. ; prys, w. *A whythré warnas vn prys*, to look on thee (for) a time, o.m. 1414 ; prey, M 1400 ; prit, pôls, termen. termvn, w. ; tyrmyn, o.m. 45. *Râg y whyrvyth an tyrmyn*, for the time shall arrive, o.m. 45 ; dermyn, w. *A-vorow devg a dermyn*, to-morrow come in time, o.m. 2843 ; tervyn (?). w. (huys, ûz. n. See AGE) ; tranc, trank, w. *Hâg a gûl trank hep worfen*, and will time without end, P.C. 1562.

TIME or OCCASION, *s.* Treveth, trefeth, w.

TIME, *s.* Tuch. *Na cous un ger tuch vyth*, nor say one word at any time, P. Pryce says " perhaps from hence comes that expression, to keep touch with anyone."

A LONG TIME. Hirenath, hyrenath, pellear, (pell-ear, *an hour*), w. ; sôl, P. *Sôl a breys*, long since, P. ; solla thyth, R.D. 2380.

A SHORT TIME. Tecen, teken, prywêth, pryg-wyth, w.

AT ANY TIME. Bysgwêth, bythêth, vythêth, besga, w. ; nevra, neffre, P.

AT THAT TIME. Ena, enna, eno, w.

THIS TIME. Torma, w.

AT THIS TIME. Breman, enûrma (*en ûr ma*, in this hour), w.

TO THIS TIME. Bet an ûrma, w.

AT ALL TIMES. Pup prys, pup preys, pyprys, bepprés, w. ; bepprez, P.

IN GOOD TIME. In prey-tha, M. 1410.

TIMID, *adj.* Ownec, ownek, w. ; ounek, P.

TIN, *s.* Stean, stên, w.

TIN-PIT. *s.* Pol-stean, D.

TINTAGEL, *s.* (The old Cornish castle). Tyndag-yel, M. 2214.

TIN SLAG or SLAG TIN, *s.* Pillion, D. This is the tin which remains in the slag after the first melting, to be separated by re-melting.

VERY FINE TIN STUFF. Floran, D The same in a state of slime is called *loob* or *loobs*, D.

LEAVINGS OF TIN. Godho, P.

A LIVING STREAM OF TIN. Beuheyl, beuheyle, P. It means a rich layer of alluvial tin ore.

REFUSE TIN (OR COPPER) ORE. Heny-ways, hennaways, P.

WOOD TIN. Costean. Tin ore is so called from its being like wood in appearance.

TINKER. *s.* Gueiduur-cober, B.

TINNER, *s.* Stênor, stêner, stynnar. *Pl.* Stenn-erion, B. ; spaliard, spadiard, spallier, D.

TIN-WORK or STREAM WORK, *s.* Hwêl stên, hwêl stean, w.; huel stean, p. For other forms of *hwêl*, see WORK, *s.*

OLD TIN WORKS. Towle Sarazin, D.

TIN MINES, *s.* Moina stean, p.

TIN STUFF, *s.* (When very fine or in powder). Floran, D.

TINY, *adj.* Greurgh, M. 1776; gruegh, M. 1692. *Orth flehys gruegl. ha byen,* towards children tiny and little, M. 1692.

TIPPLER, *s.* Harfel, p.

TIPSY, *adj.* Prill, tadly-oodly, D.

TIRE, TO BE TIRED, *v.* Tefigia, tevigia, tefighia, B.; fethé, fethy, squythé, scuythé, dho skuythi, w.; skuattya, B. *Skuattya* in Cornish is just the same as " to be knocked up," *i.e.,* to be fatigued, in English.

TIRED, WEARIED, *adj.* Squyth, scith, w.; skith, p.; sketh, scuiz, B.; louggy, D.

'TIS BUT. Nyn gew, B.

'TIS NOT. Nyn gew, B.

TITHE, TO GIVE TITHE, *v.* Degevy, w.

TITHE or TENTH PART, *s.* Dege, dhege, w.; thege, O.M. 446; deka, p.; dega, c.w. 1067; degvas, c.w. 1086.

TITMOUSE, *s.* Tscecoé, w.; tskekké'r eithin, *i.e.,* furze chatterer, p.; ekky-mowl, ekky-mal, kek-mal, hick-mal, D.

TITTLE-TATTLE, *s.* Tetyvaly, w.

TO. De, dhe, do, dho. da, dha, w.; the, tha, tur, thy, tho, p.; a. yn, w.; y. *Y sedha,* to sit, B.; u, p.; wor, B; war *War thu,* to God, N.; uorh, B.; orth, w.; uorth, worth, p. *Worth an treytor,* to the traitor, p.c. 1449; wôs, B.; sen, sin, zen, p.; chever, B.

TOAD, *s.* Cronec du, cranag diu, w.; kranag diu, B. *Lit.* A black frog. Also simply thus :—cronec, cronek, w.; kronek, B.; croinoc, w. See also FROG.

TO-DAY, *s.* Yndzedh, p.; hitheu, hythew, N. *Na moy cous thy'm hythew,* no more talk to me to-day, R.D. 1940.

TOAST, *v.* Rostia, w.

TOE, *s.* (The toe). Bis-truit, w.; bistruit, p. *Lit.* The foot finger. These words are used for the great toe, which Pryce calls *pen-brás,* which also means the thumb. *A* toe, pêz, p.; bêz, B. *Pl.* Byzias, boscias, B. These words also mean finger and fingers. Borlase gives " *boscias-truz,* the toes."

TOE-NAIL, *s.* Ewin, euin, w. Also used for a finger nail.

TOFFY, *s.* Clidgy, locus, D.

TOGETHER. Warbarth, w.; uarbarth, p.; warbarh, w.; warparth, R.D 2308; ynten, B.

TOIL, *s,* Lafur, lafyr, lavur, lavirians, w.

TOIL, *v,* Lafnryé, laviria, w.; laferrya, B.

TOKEN, *s.* Tavas, w.; thavas, p.; thavaz, B.; nôd, nôs, nôz, w,; peynye, poenis, B.

TOLD, *part.* (Said, spoken). Cowsys, cawsys, cewsys. w,; cawsés, p.

TOMB, *s.* See GRAVE.

TOM-CAT, *s.* Gurcath, w.; kurkath, B.; lawen cath, M. 3413. *Me a offren lawen cath,* I will offer a tomcat, M. 3413.

TO-MORROW, *s.* Avorow, w.; a-vorow, M. 2843; avorou, p.; yvuru, B. *Deug avar avorow,* come early to-morrow, P.C. 3240. *A-vorow devga dermyn,* to-morrow come in time, P.C. 2843.

TOMTIT, *s.* Pedn paly, w. *Lit.* Velvet-head. This name is still used in Cornwall. Also, Elecompanie, prid-prad, pridn-prall, D.

TONGS, *s.* Gevel, p.

TONGUE, TALK, PRATING, *s.* Clap, p. A word still used.

TONGUE or LANGUAGE, *s.* Tavas, w.; tavaz, p.; tavaseth, w.; tavazeth, p.; laveryans, w.; laveryanz, p.

TONGUE, *s.* (The tongue). Tavot, w.; tavés, O.M. 767. *Ny yl tavés dên yn bys,* the tongue of no man in the world can, O.M. 767; davas, w. *Yntre y thyus ha'y davas,* between his teeth and his tongue, O.M. 826.

TO-NIGHT, *s.* Hanêth. anêth, w.

TOO, *adv.* (Also). Auêdh, awêdh, aweeth, awyêtha, p.

TOO, *adv.* Re, w. *Re gót,* too short. *Re hyr,* too long.

TOO MUCH. Rè, w. *Thotho byny vye re,* for him never would it be too much, R.D. 2056; prys, p.

TOOL, *s.* Tacel, w.; takel, p.; towyll, dowyll, B.

TOOTH, *s.* Dans, w.; danz, p.; deins, dan, B.; dant, w. *Pl.* Dêns, dyns, dhyns, w.; thyns, O.M. 826; deinz, p.

TOOTHACHE, *s.* Dêns-clâv, w.; denz clâv, p.

TOOTHED, *adj.* Dênshoc, w.

TOP or SUMMIT, *s.* Gwartha, w.; guartha, O.M. 1074. *Guartha a'n gorhyl gans quêth,* the top of the ark with a cloth, O.M. 1074; gwarthav, p.; guarthav, gwarthé, B.; gwarhas, guarhas, w.; guarhaz, garhas garras, p.; tâl, w. *Tál an chy,* the top of the house. w.; coppa, B.; côp. w. *Heyl syr epscop . . . esos y'th côp owth ysethé,* Hail Sir Bishop! thou art on thy summit, sitting. P.C. 931; bar, B. *Bar an pedn,* the top of the head, B.; top, thop, w.; veen, O.M. 2444. *Ha'y veen môn ha'y scorennow,* out of its slender top and its branches, O.M. 2444.

TOP OF THE HEAD. Bar an pedn, w.; dipuleuint, P.; dysuleuuit, B.

TOP OF A PLANT. Blynthen, P.

TORCH, s. Torchan, w.

TORMENT, v. Dreynyn, a mutation of *treyneyn*, 1 pers. pl. fut. of *treynyé*, to render miserable, w.; ranny, peyné, peynyé, w.; peyny, dormont, B.; speitia, dho speitia, P.

TORMENT, s. Peyn, poan, poen, pyn, w.; câs, gâs, P.; kên, P.C. 2144.

TO BE TORN, v. Squardyé, squerdyé, w.; squerdya, P.

TORPOR, s. Vindrau, B.; uindrau, P.

TORRENT, s. Cahenryd, chahen rit, w.; kahen-ryd, B.; auan, P.

TORRID, VERY HOT, adj. Poesgys, P.

TORRID HEAT. Poesgys, P.

TORTOISE, s. Melwiogés, w.

TORTURE, v. See TORMENT, v.

TORTURE, s. Peyn, poan, pyn, w; câs, gâs, P.; kên, P.C. 2144. *Ymwyth lemman rág an kên*, preserve thyself now from the torture, P.C. 2144.

TOSS or THROW ABOUT CARELESSLY, v. Caunis, D.

TOTTER, v. Thysplevya, thysplevyas, P.

TOUCH, v. Delymmy, w.; delymhy, P.; dochyé, B.

I TOUCH. Hyndlyf, R.D. 1531. *Er na hyndlyf y golon*, until 1 touch (lay hand on) his heart, R.D. 1531.

TOWARDS. Traha, w. *Traha'n dór*, towards the ground. *Traha'n darras*, towards the door, trocha, troha, w. *Troha kén pow*, towards another country, O.M. 344; trogha, B. *Trogha'n dór*, towards the ground, O.M. 201; trôg, tiha, tyha, B. *War tyha tre*, towards home, B.; tuhé, tuag, tyag, dyag, w.

TOWEL, s. Lien duilof, lysten, w.; stollowfet, mantel, B.; hynelep, P.

TOWER, s. Tûr, tour, tûrma, w.; dour, M. 1394. *Théth dour*, to thy tower, M. 1394; turmas, kastel, B.; lug. *Origines Celticæ.* Guest, vol. 1. pp. 358, 360, note.

TOWERING, adj. Uchel, uhel, huhel, w.; ughel, yuhal, B.

TOWN, s. Tre, dre, dra, P.; trêv. trew, B. *Pl.* Trevow, N. *Tre*, says Pryce, "is the most common word prefixed to our names of places, and I believe is an original British word, it signifies the same thing in Wales, Cornwall, and Armorica." It is also a very common prefix to family names. There is the well known rhyme :—

"By Tre Pol, and Pen
You shall know the Cornishmen."

Camden ("Remains," p. 114) gives us another rhyme, *viz* :—

"By Tre, Ros, Pol, Lan, Caer, and Pen
You may know the most Cornishmen."

A FORTIFIED TOWN. Dinas, w.; dinaz, P.

THIS TOWN. Tremma, dremma, w.

TOWN-HALL, s. Odians, B.

TOWNSMAN, s. Centrevec, centrevek, contrevac, w.

TRACE or MARK, s. Ôl, ool, w.

TRACE or VESTIGE, s. Lerch, lyrch, w.

TRADER, s. Gwicur, gwiccur, gwiccor, gwecor, wecor, gwicgur, guicgur, w.; gwicher, P.; guikyr, B.; goccor, w.; guyeor, P.C. 321. *Pl.* Guycoryon (of *guycor*), P.C. 321. *Why guycoryon eugh yn mês*, ye traders, go out, P.C. 321.

TRAGEDY, s. Awayl, w. *An awdyl-ma taveth bys*, this tragedy much talked of, P.C. 551. In his *Addenda*, Williams (*Lex. Corn. Brit.*) says that the proper meaning of *awayl*, is gospel.

TRAIN-OIL, s. Seym, w.; saim, B. *Kepar ha seym py lyys haal*, like train-oil or saltmarsh mud, O.M. 2708.

TRAITOR, s. Thraytor, traytoar, B.; thrayta, trayta, P.

TRANQUILITY, s. Callamingi, w.; kallaminghi, B.; kallamingi, P.; crês, creys, w.; creez, P.; hêdh, hedwch, cesoleth, kesoleth, cysolath, w.; kysalath, P., cyzaleth, w.; kysoleth, P.

TRANQUILLIZE, v. Hêdhy. w.

TRANSGRESS, v. Pecha, peché, pehé, w.; peghy, P.; becha, beché, tremené, dremené, w. For other forms see SIN, v.

TRANSGRESSION, s. See SIN, s.

TRANSGRESSOR, s. Pechadur, pehadur, w.; pechadyr, P.

A FEMALE TRANSGRESSOR. See "a female sinner," under SINNER.

TRANSMARINE, adj. Tremôr, w.

TRANSVERSE, adj. Adrûs, trûs, w.

TRASH, s. Truck, D. A form of *trôc*, or *drók*, evil, harm.

TRAVAILS, s. (In childbirth). Golovas, P.

TRAVEL, v. Travalia, P.

TRAVERSE, v. Tremenés, dremenés, w.

TREACHEROUS, adj. Fals, fouls, w.

TREACHERY, s. Tretury, B.

TREASON, s. Dreyson, B.

TREASURY, s. Archow, w.; arghou, P.; arghov, P.C 1541.

TREAT, v. Dychyé, dhychyé, dychythyé, dygthyé, dygtyé, dhygtyé, w.; dyghty, thyghtyé, P.

TREE, *s.* Gwedhen, gwidhen, guiden, gwydhen, w. ; guydhen, B. ; guedhan, P. ; gwethan, C.W. 372 ; guethen, N. ; gvethen, O M. 29 ; guetha, B. ; wedhen, wethen, O.M. 167. *Frut a'n wethen a skyans*, the fruit of the tree of knowledge, O.M. 167 ; withen, w. ; withan, wethan, wythan wythen, P. ; weathan, c.w. 759 ; pren, bren, predn, B. *Yw hynwys pren a skyens*, which is named the tree of knowledge, O.M.82.

TREES, *s.* Guit, gwydh, w. ; gwyth, wyth, P. ; gweydh, gwêdh, w. ; gueidh, P. ; guêith, B. ; gveyth, O.M. 29 ; gueyth, N.

TREMBLE, *v.* Crenné, w. ; krenné, P.C. 2995. *Yma an dôr ow krenné*, the earth is trembling, P.C. 2995 ; krenna, P. ; crenna, krena, B. ; cerna, kerna, w. ; creuna, owerené (? *ow crené*), tiené, tyené, vrama, thegtyn, P. *Eva thysa a thegtyn*, Eve at thee will tremble, P.

TREMBLING, *s.* Vrame, P.

TRENCH, *s.* Clêdh, klêdh, glêdh, w. ; kleudh, cleuth, clawd, B. ; fôs, w. ; voze, voza, foza, fossa, P. ; pullan-troillia, w. Borlase gives *pullan troillia*, for a narrow trench or furrow. Trone, vore, D.

TRESPASS, *s.* Cam. *Pl.* Cammow, w.

TRIAL, *s.* Cabel, P. *Hep cabel*, without a trial, P.

TRIAL, *s.* (At law). Bresul, brez, P. ; brûs, P.C. 1984. *Hep brûs iustis uinytha*, without trial by a judge, P.C. 1984.

TRIBE, *s.* (A tribe, a family, *Progenies vel tribus*, Lat.) Ceid, leith, luyte, w. ; lwyth, B.

TRIBE, *s.* (A people, a nation ; people, men). Tûs, tûz, tis, tiz, tez, diz, duz, B.

TRIBE, *s.* (Retinue, a guard, clients, dependents, servants, lads, boys, children). Cosgor, kosgar, w.

TRIBE, *s.* (Kind, sort). Echen, ehen, hechen, he-hen, w. ; ehin, P.

TRICE, *s.* Lam, O.M. 885. *Bys thg'n vmma yn vn lam*, to us here, in a trice, O.M. 885.

TRICK, *s.* Cast, w. ; toul, P.C. 2920 ; pratt, c.w. 518 ; bratt, c.w. 729 ; wrynch, w. *Râk ef a wôr lyés cost*, for he knows many a trick, P.C. 1884. *Hag a aswon lyés wrynch*, and he knows many a trick, P C. 1001.

TO TRICKLE DOWN. *v.* Devery, dyvery, dyveré, w. ; dylly, P.

TRICKSTER, *s.* Kan-kayer, D.

TRIDENT, *s.* Trivorh, B.

TRIFLE, *s.* Mân, w.

TRIFLING, *adj.* Crothac, crothak, w. ; crothache, P.

TRIFLING, *s.* Flehysygow, O.M. 1868. *Ha râg an flehysygow.* and because of the trifling (childishness), O.M 1868.

TRIM, NEAT, *adj.* Fein, feyn, B.

TRINITY, THE TRINITY, *s.* Trindas, an drindas, an drensés, trensés, trinsys, trynsys, trengés, an drengés, w. ; drindaz, drendzhez, drindzhaz, an drindzhiz, P. ; drinzis, drenzhés, drynsys, drengys, w.; drendzer, B.

TRIP, *s.* Lam lithriad, w. ; clot-coffan, P.

TRIP, *v.* Trebystshya, w.

TRIPOD, *s.* Tribêdh, trebath, tribet, w.

TRIVET, *s.* The same as for Tripod, *q.v.*

TROOP *s.* Lhy, P. See MULTITUDE. Pryce calls it a company of horsemen.

TROUBLE, *s.* (Grief, misery, affliction). Ancen, anken, w. *Ny'n sparyaf awos anken*, I will not spare it because of trouble, P.C. 2556 ; dewon, w. ; dewan, dewhan, duon, P. ; câs, gâs, w. *Yn egip whyrfys câs*, in Egypt, trouble has arisen, O.M. 1415 ; kâs, P.C. 30. *Hep stryf ha kâs*, without strife or trouble, P.C. 30 ; três, B. ; govid, w. (*Pl.* of *Govid*, govidion, govigion, govegion, gividzion, w. ; govis, govys, P.); cheyson, R.D. 460. *Hep guthyl na moy cheyson*, without suffering any more trouble, R.D. 460 ; ancensy, ankensy, ankynsy, ponvos, w., ponfos, P. ; ponvotter, ponvetor, w. *Kymmys vyth an ponveter*, so great will be the trouble, P.C. 2656 ; panvotter, panveter, P. ; ponfeys, M. 1606- *Ythyv sur mur a ponfeys*, it is surely much of trouble, M. 1606. *Prâg ymons y in ponfos*, why are they in trouble? M. 1986 ; fyneas, w. ; gene, P. ; grayth, B. ; anfus, N.

TROUBLE, *v.* Dygnas, w. ; dreyny, P.

TROUBLED, VEXED, *adj.* Ponfosyc, w.; ponfosick, ponfosyk, N.

TROUGH, *s.* Laouer, B. ; tie (a large one of wood), D.

TROUT, *s.* Trud, w. ; dluzen (*Pl.* Dluz), B. ; Truff, brythall, D.

TROWEL, *s.* Geuelhorn, B. *Lit.* A work-iron.

TRUCKS, SLEDGES, *s.* Slodys, w. ; slodyys, O.M. 2319.

TRUE, *adj.* Wyr, w. ; weare, c.w. 2134 ; gwyre, c.w. 672 ; gwir, wir, gwyr, guir, w. ; guyr, N. ; defry, dheffry, deffry, devry, w.

TRUE OF SPEECH. Guirion, guerryon, P.

TRULY, *adv.* Weare, c.w. 2134 ; wyer, c.w. 2448 ; en wir, w. ; yn guyr, N. ; purguir, M. 179 ; preva, defry, dheffry, deffry, devry, w.

TRUMPET, *s.* Corn, w. ; korn, B. (*Pl.* Cernow, kernow) ; hirgorn, w. *Lit.* A long horn ; tollkorn. B. ; this is also used of a flute or fife. *Lit.* A holed horn, from *tol*, a hole. Trompour, O M, 19..6. *Trey hans harpés ha trompours*, three hundred harps and trumpets, O M. 1996.

TRUMPETER, *s.* Cerniat, w. ; kerniat, kernias, B. ; cernias, cherniat, w. ; hirgherniad, B.; hirgerniad, bardh hirgorn, w. ; barth hirgorn, P.

TRUNK or BUTT END, *s.* Bên, w.

TRUNK or BOX, *s.* Trôc, trôk, w.

TRUNK OF A TREE, *s.* Stoc, w.; boncyff, trech, B.

TRUST, *v.* Fydhyé, w.; fythy, tryst, dryst, P.; dristya, c.w. 1380. *Me a dryst yn du avan*, I trust in God above, c.w. 1380.

TRUSTY, *adj.* Laian, lén, w.; luen, lwn, B.; vên, R.D. 363. *Del ough tús vên*, as ye are trusty men, R.D. 363.

TRUST YE. Ratha (*ran tha*), P.

TRUST YE TO IT. Owh ratha, P.

TRUTH, *s.* Gwîr, wyr, vîr, w.; guir, P.; gwyr, w.; guyr, B.; guirder, P.; gwîrder, w.; guyrder, N.; gwîrioneth, w.; guîrioneth, B.; gwyryoneth, wîrioneth, w.; guyryoneth, N.; guyroneth, O.M. 702; gwreanathe, c.w. 1892; glendury, lendury, fydh, fêdh, w.; fâs, P.

TRUTH, LOYALTY, *s.* Lauté, w; leuté, O.M. 2120; lewté, leauté, louté, w.; lausé, lountée, P.

IN TRUTH. In fâs, enuir, P.; yn wys, O.M. 1545. *An tús yv marow yn wys*, the people who are dead in truth, O.M. 1545; pûr wyr, P.; yn guyryoneth, P.C. 595; yn guyrder, O.M. 1732. *Yn guyrder an thyr guelen*, in truth, the three rods, O.M. 1732; yn preva, w.; rûm laute, renlewty, rûm lewté, P.

TO SAY THE TRUTH. A leverel guyroneth, O.M. 702.

BY MY TRUTH. Rum lewté, rum lauté, P.; ru'm leuté, O.M. 2124; renlewty, P.

TRUTH-TELLING, *adj.* (Verax, *Lat.*) Gwirion, gwyryon, w.

TRY or EXAMINE, *v.* Cably, w. *Lathé dén nag yw cablys*, to kill a man who is not tried, P.C. 2434.

TRY or MAKE TRIAL OF, *v.* Sayé, P.C. 2308. *Rák the sayé me a vyn*, for I will try thee, P.C. 2308.

TRY or PROVE, *v.* Provi, provy, preva, w.; dho prêf, P.

TO TRY OUT A THING. Trebytehya, P.

TUB. *s.* Ceroin, keroin. w.; kerrin, P.; balliar, tonnel. B.

A LITTLE TUB. Kibbal, B.

TUBE, *s.* Pîb, w.

A SMALL TUBE. Piban, peban, w.; pibonoul, B.

TUCKER or FULLER, *s.* Tricciar, trikkiar, trycciar, w.; trykkiar, trikkin, B.

TUESDAY, *s.* De Merh, w.; Demer, B. *Lit.* Mars' day.

TUFT, *s.* Cop, criban, w.; kriban, B.

A TUFT OF GRASS, RUSHES, &c. Pilier, D. Perhaps from *pil*, a hillock.

TUFTED, SPIKED, *adj.* Tushoc, dushoc, w.

TO TUMBLE DOWN, *v.* Thomelly, P.

TO TUMBLE DOWN or OFF, *v.* Unchelly, P.

TUMULT. *s.* Godoryn, B.; deray, theray, P.C. 380. *Ef re ruk mur a theray*, he hath made much tumult, P.C. 380; randigal, B. *Randigal* is a word still used. See ROW and UPROAR.

TUN, *s.* Balliar, ceroin, keroin, w.; kerrin, P.; tonnel.

TUNE, *s.* Cans, kans, B.

TUNE YE. Pebouch, B.

TUNNEL, *s.* Radgel, D.

TURBOT, *s.* Brett, D.

TURF, *s.* (A turf or sod). Cesan, w.; kezan, P.; tab, D. (*Pl.* Cesow, kesow).

A SMALL PIECE OF TURF. Pednan, tabbun, D.

TURKEY, *s.* (Cock or hen). Zâr, P.

TURKEY-COCK. *s.* Kok Gini, P.

TURN, *s.* (A course or turn of time). See TIME.

TURN, *s.* (A winding, a turning). Torn, w. *Torn an vôr*, the turning of the way, w.; tro. w. (See A SUN TURN.)

TURN, *s.* Tro, w.; trettya, M. 1393. *Moys a raff trettya*, I will go in a turn, M. 1393. *Ef a wra thynny drok tro*, he will do us an ill turn, P.C. 3066.

TURNS :—BY TURNS, IN ITS TURN. Enuêdh, enwith, P.

TURN *v.* Treylé, treylyé, w.; treyl, B.; trailia, trylyé, w.; trylya, B.; troillia, w.; traillia, B. *Traillia an bêr*, to turn the spit, B.

TURN, *v.* (Twist or spin). Nedhé, w.; nethé, nedha, P.

TO TURN BACK, *v.* Treylé, trailia, P.

TO TURN ASIDE, *v.* Ommely, umhelys, w.

TO TURN or PUT OUT, *v.* Asgor, P.

TURNIP, *s.* Ervinen, B.; turnupan, tyrnypan, P.

TURTLE, *s.* Turen, turan, B.

TURTLE-DOVE, *s.* Troet, turen, w.; turan, P.

TWEAK, *v.* Grock, D.

TWELVE. Dowdhec, dowdhek, dewdhec, w.; douthek, B.; dowthack, dewthek, P. *Dewthek mys*, twelve months, P.

TWELFTH. Dowdhegvés, dowdhegvas, w.

TWELFTH-DAY, EPIPHANY, *s.* Degl stûl, deglstûl, B.; stûl, w.

TWENTIETH. Igansvés, igansvath, w.; igans vath, iganzvath, iganz vâs, P.

TWENTY. Ugans, hugens, igans, w.; iganz, nigans, B.; ugens, N.

TWENTY-ONE. Wonnen war iganz, P.; onan war ugens, N. *Lit.* One upon twenty.

TWICE. Dewêth, dewyth, w.; deuyth, dywyth, diuêth, dywêth, P.

TWIG, *s.* Guaglen, B.; prennyer, prenyer, P.

A TWIG OF HEATH. Swike, D.

TWIST, *v.* Nedhé, w.; nethé, nedha, P.

TWITCH, *s.* Squych, scwyth, skwych, w.; skwyth, pyn, P.; squitch, D.

TWO. Dew, dhew, thew, w.; deu, N.; du, w.; deaw, c.w. 1056; deau, dyw. diew, w.; dieu, B.; diw, dui, di. w. *Di* in composition, as *dibréh*, the arms, *i.e.*, the two arms.

THE TWO or BOTH. An diew, an dieu, &c.

TWO OF THEM. Deu anedho, P.

TWO-FACED, JANUS-LIKE, *adj.* Jan- jansy, D.

TWO SCORE. Dewugens, dew-ugens, w.; deuiggans, dowgans, B.

U.

"This letter in Cornish has four sounds. 1. That of the Italian *u*, or English *oo*, as *gûr*, a man; *tûr*, a tower; which are also written in Cornish, *gour, tour.*

2. That of *u*, in the English words, *burn, turn*, &c., as Cornish *umma*, here; *unna*, there.

3. That of the Welsh *u*, which is the same as that of *y*, in the English words *hungry, sundry.* Thus Cornish *tús* (written in later times *tees*), a people; *rûdh*, crimson; *úgans* (*igans*), twenty.

4. The diphthongal sound represented by *ew*, in the English words, *few, new.* Thus Cornish *pu*, who; *Du*, God; *tu*, a side; which are also written in Cornish, *pew, Dew. tew*," w. *Lex. Corn. Brit.*

UDDER, *s.* Tidi, w.; tethan, B.

UGLINESS, *s.* Hacter, c.w. 289.

UGLY, *adj.* Hager, hagar, P.; vthek (*uthek*), o.M. 798. *Best vthek hep falladow*, an ugly beast without doubt, o.M. 798.

MORE UGLY. Hagra, hacera, B.; hackra, c.w. 478.

UGLY FACES, GRIMACES, *s.* Mowys, w.

ULCER, *s.* Plûs, w.

UNABASHED, *adj.* Devêth, divêth. w.

UNANIMOUS, *adj.* Unvêr, w.

UNBELIEF, *s.* Dyscrygyans, w.; thyscregyans, M. 3299. *Galsos mûr yn dyscrygyans*, thou art gone much in unbelief, R.D. 1516. *Mentenour thyscregyans*, upholder of unbelief, M. 3299.

UNBELIEVER, *s.* Discrugyer, discrygyer, P. *Pl.* Dyscrygygyon, dysgryggyon, w.

UNBELIEVING, *adj.* Discrygye, dyscrygyc, w.; dyscrygyk, R.D. 1519. *Thomas ty yv dyscrygyk*, Thomas thou art unbelieving, R.D. 1519.

UNCHANGEABLE, *adj.* Tewlys, P.

UNCHASTE, *adj.* Squeniv, w.

UNCLAD, *adj.* Fernoyth, fernoth. These are doubtful words, w.

UNCLE, *s.* (A father's brother). Ewiter, euiter, euithr, euit, abardtat, B ; a barth ras, P.

UNCLE, *s.* (A mother's brother). Ounter, B.; abarhmam, P.

UNCONCEALED, *adj.* Apert, w.

UNCONSTRAINED, *adj.* Ruid, rid, w.

UNCOVER, *v.* Discudhé, w.; discuthé, P.; dyscudhé, w.; dhyscudhé. B.; dascudhé, disquedha, discwedha, diswedha, dyswedha, dyswedhy, dysquedhas, w.

UNCOVERED, *adj.* (Naked, bare). Nôth, w.; nooth, P.; noath, noeth, noyth, w.

UNDEFILED, *adj.* Pûr, w.

UNDER, BENEATH. Dan, tan, dhan, w.; than, N.; den, P.; yn dan, w.; dadn, ysel, yssel, P.

UNDER HIM. Dano, dadno, yndanno, w.

UNDER ME. Tanof, w.; tanov, P.

FROM UNDER. Adhan, w. (*a dhan*).

UNDERGROWTH, *s.* (As of weed in corn, &c.) Lugg, D.

UNDERSTAND, *v.* Convedhas, w.; convethas, P.; wodhfyé, uffya, w.; wothya, descy, desgy, desca, desga, dyscy, deshy, P.

UNDERSTANDING, *s.* Brês, w.; brêz, P.; brûs, w.; brûz, P.; breus, w.; vrûs, vrys, vrìs, P.; vrês, w.

UNDERTAKER, *v.* Esumsyn, w.; owerbyn, dho aulra, P.

UNDERTAKER, *s.* Aultra, P.

UNDO. *v.* (Ruin, destroy). Diswrey, w.; dizurey, diswêl. P.; dyswêl, diswul, w.; dyswul, P.; dhyswul, disil, w.; dizil, dyswrey, diswreys, dho diswrug. P.; diswruthyl, w.; dyswruthyl, dizuruthyl, dyswythyl, dystrewy, tystrywy, P.

UNDOUBTEDLY, *adv.* En dhiougel, en dhiugel, w.; diogel, diougel, P.; hepmar, B.

UNDOUBTING, *adj.* Dywysyk, P. *Pys gans colon dywysyk*, pray with undoubting heart, R.D. 1370.

UNDRESS, *v.* Digwisca, dygwysca, w.; thyguisky, P.; discy, dyscy, w.

UNEQUAL, *adj.* Anghespar, w.; anghel par, B.

UNEQUALLED, *adj.* Hepparow, w.; hepparou, P.; hepar, w.

UNEXPOSED, *adj.* Diogel, dyogel, dyhogel, dyowgel, dyougel, w.; diougel, P.

UNFAITHFUL, *adj.* Dislaian, w.

UNFORTUNATE, *adj.* Aflydys, w.

UNFORTUNATELY, *adv.* Govy, o.m. 2216. *Govy raghtho*, unfortunately for them, o.m. 2216.

UNGUENT *s.* Onement, oynment, unnient, w.; unient, p.; urat, w. For other forms see SALVE.

UNHAPPILY, *adj.* Soweth, syweth, w.

UNHAPPY, *adj.* Soweth, p. See also SAD.

UNHAPPY I. Govy, w.

UNHAPPY HE. Goef, w. *Goef nep a worth jovyn*, unhappy he who worships Jove, o.m. 1889.

UNHAPPY THEY. Goy, w.

UNHEALTHY, *adj.* Aniach, w.; aniak, b.

UNICORN, *s.* Uncorn, w.

UNITE, *v.* Yunnyé, w.; yunnyy, p.

TO BE UNITED, *v.* Yunnyé, w.; yunnyy, p.

UNITED or JOINT, *adj.* (In common). Cês, kês, kys, w.

UNITY or CONCORD, *s.* Cêsolêth, kesolêth, cysolêth, cyzalêth, w.; kyzalath, kyzauleth, b.

UNIVERSE, *s.* Bys, vys, bês, bit, w.

UNJUST, *adj.* Cam-hisic, p.; camhinsic, camhilik, b.

UNJUSTLY, *adv.* Cammen, p. *Na wrellough cammen lathé*, that ye do not unjustly slay, p.c. 2196.

UNJUST, AN UNJUST MAN, *s.* Camhilik, b.

UNKNOWN, *adj.* Uncouth, w.

UNLEAVENED, *adj.* Heb gwêl, b.

UNLEAVENED BREAD. Bara heb gwêl, b.

UNLESS. Mars, w. *Mars dre múr aur*, unless by much gold, p.c. 1964; mûrs, marny (*mar-ny*), marni, marnas, marnés, w. *Marnés drethos veronica*, unless by thee Veronica, b.d. 2220; manan (*ma-na'n*), mês, w.; mêz, p.; mâs, w.; mâz, keen, p.; kên, cên, kyn, cyn, gên, boyna, w.; pony, puni, p.; poni, w.; pini, pyni, b.; ponag, penegés, penag, w.; pynak, p.c. 681.

UNLIKE, *adj.* Anghespar, w.; anghel par, p.

UNLOCK, *v.* Dialwhedhé, dyalwhedhé, w.

UNLOOSE, *v.* Deglené, teglené, w.; louzall, b.

UNMARRIED, *adj.* Ruid, rìd, w.

AN UNMARRIED WOMAN. Benin rìd, w.

UNNATURAL, *adj.* Denatar, w.; denater, b.

UNPLEASANT, *adj.* Anwhêc, w.; anwêk, m. 451.

UNPLOUGHED LAND, *s.* Tôn, todn, w.

UNQUIET, *adj.* Difeid, w.

UNRIPE, *adj.* (Crude or green). Criv, w.; kriv, b.

UNROBE, *v.* Digwisca, dygwysca, w.; thyguisky, p.; discy, dyscy, w.

UNRULY, *adj.* Brochi, b.

UNSAVOURY, *adj.* Anwhêc, w.; anwêk, m. 451; desawer, m. 4135. *Desawer vest yv henna*, unsavoury beast is that, m. 4135.

UNSEEMLY, *adj.* Hager, w.

UNSHOD, *adj.* Diesgis, b.; diesgiz, p.

UNSWEET, *adj.* Anwhêc, w.; anwêk, m. 451; desawer, m. 4135.

UNTIE, *v.* Degylmy, b.; deglené, teglené, w.; louzall, b.

UNTIL. Erna, w. *Erna wrello tremené*, until she be dead, o.m. 2695; arna, w.; hedré, n. *Hedré vy may fo anken*, until it be that death is, o.m. 276; hysseas, w.; hyz, p.; bys, w.; bys pan, b.; byzpan, p.; pan, terebah, b.; trebé, trybo, w.; trehé, p.; spâs, w.

UNTIL THAT. Byspan, trehé, w.

UNTO, *prep.* (See TO).

UNTO THY. Dheth, dhodha, b.

UNTO YOU. Hui, huyhui, dheu, b.

UNWELL, *adj.* Aniach, w.; aniak, b,

UNWILLING, *adj.* Ambodlaun, anbodlaun, b.

I AM UNWILLING. Nem deur. (*It concerns not me*), w.

YOU ARE UNWILLING. Nôz deur, w.

UNWISE, *adj.* Anfûr, w.; unscogyon, miscogyon, b.

UNYIELDING, *adj.* Dynas, w. A doubtful word.

UP. Ban, aban, yn ban, w. *Adam saf yn ban*, Adam stand up, o.m. 65. *Bynytha na thué yn ban*, he will never come up, r.d. 2139; avan, a van, a vadna, aman, man, w.; mann, p.

UP! Insol, m. 2747. *Insol bethugh glân yesseys*, Up!, be ye clean confessed, m. 2747.

UPMOST, *adj.* Uchaf, w.

UPON. Wâr, w. *Wâr veneth (meneth)*, upon a mountain, o.m. 1281; uâr, wâr, âr, p.; êr, w.; hâr, gor, wôr, uôr, vâr, vêr, uch, ug, juh euth, p.; ord, orth, worth, yn, y, barh, barth, aberth, abervêth, aperfêth, w.; abernéth, abervadh, uhella, uhellés, uhelder, p.

UPON HER. Warnethy, n.

UPON HIM or IT. Warnodho, w.; warnetho, p.; warnotho, n.

UPON IT. Warfo, p.

UPON ME. Waraf, warnaf, w.

UPON THEE. Warnas, w.; uarnaz, p.; warnos, warnés, w.

UPON THEM. Warnedhé, w.; warnethé, n.; uarnedhé, p.; warnans, warnodhans, warnydhans, w.; uarnydzhanz, p.

UPON US. Warnan, w.; uarnan, warany, p.

UPON THE WHOLE. Warth an myns, b.

UPON YOU. Warnouch, w.; warnough, warneugh, p.; warnoch, w

UPPER, *adj.* Augh, haugh, hagh, p.

UPPER PART or SUMMIT, *s.* Pen, pyn, w.; pedn, P.

UPPERMOST, *adj.* Pennaeth, B.; uchaf, w.

UPRIGHT, *adj.* Aban, yn ban. w.; sef-ban, seban, P.; taman, ynten, B.

UPRIGHT, JUST, *adj.* Ewhinsic, euhinsic, w.

UPRIGHTLY, *adv.* Plemyk, M. 3314. *Me a leuer the plemyk,* I will tell uprightly, M. 3314.

UPROAR, *s.* Touse, B. This word is still in use. Also miggal-conpore. miggle-compore, garm, cab-a-rouse, D.

UPWARDS, *adv.* Huchot, avan, aman, man, w.; ɯann, P.; ban, w.; vyny, y vyny, P. See UP.

URGE, TO PRESS ON, *v.* Ynnya, w.

URINE, *s.* Troaz, B.; pisas, w.; pizaz, B.

URINATE, *v.* Troaza, B.

US, *pron.* An, 'n, ni, nei, ny. nyny (*nyny* is a reduplicate, form), w.; nan. *War-nan,* on us, B.; do, vy, P.; yn, w.

BY US. Drethon, N.; genen, w.; genyn, c.w. 1473; gennan, B.

FOR US. Dhynny, P.; theny, c.w. 1081; dhyn, râgon, râgon nyi, P.

FROM US. Ahanan, w.; a hanan, hanan, P.; deworthyn, dheworthyn, dyworthyn, w.; worthyn, P.; râgon, w.

IN US. Ynnon (yn-ni), w.; ynnon ni, P.

OF US. Ahanan, w.; hunnyn, B.; humy, awy (*a why*), P.

TO US. Thyn, P.; dên (*de-yn*) deyn, dheyn, dyn, w.; dhyn, dynny, w.; thynni, P.; thynny, w.; dhynny, M. 1499; dagan, P.; thagan, B.; worthyn, orthyn, w.

UNTO US. See to US.

UPON US. Warnan, N.

WITH US. Gennen, B.; genen, N.

USE, *s.* Déf. *Déf vyth,* any use, P.; dêfnydh, w.; dêfnyth P.C. 2548. *Anotho gul défnyth vas,* to make a good use of it, P.C. 2548; ous, P; gynsy, B. *The wull gynsy,* for it had use, B.

USE, *v.* Dychyé, dhychyé, dychthyé, dygthyé, dygtyé, dhygtyé, w.; dyghty, thyghtyé, P.

USED, *part.* Digthyas, B.

USAGE or CUSTOM, *s.* Desmos, P.

USUAL, *adj.* Arbednec, arbennec, w.

UTENSIL, *s.* Lofgurchel, w.; lofgurhchel, P.

UTENSILS, *s.* Cosgurhehel, daver, B.

UTMOST, *adj.* Crow, B. *Yn crow,* to the utmost, B.; diwedha, diwedhas, dywethas, w.; diuethas, B.; erow, P.

UTTER, *v.* (Speak, tell, declare). Dysmegy, dysmygy, desmygy, w.

UTTERANCE, *s.* Lavar. See also SPEAK.

UVULA, *s.* Clunker, D. From *clunk,* to swallow.

V.

" This letter, sounded as in English, is a secondary in all the Celtic dialects. It represents two characters, viz., *bh,* the soft mutation of *b*; and *mh,* the soft mutation of *m.* Thus Cornish *bara,* bread; *y vara,* his bread. *Mam,* a mother; *y vam,* his mother.

In late Cornish it was used as the secondary mutation of *f,* as *fórdh,* a way; *an vórdh,* the way." w. *Lex. Corn. Brit.*

VACANT, *adj.* Gwâg, w.; guag, B.; gwâk, w.; gwâl, B.

VACUUM, *s.* Gwâg, w.

VAGABOND, *s.* Gadlying. w. *A nyl gadlying dués yn rág,* oh, vile vagabond come forth, P.C. 1817. For other words, see RASCAL.

VAGINA, *s.* Cons, gons, w.

VAGRANT, *s.* Gwilleiw, w.; guilleia, B.; guillein, w.; losel, P.; lorel, w.

VAIN, EMPTY, *adj.* Côk, covge, cowg, w.; cowga, P.; fykyl, o.M. 234. *Na the'th fykyl lauorow,* nor thy vain words, o.M. 234.; trafyl, P.; trufyl, R.P. 1055.

VAIN, *adj.* (Of no avail) Negeris, w.; segeris, P.; guag, en guag, B.; gwâg, gwâk, w.

VALIANT, *adj.* Breseler, w.; barthesek, R.D. 109. *Hâg yn bateyl barthesek,* and in battle valiant, R.D. 109; colannac, w.; colaɲnak, P.; kollannak, B.; colanac, colenec, w.; kalonnek, B.; calonec, kalonek, P.; cylednac. cadarn, w.; cadr, ithik, gawr, B.; manerlich, w.

VALIANTLY, *adv.* Manerlich, o.M. 2200.

VALLEY, *s.* Cûm, nans, w.; nance. nantz, P.; res, rôs, B.; rose, P. *Pen rose,* the head of the valley, P.; rôsh, P.; dôl, glên, glyn, w. *Glên* and *glyn* signify a valley through which a river flows, and *dôl,* a mead with a river flowing through it, w.

A LITTLE VALLEY. Go dôl, P.

VALLUM or DITCH, *s.* Graff, B.

VALOUR, *s.* See COURAGE.

VALUE, *v.* Sensy, synsy, sendzha, dho sendzhé, w.; sindzha, P.; sensyé, sinsy, syngy, w.; sansa, sensa, P.; settya, w.; rên, rôf, roof. *Ny róf,* I value not, P.

VALUE, *s.* Prîs, prîz, prys, brys, bry, vry, w.; brêz, P.; grâs, râs, w.; râz, P.

VALUED, *part.* Dymmo, B.

VALUED, ESTEEMED, *adj.* Pryvêth, privêth, P.

VALUELESS MATERIAL ·or ORE.   Podar, P.

VALVE, *s.*   Balloc, valloc, w.

VANITY, *s.*   Uferêth, everêth, w. ; terrygy, P.C. 112.

VANNES, *s.*   Venetens, M. 2682.   *Me yv yerle in Venetens*, I am Earl in Vannes, M. 2682.

VANQUISH, *v.*   Fethé, fethy, w. ; wharfethy, P.

VARIEGATED, *adj.*   (With black and white).   Brîth, w. ; bryth, B. ; bruit, B.

VARNISH or GLAZE, *s.*   Glidder, D.

VARY, *v.*   Legria, w.

VARYING, A VARYING, *s.*   Legradz, w.

VASSAL, *s.*   Omager, M. 3482.   *Byth nynsoff the omager*, never am I thy vassal, M. 3482.

VAULT or LEAP, *v.*   Vossa, B.

VAULT or LEAP, *s.*   Vols, B. ; fût, P.

VAULT or SUMMERSAULT, *s.*   Gudrak, P.

VAULT or ARCH, *s.*   Guarrak, B.

VAUNT, *v.*   Guerha, gwertha, P.

VAUNTING, *s.*   Moureriac, w. ; moureriak, B.

VEHEMENCY, *s.*   Creys, crys, grys, w.

VEHEMENTLY, *adv.*   Lasthé, P. ; dour, M. 1749.   *Reys yv dyuyh lafurya dour*, it is for you to work vehemently (to labour hard), M. 1749.

VEIL, *s.*   Gôl, goil, goyl, goul, guil, P. ; gugl (? *guyl*), usair, B.

VEIN, *s.*   (Of the body).   Guîth, B. ; gwyth, gôth, guid, w.

VEIN or LODE, *s.*   (Of ore).   Meine, D.   A form of *mên*, stone.

VELVET, *s.*   Paly, w.

VEND, *v.*   Gwerthé, werthé, w.

VENERY, LUST, *s.*   Guenar, P.

VENGEANCE, *s.*   Dial, dyal, dyhal, w. ; dyel, M. 1596.   *Trom dyal wâr ól an veys*, heavy vengeance on all the world, O.M. 1209 ; vynions, O.M. 1498.   *Vynions créf a góth warnas*, hard vengeance will fall on thee, O.M. 1498.

VENOM, *s.*   Guenoin, P.

VENT-HOLE, *s.*   Toll y gwint, B.

VENTRILOQUIST, *s.*   Guan ascient, P.

VENTURE, *s.*   Antell, w.

VENTURE, *v.*   Lavasy, w.

I MIGHT VENTURE.   Levesyn, 1 pers. s. subj. of *lavasy*, to venture, w.

VENUS, *s.*   (Goddess of love).   Gwenar, w. ; Guenar, P.

VERACITY, *s.*   Gwîr, w. ; guîr, P. ; gwyr, gwirder, w. ; guerder, P. ; gwyrder, gwirionêth, w. ; guirionêth, B. ; gwyryonêth, w. ; gureonêth, B.

A MAN OF VERACITY.   Guirion, guerryon, guirleveriat, B.

VERBOSE, *adj.*   Tavasec, w. ; tavazek, P.

VERDANT, *adj.*   Glâs, gwêr, gwyrdh, guirt, w.

VERIER, *adj.*   Pyrra, c w. 2400.   *Pyrra foyle ne ve gwelys*, a verier fool was never seen, C.W. 2400.

VERIEST, *adj.*   Purra, w.

VERILY, *adv.*   Eredy, yredy, w. ; ên uir, B. ; ênuir, lantê, reseth (*re seth*), rum leuté, rum lancé, P. ; verement, M 2927.   See also IN TRUTH.

VERITY, *s.*   See VERACITY.

VERMIN, A VERMIN, *s.*   Prîf, pryf, prêf, prêv, w.   *Pl.* Pryvês, w.

VERY.   Pûr, pôr, pyr, pre, pêr, pâr.   *Pâr vár*, very early, P. ; bûr, O.M. 1855.   *A búr fals dyscryggyon*, oh, very false disbelievers, O.M. 1855 ; mage, kês.   *Kês-kewétha*, very familiar, P. ; hich, fêst, w.   *Wolcum fêst*, very welcome, O M. 1207 ; brâs, w.   *The colon yw calés brâs*, thy heart is very hard, O.M. 1207.   It should be noticed that *brds* and *fêst* are used after the adjective, as may be seen in the quotations given,

VERY CERTAINLY.   Gorthewyth, w.

VERY FAMILIAR.   Kêskewetha, P.

VERY MUCH.   Ithik tra, B. ; laur, P. ; caougant, B.

VERY RIGHT.   Pûr eun, P.

VERY SMALL.   Flo, B.

VERY SOON.   Dystouch, dhystouch, w. ; dystough, P,

VERY TRUE.   Pûr wyr, P.

VESPERS, *s.*   Gwesper, w.

VESSEL, *s.*   See SHIP.

VESSEL, *s.*   (As cup, dish, &c.)   Lester, lestre, kavat, B. ; cafat, P.

VESTIGE, *s.*   Lerch, lyrch, w.

VESTURE or GARMENT, *s.*   Gwisc, guisc, gwesc, guesk, P.

VEX, *v.*   Duwenhé, dewhanhé, w. ; dreyny, P. ; ranny, w. ; speitia, dho speitia, P. ; tosoanna, B. ; troplesy, w.

VEXATION, *s.*   Duwon, duwhan, dewhan, duchan, duan, duon, w.   *Dre púr anger ha duon*, for very anger and vexation, R.D. 1402 ; ponvos, ponvotter, w. ; ponfos, panveter, panvetter, P. ; ponveter, w. ; despyth, B. ; gene, P. ; cên, kên, chên, ancensy, ankensy, w.

VEXED, *adj.*   Ponfosyc, w ; ponfosick, P. ; serrys, w.

TO BE VEXED.   Huthy, P.

I AM VEXED.   Serrés, M. 1943.   *Ragtho may thoma serrés*, so that for him I am vexed, M. 1943.

VEXING, *adj.*   Raneic, rauny, B.

VICEROY, *s.* Luder, w.; lyder, B.

VICTIM, *s.* Aperth, B.

VICTORIOUS, *adj.* Budicaul, bydhygol, B.

VICTUALLER, *s.* Maidor. maithor, w.

VICTUALLING-HOUSE, *s.* Tshyi tavargn, P.

VICTUALS, *s.* Bruha, w.; breuha, P.; bygyens, vygyens, w.; vyguons, P.

VIEW, *v.* Sylly, w.

VIEW. *s.* Sell, sil, syll, sull, w.; sôll, P.; goloc, golok, woloc, w.

VIEWABLE, *adj.* (In open view). Sellic, w.

VIGOUR, *s.* Crêvder, w.; krêvder, P.; creys, greys, w.; fâs, fôs, P.

VIGOROUS, *adj.* Crêf, crêv, w.; krêv, B.; crîf, cryf, cryff, mên, vên, fên, frêth, w.

VIGOROUSLY, *adv.* Yn frêth, P.C. 1242.

VILE, *adj.* Hogen, w.; hogan, P.; acr, B.

VILELY, *adv.* See VILLAINOUSLY.

VILLAGE, *s.* Gwic, wic, w.; wick, P.; trêv, trew, B.; bounder tre, castel, w. *My a vyn gruthyl castel,* I will make a village, O.M. 1709. For *castel* see also R.D. 1471.

VILLAGES, *s.* Trevov, M. 369; trefov, 1037.

A LITTLE VILLAGE. Gwiccet, wiccet, w.; wicket, P.

VILLAGER, *s.* Trevedic, w.

VILLAIN, *s.* Bylen, w.; belan, M. 2295. *Ny a vet gans an belan,* we shall meet with the villain, M. 2295; harlot, plos (*Pl.* Plussyon), w.; drocgerut, drokgeryt, B.; gâl, M. 1244. *Gans guv the wané an gâl,* to pierce the villain with a spear, P.C 2917. *Kepar a gâl,* like a villain, M. 1244; casadow, P. *Ov ton a plos casodow,* bringing of the foul villain, O.M. 892; basadow, P.C. 452. *Me a caché an basadow,* I will catch the villain, P.C. 452. For other words see RASCAL.

VILLAINOUS, *adj.* Casadow, gasadow. plosec, plosek, w.

VILLAINOUSLY, *adv.* Vylen, velen, B. *Mar velen,* so vilely (or villainously), B.

VILLAINY, *s.* Belyny, bylyny, w.; bylen, P.; velyny. vylyny, w.

VINDICATE, *v.* Vensy, B.

VINE, *s.* Gwinbren, guinbren, w.

VINEGAR, *s.* Eysel, eysyll, guin fellet, w.

VIOLATE, *v.* Syndyé, P.C 580. *Hâg an lahés ov syndyé,* and violating the laws, P.C. 580.

VIOLENCE, *s.* Mestry, maystry, meystry, w. *War ov thyr ov gûl mestry,* over my land doing violence, O.M. 2144.

VIOLENT, *adj.* Frêth, w.

VIOLET, *s.* (The flower). Melhyonen, w.

VIOLIN or FIDDLE, *s.* Crowd, harfel, w.; fiol, P.; fylh, O.M. 1997. *Crowd* is a well known name for a fiddle, D.

VIOLINIST, *s.* See FIDDLER.

VIPER, *s.* Nader, w.; nadar, naddyr, prêv, B.

VIRGIN, *s.* Gwyrchas, wyrchas, gwyrchés, w.; gwyrghés, P.; wyrghas, O.M. 2663. *A vyth a wyrghas genys,* who shall be born of a virgin, O.M. 2663; gwerchés, werchés, gwyrhes, gwheras, wyrhés, w.; guerhays, M. 706. *Maria mam ha guerhays,* Mary, mother and virgin. M. 706; machtêth, vachtêth, w.; vaghtyth, N.; vaghtêth, P.C. 1727. *A vaghtêth gulan dynythys,* of a pure virgin born, P.C. 1727; mahteid, mahtheid, w.; mattheid, martheid, B.; maithés, w.; maithée, myrgh, P.

THE VIRGIN MARY. An wyrhés Maria, P.

VIRTUE, WORTH, *s.* Grâs, râs, w.; râz, P.

VISAGE. *s.* (The face or countenance). Fysmant, vysmant, w.

VISAGE, *s.* (The look or mien). Miras, w.; miraz, B.

VISCOUNT, *s.* Huhelvair, huhelwur, w.; huwelwair, P.; hyuelvair, huweluair, B.

VISIBLE, *adj.* Hewel, w.; heuel, B.

VISION, *s.* (A vision or a seeing). Gwêlas, welas, gwêl, wêl, gweyl, weyl, w.

VISION, *s.* (As in a dream). Besyon, M. 984. *Dre besyon,* by a vision, M. 984.

VIXEN or FOX BITCH, *s.* Lowenés, w.; lowenez, P.

VOCABULARY or WORD BOOK, *s.* Ger-lever, P.

VOICE, *s.* (Speech, utterance). Lavar, w.

A VOICE, *s.* Lêf, w.; leff, B.; leaf, C.W. 1426. *The léf arluth a glewaf,* thy voice Lord I hear, O.M. 587.

VOID or HOLLOW, *s.* and *adj.* Gwâg, w.

VOID or EMPTY, *s.* and *adj.* Noeth. noath, nôth, noyth, w.; nooth, P.; segeris, segyr, siger, B.

VOID OF, WITHOUT. Heb, w.; hep, P.; negeris, w.; segeris, P.

TO VOID EXCREMENT, *v.* Caca, w.; kakan, kah, P. *Kaka en guili,* cacavit in lecto, P. (*sic.*)

VOLUME, *s.* (Book). Levar, liver, lyvyr, caiauc, w.

VOMIT, *v.* Hweda, hwedzha, w.; huedzha, P.

VOW. *s.* Adoth, w.

VOW, *v.* Fo, vo, fe, P.

I VOW. Je vody. The French *je vous dis.*

VULGAR, THE VULGAR, THE MOB, *s.* Lû, megannu, B.; megganny, moggon, P.; mogyon, B.

VULVA, *s.* Cheber, B.

W.

" This letter is always a consonant in Cornish. In Cornish *w* is a primary and a secondary letter, when primary it is immutable, and when secondary it is a mutation of *g*, as *goloc*, sight ; *an woloc*, the sight ; *goys*, blood ; *y woys*, his blood. *Govyn, dhe wovyn*, to ask.

After certain words preceding, this mutation is further made into an aspirate *wh*. Thus *godhevys*, suffered ; *ef a whodhevys*, he suffered.

Wh is also found as an aspirate mutation of *c* in Cornish, as *colon*, a heart ; *war ow wholon*, on my heart," w. *Lex. Corn. Brit.*

WAG, *v.* Tolly, R.D. 2355. *Ye re gymmy tol ow guen*, I wag my tail at ye, R.D. 2355.

WAGES, *s.* Arféth, w. ; arvêth, M. 3201. *Awos arvéth me an gruae*, for wages I will do it, M. 3201 ; gober, gobar, gobyr, w. ; gubar, gobr, guu, gu, P. ; goober, guber, ober, B.

WAGTAIL, *s.* See WATER-WAGTAIL.

WAIL, *v.* Gwelvan, guelvan, B. ; wolé, olé, w. ; olua, P.

WAILING, *part.* Ov thola, M. 1609. *Age mammov ov thola*, their mothers wailing, M. 1609.

WAILING, *s.* Croffolas, P.

WAILINGS, *s.* Galarou, B.

WAIT, *v.* Gortes, wortos, w. ; gorlos (?), P.

TO WAIT FOR, *v.* Tregé, trega, dregé, w.

WAITER, *s.* Gonidoc, P.

A WAITER AT TABLE. Renniat, B.

A WAITING-WOMAN. Caités, P. ; caithés, kaithés, B.

TO BE WAKEFUL, *v.* Golyas, w. ; goolyas, golzyas, B. ; gologhas, P.

WAKEN, *v.* Defena, difuné, dyfuny, w. ; tefeny, P.

WALK, *v.* Cerdhés, kerdhés, w. ; kerdhez, P. ; gerdhés, w.

TO WALK ABOUT or WANDER, *v.* Gwandré, w. ; guandré, P. ; quandré, w. ; wandré, P. ; cescar, keskar, w. ; kesker, B.

WALKING QUICKLY. Janken, B.V.

WALL, *s.* Fôs, w. (*Pl.* Fosow, N.) *Ov seuel avel dyw fôs*, standing like two wall (s), O.M. 1690 ; fôz, fo, P. ; vôs, B. ; hôs, R.D. 331 ; gwâl, w. ; gual, P. ; poruit, w.

A STONE WALL. Fôs a vyin, P.

WALLED, *adj.* Gwallic, wallic, vallic, w. ; vallick, vallack, P.

WALLET, *s.* Tigan, B.

WALL-NUT, *s.* Kynyphan Frenc. *Lit.* French-nut, w.

WALLED TOWN. Dinas, dinaz, P.

WALLED TOWN or CITY. Trév, B.

WALLOW, *v.* Egruath, dho egruath, w.

WAN, *adj.* Gwyn, gwidn, w. ; guin, guidn, P. ; thurl, thirl, D.

WANDER, *v.* See TO WALK ABOUT or WANDER.

WANDER, ERR, or MISTAKE, *v.* Miscemeras, w. ; miskymeraz, P. ; meskymera, B.

WANT, *s.* (Need). Edhom, w. ; ethom, P. ; odhom, w. ; othom, P. ; otham, B. ; whans, R.D. 1517. *Ny'm bus a'th lauarow whans*, I have no want of thy words, R.D. 1517.

WANT or LACK, *s.* Fawt, w. ; faut, P. ; fowt, fout, w.

WANTON, *s.* (A wanton girl). Giglot, w. *A giglot of lynage*, Oh, wanton of lineage, P.C. 1183. *Giglot* is of often used in Cornwall for a girl who giggles.

WAR, *s.* Câd, câs, bresel, bresell, bresul, bresyl, vresyl, w.

WARDROBE, *s.* Guiscti, w. ; guisgdy, B.

WARES, *s.* (Goods). Gwara, w. ; waroe, ferna, P.

WARLIKE, *adj.* Breseler, w. ; brezeler, B.

WARM, *v.* Tomma, tumma, P. ; tubma, tubmy, B.

WARM, *adj.* Toim, tôm, tûm, tûbm, dûbm, tybm, w. ; claiar, B. ; mygil, w.

WARMED, *part.* Steuys, P. *Râg gwythé steuys*, to keep him warmed, P.

WARMTH, *s.* Tûmder, tômder, toimder, w. ; tômbder, B. ; tymder, tês, mygilder, w. ; entredés, P.

WARN, *v.* Gwarnya, w. ; guarnya, B. ; guarny, P.

WARRANT, *v.* Wrontya, wronté, P.

WARRIOR, *s.* Cadwûr, w. ; cadgûr, P.

WART, *s.* Gwennogen, gwednhogian, w.

WARY, *adj.* Fin, w. ; eruryr, eruyer, P.

WAS. Go. *Nyn go*, was not ; o, pewo, rebee, rys, tera, thera, dera, thellé, dellé, wrensé, vownas, B.

I WAS. Bema, vema, fema, buef, bûf, fuef, fûf, bêf, vêf, veve, w. ; vêv, vêva, w. ; en, esen, w. ; ezen, B. ; egen, yden, w. ; râg u, P.

THOU WAST. Ty a ve, ês, esés, ydesés, w. ; bus, N.

HE WAS. Bue, pue, vue, fue, vye, be, pe, ve, fe, veva, vefé, o, asso, esa, esé, egé, ydhé, ydho, ydhesé, ydhegé, w.

IT WAS. Vo, B.

IT WAS BEFORE. Revyé, B.

IT WAS NOT. Nawango, nago, nyngo, neung, B.

THERE WAS NOT. Na geve (*nag eve*), B.

WASH, *v.* Golchy, golhy, P. ; gulhy, w. ; gulhi, gulhya, P. ; gelchi, B. ; wolghy, wolhy, woly, wolhyia, P. ; uolhya, B. ; hambrokkia, w. ; hambronkyas, B.

HE WASHED. 1. Holhas, a mutation of *golhas*, 3 pers. s. preterite of *golhy*, to wash, w.

    2. Wholhas, the aspirate mutation of *golhas*, 3 pers. s. preter. of *golhy*, to wash, w.

HE WILL WASH. Wolch, a mutation of *golch*, 3 pers. s. fut. of *golchy*, to wash. Also written *woulch*.

WASHED, *part*. Alés, P.

WASHING, *part*. Gulhys, B.

WASP, *s*. Guhien, w.; guhyen, kuilkiorés, B.; swop, B.V.

WASSAIL, *s*. Gwyras, wyras, w.

WASTE, REFUSE, RUBBISH, *s*. Atal, attle, w. A word still in common use among miners. Scyl. skyl, scûl, skûl, w. *Néb és towle y hanow dhe skûl*, who throweth his name to waste, w.

WASTE, v. Guastia, P.

WASTED, *part*. Spendys, spengas, véz, B.

A WATCH, *s*. Guillua, B.

WATCH, *s*. Holi, holy. *Ketwell holy*, keeping watch, B.

WATCH, v. (Spy, look out). Aspyé, w.

WATCH or KEEP AWAKE, v. Golyas, w.; gollyaz, P.; goolyas, golzyas, B.; colyas, w.; kolyaz, koliaz, gologhas, P. *Golyas o agan dysyr*, it was our desire to watch, P.C. 1068.

WATCH YE. Golyough, B.

THOU WATCHEDST. Wolsys, a mutation of *golsys*, 2 pers. s. preter. of *golyas*, to watch, w.

WATCHER, *s*. Huer, D. A man on land watching for a school of pilchards.

WATCHFUL, *adj*. Hewil, hewuil, w.; heuyl, henvill (? *heuvill*), hepuil, B.

VERY WATCHFUL. Hycheul, hich hewil, B.; hich hewuil, w

WATCHFULNESS, *s*. Guillua, P.

WATCH-STATION, *s*. Guillua, w.

WATCHING, A WATCHING, *s*. Guillua, B.; golyas, w.

WATER, v. Douria, dourhi, w.

WATER, *s*. Dour, dower, douer, w.; douar, P.; dhour, w.; thower, c.w. 2164; dûr, w.; dôr, dow, P.; dofer, w.

A WATER, *s*. (As a river, brook, &c.) Gy, w.; guy, B.; gwy, P.; wy, w.; vy, P.; isge, B. See RIVER.

A STANDING WATER. Lin, lyn, polan, P.

WATER-CHANNEL, *s*. Gwerdhour, w.; guerthour, P.

WATERCRESS, *s*. Beler, w.

WATER-ELDER, *s*. Scaw-dower, D. See ELDER.

WATER-FLAG or IRIS, *s*. Elestren, B.; laister, laver, D.

WATER-LILIES, *s*. Alau, B.

WATER-LIZARD, *s*. Pedrevan an dour, w.

WATERMAN or OARSMAN, *s*. Ruifadur, ruifa dûr, ruivadur, revadur, P.

WATER-WAGTAIL, *s*. Stenor, stener, w.; tinner, D.

WATERY, *adj*. Devrac, w.

WATERY GROUND. Tir devrak, w.; devrak, P.

WATTLE, *s*. Cluit, w.; kluyd, B.; clifa, P.

A WATTLED GATE. Cluit, w.

A WATTLED HEDGE-GAP. Freath, frîth, D.

WAVE, *s*. (A great wave or surge). Armôr, tôn, w.; tûn, B.

WAX, *s*, Koir, coar, B.; côr, coir, w.

WAX-CANDLE, *s*. Tapar, P.

TO WAX ANGRY, v. Perthegy, P.

GROWN ANGRY. Perthegés, P.

WAXEN, *adj*. Taw, P.

WAY or PATH, *s* Cammen, w.; kammen, P.; gam, M. 1448, and M. 3043; arrez, B.

WAY, ROAD, PASSAGE, *s*. Fôr (*Pl*. Furu), vôr (*Pl*. Vuru), fôrdh, vôrdh, w.; fôrd, ferdh, fyrdhu, forth, P.

A HORSE WAY or HORSE ROAD. Vorver, D.

WAY or JOURNEY, *s*. Kerth, kergh, gerghen, P.; hins, w.

WAY, MANNER, SORT, *s*. Côr, w.; coore, c.w. 402. *War neb coore*, in any way, c.w. 402; kerth, P.C. 1671. *Ke yn kerth ty thesu*, go thy way thou Jesus, P.C. 1671; fôr (*Pl*. Furu), w. *Gwreuh owna 'gys furu*, mend your ways (manners), w.

IN NO WAY, NOHOW. Malbew, P.

IN THAT WAY or MANNER. Cetella, ketella, kettermen, cettermyn, ceverys, keverys, kevrys, cefrys, P.

WE, *pron*. Ni, ny, nei, 'n, w.; ow, vy, P.; thynny, B.; nyny, w. (*Nyny* is a reduplicate form of *ny*), do, agan honan, idzhin, P. *Ni idzhin a guelaz*, we see, P. Two personal pronouns for one.

WE ARE. Oan, on, B.

WE TWO. Agan deaw, P.

WE WILL. Ny a vin, w.

WEAK, INFIRM, *adj*. Gwan, gwadn, w.; guan, guadn, P.; gwedn, w.; guedrys, B.; wan. *Mar wan*, so weak, w.; wadn, c.w. 1275; aneuin, w.; anvein, aniak, B.; develo, fasow, w.; farsow, P.; palch, w. *Palch, palchy*, and *palched*, are often used of weakly persons, D.

WEAK HEART. Wecor gwan. *Lit.* Faint courage, B.

WEAKLING, *s.* Pinnick, punick, kenack, kinak, D.

WEAK OF MIND. A scient, w.

WEAKNESS, *s.* Gwander, w.; guander. N. *Råg guander ef re cothas*, for weakness he has fallen, P.C. 2618 ; garauder, P.

WEAKLY, VERY SMALL, PUNY, *adj.* Pinnikin, D.

WEAKLY, FOOLISHLY, *adv.* Sempel, M. 1994. *Ty the vynnés mar sempel,* that thou wishest so simply, M. 1994.

WEALTH, *s.* Covaith, w.; kovaith. P.; cyfoeth, liasder. B.; liastre, P ; pêth, B.; pyth, M. 2571.

WEALTHY, *adj.* Cefuidoc, covaithak, w.; kovaithak, P.; puludoc, B.

WEAPON, *s.* Arv. *Pl.* Arvow, w.; arvou, P.

WEAR, *s* (To wear clothes). Gwiscy, gwiscé, wyscé, gwesca, w.; gueska, B.; gwesga, w.; guesga, P.

WEARIED, *adj.* Annés. w.

WEARINESS, *s.* Cuêth, squytzder, B.; squythens, w. *A pup squythens y sawyé,* from all weariness cure him, P.C. 477.

WEARY, *adj.* Squyth, w.; sqwyth, C.W. 2002 ; squêth, M. 633; scîth, w.; skîth, P. *A dev kêr assoma squyth,* Oh, dear God, I am weary, O.M. 684.

WEARY, TO GROW WEARY, *v.* Squythé, scuythé, dho skuythi, w.; skuattya, P.

WEARIED, MADE WEARY. Squytheys, w. *Ov thas ev côth ha squytheys,* my father is old and wearied, O.M. 737.

WEASAND or WINDPIPE, *s.* Ritan, w.

WEASEL, *s.* Lovennan, w.; louennan, P.; codna-gwyn, codna-gwidn, w.; kodna-guidn, B. *Lit.* Whiteneck.

WEATHER, *s.* Cewar. kuer, cuer, w.; keuar, P.; auhel, awel, w.; auel, B. *Bôs sêgh ha têk awel,* that the weather is dry and fair, O.M. 1147.

BAD WEATHER. Hagar awel, w.; hagar auel, B.

FAIR or GOOD WEATHER. Awel vâs, w.; auel vâz, B ; têg awel, w.; auel teag, B.

WET WEATHER. Cewar leb, w.; keuarlêb, P.

WEAVE, *v.* Gwia, w.; gwea, guia, givia, P.; gwethy, B.; quethy, P.

WEAVED, *adj.* Gwethyn, gwethy, w.

WEAVER, *s.* Gwiader. gweiader, w.; gueadar, B.; gweader, w.

WEAVER or STING-FISH, *s.* Calcar, D.

WEAVING, *s.* (A thing woven). Gwiad, guiat, w.; guiot, P.

WEB, *s.* (Cloth woven). Gwiad, guiat, w.; guiot, P.

WEDGE, *s.* Gên, gêdn, w. The iron wedge used by the Cornish miners is familiarly known as a *gad.*

WEDGES, *s.* Genow, the *pl.* of *gen*; gwlezow, w.

WEDNESDAY, *s.* De Marhar, w.; Demarhar. B.; Dumerher, M. 2252. *Kyns ye dumerher the nos,* before it is Wednesday night, M. 2252.

WEED, *s.* Plôs, w.; myrgh, P. *Myrgh gâl,* a bad weed.

WEED, *s.* (Of standing pools). Kelin, B.

WEEK, *s.* Seithan, w: *Nessa seithan* next week, w.; zeithan, B.; sythen, M. 595. *Kyns fewy sythen omma,* though ye be a week here, M. 4568; seithyn, sythyn, seithun, seithum, w.

WEEP, *v.* Gwelvan, w.; guelvan, P.; gouelaff, B.; galarow, w.; galarou. B.; cyny, kyny, cryé, kriha, crio, w.; krio, B.; diveré, P.; wolé, w.; uolé, B.; olua, hoalea, P.; holea, olé, w.

HE SHALL WEEP. Ool, ôl, 3 pers. s. fut of *olé,* to weep, w.

WEEPING, *s.* (A weeping). Olva, w ; olah, P.; ola, C.W. 1309 ; ollna (? ollua), B.

WEPT, *part.* Wholé. B.

WEIGHT, *s.* Poes. B.; poer, poesder, P.

A WEIGHT, A BURDEN, *s.* Pouis, pois, poiys, B.

WEIGHTINESS, *s.* Pysder, B.

WEIGHTY, HEAVY, *adj.* Poys. poes, pôs, pûz, w.; powys, bos. P.; boys, w.

WEIGHTY, HEAVY, SAD, *adj.* Trom, w.

WEIGHTY, IMPORTANT, *adj.* Bysy, vysy, w.

WELCOME. Mall. *Is welcome.* Mallew (*mall-ew*), w.

WELL, *s.* Fenten, fenton, venton, funten, w.; fyntan, B.; pôl, lacca, w.; lakka B.; peeth, D.

WELL, *adv.* Benés. *Benés bôs theugh,* well be it to you, P.; ynt, B.; ynta. *Ynta a wothe,* well knew; yn fas, w.; redha, B.

WELL. Mân, lêl, leal, gamwul, P.

WELL, *adj.* (Being in health) Iach, w.; jach, B.; yach, w.

WELL BEATEN or HAMMERED. *part.* Morthelec, morthelek, w.

WELL ENOUGH. Dalour, M. 3649. *Dalour y werihés certen,* well enough thou knowest certainly, M. 3649.

WELL NIGH, *adv.* Namna, before consonants, namnag, before vowels, w.

WELSHMEN, *s.* Cembrion, w.; Kembrion, P.

THE WELSH BRITISH. Brethonek, Kembrian, P.

WEN, *s.* Gwenan, w.; guenan, P.

WENCH, *s.* Moren, moroin, w.; morain, B.

WENT. Ella, w.; gâth, thêth, B.

I WENT. Ellen, ethym, my a ethym, w.; yth, N

THOU WENTEST. Ythys, 2 pers. s. preter. of irr, v. *mós*, to go. Also written *ethys*, w.

HE WENT. E, ellas, êth, yth, 3 pers. s. of irr, v. *mós*, to go, w.; herraf, kerthaf, P.; sêth, w.

YE WENT. Etheuch, w.; etheugh, N.

THEY WENT. Ethons, ythons, w,; thevés, B.

WERE. Bonas. bonés, idzhean, P.; rebé, thesé, B. *These sethek*, were set down, B.

THOU WERT. Ezzez, B.

WE WERE. Buen, vuen, fuen, esen, oezyn, w.; fons, B.; veyn, a mutation of *beyn*, id. qd *buen*, 1 pers. pl. preter. of *bós*, to be. Vyan, a mutation of *byan*, a late form of *buen*, 1 pers. pl. preterite of *bós*, to be, w.

YOU WERE. Beugh, bugh, N.; beuch, feuch, fûch, esouch, oezyh, w.; oezy, B.; ydhesouch. Read *ydh* and *esouch*, a reduplicate form of *ouch*, 2 pers. pl. pres. of *bós*, to be, w.; esough, N.

THEY WERE. Bôns, fôns, bêns, fêns, êns, esens, esons, w.; oezenz, thens, B.; ydhens, w.; vousy (? vonsy), jové. Probably a corruption of *gevé*, he had, a mutation of *cevé*, 3 pers. s. imperf. of *cafos*, to have, w.

THEY WERE NOT. Ny won, B.

IT WERE. Vya, B.

IF IT WERE. A pe (be), N.

THAT WERE. Ven, B.

AS IT WERE. Cara, kara, w.

IF THOU WERT. Mar pês, P.

WEST, *s.* (The west). Gorlewen, w.; gorleuen, P. *En gorlewen kernow*, in the west of Cornwall, w.

WEST. (Sunset). Houlsedhas, w.; houl zedhaz, P.; houl-zethza, B.

WEST INDIES, *s.* Lollas.

WEST INDIAN SPIRIT, *i.e.*, RUM, *s.* Dour tubm lollas. *Lit.* Hot water of the West Indies.

WET, *v.* Glibbié, glybyé, w.; glibié, P.; clibbie, clybyé, klybbyé, w.

WET, *adj.* Glêb, lêb, lynnic, w.; lynnek, P.; sôg, sûg, w.

WET AND DIRTY, *adj.* (Weather, roads, &c.) Slotterée, P. This is quite a common word in Cornwall. Also *soggy*, D.

WETHER. *s.* Lodn, w.; lodon, P.

WETHER-GOAT, *s.* Cynbyc, w.; kynbyk, B.

WETHER-SHEEP, *s.* Lodon davas, w.; lodn-davas, B.; môls, moulz, mowls, w.; môlz, mowlz, B.

WITNESS, *s.* Glibor, glybor, w.; glibbor, P.

WET WEATHER. Cewar lêb, w.; keuarlêb, P.

WHALE, *s.* Môrvil. *Pl.* Môrvilow, w.

WHAT, *pron. rel.* Nêb, lêb, w.; dry, trez, P.

WHAT, *pron. sub.* Pa, pe, py, w.; pu, pyw, pew, P. *Pew an jowle pandra vyt gwyrés*, what the devil shall be done? P.; by, ba, w. *Ba dhên*, what man? w.; panna, w.; pana, M. 1501. *Pana goys aveth henna*, what blood will that be, M. 1501.

WHAT, WHY. Pandra, pendra, w.

WHAT IF. Pattel, patel, patla, fattel, fatel, fatla, fatl, fettel, fetyl, P.

WHAT THE. Pan (*pa-an*), pahan, w.; pahyn, P.

WHAT THING. Pandra, pendra, w.; pandrew, c.w. 23-9; pe dra, P.

WHAT IS. Pythiow, P.

WHAT IS IT. Pandrew? P.

WHATEVER. Penag, P.; penagh, N.; pynag, P.; pynak, N.; panak, M. 3104; ponag, pepenag, pepynag, P.; by penag, N.; pyupenag, pywpenag, piwa bennac, pyuhabennak, P.; pandra-bennak, B.; puppenac, puppenak, puppenag, py penag ol, N.; puppenagol, w.; pandra, pendra, P.; pub-er, B.; byth ol, vyth ol, N. *Dén byth ol*, any man whatever, R.D. 2169.

WHATSOEVER. See WHATEVER.

WHEAL, *s.* (From a blow). Botham, D.

WHEAT, *s.* Gwaneth, w.; guanath, P.

WHEATEN BREAD, *s.* Bara gwaneth, w.; bara guanath, P.

WHEEL, *s.* Rôs, w.; rôz, P.

A SMALL WHEEL. Bisow bezo, w.; rozellen, B.

A SMALL SOLID WHEEL. Druckshar, B.

WHEELBARROW, *s.* Gravar rôs, w.; gravar rôz, B.

WHEEL-PIT, *s.* Pûl rôz, poul rôz, P. Still used in Cornwall for the pit under the water mill-wheel.

WHELP, *s.* Coloin, w.; koloin, B.

WHEN. Pa, pan, ban, w.; po, B.; kettel, N. *Pan ruk drys y worhenwyn*, when I acted against his command, O.M. 353. *Pan cam worthybys*, when he answered rudely, P.C. 1403. *Kettel tersys an bara*, when thou didst break the bread, R D. 1319. *Po marh leddrés*, when a horse is stolen, B.

WHEN. (Since, insomuch). Aban, w.; pam, pan, P.

WHEN, AT WHAT TIME. Pa, panso, panvo, pahan, P.

WHEN IT MAY BE. Panvo (*pan-bo*), w.

WHENCE, *adv.* Apeleh, ablé, plé, pylé (*pa-lé*), w.; my, B.

WHERE, IN WHAT PLACE, *adv.* Pe, w. *Abel pe festé marbel*, Abel where hast thou been so long? O.M. 467; py, pelé, w.; py le, P.; pylé, w.; bylé, c.w. 552; pylea, c.w. 1288; palé (*pa-le*), pelea, P.;

polia, w. ; pema, P. ; ple (pa-le), w. Ple me, where
is it ? R.D. 46 ; plêch, pylêch, w. ; plex, P.   Ple is
prefixed generally, as plemonz, where they are, B.

WHERE IS. Po, B ; plemé, w. ; plema, P.

WHERE IS HE? Plema, P.

WHERE HE IS. Plema, P.

WHERE ART THOU ? Pythesta, w. ; py thestu, P.

WHERE HAST THOU BEEN ? Pefesta, pefesté, P.

WHERE ARE THEY ? Plemons, P.

WHERE THEY ARE. Plemons, P.

WHERE WAS IT ? Peveva, w.

WHEREFORE. Perâg, w. ; porâg, P. ; prâg, prâc,
praga, fraga, fra, w. ; pywough, P. ; prâgh, N. ;
prâk, P.C. 1757.

WHEREIN. Menz, B.

IN WHICH. Menz, B.

WHEREVER. Puppenac, puppenak, puppenag, w. ;
pypenag, B. ; puppenagol, w. ; pepenagol, P.C. 630 ;
pub-er, B.

WHERRY, s. Gurhal bien, P.

WHET, v. Lemma, lebma, w.

WHETHER. Py, po, bo, syns, sens, P.

WHETHER OF THEM. Panyn, B.

WHETHER WE SHALL BE. Pytheen, P.

WHETSTONE, s. Agolan, w. ; higolen, B.

WHEY, s. Meith, w.

WHICH, pron. Neb, lêb, pu, pyw, w. ; suel, sûl,
toan, ûs, P.

WHICH ? Pa, pe, py, panna, ba, w.

WHICH MAN ? Ba dhên, w.

WHICH ONE ? Panyn, w. ; paynyn, P.

WHICH OF THEM ? Panyn, B.

WHICH OF THE TWO ? Peliha, penyle, B.

WHICH IS. Pyw (pyw-yw), w.

WHICH SEE. Henz, kenz, P.

WHILE, A SPACE OF TIME, s. Pols, prys, preys,
prês, prêz, prywêth, cors, w. Rágon chy pols the
wonys, for us a while a house to dwell in, o.m. 1716.
Powesough lymmyn vn cors, rest now a while, P.C.
2146.

A LITTLE WHILE. Prygwyth, prywêth, w. ;
polge. M. 1338. ; pols byhan, o.m. 1269 ; tecen,
teken, w.

FOR A WHILE. Râg teken, P.

FOR A LITTLE WHILE. Râg token, P.

A WHILE SINCE. Agensow, agynsow, w.

WHILE or WHILST. Tre, tra, tro, try, dre, w. ;
heddré, B. ; hedré, w. Hedré vyyn ou predery, whilst
I am considering, o.m. 2035 ; cêth, kêth, w. ; bre-

dar, worthe, B. ; devone, P. Drevone bewa, whilst I
live, P. ; Awôs, auoz, entermen, spâs, P.

WHIM, s. (Odd fancy). Tarnatuan, B. ; tarnytuan,
P.

WHIMBLE, s. Tarad, tardar, w.

WHINNARD or REDWING, s. Suellak, P. ; swellack, D.

WHIP, s. Scubilen, w. Borlase gives this for a
broom.

A WHIP FOR A TOP. (To make it spin). Ging, D.

WHIPS, s. Whyppys, N. From the English.

WHIRL or WHIRL AROUND, v. Troillia, w. ;
kroddré, P.C. 882. Th'agas kroddré me a grys, to
whirl you round I believe, P C. 882.

WHIRLING, part. Wimblen, P.

WHIRLPOOL, s. Gurgés, pollan troillia, w. ; aber, P.

WHIRLWIND, s. Gwins adrô, guyns adrô, w. ;
guîns adro, P.

WHISPER, v. Huetha, P. ; wystré, w. Na ny wy-
strys yn scoforn, nor whispered it in the ears, P.C.
1254.

WHISPER, s. Hanas, w. Ny yewsyn yn tewolgow
a dryff tûs yn un hanas, I spoke not in darkness behind people in a whisper, M.C. 79.

WHISTLE, v. Huibanat, B.

WHISTLE, s. Wiban, w.

WHISTLER FISH, s. Gerrick, girrock, girac, D.

WHITE, adj. Gwên, w. ; guên, P. ; gwyn, w. ; guyn,
gwyne, guin, guyne, P. ; gwîdn, w. ; guidn, guydn,
P. ; gwydyn, B. ; huyn, uîdn, P. ; wên, w. ; wyn,
whyn, wyne, P. ; wyan, fyn, fîn, B. ; cân, w. ; kân,
gluys, gonnyon, guanath, B. ; gwanath, w. Maga
huyn, as white, P.

WHITE BREAD. Bara cân, w. ; bara kân, bara
guanath, B.

WHITE DOG. Keigwyn, P. (A family name).

WHITE NAPED, adj. Schylwyn, M. 3391. Omma
pen tarov schylwyn, here a white-naped bull's head,
M. 3391.

WHITE-PUDDING, s. Pot guidn, P. The provincial
term is white-pot.

WHITE STONES. Carrig gonnyon, B.

WHITE-THORN, s. Speruan wyn, w. ; spernan
uîdn, frîth, P.

WHITE-THROAT, s. (Bird). Codnagwyn, w. ;
codna-gwîdn, P. ; kodna-guidn, B.

WHITE THURSDAY. Jeu-whydn. It is still
called chewidden day. It is one clear week before
Christmas day. They say that on this day black
tin (the ore) was first turned into white tin (the
metal), D.

WHITEN or BLANCH, *v.* Gwynna, w.; cannu, B.

WHITENESS, *s.* Gvynder, M. 3667. *Diegrys off gans gvynder*, blinded am I by whiteness, M. 3667.

WHITHER. See WHERE.

WHITISH, *adj.* Geudnik, geudnek, geudnak, r.; widnak, B.

WHITING, *s.* (The fish). Gwynac, gwynnec, gwidnac, gwydnac, w.; guidnak, P.; guydnach, B.

WHITLOW, *s.* Veak, veach, venom, D.

WHITSUNTIDE, *s.* Pencast, w.; Penkast, P.

WHITTLE, *s.* Lêdn, w.; collel, P.

WHO, *pron. rel* Nêb, nêp, lêb, w. *Nép a marrek lên*, who was a trusty knight, N. lebba, ba, B.; a, N. *A fue genys*, who was born, N. u, ûs, P.; suel, sûl, w. *Súl a the'n nêf*, who is going to heaven, N.

WHO, *interrog. pron.* Pu, pa, pe, py, pew, pyu (*py-yu*), pyw, w. *Pyu henna*, who is that? *Pyw ough*, who are you? R.D. 196; piua, pua, pyvytho, P.

WHOEVER. Nêb, nép, lêb, penag, pynag, pynak, puppenac, puppenak, w.; pypenag, B.; pywpenag, w.; pyupenag, P.; puppenag, w.; pyuhabennak, P.; piwha bennac, w.; piua bennak, B.; pennagle, c.w. 1641; pub-er, B. *Puppenagol a vo ef*, whoever he may be, P.C. 23; kemmys, N. *Kemmys na greysa*, whoever believes not, N. See WHATEVER.

WHOLE, *adj.* (Entire). Dyen, tyen, w.; tyan, P.

WHOLE, *adj.* (Sound, healthy). Salov (*salou*), M. 4239. *Yagh ha púr salov*, healed and quite whole, M. 4239.

WHOLLY, *adv.* Yn tyen, ha heys, P.; haheyz, B.

WHOM. See WHO.

WHOMSOEVER. See WHOEVER.

WHOP or BLOW, *s.* What, wat, whaf, w.

WHORE, *s.* Drûth, hora, P.

WHORESON, *s.* Horsen, M. 3734.

WHORTLEBERRY, *s.* Iz-diu, B.

WHOSOEVER. See WHOEVER.

WHY. Prâg, w.; prâgh, N.; prâk, P.C. 1757; prâc, praga, fraga fra, perâg. w.; porâg, pywough, P.; pa, w.; chuy, P.; fôrth, nêb, nêp, nêf, B.

WICK, *s.* Porvan, D. It is made of the pith of a rush for a small lamp. One form of wick made of rag is called *booba, boobun*, and *boobus*, D.

WICKED, *adj.* Anfusyk, w.; anfugyk, P.C. 1424. *Ow bones mar anfugyk*, being so wicked, P.C. 1424; cam, gam, ham, cabm, cham. w.; camhinsic, P.; drôc, drôg, drôk, w.; gâl. gwân, P.; hager, hagar, B.; pedn dhrôg, plosec, plosek, w.; purcheniat, purkeniat, purceniat. B.; tebal, P.; tebel, debel, w. *A són a'n debel bobel*, at the noise of the wicked people, O.M 1815.

WICKED, ACCURSED. Mylygés, vylygés, w.

WICKEDLY, *adv.* Yntebel, B.

WICKED FELLOW. Gâl, w. See also RASCAL.

WICKED MAN. Purceniat, purkeniat, purcheniat, w.

A WICKED ONE. Bylen, w.

WICKED ONES. Tybelés, tebelés, debelés, w. *May whello an debelés*, that the wicked ones may see. O.M. 1849.

WICKEDNESS. *s.* Bylen, bylyny, vylyny, drôc, drôk, drôg, gâl, scherewnêth, scherewynsr, w.; scherewynêth, P.; anfûs, w. *Dun ganso er y anfús*, let us come to him, for his wickedness, P.C. 1501; cam, w. *Gans cam púr brás*, with very great wickedness, R.D. 2264.

WIDE, *adj.* Ledan, w.

WIDE AWAKE. Thyfûn, perrthyfon, P.

WIDEN, *v.* Lesé, w.

WIDOW, *s.* Gwedho, guedeu, w.; vedou, gureg uedhu, P.; gwrêg wedhu, w.

WIDOWED, *adj.* Gwedhu, wedhu, gwedho, guedeu, w.; guedho, P.

WIDOWER, *s.* Gûr gwedho, w.; guedho, P.

WIDTH, *s.* Lês, leys, w.

WIFE, *s.* Gwrêc, w. *Gwréc brederys*, a diligent wife, w.; wrêc, w.; gwreag, c.w. 877; wreage, c.w. 834; grêg, wrêg, gurêg, grueg, w.; gruêk, M. 302; gurêk, O.M. 1258; frêg, w.; vrêg. *An vrég or an urég*, the wife; freggans gûr, fryas, P.; fryés, O.M. 2187; cansgûr, B. *Pl.* Gwragedh, w.; gwregath, c.w. 2437.

WIFE or HUSBAND. *s.* (Spouse). Pryés, bryés, vryés, pryas, w.; bryas, c w. 806; priés, briés, friés. w.; freas, c.w. 1227.

GOODWIFE. Benen vâs, w.; benynvâs, c.w. 554; wrethtye, c.w. 942.

WIG. *s.* (An old scratch wig). Gozzan, D. From its rusty look.

WILD, *adj.* Alta. *Beathuige alta*, wild beasts, B.; difeid, w.; gues, B.; gwylls, w.; gwells, guelz, B.; guyls, M. 1145; gvyls, M. 7; guit, w.

A WILD BEAST. Guitfil, w.

WILD BEASTS. Beathuige alta, B.

A WILD BUCK. Cytiorch, w.

WILD CARROT. Kager, keggas, kaiyer, D.

A WILD CAT. Coidgâth, w.; koitgâth, P. *Lit.* Cat of the wood.

WILD-FOWL. Idhin guêlz, B.

WILD PARSNIP. Kager, keggas, kaiyer, D. See WILD CARROT.

WILD or MEADOW SAFFRON. Goitcenin, w.; goitkenin, B.; goickennin, P.; lodosa, hlodosa, B.

WILD THYME. Coifinel, w.

WILDERNESS. *s.* Defyth, devyth, dyveyth, w.; devêth, p; difeid, w.; guylfoys, M. 1132; guylfôs, M. 2802; guelfôs, M. 1127. *Moys then guelfôs,* to go to the wilderness, M. 1127.

WILL, *s.* Bôdh, w.; bôth, M. 2972. *Erbyn ov bôth,* against my will, M. 2972; bothe, c.w. 16; bouth, p.c. 1027; bûs, vôdh, w.; vôth, p. *Vôth agan Arluth sefryn,* the will of our sovereign Lord, o.m. 2189; vreys, vrûs, mâl, w. *Mâl yv genen the gafus,* our will is to take thee, o.m. 553; mynnas, vynnas, wl, w.; thoule, c.w. 126; thovle, M. 1168. *Rág indella yv ov thovle,* and thus is my will, M. 1168; bolungêth, bolnogêth, bolnegêth, w.; bolenegêth, blonogath, bonogath (?), p.; volnogêth, volnegêth, volungêth, w.; vlonogath, p.; vlanogathe, c w 2243; volynedzherh, volyndzherdhek, p.

WILL, *v.* Menny, minny, mynny, w.; menna. p.; mennas, vennas, mynnês, vynnês, w.; mân, mentha, mendzha, thenfyn, vedn, vynsa, p.

I WILL. Mennaf, mynnaf, manaf, madam, me vadam, vennaf, vynna, w.; vynaff, vadam, b.; fynnaf, w.; my a vydn, c.w. 1710; byn, me a byn, p.; menjam, me amenja, b.

I WILL NOT. Ny vanaff, b.

THOU WILT. Mynnyth, menta, vynnyth, fynnyth, venta, vynta, vynny, venni, w.; vinny, ti a vin, b. *Mynnyth, fynnyth, vynnyth,* are used after *na.*

IF THOU WILT. Môr menta, b. *Môr* is used for *mâr.*

WILT THOU? Mynyth, menyth, vynnyth, b.

HE WILL. Myn. *Mâr myn dew,* if God wills; mên, mân, fyn, vyʀ, vên, vêdn, w. *Myn, fyn, vyn,* are used after *a* and *ny.*

WE WILL. Mennyn, mynnyn, vennyn, vynnyn, w.

YE WILL. Mennouch, w.; menough, b.; vennouch, menno, venno, vedo, vedno, w.; wynnough, b.

WILL YE? Wynnough, b.

THEY WILL. Mennons, meddons, w.; meddonz, b.

WILLING, *adj.* Volynzhedhek, p.

WILLINGLY, *adv.* Meugh, p.

WILLOW, *s.* Heligen, helagan, hellik, helak, p.; helek, b.

WILY, *adj.* See CUNNING.

WIN, *v.* Gwaynia, guaynia, b.

WINCE, *v.* Deglené, tygly, p.; thegly, c.w. 485. *May tyglyn an tybelês* that the devils will wince, w. p.c. 3046.

HE WILL WINCE. Tyglyn, a mutation of *dyglyn,* 3 pers. s. fut. of *deglené,* to wince, w.

WIND, *s.* (The breeze). Gwens, gwins, guins, w.; guinz, b.; guenz, p.; gainz, b.; gwenz, p.; gwyns, w.; guyns, N.; wens, wenze, b. *Rak marthys yeyn yv an guyns,* for wondrous cold is the wind, p.c.

1215   The "eye of the wind" is called the *emmut,* b.

WINDFALL or LEGACY, *s.* Skuat, skuit, d.

WINDING or TURN. *s.* Torn. *Torn an vôr,* the turning of the way, w.

WINDOW, *s.* Beisder, veisder, besidar, fenester, prenest, w.

WIND-PIPE, *s.* (The trachea). Ritan, w.

WIND'S EYE or EYE OF THE WIND, *s.* Emmut. *Polwhele.*

WINDY, *adj.* Auelek, w. See also STORMY.

WINE, *s.* Gwîn, guîn, gwyn, w.; gwyne, b.; wîn, w.

A GLASS OF WINE. Gwedran a wîn, w.

A GLASS OF THE WINE. Guedran an guin, p.

WING, *s.* (Of a bird). Ascall, w.; askall, b.; asgal, asgell, escell, w.; azgran, b.

WINGS, *s.* (Of birds). Ascelli, w.; askelli, asgelli, p.; escelly, eskelly, scelli, w.; skelli, b; sgelli, w.; skerli, p.

WINKER, *s.* Brenner, d.

WINNING, *s.* (A gaining, an earning). Vangin, d.

WINNOW, *v.* Croddré, kroddré, w.

WINNOWING-FAN, *s.* Gwinzal, w.

WINNOWING-SHEET, *s.* Nothlên, w.

WINTER, *s.* Gwâv, w.; gwave, c.w. 1700; guâv, w.; gwâf, p.; guâf, gaiav (? *guiav*), b.

WINTER-CRESS, *s.* Casabully, d.

WINTERLY, *adj.* Gwavas, wavas. *Tre wavas,* a winterly place, p.

WIPE, *v.* Seché, syché, sychy, sihy, seha, zeha, w.; ystynny, p.

WISDOM, *s.* (Prudence). Furnés, w.; furnez, b.

WISDOM, *s.* (Knowledge, learning). Scient, sceans, skeans, scians, skians, skeyens, skyens, skyans, skentelêth, skentulêth, w.; skentyllur, skentyll, p.

TO BE WISE, *v.* Furaat, b.

WISE, *adj.* (Prudent, sage). Kûf, o.m. 285; cûf, p. *A mêster cûf arlûth nêf,* Oh, wise master, Lord of heaven, p.c. 869; fûr, w.; fure, c.w. 490; furre, c.w. 783; fuer, c.w. 786; fuir, M. 905; fîr, feer, w.; fyr, p.

WISE, *adj.* (Learned). Scentyl, skentyll, scyntyl, w.; skyntyll, b.; scientoc, w.; skientog, p.; skyansek, M. 377.

WISH, *s.* Plegad, w. (*Pl.* Plegadow, blegadow, w.); whans, p.c. 1092; yeues, w.; youall, merth, b.; bolnogeth, M. 310; bolenegoth, p.c. 1139. *Ha bolenegôth a'n tâs,* and the wish of the father, p.c. 1139. See also WILL, *s.*

WISH, *v.* Desef, menny, w.; menna, p.; minny, mynny, mynnés, yeuny, w.; vedn, vossaw, p. See also WILL, *v.*

IT IS WISHED. Mynner, fynner, w.

YE WILL WISH. Vynnouch, a mutation of *mynnouch*, 2 pers. pl. fut. of *mynnés*, to wish, w.

THEY WILL WISH. Vynnons, a mutation of *mynnons*, 3 pers. pl. fut. of *mynnés*, to wish, w.

HE MAY WISH. Mynno, fynno, vynno, w.

TO WIT. Ednak, B. ; en ednak, P. ; eduyn, B.

WIT, *s.* Scient, sceans, skeans, skeyens, scians, skyans, skyens, w.

WITCH, *s.* Poddrac, w. ; podrak, B. ; pestriorés, pestryorés, pystriorês, w. ; kuiliogés, cuilliogés, chuilliogés, guenoiourciat, guenoiureat, gunethiat drên, B.

WITCHCRAFT, *s.* Pystry, pystyc, pystyk, w. ; guenuyn, B.

WITCHERIES, *s.* Pystege, w.

WITCHERY, *s.* Dewnos, deunos, w.

WITH, *prep.* Cans, cens, kens, w. ; gans, P. *Gans ow tás*, with my father, P.C. 727. *Lanters gans golow*, lanterns with light, P.C. 609 ; ganz, genz, P. ; gan, gen. w. *Gen hlo*, with child, P. ; gyn, gynen, P. ; guzen, B. ; ord, orth, worth, w. ; dy, der, dre, dredh, P ; dhanna, B. *An golou dhanna*, with a light, B. ; kês, barh, B. ; barha, bara, pan, pahan, rûm, P. *Rúm trós*, with noise. *Rúm peryl*, with danger, P.

WITH HER or IT. Gynsy, w. ; ghynsi, B.

WITH HIM or IT. Ganso, w. ; ganzo, B. ; ganzha, P. ; gonzha, B. ; gansa, C.W. 805 ; gowzha, P.

WITH ME. Gynef, gyné, w.

WITH THEE. Gynés, genés, w.

WITH THEM. Gansé, gynzhans, w. ; ghynzhanz, genzynz, B.

WITH US. Genen, w. ; gennen, B. ; gynen, P.

WITH YE or YOU. Genouch, w. ; genough, P. ; ghenouch, B. ; gynouch, genoch, w. ; ghenok, genouh, B ; geneuch, gyneuch, w. ; genew, P.

WITHDRAW, *v.* Dena, dené, deny, tené, teny, w.

TO WITHDRAW ONE'S SELF, *v.* Omdena, P. ; omdenna, om-tenna, ymdenna, y'm tenna, w.

WITHER, *v.* Gwedhra, guedhra, P.

WITHERED, *part.* Sêchés, sychés, sechys, seghys, sychys, syhys, sehys, zehys, P.

WITHIN. Abervêdh, abervêth, w. *Dún abervêth*, let us come inside, O.M. 1062 ; aperfêth, w. ; abervadh, aberuêth. P. ; berth, R.D. 860. *Berth yn bysma*, within this world, R.D. 860 ; aberth, w. *Aberth yn beyth*, within the grave, R.D. 2083 ; aber, bera, barh a, en bera, w. ; ynbarth, B. ; agy, w. *Agy the lyst*, in the lists ; agey, N. ; agye, C.W. 1029 ; adzhyi, dzhyi ; yn, y, mein, meyny, w.

WITHIN ME. Ytama, P.

WITHIN US. Ynnon ni.

ARE YOU WITHIN ? Erouh hui tshyi, *i.e.*, are you within the house ? P.

WITHOLD, *v.* Ymdenné, P. ; guitha dhort, B.

WITHOUT, *adv.* (Outside). Amês, a mês, w. ; yn mêz, yn meys, yn meas, P. ; emês, w. ; emêz, P. ; emeas, mêz, B. ; vêz, vease. a vês, w. ; a vease, evêz, P. ; avês. w. ; aver, auest, P ; vez, B.V. *Avés hâg agy*, without and within. N.

WITHOUT, *prep.* Heb, w. ; hep, P. *Heb dylly*, without ceasing, B. *Hep hynny*, without denial, P. ; di, P. *Dibetti*, without pity, P. ; de, dy, w. *Dysôn*, without noise, P. ; saw, P. ; saw, N. *Saw y ober h'y thyskés*, without his work and his teaching, P.C. 57 ; hebogh, M. 2693. *Hebogh why sur na menogh*, without you surely not often, M. 2693.

WITHOUT CARE. Heb kên, P.

WITHOUT DOUBT. Hepmar, hemmar, w. ; hep thought, N. ; diougel, P.

WITHOUT END. Hep worfen, N.

WITHOUT EQUAL. Hepar, hepparow, w. ; hepparou, P.

WITHOUT FAIL. Heb fyllal, C.W. 505.

WITHOUT KNOWLEDGE. Descians.

WITHOUT ME. Heboff, M. 4546.

WITHOUT NOISE. Dysôn, w.

WITHOUT RELAXATION or CEASING. Hebdylly, P.

WITHOUT A ROAD. Hebford, w.

WITHOUT STOP or STAY. Ahanas, ahas, P.

WITHOUT YOU. Hebogh why, M. 2693.

WITHSTAND, *v.* Omdhal, w.

WITLESS, *adj.* Discient, diskient, w. ; dikrêf, B.

WITNESS, TO BEAR WITNESS, *v.* Tustuné, dustuné, dustynyé, dustyné, w.

WITNESS or TESTIMONY, *s.* Tustuny, dustuny, dustyny, w. ; destynyé, C.W. 127. *Ha henna dôk dustuny*, bear witness of that, P.C. 1272.

A WITNESS, *s.* Dustyny, P.C. 1312. *The hemma óf dustyny*, to this I am witness, P.C. 1312. (This perhaps is simply witness or *testimony*.) Tustun, dustun, tist, test, w.

A WITNESSING, *s.* Tustuny, tistuni, testyny, w. ; tistum, P. ; dustuny, dustyny, w.

WITTY, *adj.* Sceans, w. ; skeans, kydnik, P. ; avlethys. w. ; avlethis, P.

WITS, *s.* Skyans, M. 3835. *Thy skyans lemen drofa*, to his wits now bring him, M. 3835.

WIZARD, *s.* Pystryor, pystryour, w.

WOAD, *s.* (The plant). Glesin, w. ; glesyn, P.

WOODCOCK, *s.* Kyvelak, P.

WOE, *s.* Gu, gew, gwae, w.; gwêf, c,w. 1833; wew, w.; wêr, wryth. *Lena wryth,* full of woe, **P.**

WOE! *exclam.* Trew! tru! w.

WOE TO HIM. Goef, gweff, govy, w.

WOE IS ME. Govy, w.

WOE TO ME. Govy, w.

WOE TO THEE. Gogy, **M.** 3596.

WOE TO THEM. Goy, w.

WOEFUL, *adj.* Ryth, w.

WOLF, *s.* Bleidh, w.; blaidh, bleit, **P.**; blyth, **M.** 1104; blygh, c.w. 1149; bleiddie, **B.**

WOMAN, *s.* Benen, venen, bynen, vynen, bynyn, vynyn, banen, w.; benyn, c.w. 393; an venin, (the woman), **P.** *Pl.* Benenés, venenés w. *An venenés ha'n fleghys* the women and the children, o.**M.** 1575; bynynés, vynynés, w. *My onan a'y vynynés,* I am one of his women, **R.D.** 1667; bennês, **P.**; venyn (?) **B.**

A BIG WOMAN. Benen vrâs, w.

A CHATTERING WOMAN. Flattorés. *Tav flattorés na gous moy,* peace chattering woman, say no more, **R.D.** 1066.

A CROSS OLD WOMAN. Dow, **D.**

A DANCING WOMAN. Lappiorés, w.

A DRUNKEN DIRTY WOMAN. Smulk, **D.**

A DRUNKEN WOMAN. Vedho. From *medho,* to drink, **B.**

A FAT AND DIRTY WOMAN. Zess, sess, suss, **D.** (*Sus,* Lat. A sow.)

A DIRTY WOMAN or SLATTERN. Tulky, tulgy, slummock, **D.**

A CARELESS WORK-WOMAN. Slump, **D.**

A DUMPY WOMAN (or MAN). Stubbet, **D.**

A GOOD WOMAN. Bennen vâz, **P.**; benen vat, **B.V.**

WOMAN OF MY HEART. Ben ma brea, **B.V.**

THE WOMAN OF THE HOUSE. Gwrêgty, wrêgty, w.

A MARRIED WOMAN. Grêg cans gûr, gwrêc, greugh, gureg, gurak, grûk, grêg, **P.** See also WIFE.

AN ILL-TEMPERED WOMAN. Frig, **D.**

AN OLD WOMAN. Gwrah, gruah, gurah, w.

A STOUT WOMAN. Hummock, **D.**

POOR WOMAN. Gwragedh vohosugion, w.

A PROUD WOMAN. Goch, **B.**

AN UNTIDY WOMAN. Sproosen, strollop, **D.**

A WOMAN "IN THE STRAW." Bennen in golo-vas, **P.**

A WOMAN SINNER. Pehaduras, **B.**

THIS WOMAN. Homma (*hon-omma*), **P.**

THIS WOMAN HERE. Homma (*hon omma*), **B.**

WOMAN or WIFE, *s.* See WIFE.

WOMB, *s.* Brys, w.; breys, **M.** 847. *In breys a benen heb awer,* in a woman's womb, without grief, **M.** 847; mam, tor, torr, w.; nastra, **P.**; nascra, w.; *May wrûk the thôn ym nascra,* that I bore thee in my womb, **R.D.** 486.

WONDER, *s.* Marth, varth, w. *Ha henna mûr varth vye,* and that would be a great wonder, **P.C.** 1728; marthus, varthus, w.; marthys, **N.**; mestry, meystry, maystry, w.

A WONDER! *exclam.* Refaria !, **B.** This was a common expression and is the same as "By St. Mary!" See WONDERFUL!

WONDERS, *s.* Marthegion, marthegyon, varthegyon, marthogion, marthusion, maradgyon, w.; marthogyon, **N.**; maradgion, **P.**; marodgyan, c.w. 1804; marogyan, c.w. 1874.; marudgyan, c.w. 1765; marthys, **P.**

WONDERFUL, *adj.* Marthusec, marthusek, varthusec, w.; merthusy, **B.**; marthusy, marthas, **P.**; marthys, varthys, barthesec, barthusec, ethuc, ethec, ethyc, ithic, ythec, w.

WONDERFUL! *exclam.* Refaria, rafaria, rea, ria, rea rea, rea suas, rea revé, w.

WONDROUS, *adj.* Marthys. *Marthys teke,* wondrous fair. *Râk marthys yeyn yv an guyns,* for wondrous cold is the wind, **P.C.** 1215; magé. *Magé fûr,* wondrous wise, **P.**

WOOD, *s.* (A wood). Coid, koid, coyd, côd, coed, cuid, coit, w.; koit, **B.**; coet, w.; coat, **P.**; koat, kuit, **B.**; cuit, côs, cûz, w.; cûs, kûs, cooz, **P.**; coys, w.; gôd, goed, goda, gûs, gûz, gôs, gosse, guyth, gyth, govyth, wyth, **P.**; cotelle, loin, w.

A HIGH GROWN WOOD. Bali, **B.**

WOOD or TIMBER, *s.* Pren, w.; bren, **P.**; predn, w.; prin, pridn, **P.**

WOOD or FIREWOOD, *s.* Cunys, kunys, **P.** *Be cunys,* a burden of wood. *Cowethe hetheugh kunys,* comrades reach wood, **P.C.** 1219; prynner, o.**M.** 1323. *Gorré lemmyn an prynner,* put now the wood, o.**M.** 1323.

WOODCOCK, *s.* Cyvelac, w.; kyvelak, **P.**; kyvellak, w.

WOODEN, *adj.* Prenic, w.; prenick, prinik, pridnick, **P.**

WOODEN-PLATTER, *s.* Tolyer-predn, **W.F.P.** This term is still used for a *large* wooden plate.

WOODBINE, *s.* Guydhuydh, **B.**

WOOD-CORNER, *s.* Huccaner, **D.**

WOOD-DOVE, *s.* Cûdon, kylobman-kûz, **P.**

WOOD-FENNEL, *s.* Coid finel, w.

WOODMAN, *s.* Sair-pren. *Lit.* A sawer of wood, w.

WOODPECKER, *s.* Kazek-koit, kazek-koat, kazek coit, B.

A GREEN WOODPECKER. Casec coid, w.

THE GREATER or GREEN WOODPECKER. Kazek coit, P.

WOOD-PIGEON, *s.* See WOOD-DOVE.

WOOD-PILE or STACK, *s.* Tasurn, P.

WOOD-RICK, *s.* Tasurn, P.

WOOD-TIN, *s.* Costean, D. An ore of tin in structure like wood.

WOOD or WOODEN FLOOR, *s.* Plynch, P. The *ch* is soft.

WOODY or WOODEN, *adj.* See WOODEN.

WOODY, *adj.* (Abounding in trees). Gwidhenic, gwydhenic, wydhenic, withenic, w.; withenick, gyth, P.; guêlz, B.

A WOODY VALLEY. Glyn, B. See also VALLEY.

WOOL, *s.* Glân, glawn, gluan, w.; gulan, B.

WOOER, *s.* Tanter, tymarrhar. *Pl.* Tymarrhurion, B.

WORD, *s.* Gîr, gêr, B.; gear, c.w. 164; geer, M. 928; ere, c.w. 565. *Râk sawyé tûs dre vn gêr,* to save men by one word, P.C. 2972. *Covs vn geen,* speak a word, M. 928. *Râg der tha ere yth falsa,* for by thy word it seemed, c.w. 565. *Pl.* Gerryow, gyrryow, giriow, w.; gyrryraw, c.w. 638; gerryon, w,; gerennov, M. 2964. *Na wele covs gerennov,* seek not to talk words, M. 2964.

A GOOD WORD. Gâr da, P.; gervâs, B.

WORD, SAYING, or SPEECH. *s.* Lavar, w.; laver, P.C. 71. *Pl.* Lavarow, w.; lafarov, M. 2920. *Heb na herré lafarov,* without any longer words, M. 2920.

WORD-BOOK, *s.* Gerlever, w.

WORK, *v.* Gonedhy, gonethy, gonés, gonys, conys, wonys, gwethel, guthyl, gwaythé, gwethé, quethé, w.; dho wheal, dho whul, whelé, whela, whelas, wharfé, gwyl, guil, gûl, geel, geil, gil, P.; lafuryé, laviria, w.; laferrya, B.; obery, w.

HE WILL WORK. Wonés, a mutation of *gonés,* 3 pers. s. fut. of *gonys,* to work, w.

THEY WILL WORK. Wonedhons, a mutation of *gonedhons,* 3 pers. pl. fut. of *gonedhy,* to work, w.

WORK *s.* (Work or deed). Gwreans, gwryans, w.; guryans, P.; wreans, gwythrés, wythrés, w. *Hâg ól y wythrés keffrys,* and all his work also, P.C. 1443; gwaithe, gwaith, gweyth, weyth, gueid, gwyth, w.; wyth, P.; guyth, M. 785; guaith, B.; gûl, P.C. 546; obar, c.w. 1179.

A MINE WORK. Wheal, whêl, wheyl, w.; wheil, O.M. 2569; whyl, wayl, welth, w.; whela, wheela, P.; huêl, hwêl, hweyl, w.

WORK or LABOUR, *s.* Lafur, lavur, lafyr, w.; lavyr, lavut, P.; lavirians, w.; lafurye, P. *Wosé cous ha lafurye,* after talk and work, O.M. 1899; ober. *Râg an ober,* for the work, B. Eight hours work, sometimes six hours work in a mine is called a *core* or *coor,* D.

WORKER, *s.* Guythor, gueiduur, oberor, w.; oberur, H. See WORKMAN.

FULL OF WORKS. Obereth, w.

WORKFELLOW, *s.* Oberwas, w.; oberuaz, P.

WORKMAN, *s.* Gueiduur, gueidvur, w.; gueidhur, gweithiur, gwythor, w.; guythur, guidhili, P.; weidwur, gonidoc, w.; gonidog, B.; gonesig, goneseg, wonesek, wayler, vayler, vailer, P.; oberor, w.; oberur, gofail, inguinor, B.; dên huél, w.

WORKMANSHIP. *s.* See WORK or DEED,

WORKMEN, *s.* Guithorion, B.; gonesugy, wenesugy, w.

WORK-STONES, *s.* (*i.e.,* building stones). Mein wheyl, w.; mein hueyl, N.

WORKWOMAN, *s.* (?). *A careless workwoman,* Slump, D.

WORLD, *s.* Bys, w.; byz, B.; byes, c.w. 87; byese. c.w. 2371; pys, vys, beys, veys, bês, w.; beas, M 4275; beise, c.w. 1080; beis, beaz, B.; bîd, en bîd, bît, w. *The'n beys ól golowys glân,* to all the world bright lights, O.M. 34. *Bysmé,* this world, M. 153.

WORM, *s.* Cinac, cynac, w.; kinak. (*Pl.* Kinougas, P.); kenack, D.; prêv, w.; prêve, c.w. 335; prêf, w.; preaf, c.w. 502; prîf, pryf, w. *Pl.* Pryvés, w.; prevas, c.w. 111.

A SMALL WORM. Prêvan, w.

A THOUSAND WORMS. Milprêv. This, says Borlase, is the *anguinum* (the Druidical egg), "called so from the spawn of the adder inclosed in the lump; it was also called *gleinneidr* or glass serpent, which was the artificial imitation of the natural *anguinum,* made of glass, supposed a powerful amulet."

WORMS CREEPING LIKE CRABS. (? Crab-lice). Crabaliaz, P.

WORMWOOD, *s.* Fuelin, w.; fuelein, B.; felen, w.

WORRY, *v.* Dyspytyé, dhyspytyé, w.

WORSE, *adj.* Gwêth, gwethe, guêth, w.; guêyth, M. 3378; gwaeth, guyth, w.; guetha (?), N.; quêth, P.; wêth, w.; weyth, auyth, a uyth, laka, lakka, P.; lacka, B.

WORSHIP, *s.* Gordhyans, wordhyans, w.; gorthyans, worthyans, N.; gwerdhyans, gorryans, w.; guoryans, gwerthyia, gorty, gworria, P.; urria, B.

WORSHIP, *v.* Gordhy, gordhyé, cordhyé, w.; gorthé, N.; gorthy, P.; gorthya, c.w. 221; gworthya, c.w. 139; gwerthya, P.; gworria, gurria, w.; guria, P.; worria, urria, w.; worth, coly, P.

HE WORSHIPPED. Wordhyas, a mutation of *gordhyas*, 3 pers. s. preter. of *gordhyé*, to worship. w.

I SHALL WORSHIP. Cordhyaf, a regular mutation after *mâr*, of *gordhyaf*, w.

HE WILL WORSHIP. Wordh, a mutation of *gordh*, 3 pers. s. fut. of *gordhy*, to worship, w.

HE MAY WORSHIP. Wordhyo, a mutation of *gordhyo*, 3 pers. s. subj. of *gordhyé*, to worship, w.

WORSHIPPED, *part.* Gordhys, gorthys, w.

WORST, *adj.* Droca, droka, droga, gwetha, w.; guetha, p.

WORST, *v.* Gwaythy, w.; guaythé, guethé, p.; gwethé, fethy, w.

WORSTED, *part.* Gwythys, fythys, w.

WORTH, *s.* Ary, vry, prîs, prîz, prys, brys, brêz, grâs, râs, w.; râz, w.

TO BE WORTH. Bôs talvés, dâl, tâl, w.; yrvyry, p.

IT WILL BE WORTH. Dalvyth, a mutation of *talvyth*, 3 pers. s. fut. of *taly*, to pay or requite, w.

THEY WILL BE WORTH. Dalons, a mutation of *talons*, 3 pers. pl. of *taly*, to pay or requite, w.

WORTHLESS, *adj.* Casadow, gasadow, w.

WORTHY, *adj.* Gweff, gwyw, w.; guyw, p.; gyw, w.; gvyw, p.c. 481. *Dre the voth kén nag ef gvyw*, through thy will though I am not worthy, p.c. 481.

WOULD. Vynnas, fynnas, vynsé, vysé, vennyn, b.

I WOULD. Mensen, fensen, vensen, mynnys, fynnys, vynnys, w.; mennen, menzhon, b.; vynnan, w.

I WOULD RATHER. Me vedn kenz, me vendzha a kenz, b.

THOU WOULDST. Mennas, fennas, mynsys, vynsys, w.; mennyz, menzhez, b.

WOULDST THOU? Menyth, mynyth, vynnyth, b.

HE WOULD. Menné, fenné, mensé, w.; menzhé, b.; mendzha, fensé, vynsé, mynnas, fynnas, vynnas, vynné, vynna, w.; mennaz, b.

WE WOULD. Mynsyn, vynsyn, w.; mennen, b.

YE WOULD. Mennen, b.

THEY WOULD. Menuenz, b.

WOUND, *v.* Golyé, bluthyé, w.; bluthy, hertia, p.

WOUND, *s.* Goly, woly, guli. (*Pl.* Golyow, wolyow, gullyow, w.) Brew. *Pl.* Brewyon, vrewyon. Borlase gives for " wounds," *pystege, pyftege.*

WOVEN, *part.* Guethy, b. See WEAVE, *v.*

WRACK or **SEA TANG,** *s.* Gumman, gubman, w.

WRANGLE, *v.* Garey, d.

WRANGLER, *s.* Strifor, w.

WRAP, *v.* Malyé, maylé, maylyé, vaylé, w. *Hâg yn cendal glân maylyé*, and wrap him in a clean linen, p.c. 3156.

WRAPPED, *part.* Maylys, maylyés, w.; drylyas, b.

WRATH, *s.* Sôr, sorras, frôth, w.; frêth, p.

WREATH, *s.* Gaalont, plêth, w.

WREATHE, *v.* Nedhé, nedha, b.; nethé, p.

WRECK, *s.* Gurek, p.

WREN, *s.* Gwrannan, gwradnan, w.; guradnan, p.; guradn, b.

WRESTLE, *v.* Emlodh, emladh, emladha, w.; themloth, p.; ymdowla, w.; ymdoula, p. *Ov themloth may then pûr squyth*, wrestling till I was very much tired, p.c. 2509.

WRESTLER, *s.* Ymdowlur, w.; ymdoulur, b.; ymdoular, p.; kân-pûr (*f,* kân-wur), b.

WRESTLING, *s.* Umdowla, ymdoula, b.

WRETCHED, *adj.* (Miserable). Aflydhys, w.; avlethés, c.w. 1152; difrêth, dyfrêth, dyffryth, deffryth, trewyth, drewyth, trewath, w. *Lemyn dyfrêth of ha gvack*, now wretched I am, and empty, o.m. 593.

WRETCHED, *adj.* (Evil, vile). Trôc, tru, trôth, w. " We still say *an old trot*, speaking of an old miser, or covetous woman," p.

WRETCHES, *s.* (Those afflicted or miserable). Aflydhygyon, aflydhysyon, w.

WRETCHES, *s.* (Villains). Plnssyon, w. See RASCAL.

WRIGHT, *s.* Sair, w.

WRING, *v.* Strothé, w.; strothy, guryn, gurydn, p.

WRINKLE or **PERRIWINKLE,** *s.* Guihian, p.

WRINKLE, FURROW, PASSAGE. Droke, d.

WRINKLED, *part.* Squytheys, p.

WRIST, *s.* Codna brêh, w.; kodna brêh, b.; cona brêch, w.; conna brêgh, p.c. 2762. *Lit.* The arm neck.

WRITE, *s.* Screfa, scrifa, scrifé, w.; screpha, p.

WRITER, *s.* Scriviniat, w.

WRITING, *s.* (A writing). Scrife, w.; skrift, skrividh, b.; scrividh, scrivit, scriven, w. *Pl.* Scrivit, b.

WRONG, *adj.* Cam, gam, ham, cham, cabm, w.; camhinsic, p.

WRONG, *s.* (A wrong). Drôc, drôk, drôg, w.; hâs, p.

WRONG-DOER, *s.* Cam, gam, w.

TO DO WRONG, *v.* Camwul, gamwul, w.

WROUGHT, *part.* Coyntis, b.; rewruk, wharfethys, p.

WRY, *adj.* Cam, cham, cabm, w.; kabm, p.; gam, ham, w.

TO MAKE WRY, *v.* Camma, gamma, w.

WRY-NECK, s. (The disease). Pinnick, D.

Y.

"This letter is used in Cornish to express the diphthongal sound of *i*, as in the English words *wine*, *fine*, &c.

It is also constantly used in the Ordinalia for *i*; thus we find *gwyn*, *gwyr*, *gwyryoneth*, for *gwin*, *gwir*, *gwirionedh*, &c.

This letter has no place in the Armoric, Irish, and Gaelic Alphabet," W. *Lex. Corn. Brit.*

YARD, s. (A yard measure). Gwelan, W.; guelan, P.; gwelen, W.

YARD, s. (Of a ship). Delé, W.; guelan gôl, *i.e.*, sail yard, P.

YARN, s. Linyn, B.; noden, W.

A BOTTOM OF YARN. Pellen, B.

YARROW, s. Minfel, W.; milfel, nintell, B.

YE, *pron.* See YOU.

YEAR, s. Bledhen, vledhen, W.; bledhan, B.; bledhyn, bliden, blydhen, W.; blithen, blithan, P.; blythan, M. 243; blyth, M. 1537; bloth, c.w. 1976; blodh, W.; bloaz, blewen, blipen, B.

YEARS, s. Bledhynyow, bledhynnow, blenydnyow, W.; blythy (*Pl.* of Blyth), M. 1537; vledhynnow, W.; vlenydnyowe, c.w. 1915 (Ms.); vlethydnyow, c.w. 1915; vledthydnyow, c.w. 1862. *Naw cans blóth*, nine hundred years, P.

YEARLING or STEER, s. Denevoid, B.; deneuoid, loch, leauh, P.

THE YOUNG OF A COW or SHEEP. Lodn, W.; loch, leauh, P.

YEARNING, s. Hereth, M. 4515. *Hereth us orth ov grefya*, yearning is grieving me, M. 4545; hyrest, P.C. 3176; herethek, M. 4526. *War the lergh ha herethek*, after thee, and yearning, M. 4314.

YEAST, s. Burm, W.; burman, B.

YELLOW, *adj.* Melyn, melen, milin, velyn, velen, W.; mellyn, uellyn, B.

A DEEP YELLOW COLOUR. Ridhvelyn, W.; ridhvellyn, P.

YELLOW-HAMMER, s. (Bird). Gladdy, D.

YES or YEA, *adv.* Ya, yea, îa, B.; ea, M. 1546; huath, B.

YESTERDAY, s. Doy, de, W.

THE DAY BEFORE YESTERDAY. De genzhete, W.

YESTERDAY EVENING. Nehuer, neihur, W.

BEFORE YESTERDAY. Genzhete, W.

YET, *adv.* Whâth, P. *Yma dev whâth ov pewé*, there is a God yet living, O.M. 622; wâth, M. 1256. *Wâth yferne a vêth aleys*, yet hell will be wide open, M.

1256; hwâth, huâth, whêth, P.; wêth, w.; whêt, P.C. 1087; whât, vythys, bez, P.; etto, B.

YEW, s. (Tree). Hivin, W.; hiuin, B.

YIELD, v. Gwylé, P.; guella, dho ouna, B.; *Rhei an guella*, I'll yield to you. P.

TO YIELD UP, v. (Resign, deliver). Dascor, W.; thascor, P.; dastor, B.

YOKE, s. Ieu, mydzhovan, W.

A YOKE, ALSO A HORSE COLLAR. Myngar. A horse collar made of twisted straw is still called a *munger*, D.

YOLK or YELK, s. Melin-oi, melynoy, W.; melynoi, P. *Lit.* The yellow of the egg.

YOU or YE, *pron.* Why, wy, hwi, hwei, huei, huyhui, chwi, chui, chuy, a's. Borlase gives for *ye* as follows :—" *Nough*, ye ; *warnough*, on ye ; *genough*, with ye ; and suffixed to verbs, as, *vynnouch*, will ye." The variations for *nough*, after dropping the *n*, are, ouch, och, ogh, owh, o, ou, ugh, uch, ach, euch, eugh, uich, ych, euh, ew, iu, az, 's. See the following phrases, *viz* :—

BY YOU. Genouch, genoch, geneuch, W.; genough, genew, P.; drethough, N.; genawhy, c.w. 2518.

BEFORE YOU. Ragouch, W.; ragou, B.

FOR YOU. Ragouch, W.; ragough, N.; rago huei, B.

FROM YOU. Ahanouch, W.; ahanough, N.; worthyeugh, P.

IN YOU. Ynnouch (*yn-chui*), W.; ynnough, N.

OF YOU. Ahanouch, N.; worthyeugh, P.

ON YOU. Uarno, P.; uarnach, uarnaz, B.

THAN YOU. Agesouch, W.

TO or UNTO YOU. Theugh, N.; thugh, P.; deuch, deugh, N.; dheuch, P.; dheuh, dheu, deuh, W.; dhiu, B.; dyuch, W.; dhyuch, B.; dyugh, M. 807; dhuich, B.; dych, deych, dywy, dhywy, dyuwhy, wortheuch, W.; worthough, ortheugh, N.; orthowh, c.w. 704.

UPON YOU. Warnough, N.

WITH YOU. Geneugh, N.; ganso, P.; gansa, B.

YOUNG, *adj.* Iouenc, iunc, iungk, iynk, iyngk, W.; jungk, P.; iyn, B.; yonc, yonk, yync, yowync, W.; yowynk, M. 1196. *Yowynk ha hên*, young and old, P.C. 39.

YOUNG MAN, Dên iunc, dên junk, W.; dean junk, gûr iovene, P.; gûrjovene, B.; yovene, P.; jevan, B.; iyngh, iynkar, P.; iyncar, W.; yowink, P.; gwâs, guâs, B.

YOUNGEST, *adj.* Younka, c.w. 1060. *Ha abel ew ow mabe younka*, and abel is my youngest son, c.w. 1060.

YOUNGSTER, s. See YOUNG MAN.

YOUR, *pron.* Agas, agés, agez, agis, agos, agoz, agus, aguz, agys, gas, ges, gez, gos, goz, gus, guz, gys, gyz, as, es, ys.

FOR YOUR. Eâg eun, P.

OF YOURS. Aga, P.

TO YOUR. Dhys, P.; dhyz, B.

WITH YOUR. Gennys, W.; genyz, P.; ghennyz, B.

YOUR OWNSELVES Gyz honyn, P.

YOUTH or YOUNGSTER, *s.* See YOUNG MAN.

YOUNG FOLK, YOUTHS, YOUNGSTERS, *s.* Yowynkés, yowynketh, P.

YOUTH, (Adolescence), Yowyncnéth, w.; newt, M. 167. *A newt hag a henys,* in youth and in old age, M. 167.

YOUTHFUL, *adj.* Yonc, yonk, yync, younk, yowync, w.

YOUTHFUL AGE. Ooz younk, w.

YOUTHFULNESS, *s.* Yowyncnêth, w.

YOUTHFULLY, *adv.* Yowynkês, yowynkêth, P.

Z.

" This letter has properly no place in the Cornish alphabet. It is only used in late Cornish to express a softened and corrupted sound of *s*," w. *Lex. Corn. Brit.*

ZEODARY, *s.* Coste, B.

ZONE or BELT, *s.* Grugis, grigis, grygis, grigiz, w.; grygys, gwregus, grwegus, gouris, guris, grûg, cleddif, B.

THE END.   AN DIWEDH.

APPENDIX.

THE FIRST CHAPTER

OF

THE FIRST BOOK OF MOSES

CALLED

GENESIS:

Also the Lord's Prayer & Apostles' Creed, &c.

WITH A LITERAL

AND

AN INTERLINEAL TRANSLATION OF

THE ANCIENT CORNISH INTO ENGLISH.

The Ancient Cornish is according to the orthography of the Cornish Dramas, as "written in the thirteenth century, and may have been . . . . . even of the ninth century," when the Cornish Language was spoken in its purity.—(See Williams's *Lexicon Cornu-Britannicum.*)

An Censa Cabydul a'n Lyvyr an
The first Chapter of the Book the

GENESIS.
GENESIS.

1. Y'n dalleth Dew a wrûg nêf ha'n nôr.
In the beginning God (a-)created heaven and the earth.

2. Hag ydh esé an nôr heb composter ha gwag; ha tewolgow esé war enep a'n downder,
And it was the earth without form and void: and darkness was upon (the) face of the deep,
ha Spyrys Dew rûg gwaya war enep a'n dowrow.
and (the) Spirit (of) God did move upon (the) face of the waters.

3. Ha Dew a leverys, bydhens golow, hag ydh esé golow.
And God (a-)said, let there be light, and it was light.

4. Ha Dew a welas an golow may fe da; ha Dew a dhyberthas an golow dheworth an tewolgow.
And God (a-)saw the light that it was good; and God (a-)divided the light from the darkness.

5. Ha Dew a henwys an golow dŷdh, ha'n tewolgow ef a henwys nôs: ha'n gorthuer ha'n
And God (a-)named the light day, and the darkness he (a-)named night: and the evening and the
myttyn o an censa dŷdh.
morning were the first day.

6. Ha Dew a leverys, bydhens ebren y'n creys a'n dowrow, ha gwrêns e dhybarthy an
And God (a-)said, let there be (a) firmament in the midst of the waters, and let it (a-)divide the
dowrow dheworth an dowrow.
waters from the waters.

7. Ha Dew a wrûg an ebren, ha dhyberthas an dowrow esé yn dan an ebren dheworth
And God did make the firmament, and divided the waters (which) were under the firmament from
an dowrow esens a uch an ebren: hag yn delna ydh o.
the waters (which) were above the firmament: and in that manner it was.

8. Ha Dew a henwys an ebren nêf: ha'n gorthuer ha'n myttyn o an nessa dŷdh.
And God (a-)named the firmament heaven: and the evening and the morning were the second day.

9. Ha Dew a leverys, bydhens an dowrow yn dan an nêf cuntullys, warbarth dhe un tyller, ha
And God (a-)said, let be the waters under the heaven gathered together to one place, and
bydhens an tŷr sŷch dyscudhys: hag yn delna ydh o.
let be the land dry disclosed: and in that manner it was.

10. Ha Dew a henwys an tŷr sých an nor, ha ountellyans warbarth a'n dowrow ef a henwys
    And God (a-)named the land dry the earth, and (the) gathering together of the waters he (a-)named
    môr : ha Dew a welas may fe da.
    sea; and God (a-)saw that it was good.

11. Ha Dew a leverys, gwrêns an nôr dry rag gwels, ha losow ow tôn hâs, ha'n gwŷdh
    And God (a-)said, let the earth bring forth grass, and herbs (a-)bearing seed, and the trees
    ow tôn avalow warlerch aga echen, nêb usy aga hâs ynne aga honan, war an nôr: hag
    (a-)bearing fruits after their kind, such as be (with) their seed in themselves, upon the earth: and
    yn delna ydh o.
    in that manner it was.

12. Ha'n nôr a dhrôs râg gwels, an losow ow tôn hâs warlerch aga echen, ha'n gwŷdh ow
    And the earth did bring forth grass, the herbs (a-)bearing seed after their kind, and the trees (a-)
    tôn avalow, nêb usy aga hâs ynne aga honan warlerch aga echen; ha Dew a
    bearing fruits, such as be (with) their seed in themselves after their kind; and God (a-)
    welas may fe da.
    saw that it was good.

13. Ha'n gorthuer ha'n myttyn o an tressa dŷdh.
    And the evening and the morning were the third day.

14. Ha Dew a leverys, bydhens golowys y'n ebren nêf dhe dhybarthy an dŷdh dheworth
    And God (a-)said, let there be lights in the firmament (of) heaven to divide the day from
    an nôs, ha bydhens y râg tavasow, ha râg termynyow, ha râg dydhyow, ha râg bledhynnow.
    the night, and let them be for signs, and for seasons, and for days, and for years.

15. Ha bydhens y râg golowys y'n ebren nêf dhe rey golow war an nôr: hag yn
    And let them be for lights in the firmament (of) heaven to give light upon the earth: and in
    delna ydh o.
    that manner it was.

16. Ha Dew a wrûg dew golow brâs; an brassa golow dhe rewlyé an dŷdh, ha'n behanna golow
    And God did make two light(s) great; the greater light to rule the day, and the lesser light
    dhe rewlyé an nôs; ha'n stêr ef a's gwrûg yn wêdh.
    to rule the night; and the stars he them made likewise.

17. Ha Dew a's goras y'n ebren nêf dhe rey golow war an nôr.
    And God them set in the firmament (of) heaven to give light upon the earth.

18. Ha dhe rewlyé an dŷdh ha'n nôs, ha dhe dhybarthy an golow dheworth an tewolgow, ha
    And to rule the day and the night, and to divide the light from the darkness, and
    Dew a welas may fe da.
    God (a-)saw that it was good.

19. Ha'n gorthuer ha'n myttyn o an pesweré dŷdh.
    And the evening and the morning were the fourth day.

20. Ha Dew a leverys, gwrêns an dowrow dry râg pûr vêr an taclow ûs ow gwaya gans
    And God (a-)said, let the waters bring forth abundantly the things that be (a-)moving with
    bewnans, hag edhyn dhe nygé dres an nôr a lês y'n ebren nêf.
    life, and fowl to fly above the earth abroad in the firmament (of) heaven.

21. Ha Dew a wrûg an morvilow brâs, ha ceniver tra   bew   ûs ow gwaya, nêb a rûg an
And God (a-)created the   whales great, and every thing alive that is (a-)moving, which did the
dowrow dry râg pûr vêr warlerch aga echen, ha ceniver edhen gans ascal warlerch hy echen;
waters bring forth abundantly after   their kind. and every   bird with wing after   its kind;
ha Dew a welas may   fe   da.
and God (a-)saw that it was good.

22. Ha Dew a wrûg aga benygé y, ha leverys, bydhouch luen a hâs, ha drouch râg   pûr
And God   did   them   bless and said,   be ye   full of seed, and bring ye forth abun-
                                                           (_seed-full_)
vêr,   ha lenouch an dowrow y'n môr, ha gwrêns an edhyn dry râg pûr vêr y'n nôr.
dantly, and replenish the waters in the sea, and let the fowl increase abundantly in the earth.

23. Ha'n gorthuer ha'n myttyn   o   an pempes dŷdh.
And the evening and the morning were the fifth   day.

24. Ha Dew a leverys, gwrêns an nôr dry râg an taclow bew warlerch aga echen, an lodnow,
And God (a-)said,   let the earth bring forth the things living after their kind. the cattle,
ha'n taclow cramyas, ha bestes a'n   nôr warlerch aga echen; hag yn   delna   ydh o.
and the things creeping, and beasts of the earth after   their kind; and in that manner it was.

25. Ha Dew a wrûg bestes a'n nôr warlerch aga echen, ha'n lodnow warlerch aga echen, ha
And God did make beasts of the earth after   their kind, and the cattle   after   their kind, and
ceniver tra   ûs   ow cramyas war an   nôr,   warlerch aga echen; ha Dew a welas may
every thing that is (a-)creeping upon the earth,   after   their kind; and God (a-)saw that
fe   da.
it was good.

26. Ha Dew a leverys, gwrên dên yn agan del ny, warlerch agan havalder; ha gwrêns y cemeres
And God (a-)said, let us make man in our likeness, after   our similitude; and   let him   take
gallos dres an pusces a'n môr, ha dres an edhen a'n ebren, ha dres an milyow, ha dres
dominion over the fishes of the sea, and over the fowl of the sky, and over the cattle, and over
ol an nôr, ha dres ceniver tra cramyas ûs   ow cramyas war an nôr.
all the earth, and over every thing creeping that is (a-)creeping upon the earth.

27. Yn   delna Dew a wrûg dên y'n havalder y honan, y'n havalder Dew ef a's grûg;
In that manner God (a-)created man in the similitude of himself, in the likeness (of) God he him did make;
gorrow ha benow ef a's gwrûg.
male   and female he them made.

28. Ha Dew a wrûg aga benygé, ha Dew a leverys dhedhé, bydhouch luen a hâs, ha drouch râg
And God did   them bless, and God (a-)said to them, be ye   full of seed, and bring ye forth
                                                             (_seed-full_)
pûr vêr, ha lenouch an nôr, ha bydhouch dresto; ha cemerouch gallos dres   pusces
abundantly, and replenish the earth, and be ye   over it; and take ye dominion over (the) fishes
a'n môr, ha dres an edhyn y'n ebren, ha dres ceniver tra   vew   ûs ow gwaya war
of the sea, and over the fowl in the sky, and over every thing living that is (a-)moving upon
an nôr.
the earth.

29. Ha Dew a leverys, mirouch, yma reys genef vy dheuch ceniver losow ow tôn hâs, nêb ûs
And God (a-)said, behold, there is given by myself to you all herbs (a-)bearing seed, which be
war ol an nôr, ha ceniver gwedhen ûs, an avalow a'n gwedhen ynny ow tôn hâs,
upon all the earth, and every tree that is, the fruits of the tree in itself (a-)bearing seed,
dheuch y fŷdh râg boys.
to you they shall be for meat.

30. Ha dhe oll an bestes a'n nôr, ha dhe geniver edhen a'n ebren, ha dhe geniver tra
And to all the beasts of the earth, and to every bird of the sky, and to every thing
ûs ow cramyas war an nôr, ûs bewnans ynné, yma reys genef ceniver lusuan glâs
that is (a-)creeping upon the earth, that is alive in it, there is given by me every herb green
râg boys, hag yn delna ydh o.
far meat, and in that manner it was.

31. Ha Dew a welas ceniver tra esé gwreys ganso, ha mirouch, ydh o ve pûr dha; ha'n gorthuer
And God (a-)saw every thing was made by him, and behold, it was very good; and the evening
ha'n myttyn o an wheffes dŷdh.
and the morning were the sixth day.

THE LORD'S PRAYER.

Pesad a'n Arluth; po, Pader a'n Arluth.
Prayer of the Lord; or, Pater (or Paternoster) of the Lord.

Agan Tâs, nêb ûs yn nêf, bydhens uchellys dhe hanow, dêns dhe walscor, dhe vôdh re bo gwreys
Our Father, who art in heaven, be hallowed thy name, come thy kingdom, thy will be done
yn nôr cepar hag yn nêf. Ro dhynny hydhew agan pûb dŷdh bara. Ha gâf dhynny agan
in earth like as in heaven. Give to us this day our every day bread. And forgive to us our
cammow, kepar del gevyn ny nêb ûs ow cammê er agan pyn ny. Ha na dôg ny
trespasses, like as forgive we whoever be (a-) trespassing upon (us) to our disquiet. And do not lead us
yn antel, mês gwŷth ny dheworth drôc; râg genes yw an mychterneth, an crevder, ha'n
into danger, but deliver us from evil; for with the is thee dominion, the power, and the
wordhyans, râg bysqueth ha bysqueth.
glory, for ever and ever.

AMEN.
AMEN.

THE CREED.

Cregyans a'n Cannasow Cryst;
Creed of the Messengers (of) Christ;

po,

or,

An Cregyans a'n Abesteledh.
The Creed of the Apostles.

Cresaf yn Dew an Tâs Olgallosec, gwrear a'n nêf ha'n nôr: Hag yn Ihesu
I believe in God the Father Almighty, maker of the heaven, and the earth: And in Jesus
Gryst y un mâb, ef agan Arluth-ny: nêb a ve denythys dre an Spyrys Sans, genys a'n
Christ his only son, he our Lord: who was (a-)conceived by the Spirit Holy, born of the
Werches Vary, a wodhevys yn dan Pontius Pilat, a ve crowsys, marow, hag ancledhys; Ef
Virgin Mary, (a-)suffered under Pontius Pilate, was (a-)crucified, dead, and buried; He
a dhyescynnas dhe iffarn; an tressa dŷdh ef a-dhedhoras dheworth an marow; hag a-escynnas
(a-)descended into hell; the third day he a-rose from the dead; and ascended
dhe'n nêf; hag yma ow-sedhé war dorn dychow a'n Tâs Olgallosec; alena ef a-
into the heaven; and there is (a-)seated on (the) hand right of the Father Almighty; thence he will
dhue dhe vrusy bew ha marow. Cresaf y'n Spyrys Sans; an Eglos Sans dres an
come to judge (the) quick and (the) dead. I believe in the Spirit Holy: the Church Holy over the
bys; cowethyans a'n Sansow; dewyllyans pechasow; dedhoryans a'n corf; ha'n bewnans
world; communion of the Saints; forgiveness (of) sins; resurrection of the body; and the life
hep dywedh.
without end.

AMEN.
AMEN.

THE TEN COMMANDMENTS.

An Dec Arhadow;
The Ten Commands;

po,
or,

An Dec Gorhemmynadow Dew.
The Ten Commandments (of) God

Dew a gewsys an gerryow ma ha leverys; me yw an Arluth dhe Dhew, nêb a's drôs
God (a-) spoke the words here and said; I am the Lord thy God, who you brought*
dhe-vês a'n Tŷr Misraim, dhe-vês a'n chy habadin, (*alias,* gwasanaeth.)
away from the land Egypt, away from the house (of) bondage, (or, slavery.)

1. Te ny's bŷdh Dewyow erell mês ve.
   To thee shall not be Gods other than me.

2. Na wra dhys honan nêp del gravys, na havalder tra vŷth, ûs yn nêf awartha,
   Make not to thy self any image graven, nor likeness (of) anything that is in heaven above,
   po y'n nôr a-woles, po, y'n dour yn-dan an nôr. Na wra ty plegy dhe remma, na
   or in the earth below, or in the water under the earth. Do not thou bow down to these, nor
   'ga wordhyé; râg me an Arluth dhe Dhew yw Dew a-sor, hag a vyn dry pechasow
   them worship; for I the Lord thy God am (a) God of wrath and will bring sins
   a'n tasow war an flechys bŷs an tressa ha'n pesweré denythyans a'n nâb na'm
   of the fathers upon the children even to the third and the fourth generation of them who do not
   pertho ve; hag a vyn dyscudhé trueth dhe milyow a'n nêb ûs ow-caré, hag ûs
   honour me; and will shew mercy unto thousands of them who be (a-) loving, and be
   ow-gwythé ow gorhemmynadow.
   (a-) keeping my commandments.

3. Na wra cemeres hanow a'n Arluth dhe Dhew dhe scul, (*alias,* hep ethom,) râg an Arluth
   Do not take (the) name of the Lord thy God to waste, (or, without need,) for the Lord
   dhe Dhew ny vyn sensy e dipêh, nêb ûs cymeres y hanow ef dhe scul, (*alias,* yn gwâg.)
   thy God will not hold him sinless, who is taking his name to waste, (or, in vain.)

4. Perth côf dhe gwythé sans an dydh sabboth; whêh dydhyow te wra whêl, hag a wra
   Bear remembrance to keep holy the day sabbath, six days thou dost labour, and doest
   myns ûs, dhys dhe wûl, mês an sythves dydh yw an Sabboth a'n Arluth dhe Dhew.
   all that is to the to do, but the seventh day is the Sabbath of the Lord thy God.
   Yn dydh-na te nyn echen a whêl; te na dhe vâb, na dhe verch, na dhe dhên whêl,
   In that day thou not anything do; thou, nor thy son, nor thy daughter, nor thy man servant,

* Or, "brought you."

na dhe vôs whêl, na dhe lodnow, n'an dên-uncouth ûs aberth dhe dharasow. Rag
nor thy maid servant, nor thy cattle, nor the stranger that is within thy doors. For
yn whêh dydhyow Dew a wrûg an nêf, ha'n môr, ha mŷns ûs, ynné y, ha powesas
in six days God (a-)created the heaven, and the sea, and all that is therein, and rested
an sythves dŷdh, hag a'n uchellas.
the seventh day, and (a-)hallowed it.

5. Gwra perthy dhe dâs ha'th vam ; may fo dhe dhydhyow hŷr war an tŷr ûs
   Do thou honour thy father and thy mother ; that may be thy days long upon the land that is
   reys dhys gans an Arluth dhe Dew.
   given to thee by the Lord thy God.

6. Na wra ladhé mâb-dên.
   Do not slay mankind.

7. Na wra growedhé gans gwrêc dên-arall vŷth.
   Do not lie down with wife (of) another man ever.

8. Na wra ladré.
   Do not steal.

9. Na wra tyé gow erbyn dhe gontrevec.
   Do not swear false against thy neighbour.

10. Na cemer whans warlyrch ty dhe gontrevec, na cemer whans warlyrch gwrêc
    Take not (a-)longing after (the) house (of) thy neighbour, nor take (a-)longing after (the) wife
    dhe gontrevec, na'y dhên whêl, na'y vôs whêl, na'y odion, na'y asen, na
    (of) thy neighbour, nor his man servant, nor his maid servant, nor his ox, nor his ass, nor
    tra vŷth a'n pew ef.
    anything to own it.

Arluth, cemer trueth ahanan, ha scrŷf oll remma dhe arhadow aberth agan colonow, ny
Lord, take pity of us, and write all these thy commands upon our hearts, we
a'th pys.
(a-)pray thee.

Gordhyans dhe'n Tâs, ha dhe'n Mâb, ha dhe'n Spyrys Sans.
Glory be to the Father, and to the Son, and to the Spirit Holy.

Cepar del ve y'n dalleth yma yn ûr-ma, hag y fŷdh bŷth-tranc hep warfen.
Like as was in the beginning there is in this hour, and it shall be evermore without end.

Gras agan Arluth Ihesu Grist, ha cerensé Dew, ha cowethyans a'n Spyrys
The) grace (of) our Lord Jesus Christ, and (the) love (of) God, and (the) fellowship of the Spirit
Sans, re-bo genen ny oll bŷs venytha.
Holy, be with us all ever, for ever.

Amen. Yn delna re bo.
Amen. In that manner be it.

ENGLISH CHANGES OF CELTIC CORNISH NAMES

DURING the long period that the ancient Cornish language was gradually decaying, many names of farms, fields, hills, valleys, etc., underwent a curious change; old Cornish names took an English form, and the original meanings of many of them have been completely lost.

Under this process the old words have assumed a phonetic disguise in English, and Celtic Cornish names, which are very descriptive, and were easily understood by the old Cornish people, have become quite metamorphosed by English use and interpretation.

The following list is given as an illustration of the constancy with which names are handed down from generation to generation. It will, however, be seen that such names, permanent as they are in themselves, rapidly lose their true signification when they become a part of another language. Such has been the fate of a very large number of Celtic Cornish names of places.

In the examples given below, the definitions are mostly according to Dr. Bannister, but with some variations. (See his *Glossary of Cornish Names*.)

Although many names of places admit of various explanations, yet the following list will afford singular instances of the phonetic changes of Cornish names into English—a mere glance will show how utterly different the English names are from the Celtic Cornish terms and meanings. All the words in the following list have been compared with those of the *Archæologia Cornu-Britannica* of Pryce, and the *Lexicon Cornu-Britannicum* of Williams. The spelling of the latter has been generally followed.

ARROW PARK.—*Garow* Park. The rough park or field : from *garow*, rough, *parc*, a field or close.

BACCHUS PARK.—*Bagas* Park. The bush park or field : from *bagas*, bush, *parc*, a field or close.

BACON PARK.—*Bechan* Park. The little park or field : from *bechan*, little, small, *parc*, a field or close.

BARBARY.—*Bar bre*. The top of the hill : from *bar*, the top or summit, *bre* a hill, a mountain.

BEAGLE MOOR.—*Bigal* Moor. The shepherd's moor or common : from *bigal*, shepherd.

BRAN PARK.—*Byhan* Park. The little park or field : from *byhan*, little, small, *parc*, a field.

BILLOWS FIELD.—*Pilez* Field. The bare field : from *pilez*, bare, bald.

BLISS PARK.—*Pilez* Park. The bare or barren field : from *piléz*, bare, bald.

BLUE PARK.—*Plew* Park. The parish park or field : from *plew*, parish, *parc*, a close or field.

BOLSTER —*Bol tir*. The earth pit : from *bol*, a pit, a hole, *tir*, land, earth, soil, ground.

BONY —A Celtic Cornish word for an axe, a hatchet.

BOOSY.—*Boudshi*. A cow-house.

BRANDY.—*Branty*. The crow's house : from *bran*, a crow, *ty* or *ti*, a house.

BUGLE INN.—*Bugel* Inn. The herdsman's or shepherd's inn : from *bugel*, a herdsman or shepherd.

BUTTON.—*Bod oon*. The dwelling-house on the down or common : from *bod*, a dwelling-house, *oon* or *gwon*, a down, common, or field.

CAMEL FIELD.—*Cammen* Field. The path field : from *cammen*, a way, a path; or, the chamomile field. Chamomile flowers are called camels in Cornwall.

CANE PARK.—*Kein* Park. The ridge park or field : from *kein*, the ridge of a hill, *parc*, a field.

CAVIL CLOSE.—*Kevil* Close. The horse field : from *kevil*, a horse.

CHANNEL CROFT.—*Tshei an hal* Croft. The moor-house croft : from *tshei*, house, *hal*, moor,

CHIN PARK.—*Chy wyn* Park. The white house park or field : from *chy*, house, *wyn*, white, *parc*, a field.

COAL PARK.—*Caol* Park. The cabbage close or field : from *caol* or *caul*, cabbage, *parc*, a close or field.

COD PARK.—*Coid* Park. The wood close or field : from *coid*, a wood.

COLD HARBOUR.—*Col ar burg*. The narrow neck over the camp : from *col*, a neck, *ar*, over, above, upon.

COME TO GOOD.—*Cum ty coed*. The wood house valley : from *cum*, valley, *ty* or *ti*, house, *coed*, a wood.

CONEY EAR.—*Goon y hir*. The long down or common : from *goon*, a down, *hir*, long.

CORNHILL.—*Carn heul*. The sun rock : from *carn*, a rock, *heul*, the sun.

COTTON.—*Coit oon*. The down or commons wood : from *coit* or *coed*, wood, *oon*, *goon*, or *wón*, a down.

CRACKER.—*Carrag hir*. The long stone : from *carrag* a rock or stone, *hir*, long.

CUT PARK.—*Coit* Park. The wood park or field : from *coid*, *coid*, *coed*, or *cuit*, a wood, *parc*, a field.

DARKEY.—*Dour chy*. Water house : from *dour*, water, *chy*, a house.

DICE MEADOW.—*Diz* Meadow. The people's meadow : from *dis* or *diz*, the people.

DINAH'S HILL.—*Dinas* Hill. The fort hill : from *dinas*, a fort, fortress, fortified town, a city.

DIPPER PARK.—*Dippa* Park. The pit close or field : from *dippa*, a pit, *parc* a field

DOOR DOWNS.—*Dour* Downs. Water downs : from *dour*, water.

DORCAS.—*Dor cus*. The forest or wood land : from *dor*, land, *cus*, a forest.

DOWER PARK.—*Dour* Park. The water park or field : from *dour*, water, *parc*, a field.

DRY FIELD.—*Adré* Field. The home field : from *adré*, homewards.

GALLOWS PARK.—*Golez* Park. The lowest, or bottom close or field : from *golés* or *golez*, the bottom, the lowest part.

GOLD ARROWS.—*Gweal daras*. The field by the door : from *gweal*, field, *daras*, door.

GOOD GRACE.—*Coed cres*. The middle wood : from *coed*, a wood, *crés*, middle.

GOOSE FORD.—*Cús fordh*. The way by the wood : from *cús*, wood, *fordh*, a way.

GROAN FIELD. *Grow* or *growan* Field. The sand field : from *grow* or *growan*, sand, gravel.

GROUSE CROFT.—*Crows* Croft. The cross field : from *crows*, a cross.

GRUMBLER.—*Grambla*. A climbing place : from *grambla*, to climb.

GULL's PARK.—*Golés* Park. The bottom close or field : from *golés*, the bottom, the lowest part.

GUN.—*Goon*. The down or common.

GUN PARK.—*Goon* Park. The down park or common : from *goon*, a down, *parc*, a field or close.

GUN POOL.—*Goon* Pool. The down pool, or pool on the common : from *goon*, down or common, *pol*, **pond**, pool, stagnant water.

HAWKEY'S PRAISE.—Hawkey's *prás*. Hawkey's meadow : from *prás*, a meadow.

KISSING CLOSE.—*Kesan* Close. The turf close, or field : from *kesan*, a turf, a sod.

LAWYER.—*Lau hir*. Long hand : from *lau*, hand *hir*, long.

LAUGHER.—*Lan veor*. The great enclosure : from *lan*, inclosure (also, a church), *veor*, great.

LOSTWITHIEL.—*Les uthiel*, or *uhel*. The high court or hall : from *les*, a court, a hall, *uthiel*, *uthell*, *uhel*, high.

MAIDEN BOWER.—*Maen veur*. The great stone : from *maen*, stone, *veur*, great.

MANACLES.—*Maen eglos*. The church rock : from *maen*, rock or stone, *eglos*, church.

MAN OF WAR.—*Maen veur*. The great stone : from *maen* stone, *veur*, great.

MEN PARK.—*Maen* Park. The stone park or field : from *maen*, a stone, *parc*, a close or field.

MERRY MAIDENS.—*Meur meyn*. The great stones : from *meur*, great, *meyn*, stones.

NINE MAIDENS.—*Naw meyn*. The nine stones : from *naw*, nine, *meyn*, stones.

ONE AND ALL (a place so named).—*Gwon an hal*. The moor field : from *gwon*, field, *hal*, a moor.

ONE FIELD.—*Oon* field. The down field : from *oon* or *goon*, a down or common.

PARSLEY (Park).—*Park isella.*   The lower field or close : from *parc,* a field, *isella,* lower.

PAUL PRY.—*Pol Pry.*   Muddy pool : from *pol,* pool, *pri* or *pry,* earth, clay.

PEACH FIELD.—*Bech* field.   The little field : from *bechan,* little, small.

PENNY BALL.—*Pen y Bal.*   The head of the mine : from *pen,* head, extremity, summit, *bal,* a mine, a parcel of Tinworks.

PENNY-COME-QUICK.—*Pen y cum gwic.*   The head (or end) of the creek-coomb : from *pen,* the head or end, *cum,* a coomb or valley, and *gwic,* a creek or inlet of the sea.

PERICLES COVE.—*Porth eglos* Cove.   The church cove : from *porth,* a port, a bay, *eglos,* a church.

PITCH PARK.—*Bech* Park.   The little field or close : from *bechan,* little, small.

PLAYER.—*Pol heir.*   The battle pool ; or *Pol hir,* the long pool : from *pol,* a pool, *heir,* battle, or *hir,* long.

POLL BRANDY.—*Pol bran ti.*   The crow house pool : from *pol,* a pool, *bran,* a crow, *ti* or *ty,* a house.

POLL BROWN.—*Pol bruin.*   The rush pool : from *pol,* a pool, *bruin,* a rush.

POLICY.—*Pol* Issey.   St. Issey's pool.

POLL PARK.—*Pol parc.*   The field pool : from *pol,* a pool, *parc,* a close or field.

POLL PRY.—*Poll pri.*   Muddy pool : from *pol,* pool, *pri,* clay or mud.

POLL QUICK.—*Pol gwic.*   The village pool or creek : from *pol,* a pool, *gwic,* a village, a creek.

POLL ROSE.—*Pol ros.*   The wheel pit : from *pol,* a pit, *ros,* a wheel.

PROCLAIM.—*Parc clam.*   The footbridge field : from *parc,* a field, *clam,* a footbridge.

PULL MAIN.—*Pol maen*   The stone pit : from *pol,* a pit, *maen,* a stone.

PURGATORY.—*Parc a dourie.*   The watery park or field : from *parc,* field, *dour,* water.

PURSE HILL.—*Parc isal.*   The low close or field : from *parc,* a field, *isal,* low.

PUSSEY.—*Pos* Hay.   The post close : from *pos,* a post.

QUEEN PARK.—*Gwin* Park.   The white field : from *parc,* a field, *gwin,* white.

READER.—*Rid hir.*   The long ford : from *rid* or *ryd,* a ford, *hir,* long.

RED TYE.—*Rid ty.*   The house ford : from *rid* or *ryd,* a ford, *ty,* a house.

ROSY.—*Ros hay.*   The net field : from *ros,* a net.

SHAKE'S MOOR.—Shag's moor : from *shagga,* a shag or cormorant.

SKIN FIELD.—*Heskin* Field.   The sedge field : from *hesken,* sedge.

TAR PARK.—*Dar* Park.   The oak close or field : from *dar,* an oak tree.

TINKER'S LAKE.—*Tan caer* Lake.   The fire castle lake : from *tan,* fire, *caer,* a castle.

TODDY WELL.—The tadpole well ; from the provincial word *tomtoddy,* a tadpole.

TRY CORNER FIELD.—*Tri* Corner Field.   Three corner field : from *tri,* three.

TURKEY PARK.—*Dourgi* Park.   The otter close or field : from *dourgi,* an otter, *parc,* a field.

TURNAVORE —*Tur an veur.*   The great tower : from *tur,* a tower, *veur,* great.

TURN A PENNY.—*Turnupan* Hay.   The turnip field : from *turnupan,* a turnip.

WELL MAN.—*Gweal maen.*   The stone field : from *gweal,* a field, *maen,* a stone.

WHISTLE PARK.   *Isel* Park.   The low field : from *isel,* low, *parc,* a close or field.

PRINCE L. L. BONAPARTE'S LETTER

ACCUSING PRYCE OF PLAGIARISM.

To the Publisher of the Cambrian Journal,

LONDON, Nov. 30, 1861.

DEAR SIR,

When you asked me some time ago to send you some papers on the Celtic Languages, I promised on the first occasion when I had a leisure moment to comply with your wish. My intention was to send you a very particularized description of a previous manuscript containing a Cornish Vocabulary by Tonkin and Gwavas, the same that Pryce unscrupulously printed at Sherborne. in 1790 under his own name, and whose real performance took place at least fifty years previously. This manuscript is preceded by a very interesting correspondence between Tonkin and Gwavas on the Cornish language, as it was still spoken in their time in some of the western parishes of Cornwall, and would not fail to give great pleasure to every one that takes interest in the Celtic and particularly in the Cornish literature.

Still, as I have no immediate prospect of printing the aforesaid valuable correspondence, and as the production of the evidence of the plagiate of Pryce is by itself a rather interesting bibliographical fact, I hope you will excuse me, if for the present I limit myself to send you an exact copy of the dedication of Tonkin to Gwavas, preceding his Vocabulary, which your numerous readers may compare with Pryce's Preface.

You will perceive by the terms in which the dedication of Tonkin is couched, the contrast between the unassuming style of one of the real authors, and the conceited one of the self-styled.

Had Mr. Edwin Norris, the clever Editor of the *Cornish Dramas*, seen the whole of the Preface in question when I had the pleasure to point out to him in my library the plagiate of Mr. Pryce, I do not doubt that he would not have attributed to the celebrated Lhuyd the authorship of this work.

And believe me, yours sincerely,

L. L. BONAPARTE.

To William Gwavas of Gwavas, in the County of Cornwall Esquire.

DEAR SIR,

In dedicating the two following articles to you, *viz.,* Title VIII, A collection of modern Cornish Pieces—and, Title IX, A Cornish Vocabulary—I do but in a manner restore to you what in a great measure belonged to you before, since 'tis what you have, in the first of these, for the best and greatest part, supply'd me with out of your own store and compositions; and as for the latter, *viz.* The Vocabulary, I must always acknowledge that without your kind assistance, I should never have been able to have gone through with it, especially in the Modern or Vulgar Cornish. It is therefore but common justice to lay before you these parts of the present undertaking, in which you have so large a share, and to whom must be owing their appearing, if not in perfection, at least without any great and notorious errors. I wish indeed it had been in either of our powers to have made the Vocabulary more compleat : but such as it is, I fear it is the utmost that can be done in it.   There are, that ever I could here of, no other Cornish manuscripts to be mett with any where, than those which are published in this present volume, out of which I have extracted those words in the Vocabulary, which are to be found in them, and to which I have severally refer'd in my quotations. And as for the vulgar Cornish now spoken (except what I have taken out of Mr. Lhuyd's Archæologia) it is reduced to such a small nook of the country, and those ancient persons that still speak it, are even there so few, the language itself so corrupted, and they too for the most part such illiterate people, that I cannot sufficiently commend your great industry in gathering together so much of it, and that so correct, as you have now enabled me to set forth; since, what it has been my fortune to collect myself has been so little in comparison, as not to deserve the naming separately.   I may add too, that very few of those that speak the language, can give any tolerable account of the orthography, much less of the etymology, or derivation of those words which they make use of, and are many times apt to jumble two or three words together, making but one of them all, tho' they pronounce them rightly enough.   Of this you were pleased to give me lately some instances—as in *merastadu*, which they thus pronounce in one breath, as if it had been but one word, whereas it is a contraction of four, *meor 'ras tha Dew*, much thanks to God, and anciently written, *maur gras tha Deu*, and *merastawhy*, much thanks to you, a contraction of *meor 'ras tha why*.

If there had been the least prospect left of recovering Mr. Lhuyd's papers, especially his *Cornish Vocabulary* (which he tells us in his Archæologia pag. 253. he had by him ready for the press) I should have defer'd the publishing this, yet for some time longer; but as I have long since given over my hopes of it, so I doubt the death of S[r]. Thomas Sebright[1] (in whose hands, you know, all *Mr. Lhuyd's* manuscript collections were) will put a full end to those, which you had so justly conceiv'd from S[r]. W[m]. Carew's late promises to you, and the fresh assurance of his assistance in procuring them for you, the heir being a minor of tender years, and the difficulties which attend such a state, from trustees, &c., not leaving you any probability of suceeding in it. And here I cannot forbear bewailing my own misfortune in having, by being imposed upon myself, been in a great degree the occasion of his delaying the publication of it which you will find a hint of in one of his letters, p. 49, and my remark under it, since I was the person who gave him the information mentioned in the preface to his Archæologia, "that a gentleman near *Truro* was composing a Cornish Vocabulary," and had " some thoughts of publishing it."—And indeed being then but young, and wholly a stranger to his character, I believ'd his mighty pretences, which I had soon reason to repent of.—But I shall forbear saying any more in this place, for I have not corresponded with him for these many years, and shall only give him this friendly admonition, that, if he still entertains thoughts of publishing his *An Laymer ay Kernow*, and (what he calls) his *Parochial Antiquities of Cornwall*, he would do well to have them carefully revis'd by some learned discreet persons. especially the latter, which the late very ingenious *Dr. Kestell*, not long before his death, telling me he had seen, was pleas'd to add of it (altering only one word) that noted saying of Juvenal.

Quicquid errant homines ————
———— Nostri est farrago libelli.

For, said the Doctor, *he has scrap'd together all the scandal, ordure, and filth that he could possibly meet with of any person or family.*—

This disappointment to the learned, and curious in ancient languages, which I was so inadvertently the occasion of, has made me the more desirous of endeavouring at some amends for it ; and since both those pieces have pass'd under your correction and review, I flatter myself that they will be candidly receiv'd by the publick, especially our own countrymen, for whom this whole collections chiefly design'd, and that, since you have so kindly lent me your helping hand, they may in some measure supply the loss of what we had, with confidence, reason to expect from that most learned and judicious antiquary.—

1 He died April the 11tb, 1736.

I have in my preface in the beginning given an account of the present undertaking, and the reasons which induced me to print it, and shall therefore detain you no longer than to return you my thanks for all your favors and to subscribe my self,

Dear Sir, Your very affectionate humble servant,

Tho: Tonkin.

Pol Gorran, July ye 19th
1736.—

The following is the concluding part of Pryce's preface : —

"As for the vulgar Cornish now spoken, it is so confined to the extremest corner of the county, and those ancient persons who still pretend to jabber it, are even there so few ; the speech itself is so corrupted, and the people, too, for the most part, are so illiterate, that I cannot but wonder at my patience, and assume some merit to myself, for my singular industry in collecting the words which I have accumulated from oral intelligence, especially, as hardly any of the persons whom I have consulted, could give a tolerable account of the orthography, much less of the etymology, or derivation of those words which they use ; for they often join, or rather run, two or three words together, making but one of them all, though their pronunciation is generally correct, as, for instance, "*Merastadu*," which they pronounce in one breath, as if it were a single word, whereas it is a contraction of four, "*Meor 'ras tha Dew*," many thanks to God, anciently written, "*Maur gras tha Dew*," and, "*Merastawhy*, many thanks to you, a contraction of "*Maur 'ras tha why*."

As the above letter of Prince L. L. Bonaparte contains only a part of Pryce's preface, it will be more fair to Pryce to give the whole. A verbation copy of the preface to the Archæologia Cornu-Britannica is therefore inserted here to serve as Pryce's defence, and also because of the information the preface contains. It is very probable that there were more words and phrases of the ancient language of Cornwall known, and used about a century ago, than Prince L. L. Bonaparte seems to be aware of. This may be the reason why Pryce felt justified in appropriating what Tonkin wrote to Gwavas, applying the words to his own time, about 1790. Even now there are men living (Mr. Bernard Victor, of Moushole, and Mr. W. F. Pentreath, of Newquay, to wit), who know many Cornish words quite apart from books ; words which have been handed down, and are not yet dead. Furthermore, the Cornish dialect is to this day full of Celtic Cornish words. But let Pryce's preface speak for itself.

PRYCE'S PREFACE

TO THE

ARCHÆOLOGIA CORNU-BRITANNICA.

I own it may appear unnecessary to the learned at this period to attempt an investigation of the high antiquity of the British language, of which the Cornish is most incontestably a very pure dialect. The subject hath been already successfully treated by many diligent and able writers, to the entire satisfaction of those who delight in researches of this kind.

Yet, it must be acknowledged, that a local inquiry and disquisition into the antiquity of our Cornu-British language has not been so particularly attended to as it deserves. And as the discovery of an original language is the first and leading step to the progressional examination of all other antiquities of a country, it follows of course, that the oldest tongue ought to be studied and understood previously to our entering upon the remains of less remote ages.

On this consideration I am inclined to believe, that a work of this tendency will be very acceptable, both to the Antiquarian and the Philologist; especially as I can safely assert, that the old Cornish-British, which is here distinguished very precisely from the modern Cornish dialect, is the most pure and nearest the original of any speech now used in Armorica, or the northern provinces of France, Great Britain, and Ireland.

The Chaldean, Syriac, Egyptian, Arabic, Phenician, Celtic, Gaulish, Welsh, and Cornish languages are all derived from the original Hebrew tongue; and in their descent one from the other, in travelling from the East to the West, have branched themselves into so many different dialects from one and the same root.

The Hebrew and Chaldee are very nearly the same; and the Syriac is next to the latter. The former flourished from the beginning of the world to the Babylonish captivity, 3400 years: But in our Saviour's time the Jews spoke the Syriac language, and Christ and his Apostles conversed in it.

As from the Hebrews to the Canaanites or Phenicians, so from the Phenicians to the Greeks came letters and arts: And accordingly, from the Phenician character, the Greeks appear to have composed their letters, and the Latins progressively from the Greeks.

So likewise, our ancient and true Cornish appears to be mostly derived from the Greek and old Latin tongues, as it participates much of their cadence and softness, with less of the guttural harshness peculiar to the Hebrew and Chaldee. This is the more easily accounted for, as the Phenicians, about the time of the Trojan war, first discovered the Scilly Islands, and the western shores of Cornwall; with the natives of which they traded for tin, and sold it to the Greeks. The language at that time spoken in other parts of this island, having travelled across a vast continent, was compounded and impure, and therefore we may boldly infer, that the superior purity of the ancient Cornish is chiefly to be ascribed to its genuine introduction from the shores of Greece and Sidon.

It is affirmed by writers, that the inland parts of our island were first planted from the German continent, about eight hundred years after the Flood, and not from the Gauls: And indeed it is very possible that the body of the south-western part of the island was peopled from the Belgic, and Gaulish countries both, on account of their propinquity to our opposite coasts and inlets of safety. Nevertheless, our dialect in Cornwall must certainly have obtained that purity, for which it is celebrated, from its immediate introduction by the Phenician navigators; especially as the character and orthography are so greatly softened and the language is divested of that rough guttural pronunciation, which is retained to this time by the Cambro-Britons. In fact, the Cornish and the Armoric dialects are the most nearly allied in character, orthography, and sound, of any two of the British dialects. The Welsh, Irish, and Erse differ from each other greatly; and the two latter differ from the Cornish and Gaulish very much. Indeed the Welsh is closely related to us, and would appear more so, if it were deprived of those numerous combinations of consonants, with which it is, to us, perplexed and entangled.

Hence we may easily account for the similarity existing between the Cornish and Armoric-British; for the coasts of Bretagne, Normandy, and Picardy, are opposite to the shores of Cornwall, Devon, &c., so that the first commercial discoverers of those lands, in their sailing up the British Channel, had equal opportunities of communicating their Grecian and Roman dialects of the Syriac root. This is evidenced by the colloquial resemblance to this day subsisting betwixt the Cornish on the south-western margin of the county, and their opposite neighbours at Morlaix, and other parts of Bas Bretagne, where the low French and the Cornish seem almost one and the same dialect. If I had not been otherwise well apprized of this fact, yet my opinion would have been confirmed by what I have heard from a very old man now living at Moushole, near Penzance, who, I believe, is, at this time, the only person capable of holding half an hour's conversation on common subjects in the Cornish tongue. He tells me, that above threescore years ago, being at Morlaix on board a smuggling cutter, and the only time he was ever there, he was ordered on shore with another young man to buy some greens, and not knowing a word of French, as he thought, he was much surprised to find that he understood a great part of the conversation of some boys at play in the street; and upon further inquiry, he found that he could make known all his wants in Cornish, and be better understood than he could be at home, when he used that dialect. I am well satisfied of the fact, as he is quite an illiterate man, and could have neither the temptation nor the ingenuity to invent a story so useless to himself.

So many centuries having elapsed since the ancient and true dialect hath been spoken, it is now become altogether obsolete, if not totally dead. I have therefore made a distinction between the ancient and modern Cornish in some pieces, such as the Creed, Lord's Prayer, Proper Names of Places, &c., as more notorious and useful for critical inspection: And in the Vocabulary throughout, I have sedulously preferred and extracted from the MSS. which I have collected, all the ancient Cornish I could find in them, divested of Saxon words with Cornish accents and terminations, imposed by oral and illiterate tradition.

The old British language being superseded by the adoption and general cultivation of the Teutonic or Saxon tongue, in process of time became unintelligible and useless in the body and bulk of this island, whence it was driven to the borders and extremities, such as Scotland, Wales, and Cornwall, where it still maintains a reverence and footing among the respective inhabitants, in the dress of differing dialects. Indeed, the veneration in which it is held in Wales is sufficiently shewn by the preservation of it among the natives; many thousands of the peasantry scarcely knowing how to make themselves understood in the Saxon or English.

To such a height of enthusiasm is it revered by many of the inland inhabitants, that they hold all other speech in the utmost contempt; preferring their own predilection with the most stubborn perverseness, and shunning in the most contumaceous manner every sort of interlocution and communion with any other tongue, till overcome by the pressure of their necessities, and the unavoidable intercourse of mankind in trade and business.

Had the Cornish been equally pertinacious with them, we should not have had reason to lament the loss of our native language for those many ages during which it has been almost sunk into oblivion among us, but such has been the neglect of our ancestors, and the depredation of time, that our primitive speech was nearly annihilated before the Art of Printing could perpetuate the memory of it to posterity.

So habitually inattentive were they, that many years after the discovery of this Art, they never adverted to the preservation of the MSS. in their language, so that the only MS. extant, was that found in the Cotton Library, now about 800 years old, from which time no other MS. appears, till about the fifteenth century, when we meet with one, which exhibits three Ordinalia or Interludes taken from Holy Writ :—1. *De origine mundi* : 2. *Of the passion of our Lord* ; 3. *Of the Resurrection*. The originals of these are all in the Bodleian Library ; as likewise one Ordinale, Of the creation of the world and the deluge, by William Jordan, of Hellaston, anno 1611. The 5th and last book is a poem, entitled Mount Calvary, On the passion and resurrection of our Lord and Saviour. This MS. written on vellum, was given by Mr. Anstis, Garter King at Arms, to Mr. Lhuyd ; but when or by what author it was written is wholly uncertain, though this copy, by the hand writing, may also be attributed to the fifteenth century.

The late Rev. Dr. William Borlase, my learned friend and relation, received a copy of this poem (which is the best of the whole in the Cornish tongue) from the Rev. Dr. Lyttleton, Dean of Exeter, afterwards Bishop of Carlisle ; which was written under the direction of Mr. Scawen, of Molinick, who says " That he had long had a proposal and a desire for the recovery of our primitive tongue ; and that at the last assizes, 1678, that he was able to be at in Launceston to perform his duty to his King and country, there in the Judges' chambers happened some speech to be of things memorable in Cornwall, and particularly concerning the ancient Cornish tongue ; for the loss or decay whereof Sir Francis North, then Lord Chief Justice, afterwards Lord Keeper, seemed to be concerned ; blaming us all then present ; Enquiring also whether there were anything written in it now remaining. I told his Lordship, I had an old Cornish piece long in my keeping, *viz.*, The passion of Christ described in Cornish heroic metre. His Lordship was earnest for a sight of it. This, spoken by such a person, a stranger to our country (and I having thereupon promised it to him, at his next coming in circuit) it put me into more serious thoughts concerning it than formerly.

" Accordingly I prepared it with some additions thereon, as well as I could, (without help of fit books, and men living, and good associates by me), but then by reason of grievous infirmities grown upon me, in the mean time, expressed by syncopes and other distempers. I was not able to present it to his Lordship as I intended ; together with the discourse which takes its rise from the aforementioned conference in 1678, since which time it hath layen upon my hands.

" I do not know any Cornish writing else extant, and this hath been a long time reserved by me as a precious relict.* How ancient it is may be in part guessed at, but not clearly made out by demonstration. But as to the speech itself preserved in this writing, it is such as the common speakers of he Cornish now used here. and in Wales, and Armorica do not understand it ; nor any but such as will be studious in it : No more, than the common speakers of the vulgar tongue of the Greeks do at this day Homer's Iliads. Words of one another, 'tis true, all those three sorts of people do understand alternately ; not all, but mostly such as are radical. Colloquies of one another they do not enjoy, nor distinguish the several dialects ; and least of all do our common speakers understand this MS. but such of them as, upon study, come to the knowledge of it, commend the elegancy thereof extremely.

" If I should say, that these endeavours of mine, would be totally useful and successful to the recovery of the speech, as ill qualified as I am, I know well it must be thought more vain and censurable in me, now at 84, than it was in Tully to attempt the Greek tongue at 60 years. For me it will suffice me, if I do but, *hoc digito monstrare viam*."

---

* By this it appears, that Mr. Scawen had never seen the plays before mentioned.—(*Note by Pryce.*)

Unfortunately this was the case; for in the same year, that worthy old gentleman departed this life, and left his papers on our subject in a very disordered condition, together with several others on Stannary business, he being also Vice-Warden of the Stannaries many years before his death.

Here a pause succeeds to any further inquiries into our subject for more than twenty years; when Mr. Lhuyd coming into Cornwall professedly on this business, it made Mr. Tonkin, Mr. Keigwin, Mr. Gwavas, and several other Cornish gentlemen, very solicitous to promote his success, by all the assistance in their power, which was not inconsiderable, as from a strong prepossession in favour of their native language, they were exceedingly zealous in the cause, and diligent in their endeavours to restore this object of their veneration to its former honours.   Accordingly we find in the correspondence of Mr. Lhuyd and Mr. Tonkin, about the commencement of the present century, that Mr. Lhuyd had gone great lengths towards the formation of a Cornish-British Vocabulary, as he says at the end of his Cornish Grammar, p. 253.—That looking over the sheets of his said Grammar he must recall the promise made in his preface, p. 222, of a Cornish-English Vocabulary, there being no room for it in that Volume of Glossography, and therefore must defer it 'till the next.   Mr. Lhuyd's death about the year 1709 frustrated his good intention, which must have been the greatest loss to this pursuit that it ever had, or ever will meet with, on account of his profound learning and singular attachment to the recovery of our primitive language.   In his hands, particularly fitted as he was for the undertaking, and supplied with every essential article of erudition from surrounding libraries, not only the recovery of this dialect would have been affected, but it would have been adorned with every elegancy and improvement, from the unceasing labours of such a consummate Philologist.

Soon after the death of Mr. Lhuyd, all his MS. collections were surrendered to the custody of Sir Thomas Sebright, who died in 1736.   His heir being a minor of tender years, and the trustees unmindful of such things as were not obviously and immediately connected with the benefit of their charge, those collections were eventually buried, and lost to all future publick inspection.*

Here I should observe also that about the 15th year of this century, the publick expectation was turned towards Mr. Hals, of Fenton Gymps, who professed a warm affection for the dialect of his country and took uncommon pains to heap together a mass of words which he entitled *Lhadymer ay Kernow*, or the Cornish Interpreter; which I discovered, some years since, by certain notices found among Mr. Tonkin's writings, to be in the custody of the Rev. Henry Hawkins Tremayne.   Mr. Tremayne, on my application, found the MS. and lent it to me for a considerable time.

Mr. Hals's *Lhadymer* is a most strange hodge-podge of Hebrew, Greek, Latin, and British words, confusedly heaped together, and in such a manner as not only to shew his want of method, but also to expose his great deficiency in those learned languages, which he lugged in to support and illustrate his etymology; it being common with him to write *Tempore regnum Augustus; ostium fluvius*, &c.   Indeed all his knowledge of those languages appears to have been derived from some books, with which he was furnished by his first wife, the widow of one Code, a schoolmaster of St. Wenn.   However, as this farrago contained some intelligence not unworthy my notice, I took particular care to select all that was valuable and proper for my purpose.

About the time of Mr. Lhuyd's demise, Messrs. Tonkin, Keigwin, and Gwavas, with other associates, kept up a correspondence in their native tongue, as well as they could, by collecting all the mottoes, proverbs, and idioms, on which they could lay their hands.

In this collection Mr. Tonkin took the lead, being determined to publish a Cornish Word-Book in his then proposed History and Antiquities of Cornwall illustrated, in three volumes, quarto.   But being a person of a

---

* It may not be too late even now to recover the lost or "buried" papers left by Lhuyd.   I do not know that any strict search has ever been made.   Will the Philological Society make an effort for this purpose? F.W.P.J.

desultory turn, and meeting with many vexations and difficulties in the world, he died before he had com-pleated the work. He left, indeed, a large mass of MS. books, but they were thrown together without any sort of order or connection. Had this gentleman been as happy and steady in his disposition, as he was distinguished by his learning and genius, his abilities would have ensured applause far superior to the coldness of simple approbation.

Mr. Tonkin was assisted in his undertaking by the critical knowledge and industry of William Gwavas, Esq., who was indefatigable in collecting and ascertaining words for his use and arrangement. Mr. Martin Keigwin likewise, and his son Mr. John Keigwin, both inhabitants of the little fishing village of Mousbole, and who had sucked in the broken dialect with their milk, were ready upon all occasions to clear up any doubts that might arise, and were generally fortunate in removing those difficulties, which embarrassed the other gentlemen.

The result of this coalition was an alphabetical arrangement of words; not, however, in the manner of the Vocabulary found in the Cotton Library, which is exceedingly devious and irregular, being written throughout in continued lines, without any respect to order and verbal distribution. In consequence of the death of Mr. Tonkin, this collection must have lain some time subject to the caprice of his descendants, who were illiterate women, and was therefore liable to much loss and mutilation, till it was taken into the protection of the late Robert Hoblyn, of Nanswhidden, Esq., in whose celebrated library it met with a safe asylum. It was afterwards taken thence, and committed to my trust by favour of the late John Quicke, Esq., who married the relict of Mr. Hoblyn, and who, with reiterated expressions of his wish to see it warmed into life, consigned it to my care for correction, additions, and publication; to which end I pledged my diligence and application, with whatever assistance I could procure from the MSS. before mentioned, together with some detached papers from Mrs. Veal, the daughter of Mr. Gwavas; from Mrs. Mary Ustick, the widow of the Rev. Henry Ustick, of Breage; and from the papers of Mr. John Bosons, of Newlyn. I also applied to Miss Foss, the representative of her grandfather, Thomas Tonkin, Esq., for the use of his other MSS. to which I had access, and from which I extracted all that I could find valuable in that rich mass of indigested materials.

The manuscript ground-work of my undertaking being thus acknowledged, I must also confess my implicit submission to the works of Mr. Lhuyd, and of the late Dr. Wm. Borlase, who, in the interval betwixt the death of Mr. Tonkin, and his papers being delivered into my custody, published at the end of his *Antiquities of Cornwall* an epitomised Vocabulary, which has furnished a few useful additions to my larger collection. It is likewise with singular satisfaction that I acknowledge my obligations to the Rev. Mr. Whitaker, of Ruan Lanyhorn, for his communications, and his criticisms on the British language; a Gentleman, whose warm defence of our ancient tongue deserves the grateful applause of his country.

After much consideration how to render my performance so full and complete as to engage the approbation of the publick, and as the curious nature of the undertaking demands, I determined to make it a digest of the Cornish-British language, by introducing in the First Part the marrow of Mr. Lhuyd's Grammar, with some additions, in which are incorporated his instructions for the reading of old British MSS. I hope this very learned Introduction to Philology, which I have reprinted at the entrance of my book, will not be found out of its place. The Second Part contains my Vocabulary, consisting of several thousand words, collected and arranged from the materials already mentioned. This hath employed the labour of many years; and perhaps, a work of a drier kind hath seldom been undertaken by any harmless drudge whomsoever.* As the whole of the Cotton Vocabulary is inserted, I have taken care to note each word from that ancient remain, with this mark †. The Third and last Part consists of the Cornish Proper Names of Hundreds, Parishes, Villages, &c., with their distinctions of the old and modern Cornish set forth in the concisest manner I could adopt, so that

* See Dr. Johnson on the word Lexicographer.—(*Note by Pryce.*)

the reader may, at a single glance, apprehend the difference. This is followed by the Creed, Pater Noster, and Decalogue in both Ancient and Modern Cornish, and also Mottoes, Proverbs, and Sayings in the vulgar Cornish; with the last correspondence between Mr. Lhuyd and Mr. Tonkin.

I wish, indeed, it had been within the compass of my knowledge, to have rendered the Vocabulary perfect and complete; but the scanty and limited materials I had to consult, rendered every hope of that kind abortive; For according to the best information I have been able to procure, there are no other Cornish MSS. to be met with any where, beside those I have already mentioned; from which I have extracted those words in the Vocabulary, which are to be found in them, illustrated by numerous quotations from them, which are familiar to the language of scripture and the popular idiom.

As for the vulgar Cornish now spoken, it is so confined to the extremest corner of the county, and those ancient persons who still pretend to jabber it, are even there so few; the speech itself is so corrupted, and the people too, for the most part, are so illiterate, that I cannot but wonder at my patience, and assume some merit to myself, for my singular industry, in collecting the words which I have accumulated from oral intelligence; especially, as hardly any of the persons whom I have consulted, could give a tolerable account of the orthography, much less of the etymology, or derivation of those words, which they use; for they often join, or rather run two or three words together, making but one of them all, though their pronunciation is generally correct:—As for instance, *Merastadu*, which they pronounce in one breath, as if it were a single word, whereas it is a contraction of four, *Meor 'ras tha Dew*; "Many thanks to God," anciently written, *Maur gras tha Deu*, and, *Merasthawhy*, "Many thanks to you," a contraction of *Maur 'ras tha why*.

ERRATA.

In the Introduction it is said that Dr. Bannister's unfinished MS. of an English-Cornish Dictionary lies buried in the British Museum. This is true, but it should be explained that since the first part of this book was printed, Dr. James Jago, of Truro, has informed me that "The Royal Institution of Cornwall is in possession of a copy of Dr. Williams's *Cornish-British Lexicon*, presented by the widow of Dr. Bannister, and containing on interleaves of writing-paper free from print, plentiful notes from his hand, varied and elaborate, and ranging throughout the work."

It is to be hoped that one day Dr. Bannister's MSS. will be printed. They cannot but be valuable, coming as they do, from one so well acquainted with Ancient Cornish.

In the Introduction, p. IV., line 9, for gentlemen, *read* gentleman.

On p. 41, line 16, for VOILENT, *read* VIOLENT.

Under the following " words " (in capitals) the corrections are :—

(ABLE.) YE MIGHT BE ABLE. For 2 pers. s., *read* 2 pers. pl.

ABOVE. For ahueh, *read* ahuch.

AFTER or BEHIND. For adhethar, *read* adhelhar.

AMAZED. For muscoe, museok, *read* muscoc, muscok.

ANCESTORS. For henlasou, *read* hendasou (Pl.).

ANXIETY. For fyenesow, *read* fyenasow.

APRON. For *goul and guns*, read *goul an guns.*

AS WELL. For *Lath ny gansé ta*, read *Lath ny gansé magé ta.*

AS MANY AS. For hynifer, *read* kynifer.

BACK. (Of the body). For War an aywen, *read* War an dywen.

(BIT.) A SMALL BIT or PIECE. For *Den vythol na thovtgans*, read *Den vythol na thovtgans peg.*

BLESSED, *part.* and *adj.* For blesssed God, *read* blessed God.

BRAGGING. For *tás ha trós*, read *fás ha trós.*

BUTTOCKS. For pedennow, *read* pedrennow.

HE CAN. For neth read nerth.

CAUSE or REASON. For tell use the cause, *read* tell us the cause.

CHAMPION. For Côdwûr, *read* Cadwûr.

DEBTOR. For keudoner, *read* kendoner.

DELUGE. For kyel, *read* dyel.

DESPATCH. For toysh, *read* toyth.

(DESTROY.) For THOU WOULSDT DESTROY, *read* THOU WOULDST DESTROY.

DISPUTE. For *he* (the last word), read *here.*

DOOR-POST. For dnrn, *read* durn.

DRINK. (Liquor, beer). "Eveugh, P.;" is misplaced. It means drink, or drink ye, the 2 pers. pl. imper. of *eva*, to drink.

FALSEHOOD. *Stram* is singular, not plural.

HE MAY FETCH. For cervho, *read* cercho.

(FASTEN.) For HE SHALY FASTEN, *read* HE SHALL FASTEN.

FINE. (Slender, thin). For moiu, *read* moin.

FIRMAMENT. For fyrvan, *read* fyrvav (fyrvau).

FISH-POND. For Hisclîn, *read* Pisclîn.

FULFIL. For konlenuel, *read* kovlenuel.

FURY, A SHE DEVIL. For dzhonlés, *read* dzhoulés.

GENTLE. (Easy). For Hêkh, *read* Hêdh.

GIRL. For morion, *read* moroin.

HOW. For fetiyl, *read* fettyl.

ILL-DEED. For dhroloceth, *read* dhrocoleth.

For IMMEDIATLY, *read* IMMEDIATELY.

For INSUMENT, *read* INSTRUMENT.

KEEN. For dyn, *read* dyn, B. ; and for feyn, *read* tyen, P.

LAMENT, *v.* For garlarow, *read* galarow.

LAMENTATION. For dhnan, *read* dhuan, and for croffolae, *read* croffolas.

LOOK, LOOK. For *wér*, read *mér.*

METHUSALEH. For 1435, *read* c.w. 1435.

TO MAKE A NET. For Lreedy, *read* Breedy.

OWNER. For *Ystym thym*, read *Ystyn thym.*

RECONCILE. For *s.*, read *v.* (verb).

RIGHT, *adj.* (Correct). For *evu hys*, read *evn (eun) hys.*

ROLL, *v.* For Rgruatt, *read* Egruatt.

RUBBISH. For head or rocky, *read* hard or rocky.

A FEMALE RULER. For Luifanés, *read* Ruifanés,

SERVANT. For gnâs, *read* guâs.

SHAME, *s.* (Bashfulness). The quotation, *Ty a feth méth*, should have been under SHAME, *s.* (Infamy)

WITH THEM. For gansy, c.w. 1452, *read* ganssy, c.w. 1452.

(WOMAN.) For POOR WOMAN, *read* POOR WOMEN.

Page 196.—In the Lord's Prayer. For " with the is thee dominion," *read* " with thee is the dominion."

Genesis.—In the 7th verse, for *an dowrow esé*, read *an dowrow esens.*

In the 4th Commandment, for "all that is to the to do," *read* "all that is to thee to do," and in the 10th Commandment, for "warfen, *read* "worfen."

Page 204, line 14 from the bottom, for *Laymer*, read *Lhadymer.*

LIST OF SUBSCRIBERS.

Bennett, W. S., Esq., Escot, Penzance.

Boase, Charles W., Esq., Exeter College, Oxford.

Boase, George Clement, Esq., 15, Queen Anne's Gate, Westminster, S.W.

Bolitho, William, jun., Esq., Ponsandane, Penzance.

Bond, Kinton, Esq., The Crescent, Plymouth.

Boyle, Thomas, Esq., Newquay, Cornwall.

Bonython, J. L., Esq., Adelaide, South Australia.

Brushfield, T. N., Esq., M.D., The Cliff, Budleigh-Salterton.

Burnard, Robert, Esq., 3, Hillsborough, Mannamead.

Carew, W. F. Pole, Esq., Antony House.

Courtney, Leonard, Esq., M.P., 15, Cheyne Walk, Chelsea.

Clyma, Mr. W. J., St. Nicholas Street, Truro.

Coode, Edward, Esq., Polapit, Tamar, Launceston.

Curgenven, J. Brenden, Esq., 12, Craven Hill Gardens, London, W.

Cornwall County Library, Truro, Edward Parkyn, Esq., Librarian

Crofts, E. Whitfield, Esq., Alverton Lodge, Penzance.

Fisher, Edward, Esq., Abbotsbury, Newton Abbot.

Foster, Richard, Esq., Lanwithan, Lostwithiel.

Free Public Library, Whimple Street, Plymouth, W. H. K. Wright, Esq., Librarian.

Free Public Library, Birkenhead, W. May, Esq., Librarian.

Free Library, Dundee, N.B., J. F. Meare, Esq., Chief Librarian.

Gilbert, C. Davies, Esq.

Harrison, Rev. David J., Ludgvan Rectory, Penzance.

Holman, Frederick, Esq., 9, North Parade, Penzance.

Jago, John Rowse, Esq., Lynher Cottage, St. Germans.

Jago, Richard, Esq., Halwell House, Plymouth.

Kevern, J. T., Esq., Penzance.

Latimer, I., Esq., Glen View, Mannamead, Plymouth.

Luke, Mr. W. H., Bedford Street, Plymouth.

Library of the Corporation of the City of London, W. H. Overall, Esq., Librarian.

Library of the Supreme Council for the Southern Jurisdiction, Washington, America, Albert Pike, Esq., Curator of the Library.

Library of the Royal Institution of Cornwall, Truro.

Mount Edgcumbe, The Right Honourable the Earl of.

Mayne, Rev. James, Pons a Verran, Constantine, near Penryn.

Moore, Rev. Charles, Garlenick, Grampound, Cornwall.

Magor, Mr. M., 24, Chapel Street, Penzance.

Martin, T., Esq., Alston, Plympton.

Moore, A. W., Esq., Editor of the *Manx Note Book*, Isle of Man.

Matthews, J. H., Esq., Grosvenor Place, Ripley, Derby.

Meeres, Dr., St. Andrew's Terrace, Plymouth.

Millett, G. B., Esq., Penzance.

Penny, Rev. Edward L., D.D., Coryton, Plymouth.

Peter, Richard, Esq., The Cottage, Launceston.

Pye, Rev. Francis W., Rectory, Blisland.

Pethybridge, John, Esq., Bodmin, Cornwall.

Pattison, Dr. W. T. A., Bath.

Pearce, Gilbert P., Esq., Hayle, Cornwall.

Pearce, Mark Guy, Esq., 21, Cotham New Road, Bristol.

Penberthy, Professor John, Royal Veterinary College, Camden Town, London, N.W.

Penzance Public Library, P. Hedgeland, Esq., Hon. Sec.

Plymouth Proprietary Library, Cornwall St., Plymouth.

Public Library, Leeds, James Yates, Esq., Librarian.

Rashleigh, Jonathan, Esq., Menabilly, Par Station, Cornwall.

Rhys, John, Esq., Professor of Celtic University, Oxford.

Rogers, Dr. James, Saltash, Cornwall.

St. Aubyn, Edward, Esq., Manor Lodge, Devonport.

Szyrma, Rev. W. S. Lach, 4, Canterbury Street, Liverpool.

Smith, G. S., Esq., Trevu, Camborne, Cornwall.

Stokes, Whitley, Esq., LL.D., 15, Grenville Place, London, S.W.

Trelawny, Jago, Major General, Coldrenick, Liskeard.

Tremayne, John, Esq., Heligan, St. Austell.

Tresidder, T. J., Esq., Corfield, St. Dye, Cornwall

Thomas, S. V., Esq., F.R.H.S., West Parley Curacy, Winbourne Minster.

Tremenheere, H. S., Esq., 43, Thurloe Square, London, S.W.

Treweeke, G. Esq., St. Ives, Cornwall.

Truscott, C., Esq., Cusgarne, St. Austell.

Torquay Natural History Society, W. Pengelly, Esq., Hon. Sec.

Victor, Mr. Burnard, Mousehole, Cornwall.

Williams, B., Esq., 17, River Street, Truro.

Wright, W. H. K., Esq., Headland Park, Plymouth.

Printed in Great Britain
by Amazon

42173002R00137